ECONOMICS

an introduction to
traditional and radical views

E. K. Hunt and Howard J. Sherman
UNIVERSITY OF CALIFORNIA, RIVERSIDE

HARPER & ROW, PUBLISHERS

New York   Evanston   San Francisco   London

ECONOMICS
an introduction to
traditional and radical views

Standard book number: 06–043019–2

Library of congress catalog card number: 70–184939

TO LINDA AND BARBARA

contents

foreword

by John G. Gurley

At last! Beginning economics students for too long have been denied
a thoroughly critical analysis of the society in which they live. Hunt
and Sherman have now provided these students with such a critique,
and at the same time they have supplied professional expositions of
traditional economic theory. Other authors of elementary textbooks
have presented this aspect or that of traditional theory as well as
or even better or more fully than Hunt and Sherman have, good as
their treatment generally is, but no authors, to my knowledge, have
given elementary economics students a truer picture of modern
capitalism, in its national and world dimensions. There are many
ways to present traditional economic theory, and each instructor
undoubtedly has his favorites, but the theory presented in this book
is by *social critics* rather than by apologists for the system, and that
should make all the difference to students who truly wish to gain a
deeper understanding of what is going on in the world today.

Radical economists are dissatisfied, to put the point gently, with
the conventional approach to economics, which takes the capitalist
system for granted, considering it to be more or less eternal, and so
skimps on the history of both the system and its ideology. Accordingly, conventional textbooks serve capitalism to the students on a
platter, as though there was nothing else in the kitchen or ever would
be. Hunt and Sherman break with that approach, right off the bat, by

devoting Part I of their book to the evolution of economic institutions and ideologies. Joseph Schumpeter once wrote that "Nobody can hope to understand the economic phenomena of any, including the present, epoch who has not an adequate command of historical facts and an adequate amount of historical sense . . ." The authors of this book have taken those words seriously.

There is another reason for discontent with the conventional approach. It distorts reality by assuming harmonies of interest throughout society, ignoring the deep class conflicts that prevail in our society. Such sweetness and light enable conventional economists to refer to "the general interest," "the public welfare," "the common good," and other equally soothing expressions, and to assume that the State represents everyone's interests. Hunt and Sherman, I am pleased to say, look upon their discipline as "political economics," rather than economics in the narrow sense, and so throughout the book they study economic problems within the context of ruler-subject relations—always sensitive to the fact that there are pervasive relations of domination and servitude throughout our society. That this makes a difference can easily be seen by comparing their analyses of income distribution, discrimination, economic waste, international finance, and development of poor countries with corresponding treatments in other textbooks. Hunt and Sherman come out on top because their conception of the world —which includes power, conflict, and disruptive change within a historical setting—is more accurate than the paradigms used by bourgeois economists.

Do we have to put up with the misinformation in the thin and slanted chapters in one elementary textbook after another, which are supposed to pass for serious analyses of socialism, communism, and Marxism? Not any longer. I do not mean that Hunt and Sherman have given us glowing accounts of the supreme joy of living in the Soviet Union and in China, for they have not. What I mean is that we now have a serious discussion of alternative economic systems by experts who have more than their share of critical faculties. The five chapters that comprise the last part of the book will inform and stimulate a large number of beginning economics students.

Radical economics still has a long way to go, as Hunt and Sherman well know, before it can sweep away most of the rubbish in present-day bourgeois economics. This book is an excellent contribution toward that end.

preface

This book is *very* different from the traditional elementary
economics text.

We do present the traditional economic theory. In addition, we
present radical critiques and radical theories. In the traditional
economics category we include economists who are generally
classified as liberal as well as those generally considered to be
conservative. The traditional view rests on Adam Smith's notion that
in a market economy the forces of supply and demand act as an
"invisible hand" to guide resources into their most efficient uses and
to distribute the proceeds of the productive process in a reasonably
fair manner.

Most economists realize that the forces of supply and demand do
not always maximize social welfare. In some circumstances, they
might even be pernicious. In these instances, it is necessary for the
government to intervene in the market to ensure a socially
acceptable outcome. Varying assessments of the extent and significance of these "special cases" differentiate liberals and conservatives. Liberals believe that promoting the society's welfare
requires relatively frequent government intervention into market
processes. Conservatives believe that these interventions should be
relatively less frequent. Neither liberals nor conservatives seriously
question the basic institutional framework of the private-property,
market-capitalist economy within which the forces of supply and
demand operate.

Radicals, however, subject these institutions to critical scrutiny. In this book, we shall use the term *radical* in its traditional meaning. Traditionally, the adjective *radical* has referred to "leftist" or "socialist" criticisms or actions, and the noun *radical* has referred to these leftists and socialists. In recent times, particularly since the 1964 American presidential election, references have been made to the *radical right.* Included in the radical right have been various political conservatives, reactionaries, and assorted cranks. We do not refer to these right-wing radicals when we use the term. We mean only radicals of the left.

Thus, in this book, we shall be concerned with radical criticism of the fundamental institutions of capitalism as well as the orthodox views on how the market capitalist system functions.

a historical approach

In Part I, we introduce economics by way of a history of the great economists (some of them wild and wonderful). We present their ideas as set within the context of the institutions of their times, and therefore sketch out an economic history.

There is no easier and more pleasant way of learning economics than to follow the evolution of the main ideas of the great thinkers in the field. This will also impress upon the reader, as nothing else could, that there are at least two (and usually more) views on every subject in economics.

It is interesting to see how our modern economic institutions slowly evolved from feudal times. The usual textbooks start off cold from the present situation. We believe it is much more meaningful to witness all of the curious zigzags and the fighting that occurred in the development of our present institutions. How things developed in the past gives us a key to understanding the present and, hopefully, the future.

The history of economic ideas and the history of economic institutions are not totally independent of each other. In reality, they are very closely related, each affecting the other at all times. Thus, we shall see that the specific problems and interests of various groups gave rise to very specific economic ideologies, and that these ideologies served as an excuse for the status quo or as a call for drastic change. For example, we shall see in the first few chapters that the dominant ideology in the medieval period fully supported the feudal economic system as just and correct and eternal. Eventually, however, the contrary ideas of the new groups of merchants and industrialists were reflected in new economic ideologies, which then helped to overturn the old restrictive feudal order.

teaching economic theory

The traditional approach concentrates on explaining how the consumer may maximize his satisfaction from spending, how the businessman may maximize his profits, and how the government may aid private business to maximize growth. This approach is often dull and mechanical. We include these usual and somewhat mechanical subjects, but to a lesser degree, focusing on the more exciting, present-day social and political issues. In fact, ours is more of a *political*-economics text than a purely economics text.

Thus, in Part II, we discuss the traditional *microeconomic* problems of the individual consumer and the individual business firm. We also investigate often neglected problems—for example, poverty, racism, sexual discrimination, monopoly power, unequal education opportunities, and tax loopholes.

Similarly, in Part III, we discuss the usual *macroeconomic* problems of the economy as a whole, including the standard questions of economic growth and unemployment. In addition, we examine such problems as inflation, pollution and waste, population, war spending, the underdeveloped countries, and imperialism.

objectivity

Some traditional economists will complain that we do not present the conservative or traditional views completely enough. We do try, especially in the historical presentations of Part I, to state both the traditional and radical views as impartially as possible. Of course, no one is impartial, so we undoubtedly state the radical view somewhat more effectively. In Parts II and III, we again state the traditional views first, before giving the radical view, but our sympathy with the radical view will be quite apparent.

Some radical economists who have read this book before publication have complained of the opposite. They said that we sound too impartial between the conservative and radical views, especially in their historical presentation.

Other radicals have complained that it is not necessary to state the orthodox views at all, since they are wrong. We believe, first, that students should be acquainted with all views; second, that present radical views can only be understood in their historical context, which definitely includes the traditional theories, the criticism of which led to the radical theories; and third, we do not like a know-nothing radicalism of the type that says: poverty and racism are bad, so we should just go out and demonstrate against them, and toss tomatoes at their defenders. On the contrary, we believe that one must put some hard study into political economics in order to understand the causes of poverty and racism and other evils and their possible cures.

a comparative approach

In Part IV, we take the reader on an excursion through some of the countries that call themselves socialist, particularly Russia, China, and Yugoslavia. Various chapters examine their historical development, current institutions, and current problems. Their development and institutions are compared with those of the Western capitalist countries. This does not merely give us an idea of what the rest of the world looks like. It is also important because the comparisons bring out more clearly many of the features of the Western capitalist countries. For example, in studying the market process of the United States, it is very interesting and helpful to compare it with the planned nonmarket economies of eastern Europe.

some other special features

The usual elementary economics text is filled with nothing but graphs and mathematics. We have used graphs only where necessary to illustrate a point, but have always explained it first in ordinary English, and have kept the graphs as simple as possible.

For the convenience of students, summaries are provided at the end of each chapter. Warning: No summary can explain a chapter, it may merely remind you of the most important points. Another warning: No summary can be very accurate because it is too short to include all the necessary qualifications.

For instructors accustomed to the standard textbooks, we have presented most theory in its usual order and covered the usual topics. In a few places, that is not so. For example, international trade is sometimes placed in the microeconomics part, even though it always contains many macroeconomic observations. Because we found that the macroeconomic issues in international trade are the most interesting, we have emphasized them, and put the discussion in that part. (It is independent enough of the surrounding chapters that it can be used at a different point.) Also, we have omitted production functions, a traditional topic, because we approach the subject differently, and believe that recent theory has shown this approach to be based on indefensible assumptions.

how to use this book

This book has been designed so that it may be used as the main text for a one-year course, but with the plentiful use of supplements. Many good collections of readings are available. It may also be used for a one-semester or one-quarter course if one wishes to cover the material somewhat lightly or emphasize some particular areas.

Most instructors prefer to teach macroeconomics before microeconomics. That is understandable because microeconomic theory is usually especially dull and lifeless in most texts. This text is so arranged that the instructor may, if he wishes, teach the macroeconomics first, even though it comes second in this book. In other words, the two parts are sufficiently independent, even though they refer to each other at the appropriate points.

After some heated discussion between the authors, we decided to put the microeconomics part first. For one, we believe that our microeconomics section is much more interesting than the average. We go through the usual supply and demand graphs, although as simply as possible. But the section also emphasizes the radical views on poverty, government behavior, and racial and sexual discrimination—all of which, we believe, the reader will find exciting. We also present the usual graphs on monopoly theory, but give a great deal more attention than most books to the history and facts of monopoly in the United States. We believe that the material on income distribution and monopoly is particularly important in understanding the later macro material on waste and cyclical unemployment in the United States. (But again, we emphasize that the instructor could conceivably teach Part III ahead of Part II, if he so desired.)

Finally, the book may be used in special ways in one-quarter or one-semester courses emphasizing only one aspect of economics. First, in a macroeconomics course, we would suggest that Part I on history be assigned so as to be read lightly in the first few weeks. (Chapter 10 on Keynes could be emphasized.) Then jump to Part III on macroeconomics; this is a lengthy part and will give plenty of meat, although a supplement could certainly be used as well (several paperbacks go more fully into the traditional subjects of income accounting and determination).

Second, in a course on microeconomics, we would again suggest beginning with Part I so that the student sees how microeconomics developed through the history of thought (particularly emphasizing the chapters on the neoclassical economists and on Marx). Part II will then follow naturally. Since Part II is fairly short, you may have time for the comparative material of Part IV, which examines several microproblems in the context of economic planning. You should also have time to include a supplement.

Third, some courses emphasize history and institutions, and deemphasize theory. We believe that our book is better suited for such a course than any other available complete text. All of Part I could be emphasized. In Part II, most of Chapters 13 through 17 could be omitted, although 13 gives a very simple introduction, and the material on poverty at the beginning of Chapter 15 should surely be emphasized. Also, Chapters 18, 19, and 20 are mainly institutional. In Part III, Chapters 23, 24, and 25 could be omitted. The other chapters are mainly institutional, although certain sections referring to multipliers might be omitted. In Part IV, Chapter 36 is somewhat theoretical and could be omitted. The rest of this part is heavily historical and institutional.

E. K. Hunt
Howard J. Sherman

acknowledgments

We are profoundly grateful to those whose teaching or direct help made this book possible: Professors Sidney Coontz, William Davisson, Douglas Dowd, Robert Edminster, David Felix, John Gurley, J. W. Hanks, Kiyotoshi Iwamoto, Robert Lekachman, Lawrence Nabors, Andreas Papandreou, Lynn Turgeon, Benjamin Ward, Thomas Weisskopf, and Stephen Worland. Extensive research help, for which we express our thanks, was furnished by Professor Maryanna Boynton.

We also wish to thank various publishers for giving us permission to use certain materials from our previous books: Hunt, *Property and Prophets* (Harper & Row, 1972); Sherman, *Elementary Aggregate Economics* (Appleton-Century-Crofts, 1966); Sherman, *The Soviet Economy* (Little, Brown, 1969); Sherman, *Profit Rates in the United States* (Cornell University Press, 1968); and Sherman, *Radical Political Economy* (Basic Books, 1972).

part one

property and prophets: the evolution of economic institutions and ideologies

chapter 1
the ideology of
precapitalistic europe

Human beings must exist in societies in order to survive. Unlike some
species of animals, whose individual members can exist fairly
adequately in relative isolation, human beings are not equipped by
nature with the physical prowess individually to provide the material
requisites of life. Humans survive and indeed prosper because by
living in groups, they have learned to subdivide tasks and use tools.
It was this division of labor and the accumulation of more and better
tools (or capital) that made possible the impressive increases in
man's control over nature, or increases in man's potential to produce
the material necessities of life.

   This division of labor also resulted, of necessity, in a differentiation
of the roles that the different members of a society occupy. This
differentiation was probably purely functional in earliest times; that
is, when productivity was low, all members of a society lived near
the subsistence level and social class, or hierarchical, differentiation
was absent. Increasingly elaborate divisions of tasks, combined with
more sophisticated tools, however, led to higher productivity which
made possible the escape from the drudgery of everyday toil for at
least a small part of society.

   A small leisure class could be supported because with higher
per capita productivity, the labor of a smaller number of persons
could support the entire society at its customary standard of living
or at an even higher standard. When this occurred, societies began
to differentiate among their members according to social class. This

hierarchical class differentiation was generally economic in nature. Those who worked were usually assigned to the lowest classes; those who escaped the burdens of ordinary labor were of higher class standing. Although these higher-class persons no longer were directly connected with the production of everyday necessities, they often performed rites, rituals, or extensive duties, some of which were undoubtedly beneficial to the society.

As human productive and social relations became more complex, an economic system evolved. An *economic system* is a set of principles, laws, or customs by which society assures itself that persons with appropriate skills are available to perform the necessary productive tasks at the proper place and time. The economic system also provides a mechanism to allocate properly the produced goods and services among the different social classes. Moreover, the system determines the size of the shares going to different persons within the various classes.

Such a system could not continue to exist for long if the majority of its members did not share common feelings about the proper way of conducting economic and social affairs. These common feelings and values, which generally stemmed from a common world view, or system of metaphysics, justified both the division of productive tasks and the class differentiation that existed. These common feelings and values were expressed in ideologies.

An *ideology,* as the term is used in this book, refers to those ideas and beliefs that tend to justify morally a society's social and economic relationships. Most members of a society internalize the ideology and thus believe that their functional role as well as the functional roles of others are morally correct and that the method by which society divides its produce is fair. This common belief gives society its cohesiveness and viability. Lack of it creates turmoil and strife—and ultimately revolution, if the differences are deep enough!

This book is primarily concerned with our present economic system: capitalism. We sketch the broad outlines of the evolution of this system. In doing so, we focus on conflicts and social antagonisms and examine the ideologies with which the capitalist system attempted to mitigate these conflicts and to promote social cohesiveness.

From its beginning, the capitalist system created a large class of rebels, dreamers, and visionaries who rejected it. They mentally constructed utopian schemes of how a good society should be organized and used these schemes as the basis for moral attacks on the excesses and suffering they saw in the capitalist system. Throughout most of its history, the socialist movement was no more than anticapitalist ideas, writings, propaganda, and agitation. Only in the twentieth century has the term *socialism* been used to describe an actual, existing economy.

Throughout most of this book, we shall be concerned with the economic, social, and ethical views that have been used either to defend or to attack capitalism. By way of background, we shall first examine the code of ethics that can be traced from its biblical Judeo-Christian origins to its zenith in medieval feudal society. Feudal society was the social and economic system from which capitalism evolved. The Judeo-Christian tradition, which was the basis of medieval ideology, proved to be incompatible with many of the institutions and practices necessary for the maintenance of capitalism. This conflict of the traditional religious and moral code with the emerging economic and social system, and the ways in which men sought to resolve this conflict, provides a framework that is helpful in understanding the later critiques and defenses of capitalism.

Men who sought to provide an intellectual defense for the new capitalist system proceeded along two separate paths. Some tried to modify and alter certain key elements of the Judeo-Christian ethic. Others abandoned that ethical and philosophical tradition completely and embraced a new philosophical world view compatible with capitalism. The conflicts between these two basic types of capitalist ideologies will be explored in later chapters.

There was still another way of reconciling the conflict between the Judeo-Christian ethical tradition and the emerging capitalist system. One could reject the institutions and practices of capitalism that conflicted with the ethical tradition. This course of thought gave impetus to the socialist movement, and certain elements of the Judeo-Christian ethic had (and still have) a very important influence in the formation of socialist as well as capitalist ideologies.

the christian corporate ethic

The Judeo-Christian moral code will be called the *Christian corporate ethic* in this book. It can be understood most easily by comparing society with a family. Those with positions of power and wealth can be likened to the father or keeper of the family. They have strong paternalistic obligations toward the common people, the poor, or in our analogy, the children. The common man, however, is expected to accept his place in the society and to subordinate himself willingly to the leadership of the wealthy and the powerful in much the same way that a child accepts the authority of his father.

The Old Testament Jews[1] quite literally regarded themselves as the children of one God. This relationship meant that all Jews were

1 This account relies on Alexander Gray, *The Socialist Tradition* (London: Longmans, 1963), chap. 2.

brothers; the Mosaic law was intended to maintain this feeling of membership in one big family. This brotherhood was one of grown children who acknowledged their mutual obligations, even though they no longer shared possessions.

From the confused mass of duties and regulations governing the early Jews, the most salient feature is the large number of provisions made for the prevention and relief of poverty. Their humane treatment of debtors was also notable. Each Jew was to be his brother's keeper; indeed, the obligations extended to caring for his neighbor's animals should they wander his way.[2] The first duty of all, however, and even more particularly of the wealthy, was the caring for the poor: "Thou shalt open thine hand wide unto thy brother, to the poor, and to the needy, in the land."[3] An important element in this paternalistic code was the sanction against taking a worker's tools as a means of satisfying a debt: "No man shall take the nether or the upper millstone to pledge: for he taketh a man's life to pledge."[4] The same point was made elsewhere in the Old Testament: "He that taketh away his neighbor's living slayeth him."[5]

All Jews did not, of course, live up to these lofty professions. Great extremes of wealth and poverty existed that would have been impossible had the Mosaic law been strictly observed. Many of the prophets, who were often radical champions of the poor, eloquently denounced the rich for their abuse of their wealth, for their wicked, slothful luxury and general unrighteousness. The important point is not that they failed to live up to the code, but that the moral code of this small tribe left so important an imprint on much of subsequent history.

The teachings of Christ in the New Testament carry on part of the Mosaic tradition relevant to economic ideology. He taught the necessity of being concerned with the welfare of one's brother, the importance of charity and almsgiving, and the evil of selfish acquisitiveness and covetousness. His emphasis on the special responsibilities and obligations of the rich is even more pronounced than that of the earlier Jewish writers. In fact, on the basis of a reading of the Gospel of Luke, one might conclude that Christ condemned the rich simply because they were rich and praised the poor simply because they were poor: "Woe unto you that are rich! . . . Woe unto you that are full! for ye shall hunger. Woe unto you that laugh now! for ye shall mourn and weep."[6] However, on

2 Deut., 22:1–4.
3 Deut., 15:7–11.
4 Deut., 24:6.
5 Eccles., 34:22.
6 Quoted in Gray, op. cit., p. 41.

examining the other Gospels, it must be concluded, that this probably is Luke speaking, not Christ. Luke must be seen as the radical "leveller among the apostles."[7]

In the other Gospels, there are warnings that wealth may be a stumbling block in getting to heaven, but there is no condemnation of wealth as such. The most important passages in this regard deal with the wealthy young man who wants to know what he must do to attain eternal life.[8] Christ's first answer amounts to nothing more than a brief statement of the Ten Commandments. It is only after being pressed further that Christ goes beyond the binding, universal moral requirements to a counsel of perfection. "If thou wilt be perfect"[9] begins the statement in which he tells the young man to sell whatever he has and give to the poor.

The Christian corporate ethic, with its paternalistic obligations of the wealthy toward the poor, was developed more specifically and elaborately by most of the later Christian fathers. The writings of Clement of Alexandria are a reasonably good reflection of the traditional attitudes of the early church. He emphasized the dangers of greed, love of material things, and acquiring of wealth. Those who had wealth were under a special obligation to treat it as a gift of God and to use it wisely in the promotion of the general well-being of others.

Clement's *The Rich Man's Salvation* was written in order to free the rich of the "unfounded despair" they might have acquired from reading passages in the Gospels, such as those found in Luke. Clement began by asserting that contrary to anything one might find in Luke, "it is no great or enviable thing to be simply without riches." Those who were poor would not for that reason alone find God's blessedness. In order to seek salvation, the rich man need not renounce his wealth, but need merely "banish from the soul its opinions about riches, its attachment to them, its excessive desire, its morbid excitement over them, its anxious cares, the thorns of our earthly existence which choke the seed of the true life."[10]

Not the possession of wealth, but the way in which it was used was important to Clement. The wealthy were given the responsibility of administering their wealth, on God's behalf, to alleviate the suffering and promote the general welfare of their brothers. In decreeing that the hungry should be fed and the naked should be clothed, God certainly had not willed a situation in which no one could carry out these commandments for lack of sufficient material prerequisites.

7 Ibid., p. 42.

8 Matt., 19:16–26; Mark, 10:17–27; Luke, 18.

9 Matt., 19.

10 Quoted in Gray, op. cit., p. 48.

It followed, thus, that God had willed that some men should have wealth, but had given them the important function of paternalistically caring for the well-being of the rest of society.

In a similar vein, Ambrose wrote that "riches themselves are not blamable" as long as they are used righteously. In order to use wealth righteously, "we ought to be of mutual help one to the other, and to vie with each other in doing duties, to lay all our advantages . . . before all, and . . . to bring help one to the other."[11]

The list of Christian fathers who wrote lengthy passages to the same effect could be expanded greatly. Suffice it to say that by the early feudal period, the Christian corporate ethic was thoroughly entrenched in western European culture. Greed, avarice, materialistic self-seeking, the desire to accumulate wealth—all such individualistic and materialistic motives—were sharply condemned. The acquisitive, individualistic person was considered the very antithesis of the good man, who concerned himself with the well-being of all his brothers. The wealthy man had the potential to do either great good or great evil with his wealth and power, and the worst evil resulted when wealth was used either exclusively for self-gratification or as a means of continually acquiring more wealth for its own sake. The righteously wealthy were those who realized that their wealth and power were God's gift, that they were morally obligated to act as paternalistic stewards, and that they were to administrate worldly affairs in order to promote the welfare of all.

This Christian corporate ethic reached its zenith during the feudal period of European history. Because the feudal manorial system was the social and economic system that immediately preceded capitalism, the evolution of capitalism can best be understood if the feudal manorial society and its Christian ideology are examined first.

feudalism

The decline of the western part of the old Roman Empire left Europe without the laws and protection that the empire had provided. The vacuum was filled by the creation of a feudal hierarchy. In this hierarchy, the serf, or peasant, was protected by the lord of the manor, who in turn owed allegiance to and was protected by an overlord, who himself owed allegiance to and was protected by a higher overlord. And so the system went, ending eventually with the king. The strong protected the weak, but they did so at a high price. In return for payments of money, food, labor, or military allegiance,

11 Ibid., p. 49.

overlords granted the fief, or feudum—a hereditary right to use land—to their vassals. At the bottom was the serf, a peasant who tilled the land. The vast majority of the population raised crops for food or clothing or tended sheep for wool and clothing.[12]

Custom and tradition are the key to understanding medieval relationships. In place of laws as we know them today, the *custom of the manor* governed. There was no strong central authority in the Middle Ages that could have enforced a system of laws. The entire medieval organization was based on a system of mutual obligations and services up and down the hierarchy. Possession or use of the land obligated one to certain customary services or payments in return for protection. The lord was as obligated to protect the serf as the serf was to turn over a portion of his crop to or perform extensive labor for the lord.

Customs were broken, of course; no system always operates in fact as it is designed to operate in theory. One should not, however, underestimate the strength of custom and tradition in determining the lives and ideas of medieval people. Disputes between serfs were decided in the lords' courts according to both the special circumstances of each case and the general customs of the manor for such cases. Of course, a dispute between a serf and a lord would usually be decided in his own favor by the lord. Even in this circumstance, however, especially in England, an overlord would impose sanctions or punishments on a lord who, as his vassal, had persistently violated the customs in his treatment of serfs. This rule by the custom of the manor stands in sharp contrast to the legal and judicial system of capitalism. The capitalist system is based on the enforcement of contracts and universally binding laws, which are only rarely softened by the possible mitigating circumstances and customs that often swayed the lord's judgment in medieval times.

The extent to which the lords could enforce their "rights" varied greatly from time to time and from place to place. It was the strengthening of these obligations and the nobleman's ability to enforce them through a long hierarchy of vassals and over a wide area, that eventually led to the emergence of the modern nation-states. This process occurred during the period of transition from feudalism to capitalism. Throughout most of the Middle Ages, however, many of the claims were very weak because political control was very fragmented.

The basic economic institution of medieval rural life was the manor, which contained within it two separate and distinct classes: noble-

---

12 For a more complete discussion of the medieval economic and social system, see J. H. Claphan and Eileen E. Power, eds., *The Agrarian Life of the Middle Ages*, 2nd ed, The Cambridge Economic History of Europe, vol. I (London: Cambridge University Press, 1966).

men, or lords of the manors, and the serfs (from the Latin word *servus,* or "slave"). Serfs were not really slaves. Unlike a slave, who was simply property to be bought and sold at will, the serf could not be parted from either his family or his land. If his lord transferred possession of the manor to another nobleman, the serf simply had another lord. In varying degrees, however, obligations were placed upon the serfs that were sometimes very onerous and from which there was often no escape. Usually, they were far from being "free."

The lord lived off the labor of the serfs who farmed his fields and paid taxes in kind and money according to the custom of the manor. Similarly, the lord gave protection, supervision, and administration of justice according to the custom of the manor. It must be added that although the system did rest on reciprocal obligations, the concentration of economic and political power in the hands of the lord led to a system in which, by any standard, the serf was exploited in the extreme.

The Catholic church was by far the largest owner of land during the Middle Ages. While bishops and abbots occupied much the same place as counts and dukes in the feudal hierarchy, there was one important difference between the religious and the secular lords. Dukes and counts might shift their loyalty from one overlord to another (depending on the circumstances and the balance of power involved), but the bishops and abbots always had (in principle at least) a primary loyalty to the church in Rome. This was also an age during which the religious teaching of the church had a very strong and pervasive influence throughout western Europe. These factors combined to make the church the closest thing to a strong, central government throughout this period.

Thus, the manor might be secular or religious (many times secular lords had religious overlords and vice versa), but the essential relationships between the lords and the serfs were not significantly affected by this distinction. There is little evidence that serfs were treated any less harshly by religious lords than by secular lords. The church lords and the secular nobility were the joint ruling classes; they controlled the land and the power that went with it. In return for very onerous appropriations of the serfs' labor, produce, and money, the nobility provided military protection and the church provided spiritual aid.

In addition to manors, medieval Europe had many towns, which were important centers of manufacturing. Manufactured goods were sold to manors and, sometimes, were traded in long-distance commerce. The dominant economic institutions in the towns were the guilds—craft, professional, and trade associations that had existed as far back as the Roman Empire. If anyone wanted to produce or sell any good or service, he had to join a guild.

The guilds were as involved with social and religious as with economic questions. They regulated their members' conduct in all their activities: personal, social, religious, and economic. Although the guilds did regulate very carefully the production and sale of commodities, they were less concerned with making profits than with saving their members' souls. Salvation demanded that the individual lead an orderly life based upon church teachings and custom. Thus, the guilds exerted a powerful influence as conservators of the status quo in the medieval towns.

the anticapitalist nature of feudal ideology

The philosophical and religious assumptions upon which medieval people acted were extensions of the Christian corporate ethic. The many particular additions to the ethic were profoundly conservative in purpose and content. Both the continuity in and conservative modifications of the ethic can be seen in the writings of Thomas Aquinas, the preeminent spokesman of the Middle Ages.

Tradition was upheld in his insistence that private property could be justified *morally* only because it was a necessary condition for almsgiving. The rich, he asserted, must always be "ready to distribute, . . . [and] willing to communicate."[13] Aquinas believed, with the earlier fathers, that "the rich man, if he does not give alms, is a thief."[14] The rich man held wealth and power for God and for all society. He administered his wealth for God and for the common good of mankind. Without proper use and administration of this wealth, it could no longer be religiously and morally justified, in which case the wealthy man was to be considered a common thief.

Aquinas' and, indeed, most of the medieval church fathers' profoundly conservative addition to the Christian corporate ethic was their insistence that the economic and social relationships of the medieval manorial system reflected a natural and eternal ordering of these relationships. Indeed, these relationships were ordained by God. They stressed the importance of a division of labor and effort, with different tasks assigned to the different classes, and insisted that the social and economic distinctions between the classes were necessary to accommodate this specialization.

If one was in the position of a lord (secular or religious), it was necessary to have an abundance of material wealth in order to do

13 Gray, op. cit., p. 57.
14 Ibid.

well the tasks that providence had assigned. Of course, it took almost nothing to perform the tasks expected of a serf. It was every person's duty to labor unquestioningly at the task to which providence had assigned him, to accept the station into which he was born, and to accept the rights of others to have and do those things appropriate to their stations in life. Thus, despite its paternalism, the Christian corporate ethic could be used (and was used) to defend as natural and just the great inequities and intense exploitation that flowed from the concentration of wealth and power in the hands of the church and nobility.

Any account of medieval social and economic thought must also stress the great disdain with which they viewed trade and commerce and the commercial spirit. The medieval way of life was based upon custom and tradition; its viability depended upon the members of society accepting that tradition and their place within it. Where the capitalist commercial ethic prevails, greed, selfishness, covetousness, and the desire to better oneself materially or socially are accepted by most people as innate qualities. Yet they were uniformly denounced and reviled in the Middle Ages. The serfs (and, sometimes, the lower nobility) tended to be dissatisfied with the traditions and customs of medieval society, and thus threatened the stability of the feudal system. It is not surprising, therefore, to find pervasive moral sanctions designed to repress or to mitigate the effects of these motives.

One of the most important of such sanctions, which was repeated over and over throughout this period, was the insistence that it was the moral duty of merchants and traders to transact all trade or exchanges at the just price. This notion illustrates the role that paternalistic social control played in the feudal era. A *just price* was one that would compensate the seller for his efforts in transporting the good and in finding the buyer at a rate that was just sufficient to maintain the seller at his *customary* or *traditional* station in life. Prices above the just price would, of course, lead to profits, which would be accumulated as material wealth.

It was the lust for wealth that the Christian corporate ethic consistently condemned. Thus, the doctrine of the just price was intended as a curb on such acquisitive and socially disruptive behavior. Then as now, the accumulation of material wealth was a passport to greater power and upward social mobility. This social mobility was eventually to prove totally destructive of the medieval system because it put an end to the status relationships that were the backbone of medieval society.

Another example of this condemnation of acquisitive behavior was the prohibition on usury, or the loaning of money at interest. A "bill against usury" that was passed in England reflected the attitudes of most of the people of those times. It read in part:

> But forasmuch as usury is by the word of God utterly prohibited, as a vice most odious and detestable . . . which thing, by no godly teachings and persuasions can sink in to the hearts of divers greedy, uncharitable and covetous person of this Realm . . . be it enacted . . . that . . . no person or persons of what Estate, degree, quality or condition so ever he or they be, by any corrupt, colorable or deceitful conveyance, sleight or engine, or by any way or mean, shall lend, give, set out, deliver or forbear any sum or sums of money . . . to or for any manner of usury, increase, lucre, gain or interest to be had, received or hoped for, over and above the sum or sums so lent . . . as also of the usury . . . upon pain of imprisonment.[15]

The church believed that usury was the worst sort of acquisitive behavior because most loans upon which interest was charged were granted to poor farmers or peasants after a bad crop or some other tragedy had befallen them. Thus, interest was a gain made at the expense of one's brother at a time when he was most in need of help and charity. Of course, the Christian ethic strongly condemned such rapacious exploitation of a needy brother.

Many historians have pointed out that bishops and abbots as well as dukes, counts, and kings often flagrantly violated these sanctions. They themselves granted loans at interest, even while they were punishing others for doing so. We are more interested, however, in the values and motives of the period than in the sins and infractions of the rules. The values of the feudal system stand in stark, antithetical contrast to those that were shortly to prevail under a capitalist system. The desires to maximize monetary gain, to accumulate material wealth, and to advance oneself socially and economically through acquisitive behavior were to become the dominant motive forces in the capitalist system.

The sins that were most strongly denounced within the context of the Christian corporate ethic were to become the behavioral assumptions upon which the entire capitalist market economy was to be based. It is obvious that such a radical change would render the Christian corporate ethic, at least in its medieval version, inadequate as the basis of a moral justification of the new capitalist system. The ethic would have to be modified drastically or rejected completely in order to elaborate a defense for the new system. Attempts to do both are explored in subsequent chapters.

15 Quoted in Leo Huberman, *Man's Worldly Goods* (New York: Monthly Review Press, 1961), p. 39.

summary

Economic systems organize human effort to transform the resources given in nature into usable articles, or economic goods. Ideologies are systems of ideas and beliefs that are used to justify morally the economic and social relationships within an economic system.

The Christian corporate ethic was used to justify the feudal economy and its attendant social and economic relationships. This ideology contained elements that were antithetical to the functioning of a capitalist market system. In later chapters, we shall examine the ways in which men attempted to substitute new ideologies for the older Christian corporate ethic or to modify this ethic in such a way that it could be used to provide a moral justification of a capitalist market economic system.

chapter 2
the transition to early capitalism and the beginnings of the mercantilist view

The medieval society was an agrarian society. The social hierarchy was based on individuals' ties to the land, and the entire social system rested on an agricultural base. Yet, ironically, increases in agricultural productivity were the original impetus to a series of profound changes. These changes, occurring over several centuries, resulted in the dissolution of medieval feudalism and the beginnings of capitalism.

changes in technology

The most important technological advance in the Middle Ages was the replacement of the two-field system of crop rotation with the three-field system. Although there is evidence that the three-field system was introduced into Europe as early as the eighth century, its use was probably not widespread until around the eleventh century.

Yearly sowing of the same land would deplete the land and eventually make it unusable. Consequently, in the two-field system, one-half of the land was always allowed to lie fallow in order to recover from the previous year's planting.

With the three-field system, arable land was divided into three equal fields. Rye or winter wheat would be planted in the fall in the first field. Oats, beans, or peas would be planted in the spring in the second field. The third field would lie fallow. In each subsequent year there was a rotation of these positions. Any given piece of land would have a fall planting one year, a spring planting the next year, and would lie fallow the third year.

A dramatic increase in agricultural output resulted from this seemingly simple change in agricultural technology. With the same amount of arable land, the three-field system could increase the amount under cultivation at any particular time by as much as 50 percent.[1]

The three-field system led to other important changes. Spring sowing of oats and other fodder crops enabled the people to support more horses, which began to replace oxen as the principal source of power in agriculture. Horses were much faster than oxen, and consequently, the region under cultivation could be extended. Larger cultivated areas enabled the countryside to support more concentrated population centers. Transportation of men, commodities, and equipment was much more efficient with horses. Greater efficiency was also attained in plowing: A team of oxen required three men to do the plowing; a horse-drawn plow could be operated by one man. The costs of transporting agricultural products was substantially reduced in the thirteenth century, when the four-wheeled wagon with a pivoted front axle replaced the two-wheeled cart.

These improvements in agriculture and transportation contributed to two important and far-reaching changes. First, they made possible a rapid increase in population growth. The best historical estimates show that the population of Europe doubled between 1000 and 1300.[2] Second, closely related to the expansion of population was a rapid increase in urban concentration. Prior to the year 1000, most of Europe, except for a few Mediterranean trade centers, consisted of only manors, villages, and a few small towns. By 1300, there were many thriving cities and larger towns.

The growth of towns and cities led to a growth of rural–urban specialization. With urban workers severing all ties to the soil, the output of manufactured goods increased impressively. Along with increased manufacturing and increased economic specialization came many additional gains in human productivity. Interregional, long-distance trade and commerce was also a very important result of this increased specialization.

1 Lynn White, Jr., *Medieval Technology and Social Change* (Oxford: Clarendon, 1962) pp. 71–72.

2 Harry A. Miskimin, *The Economy of Early Renaissance Europe, 1300–1460* (Englewood Cliffs, N.J.: Prentice-Hall, 1969) p. 20.

the increase in long-distance trade

The single most persistent force that led to the disintegration of medieval traditions and customs was the spread of trade and commerce. The expansion of trade, particularly long-distance trade in the early period, led to the establishment of commercial and industrial towns that serviced this trade. And the growth of these cities and towns, and their increased domination by merchant capitalists, led to important changes in both industry and agriculture. Each of these areas of change, particularly the latter, brought about a weakening and ultimately a complete dissolving of the traditional ties that held together the feudal economic and social structure.

From the earliest part of the medieval period, some long-distance trade had been carried on throughout many parts of Europe. This trade was very important in southern Europe, on the Mediterranean and Adriatic seas, and in northern Europe, on the North and Baltic seas. Between these two centers of commercialism, however, the feudal manorial system in most of the rest of Europe was relatively unaffected by commerce and trade until the later Middle Ages.

From about the eleventh century onward, the Christian Crusades in southern Europe and the piracy and commerce of the Vikings in northern Europe gave the impetus to a marked expansion of commerce from both directions. This development led to the great trade fairs that flourished from the twelfth through the late fourteenth centuries. Held annually in the principal European trading cities, these fairs usually lasted from one to several weeks. Northern European merchants exchanged their grain, fish, wool, cloth, timber, pitch, tar, salt, and iron for the spices, silks, brocades, wines, fruits, and gold and silver that were the dominant items in southern European commerce.[3]

By the fifteenth century, the fairs were being replaced by commercial cities where year-round markets thrived. The trade and commerce of these cities was incompatible with restrictive feudal customs and traditions. Generally, the cities were successful in gaining independence from church and feudal lords. Within these commercial centers there arose complex systems of currency exchange, debt-clearing, and credit facilities, and modern business instruments such as bills of exchange came into widespread use. New systems of *commercial law* developed. Unlike the system of

[3] For a more complete discussion of the rise of trade and commerce, see Dudley Dillard, *Economic Development of the North Atlantic Community* (Englewood Cliffs, N.J.: Prentice-Hall, 1967), pp. 3–178.

paternalistic adjudication based upon custom and tradition that prevailed in the manor, the commercial law was fixed by precise code. Hence, it became the basis of the modern capitalistic law of contracts, negotiable instruments, agency sales, and auctions.

In the manorial handicraft industry, the producer (the master craftsman) was also the seller. The industries that burgeoned in the new cities, however, were primarily export industries in which the producer was distant from the final buyer. Craftsmen sold their goods wholesale to merchants, who, in turn, transported and resold them. Another important difference was that the manorial craftsman was also generally a farmer. The new city craftsman gave up farming to devote himself to his craft, with which he obtained a money income that could be used to satisfy his other needs.

the putting-out system
and the birth of capitalist industry

As trade and commerce thrived and expanded, the need for more manufactured goods and greater reliability of supply led to increasing control of the productive process by the merchant-capitalist. By the sixteenth century, the handicraft type of industry, in which the craftsman owned his workshop, tools, and raw materials and functioned as an independent, small-scale entrepreneur, had largely been replaced in the exporting industries by the putting-out system. In the earliest period of the *putting-out system,* the merchant-capitalist would furnish an independent craftsman with raw materials, and pay him a fee to work the materials into finished products. In this way, the capitalist owned the product throughout all stages of production, although the work was done in independent workshops. In the later period of the putting-out system, the merchant-capitalist owned the tools and machinery and often owned the building in which the production took place. He hired workers to use these tools, furnished them with the raw materials, and took the finished products.

The worker no longer sold a finished product to the merchant. Rather, he sold only his labor power. The textile industries were among the first in which the putting-out system developed. Weavers, spinners, fullers, and dyers found themselves in a situation where their employment, and hence their ability to support themselves and their families, depended upon the merchant-capitalists who had to sell what the workers produced at a price that was high enough to pay wages and other costs and still make a profit.

Capitalist control was, then, extended into the process of production. At the same time, a labor force was created that owned little or no capital and had nothing to sell but its labor power. These two features mark the appearance of the economic system of capitalism. Some writers and historians have defined capitalism as existing when trade, commerce, and the commercial spirit expanded and became more important in Europe. Trade and commerce, however, had existed throughout the feudal era. Yet as long as feudal tradition remained the organizing principle in production, trade and commerce were really outside the social and economic system. The market and the search for money profits replaced custom and tradition in determining who would perform what task, how the task would be performed, and whether a given worker could find work to support himself. When this occurred, the capitalist system was created.[4]

Capitalism became dominant with the extension to most lines of production of the relationship that existed between capitalists and workers in the sixteenth-century export industries. For such a system to evolve, the economic self-sufficiency of the feudal manor had to be broken down and manorial customs and traditions had to be undermined or destroyed. Agriculture had to become a capitalistic venture in which workers would sell their labor power to capitalists, and capitalists would buy labor only if they expected to make a profit in the process.

A capitalist textile industry existed in Flanders in the thirteenth century. When, for various reasons, its prosperity began to decline, the wealth and poverty it had created led to a long series of violent class wars, starting around 1280, that almost completely destroyed the industry. In the fourteenth century, a capitalist textile industry flourished in Florence. There, as in Flanders, adverse business conditions led to tensions between a poverty-stricken working class and their affluent capitalist employers. The results of these tensions were violent rebellions in 1379 and 1382. Failure to resolve these class antagonisms significantly worsened the precipitous decline in the Florentine textile industry, as it had done earlier in Flanders.

In the fifteenth century, England dominated the world textile market. Its capitalist textile industry solved the problem of class conflict by ruralizing the industry. Whereas the earlier capitalist textile industries of Flanders and Florence had been in the densely populated cities, where the workers were thrown together and organized resistance was easy to initiate, the English fulling mills were scattered about the countryside. This meant that the workers were isolated from all but a small handful of other workers, and effective organized resistance did not develop.

4 See Maurice H. Dobb, *Studies in the Development of Capitalism* (London: Routledge & Kegan Paul, 1946), particularly chap. 4.

The later system, however, in which wealthy owners of capital employed propertyless craftsmen, was usually a phenomenon of the city rather than of the countryside. From the beginning, these capitalistic enterprises sought monopolistic positions from which to exploit the demand for their products. The rise of livery guilds, or associations of merchant-capitalist employers, created a host of barriers to protect their position. Different types of apprenticeships, with special privileges and exemptions for the sons of the wealthy, excessively high membership fees, and other barriers, prevented ambitious poorer craftsmen from competing with, or entering, the new capitalist class. Indeed, these barriers generally resulted in the transformation of poorer craftsmen and their sons into a new urban working class that lived exclusively by selling its labor power.

the decline of the manorial system

Before a complete system of capitalism could emerge, however, the force of capitalist market relations had to invade the rural manor, the bastion of feudalism. The vast increase of population in the new trading cities led to this penetration into the manor. Large urban populations depended upon the rural countryside for food and much of the raw materials for export industries. These needs fostered a rural–urban specialization and a large flow of trade between the rural manor and the city. The lords of the manors began to depend on the cities for manufactured goods and increasingly came to desire luxury goods that merchants could sell to them.

The peasants on the manor also found they could exchange surpluses for money at the local grain markets, which could be used by the peasants to purchase commutation of their labor services.[5] Commutation often resulted in a situation in which the peasant became very nearly an independent small businessman. He might rent the land from the lord, sell the produce to cover the rents, and retain the remaining revenues himself. This system gave peasants a higher incentive to produce and thereby increased their surplus marketings, which led to more commutations, more subsequent marketings, and so forth. The cumulative effect was a very gradual breaking down of the traditional ties of the manor and a substitution of the market and the search for profits as the organizing principle of production. By the middle of the fourteenth century, money rents in many parts of Europe exceeded the value of labor services.

Another force that brought the market into the countryside and

[5] Commutation involved the substitution of money rents for the labor services required of the serf.

that was closely related to commutation was the alienation of the lords' demesnes. The lords who needed cash to exchange for manufactured goods and luxuries began to rent their own lands to peasant farmers, rather than having them farmed directly with labor-service obligations. This process led increasingly to a situation in which the lord of the manor was simply a landlord in the modern sense of that term. In fact, he very often became an absentee landlord, as many lords chose to move to the cities or were away fighting battles.

The breakup of the manorial system, however, stemmed more directly from a series of catastrophies in the late fourteenth and fifteenth centuries. The Hundred Years' War between France and England (1337–1453) created general disorder and unrest in those countries. The Black Death was even more devastating. On the eve of the plague of 1348–1349, England's population stood at 4 million. By the early fifteenth century, after the effects of the wars and the plague, England had a scant 2.5-million population. This was fairly typical of trends in other European countries. The depopulation led to a desperate labor shortage, and wages for all types of labor rose abruptly. Land, now relatively more plentiful, began to rent for less.

These facts led the feudal nobility to attempt to revoke the commutations they had granted and to reestablish the labor-service obligations of the serfs and peasants (peasants were former serfs who had attained some degree of independence and freedom from feudal restrictions). They found, however, that the clock could not be turned back. The market had been extended into the countryside, and with it had come greater freedom, independence, and prosperity for the peasants. They bitterly resisted efforts to reinstate the old obligations. Their resistance did not go unchallenged.

The result was the famous peasant revolts that broke out all over Europe from the late fourteenth through the early sixteenth centuries. These rebellions were extreme in their cruelty and ferocity. A contemporary French writer described a band of peasants who killed a "knight and putting him on a broach, roasted him over a fire in the sight of his wife and children. Ten or twelve of them ravished the wife and then forced her to eat of her husband's flesh. Then they killed her and her children. Wherever these ungracious people went they destroyed good houses and strong castles."[6] Rebellious peasants were ultimately slaughtered with equal or greater cruelty and ferocity by the nobility.

England experienced a series of such revolts in the late fourteenth and fifteenth centuries. But the revolts that occurred in Germany in the early sixteenth century were probably the bloodiest of all. The

[6] N. S. B. Gras, *A History of Agriculture in Europe and America* (New York: Appleton, 1940), p. 108.

peasant rebellion in 1524–1525 was crushed by the Imperial troops of the Holy Roman emperor, who slaughtered peasants by the tens of thousands. Over 100,000 persons probably were killed in Germany alone.

These revolts are mentioned here to illustrate the fact that fundamental changes in the economic and political structure of a social system are often achieved only after traumatic and violent social conflict. Any economic system generates a class or classes whose privileges are dependent on the continuation of that system. Quite naturally, these classes go to great lengths to resist change and to protect their positions. The feudal nobility fought a savage rearguard action against the emerging capitalist market system, but the forces of change ultimately swept them aside. Although the important changes were brought about by aspiring merchants and minor noblemen, the peasants were the pathetic victims of the consequent social upheavals. Ironically, the peasants were usually struggling to protect the status quo.

other forces in the transition to capitalism

The early sixteenth century is a watershed in European history. It vaguely marks the dividing line between the old, decaying feudal order and the rising capitalist system. After 1500, important social and economic changes began to occur with increasing frequency, each reinforcing the other, and together having the cumulative effect of ushering in the system of capitalism. The population of western Europe, which had been relatively stagnant for a century and a half, increased by nearly a third in the sixteenth century and stood at about 70 million in 1600.

The increase in population was accompanied by the *enclosure movement,* which had begun in England as early as the thirteenth century. The feudal nobility, in ever-increasing need of cash, fenced off, or enclosed, lands that had formerly been used for communal grazing. Enclosed lands were used to graze sheep to satisfy the booming English wool and textile industries' demand for wool. The sheep brought good prices, and a minimal amount of labor was needed to herd them.

The enclosure movement reached its peak in the late fifteenth and sixteenth centuries when, in some areas, as many as three-fourths to nine-tenths of the tenants were forced out of the countryside and into the cities to try to support themselves. The enclosures and the increasing population further destroyed the remaining feudal ties, creating a large, new labor force—a labor force without land, without any tools or instruments of production, and with only their labor power to sell. This migration to the cities meant more labor for the capitalist industries, more men for the armies and navies, more men to colonize new lands, and more potential consumers, or buyers of products.

Another important source of change was the intellectual awakening of the sixteenth century, which fostered scientific progress that was promptly put to practical use in navigation. The telescope and the compass enabled men to navigate much more accurately for much greater distances. Hence, the "Age of Exploration." Within a short period of time, Europeans had charted sea routes to India, Africa, and the Americas. These discoveries had a twofold importance. First, they resulted in a rapid and large flow of precious metals into Europe, and second, they ushered in a period of colonization.

Between 1300 and 1500, European gold and silver production had stagnated. The rapidly expanding capitalist trade and the extension of the market system into city and countryside had led to an acute shortage of money. Because money consisted primarily of gold and silver coin, the need for these metals was critical. Beginning around 1450, this situation was alleviated somewhat when the Portuguese began extracting metals from the African Gold Coast, but the general shortage continued until the middle of the sixteenth century. After that date, there occurred such a large inflow of gold and silver from the Americas that Europe experienced the most rapid and long-lasting inflation in history.

During the sixteenth century, prices rose in Europe between 150 and 400 percent, depending upon the country or region chosen. Prices of manufactured goods rose much more rapidly than either rents or wages. In fact, the disparity between prices and wages continued until late in the seventeenth century. This meant that the landlord class (or feudal nobility) and the working class both suffered, because their income rose less rapidly than did their expenses. The capitalist class was the great beneficiary of the price revolution. They received larger and larger profits as they paid lower real wages and bought materials that appreciated greatly as they held them as inventories.

These larger profits were accumulated as capital. *Capital* refers to the materials that are necessary for production, trade, and commerce. It consists of all tools, equipment, factories, raw materials and goods in process, means of transporting goods, and money. The essence of the capitalist system is the existence of a class of capitalists who own the capital stock. It is by virtue of their ownership of this capital that they derive their profits. These profits are then plowed back, or used to augment the capital stock. The further accumulation of capital leads to more profits, which leads to more accumulation, and the system continues in an upward spiral.

The name *capitalism* describes this system of profit-seeking and accumulation very well. Capital is the source of profits and hence the source of further accumulation of capital. But this chicken–egg process had to have a beginning. The substantial initial accumulation, or *primitive accumulation,* of capital took place in the period under consideration. The four most important sources of the initial accumulation of capital were (1) the rapidly growing volume of trade and commerce, (2) the putting-out system of industry, (3) the enclosure movement, and (4) the great price inflation. There were several other sources of initial accumulations, some of which were somewhat less respectable and often forgotten, for example, colonial plunder, piracy, and the slave trade.

During the sixteenth and seventeenth centuries, the putting-out system was extended until it was common in most types of manufacturing. Although this was still not the modern type of factory production, the system's increased degree of specialization led to significant increases in productivity. Technical improvements in shipbuilding and navigation also lowered transportation costs. Thus, during this period, capitalist production and trade and commerce thrived and grew very rapidly. The new capitalist class (or middle class or bourgeoisie) slowly but inexorably replaced the nobility as the class that dominated the economic and social system.

The emergence of the new nation-states signaled the beginnings of the transition to a new dominant class. The new monarchs usually drew on the bourgeois capitalist class for support in their efforts to defeat feudal rivals and unify the state under one central power. This unification freed the merchants from the feudal maze of different rules, regulations, laws, weights and measures, and moneys; consolidated many markets; and provided military protection for commercial ventures. In return, the monarch relied on the capitalists for much-needed sources of revenues.

Although England was nominally unified much earlier, it was not until Henry VII (1485–1509) founded the line of Tudor monarchs that England was unified in fact. Henry VIII (1509–1547) and Elizabeth I (1558–1603) were able to complete the work of nation-building only because they had the support of Parliament, which represented the middle classes of the shires and boroughs. In the revolutions of 1648 and 1688, the supremacy of Parliament, or of the bourgeois middle classes, was finally established.

The other important early capitalist nation-states also came into existence in this same period. In France, Louis XI (1461–1483) was the first king to unify France effectively since the time of Charlemagne.

The marriage in 1469 of Ferdinand of Aragon and Isabella of Castile, and their subsequent defeat of the Moors, led to the unification of Spain. The Dutch republic, the fourth of the important early nation-states, did not win its independence until 1690, when they finally expelled their Spanish oppressors.

By the late sixteenth and early seventeenth centuries, most of the large cities in England, France, Spain, and the Low Countries (Belgium and Holland) had been transformed into thriving capitalist economies, dominated by the merchant-capitalists who controlled not only commerce but also much of the manufacturing. In the modern nation-states, coalitions of monarchs and capitalists had wrested effective power from the feudal nobility in many important areas, especially those related to production and commerce. This period of early capitalism is generally referred to as *mercantilism.*

mercantilism: feudal paternalism in early capitalism

The earliest phase of mercantilism, usually called *bullionism,* originated in the period (discussed above) during which Europe was experiencing an acute shortage of gold and silver bullion, and hence there was not enough money to service the rapidly expanding volume of trade. Bullionist policies were designed to attract a flow of gold and silver into a country and to keep them there by prohibiting their export. These restrictions lasted from the late Middle Ages into the sixteenth and seventeenth centuries.

Spain, the country into which most of the gold from the Americas flowed, applied bullionist restrictions over the longest period and imposed the most severe penalty for the export of gold and silver: death! Yet the needs of trade were so pressing and such large profits could be made by importing foreign commodities that even in Spain merchant-capitalists succeeded in bribing corrupt officials or in smuggling large quantities of bullion out of the country. Spanish bullion rapidly found its way all over Europe and was, to a large extent, responsible for the long period of inflation described above. Spain did not legalize the export of gold and silver until long after the bullionist restrictions had been removed in England and Holland in the middle of the sixteenth century.

After the bullionist period, the mercantilists' desire to maximize the gold and silver within a country took the form of attempts by the government to create a favorable balance of trade. A *favorable balance of trade* meant to them that money payments into the country would be greater than money flowing out of the country. Thus exports of goods as well as such things as shipping and insuring, when they were performed by countrymen and paid for by foreigners, were encouraged, and imports of goods and shipping and insurance charges paid to foreigners were discouraged. A favorable balance of trade would ensure the augmentation of the country's treasure. Even though some gold and silver would be paid out in the process, more would come in than would leave.

One of the most important types of policies designed to increase the value of exports and decrease the value of imports was the creation of monopolies of trade. A country such as England could buy most cheaply (from a backward area, for example) if only one English merchant bargained with the foreigners involved, rather than having several competing English merchants bidding the price up in an effort to capture the business. Similarly, English merchants could sell their goods to foreigners for much higher prices if there was only one seller rather than several sellers bidding the price down to attract each other's customers.

The English government could prohibit English merchants from competing in an area where such a monopoly had been established. It was much more difficult, however, to keep out French, Dutch, or Spanish merchants. Various governments attempted to exclude such rival foreign merchants by establishing colonial empires that could be controlled by the mother country to ensure a monopoly of trade. Colonial possessions could thereby furnish cheap raw materials to the mother country and purchase expensive manufactured goods in return.

In addition to the creation of monopolies, all the western European countries (with the exception of Holland) applied extensive regulations to the businesses of exporting and importing. These regulations were probably most comprehensive in England, where exporters who found it difficult to compete with foreigners were given tax refunds or, if that was not enough, they were subsidized. Export duties were placed on a long list of raw materials to keep them within England. Thus, the price English merchant-manufacturers would have to pay for these raw materials would be minimized. Sometimes, when these items were in short supply for British manufacturers, the state would completely prohibit their export. The English textile industry received this type of protection. In the early eighteenth century, it accounted for about one-half of that country's exports. The English prohibited the export of most raw materials and semifinished products such as sheep, wool, yarn, and worsted, which were used by the textile industry.

Measures aimed at discouraging imports were also widespread. The importation of some commodities was prohibited, and other commodities had such high duties that they were nearly eliminated from trade. Special emphasis was placed on protecting England's principal export industries from foreign competitors attempting to cut into the export industries' domestic markets.

Of course, all these restrictions profited some capitalists and harmed others. As would be expected, coalitions of special-interest groups were always working to maintain the restrictions or to extend them into different areas in different ways. Attempts such as the English Navigation Acts of 1651 and 1660 were made to promote the use of British ships (both British-made and British-manned) in both import and export trade. All these types of regulations of foreign trade and shipping were designed to augment the flow of money into the country while decreasing the outflow. Needless to say, many of the measures also stemmed from appeals and pressures by special interests.

In addition to these restrictions on foreign trade, there was a maze of restrictions and regulations aimed at controlling domestic production. Besides the tax exemptions, subsidies, and other privileges used to encourage larger output by industries that were important exporters, the state also engaged in extensive regulation of production methods and of the quality of produced goods. In France, the regime of Louis XIV codified, centralized, and extended the older decentralized guild controls. Specific techniques of production were made mandatory, and extensive quality control measures were enacted, with inspectors appointed in Paris charged with enforcing these laws at the local level. Jean Baptiste Colbert, Louis XIV's famous minister and economic advisor, was responsible for the establishment of extensive and minute regulations. In the textile industry, for example, the width of a piece of cloth and the precise number of threads contained within it were rigidly specified by the government.

In England, the Statute of Artificers (1563) effectively transferred to the state the functions of the old craft guilds. It led to central control of the training of industrial workers, of conditions of employment, and of allocation of the labor force among different types of occupations. The regulation of wages, of the quality of many goods, and of other details of domestic production was also tried in England during this period.

What was the source of this extensive state control of trade, commerce, and domestic production? It might seem at first glance that the state was merely using its powers to promote the special interests of capitalists. This view is reinforced by the fact that most of the important writers of this period who dealt with economic issues were either merchants or employees of merchants. Undoubtedly, many of the particular statutes and regulatory measures were backed by special interests who benefited handsomely from these measures.

However, the rising new middle class of merchant and industrial capitalists were often constrained in their pursuit of profits by the maze of state regulations. Therefore, throughout the period, one finds extensive arguments advanced by these capitalists and their spokesmen for greater freedom from state controls. Economic regulation increasingly became anathema to the capitalists and their spokesmen. In fact, the mercantilist period represents an era in which an outdated economic ideology, the medieval version of the Christian corporate ethic, came into increasingly sharp conflict with a new social and economic order with which it was incompatible. It is this conflict with which Chapter 3 will be concerned.

summary

A series of profound changes resulted in the decline of feudalism and the rise of a new, market-oriented economy. Perhaps the most important of these changes was the improvements in agricultural technology that occurred between the eleventh century and the end of the thirteenth century. These improvements in farming techniques were the original force that set into motion a centuries-long chain of events that ushered in capitalism.

Population grew rapidly and urban concentration increased, which led to a resurgence of long-distance trade. In the cities, the putting-out system was created to produce items that were sold in this trade. This, in turn, led to an urban–rural specialization that could only be accomplished by the monetization of economic tasks and productive activities. The transformation of feudal social relationships into market cash relations destroyed the social base of feudalism. Attempts to preserve the feudal system resulted in bloody suppressions of peasant revolts.

The new capitalist market system was ushered in by the enclosure movement, the intellectual awakening, world exploration, the discovery of large quantities of precious metals, the price inflation of the sixteenth and seventeenth centuries, and the creation of the new nation-states.

In the early stages of capitalism, mercantilist policies resulted in extensive government intervention into market processes, particularly those related to international commerce. These policies were generally aimed at securing high profits for the great merchant trading companies, raising revenues for national governments, and more generally, bringing a maximum of precious metal into the country concerned.

chapter 3
the conflict
in mercantilist thought

The Christian corporate ethic, with its condemnation of acquisitive behavior, conflicted with the interests of merchants throughout the feudal period. As the importance of trade and commerce grew, the intensity of the conflict grew. There were two principal themes underlying the development of English mercantilism.[1] "One was the biblical injunction to promote the general welfare and common good of God's corporate world and its creatures. The second was the growing propensity to define God's estate as the civil society in which the Christian resided."[2] During this period, the state began to take over the role of the church in interpreting and enforcing the Christian corporate ethic. The basic issue for the earliest formulators of mercantilist policies was whether the growing merchant class was to be allowed to pursue its profits recklessly, regardless of the social and economic consequences of that pursuit. The Christian ethic demanded that the activities of the merchants be checked and controlled in the interest of the welfare of the entire community.

[1] We will concentrate primarily on English mercantilism in this chapter because industrial capitalism developed first in England and because most of the ideas in the capitalist ideology that we will discuss in Chapter 4 were developed in England.

[2] William Appleman Williams, *The Countours of American History* (Chicago: Quadrangle Books, 1966), p. 33.

the medieval origins
of mercantilist policies

The first indications of a mercantilistic type of economic policy can be traced to Edward I (1272–1307), who evicted several foreign economic enterprises from England, established the English wool trade in Antwerp, and made various attempts to control commerce within England. A short time later, Edward III significantly extended these policies of economic control. The long war with France (1333–1360) led him to attempt to mitigate the harsh effects that the wartime inflation was having on the laborers. He did this by fixing wages and prices in a ratio that was more favorable to the laborers. In return for this aid, Edward required all men to work at whatever jobs were available. "As this *quid pro quo* indicates, mercantilism was grounded in the idea of a mutual, corporate responsibility. God's way was based on such reciprocal respect and obligation, and Jerusalem provided the example to be followed."[3]

Richard II (1377–1399) extended and systematized his predecessors' policies. The principal problems facing England during his reign were the social and economic conflict that led to the Peasant's Rebellion of 1381 (see Chapter 2) and the necessity of countering foreign competition more effectively. The latter problem led to the Navigation Act of 1381, which was designed to favor English shippers and traders and to bring gold and silver into England. This money was needed for his program of building England into a "well and rightly governed kingdom" in which greater economic security for all would mitigate the social tensions that existed.

Henry VII (1485–1509) renewed these policies. He commissioned numerous voyages of explorers and adventurers and attempted in various ways to secure legislation and negotiate treaties advantageous to English merchants. At the same time, he subjected merchants to many controls and regulations imposed by the crown, for he believed that the unlimited pursuit of self-interest in the quest for profits was often harmful to general social interests and harmony.

Henry was still balancing feudal and capitalist interests; neither was dominant enough to persuade him to favor one over the other. The rapid growth of mining and wool-raising during his reign led to an unfortunate neglecting of food production. Moreover, the general excesses of the merchants had alienated both the peasants and the

---

[3] Williams, op. cit., p. 34. The following several pages draw heavily on Williams' excellent book.

agrarian aristocracy. The merchants seemed to understand these problems and accepted a relationship in which, in return for crown policies that would benefit them in foreign dealings, they submitted to domestic regulation of manufacturing and commerce.

the secularization of church functions

During the reign of Henry VIII, England broke with Roman Catholicism. This event was significant because it marked the final secularization (in England at least) of the functions of the medieval church. Under Henry, "the state in the form of God's monarchy assumed the role and the functions of the old universal church. What Henry had done in his own blunt way was to sanctify the processes of this world."[4] During his reign as well as during those of Elizabeth I, James I, and Charles I (1558–1649) there was widespread social unrest. The cause of this unrest was poverty, and the cause of much of the poverty was unemployment.

The enclosure movements (discussed in Chapter 2) were responsible for much of the unemployment. Another factor, however, was the decline in the export of woolens in the last half of the sixteenth century, which created a great deal of unemployment in England's most important manufacturing industry. There were also frequent commercial crises similar to, but without the regularity of, the depression phase of later business cycles. In addition to these factors, seasonal unemployment put many workers out of work for as many as four months of the year.

The people could no longer look to the Catholic church for relief from widespread unemployment and poverty. Destruction of the power of the church had eliminated the organized system of charity. The state attempted to assume responsibility for the general welfare of society. In order to do this, "England's leaders undertook a general, coordinated program to reorganize and rationalize . . . industry by establishing specifications of standards of production and marketing."[5] All these measures were designed to stimulate English trade and alleviate the unemployment problem.

In fact, it appears that the desire to achieve full employment is the unifying theme of most policy measures advocated by mercantilist writers. The mercantilists preferred measures designed to stimulate foreign rather than domestic trade "because they believed it contributed more to employment, to the nation's wealth and to

4 Ibid., p. 36.
5 Ibid., p. 40.

national power. The writers after 1600 stressed the inflationary effect of an excess of exports over imports and the consequent increase in employment which inflation produced."[6]

Among the other measures taken to encourage industry during this period was the issuance of patents of monopoly. The first important patent was granted in 1561, during the reign of Elizabeth I. Monopoly rights were given in order to encourage inventions and to establish new industries. These rights were severely abused, as might be expected. Moreover, they led to a complex system of special privileges and patronage and a host of other evils, which outraged most mercantilist writers every bit as much as similar abuses outraged late nineteenth-century American reformers. The evils of monopoly led to the Statute of Monopolies of 1624, which outlawed all monopolies except those that involved genuine inventions or that would be instrumental in promoting a favorable balance of payments. Of course, these loopholes were large, and abuses continued almost unchecked.

The Statute of Artificers (1563) specified conditions of employment and length of apprenticeships, provided for periodic wage assessments, and established maximum rates that could be paid to laborers. The statute is important because it illustrates the fact that the crown's paternalistic ethic never led to any attempt to elevate the status of the laboring classes. Monarchs of this period felt obliged to protect the working classes but, like their predecessors in the Middle Ages, believed that the working classes should be kept in their proper place. Maximum wage rates were designed to protect the capitalists, and furthermore, the justices who set these maximums and who enforced the statute generally belonged to the employing class themselves. It is probable that these maximums reduced the real wages of laborers because prices generally rose faster than wages during the succeeding years.

Poor laws passed in 1531 and 1536 attempted to deal with the problems of unemployment, poverty, and misery then widespread in England. The first sought to distinguish between "deserving" and "undeserving" poor: Only the deserving poor were allowed to beg. The second decreed that each individual parish throughout England was responsible for its poor and that the parish should, through voluntary contributions, maintain a poor fund. This proved to be completely inadequate, and the "pauper problem" grew increasingly severe.

Finally, in 1572, the state accepted the principle that the poor would have to be supported by tax funds and enacted a compulsory "poor rate." And in 1576, "houses of correction" for "incorrigible vagrants"

[6] William D. Grampp, *Economic Liberalism*, vol. 1 (New York: Random House, 1965), p. 59.

were authorized and provisions were made for the parish to purchase raw materials to be worked up by the more tractable paupers and vagrants. Between that time and the close of the sixteenth century, several other poor law statutes were passed.

The Poor Law of 1601 was the Tudor attempt to integrate all these into one consistent framework. Its main provisions included the formal recognition of the right of the poor to receive relief, the imposition of compulsory poor rates at the parish level, and the provision for differential treatment for various classes of the poor. The aged and the sick could receive help in their homes; pauper children who were too young to be apprenticed in a trade were to be boarded out; the deserving poor and unemployed were to be given work as provided for in the act of 1576; and incorrigible vagrants were to be sent to houses of correction and prisons.[7]

From the foregoing discussion, it is possible to conclude that the period of English mercantilism that preceded the English civil war was characterized by an acceptance, in the spirit of the Christian corporate ethic, of the idea that "the state had an obligation to serve society by accepting and discharging the responsibility for the general welfare."[8] The various statutes passed during this period "were predicated upon the idea that poverty, instead of being a personal sin was a function of the economic system."[9] They acknowledged that those who were the victims of the deficiencies of the economic system should be cared for by those who benefited from the system.

the rise of individualism

After the Glorious Revolution of 1688, the English government was dominated by the gentry and the middle-class capitalists. The medieval world view that underlay the Christian corporate ethic was eclipsed. A fundamental shift in the philosophy of the role of the state in society took place over the next 100 years. In 1776, with the publication of Adam Smith's *The Wealth of Nations,* a new individualistic philosophy—classical liberalism[10]—had definitely gained the ascendancy in England. This individualistic philosophy

---

[7] For an extension of this discussion of the poor laws, see Arthur Birnie, *An Economic History of the British Isles* (London: Methuen, 1936), chaps. 12 and 18.

[8] Williams, op. cit., p. 41.

[9] Ibid., p. 44.

[10] We use the adjective *classical* to differentiate the traditional liberal world view from what is called liberalism in the twentieth century. This distinction is further clarified in Chapter 4.

had existed throughout the mercantilist period, struggling to break the hold of the older corporate world view. In the end, the new classical liberalism prevailed because it, not the older, essentially medieval world view, reflected the needs of the new capitalist order.

In condemning greed, acquisitive behavior, and the desire to accumulate wealth, the medieval Christian corporate ethic condemned what had become the capitalist order's dominant motive force. The capitalist market economy, which had been extended by the late eighteenth century to almost every phase of production, demanded self-seeking, acquisitive behavior for its successful functioning. In this context new theories about human behavior began to emerge. Writers began to assert that selfish, egoistic motives were the primary if not the only motives that moved men to action.

This interpretation of man's behavior is expressed in the writings of many important thinkers of the period. Many philosophers and social theorists began to assert that every human act was related to self-preservation and hence was egoistic in the most fundamental sense. The English nobleman Sir Robert Filmer was greatly alarmed by the large number of people who spoke of "the natural freedom of mankind, a new, plausible and dangerous opinion" with anarchistic implications.[11] Thomas Hobbes' *Leviathan,* published in 1651, trenchantly articulated a widely held opinion—that all human motives stem from a desire for whatever promotes the "vital motion" of the organism (man). Hobbes believed that all men were, by nature, self-seeking and egoistic, and that all man's motives, even compassion, were merely so many disguised species of self-interest: "Grief for the calamity of another is *pity,* and ariseth from the imagination that the like calamity may befall himself; and therefore is called . . . *compassion,* and . . . fellow-feeling. . . ."[12]

Except for the few special interests that benefited from the extensive restrictions and regulations of commerce and manufacturing during this period, most capitalists felt constrained and inhibited by state regulations in their quest for profits. The individualistic and egoistic doctrines were eagerly embraced by such men. This view began to dominate economic thinking, even among the mercantilists. One careful history asserts: "most of the mercantilist . . . policy assumed that self-interest governs individual conduct. . . ."[13]

The majority of mercantilist writers were either capitalists or employees of the great capitalist trading companies. It was quite

[11] Lee Cameron McDonald, *Western Political Theory: The Modern Age* (New York: Harcourt Brace Jovanovich, 1962), p. 29.

[12] Quoted in Harry K. Girvetz, *The Evolution of Liberalism* (New York: Colliers, 1963), pp. 28–29.

[13] Grampp, op. cit., p. 69.

natural for them to perceive the motives of the capitalists as universal. From the capitalists' views of the nature of man and from their needs to be free of the extensive economic restrictions that inhibited them in the conduct of their everyday business grew the philosophy of individualism that provided the basis of classical liberalism. Against the well-ordered, paternalistic view that Europe had inherited from the feudal society, they asserted "the view that the human person ought to be independent, self-directing, autonomous, free—ought to be, that is, an individual, a unit distinguished from the social mass rather than submerged in it."[14]

protestantism and the individualistic ethic

One of the most important examples of this individualistic and middle-class philosophy was the Protestant theology that emerged from the Reformation. The new middle-class capitalists wanted to be free not only of economic restrictions that encumbered manufacturing and commerce but also of the moral opprobrium that the Catholic church had heaped upon their motives and activities. Protestantism not only freed them from religious condemnation but eventually made virtues of the selfish, egoistic, and acquisitive motives the medieval church had so despised![15]

The principal originators of the Protestant movement were quite close to the Catholic position on such questions as usury and the just price. On most social issues they were deeply conservative. During the German peasant revolt of 1524, Luther wrote a virulent pamphlet, *Against the Murdering Hordes of Peasants,* in which he said princes should "knock down, strangle and stab. . . . Such wonderful times are these that a prince can merit heaven better with bloodshed than another with prayer." His advice contributed to the general atmosphere in which the slaughter of over 100,000 peasants was carried out with an air of religious righteousness.

Yet despite the conservatism of the founders of Protestantism, this religious outlook contributed to the growing influence of the new individualistic philosophy. The basic tenet of Protestantism, which laid the groundwork for religious attitudes that were to sanction middle-class business practices, was the doctrine that men were justified by faith rather than by works. The Catholic church had

14 McDonald, op. cit., p. 16.

15 The classic studies of the relationship between Protestantism and capitalism are Max Weber, *The Protestant Ethic and the Spirit of Capitalism* (New York: Scribner's, 1958), and Richard H. Tawney, *Religion and the Rise of Capitalism* (New York: Mentor Books, 1954).

taught that men were justified by *works,* which generally meant by ceremonies and rituals. In the Catholic view, no man could be justified on his own merit alone. "Justification by works . . . did not mean that an individual could save himself: it meant that he could be saved through the Church. Hence the power of the clergy. Compulsory confession, the imposition of penance on the whole population . . . together with the possibility of withholding absolution, gave the priests a terrifying power."[16] These powers also created a situation in which the medieval doctrines of the Catholic church were not easily abandoned and in which the individual was still subordinated to society (as represented by the church).

The Protestant doctrine of justification by faith asserted that *motives* were more important than specific acts or rituals. Faith was "nothing else but the truth of the heart."[17] Each man had to search his own heart to discover if his acts stemmed from a pure heart and faith in God. Each man had to judge for himself. This individualistic reliance on each person's private conscience appealed strongly to the new middle-class artisans and small merchants. "When the business man of sixteenth and seventeenth century Geneva, Amsterdam or London looked into his inmost heart, he found that God had planted there a deep respect for the principle of private property. . . . Such men felt quite genuinely and strongly that their economic practices, though they might conflict with the traditional law of the old church, were not offensive to God. On the contrary: they glorified God."[18]

It was through this insistence on the individual's own interpretation of God's will that the "Puritans tried to spiritualize [the new] economic processes" and eventually came to believe that "God instituted the market and exchange."[19] However, it was only a matter of time before the Protestants expounded dogma that they expected everyone to accept. But the new dogma was radically different from medieval doctrines. The new doctrines stressed the necessity of doing well at one's earthly calling as the best way to please God and emphasized diligence and hard work.

The older Christian distrust of riches was "translated" into a condemnation of extravagance and needless dissipation of wealth. Thus, the Protestant ethic stressed the importance of asceticism and abstemious frugality. A theologian, who has studied the connection between religion and capitalism, summed up the relationship in this way: "The religious value set upon constant, systematic, efficient

[16] Christopher Hill, "Protestantism and the Rise of Capitalism," in D. S. Landes, ed., *The Rise of Capitalism* (New York: Macmillan, 1966), p. 43.

[17] Ibid.

[18] Ibid., pp. 46–47.

[19] Ibid., p. 49.

work in one's calling as the readiest means of securing the certainty of salvation and of glorifying God became a most powerful agency in economic expansion. The rigid limitations of consumption on the one hand and the methodical intensification of production on the other could have but one result—the accumulation of capital."[20] Thus, although neither Calvin nor Luther was a spokesman for the new middle-class capitalist, within the context of the new religious individualism the capitalists found a religion in which, over time, "profits . . . [came to be] looked upon as willed by God, as a mark of his favor and a proof of success in one's calling."[21]

the economic policies of individualism

Throughout the mercantilist period, this new individualism led to innumerable protests against the subordination of economic affairs to the will of the state. From the middle of the seventeenth century, almost all mercantilist writers condemned state-granted monopolies and other forms of protection and favoritism in the internal economy (as opposed to international commerce). Many believed that in a competitive market that pitted buyer against buyer, seller against seller, and buyer against seller, society would benefit most greatly if the price were left free to fluctuate and find its proper (market equilibrating) level. One of the earliest mercantilist writers of importance, John Hales, argued that agricultural productivity could best be improved if the husbandmen were allowed to

> have more profit by it than they have, and liberty to sell it at all times, and to all places, as freely as men may do their other things. But then no doubt, the price of corn would rise, specially at the first more than at length; yet that price would provoke every man to set plough in the ground, to husband waste grounds, yes to turn the lands which be enclosed from pasture to arable land; for every man will gladder follow that wherein they see the more profit and gains, and thereby must need ensue both plenty of corn, and also much treasure should be brought into this realm by occasion thereof; and besides that plenty of other victuals increased among us.[22]

This belief—that restrictions on production and trade within a nation were harmful to the interests of everyone concerned—became

[20] Kemper Fullerton, "Calvinism and Capitalism; an Explanation of the Weber Thesis," in Robert W. Green, ed., *Protestantism and Capitalism: The Weber Thesis and Its Critics* (Lexington, Mass.: Heath, 1959), p. 19.

[21] Ibid., p. 18.

[22] Quoted in Grampp, op. cit., p. 78.

increasingly widespread in the late seventeenth and early eighteenth centuries. Numerous statements of this view can be found in the works of such writers as Malynes, Petty, North, Law, and Child.[23] Of these men, perhaps Sir Dudley North (1641–1691) was the earliest clear spokesman for the individualistic ethic that was to become the basis for classical liberalism. North believed that all men were motivated primarily by self-interest and that they should be left alone to compete in a free market if the public welfare were to be maximized. He argued that whenever merchants or capitalists advocated special laws to regulate production or commerce, "they usually esteem the immediate Interest of their own to be the common Measure of Good and Evil. And there are many, who to gain a little in their own Trades, care not how much others suffer; and each man strives that all others may be forced in their dealings to act subserviently for his Profit, but under the cover of the Publick."[24] The public welfare would best be served, North believed, if most of the restrictive laws that bestowed special privileges were entirely removed.

In 1714, Bernard Mandeville published *The Fable of the Bees: or Private Vices, Publick Benefits,* in which he put forth the seemingly strange paradox that the vices most despised in the older moral code, if practiced by all, would result in the greatest public good. Selfishness, greed, and acquisitive behavior, he maintained, all tended to contribute to industriousness and a thriving economy. The answer to the paradox was, of course, that what had been vices in the eyes of the medieval moralists were the very motive forces that propelled the new capitalist system. And in the view of the new religious, moral, and economic philosophies of the capitalist period, these motives were no longer vices.

The capitalists had struggled throughout the mercantilist period to free themselves from all restrictions in their quest for profits. These restrictions had resulted from the paternalistic laws that were the remnants of the feudal version of the Christian corporate ethic. The paternalistic Christian ethic was simply not compatible with the new economic system that functioned on the basis of strict contractual obligations between persons rather than on that of traditional personal ties. Merchants and capitalists who invested large sums in market ventures could not depend on the forces of custom to protect their investment.

Profit-seeking could only be effective in a society based on the protection of property rights and the enforcement of impersonal contractual commitments between individuals. The new ideology that

23 Ibid., pp. 77–81.

24 Quoted in Robert Lekackmen, ed., *The Varieties of Economics,* vol. I (New York: Meridian, 1962), p. 185.

was firmly taking root in the late seventeenth and eighteenth
centuries justified these motives and relations between individuals.
It is to a consideration of this new individualistic philosophy of
classical liberalism that we turn in Chapter 4.

summary

There is a basic continuity between medieval and mercantilist social
thought. State intervention into economic processes was originally
justified in terms of the medieval Christian notion that those to whom
God had given power were obligated to use this power to promote the
general welfare and common good of all society. In early capitalism,
the state began to assume many of the roles that the church had
formerly held.

The Christian corporate ethic, however, had thoroughly condemned
the acquisitive behavior that was to become the dominant motive
force of the new capitalist system. It was, therefore, necessary to
create a new philosophical and ideological point of view that morally
justified individualization, greed, and profit-seeking.

Protestantism and the new philosophies of individualism furnished
the bases for this new ideology. The economic writings of the
mercantilists reflected this new individualism. The new point of view
emphasized the need for greater freedom for capitalists to seek
profits, and hence the need for less government intervention in the
market. Thus, the presence of two fundamentally different general
points of view in mercantilist writings created an intellectual conflict
that was not resolved until the classical liberal philosophy, including
classical economics, effectively ferreted out all remnants of the
medieval Christian corporate ethic. In Chapter 4, we shall examine
the industrial revolution and the ascendance of the classical liberal
ideology of capitalism.

chapter 4
classical liberalism and the triumph of industrial capitalism

A single theme runs through the works of the mercantilist writers (considered in the latter part of Chapter 3) that distinguishes them from the later classical liberal writers. They argued for a minimum of internal restriction and regulation, *but* they favored an active governmental policy designed to further England's commerce in the international trading markets. The classical liberals, however, advocated free trade internationally as well as domestically. In this chapter, we examine the changes in England's commercial position that encouraged her economists to favor free trade.

the industrial revolution

Between 1700 and 1770, the foreign markets for English goods grew much faster than her domestic markets. During the period 1700–1750, output in domestic industries increased by 7 percent, while that in export industries increased by 76 percent. For the period 1750–1770, the figures are 7 percent and 80 percent. This rapidly increasing foreign demand for English manufactures was the single most important cause of the most fundamental transformation of human life in history: the industrial revolution.

Eighteenth-century England was an economy with a well-developed market and one in which the traditional anticapitalist market bias in attitudes and ideology had been greatly weakened. In this England, larger outputs of manufactured goods produced at lower prices meant ever-increasing profits. Thus, profit seeking was the motive that, stimulated by increasing foreign demand, accounts for the virtual explosion of technological innovations that occurred in the late eighteenth and early nineteenth centuries—and radically transformed all England and eventually most of the world.

The textile industry was the most important in the early industrial revolution. In 1700, the woolen industry had persuaded the government to ban the import of Indian-made "calicoes" (cotton), and thus had secured a protected home market for domestic producers. As outlined above, rising foreign demand spurred mechanization of the industry.

More specifically, an imbalance between the spinning and weaving processes led to many of the innovations. The spinning wheel was not as productive as the hand loom, especially after the 1730s, when the flying shuttle was invented and the weaving process was speeded up considerably. This imbalance led to three inventions that reversed it: the spinning jenny, developed in the 1760s, with which one person could spin several threads simultaneously; the water frame, invented in 1768, which improved spinning by using both rollers and spindles in the process; and the mule, developed in the 1780s, which combined features of the other two and permitted the application of steam power. These new inventions could be used most economically in factories near the source of the water power (and later steam power). Richard Arkwright, who claimed to be the inventor of the water frame, raised sufficient capital to put a great many factories into operation, each employing anywhere from 150 to 600 persons. Others followed his example, and textile manufacturing in England was rapidly transformed from a cottage to a factory industry.

The iron industry was also very important in the early drive to mechanized factory production. In the early eighteenth century, England's iron industry was quite inconsequential. Charcoal was still used for smelting, as had been done since prehistoric times. By this time, however, the forests surrounding the iron mines were almost completely depleted. England was forced to import pig iron from her colonies, as well as from Sweden, Germany, and Spain. In 1709, Abraham Darby developed a process for making coke from coal for use in the smelting process.

Despite the relative abundance of coal near the iron mines, it was not until the latter part of the eighteenth century (when the military demands on the arms and munitions industries were very great) that the iron industry began using coke extensively. This increased demand led to the development of the puddling process, which eliminated the excess carbon left by the coke. A whole series of innovations followed, including the rolling mill, the blast furnace, the steam hammer, and metal-turning lathes. All these inventions led to a very rapid expansion of the iron and coal-mining industries, which permitted the increasingly widespread use of machines made of iron in a great variety of industries.

Entrepreneurs in many other industries saw the possibilities for larger profits if they could increase output and lower costs. In this period, there was a "veritable outburst of inventive activity":

> During the second half of the eighteenth century, interest in technical innovations became unusually intensive. For a hundred years prior to 1760, the number of patents issued during each decade had reached 102 only once, and had otherwise fluctuated between a low of 22 (1700–1709) and a high of 92 (1750–1759). During the following thirty-year period (1760–1789), the average number of patents issued increased from 205 in the 1760's to 294 in the 1770's and 477 in the 1780's.[1]

Undoubtedly the most important of these innovations was the development of the steam engine. Industrial steam engines had been introduced in the early 1700s, but mechanical difficulties had limited their use to the pumping of water in mines. In 1769, James Watt designed an engine with such accurate specifications that the straight thrust of a piston could be translated into rotary motion. A Birmingham manufacturer named Boulton formed a partnership with Watt, and with Boulton's financial resources they were able to go into large-scale production of steam engines. By the turn of the century, steam was rapidly replacing water as the chief source of power in manufacturing. The development of steam power led to profound economic and social changes.

> With this new great event, the invention of the steam engine, the final and most decisive stage of the industrial revolution opened. By liberating it from its last shackles, steam enabled the immense and rapid development of large-scale industry to take place. For the use of steam was not, like that of water, dependent on geographical position and local resources. Whenever coal could be bought at a reasonable price a steam engine could be erected. England had plenty of coal, and by the end of the eighteenth century it was already applied to many different uses, while a network of waterways, made on purpose, enabled it to be carried everywhere very cheaply: the whole country became a privileged land, suitable above all others for

---

1 Reinhard Bendix, *Work and Authority in Industry* (New York: Harper & Row, Torchbooks, 1963), p. 27.

the growth of industry. Factories were now no longer bound to the valleys, where they had grown up in solitude by the side of rapid-flowing streams. It became possible to bring them nearer the markets where their raw materials were bought and their finished products sold, and nearer the centers of population where their labor was recruited. They sprang up near one another and thus, huddled together, gave rise to those huge black industrial cities which the steam engine surrounded with a perpetual cloud of smoke.[2]

The growth in the major manufacturing cities was truly spectacular. For example, the population of Manchester rose from 17,000 in 1760 to 237,000 in 1831 and to 400,000 in 1851. Output of manufactured goods approximately doubled in the last half of the eighteenth century and grew even more rapidly in the early nineteenth century. By 1801, nearly 30 percent of the English work force was employed in manufacturing and mining; by 1831, this figure had risen to over 40 percent. Thus, the industrial revolution transformed England into a country of large urban manufacturing centers, where the factory system was dominant. The result was a very rapid growth of productivity that vaulted England into the position of the greatest economic and political power of the nineteenth century. The effects of the industrial revolution on the lives of the English people will be discussed in Chapter 5.

the rise of classical liberalism

It was during this period of industrialization that the individualistic world view of classical liberalism became the dominant ideology of capitalism.[3] Many of the ideas of classical liberalism had taken root and even gained wide acceptance in the mercantilist period, but it was in the late eighteenth and nineteenth centuries that classical liberalism most completely dominated social, political, and economic thought in England. The Christian corporate ethic was still advanced in the writings of many of the nobility and their allies as well as many socialists, but in this era these expressions were, by and large, dissident minority views.

2 Paul Mantoux, *The Industrial Revolution in the Eighteenth Century* (New York: Harcourt Brace Jovanovich, 1927), pp. 344–345.

3 This account of classical liberalism relies heavily on Harry K. Girvetz, *The Evolution of Liberalism* (New York: Collier, 1963), pp. 1–149.

the psychological creed

Classical liberalism's psychological creed was based upon four assumptions about human nature. People were believed to be egoistic, intellectualistic, essentially inert, and atomistic. (See Chapter 3 for a discussion of the egoistic theory of human nature.) The egoism argued by Hobbes furnished the basis for this view, and, in the works of later liberals, especially Jeremy Bentham, it was blended with psychological hedonism: the view that all actions are motivated by the desire to achieve pleasure and avoid pain.

"Nature," Bentham wrote, "has placed mankind under the governance of two sovereign masters, *pain,* and *pleasure.* . . . They govern us in all we do, in all we say, in all we think."[4] Pleasures differed in intensity, Bentham believed, but there were no qualitative differences. He argued that "quantity of pleasure being equal, pushpin is as good as poetry." This theory of human motivation as selfish is found in the writings of many of the most eminent thinkers of the period, including John Locke, Bernard Mandeville, David Hartley, Abraham Tucker, and Adam Smith. Smith's ideas will be examined in some detail later in this chapter.

Man's intellect played a significant role in the classical liberal's scheme of things. Although all motives stemmed from pleasure and pain, the decisions people made about what pleasures or pains to seek or avoid were based on a cool, dispassionate, and rational assessment of the situation. Reason would dictate that all alternatives in a situation be weighed in order to choose that which would maximize pleasure or minimize pain. It is this emphasis on the importance of rational calculation of pleasures and pains (with a corresponding deemphasis of caprice, instinct, habit, custom, or convention) that forms the intellectualistic side of the classical liberal's theory of psychology.

The view that individuals were essentially inert stemmed from the notion that pleasure or the avoidance of pain were men's only motives. If men could see no activities leading to pleasurable conclusions or feared no pain, then they would be inert, motionless, or in simpler terms, just plain lazy. Any kind of exertion or work was viewed as painful and therefore would not be undertaken without the promise of greater pleasure or the avoidance of greater pain. "Aversion," wrote Bentham, "is the emotion—the only emotion—

4 Jeremy Bentham, "An Introduction to the Principles of Morals and Legislation," in A. I. Melden, ed., *Ethical Theories* (Englewood Cliffs, N.J.: Prentice-Hall, 1955), p. 341.

which labor, taken by itself, is qualified to produce: of any such emotion as *love* or *desire, ease,* which is the *negative* or *absence* of *labor*—ease, not labor—is the object."[5]

The practical outcome of this doctrine (or perhaps the reason for it) was the widespread belief of the time that laborers were incurably lazy. Thus, only a large reward or the fear of starvation and deprivation could force them to work. The Reverend Joseph Townsend put this view very succinctly: "Hunger is not only peaceable, silent and unremitted pressure, but, as the most natural motive to industry and labor, it calls forth the most powerful exertions." Townsend believed that "only the experience of hunger would goad them [laborers] to labor."[6]

This view differed radically from the older, paternalistic ethic which had led to the passage of the Elizabethan Poor Relief Act of 1601. The paternalistic concern for the poor had lasted for two centuries and had culminated in 1795 in the *Speenhamland system,* which guaranteed everyone, able-bodied or not, working or not, a minimal subsistence to be paid by public taxes. It was against this system that the classical liberals railed. They eventually succeeded in passing the Poor Law of 1834, the object of which, according to Dicey, "was in reality to save the property of hard-working men from destruction by putting an end to the monstrous system under which laggards who would not toil for their support lived at the expense of their industrious neighbors. . . ."[7]

Classical liberals were persuaded, however, that the "higher ranks" of men were motivated by ambition. This differentiation of men into different ranks betrayed an implicit elitism in their individualistic doctrines. In order to assure ample effort on the part of the "elite," the classical liberals believed that the state should put the highest priority on the protection of private property. Although the argument began "as an argument for guaranteeing to the worker the fruits of his toil, it has become one of the chief apologies for the institution of private property in general."[8]

The last of the four tenets was atomism which held that the individual was a more fundamental reality than the group or society. "Priority . . . [was] . . . assigned to the ultimate components out of which an aggregate or whole . . . [was] . . . composed; they constituted the fundamental reality."[9] With this notion, the classical liberals rejected the concept, implicit in the Christian corporate

5 Quoted in Girvetz, op. cit., p. 38.

6 Bendix, op. clt., p. 74.

7 Albert V. Dicey, *Law and Public Opinion in England* (2d. ed.; London: Macmillan, 1926), p. 203.

8 Girvetz, op. cit., p. 50.

9 Ibid., p. 41.

ethic, that society was like a family and that the whole and the relationships that made up the whole were more important than any individual. The liberal's individualistic beliefs were inconsistent with the personal and human ties envisioned in the Christian corporate ethic. The group was, for them, no more than the additive total of the individuals that constituted it. They believed that restrictions placed upon the individual by society were generally evil and should be tolerated only when an even worse evil would result without them.

This atomistic psychology can be contrasted to a more socially oriented psychology that would lead to the conclusion that most of the characteristics, habits, ways of perceiving and thinking about the life processes, and the individual's general personality patterns are significantly influenced, if not determined, by the social institutions and social relationships of which he is a part. Atomistic psychology, however, sees the makeup of the individual as somehow independently given. It therefore regards social institutions as both tools for and the handiwork of these individuals. In this view, society exists only because it is useful, and if it were not for this usefulness, each individual could go his own way, discarding society much as he would discard a tool that no longer served its purpose.

the economic creed

Several explanations are necessary for an understanding of why the classical liberals thought society to be so useful. For example, they talked about the "natural gregariousness of men," the need for collective security, and the economic benefits of the division of labor, which society makes possible. The latter was the foundation of the economic creed of classical liberalism, and the creed was crucial to classical liberalism because this philosophy contained what appear to be two contradictory or conflicting assumptions.

On the one hand, the assumption of man's innate egoism had led Hobbes to assert that in the absence of restraints, men's selfish motives would lead to a "natural state" of war, with each man pitted against all others. In this state of nature, Hobbes believed that the life of man was "solitary, poor, nasty, brutish, and short." The only escape from brutal combat was the establishment of some source of absolute power—a central government—to which each man submitted in return for protection from all other men.[10]

On the other hand, one of the cardinal tenets of classical liberalism was that men (or more particularly businessmen) should be free to

[10] Hobbes, "Leviathan," reprinted in Melden, op. cit., pp. 192–205.

give vent to their egoistic drives with a minimum of control or restraint imposed by society. This apparent contradiction was bridged by the liberal economic creed which asserted that if the competitiveness and rivalry of unrestrained egoism existed in a capitalist market setting, then this competition would benefit the individuals involved and all society as well. This view was put forth in the most profound single intellectual achievement of classical liberalism: Adam Smith's *The Wealth of Nations,* published in 1776.

Smith believed that "every individual . . . [was] continually exerting himself to find out the most advantageous employment for whatever capital he can command."[11] Those without capital were always searching for that employment at which the monetary return for their labor would be maximized. If both capitalists and laborers were left alone, self-interest would guide them to use their capital and labor where they were most productive. The search for profits would ensure that what was produced would be what people wanted most and were willing to pay for. Thus, Smith and classical liberals in general were opposed to having some authority or law determine what should be produced. "It is not from the benevolence of the butcher, the brewer, or the baker, that we expect our dinner, but from their regard to their own interest,"[12] wrote Smith. Producers of various goods must compete in the market for the dollars of consumers. That producer who offered a better-quality product would attract more consumers. He therefore would be led by his self-interest to constant improvement of the quality of his product. The producer could also increase profits by cutting his costs of production to a minimum.

Thus, a *free market,* in which producers competed for consumers' dollars in an egoistic quest for more profits, would guarantee the direction of capital and labor to their most productive uses and would ensure the production of the goods consumers wanted and needed most (as measured by their ability and willingness to pay for them). Moreover, the market would lead to a constant striving to improve the quality of products and to organize production in the most efficient and least-costly manner possible. All these beneficial actions would stem directly from the competition of egoistical men, each pursuing his self-interest.

What a far cry from the "solitary, poor, nasty and brutish" world Hobbes thought would result from man's competitiveness. The wonderful social institution that could make all this possible was the free and unrestrained market, the forces of supply and demand. The market, Smith believed, would act as an "invisible hand"

11 Adam Smith, *The Wealth of Nations* (New York: Modern Library, 1937), p. 421.
12 Ibid., p. 14.

channeling selfish, egoistic motives into mutually consistent and complementary activities that would best promote the welfare of all society. And the greatest beauty of it was the complete lack of any need for paternalistic guidance, direction, or restrictions. Freedom from coercion in a capitalist market economy was compatible with a natural orderliness in which the welfare of each, as well as the welfare of all society (which was, after all, only the aggregate of the individuals that constitute it), would be maximized. In Smith's words, each producer

> intends only his own security; and by directing that industry in such a manner as its produce may be of the greatest value, he intends only his own gain, and he is in this, as in many other cases, led by an invisible hand to promote an end which was no part of his intention. Nor is it always the worse for the society that it was not part of it. By pursuing his own interest he frequently promotes that of society more effectually than when he really intends to promote it. I have never known much good done by those who affected to trade for the public good. It is an affectation, indeed, not very common among merchants, and very few words need be employed in dissuading them from it.[13]

With this statement it is evident that Smith had a philosophy totally antithetical to the paternalism of the Christian corporate ethic. The Christian notion of the rich promoting the security and well-being of the poor through paternalistic control and almsgiving contrasts sharply with Smith's picture of a capitalist who is concerned only with "his own advantage, indeed, and not that of the society. . . . But the study of his own advantage naturally, or rather necessarily leads him to prefer that employment which is most advantageous to the society."[14]

Not only would the free and unfettered market channel productive energies and resources into their most valuable uses, but it would also lead to continual economic progress. Economic well-being depended upon the capacity of an economy to produce. Productive capacity in turn depended upon the accumulation of capital and the division of labor. When one man produced everything he needed for himself and his family, production was very inefficient. But if men subdivided tasks, each producing only that commodity for which his own abilities best suited him, productivity increased. For such a subdivision of tasks, a market was necessary in order to exchange goods. In the market, each person could get all the items he needed but did not produce.

13 Ibid., p. 423.
14 Ibid., p. 421.

This increase in productivity could be extended further if the production of each commodity were broken down into many steps or stages. Each person would then work on only one stage of the production of one commodity. In order to achieve a division of labor of this degree, it was necessary to have many specialized tools and other equipment. It was also necessary that all the stages of production for a particular commodity be brought together and coordinated as, for example, in a factory. Thus, an increasingly fine division of labor required the accumulation of capital in the form of tools, equipment, factories, and money. This capital would also provide wages to maintain workers during the period of production before their coordinated efforts were brought to fruition and sold on the market.

The source of this capital accumulation was, of course, the profits of production. As long as demand was brisk and more could be sold than was being produced, capitalists would invest their profits in order to expand their capital, which would lead to an increasingly intricate division of labor. The increased division of labor would lead to greater productivity, higher wages, higher profits, more capital accumulation, and so forth, in a never-ending, upward-moving escalator of social progress. The process would be brought to a halt only when there was no longer sufficient demand for the products to warrant further accumulation and more extensive division of labor. Government regulation of economic affairs, or any restrictions on the freedom of market behavior, could only decrease the extent of demand and bring the beneficial process of capital accumulation to a halt before it would have ended otherwise. So, here again, there was no room for paternalistic government meddling in economic affairs.

the theory of population

Thomas Robert Malthus' population theory was an important and integral part of classical liberal economic and social doctrines. He believed that most men were driven by an insatiable desire for sexual pleasure, and that consequently, natural rates of human reproduction, *when unchecked,* would lead to geometrical increases in population —that is, population would increase each generation at the ratio of 1, 2, 4, 8, 16, and so forth. But, food production, at the very best, increases at an arithmetical rate—that is, it can only increase each generation at a rate such as 1, 2, 3, 4, 5, and so on.

Obviously, something would have to hold the population in check. The food supply could not support a population that was growing at a geometrical rate. Malthus believed there were two general kinds of checks that limited population growth: preventive checks and positive checks. Preventive checks reduced the birth rate, whereas positive checks increased the death rate.

Moral restraint, vice, and birth control were the primary preventive checks. Moral restraint was the means by which the higher ranks of men limited their family size in order not to dissipate their wealth among larger and larger numbers of heirs. For the lower ranks of men, vice and birth control were the preventive checks, but they were grossly insufficient to curb the vast numbers of the poor.

Famine, misery, plague, and war were the positive checks. The fact that preventive checks did not succeed in limiting the numbers of lower-class people made these positive checks inevitable. Finally, if the positive checks were somehow overcome, the growing population would press upon the food supply until starvation—the ultimate and unavoidable check—succeeded in holding the population down.

Before starvation set in, Malthus advised that steps be taken to help the positive checks do their work:

> It is an evident truth that, whatever may be the rate of increase in the means of subsistence, the increase in population must be limited by it, at least after the food has once been divided into the smallest shares that will support life. All the children born, beyond what would be required to keep up the population to this level, must necessarily perish, unless room be made for them by the deaths of grown persons. . . . To act consistently therefore, we should facilitate, instead of foolishly and vainly, endeavouring to impede, the operation of nature in producing this mortality; and if we dread the too frequent visitation of the horrid form of famine, we should sedulously encourage the other forms of destruction, which we compel nature to use. Instead of recommending cleanliness to the poor, we should encourage contrary habits. In our towns we should make the streets narrower, crowd more people into the houses, and court the return of the plague. In the country, we should build our villages near stagnant pools, and particularly encourage settlements in all marshy and unwholesome situations. But above all, we should reprobate specific remedies for ravaging diseases; and those benevolent, but much mistaken men, who have thought they were doing a service to mankind by projecting schemes for the total extirpation of particular disorders. If by these and similar means the annual mortality were increased . . . we might probably every one of us marry at the age of puberty, and yet few be absolutely starved.[15]

15 Thomas Robert Malthus, *Essay on the Principle of Population,* vol. 2 (New York: Dutton, 1961), pp. 179–180.

The masses of men, in Malthus' opinion, were incapable of exer-
cising moral restraint, which was the only real remedy for the
population problem. They were, therefore, doomed to live perpetually
at a bare minimum subsistence level. If all income and wealth were
distributed among them, it would be totally dissipated within one
generation because of profligate behavior and population growth,
and they would be as poor and destitute as ever.

Paternalistic attempts to aid the poor were, thus, doomed to
failure. Furthermore, they were a positive evil because they drained
wealth and income from the higher (more moral) ranks of men. These
higher-class individuals were responsible, either in person or by
supporting others, for all the great achievements of society. Art,
music, philosophy, literature, and the other splendid cultural attain-
ments of Western civilization owed their existence to the good taste
and generosity of the higher classes of men. Taking money from
them would dry up the source of such achievement; using the money
to alleviate the conditions of the poor was a futile foredoomed
exercise.

It is obvious that the Malthusian population theory and the liberal
economic theories led to the same conclusion: Paternalistic government should avoid any attempt to intervene in the economy on behalf
of the poor.

the political creed

The economic and population doctrines of classical liberalism gave
rise quite naturally to a political creed that rejected the state, or
government, as an evil to be tolerated only when it was the sole
means of avoiding a worse evil. Much of this antipathy stemmed
directly from the many corrupt, despotic, capricious, and tyrannical
actions of several European kings, as well as from the actions of the
English Parliament, which was notoriously unrespresentative and
often despotic. The liberal creed was not put forward as an objection
against particular governments, however, but against governments
in general. Thomas Paine reflected the sentiment of classical liberals
when he wrote: "Society in every state is a blessing, but government,
even in its best state, is but a necessary evil; in its worst state an
intolerable one. . . ."[16]

What were the functions that classical liberals thought should be
given to governments? In *The Wealth of Nations,* Adam Smith listed
three: the protection of the country against foreign invaders, the

16 Quoted in Girvetz, op. cit., p. 66.

protection of citizens against "injustices" suffered at the hands of
other citizens, and the "duty . . . of erecting and maintaining those
public institutions and those public works, which, though they may
be in the highest degree advantageous to a great society, are,
however, of such a nature, that the profit could never repay the
expense to any individual or small number of individuals, and which
it therefore cannot be expected that any individual or small number
of individuals should erect and maintain."[17]

This list is very general, and almost any kind of government action
could be justified under one of these three functions. In order to
understand the specific functions the liberals believed government
should have, it is necessary to deal first with an objection that is
frequently raised when the writings of Adam Smith are said to
comprise a part of an ideology justifying capitalism. It is often
pointed out that not only was Smith *not* a spokesman for the
capitalists of his day, but also that many of his passages show that
he was in general suspicious and distrustful of capitalists.[18] This
contention is certainly true. Nevertheless, capitalists used the arguments put forward by Smith to justify their attempts to eliminate the
last vestiges of paternalistic government when these stood in the
way of their quest for profits. It was Smith's rationale that enabled
them to quiet their consciences when their actions created widespread hardship and suffering. After all, they were only following his
advice and pursuing their own profits; and this was the way in which
they should act if they wished to be of the greatest service to society.

Finally, most classical liberals interpreted Smith's theory of the
three general governmental functions in a way that showed they were
not hesitant about endorsing a paternalistic government when they,
the capitalists, were the beneficiaries of the paternalism. Thus,
"the original doctrine of laissez faire . . . passed, for the most part,
from the care of intellectuals like Adam Smith . . . into the
custodianship of businessmen and industrialists and their hired
spokesmen."[19]

First, the requirement that the government protect the country
from external threats was often extended in the late nineteenth
century to a protection or even enlargement of foreign markets
through armed coercion. Second, protection of citizens against
"injustices" committed by other citizens was usually defined to mean
the protection of private property, the enforcement of contracts, and

---

[17] Smith, op. cit., p. 681.

[18] For a statement of this view, as well as a scholarly inquiry into classical
economics from a viewpoint that differs from the one presented in this book, see
Lionel Robbins, *The Theory of Economic Policy in English Classical Political
Economy* (London: Macmillan, 1953).

[19] Girvetz, op. cit., p. 81.

the preservation of internal order. Protection of private property, especially ownership of factories and capital equipment, is, of course, tantamount to protection of that which is the sine qua non of capitalism. It was their ownership of the means of production that gave the capitalists their economic and political power. Giving the government the function of protecting property relations meant giving the government the job of protecting the source of power of the economically and politically dominant class: the capitalists.

Contract enforcement was also essential for the successful functioning of capitalism. The complex division of labor and the necessity of complex organizing and coordinating in production, as well as the colossal size of capital investments necessary in many commercial ventures, meant that capitalists had to be able to depend on people meeting contractual commitments. The medieval notion that custom and the special circumstances of a case defined an individual's obligations was just not compatible with capitalism. Therefore, the duty to enforce contracts amounted to governmental coercion of a type necessary for capitalism to function.

The preservation of internal order was (and is) always necessary. In the late eighteenth and early nineteenth centuries, however, it often meant brutally crushing labor-union movements or the English Chartist movement, which capitalists considered to be threats to their profit-making.

Finally, the function of "erecting and maintaining those public institutions and those public works" that were in the public interest generally was interpreted to mean the creation and maintenance of institutions that fostered profitable production and exchange. These included the provision of a stable and uniform currency, standard weights and measures, and the physical means necessary for conducting business. Roads, canals, harbors, railroads, the postal services, and other forms of communication were among the prerequisites of business. Although these were often privately owned, most capitalist governments were extensively involved in their erection and maintenance either through financial subsidies to private businesses or through the direct undertaking of these projects by the governments.

Thus, it may be concluded that the classical liberals' philosophy of laissez faire was opposed to government interference in economic affairs *only if* such interference was harmful to the interests of capitalists. They welcomed and even fought for those paternalistic interferences in economic affairs that stabilized business or made larger profits possible.[20]

---

[20] Considerable evidence for this assertion can be found in Warren J. Samuels, *The Classical Theory of Economic Policy* (New York: World Publishing, 1966).

classical liberalism and industrialization

The industrial revolution and the triumph of the classical liberal capitalist ideology occurred together during the late eighteenth and early nineteenth centuries. Liberalism was the philosophy of the new industrial capitalism, and the new liberal ideas created a political and intellectual atmosphere in eighteenth-century England that fostered the growth of the factory system.

In its medieval version, the paternalistic Christian corporate ethic had led to a pervasive system of restrictions on the behavior of capitalists during the mercantilist period. Capitalists and their spokesmen opposed most of these restrictions with a new individualistic philosophy which advocated greater freedom for the capitalist to seek profits in a market free of encumbrances and restrictions. It is not surprising that the triumph of this philosophy should coincide with the greatest achievement of the capitalist class: the industrial revolution. The industrial revolution vaulted the capitalist class into a position of economic and political dominance, and this fact goes far in explaining the triumph of classical liberalism as the ideology of the new age of industrial capitalism.

summary

The pressure of rapidly increasing demand, and the prospect of larger profits, led to a "veritable outburst of inventive activity" in the late eighteenth and early nineteenth centuries. This period of widespread innovation—the industrial revolution—transformed England (and later western Europe and North America) into urban societies dominated by great manufacturing cities in which large numbers of workers were subjected to the dehumanizing discipline of factory production.

During this period, the classical liberal ideology of capitalism came to dominate social and economic thinking. The new ideology pictured individuals as egoistic, intellectualistic, lazy, and generally existentially independent of the society of which they were a part. Adam Smith's analysis of the market as an "invisible hand" that channeled egoistic drives into the most socially useful activities supported a doctrine of laissez faire. The only functions that this philosophy assigned to the government were those that would support and encourage profit-making.

Finally, the Malthusian theory of population taught that social action designed to mitigate the suffering of the poor was not only useless, but even had socially deleterious effects. Acceptance of this view necessitated the complete abandonment of the Christian corporate ethic.

chapter 5
socialist protest amid the industrial revolution

The industrial revolution brought about increases in human
productivity that were without precedent in history. The widespread
construction of factories and the extensive use of machinery
represented the mechanical basis of this increase. In order to
channel the economy's productivity capacity into the creation of
capital goods, however, it was necessary to devote a relatively much
smaller part of this capacity to the manufacture of consumer goods.
Capital goods had to be purchased at a social cost of mass
deprivation.

the social costs
of the industrial revolution

Historically, in all cases where society has had to force a bare
subsistence existence on some of its members, it has always been
those with the least economic and political power who have made
the sacrifices. And so it was in the industrial revolution in England.
The working class lived at near the subsistence level in 1750, and
their standard of living (measured in terms of the purchasing power
of wages) deteriorated during the last half of the eighteenth century.
The trend of working-class living standards in the first several
decades of the nineteenth century is a subject of dispute among

historians. The fact that many eminent scholars find sufficient evidence to argue that the living standard failed to increase, or even decreased, leads to the conclusion that any increase during this period was slight at best.

Throughout the period of the industrial revolution, there is no doubt that the standard of living of the poor fell precipitously in relative terms. A detailed analysis shows that "relatively the poor grew poorer, simply because the country, and its rich and middle class, so obviously grew wealthier. The very moment when the poor were at the end of their tether . . . was the moment when the middle class dripped with excess capital, to be wildly invested in railways and spent on the bulging opulent household furnishings displayed at the Great Exhibition of 1851, and on palatial municipal constructions . . . in the smoky northern cities."[1] There can be no doubt about which class paid the social costs in terms of the sacrificed consumption that was necessary for industrialization.

Yet the costs in terms of decreased consumption were by no means the only, and perhaps not even the worst, hardships forced upon the laboring class by the industrial revolution. The new factory system completely destroyed the laborers' traditional way of life, throwing them into a nightmare world with which they were completely unprepared to cope. They lost the pride of workmanship and close personal relationships that had existed in handicraft industries. Under the new system, their only relationship with their employer was through the impersonal market, or *cash nexus.* They lost any direct access to the means of production and were reduced to mere sellers of labor power totally dependent upon market conditions for their livelihood.

Perhaps worse than any of these was the monotonous, mechanical regularity imposed upon the worker by the factory system. In pre-industrial Europe, the worker's tasks were not so specialized. He went from one task to another, and his work was interrupted by variations in the seasons or the weather. When he felt like resting or playing or changing the pace of his work routine, he had a certain amount of freedom to do so. Factory employment brought the tyranny of the clock. Production was mechanized. Absolute regularity was necessary to coordinate the complex interaction of processes and to maximize the use of the new, expensive machinery. The pace of work was no longer decided by the man, but by the machine.

The machine, which had formerly been an appendage to the man, was now the focal point of the productive process. Man became a mere appendage to the cold, implacable, pacesetting machine.

1 E. J. Hobsbawm, *Industry and Empire: An Economic History of Britain Since 1750* (London: Weidenfeld & Nicolson, 1968), p. 72. Several of Hobsbawm's ideas appear in this chapter.

During the late eighteenth and early nineteenth centuries, a spontaneous revolt against the new factory system saw bands of workers
smashing and destroying machines and factories, which they believed
were responsible for their plight. These revolts, called the Luddite
revolts, ended in 1813 when large numbers of workers were hanged
or deported for their activities.

The extensive division of labor in the factory made much of the
work so routine and simple that untrained women and children could
do it as well as men. Because women and children could be hired for
much lower wages than men, and because in many cases entire
families had to work in order to earn enough to eat, women and
children were employed widely. Many factory owners preferred
women and children because they were weaker and could be reduced
to a state of passive obedience more easily than men.

Children were bound to factories by indentures of apprenticeship
for seven years or until they were twenty-one. In these cases, almost
nothing was given the children in return for long hours of work under
the most horrendous conditions. Poor-law authorities could indenture
the children of paupers. This led to "regular bargains . . . [where]
children . . . were dealt with as mere merchandise . . . between
the spinners on the one hand and the Poor Law authorities on the
other. Lots of fifty, eighty or a hundred children were supplied and
sent like cattle to the factory, where they remained imprisoned for
many years."[2]

These children endured the cruelest servitude. They were totally
isolated from anyone who might take pity on them and were thus at
the mercy of the capitalists or their hired managers, whose main
concern was the challenge of competitive factories. The children's
workday was from 14 to 18 hours or until they dropped from complete
exhaustion. The foremen were paid according to how much the
children produced and therefore pushed them mercilessly. In most
factories, the children had hardly more than 20 minutes a day for
their main (and often only) meal. "Accidents were very common,
especially towards the end of the overlong day, when the exhausted
children almost fell asleep at their work. The tale never ended of
fingers cut off and limbs crushed in the wheels."[3] The children were
disciplined in such savage and brutal ways that a recitation of the
methods used would appear completely incredible to the reader of
today.

Women were mistreated almost as badly. Work in a factory was
long, arduous, and monotonous. Discipline was harsh. Many times the
price of factory employment was submission to the sexual advances

[2] Paul Mantoux, *The Industrial Revolution in the Eighteenth Century* (New York:
Harcourt Brace Jovanovich, 1927), pp. 410–411.

[3] Ibid., p. 413.

of employers and foremen.[4] Women in the mines toiled 14 to 16 hours a day, stripped naked to the waist, working with men and doing the work of men. There were reports of women who came out of the mines to bear children and who were back in the mines within days after the births. Many accounts have been written of the fantastically cruel and dehumanizing working conditions for women during this period. And, of course, the working men were not much better off than the women or the children. Our sympathies are perhaps more deeply touched by narratives of the depredations suffered by women and children, but industrialization was stern, harsh, and cruel in the extreme for men as well.

Another important consideration in assessing the living standard of the working class during the period of capitalist industrialization was the rapid urbanization that took place. In 1750, only 2 cities in Britain had populations of 50,000 persons. In 1850, there were 29. By this latter date, nearly one person in three lived in a city with over 50,000 inhabitants.

Conditions in the cities of this period were terrible:

> And what cities! It was not merely that smoke hung over them and filth impregnated them, that the elementary public services— water-supply, sanitation, street-cleaning, open spaces, etc.—could not keep pace with the mass migration of men into the cities, thus producing, especially after 1830, epidemics of cholera, typhoid and an appalling constant toll of the two great groups of nineteenth-century urban killers—air pollution and water pollution, or respiratory and intestinal disease. . . . The new city populations . . . [were] pressed into overcrowded and bleak slums, whose very sight froze the heart of the observer. "Civilization works its miracles" wrote the great French liberal de Tocqueville of Manchester, "and civilized man is turned back almost into a savage."[5]

Included in these slums was a district of Glasgow that, according to a report of a government commissioner, housed

> a fluctuating population of between 15,000 and 30,000 persons. This district is composed of many narrow streets and square courts and in the middle of each court there is a dunghill. Although the outward appearance of these places was revolting, I was nevertheless quite unprepared for the filth and misery that were to be found inside. In some bedrooms we visited at night, we found a whole mass of humanity stretched on the floor. There were often 15 to 20 men and women huddled together, some

4 Ibid., p. 416.
5 Hobsbawm, op. cit., pp. 67–68.

being clothed and others naked. There was hardly any furniture there and the only thing which gave these holes the appearance of a dwelling was fire burning on the hearth. Thieving and prostitution are the main sources of income of these people.[6]

The total destruction of the laborers' traditional way of life and the harsh discipline of the new factory system, combined with deplorable living conditions in the cities, generated social, economic, and political unrest. Chain reactions of social upheaval, riots, and rebellion occurred in the years 1811–1813, 1815–1817, 1819, 1826, 1829–1835, 1838–1842, 1843–1844, and 1846–1848. In many areas, these were purely spontaneous and primarily economic in character. In 1816, one rioter from the Fens exclaimed: "Here I am between Earth and Sky, so help me God. I would sooner lose my life than go home as I am. Bread I want and bread I will have."[7] In 1845, an American named Colman reported that the working people of Manchester were "wretched, defrauded, oppressed, crushed human nature lying in bleeding fragments all over the face of society."[8]

There can be no doubt that industrial capitalism was erected on the base of the wretched suffering of a laboring class denied access to the fruits of the rapidly expanding economy and subjected to the most degrading of excesses to increase the capitalists' profits. The basic cause of the great evils of this period was "the absolute and uncontrolled power of the capitalist. In this, the heroic age of great undertakings, it was acknowledged, admitted and even proclaimed with brutal candor. It was the employer's own business, he did as he chose and did not consider that any other justification of his conduct was necessary. He owed his employees wages and once those were paid the men had no further claim on him."[9]

liberal social legislation

From the earliest introduction of factory production in the textile industries, workmen tried to band together to protect their interests collectively. In 1787, during a period of high unemployment, the Glasgow muslin manufacturers attempted to lower the piece rates they were paying. The workers resisted collectively, refused to work below a certain minimum rate, and organized a boycott of those

6 Quoted in F. Engels, *The Condition of the Working Class in England in 1844* (New York: Macmillan, 1958), p. 46.

7 Quoted in Hobsbawm, op. cit., p. 74.

8 Ibid., p. 75.

9 Mantoux, op. cit., p. 417.

manufacturers who would not pay the minimum rate. The struggle led to open rioting and shooting, but the workingmen proved to have a strong and well-disciplined group, and they built a strong union. In 1792, a union of weavers forced a collective agreement upon Bolton and Bury Manufacturers.

Labor organizations spread rapidly in the 1790s. As a result of this and the concurrent growth of social and economic discontent, the upper classes became very uneasy. The memory of the French Revolution was fresh in their minds, and they feared the power of united workingmen. The result was the Combination Act of 1799, which outlawed any combination of workers whose purpose was to obtain higher wages, shorter hours, or the introduction of any regulation constraining the free action of their employers. Proponents couched their arguments in terms of the necessity of free competition and the evils of monopolies—cardinal tenets of classical liberalism— but did not mention combinations of employers or monopolistic practices of capitalists. The effects of this legislation have been summarized as follows:

> The Combination Laws were considered as absolutely necessary to prevent ruinous extortions of workmen, which, if not thus restrained, would destroy the whole of the trade, manufactures, commerce and agriculture of the nation. . . . So thoroughly was this false notion entertained, that whenever men were prosecuted to conviction for having combined to regulate their wages or the hours of working, however heavy the sentence passed upon them was, and however rigorously it was inflicted, not the slightest feeling of compassion was manifested by anybody for the unfortunate sufferers. Justice was entirely out of the question: They could seldom obtain a hearing before a magistrate, never without impatience or insult . . . could an accurate account be given of proceedings, of hearings before magistrates, trials at sessions and in the Court of King's Bench, the gross injustice, the foul invective, and terrible punishments inflicted would not, after a few years have passed away, be credited to any but the best evidence.[10]

Another cause for which the classical liberals campaigned vigorously was the abolition of the Speenhamland system of poor relief that had come into existence in 1795. This system was (continuing in the tradition of the Elizabethan Statute of Artificers) the result of the paternalistic tradition of the Christian corporate ethic. It held that unfortunates would be entitled to a certain minimum living standard whether employed or not. To be sure, the system had serious

[10] Quoted in ibid., p. 449.

drawbacks: It actually depressed wages below the relief level in many cases (with the parish taxes making up the difference), and severely limited labor mobility at a time when greater mobility was needed.

The important issue, however, is not the deficiencies of the Speenhamland system, but rather the type of legislation the liberals enacted in its place when they succeeded in abolishing it in 1834. The view of the classical liberals was that workers should accept any job the market offered, regardless of the conditions or pay involved. Any person who would not or could not do so should be given just enough to prevent physical starvation. His dole should be substantially lower than the lowest wage offered in the market, and his general situation should stigmatize him sufficiently to motivate him to seek gainful employment. Thus, the new law

> was an engine of degradation and oppression more than a means of material relief. There have been few more inhuman statutes than the Poor Law Act of 1834, which made all relief "less eligible" than the lowest wage outside, confined it to the jail-like workhouse, forcibly separated husbands, wives and children in order to punish the poor for their destitution, and discourage them from the dangerous temptation of procreating further paupers.[11]

the paternalism of the tory radicals

It might seem from this discussion that the paternalism of the Christian corporate ethic was completely eclipsed during the industrial revolution. This was not so. Among the landed or aristocratic wealthy there were many Tory radicals, men who often had a "gentleman's disdain" for the "vulgar, money grubbing" middle-class merchants and manufacturers. They asserted that it was the obligation of the "higher classes" to think for and protect the poor. Some of the most vivid descriptions and outspoken denunciations of the excesses of the factory managers came from the pens of Tory radicals.

The ideas of the traditionalist Tories were summarized by John Stuart Mill (who was critical of the point of view he was summarizing). According to Mill, the traditionalists believed that

> the lot of the poor, in all things which affect them collectively, should be regulated *for* them, not *by* them. They should not be required or encouraged to think for themselves, or give to their

11 Hobsbawm, op. cit., pp. 69–70.

own reflection or forecast an influential voice in the determination of their destiny. It is supposed to be the duty of the higher classes to think for them, and to take the responsibility of their lot, as the commander and officers of an army take that of the soldiers composing it. This function, it is contended, the higher classes should prepare themselves to perform conscientiously, and their whole demeanour should impress the poor with a reliance on it, in order that, while yielding passive and active obedience to the rules prescribed for them, they may resign themselves in all other respects to a trustful *insouciance,* and repose under the shadow of their protectors. The relationship between the rich and poor, according to this theory should be only partly authoritative; it should be amiable, moral and sentimental: affectionate tutelage on the one side, respectful and grateful deference on the other.[12]

Most of these traditionalists believed that the greedy profit-seeking of the vulgar, unrefined, acquisitive middle classes was responsible for the social ills of the industrial revolution. Capitalism would function properly, in their opinion, only when capitalists functioned as gentlemen rather than moneygrubbers. These ideas were put into practice in several industrial enterprises owned either by the aristocracy or by humane middle-class capitalists with traditionalist views. Perhaps the most famous of the latter was Robert Owen.

Born in 1771, Owen served as a draper's apprentice from the age of ten. At twenty, he was the manager of a large mill. Wise business decisions and good luck soon resulted in the acquisition of a considerable fortune. Owen was a perfect example of a benevolent autocrat. His factory at New Lanark became known throughout all England because he insisted on decent working conditions, livable wages, and education for working-class children. His workers received "affectionate tutelage" from him, and he thought of himself as their trustee and steward.

This paternalistic attitude did *not* interfere with Owen's very strict organizational discipline in his factory. Owen has described one of his methods of maintaining discipline:

> that which I found to be the most efficient check upon inferior conduct was the contrivance of a silent monitor for each one employed in the establishment. This consisted of a four-sided piece of wood, about two inches long and one broad, each side colored—one side black, another blue, the third yellow, and the fourth white, tapered at the top, and finished with wire eyes, to hang upon a hook with either side to the front. One of these

12 John Stuart Mill, *Principles of Political Economy* (New York: Augustus M. Kelley, 1965 [first published in 1848]), p. 753.

was suspended in a conspicuous place near to each of the
persons employed, and the color at the front told the conduct
of the individual during the preceding day, to four degrees of
comparison. Bad, denoted by black and No. 4; indifferent by blue,
and No. 3; good by yellow, and No. 2; and excellent by white,
and No. 1. Then books of character were provided, for each
department, in which the name of each one employed in it was
inserted in the front of succeeding columns, which sufficed to
mark by the number the daily conduct, day by day, for two
months; and these books were changed six times a year, and
were preserved; by which arrangement I had the conduct of each
registered to four degrees of comparison during
every day of the week, Sundays excepted, for every
year they remained in my employment.[13]

So in his life and deeds, Owen, like other capitalists of his era,
strove to maximize his profits. He believed that his competitors'
harsh treatment of their workers was stupid and shortsighted, and he
based his life on the assumption that the paternalism of the Christian
corporate ethic was compatible with the capitalist system, at least at
the factory level. In his own words: "My time, from early to late, and
my mind, were continually occupied in devising measures and
directing their execution, to improve the condition of the people,
and to advance at the same time the works and the machinery as a
manufacturing establishment."[14]

the socialist version
of the christian corporate ethic

Although Owen's life and actions did not differentiate him from many
of the conservative Tory radicals of his time, some of his ideas did.
He did not believe that any society in which one class was elevated
to a position of power and used this power to exploit the lower
classes could ultimately become a truly good society. Private
ownership of the means of production (factories, machinery, tools)
was the social institution by which one small class in the existing
economic system gained immense power over the mass of farmers
and workers. The profit motive was the force that drove this small
class to use this power to exploit the workers and farmers to gain
profits.

Owen believed that in an ideal society, the people could most

[13] M. Beer, ed., *Life of Robert Owen* (New York: Knopf, 1920), p. 111.
[14] Ibid., p. 112.

effectively control nature, because they would reap the greatest collective benefit if they cooperated. This cooperation should take the form of self-governing industrial and agricultural communities. In such communities, private ownership of the means of production would be abolished and the selfish quest for profits would be eliminated. He maintained that only when such a society was established would it be true that

> One portion of mankind will not, as now, be trained and placed to oppress, by force or fraud, another portion, to the great disadvantage of both; neither will one portion be trained in idleness, to live in luxury on the industry of those whom they oppress, while the latter are made to labor daily and to live in poverty. Nor yet will some be trained to force falsehood into the human mind and be paid extravagantly for so doing while other parties are prevented from teaching the truth, or severely punished if they make the attempt.[15]

There was something in these writings that differed very radically from his description of the way in which he ran his own factory at New Lanark. The ideal society, for Owen, would be one in which the paternalism of the traditional Christian ethic would be expressed as a *brotherhood of equals,* a considerable shift from the parent–child type of subordination expressed in the medieval and Tory radical versions of the Christian corporate ethic.

The feudal version of the ethic had accepted a hierarchical society. In it, those at the top lived lavishly (by standards of the day, at least), and they did so by exploiting those at the bottom. Chaucer's parson's description of the medieval view is apt: "God has ordained that some folk should be more high in estate and degree and some folk more low, and that everyone should be served in his estate and his degree."[16] This traditional feudal ethic seemed to most capitalists to be incompatible with the capitalist order, and it was gradually replaced by the new individualist philosophy of classical liberalism.

Classical liberalism, however, was a two-edged sword. It became an ideology justifying the new capitalist order (see Chapter 4). But the individualistic assumptions of classical liberalism were very radical. If the old feudal aristocracy had no inherent superiority over the middle class, and if any member of the middle class was to be freed of the old restraints, and if each individual should be the best judge in deciding his own affairs, then how could one stop short of

---

15 Robert Owen, "The Book of the New Moral World," reprinted in part in Carl Cohen, ed., *Communism, Fascism and Democracy* (New York: Random House, 1962), pp. 47–48.

16 Quoted in J. L. and Barbara Hammond, *The Rise of Modern Industry* (New York: Harper & Row, Torchbooks, 1969), p. 215.

asserting the same rights and advantages for the lowest classes? The ideal that each individual ought, in some abstract way, to be considered as important as any other individual was radical indeed.

If individualism seemed to imply equality in theory, however, it certainly did not lead to it in practice. The rugged battles for more profits led not only to the social misery described above but also to a new class division of society, which was as sharply defined and as exploitative in nature as the medieval class structure. Membership in the higher class of the new system depended not on genealogy but on ownership. Capitalists derived their income and their power from the ownership of the means of production.

Socialism, then, was a protest against the inequalities of capitalism and the social evils resulting from these inequalities. The inequalities themselves, in the opinion of socialists from the earliest times to the present, resulted inevitably from the institution of private property in the means of production. Hence, socialism asserted as its most cardinal tenet that social justice demanded the abolition of private ownership of capital.

Intellectually, socialism was a wedding of the liberal notion of the equality of all men to the notion inherent in the traditional Christian corporate ethic that every man should be his brother's keeper. Incorporating the egalitarian elements of classical liberalism into the traditional Christian ethic made this a utopian ethic, in comparison with which existing society was criticized. Without this egalitarian element, the Christian ethic served well as an ideological justification of the hierarchical class system of the Middle Ages and was sometimes used to defend the capitalist system, particularly in the late nineteenth and twentieth centuries (of which more will be said later).

important pre-marxist socialists

When Owen asserted that in the ideal society, private property and acquisitive profit-seeking would be eliminated, he became part of a socialist tradition that had already been firmly established by his time. One of the first voices of socialist protest against capitalist property relations was that of Gerrard Winstanley (1609–1652), a cloth merchant who had been bankrupted in the depression of 1643. He blamed his own misfortune as well as that of others on the "cheating art of buying and selling."[17] In 1649, he led a strange band of followers from London to Saint George's Hill, Surrey. There they

17 Quoted in Lee Cameron McDonald, *Western Political Theory: The Modern Age* (New York: Harcourt Brace Jovanovich, 1962), p. 63.

occupied unused crown lands, which they cultivated in common and, in general, shared a communal existence.

In that same year, Winstanley published *The True Levellers Standard Advanced,* in which he rebuked "the powers of England" and "the powers of the world" for their failure to realize that "the great creator . . . made the Earth a common treasury for beasts and man."[18] He asserted that all those who derived their incomes in part or in full from property ownership were violating God's commandment "Thou shalt not steal." "You pharaohs, you have rich clothing and full bellies, you have your honors and your ease; but know the day of judgment is begun and that it will reach you ere long. The poor people you oppress shall be the saviours of the land."[19]

Throughout the eighteenth and nineteenth centuries, a large number of writers argued that private property was the source of the inequities and exploitation that existed in the capitalist economy. In this chapter, we can mention only a few of the better known among them. One of the most interesting was the Frenchman Gracchus Babeuf (1760–1797). Babeuf argued that nature had made all men equal in rights and needs. Therefore, the inequalities of wealth and power that had developed should be redressed by society. Unfortunately, most societies did the opposite: They set up a coercive mechanism to protect the interests of the property holders and the wealthy. For Babeuf, the presence of inequality meant, of necessity, the presence of injustice. Capitalist commerce existed, he said, "for the purpose of pumping the sweat and blood of more or less everybody, in order to form lakes of gold for the benefit of the few."[20] The workers who created the wealth of society got the least, and until private property was eliminated, the inequalities in society could never be redressed.

Babeuf led the extreme left wing of the French revolutionary movement. After the fall of Robespierre, he masterminded a conspiracy to destroy the French government and replace it with one dedicated to equality and brotherhood. The plot was betrayed by Georges Grisel, and its leaders were arrested. Babeuf and his lieutenant, Darthe, were condemned to death and executed on February 24, 1797.

Babeuf is important in the socialist tradition because he was the first to advance the notion that if an egalitarian socialist state is to be achieved, the existing government must be toppled by force. The issue of whether socialism can be achieved peacefully has divided

18 Ibid.
19 Ibid.
20 Alexander Gray, *The Socialist Tradition* (London: Longmans, Green, 1963), p. 105.

socialists since Babeuf's time. Babeuf also believed that if his revolt were successful, a period of dictatorship during the transition from capitalism to the communist democracy he envisioned would be necessary to extirpate the surviving remnants of the capitalist system. Thus, in several important ways Babeuf was a precursor of the twentieth-century Russian Bolsheviks.

Other important ideas in the socialist critique of capitalism can be seen in the writings of the Englishman William Godwin (1756–1836). Whereas the classical liberals were bemoaning the natural laziness and depravity of the lower classes, Godwin argued that the defects of the working class were attributable to corrupt and unjust social institutions. The capitalist society, in Godwin's opinion, made fraud and robbery inevitable: "If every man could with perfect facility obtain the necessaries of life . . . temptation would lose its power."[21] Men could not always obtain the necessities because the laws of private property created such great inequalities in society. Justice demanded that capitalists property relations be abolished and that property belong to that person whom it would benefit most:

> To whom does any article of property, suppose a loaf of bread, justly belong? To him who most wants it, or to whom the possession of it will be most beneficial. Here are six men famished with hunger, and the loaf is, absolutely considered, capable of satisfying the cravings of them all. Who is it that has a reasonable claim to benefit by the qualities with which the loaf is endowed? They are all brothers perhaps, and the law of primogeniture bestows it exclusively to the eldest. But does justice confirm this award? The laws of different countries dispose of property in a thousand different ways; but there can be but one way which is most conformable to reason.[22]

That one way, of course, must be based upon the equality of all men. To whom could the poor turn to correct the injustices of the system? In Godwin's opinion, it most certainly would not be the government. With economic power went political power. The rich are "directly or indirectly the legislators of the state; and of consequence are perpetually reducing oppression into a system."[23] The law, then, is the means by which the rich oppress the poor, for "legislation is in almost every country grossly the favorer of the rich against the poor."[24]

These two ideas of Godwin's were to be voiced again and again by

[21] William Godwin, An Inquiry Concerning Political Justice, pp. 33 and 34. Quoted in Gray, op. cit., p. 119.

[22] Ibid., p. 131.

[23] Ibid., p. 119.

[24] Ibid.

nineteenth-century socialists: (1) that capitalist social and economic institutions, particularly private property relations, were the causes of the evils and suffering within the system, and (2) that the government in a capitalist system would never redress these evils because it was controlled by the capitalist class. But Godwin had an answer to this seemingly impossible situation. He believed that human reason would save society. Once men became educated about the evils of the situation, they would reason together and arrive at the only rational solution. As Godwin saw it, this solution entailed the abolition of government, the abolition of laws, and the abolition of private property. For this radical social transformation, Godwin believed that socialists could rely, primarily, on education and reason. Most subsequent socialists argued that education and reason alone were insufficient. Education, they believed, should be only a part of the larger objective of creating a mass socialist movement. The importance of education and intellectual persuasion in attaining socialist ends has remained a much-debated issue to this day.

Other important socialist ideas were advanced by Henri de Saint-Simon (1760–1825), who was actually closer to the Tory radicals than the socialists in many ways. He came from an impoverished family of nobility, and his writings show an aristocrat's disdain for the antisocial egoism of the rich capitalists.

He also condemned the idle rich who lived off the labor of the poor but contributed nothing to society's well-being:

> Suppose that France preserves all the men of genius that she possesses in the sciences, fine arts and professions, but has the misfortune to lose in the same day Monsieur the King's brother [and all of the other members of the royal household]. . . . Suppose that France loses at the same time all the great officers of the royal household, all the ministers . . . all the councillors of state, all the chief magistrates, marshals, cardinals, archbishops, bishops, vicars-general, and canons, all the prefects and subprefects, all the civil servants, and judges, and, in addition, ten thousand of the richest proprietors who live in the style of nobles. This mischance would certainly distress the French, because they are kind-hearted, and could not see with indifference the sudden disappearance of such a large number of their compatriots. But this loss of thirty thousand individuals . . . would result in no political evil for the state.[25]

Saint-Simon was the first to emphasize the efficiency of huge industrial undertakings and argued that the government should actively intervene in production, distribution, and commerce in the

25 F. M. H. Markham, ed., *Henri Comte de Saint-Simon, Selected Writings* (Oxford: Blackwell, 1952), pp. 72–73.

interest of promoting the welfare of the masses. He sanctioned both private property and its privileges as long as they were used to promote the welfare of the masses.

Many of his followers were more radical. They wrote endless pamphlets and books exposing abuses of capitalism, attacking private property and inheritance, denouncing exploitation, and advocating government ownership and control of economic production in the interest of the general welfare. It was from Saint-Simon and his followers that socialism inherited the idea of the necessity of government administration of production and distribution in a socialist economy.

There were many other famous socialists in the first half of the nineteenth century. The Frenchman Charles Fourier popularized the idea of cooperatives (or "phalanxes," as he called them). He attempted to change society by encouraging the formation of phalanxes. His failure proved to many socialists that capitalism could not be reformed by the mere setting of examples. He was also one of the first socialists to predict that competition among capitalists would lead inevitably to monopoly:

> Among the influences tending to restrict man's industrial rights, I will mention the formation of privileged corporations which, monopolizing a given branch of industry, arbitrarily close the doors of labour against whomsoever they please. . . . Extremes meet, and the greater the extent to which anarchical competition is carried, the nearer the approach to *universal monopoly,* which is the opposite excess. . . . Monopolies, . . . operating in conjunction with the great landed interest, will reduce the middle and labouring classes to a state of commercial vassalage. . . . The small operators will be reduced to the position of mere agents, working for the mercantile coalition. We shall then see the reappearing of feudalism in an inverse order, founded on mercantile leagues, and answering to the Baronial Leagues of the Middle Ages.[26]

Fourier believed that in a capitalist economy, only one-third of the people really did socially useful work. The other two-thirds were directed, by the corruption and distortion caused by the market system, into useless occupations or were useless, wealthy parasites. He divided these wastes into four categories:

First Waste: Useless or destructive labour. (1) the army (2) the idle rich (3) ne'er-do-wells (4) sharpers (5) prostitutes (6) magistrates (7) police (8) lawyers (9) philosophical

---

[26] Quoted in Sydney H. Coontz, *Productive Labor and Effective Demand* (New York: Augustus M. Kelley, 1966), p. 54.

cranks (10) bureaucrats (11) spies (12) priests and clergymen.

Second Waste: Misdirected work, since society makes it repellent, and not a vehicle of man's personality, attractive to him.

(a) Deflection of the passions into greed and morbidity, instead of being utilized as society's motors.

(b) Scale of production too small to utilize labour properly.

(c) No co-operation.

(d) No control of production.

(e) No adjustment of supply to demand, except by the mechanism of the "blind" market.

(f) The family: this economic and educational unit is absurdly small.

Third Waste: Commerce dominated by middlemen. It takes a hundred men to do what society, with warehouses, distributed according to need, could do with one. A hundred men sit at counters, wasting hours waiting for someone to enter, a hundred people write inventories, etc., competitively. These hundred wasted merchants eat without producing.

Fourth Waste: Wage labour in indirect servitude; cost of class antagonisms. Since class interests are opposed, the cost keeping men divided are greater than the gains in making them co-operate.[27]

Most socialists agreed that capitalism was irrational and wasteful and that it led to extreme inequalities and, hence, was unjust and immoral. They disagreed, however, on the tactics that they should use to achieve socialism. Many famous socialists, such as Louis Blanc (1811–1882), believed that the government could be used as an instrument of reform and that socialism could be achieved through gradual, peaceful, piecemeal reform. Others, such as Auguste Blanqui (1805–1881), the pupil of Babeuf, based his ideas on the assumption that capitalism involved a constant class war between capitalists and workers. He believed that as long as capitalists occupied the position of power, which ownership of capital gave them, they would exploit the workers, and the government and laws would be weapons to be used in this exploitation. He therefore saw no hope through gradual political reform. Revolution was, for him, the only answer.

Pierre Joseph Proudhon (1809–1865), in his well-known book,

27 Ibid., p. 55.

What is Property?, answered the question posed in the title with a slogan that made him famous: "Property is theft." He believed that property was "the mother of tyranny." The primary purpose of the state was the enforcement of property rights. Because property rights were simply sets of special privileges for the few and general restrictions and prohibitions for the masses, they involved coercion, of necessity, in their establishment and their continued enforcement. Hence, the primary function of the state was to coerce.

"Every state is a tyranny," declared Proudhon. The state was the coercive arm of the ruling class, and Proudhon advocated resistance rather than servitude: "Whoever lays a hand on me to govern me is a usurper and a tyrant. I declare him to be my enemy." There could be no justice until property relations were abolished and the state was made unnecessary:

> To be governed is to be watched over, inspected, spied on, directed, legislated, regimented, closed in, indoctrinated, preached at, controlled, assessed, evaluated, censored, commanded; all by creatures that have neither the right, nor wisdom, nor virtue. . . . To be governed means that at every move, operation, or transaction one is noted, registered, entered in a census, taxed, stamped, priced, assessed, patented, licensed, authorized, recommended, admonished, prevented, reformed, set right, corrected. Government means to be subjected to tribute, trained, ransomed, exploited, monopolized, extorted, pressured, mystified, robbed; all in the name of public utility and the general good. Then, at the first sign of resistance or word of complaint, one is repressed, fined, despised, vexed, pursued, hustled, beaten up, garroted, imprisoned, shot, machine-gunned, judged, sentenced, deported, sacrificed, sold, betrayed, and to cap it all ridiculed, mocked, outraged, and dishonored. That is government, that is its justice and its morality! . . . O human personality! How can it be that you have cowered in such subjection for sixty centuries?"[28]

Property rights were not only the source of tyranny and coercion, they were also the source of economic inequality. Whereas the amount of labor expended determined how much was produced in a capitalist society, ownership of property determined how that produce was divided. It was divided in such a way that those who produced got almost nothing of what they produced; whereas those who owned property used the laws of private ownership to "legally steal" from the workers. In Proudhon's ideal state, he rejected not only capitalist property relations but industrialization as well. Like

---

[28] Quoted in Daniel Guerin, *Anarchism* (New York: Monthly Review Press, 1970), pp. 15–16; the quotations in the preceding paragraph are from the same source.

Thomas Jefferson, he envisioned a golden age of small-scale agriculture and handicraft production, in which each farmer and worker owned his own capital, and no one lived through property ownership alone.

The list could be continued, but we have included most of the important pre-Marxian socialist ideas and have introduced some of the most famous socialist thinkers. Unquestionably the most influential socialist thinker was Karl Marx, and it is to a summary of his ideas that we turn in Chapter 6.

summary

The workers bore the social costs of industrialization. The new factory system reduced most of them to poor, unhealthy, dehumanized wretches. Classical liberalism was not only impervious to their plight, it even taught that the desire to improve the conditions of the poor was quixotic and doomed to failure. Two groups of thinkers, the Tory radicals and the socialists, took strong exception to this view.

The Tory radicals had a gentleman's disdain for the "vulgar, money-grubbing" middle-class merchants and manufacturers. They clung to an essentially reactionary, paternalistic version of the Christian corporate ethic—reactionary because it seemed to assume that they could ignore industrialism and go back to an earlier agrarian way of life.

The socialists protested the inequalities of capitalism. They believed that by eliminating private ownership of capital, they could create an industrial society in which every man was treated with dignity and in which the fruits of production were equitably divided.

chapter 6
socialist protest:
the economics of marx

Karl Marx (1818–1883) has been the most influential of all socialists.
His writings have had, and continue to have, a profound impact not
only on socialist thought but also on policy decisions that affect a
large percentage of the world's population. Although he worked in
close collaboration with Friedrich Engels (1820–1895) and was
unquestionably deeply influenced by Engels, Marx was the intellectual
leader in most matters of political economy, so no attempt is made in
this chapter to distinguish Engels' separate contributions.

historical materialism

Marx believed that most of the late eighteenth- and early nineteenth-
century socialists were humanitarians who were rightly indignant
about the harsh exploitation that accompanied early capitalism.
Despite his admiration for many of them, he gave to them the derisive
label "utopian socialists." He believed most of them to be quixotic
utopians who hoped to transform society by appealing to the
rationality and moral sensibilities of the educated class. In Marx's
view, educated men were usually members of the upper classes, and
thus they owed their position, prosperity, and superior knowledge and
education to the privileges inherent in the capitalist system.
Therefore, they would generally do everything within their power to

preserve that system. The few heretics and humanitarians among them would certainly never constitute the power base from which a transition from capitalism to socialism could be effected. Yet Marx had an undying faith that such a social and economic transition would occur. This faith was not the result of his belief in the rationality and humanity of men but rather was based on an analysis of capitalism. He concluded that internal contradictions and antagonisms within the capitalist system would eventually destroy it.

Marx based his study of capitalist society on a historical approach that has been called *historical materialism.* When he looked at the mass of ideas, laws, religious beliefs, mores, moral codes, and economic and social institutions that were present in all social systems, he tried to simplify the complex cause–effect relations that existed among these many facets of social systems. Such a simplification, he believed, would enable him to focus his attention on those relationships that were most fundamental in determining a social system's overall direction of movement and change.

Although all social institutions and intellectual traditions were reciprocally related in a complex web of cause–effect relations (each affecting and in turn being affected by the other), he believed that a society's economic base, or mode of production, exerted the most powerful influence in determining the other social institutions as well as social and religious thought. The *mode of production* consisted of two elements: (1) the forces of production and (2) the relations of production. The *forces of production* included tools, factories, equipment, production skills and knowledge of the labor force, natural resources, and the general level of technology. The *relations of production* were the social relationships between men, particularly the relations of each class of men to the means of production, which included the ownership of productive facilities and the division of the fruits of productive activity. The whole economic system, or mode of production, Marx called the *base,* or *substructure.* The religions, ethics, laws, mores, and institutions of society he called the *superstructure.*

Although the mode of production and the superstructure interacted reciprocally as both cause and effect, the mode of production was the base upon which the superstructure was built. Therefore, the line of causation running from this economic base to the superstructure was much more powerful and important than the reverse line of causation. To argue that Marx believed that the economic base determined, completely and rigidly, every aspect of the superstructure is grossly inaccurate (although it is often done). He did assert, however, that the mode of production was the most important single aspect in determining not only the present social superstructure but also the direction of social change.

When he referred to the relations of production Marx meant the class structure of society, the most important single aspect of the mode of production. The antagonisms between social classes were, for Marx, the propelling force in history. "The history of all hitherto existing society is the history of class struggles."[1] he proclaimed. The importance of the mode of production and the class antagonisms it engendered have been summarized by Marx in a famous passage:

In the social production which men carry on they enter into definite relations that are indispensable and independent of their will; these relations of production correspond to a definite stage of development of their material powers of production. The sum total of these relations of production constitutes the economic structure of society —the real foundation, on which rise legal and political superstructures and to which correspond definite forms of social consciousness. The mode of production in material life determines the general character of the social, political, and spiritual processes of life. It is not the consciousness of men that determines their existence, but, on the contrary, their social existence determines their consciousness. At a certain stage of their development, the material forces of production in society come into conflict with the existing relations of production, or—what is but a legal expression for the same thing—with the property relations within which they had been at work before. From forms of development of the forces of production these relations turn into their fetters. Then comes the period of social revolution. With the change of economic foundation the entire immense superstructure is more or less rapidly transformed. In considering such transformations the distinction should always be made between the material transformation of the economic conditions of production which can be determined with the precision of natural science, and the legal, political, religious, aesthetic, or philosophic—in short ideological forms in which men become conscious of this conflict and fight it out.[2]

Marx identified four separate economic systems, or modes of prcduction, through which the European civilization had evolved: (1) primitive communal, (2) slave, (3) feudal, and (4) capitalist. In any one of these economic systems, there was a unique mode of production which included forces of production as well as a particular class structure, or relations of production. Increasing demands for more production inevitably led to changes in the forces of production, yet the relationships of production, or class positions, remained

1 Karl Marx and Friedrich Engels, "The Communist Manifesto," in Arthur P. Mendel, ed., *Essential Works of Marxism* (New York: Bantam, 1965), p. 13.

2 Karl Marx, *Critique of Political Economy*, reprinted in part in Howard Selsam and Harry Martel, eds., *Reader in Marxist Philosophy* (New York: International Publishers, 1963), pp. 186–187.

fixed and were fiercely defended. Therefore, there were conflicts, tensions, and contradictions between the changing forces of production and the fixed social relations (and vested interests) of production. These conflicts and contradictions grew in intensity and importance until a series of violent social eruptions destroyed the old system and created a new system which would have new class relationships compatible (for a time at least) with the changed forces of production.

In each mode of production, the contradictions that developed between the forces of production and the relations of production showed themselves in the form of a class struggle. The struggle raged between the class that controlled the means of production and received most of the benefits and privileges of the system (e.g., the Roman slaveholders) and the much-larger class that they controlled and exploited (e.g., the Roman slaves). In all economic systems prior to capitalism, this class struggle had destroyed one system only to create a new system based upon exploitation of the masses by a new ruling class, and hence the beginning of a new class struggle. Capitalism, however, was, in Marx's opinion, the last mode of production that would be based upon the existence of antagonistic classes. The capitalist class, which ruled by virtue of its ownership of the means of production, would be overthrown by the proletariat, or working class, which would establish a classless society in which the means of production were owned in common by all. The transition from capitalism to socialism will be discussed in greater detail below. Before proceeding further, however, it is necessary to examine the basis of Marx's moral condemnation of capitalism.

marx's moral critique of capitalism

According to Marx, two most important features define capitalism and distinguish it from other economic systems: (1) The separation of the worker from the means of production created a class of owners and a class of workers; (2) the market, or cash nexus, was extended into all human relationships involved in production and distribution. Like most socialists before him, Marx deplored the extremes of wealth and poverty that this class relationship created.

His moral condemnation of capitalism, however, went beyond an ethical rejection of these great inequalities. His most important criticism of capitalism involved the idea that within a capitalist system, men could not develop their innate potentialities. They could not become emotionally or intellectually fully developed men.

Man differed from animals because in order to satisfy his needs, he created tools and worked with them to shape and control his environment. Man's senses and intellect were developed and refined through working. Through his relations with what he produced, man achieved both pleasure and self-realization. In precapitalist social systems such as feudalism, man could achieve this self-realization through work despite an exploitative class structure. Because the exploitative social relations were also personal and paternalistic, work was not merely a means of making money.

This changed with capitalism, when, in Marx's opinion:

> the bourgeoisie, wherever it has got the upper hand, has put an end to all feudal patriarchal, idyllic relations. It has pitilessly torn asunder the motley feudal ties that bound man to his "natural superiors," and has left remaining no other nexus between man and man than naked self-interest, than callous "cash payment." It has drowned the most heavenly ecstasies of religious fervor, of chivalrous enthusiasm, of philistine sentimentalism, in the icy water of egotistical calculation. It has resolved personal worth into exchange value. . . .[3]

In a capitalist society, the market separated and isolated "exchange value," or money price, from the qualities that shaped man's relation with things as well as with other human beings. This was especially true in the work process. To the capitalist, wages were merely another expense of production to be added to the costs of raw materials and machinery in the profit calculation. Labor became a mere *commodity* to be bought if a profit could be made on the purchase. Whether the laborer could sell his labor power was completely beyond his control. It depended on the cold and totally impersonal conditions of the market. The product of this labor was likewise totally outside of the laborer's life, being the property of the capitalist.

Marx used the term *alienation* to describe the condition of men in this situation. They felt alienated or divorced from their work, from their institutional and cultural environment, and from their fellow men. The conditions of work, the object produced, and indeed the very possibility of working were determined by the numerically small class of capitalists and their profit calculations, not by human need or aspirations. The effects of this alienation can best be summarized in Marx's own words:

> What, then, constitutes the alienation of labour?
> First, the fact that labour is external to the worker, i.e., it does not belong to his essential being; that in his work, therefore, he does not affirm himself but denies himself, does not feel content but unhappy, does not develop freely his physical and mental energy but mortifies

3 Marx and Engels, "The Communist Manifesto," op. cit., p. 15.

his body and ruins his mind. The worker therefore only feels himself outside his work, and in his work feels outside himself. He is at home when he is not working, and when he is working he is not at home. His labour is therefore not voluntary but coerced; it is *forced labour.* It is therefore not the satisfaction of a need; it is merely a *means* to satisfy needs external to it. Its alien character emerges clearly in the fact that as soon as no physical or other compulsion exists, labour is shunned like the plague. External labour, labour in which man alienates himself, is a labour of self-sacrifice, or mortification. Lastly, the external character of labour for the worker appears in the fact that it is not his own, but someone elses, that it does not belong to him, that in it he belongs, not to himself, but to another. . . . As a result, therefore, man (the worker) no longer feels himself to be freely active in any but his animal functions—eating, drinking, procreating, or at most in his dwelling and in dressing up, etc.; and in his human functions he no longer feels himself to be anything but an animal. What is animal becomes human and what is human becomes animal.[4]

It was this degradation and total dehumanization of the working class, thwarting man's personal development and making an alien market commodity of man's life-sustaining activities, that Marx most thoroughly condemned in the capitalist system. Thus, his moral critique went far beyond those of most of his socialist precursors. His faith in the possibility of a better future for the working class, however, was not based on the hope that ever-increasing numbers of people would share his moral indignation and therefore attempt to reform the system. Rather, he believed that the capitalist mode of production and the class conflict inherent in it would lead to the destruction of capitalism. Capitalism, like all previous modes of production in which class conflicts were present, would destroy itself. In order to understand the basis for this faith, it is necessary to examine his economic theory, in which he attempted to analyze the "laws of motion" of capitalism.

the labor theory of value and surplus value

Because, for Marx, the capitalist mode of production was based upon the opposition of labor and capital, he began by analyzing the capital-labor relation. This relation was essentially one of exchange. The worker sold his labor power to the capitalist for money, with which the worker bought the necessities of life. Thus, this exchange

4 Karl Marx, *Economic and Philosophic Manuscripts of 1844* (Moscow: Progress Publishers, 1959), p. 69.

relation was obviously merely a special case of the general problem
of exchange values within a capitalist market economy. Marx,
therefore, began volume 1 of *Capital* with a section entitled
"Commodities" in which, he defined *commodities* as objects that are
usually intended for exchange rather than for the direct personal use
of the producer. He then attempted to analyze the basic determinant
of the exchange value of commodities. In other words, he analyzed
the ratio in which commodities could be exchanged for other
commodities, as opposed to use value which was a measure of the
usefulness of commodities to their possessor.

Like Adam Smith, David Ricardo (Smith's most important disciple),
and most of the pre-Marxian classical economists, Marx believed
that the exchange value of a commodity was determined by the
amount of labor time necessary for its production. His theory is,
therefore, usually called the *labor theory of value.* He recognized that
laborers differed in abilities, training, and motivation, but he believed
that skilled labor could be calculated as a multiple of unskilled labor.
Thus, all labor time could be reduced to a common denominator:
abstract labor.

He also realized that labor time expended in the production of a
useless commodity (one for which there was no demand) would not
create a commodity with an exchange value equal to the labor time
embodied in it. The desire of capitalists to maximize their profits
would, however, prevent the production of objects for which there
was no demand. Capitalists would produce only those commodities
for which market demand would permit the realization of at least
their costs of production. Market demand would determine not only
what commodities were produced but also the relative quantities in
which they were produced.

Marx began by describing a system of *simple commodity
production,* in which each producer owned his own means of
production and sold the commodities he produced. The producer
would exchange his commodities for money, with which he would
buy other commodities for his own use. Simple commodity production
was then contrasted with *capitalist commodity production,* in which
the capitalist begins the process with only money. He buys the means
of production and the labor power, and when the laborers complete
the production process, he sells the commodities for more money.
Thus, the money with which he ends is greater than that with which
he started. This difference is what Marx called *surplus value.* He
considered it to be the source of capitalist profits.

Surplus value originated in the fact that capitalists bought one
commodity—labor power—and sold a different commodity—that
which labor produced in the production process. Profits were made
because the value of labor power was less than the value of the

commodities produced with the labor power. The value of labor power was "determined, as in the case of every other commodity, by the labor time necessary" for its maintenance and reproduction, which meant that "the value of labor power . . . [was] the value of the means of subsistence necessary for the maintenance of the laborer at a socially defined minimal standard of living."[5] The fact was that the average length of the working day exceeded the time necessary for a laborer to produce the value-equivalent of his subsistence wage, which enabled the capitalist to appropriate the surplus produced over and above this subsistence.

the accumulation of capital

The capitalist gained his profits because of his ownership of capital. Most of these profits were plowed back to increase his capital and hence increase future profits, which could then be plowed back into more capital, and so forth. This was the process of capitalist accumulation: Capital led to profits, which led to more capital. When and how did the process originate? Many classical economists and liberals, particularly the English economist Nassau Senior (1790–1864), had answered this question in a way favorable to the capitalist, arguing that through hard, diligent work and abstemious behavior, the capitalist had begun a modest saving program, which enabled him to accumulate slowly the fortunes that many nineteenth-century capitalists owned. Laborers, on the contrary, rather than devoting themselves to working and living abstemiously, had profligately squandered their earnings.

Marx accused these defenders of the capitalist system of being totally ignorant of history. In a famous passage, which gives the flavor of some of his most colorful writing, Marx described the process of "primitive accumulation" by which the fortunes were originally made:

> This primitive accumulation plays in Political Economy about the same part as original sin in theology. Adam bit the apple, and thereupon sin fell on the human race. Its origin is supposed to be explained when it is told as an anecdote of the past. In times long gone by there were two sorts of people; one, the diligent, intelligent, and above all, frugal elite; the other, lazy rascals, spending their substance, and more, in riotous living. . . . Thus it came to pass that the former sort accumulated wealth, and the latter sort had nothing

[5] Karl Marx, *Capital,* vol. 1 (Moscow: Foreign Language Publishing House, 1961), pp. 170–171.

to sell except their own skins. And from this original sin dates the poverty of the great majority that, despite all its labour, has up to now nothing to sell but itself, and the wealth of the few that increases constantly although they have long ceased to work. Such insipid childishness is every day preached to us in the defence of property. . . . As soon as the question of property crops up, it becomes a sacred duty to proclaim the intellectual food of the infant as the one thing fit for all ages and for all stages of development. In actual history it is notorious that conquest, enslavement, robbery, murder, briefly force, play the great part. . . . The methods of primitive accumulation are anything but idyllic.[6]

Marx listed the important forms of primitive accumulation as the enclosures and the dislocation of the feudal agrarian population, the great price inflation, monopolies of trade, colonies, "the extirpation, enslavement and entombment in mines of the aboriginal population, the beginning of the conquest and looting of the East Indies, [and] the turning of Africa into a warren for the commercial hunting of black skins."[7]

Once this initial accumulation of capital had taken place, the drive to acquire more capital became the moving force of the capitalist system. The capitalist's social standing and prestige as well as his economic and political power depended on the size of the capital he controlled. He could not stand still; he was beset on every side by fierce competition. The system demanded that he accumulate and grow more powerful in order to outdo his competitors, or else his competitors would force him to the wall and take over his capital. Competitors were constantly developing new and better methods of production. Only by accumulating new and better capital equipment could this challenge be met. Thus, Marx believed that the capitalist

shares with the miser the passion for wealth as wealth. But that which in the miser is a mere idiosyncrasy, is in the capitalist the effect of the social mechanism of which he is but one of the wheels. Moreover, the development of capitalist production makes it constantly necessary to keep increasing the amount of capital laid out in a given industrial undertaking, and competition makes the immanent laws of capitalist production to be felt by each individual capitalist as external coercive laws. It compels him to keep constantly extending his capital, in order to preserve it, but extend it he cannot except by means of progressive accumulation.[8]

6 Ibid., pp. 713–714.
7 Ibid., p. 751.
8 Ibid., p. 592.

sectoral imbalances and economic crises

It was this ceaseless drive to accumulate more capital that created many of the contradictions of capitalist development. The capitalist would begin with the acquisition of more machines and tools of the types that were currently being used. This would require a proportional increase in the number of workers employed in order to operate the new equipment. But the capitalists had been able to keep the wage rate at the subsistence level only because there existed what Marx called an "industrial reserve army" of unemployed labor, which was living at below subsistence and striving to take jobs that would pay a mere subsistence wage. Therefore capitalists usually had no problem in keeping wage rates down. As the industrial expansion took place, however, the increasing demand for labor soon depleted the ranks of the reserve. When this happened, the capitalist began to find that he had to pay higher wages to get enough labor.

The individual capitalist took the wage level as given and beyond his power to change, so he attempted to make the best of the situation. The most profitable course of action seemed to be changing the techniques of production by introducing new labor-saving machinery so that each laborer would then be working with more capital and output per laborer could be increased. This labor-saving investment would enable the capitalist to expand output with the same or an even smaller work force. When all or most of the capitalists, acting individually, did this, the problem of high wages was temporarily alleviated as the reserve army was replenished by workers displaced by the new productive techniques. The creation of technological unemployment saved the day. But not without introducing new problems and contradictions.

Labor-saving expansion permitted increases in total production without increasing the wages paid to workers. Therefore, while new goods were flooding the market, workers' wages were being restricted, with the result that consumer demand was limited. As Marx put it, the workers were still producing more profits in the form of goods, but the capitalists could not "realize" the profits by selling these goods in the market because of lack of consumer demand.

In order to clarify this process further, Marx divided the capitalist economy into two sectors, one producing consumer goods and the other producing capital goods. Lack of consumer demand meant that capitalists in the consumption-goods sector would find they could not sell their entire output and thus would lower their expectations of profits and would certainly *not* want to add to their productive facilities. They would, therefore, cancel any plans to add to their already excessively large capital stock. These decisions would, of course, significantly reduce the demand for capital goods, which would result in a decrease in production in the capital-goods sector. Unlike the naïve underconsumptionist theories of the earlier socialists, Marx noted that the first obvious sign of a depression might thus appear in the capital-goods sector.

The actual decrease in capital-goods production would mean that some workers in that sector would be fired, which would lower total wages, decrease national income, and reduce consumer demand. Thus, there would be a cutback in consumer-goods production, and layoffs of workers would spread to those industries. Wages and incomes would then be further reduced, causing a glut, or surfeit, of consumer goods. The entire process of successive repercussions in both sectors would then be one of economic collapse.

The resulting depression would more than restore the reserve army of unemployed and push labor's standard of living back to or below the subsistence level. Marx, however, was not a "stagnationist" —that is, he did not believe that capitalism would suffer one long depression or that mass unemployment at high levels would last forever. In the depression, workers' wages would fall, but not as rapidly as the output of goods. Thus, eventually supply would be lower than consumer demand, and therefore recovery would occur. Marx believed that capitalism does grow, but jerkily, in cycles of boom and bust, with periodic high levels of unemployment for the workers.

economic concentration

Concentration of wealth and economic power in the hands of fewer and fewer capitalists was another important consequence of capital accumulation. This concentration was the result of two forces. First, competition between capitalists tended to create a situation in which the strong either crushed or absorbed the weak. "Here competition rages in direct proportion to the number, and in inverse proportion to the magnitudes, of the antagonistic capitals. It always ends in the ruin of many small capitalists, whose capitals partly pass into the hands of their conquerors, partly vanish."[9]

Second, as technology improved, there was "an increase in the minimum amount of . . . capital necessary to carry on a business

9 Ibid., p. 626.

under its normal conditions." In order to remain competitive a firm would constantly have to increase the productivity of its laborers. The "productiveness of labor . . . [depended] on the scale of production."[10] Thus, changing technology as well as competition among capitalists created an inexorable movement of the capitalist system toward larger and larger firms owned by fewer and fewer capitalists. In this way, the gulf between the small class of wealthy capitalists and the great majority of society, the proletariat, continually widened.

the immiserization of the proletariat

At the same time that this increasing concentration of capital was taking place, the misery of the proletariat grew constantly worse. In his famous "doctrine of increasing misery" (immiserization), Marx argued that the conditions of labor would worsen, relative to the affluence of the capitalists, until the laborers could stand no more. And then revolution was inevitable. Because Marx's doctrine of immiserization is very often misrepresented, we will quote his own writings on this point:

> within the capitalist system all methods for raising the social productiveness of labour are brought about at the cost of the individual labourer; all means for the development of production transform themselves into means of domination over, and exploitation of, the producers; they mutilate the labourer into a fragment of a man, degrade him to the level of an appendage of a machine, destroy every remnant of charm in his work and turn it into hated toil; they estrange from him the intellectual potentialities of the labour-process in the same proportion as science is incorporated in it as an independent power; they distort the conditions under which he works, subject him during the labour-process to a despotism the more hateful for its meanness; they transform his life time into working time, and drag his wife and child beneath the wheels of the Juggernaut of capital. But all methods for the production of surplus-value are at the same time methods of accumulation; and every extension of accumulation becomes again a means for the development of those methods. It follows therefore that in proportion as capital accumulates, the lot of the labourer, be his payment high or low, must grow worse. The law . . . establishes an accumulation of misery, corresponding with accumulation of capital. Accumulation of wealth at one pole is, therefore, at the same time accumulation of

[10] Ibid.

> misery, agony of toil, slavery, ignorance, brutality [and] mental
> degradation at the opposite pole. . . .[11]

It should be noted that Marx asserted that the laborer would become worse off even if his wages increased. There were two reasons for this. First, Marx believed that even if workers' wages increased, they would not increase by as much as capitalists' profits increased. The worker would, therefore, become continuously worse off, *relative* to the capitalist. Second, Marx correctly foresaw that as the capitalist system progressed, there was to be an increasingly minute division of labor.

A finer division of labor makes the worker's activities less varied, and his job becomes more repetitious and tedious. Marx agreed with Adam Smith, who had stated that "the man whose whole life is spent in performing a few simple operations . . . generally becomes as stupid and ignorant as it is possible for a human creature to become."[12] Forced into a condition of stupor, and increasingly severely alienated, "the lot of the labourer *be his payment high or low,* must grow worse."[13]

the capitalist state

Marx rejected the notion that socialism could be created through gradual, piecemeal reforms undertaken by the state. By *the state,* Marx meant something more than simply any government: ". . . we may speak of a state only where a special public power of coercion exists which, in the form of an armed organization, stands over and above the population."[14]

Many socialists believed that the state was (or could be) an impartial arbiter in the affairs of society, and they had faith in moral and intellectual appeals to the state. Marx rejected this idea. "Political power," he declared in the *Communist Manifesto,* "is merely the organized power of one class for oppressing another." During each period of history, or for each mode of production, the state is the coercive instrument of the ruling class.

Friedrich Engels has summarized the Marxist argument:

> Former society, moving in class antagonisms, had need of the state,
> that is, an organization of the exploiting class at each period for

11 Ibid., p. 645.

12 Adam Smith, *The Wealth of Nations,* ed. Andrew Skinner (London: Penguin Books, 1970), p. 80.

13 Marx, *Capital,* op. cit., p. 645.

14 Sidney Hook, *Towards the Understanding of Karl Marx* (New York: Day, 1933), p. 256.

the maintenance of external conditions of production; that is, therefore, for the forcible holding down of the exploited class in the
conditions of oppression (slavery, villeinage or serfdom, wage labor)
determined by the existing mode of production. The state was the
official representative of society as a whole, its embodiment in a
visible corporation; but it was this only in so far as it was the state of
that class which itself, in its epoch, represented society as a whole;
in ancient times, the state of the slave-owning citizens; in the Middle
Ages, of the feudal nobility; in our epoch, of the bourgeosie.[15]

Thus, the state is simply a dictatorship of the ruling class over the
remainder of society.

In the capitalist system, the state has two functions. First, it has
the traditional function of enforcing the dictatorship of the capitalists
over the rest of society. The state achieves this, primarily, by
enforcing propery rights, the source of the capitalists' economic
power. It also serves in innumerable other ways—for example,
jailing or harassing critics of capitalism, fighting wars to extend
capitalists' markets, and providing roads, railroads, canals, postal
service, and hundreds of other prerequisites for the conduct of
profitable commerce. Second, the government acts as the arbiter of
the rivalries between capitalists. Each capitalist is interested only in
his own profits, and, therefore, it is inevitable that the interests of
capitalists will clash. If not resolved, many of these clashes would
threaten the very existence of the system. Thus, the government
intervenes, and in doing so, it protects the viability of the capitalist
system. This is why it is sometimes possible to observe the government acting in a way that is contrary to the interests of *some* of the
capitalists. But the government never acts in a way that is contrary
to the interests of *all* capitalists, taken as a class.

For these reasons, Marx rejected the notion that socialists could
rely upon the government for help in bringing about the transition
from capitalism to socialism. The establishment of socialism, in
Marx's opinion, would require a revolution.

the socialist revolution

In his overall view of capitalism, Marx saw the process of capital
accumulation as inevitably involving several steps. Business cycles
or crises would occur regularly and with increasing severity as the
capitalist economy developed. There would be a long-run tendency
for the rate of profit to fall, which would exacerbate the other

15 Friedrich Engels, "Anti-Duhring," in *Handbook of Marxism* (New York: Random
House, 1935), p. 295.

problems of capitalism. Industrial power would become increasingly concentrated in fewer and fewer giant monopolistic and oligopolistic firms, and wealth would become concentrated in the hands of fewer and fewer capitalists. The plight of the laborer would steadily deteriorate.

Given these increasingly bad conditions, the system could not be perpetuated. Eventually, life under capitalism would become so intolerable that workers would revolt, overthrow the whole system, and create a more rational socialist economy.

> Along with the constantly diminishing number of magnates of capital, who usurp and monopolize all advantages of this process of transformation, grows the mass of misery, oppression, slavery, degradation, exploitation; but with this too grows the revolt of the working-class, a class always increasing in numbers, and disciplined, united, organized by the very mechanism of the process of capitalist production itself. The monopoly of capital becomes a fetter upon the mode of production, which has sprung up and flourished along with, and under it. Centralization of the means of production and socialization of labour at last reach a point where they become incompatible with their capitalist integument. This integument is burst asunder. The knell of capitalist private property sounds. The expropriators are expropriated.[16]

In subsequent chapters, we shall examine the defenses of capitalism offered in opposition to Marx, as well as the further development of socialist thought after Marx.

summary

Karl Marx, the most influential of all socialists, based his economic analysis on a theory of history called historical materialism. Most social and political institutions, he believed, were significantly shaped by the economic base of society: the mode of production. Over time, conflicts developed between the forces of production and the relations of production. The working-out of these conflicts was the most important element in the historical evolution of society.

Marx's economic writings were aimed at understanding the conflicts between the class system (or private property system) of capitalism and the methods of production and commodity exchange under capitalism. The conflicts, he believed, would ultimately lead to the overthrow of capitalism and its replacement by a classless, socialist society.

16 Marx, *Capital,* op. cit., p. 763.

chapter 7
the rise of corporate capitalism and the defense of laissez faire

The period from the mid-1840s to 1873 (the year that marked the beginning of the Long Depression in Europe) has been called the golden age of competitive capitalism.[1] These were years of rapid economic expansion throughout most of Europe. Industrialization was getting under way in the United States and continental Europe. The new capital goods necessary for industrialization were, to a large extent, imported from England. Between 1840 and 1860, England experienced an expansion of her exports that was more rapid than it had ever been before or has been since that period. Capital goods increased from 11 percent of English exports to 22 percent, and exports of coal, iron, and steel also rose sharply.

Between 1830 and 1850, England experienced a railroad-building boom in which some 6,000 miles of railroads were constructed. This railroad-building created a strong demand for iron, the production of which doubled between the mid-1830s and the mid-1840s. During the next 30 years, the increases in industrial production were also very impressive. Between 1850 and 1880, the production of pig iron increased from 2,250,000 to 7,750,000 tons per year; steel production went from 49,000 to 1,440,000 tons; and coal increased by 300 percent, to 147,000,000 tons. The Bessemer converted (in the 1850s), the open-hearth furnace (in the 1860s), and the basic process (in the 1870s) completely revolutionized the steel industry, making large-

1 Dudley Dillard, *Economic Development of the North Atlantic Community* (Englewood Cliffs, N.J.: Prentice-Hall, 1967), p. 363.

scale mass production of high-quality steel possible at much lower costs. The capital-goods industries also prospered in the last half of the nineteenth century. The production of machines, ships, chemicals, and other important capital goods employed twice as many men in 1881 as in 1851.

the concentration of corporate power

Just as competitive capitalism seemed to be achieving its greatest successes, the forces that Marx had predicted would lead to the concentration of capital began to show themselves. Improvements in technology were such that larger-sized plants were necessary to take advantage of the more efficient methods of production. Competition became so aggressive and destructive that small competitors were eliminated. Large competitors, facing mutual destruction, often combined in cartels, trusts, or mergers in order to assure their mutual survival. In the United States, this competition was particularly intense (it is described in greater detail in Chapter 8).

A factor that Marx had nearly overlooked, the revolutionary changes in transportation and communication, led to ever-widening markets that could be efficiently supplied by single companies or corporations. The joint-stock company, or corporation, became an effective means by which a single business organization could gain control over vast amounts of capital. And a large, well-organized money market evolved in Europe and North America, which success-fully channeled the smaller capital holdings of many thousands of individuals and small businesses into the hands of large corporations.

In the late nineteenth-century world of giant corporations, in which articles were mass-produced for nationwide or worldwide markets, price competition (and indeed sometimes any kind of competition) proved to be so destructive that it was abandoned almost completely in the large and important industries. There was an inexorable trend toward monopoly, or at least toward collusive oligopoly, which amounted to much the same thing. Many business giants entered into voluntary combinations in which each firm remained somewhat autonomous (e.g., cartels and pools). Other combinations used a financial enterprise such as a trust or holding company to control the voting stock of the corporations involved. Still others used direct mergers and amalgamations from which a single unified corporation emerged.

THE ENGLISH CASE

England, where the classical liberal laissez faire philosophy had taken root most firmly, was perhaps least affected by this movement to corporate monopolies. Advances in technology led to a steel industry made up of very large producers. Nevertheless, the fact that England had very few restrictions on imports prevented the industry from combining into an effectively coordinated group until after the trade restrictions of 1932. The producers of some heavy steel products, such as ship and boiler plate, however, were able to create effective monopolies much earlier.

In other industries, amalgamations led to heavy concentrations. English railroads were combined very early into four main companies. Banking was consolidated until five large commercial banks dominated the industry by the time of World War I. In 1896, the five rivals in the cotton sewing-thread industry had merged into a single monopoly (J. & P. Coats), which came to dominate the entire world market for that commodity and regularly made profits of 20 percent or more. The firm of Lever Brothers, through amalgamations, gained dominance over the soap business in England as well as in several other countries. Monopolies or closely coordinated oligopolies came to control the wallpaper, salt, petroleum, and rubber industries. Many other industries were either dominated or strongly influenced by a few large firms.

THE GERMAN CASE

In Germany, the classical liberal ideology had never really taken root. During Germany's rapid rise to industrial power during the last half of the nineteenth century, there were neither philosophical nor ideological nor legal barriers to large-scale monopolistic industries. It is, therefore, not surprising that monopolies and combinations were more widespread in Germany than in any other country in Europe. The cartel was the main type of monopolistic business combination in Germany. There were approximately 16 cartels in 1879; the figure rose to 35 by 1885, to 300 by 1900, to 600 by 1911, to 1,000 by 1922, and to 2,100 by 1930.

Thus, by the early twentieth century, monopolistic cartels completely dominated almost all the important sectors of the German capitalist economy. (The legal and philosophical justifications of these monopolistic German cartels will be discussed in Chapter 8.)

THE AMERICAN CASE

In the United States, the Civil War gave a great stimulus to industrialization. The war not only increased the demand for industrially produced commodities but also led to the passage of laws that were beneficial to the newly emerging corporations which were soon to dominate American industry.

In an effort to provide civil and political rights for all Americans, Congress had passed the first Civil Rights Act in 1866. By 1868, the Fourteenth Amendment to the U.S. Constitution had been ratified by the states. The ostensible aim of these laws was to confer citizenship and equal rights on American blacks. The Civil Rights Act declared that citizens "of every race and color" were to have equal rights to make contracts, to sue, and to enjoy "full and equal benefit of all laws and proceedings for the security of person and property."[2]

Most of the Civil Rights Act was incorporated into the Fourteenth Amendment. The Amendment also included the famous due process clause, which prohibited any state government from depriving "any person of life, liberty, or *property,* without due process of law."[3]

For decades after its ratification, the Fourteenth Amendment had no effect at all on the civil rights of American blacks; many of them were thrust into situations that were worse than slavery. Rather, most court decisions based on the Fourteenth Amendment involved corporations. The courts ruled that corporations were persons and as such, were protected under the due process clause.

Each time a state government attempted to curb the extravagant excesses of corporations by passing regulatory legislation, the federal courts would invalidate the legislation because it violated the due process clause of the amendment. State governments became powerless before the growing strength of large corporations.

Representative John A. Bingham, who had written the due process clause, later admitted that he had phrased it "word for word and syllable for syllable" to protect the rights of private property and the corporations. Representative Roscoe Conkling, who had also helped frame the Amendment, later declared: "At the time the Fourteenth Amendment was ratified, individuals and *joint stock companies* were appealing for congressional and administrative protection against invidious and discriminating state and local taxes. . . . [the Fourteenth amendment embodies] the Golden Rule, so entrenched

---

[2] Quoted in Kenneth M. Stampp. *The Era of Reconstruction, 1865–1877* (New York: Random House, Vintage Books, 1967), p. 136.

[3] Ibid.; italics added.

as to curb the many who would do to the few as they would not have the few do to them."[4]

With the knowledge that they could go to almost any lengths in their pursuit of profits, without fear of state government controls, the corporations thrived. They grew through internal expansion and, more importantly, through absorbing their competitors. As the giant corporations flourished, the entire American economy thrived and grew.

By the turn of the century, the United States had become the leading industrial power in the world. By 1913, when the American economy produced over one-third of the world's industrial output—more than double that of its closest competitor, Germany—most of the strategic industries (railroads, meat-packing, banking in the large cities, steel, copper, and aluminum) and important areas of manufacturing were dominated by a relatively small number of immensely powerful corporations.

With the exception of the railroads, most industries in the immediate post-Civil War years had been relatively atomistic by present-day standards. Although accurate statistics are not available for this early period, it has been estimated that the largest 200 nonfinancial enterprises would have controlled a very minor and inconsequential percentage of all business assets. By the end of the 1920s, this had grown to 33 percent of all assets.[5]

The primary cause of this concentration was the wave of combinations and mergers that took place at an unprecedented rate during the last quarter of the nineteenth century. This merger movement was the outgrowth of the particularly severe competition that had ravaged and destroyed scores of businesses. During this period, many people began to question seriously the liberal notion of the invisible hand. It seemed to them that unrestrained individualism had led to unrestrained warfare.

> As growing giant businesses locked horns, railroad against railroad, steel mill against steel mill, each sought to assure the coverage of its fixed expenses by gaining for itself as much of the market as it could. The outcome was the steady growth of cutthroat competition among massive producers. . . . On the railroads for example, constant rate-wars were fought in the 1870s. In the oil fields, the coal fields, among the steel and copper producers, similar price-wars repeatedly broke out as producers sought to capture the markets.[6]

4 Ibid., p. 137.

5 Joe S. Bain, *Industrial Organization* (New York: John Wiley, 1959), pp. 191–192.

6 Robert L. Heilbroner, *The Making of Economic Society* (Englewood Cliffs, N.J.: Prentice-Hall, 1962), p. 120.

The outcome of such competition was the destruction or absorption of the small competitors. Eventually, only giants remained, and at this point, further competition was immensely destructive to all competitors. The merger movement represented the means whereby the surviving firms could escape this competition.

The scope of the merger movement was so great that by 1904 it had basically altered the structure of American industry. By the beginning of that year there were over three hundred large industrial combinations with a combined capitalization in excess of $7,000,000,000. They controlled more than two-fifths of the manufacturing capital of the country and had affected about four-fifths of important American industries.[7]

the concentration of income

Accompanying this concentration of industry was an equally striking concentration of income in the hands of a small percentage of the population. Despite the fact that no accurate statistics for the early part of the period exist, it seems reasonably certain that the degree of concentration increased substantially between 1870 and 1929. By 1929, just 5 percent of the population received 34 percent of personal, disposable income in the United States.[8] The degree of concentration had probably reached this extreme as early as 1913. By the end of the 1920s, the highest one-fifth of "families and unattached individuals" were receiving in excess of 50 percent of all personal income.[9]

the reemergence of
the classical liberal ideology

With this immense concentration of economic power in the hands of a small number of giant firms and a small percentage of the population, it would seem that the classical liberal ideology of capitalism would have been abandoned. The economic creed of classical

7 Joe S. Bain, "Industrial Concentration and Anti-Trust Policy," in Harold F. Williamson, ed., Growth of the American Economy (2d ed.; Englewood Cliffs, N.J.: Prentice-Hall, 1951), p. 619.

8 U.S. Department of Commerce, Historical Statistics of the United States (Washington, D.C.: U.S. Government Printing Office, 1961), p. 167.

9 Ibid., the data for 1913 do not give a figure for the income going to the top 5 percent. The amount going to the top 1 percent, however, was 14.98 percent in 1913 and 14.94 percent in 1928.

liberalism, as developed by Adam Smith and refined by such well-known classical economists as David Ricardo, Nassau Senior, and J. B. Say, was based on an analysis of an economy composed of many small enterprises. In such an economy, no individual enterprise could exercise a significant influence on the market price or on the total amount sold in the market. The actions of any firm were dictated to it by consumer tastes as registered in the marketplace and by the competition of innumerable other small firms, each vying for the consumers' dollars.

As wide as the gulf between classical economic theory and late nineteenth-century economic reality seems to have been, the economic creed of classical liberalism did not fall by the wayside in this later period. Rather, it was combined with Benthamite utilitarianism (which was already implicit in Adam Smith's normative model of the invisible hand) and refurbished within an elaborate and esoteric framework of algebra and calculus. This resurgence of the classical liberal economic creed was accomplished by a new school of economic thinkers known as *neoclassical* economists.

the neoclassical theory of utility and consumption

During the early 1870s, at precisely the time the drive toward the economic concentration of corporate capitalism was taking place, three very famous economics texts were published. William Stanley Jevons's *The Theory of Political Economy*[10] and Karl Menger's *Grundsätze der Volkswirtschaftslehre*[11] both appeared in 1871, and three years later, Léon Walras's *Eléments d'économie politique pure* was published.[12] Although there were many differences between the analyses of these men, the similarities in both approach and content of these books were striking.

Their theories pictured an economy made up of large numbers of small producers and consumers, each having insufficient power to influence the market significantly. The business firms hired or bought factors of production; they utilized the factors in the production process in such a way that their profits were maximized. Prices of the final products and factors of production were taken as given and

---

10 William Stanley Jevons, *The Theory of Political Economy* (1st ed.; London: Macmillan, 1871).

11 Karl Menger, *Grundsätze der Volkswirtschaftslehre* (Vienna: Braumuller, 1871), translated as *Principles of Economics* (New York: Free Press, 1950).

12 Léon Walras, *Eléments d'économie politique pure* (Lausanne: Corbaz et Cie, 1874); translated as *Elements of Pure Economics* (Homewood, Ill.: Irwin, 1954).

beyond their control. The firms could control only the productive process chosen and the amount produced.

Households likewise sold their land and capital, as well as their labor, at prices determined in the market and used the receipts (their incomes) to buy goods and services. Consumers apportioned their income among the various commodities they wished to purchase in a way that maximized the utility they received from these commodities.

Commodities were the ultimate source of pleasure or utility, and the utility they yielded was assumed to be quantifiable. Jevons wrote: "A unit of pleasure or pain is difficult even to conceive; but it is the amount of these feelings which is continually prompting us to buying and selling, borrowing and lending, laboring and resting, producing and consuming; *and it is from the quantitative effects of the feelings that we must estimate their comparative amounts.*"[13]

Walras was less ambiguous in arguing that utility was quantifiable: "I shall, therefore, assume the existence of a standard measure of intensity of wants or intensive utility, which is applicable not only to similar units of the same kind of wealth but also to different units of various kinds of wealth."[14]

These economists, having presumably quantifiable magnitudes with which to work, next set up general mathematical formulas purporting to show a functional relationship between the utility a consumer received and the amounts of the various commodities he consumed. The problem then was to show how the consumer could get the maximum utility, given his income and the commodity prices prevailing in the market.

Consumers maximized utility when the increase in utility derived from the last unit consumed, expressed as a ratio over the price of that commodity, was an equal proportion for all other commodities. In other words, the last dollar spent on a commodity should yield the same increase in the utility derived by the consumer as the last dollar spent on any other commodity. Jevons explained the same thing in a different way, stating that the consumer maximized utility because he "procures such quantities of commodities that the final degrees of utility of any pair of commodities are inversely as the ratios of exchange [prices] of the commodities."[15]

Suppose that there was a free market in which consumers could freely exchange their incomes for commodities. They would be led by their self-interest to maximize utility. Therefore, it was concluded that consumers distributed their income among the purchases of commodities in such a way that the welfare of all

[13] Jevons, op. cit., p. 11.
[14] Walras, op. cit., p. 117.
[15] Jevons, op. cit., p. 139.

would be maximized, given the existing distribution of wealth and income.

the neoclassical theory of production

In neoclassical production theory, the analysis of the business firm was perfectly symmetrical to the analysis of consumer behavior. In order to maximize profits, the firm would operate at its highest efficiency and hence produce at the lowest possible cost. It purchased factors of production (such as labor) up to the point where the amount added to production by the last unit of each factor of production, expressed as a ratio over the price of the factor, was an equal proportion for all factors. The last dollar spent on each factor should yield the same increase in production from all factors. In a free market, firms would always attempt to maximize efficiency in order to maximize profits. Therefore this condition would always hold. Thus, the factors of production would all be used in such a way that no possible reorganization of production (given the existing technology) could result in a more efficient use of the factors of production.

Neoclassical economists also believed that if an economy were characterized by a free market with many small competitive firms, then each commodity would be produced in such quantities and with such methods that it would be impossible to shift resources from the production of one commodity to the production of a different commodity without diminishing the total value of what was produced in the market economy.

laissez faire

Thus, the neoclassical economists gave a very elaborate and esoteric analytical defense of Adam Smith's notion of the invisible hand of market competition and the economic policy of laissez faire. They showed that in a competitive market economy made up of innumerable small producers and consumers, the market would guide consumers in such a way that they would end up with an optimal mix of commodities, *given their original income and wealth*. Factors of production would be used in the most efficient way possible. Moreover, commodities would be produced in amounts that would maximize the value of society's production. This optimal result depended, however, on a minimum of interference by government in the processes of the free market.

They recognized that this result was optimal only if one accepted the existing distribution of income. Some (particularly the American economist John Bates Clark) tried to defend the distribution of income that obtained in a free-market economy. They argued that the principles of profit maximization would lead to a situation in which each category of productive factors would be paid an amount equal to the value of its marginal contribution to the productive process. This seemed to them to be a model of distributive justice, with each unit of the productive factors being paid an amount equal to what it produced. Critics were quick to point out, however, that units of productive factors were not people (at least as far as land, natural resources, and capital were concerned). In order for such a system to be fair, these critics insisted, an equitable distribution of owner-ship of the factors of production would be necessary.

Nevertheless, the neoclassical economists did succeed in erecting an impressive intellectual defense of the classical liberal policy of laissez faire. But they did it by creating a giant chasm between economic theory and economic reality. From the 1870s until today, many economists in the neoclassical tradition have abandoned any real concern with the existing economic institutions and problems. Instead, many of them have retired to the rarefied stratosphere of mathematical model-building, constructing endless variations on esoteric trivia.

subsequent modifications of neoclassical theory

Some economists in the second and third generations of neoclassical analysis recognized the need to make the theory more realistic. The economic system was *not* characterized by "perfect competition"; it had flaws. The principal admitted weaknesses were as follows:
(1) Some buyers and sellers *were* large enough to affect prices, and, moreover, the economies of large-scale production seemed to render this inevitable. (2) Some commodities should be "consumed socially," and their production and sale might never be profitable in a laissez faire capitalist economy, even though they might be deemed highly desirable by most citizens (e.g., roads, schools, armies).
(3) The costs to the producer of a commodity (such as automobiles) might differ significantly from the social costs (such as smog) of producing that commodity. In such a case, it was possible that for society as a whole, the costs of production might exceed the benefits of production for the commodity, even though the producer still

profited from making and selling it. For example, consider the poisoning of the water and air by producers making profits but doing little or nothing about this evil, even though its side effects could endanger human life itself. (4) An unrestrained free-market capitalist system appeared to be quite unstable, being subject to recurring depressions that incurred enormous social waste.

It was generally agreed that such flaws did exist and did disrupt the otherwise-beneficial workings of the capitalist system, but they could only be corrected by some amount of government intervention into the market system. Government antitrust actions, it was argued, could force giant firms to act as if they were competitive, and something called "workable competition" could be achieved. Roads, schools, armies, and other socially consumed commodities could be provided by the government. Extensive systems of special taxes and subsidies could be used to equate private and social costs where they differed. Finally (especially after the 1930s), it was believed that through the wise use of fiscal and monetary policy, the government could eliminate the instability of the system. (This last point will be discussed in more detail in Chapter 10.)

The flaws were thus seen as minor and ephemeral. An enlightened government could correct them and free the invisible hand once again to create the best of all possible worlds. There did develop, however, an inability to agree on the extent and significance of the flaws. Those who believe them to be fairly widespread and quite significant have, during the course of the twentieth century, become known as *liberals*. They have sometimes advocated fairly extensive government intervention in the economic system, but most have continued to use neoclassical economic theory as an ideology to defend the private-ownership, capitalist market economic system.

Economists who see the flaws as minor and unimportant continue to advocate a minimum of government intervention in the market economy. Despite the fact that the laissez faire policies advocated by these economists have been much closer to those advocated by the nineteenth-century classical liberals, they have become known in the twentieth century as *conservatives*. Both liberals and conservatives, as we have described them here, have used neoclassical economic theory to justify the capitalist system.

laissez faire and the social darwinists

Before leaving the topic of late nineteenth- and early twentieth-century advocates of laissez faire capitalism, a brief discussion of *social Darwinism* is necessary. Social Darwinists believed the government should allow capitalists to compete freely in the marketplace with a minimum of government restrictions and, in general, favored as little government intervention as possible in all spheres of life. Therefore, many people have imagined their defense of laissez faire capitalism to be similar to that of the neoclassical economists. This is not so. Their policy recommendations were based on a substantially different theoretical framework.

The social Darwinists took Darwin's theory of evolution and extended it to a theory of social evolution (in a manner that Darwin himself strongly disapproved, it may be added). Competition, they believed, was a teleological process in which each succeeding generation was superior to the preceding generation. This upward progress was made possible because those least fit to survive did not succeed in maintaining themselves and procreating. Greater ability to survive was equated with a biological as well as a moral superiority.

Herbert Spencer (1820–1903), the father of social Darwinism, based his evolutionary theory as well as his moral theory on what he called the *law of conduct and consequence*. He believed the survival of the human species could be assured only if society distributed its benefits in proportion to a person's merit, which was measured by his power to sustain himself. Each person ought to reap the benefits or suffer the evil results of his own actions. Thus, the persons most adapted to their environment would prosper, and those least adapted would be weeded out—provided that the laws of conduct and consequence were observed. If the government, wishing to mitigate the inequalities of wealth and income in society, took "from him who . . . [had] prospered to give to him who . . . [had] not, it [violated] its duty towards the one to do more than its duty towards the other."[16] This type of action slowed social progress and could, if carried to excess, destroy the human species. Survival and progress could be assured only if the weak were weeded out and destroyed by the impersonal forces of social evolution.

In Spencer's opinion, "the poverty of the incapable, the distresses that come upon the imprudent, the starvation of the idle, and those shoulderings aside of the weak by the strong . . . are the decrees of a large, far-seeing benevolence."[17] Spencer categorically opposed any action by the government that interfered with trade, commerce, production, or the distribution of wealth or income. He rejected welfare payments of any kind, attempts to decrease the economic insecurity of workers, and government's provision of schools, parks, or libraries as detrimental to human progress. His laissez faire was

[16] Quoted in Sidney Fine, *Laissez Faire and the General Welfare State* (Ann Arbor, Mich.: University of Michigan Press, 1964), p. 38.
[17] Ibid.

thus much more extreme than that of the classical economists or most of the conservative neoclassical economists.

Social Darwinists accepted the large monopolistic and oligopolistic industries as the beneficent result of evolution. Neoclassical economists, if they did not simply define away or ignore the concentrations of economic power, believed that government should attempt to create a more competitive and atomistic market situation. Thus, in this very important respect, the two theories were quite antagonistic.

laissez faire and the ideology of businessmen

Most businessmen, however, were not very concerned with intellectual consistency. They feared radical and socialist reformers who wanted to use the government as a means of achieving greater equality; and they welcomed any theory that concluded that the government should not intervene in the economic process. Even though they themselves used the government extensively to promote their own interests (through special tariffs, tax concessions, land grants, and a host of other special privileges), they relied on laissez faire arguments when threatened with any social reform that might erode their status, influence, wealth, or income. Thus, in the ordinary businessman's ideology of the late nineteenth and early twentieth centuries, there was a general attempt to combine neoclassical economics and social Darwinism.

In this ideology, the accumulation of wealth was considered de facto proof of evolutionary superiority, whereas poverty was believed to be evidence of evolutionary inferiority. Success, asserted writer Benjamin Woods, was "nothing more or less than doing thoroughly what others did indifferently." Andrew Carnegie equated success with "honest work, ability and concentration"; another businessman argued that "wealth has always been the natural sequence to industry, temperance, and perseverance, and it will always so continue." At the same time, S. C. T. Dodd, solicitor for Standard Oil, maintained that poverty existed "because nature or the devil has made some men weak and imbecile and others lazy and worthless, and neither man nor God can do much for one who will do nothing for himself."[18]

The beneficial results of competition in neoclassical economic theory seemed to reinforce reliance on the "survival of the fittest" in the "struggle for survival." "Competition in economics," asserted

18 All quotations in this paragraph are cited in Fine, op. cit., p. 98.

Richard R. Bowker, "is the same as the law of . . . 'natural selection' in nature."[19]

Although some businessmen and their spokesmen were trying to perpetuate the laissez faire conclusions of the classical liberal ideology of capitalism, many defenders of the capitalist system believed that in the new age of mass production (with gigantic concentrations of wealth and power in the hands of so few corporations and capitalists), the older, individualistic, laissez faire ideology was no longer appropriate. The late nineteenth century witnessed a rebirth of the older paternalistic ethic. In Chapter 8, we will examine a new ideology of capitalism that was based, in many essential respects, on a new version of the Christian corporate ethic.

summary

In the late nineteenth century, capitalism was characterized by the growth of giant corporations. Control of most of the important industries became more and more concentrated. Accompanying this concentration of industry was an equally striking concentration of income in the hands of a small percentage of the population.

In view of these facts, it would seem that the classical liberal ideology (which was based on an analysis of an economy based on many small, relatively powerless enterprises) would have to be abandoned. The gulf that separated the theory from reality had widened into a giant chasm. But the idea that the market economy channeled acquisitive profit-seeking into socially benevolent practices was simply too elegant an apologia for unrestrained profit-making. So the classical liberal ideology of capitalism was even more assiduously disseminated in a new school of neoclassical economics.

An elaborate deductive theory permitted the neoclassical economists to defend the classical policy prescription of laissez faire. Conservative neoclassical economists assigned to the government only those tasks that would directly or indirectly promote business profits. Liberal neoclassical economists also believed the government should enter a limited number of other areas in which the operation of the free market did not maximize the social welfare. Whether in the hands of the conservative or the liberal faction, neoclassical economics remained essentially an ideological defense for the status quo.

Finally, social Darwinist ideology and the ideology of most businessmen defended many of the neoclassical economists' con-

19 Ibid., p. 100.

clusions. They did so, however, on entirely different grounds. They accepted the fact that corporate power, personal wealth, and personal income were highly concentrated. This, they believed, was evidence of the evolutionary superiority of the wealthy and, as such, was socially beneficial.

chapter 8
the consolidation of monopoly power and the new christian corporate ethic

The process of industrialization in the United States after the Civil War involved, in its initial stages, a competition among industrial and financial capitalists that was unique in its ferocity. From 1860 until the early 1880s, the strongest and shrewdest businessmen built great empires with the fruits of economic conquest. The great improvements in transportation that occurred in the period, the rise of standardization in parts and finished products, and the increased efficiency in large-scale mass production created the possibility of nationwide markets. The stakes in the economic struggle were very large, and the participants neither asked for nor received quarter.

competition as industrial warfare

Examples of the industrial warfare have filled many books.[1] In the oil industry, for example, John D. Rockefeller and Henry M. Flagler shipped so much oil that they were able to demand large concessions from the railroads. With this cost advantage, they could undersell competitors. Their company (which was incorporated in 1870 under the name of Standard Oil Company of Ohio) was able to force many

[1] See, for example, Matthew Josephson, *The Robber Barons* (New York: Harcourt Brace Jovanovich, Harvest Books, 1962), for a fascinating account of the exploits of the capitalists of this era.

competitors to the wall and to achieve regional monopolies, at which point the price could be substantially increased without fear of competition. After securing their large rebates on transport costs, Standard Oil's share in the petroleum industry quickly increased from 10 to 20 percent. But they did not stop there. They next succeeded in forcing the railroads to give them rebates on their *competitor's* shipments as well as "all data relating to shipper, buyer, product, price and terms of payment," a scheme that "provided Rockefeller and his associates with rebates on all their own shipments, rebates on all shipments by their competitors, and in addition a complete spy system on their competitors."[2] With this power, Rockefeller was able to smash most of his competitors. By 1879, only nine years after incorporation, Standard Oil controlled between 90 and 95 percent of the nation's output of refined petroleum. A sympathetic biographer of Rockefeller has written: "Of all the devices for the extinction of competition, this was the cruelest and most deadly yet conceived by any group of American industrialists."[3]

Competition among the railroad magnates was particularly intense. Rate wars were common, forcing weaker competitors out of business and giving stronger competitors monopoly powers over large regions. The battles sometimes got so brutal that locomotives were crashed into each other and track was destroyed. The railroads also extorted money from towns along proposed railroad lines. A member of the California Constitutional Convention of 1878 described the technique:

> They start out their railroad track and survey their line near a thriving village. They go to the most prominent citizens of that village and say, 'If you will give us so many thousand dollars we will run through here; if you do not we will run by.' And in every instance where the subsidy was not granted this course was taken and the effect was just as they said, to kill off the little town.[4]

According to that same report, the railroad "blackmailed Los Angeles County for $230,000 as a condition of doing that which the law compelled them to do." The railroads also manipulated connections with politicians to get government handouts of public lands. It is estimated that these giveaways amounted to 158,293,000 acres—more land than is contained in some whole countries.[5] The

---

2 Dudley Dillard, *Economic Development of the North Atlantic Community* (Englewood Cliffs, N.J.: Prentice-Hall, 1967), p. 410.

3 Allan Nevins, *John D. Rockefeller, The Heroic Age of American Enterprise,* vol. 1 (New York: Scribner's, 1940), p. 325.

4 Quoted in Josephson, op. cit., pp. 84–85.

5 Ibid., p. 79.

railroads were certainly not in favor of a laissez faire policy
in practice.

The great entrepreneurs of that age were definitely not men of
estimable social conscience. Many founded their fortunes on the
Civil War. When shortages of supplies became desperate, they
received high prices for selling to the army "shoddy blankets, so
many doctored horses and useless rifles, [and] . . . stores of
sickening beef."[6] In order to eliminate their competitors, they did
not hesitate to use hired thugs, kidnappings, and dynamiting. Likewise, they stopped at nothing as they mulcted the public of millions
of dollars through stock frauds, schemes, and swindles. Some of
these actions were legal and some were not, but the dominant mood
of these capitalist entrepreneurs was expressed by Cornelius
Vanderbilt, who, when cautioned about the questionable legality of a
desired course of action, exclaimed, "What do I care about the law?
Hain't I got the power?"[7] Much the same idea was expressed by
William Vanderbilt during a public outcry against one of his policy
decisions: "The public be damned. I am working for my stockholders."[8]

business collusion
and government regulation

After a few years of this type of competition, however, most of the
remaining business firms were battle-tested giants. Continuing such
competition would have been ruinous for all. So, whereas competition
was the road to large profits before 1880, after that date, it became
obvious that cooperative collusion would be more beneficial for the
remaining firms. In that way, they could exercise monopolistic power
for their mutual benefit. Thus, pools, trusts, and mergers (described
in Chapter 7) were the consequence of the earlier competition.
Increasingly, as the turn of the century neared, the neoclassical
vision of many small competing firms diverged from the reality of
massive corporations acting cooperatively to maximize their joint
profits.

With the rise of big corporations, there was a parallel growth of
grass-roots popular opposition to these companies and their blatant
disregard for the public welfare. This popular antagonism became so

6 Ibid., p. 67.
7 Ibid., p. 72.
8 Ibid.

widespread and intense that in the presidential campaign of 1888, both the Democrats and the Republicans advocated federal laws to curb the abuses of big corporations.

After the 1888 election, both parties became extremely reluctant to take any such action. Many of the most important Republicans controlled the very corporations they had promised to curb, and the Democrats were but slightly less involved with big business. Only when public pressure reached incredible heights did Congress respond, in December 1889, by passing the Sherman Antitrust Act. The act, an obvious concession to an aroused public opinion, passed both houses of Congress with only a single dissenting vote. But the law was so weak and vaguely worded that it appeared to be designed to insure that it would be ineffective. Another proposal that recommended meaningful punishment of firms who violated the law was overwhelmingly defeated.

The law proscribed "every contract, combination in the form of a trust or otherwise, or conspiracy, in restraint of trade or commerce among the several states or with foreign nations. . . ." It also declared a person guilty of a misdemeanor if he attempted "to monopolize, or combine or conspire with any other person . . . to monopolize any part of the trade or commerce among the several states, or with foreign nations. . . ."

The primary effect of the Sherman Act over the next few decades was to weaken labor unions. What had begun as a concession to the public's hatred of big business' abuses became an antilabor law as the courts ruled that many union strikes constituted constraints of trade.

While President McKinley was in office, there were only five cases initiated under the Sherman Act, despite the fact that there were 146 major industrial combinations formed between the years 1899 and 1901 alone. One of these was the massive United States Steel Corporation, which in 1901 controlled or acquired 785 plants worth a whopping $1,370,000,000.

Staggeringly high profits, graft, corruption, and discriminatory practices on the part of the nation's railroads led to the establishment of the first federal government regulatory agency. The Interstate Commerce Act of 1887 established the Interstate Commerce Commission (ICC), which was designed to regulate the railroads in order to protect the public interest.

Competition among the railroads had been so destructive that the railroads themselves were the leading advocates of extended federal regulation. A few years after the passage of the Interstate Commerce Act, U.S. Attorney General Olney wrote a letter to a railroad president that read, in part: "The Commission [ICC] . . . is, or can be made, of great use to the railroads. It satisfies the popular clamor for a government supervision of railroads, at the same time that supervision is almost entirely nominal. Further, the older such a commission gets to be, the more inclined it will be found to take the business and railroad view of things. . . ."[9]

The attorney general's prediction has certainly been borne out by the facts. In the years since the establishment of the ICC, many other federal regulatory agencies have been established. The Federal Communications Commission (FCC), the Civil Aeronautics Board (CAB), and the Securities Exchange Commission (SEC) were among the federal agencies that joined the ICC as "protectors" of the public interest. Most serious students of government regulation would agree that "the outstanding political fact about the . . . regulatory commissions is that they have in general become promoters and protectors of the industries they have been established to regulate."[10]

Thus, in many oligopolistic industries, there was an inability to cooperate and to act collectively as a monopoly. For these industries, there is a considerable body of evidence indicating that they turned to the government and to federal regulatory agencies as a means of achieving this monopolistic coordination.[11] Regulatory agencies have generally performed this function very effectively.

The collusive behavior of the oligopolistic businesses seemed to go unnoticed by neoclassical economists. They continued to frame their analyses in terms of innumerable small, competing business firms. In their advocacy of laissez faire policies, they failed to see that it was primarily big business that supported active government intervention.

Neoclassical economists also continued to accept the classical economists' view that as long as free competition prevails, the economy will tend toward a full utilization of its productive capacity and full employment will more or less continuously prevail. During the last half of the nineteenth century, however, economic depressions became more frequent and more severe. During the first half of the nineteenth century, the United States had had two economic crises (in 1819 and 1837), and England had had four (in 1815, 1825, 1836, and 1847). During the last half of the century, the number increased to five in the United States (in 1854, 1857, 1873, 1884, and 1893), and six in England (in 1857, 1866, 1873, 1882, 1890 and 1900). Thus, the neoclassical economic ideology was as poor a

---

[9] Quoted in Grant McConnell, "Self-Regulation, The Politics of Business," in D. Mermelstein, ed., *Economics: Mainstream Readings and Radical Critiques* (New York: Random House, 1970), p. 197.

[10] Ibid., p. 199.

[11] The most thoroughly documented defense of this assertion can be found in Gabriel Kolko, *The Triumph of Conservatism* (New York: Free Press, 1963).

reflection of economic performance as it was of industrial concentration.

a new christian corporate ethic

The distance separating the neoclassical liberal ideology of capitalism and economic reality impressed itself on the minds of many academicians and businessmen. The result was a new ideology for the new age of corporate capitalism. Just as the new industrial and financial entrepreneurs came to resemble the feudal robber barons, so the new ideology resembled the feudal version of the Christian corporate ethic. It emphasized the natural superiority of a small elite (the new industrial and financial magnates) and the paternalistic functions of that elite in caring for the masses.

The new ideology reflected the fact that many of the wealthy capitalists of the era were becoming something of folk heroes among the general public. The last two decades of the nineteenth century and the first three of the twentieth were an age during which the businessman became the most admired social type. Their success was viewed as de facto proof that they possessed virtues superior to those of the ordinary man. This version of success was the theme of the biographies of William Makepeace Thackeray and the novels of Horatio Alger. These men and other writers created a cult of success that viewed the increase of industrial concentration as proof of a Darwinian superiority of the industrialists, glorified the self-made man, and kept the Horatio Alger myth of rags to riches constantly in the public mind.

This veneration of businessmen, added to the strong rejection of destructive competition by both the businessmen and the general public, led to a new conservative version of the Christian corporate ethic, which resembled the philosophy of the Tory radicals of the late eighteenth and early nineteenth centuries. The unfortunate plight of the poor received prominent mention in the new writings. This problem as well as that of economic instability could best be solved, according to the new ideology, by encouraging cooperation among the leaders of the giant corporations. Competition was viewed as antisocial. Through cooperation, business cycles could be eliminated and the plight of the poor could be improved.

This new version of the Christian corporate ethic received the support of Pope Leo XIII (1810–1903). Between 1878 and 1901, the pope sought to analyze the problems of corporate capitalism and to suggest remedies in a series of encyclicals. In *Rerum novarum* (1891), he argued that "a remedy must be found . . . for the misery and

wretchedness which press so heavily at this moment on the large
majority of the very poor." He continued with a condemnation of
unrestrained laissez faire competition.

> Working men have been given over, isolated and defenseless, to
> the callousness of employers and the greed of unrestrained
> competition. The evil has been increased by rapacious usury . . .
> still practiced by avaricious and grasping men. And to this must
> be added the custom of working by contract, and the concentration
> of so many branches of trade in the hands of a few individuals,
> so that a small number of very rich men have been able to lay upon
> the masses of the poor a yoke little better than slavery itself.[12]

This passage, which sounds so socialist in tone and content, was
followed by a strong condemnation of socialism and a defense of
private property. The pope hoped the problems could be corrected
by rejection of competition and a return to the Christian virtues of
love and brotherhood, with the leaders of business and industry
leading the way to a new Christian paternalism within the context
of a private property capitalist system.

THE GERMAN VERSION

The new paternalistic ideology was probably strongest in Germany,
where classical liberalism had really never gained a good hold and
where industrial concentration was most pronounced. A famous
German economist expressed the very widely held view that

> the proper kind of cartelization creates more or less a system of
> justice and equity. . . . The directors of the cartels are educators
> who wish to bring about the triumph of wide interests of a branch
> of industry over the egoistic interests of the individual. . . . The
> cartel system is, like a co-operative or merchants' association,
> an important element in the education of commercial and
> technical officials who want to make money but who have also
> learned to put themselves in the service of general interests and to
> administer the property of others in a loyal and honorable fashion.[13]

Cartels were also widely justified as means of eliminating economic
crises. A German court decision, one of several that formed the
legal justification of the cartel system in that country, stated:
"Indeed the formation of syndicates and cartels . . . has repeatedly
been considered a device especially useful for the economy as a

---

12 Quoted in Daniei R. Fusfeld, *The Age of the Economist* (Glenview, Ill.: Scott,
Foresman, 1966), p. 86.

13 Gustave Schmoller, quoted in Koppel S. Pinson, *Modern Germany: Its History and
Civilization* (New York: Macmillan, 1954), p. 236.

whole, since they can prevent uneconomic overproduction and ensuing catastrophe."[14]

THE AMERICAN VERSION

In the United States, as was mentioned above, the new ideology thrived in an atmosphere that venerated the successful businessman and was extremely weary of destructive competition. The view of many American industrial and financial magnates was expressed by Andrew Carnegie (one of the most successful of the magnates):

> Not evil, but good, has come to the race from the accumulation of wealth by those who have the ability and energy that produce it. . . .
> We have the true antidote for the temporary unequal distribution of wealth, the reconciliation of the rich and the poor—a reign of harmony—another ideal, differing, indeed, from that of the Communist in requiring only further evolution of existing conditions, not the total overthrow of our civilization. . . .
> Under its sway we shall have an ideal state, in which the surplus wealth of the few will become in the best sense, the property of the many, because administered for the common good, this wealth passing through the hands of the few can be made a more potent force for the elevation of our race than if it were distributed in sums to the people themselves.[15]

Carnegie argued, and many businessmen and their spokesmen agreed, that the millionaire would be "a trustee for the poor, entrusted for a season with a great part of the increased wealth of the community, but administering it for the community far better than it could or would have done for itself."[16]

The Right Reverend William Lawrence gave the new elitist view the sanction of religion. "In the long run, it is only to the man of morality that wealth comes. . . . Godliness is in league with riches."[17] And railroad President George F. Baer had the same idea in mind when he tried to assure railroad workers that "the rights and the interests of the laboring man will be protected and cared for, not by the labor agitators, but by the Christian men to whom God in his infinite wisdom, has given control of the property interests of the country."[18]

14 Quoted in Dillard, op. cit., p. 396.

15 Andrew Carnegie, "Wealth," in Gail Kennedy, ed., *Democracy and the Gospel of Wealth* (Lexington, Mass.: Raytheon/Heath, 1949), pp. 3, 5, and 6.

16 Cited in Kennedy, op. cit., p. xii.

17 Ibid.

18 Ibid.

simon patten's economic basis for the new ethic

Perhaps the most influential academic spokesman for the new corporate ideology was Dr. Simon N. Patten, professor of economics at the University of Pennsylvania from 1888 to 1917 and one of the founders of the American Economic Association.[19] In keeping with the paternalistic element of the new ideology, Patten denounced the poverty and economic exploitation of his era. The following passage could almost have been written by a Marxist of that era:

> There have flowed then, side by side, two streams of life, one bearing the working poor, who perpetuate themselves through qualities generated by the stress and mutual dependence of the primitive world, and the other bearing aristocracies, who dominate by means of the laws and traditions giving them control of the social surplus.[20]

in the same vein, fifteen years later, he wrote that

> The glow of Fifth Avenue is but the reflection of a distant hell into which unwilling victims are cast. Some resource is misused, some town degraded, to create the flow of funds on which our magnates thrive. From Pennsylvania, rich in resources, trains go loaded and come back empty. For the better half no return is made except in literary tomes designed to convince the recipients that exploitation is not robbery. . . . But Nature revolts! Never does the rising sun see children yanked from bed to increase the great Strauss dividends, nor the veteran cripples of the steel mill tramping in their beggar garb, but that it shrivels, reddens, and would strike but for the sight of happier regions beyond.[21]

This poverty and exploitation were, in Patten's opinion, the last vestiges of an earlier age characterized by scarcity. In the economy of scarcity, capitalists aggressively competed with each other, with the result that laborers as well as the general public suffered. The fierce competition of the robber barons, however, had marked a watershed in history. The merger movement that followed this competition was the beginning of a new era, an era of plenty rather

---

[19] For a more complete account of Patten's ideas see E. K. Hunt, "Simon N. Patten's Contribution to Economics," *Journal of Economic Issues* (December 1970), pp. 38–55.

[20] Simon Nelson Patten, *The New Basis of Civilization* (New York: Macmillan, 1907), p. 39.

[21] Simon Nelson Patten, *Mud Hollow* (Philadelphia: Dorrance, 1922), p. 226.

than of scarcity. Capitalists were becoming socialized. They were putting the public welfare ahead of their pursuit of profits, and in doing this, they eschewed competition, recognizing that the public welfare could be best promoted by cooperation.

Evidence that the conditions of economic prosperity at the turn of the century were socializing capitalists could be gotten from the fact that "hospitals . . . [were] established, schools . . . [were] made free, colleges . . . [were] endowed, museums, libraries, and art galleries . . . [received] liberal support, church funds . . . [grew] and missions . . . [were] formed at home and abroad."[22] On almost every policy issue of his day, Patten took a strongly proindustrial capitalist position. He viewed the late nineteenth-century captains of industry as a paternally beneficent elite:

> The growth of large-scale capitalism has resulted in the elimination of the unsocial capitalist and the increasing control of each industry by the socialized groups. . . . At bottom altruistic sentiment is the feeling of a capitalist expressing itself in sympathy for the laborer. This desire of upper class men to improve the conditions of lower classes is a radically different phenomenon from the pressure exerted by the lower classes for their own betterment. The lower class movement stands for the control of the state by themselves in their own interests. The upper class movement directs itself against the bad environmental conditions preventing the expression of character.[23]

He believed that competition should be discouraged by taxing competitive firms and exempting trusts and monopolies from these taxes. This would benefit all society by eliminating the extensive waste created by competition. In *The Stability of Prices,* he argued that competition was largely responsible for the economic instability of the late nineteenth century. When the movement toward trusts and monopolies had been completed, production would be controlled and planned in such a way that this instability would be eliminated.

Patten's paternalistic ideology was, like the liberal ideology of capitalism, ultimately a plea for a minimum of government interference with the actions of businessmen. The government was to interfere in the economy only by encouraging trusts and monopolies and discouraging competition. In Patten's scheme, all important social and economic reforms were to be carried out voluntarily by the socialized capitalists in a system of cooperative corporate collectivism.

[22] Simon Nelson Patten, *The Theory of Prosperity* (New York: Macmillan, 1902), p. 170.

[23] Simon Nelson Patten, "The Reconstruction of Economic Theory," reprinted in Simon Nelson Patten, *Essays in Economic Theory,* ed. Rexford Guy Tugwell (New York: Knopf, 1924), p. 292.

the new paternalism and the new deal[24]

Patten's version of the new ideology of corporate capitalism was to be very important historically. When the Great Depression of the 1930s struck, two of Patten's students and devotees, Rexford Guy Tugwell and Frances Perkins, had influential positions as members of Roosevelt's original cabinet. Tugwell had asserted that Patten's views "were the greatest single influence on my thought. Neither Veblen nor Dewey found their orientation to the future as completely and instinctively as did Patten. The magnificence of his conceptions and the basic rightness of his vision become clearer as time passes. I am eternally grateful to him."[25] Miss Perkins believed her former teacher to be "one of the greatest men America has ever produced."[26]

Through these two former students, Patten exerted a considerable influence on the economic policies of the early phase of the New Deal. His ideas helped to create the intellectual basis of the National Industrial Recovery Act of 1933 (NIRA).[27] Patten was not, of course, the only source of these ideas. During World War I, the War Industries Board had generated enthusiasm for corporate collectivism. Throughout the 1920s, trade associations prospered, and the doctrine of business self-government gained many adherents in the busines world. In 1922, Franklin Roosevelt had been president of one such association: the American Construction Council. However, Patten's teachings were unquestionably influential. His two protégés, Tugwell and Perkins, were both instrumental in the actual framing of the NIRA.

The National Industrial Recovery Act proclaimed the intent of Congress "to promote the organization of industry for the purpose of cooperative action among trade groups."[28] The bill contained sections providing for codes of fair competition that permitted and even encouraged cooperative price-fixing and market-sharing and for virtually complete exemption from antitrust laws. Section 7A was designed to promote labor organization but was so diluted that very

---

[24] For a more complete discussion of the material covered in this section, see E. K. Hunt, "A Neglected Aspect of the Economic Ideology of the Early New Deal," *Review of Social Economy* (September 1971), pp. 180–192.

[25] Quoted in Allan G. Gruchy, *Modern Economic Thought: The American Contribution* (New York: Augustus M. Kelley, 1967), p. 408.

[26] Quoted in Arthur M. Schlesinger, Jr., *The Coming of the New Deal* (Boston: Houghton Mifflin, 1965), p. 229.

[27] Schlesinger, op. cit., p. 98.

[28] Quoted in ibid., pp. 98–99.

often it promoted the formation of company unions. "If it [the NIRA] worked, Tugwell thought, each industry would end with a government of its own under which it could promote its fundamental purpose ('production rather than competition'). NRA could have been administered, Tugwell later wrote, so that a 'great collectivism' would have channeled American energy into a disciplined national effort to establish a secure basis for well-being."[29]

In explaining the bill to the National Association of Manufacturers, General Hugh S. Johnson, the first head of the National Recovery Administration (NRA) declared that "NRA is exactly what industry organized in trade associations makes it." He further asserted that before the NRA, the trade associations had about as much effectiveness as an "Old Ladies' Knitting Society; now I am talking to a cluster of formerly emasculated trade associations about a law which proposes for the first time to give them power."[30]

Most of the economic literature which appeared in 1934 recognized that the early New Deal reforms had not significantly extended government control over business. On the contrary, it had given voluntary trade associations the support of the government in forcing the controls of the trade associations on all industry.[31]

This experience in business self-government proved to be disastrous. The distinguished historian Arthur M. Schlesinger, Jr., has assessed the success of this phase of the early New Deal. With Schlesinger, we concur:

> And the result of business self-government? Restriction on production, chiseling of labor and of 7A, squeezing out of small business, savage personal criticism of the President, and the general tendency to trample down every one in the rush for profits. Experience was teaching Roosevelt what instinct and doctrine has taught Jefferson and Jackson; that, to reform capitalism you must fight the capitalists tooth and nail.[32]

The early New Deal philosophy underlying the NIRA was very quickly abandoned, and the NIRA was declared unconstitutional. The new paternalistic ideology of capitalism, however, was to receive more elaborate statements after World War II. (These

---

[29] Ibid., p. 108.

[30] General Hugh S. Johnson, quoted in ibid., p. 110.

[31] See Leo Rogin, "The New Deal: A Survey of Literature," *Quarterly Journal of Economics* (May 1935), pp. 338, 346, and 349–355. Typical of the comments of supporters of the early New Deal is this quotation from Tilly: "Here *industry* is setting up a legal and enforceable Golden Rule." Ibid., p. 351.

[32] Arthur M. Schlesinger, Jr., "The Broad Accomplishments of the New Deal," in Edwin C. Rozwenc, ed., *The New Deal: Revolution or Evolution* (Lexington, Mass.: Raytheon/Heath, 1959), pp. 30–31.

statements and the later New Deal policies will be discussed in subsequent chapters.)

summary

The industrial warfare of the late nineteenth century led to an era of mergers and collusion among the giant corporations. Through collusion, the few corporations that controlled an industry could act effectively as monopolists and maximize their joint profits. Where collusion was difficult, the corporations relied heavily on government regulatory agencies to help enforce mutual cooperation.

Within this economic and political context, many ideologists of capitalism rejected classical liberalism because of its unrealistic assumptions. These thinkers created a new version of the Christian corporate ethic that pictured the new industrial and financial magnates as beneficent, paternalistic protectors of the public welfare.

This new ethic was to become particularly influential in the social and economic legislation of the early New Deal of the 1930s.

chapter 9
evolutionary socialism and imperialism

In the late nineteenth and early twentieth centuries, the socialist analysis of capitalism was profoundly affected by two developments: (1) the economic and political gains made by the working class and (2) the imperialistic carving-up of the economically less-developed areas of the world by the major capitalist powers.

the economic and political gains of the working class

During the last half of the nineteenth century, the real income of workers rose throughout the capitalist world. In England, the average real wage increased rapidly throughout the 1860s and early 1870s. By 1875, it was 40 percent higher that it had been in 1862. After ten years in which wages sagged, they again rose sharply between 1885 and 1900. By 1900, the average real wage was 33 percent higher than in 1875 and 84 percent higher than in 1850. Most of the gains in real wages are attributable to the advent of mass-production techniques which permitted prices of many commodities laborers consumed to be lowered. With the new methods of producing and labor's greater purchasing power, there was a fundamental change in patterns of consumption. Workingmen began to eat more meats, fruits, and sweets. Cafés, mass-produced shoes and clothing, furniture, newspapers, bicycles, and other new products came to be within the reach of many. Unquestionably, the average workingman's lot improved substantially during the period.

It should be mentioned, however, that averages can be misleading. Two late nineteenth-century social surveys revealed that about 40 percent of the working class in London and York still lived in abject poverty. The fact that this could be so after a half century of rapid increases in average real wages gives an indication of the truly pitiful conditions that must have existed in the early nineteenth century.

Similar gains were being made in western Europe and the United States during the period, and the economic gains were accompanied in most of the countries by political gains. Most of the industrialized capitalist countries had nearly complete male suffrage by the early twentieth century. Political parties were created that were devoted to furthering the cause of workingmen. Despite at times harsh efforts to repress them, the German Social Democratic party, most of whose leaders professed to be Marxists, polled 549,000 votes in 1884 and 763,000 votes in 1887; by 1890, they were the largest single party in the Reichstag, having polled 1,427,000 votes.

the fabian socialists

In England, despite the brilliant achievements of individual Marxists such as William Morris, the socialist movement was largely non-Marxist. The Fabian Society was the primary influence on English socialism, and they rejected Marx's analysis completely. In their economic analysis, the Fabians used orthodox neoclassical utility theory. Labor received, they believed, an amount equal to what it produced, and capitalists and landlords received the value of what was produced with their capital and land. The chief cause of injustice was not that labor's surplus value was appropriated by capitalists, but rather that all the income from ownership accrued to a tiny percentage of the population. The only way to achieve an equitable society would be to divide the income from ownership equally, and this could be done only through government ownership of the means of production.

On the issue of the nature and role of the government, the Fabians differed radically from Marx. For Marx, the government was an instrument of coercion controlled and used by the ruling class to perpetuate the privileges inherent in the capitalist system. The Fabians believed that in a parliamentary democracy based upon universal suffrage, the state was a neutral agency which could be freely used by the majority to reform the social and economic system. Because the working class was the majority in a capitalist economy, they were confident that, step by step, piecemeal reforms would strip away the privileges of the owning class and result in socialism achieved by peaceful evolution rather than violent revolution.

The Fabian Society gradually succeeded in gaining influence in the parliamentary Labour party. By 1918, the Labour party adopted a socialist program that reflected the Fabian Society's views and attitudes. By the 1920s, the Labour party had formed a government, and the cause of socialism via the voting booth seemed to many to be on the road to triumph.

The Fabians had never wanted to be a mass-membership society. A small, select group, they hoped to educate the middle class to accept socialism. They published innumerable tracts exposing the poverty and injustice they found in early twentieth-century England. Remedies for these evils would be forthcoming through paternalistic government actions and programs, they believed, once the government was made truly democratic and the people were made aware of these conditions.

However debatable their certainty that socialism could be achieved through education, it is undeniable that the Fabians offered an impressive group of teachers. Some of the most brilliant of the English intellectual elite were members of the society, including Sidney and Beatrice Webb, George Bernard Shaw, H. G. Wells, Sydney Olivier, and Graham Wallas. With such sponsorship, the Fabians' reformist, evolutionary socialism became eminently respectable. One could espouse socialism and still remain completely secure in one's comfortable middle-class niche in English capitalistic society.

the german revisionists

The German counterparts of the English Fabians were the revisionists. At the turn of the century, the Social Democratic party was nominally a Marxist party. A large segment of the membership, however, argued that the course of history had proven Marx wrong on many issues and that a "revision" of Marx's ideas was necessary to make them relevant to German economic and social life. The most famous of the revisionists was Eduard Bernstein, who presented a detailed critique of Marxist ideas in his best-known work, *Evolutionary Socialism,* which was published in 1899. Bernstein maintained that capitalism was not approaching any kind of crisis or collapse, and indeed that it had never been more viable. Marx was also wrong, Bernstein declared, in predicting the concentration of all industries in the hands of a few giant firms. He argued that enterprises of all sizes thrived and would continue to do so (despite the fact that corporate concentration and the cartel movement were more extreme in Germany than in any other capitalist country). Even if large trusts did dominate the economy, Bernstein insisted, there would be a "splitting up of shares," making petty capitalists of a very large percentage of the population, including many workers. He believed the economy had already gone far in this direction: "The number of members of the possessing classes is today not smaller but larger. The enormous increase of social wealth is not accompanied by a decreasing number of large capitalists, but by an increasing number of capitalists of all degrees."[1]

Thus, in continental Europe, as well as in England, the idea that a democratic government in a capitalist country could be used to effect a gradual and peaceful transition from capitalism to socialism received widespread support, and evolutionary socialism appeared to be displacing the revolutionary socialism of the Marxists. However, events of the late nineteenth and early twentieth centuries significantly weakened the solidarity of the evolutionary socialists, particularly the Fabians. This was the period during which European economic imperialism was most intensive. The nature and importance of and the appropriate socialist response to imperialism were issues that created a profound division of socialist opinion—and one that persists to this day.

european imperialism

India was one of the earliest and most dramatic cases of European imperialism. The East India Company had traded extensively in India for 150 years prior to the conquest of Bengal in 1757. During this period, India was relatively advanced economically. Her methods of production and her industrial and commercial organization could definitely be compared with those prevailing in western Europe. In fact, India had been manufacturing and exporting the finest muslins and luxurious fabrics since the time when most western Europeans were backward, primitive peoples.

But after the conquest, the East India Company became the ruling

[1] Eduard Bernstein, *Evolutionary Socialism* (New York: Schocken Books, 1961 [first published in 1899]), p. xii.

power in much of India, and the trade of the previous 150 years turned to harsh exploitation. It has been estimated that between 1757 and 1815, the British took between £500 million and £1,000 million of wealth out of India.[2] The incredible magnitude of this sum can only be appreciated when compared with the £36 million that represented the total capital investment of all the joint-stock companies that were operating in India.[3]

The policy of the East India Company in the last decades of the eighteenth century and in the early nineteenth century reflected two objectives. First, in the short run, the myriad of greedy officials sought personal fortunes overnight: "These officials were absolute, irresponsible and rapacious, and they emptied the private hoards. Their only thought was to wring some hundreds of thousands of pounds out of the natives as quickly as possible, and hurry home to display their wealth. Enormous fortunes were thus rapidly accumulated at Calcutta, while thirty millions of human beings were reduced to the extremity of wretchedness."[4]

A British observer described this ruthless quest for wealth in similar terms: "No Mahratta raid ever devastated a countryside with the thoroughness with which both the Company [East India Company] and, above all, the Company's servants in their individual capacities, sucked dry the plain of Bengal. In fact, in their blind rage for enrichment they took more from the Bengali peasants than those peasants could furnish and live. And the peasants duly died."[5]

The second was a long-run goal: to discourage or eliminate Indian manufacturers and to make India dependent on British industries by forcing the Indians to concentrate on raw materials and export them to supply the textile looms and other British manufacturers. The policy was brutally and methodically—and successfully—executed.

The total effect of this was that the British administration of India systematically destroyed all the fibres and foundations of Indian society. Its land and taxation policy ruined India's village economy and substituted for it the parasitic landowner and moneylender. Its commercial policy destroyed the Indian artisan and created the infamous slums of the Indian cities filled with millions of starving and diseased paupers. Its economic policy broke down whatever beginnings there were of an indigenous industrial development and promoted the proliferations of speculators, petty businessmen,

2 Paul A. Baran, *The Political Economy of Growth* (New York: Monthly Review Press, 1962), p. 145.

3 Ibid.

4 Brooks Adams, *The Law of Civilization and Decay, An Essay on History* (New York: 1896); quoted in Baran, op. cit., p. 146.

5 John Strachey, "Famine in Bengal" in Robert Lekachman, ed., *The Varieties of Economics* vol. 1 (New York: Meridian, 1962), p. 296.

agents, and sharks of all descriptions eking out a sterile and precarious livelihood in the meshes of a decaying society.[6]

It was only later, however, after the period of extensive railroad construction, which began in 1857, that the British thoroughly penetrated the interior of India. British investors who sank money into these railroads were guaranteed a 5 percent return by the government which enforced a provision that if profits fell below 5 percent, the Indian people would be taxed to make up the difference. Thus, Indians were taxed to ensure that British investors would have adequate transport for the further economic exploitation of the Indian interior.

Despite such harsh measures, the age of European imperialism really did not get under way on a broad, pervasive front until the last quarter of the nineteenth century. Between 1775 and 1875, the European countries had lost about as much colonial territory as they had won. The opinion was widely held that colonies were expensive luxuries.

All this changed suddenly and drastically after 1875. By 1900, Great Britain had grabbed 4,500,000 square miles, which she added to her empire; France had gobbled up 3,500,000; Germany, 1,000,000; Belgium, 900,000; Russia, 500,000; Italy, 185,000; and the United States, 125,000. Imperialism ran rampant as one-fourth of the world's population was subjugated and put under European and American domination.

IMPERIALISM IN AFRICA

By 1800, the Europeans had hardly penetrated beyond the coastal areas of Africa. By the early twentieth century, after a 100-year orgy of land-grabbing and empire-building, they controlled over 10 million square miles, or about 93 percent of the continent. In that gigantic rape, various European powers sought to acquire the abundant minerals and agricultural commodities of the Dark Continent.

The brutality of the European exploitation of Africa was perhaps the most severe in the Belgian Congo. Belgian King Leopold II had sent H. M. Stanley into central Africa in 1879. Serving a private, profit-seeking company headed by Leopold and some of his associates, Stanley had a network of trading posts constructed and also duped native chiefs into signing "treaties" that established a commercial empire stretching over 900,000 square miles. Leopold set himself up as sovereign ruler of the Congo Free State and proceeded to exploit the natural and human resources of the area for the profits of his company.

6 Baran, op. cit., p. 149.

The exploitation was ruthless. Natives were forced, through outright physical coercion, to gather rubber from the wild rubber trees and ivory from the elephants. Leopold confiscated all land that was not directly cultivated by the natives and placed it under "government ownership." Atrocities of the worst sort were committed to force the natives to submit to a very burdensome tax system which included taxes payable in rubber and ivory as well as in labor obligations.

By the twentieth century, the Congo had also become a rich source of diamonds, uranium, copper, cotton, palm oil, palm kernels, and coconuts. In general, it can be said that the Congo was one of the most profitable of European imperialistic exploits as well as one of the most scandalous.

The British grabbed the most populous and also the richest holdings in Africa. In 1870, Cecil Rhodes went to South Africa for his health. Within two years, his genius for organizing and controlling joint-stock companies and his ability to corner the market on diamonds had made him a millionaire. In later years, the British South Africa Company, which Rhodes headed, came to control South Africa completely. Although a private, profit-seeking company, it had all the power of a government, including the authority (given in its charter of 1889) to "make treaties, promulgate laws, preserve the peace, maintain a police force, and acquire new concessions."

The expansionist policies of the British South Africa Company led to the Boer War (1899–1902), which crushed the Dutch republics (the Orange Free State and the Transvaal republic) and gave Britain complete control over all South Africa. South Africa proved to be a rich mining region. But the legacy of British and Dutch imperialism is most vividly seen today in the suppression of the blacks who constitute the vast majority of the population.

The other instances of imperialism in Africa are no less deserving of study. It must suffice in this short account, however, to mention that on the eve of World War I, France held about 40 percent of Africa (much of it within the Sahara desert), England controlled 30 percent and the remaining roughly 23 percent was divided among Germany, Belgium, Portugal, and Spain.

IMPERIALISM IN ASIA

The results of the British take-over of India were evident by the turn of the twentieth century. In 1901, the per capita income was less than $10 per year; over two-thirds of the population were badly undernourished; most native Indian manufacturing had been either ruined or taken over by the British. Nearly 90 percent of the population struggled to subsist in villages where the average holding was only 5 acres and where farming techniques were primitive. Much of the meager produce was paid out in taxes, rents, and profits which accrued to the British. Famine, disease, and misery were rife. In 1891, the average Indian lived less than 26 years and usually died in misery.

Much of the rest of Asia was also subjugated during this period. In 1878, the British overran Afghanistan and placed it under the Indian government, and in 1907, Persia was divided between Russia and Britain.

In 1858, the French had used the murder of a Spanish missionary as the rationalization for invading Annam, a tributary state of China. They soon established a French colony in what is now Vietnam. With this toehold, the French succeeded, through war and intrigue, in bringing all the territory of Indochina under their domination by 1887.

The Malay Peninsula and the Malay Archipelago (which stretches for nearly 3,000 miles) were also carved up. The British grabbed Singapore and the Malay States, the northern part of Borneo, and southern New Guinea. Another part of New Guinea was taken by the Germans, and most of the remaining islands (an area comprising about 735,000 square miles) went to the Dutch.

american imperialism

Throughout much of the nineteenth century, American imperialism channeled all its energies in conquering the continent and exterminating the native American Indian population. The Samoa Islands were America's first overseas imperialist grab. In 1878, the natives of Pago Pago granted the Americans the right to use their harbor. Eleven years later, the islands had been conquered and divided between the United States and Germany.

Similarly, Pearl Harbor, in the Hawaiian Islands, became a U.S. naval station in 1887. It was but a very short time before American capitalists controlled most of Hawaii's sugar production. The tiny minority of white Americans soon revolted against Queen Liliuokalani's rule and, with the help of U.S. Marines, subjugated the native population. In 1898, Hawaii was officially annexed by the United States.

It was also in 1898 that the United States used the convenient sinking of the battleship *Maine* as an excuse to declare war on Spain and "liberate" the Cubans from Spanish oppression. Recognizing that it was no match for the United States, the Spanish government accepted every American demand, but the United States declared war anyway as a "measure of atonement" for the *Maine*. The American victory gave her Puerto Rico, Guam, and the Philippine

Islands outright, and the newly "independent" Cubans soon found American capitalists taking over most of their agriculture and commerce. Cuban independence had been restricted by a provision that the United States could intervene at its own discretion into Cuba's internal affairs "for the protection of life, property and individual liberty," a slogan that has been used to justify imperialism more than a few times. American troops invaded Cuba in 1906, 1911, and 1917, before secure control was finally established.

The Filipinos, who had been fighting for their independence from Spain, discovered the American brand to be no better than Spanish domination. President McKinley had decided that Americans were obligated "to educate the Filipinos and uplift and Christianize them," but the Filipinos, who had been Roman Catholics for centuries, resisted this American "Christianization." It took 60,000 American troops, as well as endless atrocities and concentration camps, before the Filipinos were finally "uplifted" and "educated."

In 1901, when the republic of Colombia refused to sell a strip of land (on which the Panama Canal was to be constructed) to the United States, President Roosevelt took action. A Panamanian insurrection was organized with American approval and help. United States warships were strategically placed to prevent Colombian troops from moving in to suppress the rebellion. The revolt started on November 3, 1903; on November 6, the United States extended diplomatic recognition to the "new nation"; on November 18, the United States had the Canal Zone on much more favorable terms than they had originally offered.

In 1904, President Roosevelt announced that the United States believed in the principle of self-determination for nations that acted "with reasonable efficiency and decency in social and political matters." He added, however, that "chronic wrongdoing, or any impotence which results in a general loosening of the ties of civilized society, may in America, as elsewhere, ultimately require intervention by some civilized nation. . . ."[7]

In 1909, U.S. Marines invaded Nicaragua to overthrow José Santos Zelaya, who had threatened American economic concessions there. In 1912, American troops were back in Nicaragua again. In 1915, American Marines invaded Haiti, and in 1916, American troops overwhelmed the Dominican Republic and established a military government there.

By World War I, the United States had seized or otherwise controlled Samoa, Midway Island, Hawaii, Puerto Rico, Guam, the Philippines, the island of Tutuila, Cuba, Santo Domingo, Haiti, Nicaragua, and the Panama Canal Zone.

[7] Quoted in G. C. Fite and J. E. Reese, *An Economic History of the United States* (2d ed.; Boston: Houghton Mifflin, 1965), p. 472.

imperialism and evolutionary socialism

The Boer War jolted British public opinion and resulted in strong conflicts among many radicals and socialists. On the one hand, it produced an abundance of jingoist sentiment and imperialist ideology that influenced some socialists, but on the other, J. A. Hobson's *Imperialism: A Study* caustically ridiculed this sentiment and ideology and advanced a theory of imperialism that was to have a profound influence on Marxists and many non-Marxist socialists.

Imperialism, according to Hobson, was a struggle for political and economic domination of areas of the world occupied by "lower races." Its "economic tap-root" was the necessity for advanced capitalist countries to find markets for the goods and capital produced domestically but for which there was inadequate domestic demand. Evoking traditions of nationalism and militarism, it could "appeal to the lust of quantitative acquisitiveness and of forceful domination surviving in a nation from early centuries of animal struggle for existence."[8]

The basic cause of the deficiency in domestic demand was, Hobson believed, a severely inequitable distribution of income which resulted in a distorted allocation of resources which led in turn to the quest for foreign markets. Hobson argued that the imperialist tendencies of the late nineteenth and early twentieth centuries could be reversed only by reform radical enough to effect a more equitable distribution of income. He summarized his position succinctly in the following passage:

> There is no necessity to open up new foreign markets; the home markets are capable of indefinite expansion. Whatever is produced in England can be consumed in England, provided that the "income," or power to demand commodities, is properly distributed. This only appears untrue because of the unnatural and unwholesome specialization to which this country has been subjected, based upon a bad distribution of economic resources, which has induced an overgrowth of certain manufacturing trades for the express purpose of effecting foreign sales. If the industrial revolution had taken place in an England founded upon equal access by all classes to land, education and legislation, specialization in manufactures would not have gone so far. . . . ; foreign trade would have been less important though more steady; the standard of life for all portions of the

---

8 Quotations in this paragraph from J. A. Hobson, *Imperialism: A Study* (London: Allen and Unwin, 1938 [first published in 1902]), p. 368.

population would have been high, and the present rate of national consumption would probably have given full, constant, remunerative employment to a far larger quantity of private and public capital than is now being employed.[9]

The issue of whether publicly to denounce English imperialism bitterly divided the Fabians. Sydney Olivier's insistence that the society's executive committee issue a pronouncement condemning the Boer War in particular and imperialism in general was rejected by one vote, but the committee agreed to the demand that the issue be put to a general vote.

Led by George Bernard Shaw, the proimperialist faction argued that small, backward nations could not manage their own affairs and should not be considered as nations at all and that the advanced European nations thus had a duty to police and manage the internal affairs of these backward peoples—for their own welfare. The debate was bitter. Finally, 45 percent of the membership voted to condemn English imperialism, and 55 percent opted to approve of or ignore imperialism. Immediately, 18 members of the society, including several of its most prominent personalities, handed in their resignations.

The sentiments of the German revisionists were similar to those of the Fabians, the majority either approving of European imperialism or not considering it a proper issue upon which to take a stand. Bernstein, for example, wrote: "only a conditional right of savages to the land occupied by them can be recognized. The higher civilization ultimately can claim a higher right."[10] Orthodox Marxists, however, were virtually unanimous in condemning imperialism which they analyzed as only the latest stage in the historical development of capitalism: Capitalists were forced by the mounting contradictions of the economic system to turn frantically to economic exploitation of more backward areas.

lenin's analysis of imperialism

The most famous and influential socialist analysis was contained in Lenin's pamphlet *Imperialism: The Highest Stage of Capitalism,* published in 1916. Lenin attempted "to show, as briefly and as popularly as possible, the principal economic characteristics of imperialism."[11] The most important was that in the imperialistic phase

[9] Ibid., pp. 88–89.

[10] Bernstein, op. cit., p. 179.

[11] *Imperialism: The Highest Stage of Capitalism* (London: Lawrence & Wishart, 1939), p. 1.

of capitalist development, the capitalist economies were thoroughly dominated by monopolies, a development that Marx had correctly foreseen. By monopolies, Lenin did not mean industries that consisted of only one firm (the modern economic definition of monopoly), but rather he referred to industries dominated by trusts, cartels, combinations, or by a few large firms.

Drawing heavily on the German experience, Lenin argued that the development of monopolies was closely related to important changes in the banking system. Banks had assumed a position of central importance in the drive toward cartelization and had come to exercise considerable control over many of the most important industrial cartels. This control was so extensive that Lenin spoke of the imperialistic phase of capitalism as the age of "finance capital."

Banks were able to mobilize huge sums of money for investment, but persistent downward pressures on domestic profit rates dictated that investment outlets be sought outside the home country. Lenin, unlike Hobson, did not believe that the necessity to export commodities was the most important economic cause of imperialism. Rather, it was the necessity to export capital. Backward areas offered a large and inexpensive labor force and lucrative investment prospects.

In the imperialist phase of capitalism, the various governments fought to gain access to privileged and protected markets for the combines and cartels within their own political boundaries. At the same time, these national combines and cartels sought to partition the world markets through international cartels. Deep-seated rivalry and competition, however, were more important than the opportunistic short-run collaborations. Persistent national conflicts and wars were the inevitable result. In Lenin's words:

> The epoch of the newest capitalism shows us that certain relations are being established between capitalist combines, *based* on the economic division of the world; while parallel with this and in connection with it, certain relations are being established between political alliances, between states, on the basis of the territorial division of the world, of the struggle for colonies, of the "struggle for economic territory."[12]

Such a situation was, Lenin believed, inherently unstable. Imperialism would lead to wars among the advanced capitalist countries and to rebellions and revolutions in the exploited areas. As long as the capitalist system could support its imperialistic thrust, however, it would prolong its existence by providing outlets for excess investment funds. The extra profits that imperialism secured

12 Ibid., p. 69.

for the home country meant that wages paid its workers could be raised. Thus, because it shared in the spoils, labor would at least temporarily be sapped of its revolutionary potential and controlled by right-wing labor leaders, "justly called social imperialists."[13]

If imperialism expanded the domain of capitalism and in doing so prolonged the system's existence, the tensions and conflicts it engendered were, Lenin believed, more severe than those of the competitive capitalism about which Marx wrote. Capitalism was still doomed, and socialism was still the wave of the future.

summary

During the late nineteenth and early twentieth centuries, workingmen made important economic and political gains throughout the capitalist world. This led many socialists to believe that capitalism could be transformed into socialism through gradual, peaceful political reform.

The same period witnessed the imperialistic carving-up of most of the world's economically underdeveloped areas. The inhabitants of these areas were harshly and cruelly exploited for the profits of large corporations in the advanced capitalist countries.

The issue of imperialism split the evolutionary socialist movement. Many of the reform socialists, for example, George Bernard Shaw and Eduard Bernstein, were strongly proimperialist. Others, among them J. A. Hobson, were strongly antiimperialist as were virtually all the Marxist socialists. Lenin's *Imperialism: The Highest Stage of Capitalism* was the most influential Marxist condemnation of imperialism.

---

[13] Ibid., p. 99.

chapter 10
keynesian economics and the great depression

While the period from the Civil War to 1900 was one of rapid
economic expansion in the United States, these accomplishments
were dwarfed by the growth from 1900 to 1929. The following
figures show the percentage increase in value added by manufacture
in several key industries between 1899 and 1927.[1]

Chemicals, etc.	239%
Leather and products	321%
Textiles and products	449%
Food products	551%
Machinery	562%
Paper and printing	614%
Steel and products	780%
Transportation and equipment	969%

In 1900, it has been estimated, U.S. wealth (the market values of
all economic assets) was $86 billion; in 1929, it was $361 billion.
    This spectacular growth gave the United States a huge edge
over all other countries in manufacturing output. The American
prosperity of the 1920s was based on high and rising levels of output.

[1] Figures taken from Leo Huberman, *We the People* (New York: Monthly Review
Press, 1964), p. 254.

Real gross national product (GNP), adjusted for price changes, increased by 62 percent from 1914 to 1929. Only 3.2 percent of the labor force was unemployed in 1929, and labor productivity rose during that decade at least as fast as wages. Between 1921 and 1929, total automobile registrations increased from less than 11 to more than 26 million; consumers spent tens of millions of dollars on radios, refrigerators, and other electric appliances that had not been available before. American manufacturing seemed, to most, to be a permanent cornucopia destined to create affluence for all.

This leadership in manufacturing was associated with financial leadership in the world economy. The American economic empire began to rival that of England. By 1930, American businessmen owned large investments around the world. The following figures give the values of these investments in 1930:[2]

Canada	$3,942,000,000
Europe	4,929,000,000
Mexico and Central America	1,000,000,000
South America	3,042,000,000
West Indies	1,233,000,000
Africa	118,000,000
Asia	1,023,000,000
Oceania	419,000,000

the great depression

But this era of rapid growth and economic abundance came to a halt on October 24, 1929. On that "Black Thursday," the New York stock market saw security values begin a downward plummet that eventually was to destroy all confidence in business. Their confidence undermined, businessmen cut back production and investment. This decreased national income and employment, which, in turn, worsened business confidence even more. Before the process came to an end, thousands of corporations had gone bankrupt, millions were unemployed, and one of the worst national catastrophes in history was under way.

Between 1929 and 1932, there were over 85,000 business failures; more than 5,000 banks suspended operations; stock values on the New York Exchange fell from $87 billion to $19 billion; unemployment rose to 12 million, with nearly one-fourth of the population having no means of sustaining themselves; farm income fell by more than

2 Ibid., p. 251.

half; and manufacturing output decreased by almost 50 percent.[3]

America had plunged from the world's most prosperous country to one in which tens of millions lived in desperate, abject poverty. Particularly hard-hit were the blacks and other minority groups. The proportion of blacks among the unemployed was from 60 to 400 percent higher than the proportion of blacks in the general population.[4] Certain geographical areas suffered more than others. Congressman George Huddleston of Alabama reported in January 1932:

We have about 108,000 wage and salary workers in my district. Of that number, it is my belief that not exceeding 8,000 have their normal incomes. At least 25,000 men are altogether without work. Some of them have not had a stroke of work for more than 12 months, maybe 60,000 or 75,000 are working one to five days a week, and practically all have had serious cuts in their wages and many of them do not average over $1.50 a day.[5]

Many cities reported that they could give relief payments for only a very short time, often one week, before people were forced to their own devices to subsist. The executive director of the Welfare Council of New York City described the plight of the unemployed.

when the breadwinner is out of a job he usually exhausts his savings if he has any. Then, if he has an insurance policy, he probably borrows to the limit of its cash value. He borrows from his friends and from his relatives until they can stand the burden no longer. He gets credit from the corner grocery store and the butcher shop, and the landlord foregoes collecting the rent until interest and taxes have to be paid and something has to be done. All of these resources are finally exhausted over a period of time, and it becomes necessary for these people, who have never before been in want, to ask for assistance.

The specter of starvation faces millions of people who have never before known what it was to be out of a job for any considerable period of time and who certainly have never known what it was to be absolutely up against it.[6]

The abject despair of these millions of people is at best suggested by a 1932 report describing the unloading of garbage in the Chicago

---

3 Figures taken from Louis M. Hacker, *The Course of American Economic Growth and Development* (New York: Wiley, 1970), pp. 300–301.

4 See Lester V. Chandler, *America's Greatest Depression* (New York: Harper & Row, 1970), pp. 40–41.

5 U.S., Congress, Senate Hearings before a subcommittee of the Committee on Manufactures, 72d Cong., 1st sess., p. 239.

6 Quoted in Chandler, op. cit., pp. 41–42.

city garbage dumps: "Around the truck which was unloading garbage and other refuse were about 35 men, women and children. As soon as the truck pulled away from the pile all of them started digging with sticks, some with their hands, grabbing bits of food and vegetables."[7]

What had happened to reduce the output of goods and services so drastically? Natural resources were still as plentiful as ever. The nation still had as many factories, tools, and machines. The people had the same skills and wanted to put them to work. And yet millions of workers and their families begged, borrowed, stole, and lined up for a pittance from charity, while thousands of factories stood idle or operated at far below capacity. The explanation lay within the institutions of the capitalist market system. Factories could have been opened and men put to work, but they were not because it was *not profitable* for businessmen to do this. And in a capitalist economy, production decisions are based primarily on the criterion of profits— not on peoples' needs.

the economics of keynes

The socialist cause gained many enthusiasts in the 1930s. While the capitalist world was suffering what was, perhaps, its most severe depression, the Soviet economy was experiencing rapid growth. When the depression struck, it was a traumatic shock to many Americans, who had come to believe that their country was destined to achieve unparalleled and unending increases in material prosperity.

The capitalist economic system seemed to be on the verge of total collapse. Drastic countermeasures were essential, but before the system could be saved, the malady had to be better understood. And to that task came one of the most brilliant economists of this century: John Maynard Keynes (1883–1946). In his famous book *The General Theory of Employment, Interest and Money,* Keynes attempted to show what had happened to capitalism so that it could be preserved.

Keynes began his analysis by looking at the process of production. In a given production period, a firm produces a certain dollar volume of goods. From the proceeds of the sale of these goods, the firm pays its costs of production which include wages, salaries, rent, supplies and raw materials, and interest on borrowed funds. What remains after these costs are paid is profit.

[7] Quoted in Huberman, op. cit., p. 260.

The important point to remember is this: What is a cost of production to the business firm represents income to an individual or another firm. The profit is also income—the income going to the owners of the firm. Because the value of production is exhausted by the costs of production and profits, and all these are income, it follows that the value of what has been produced must be equal to the incomes generated in producing it.

In terms of the entire economy, the aggregate picture is the same as that for the individual firm: The value of everything produced in the economy during any period is equal to the total of all incomes received in that period. Therefore, in order for businesses to sell all that they have produced, people must spend in the aggregate all their incomes. If an amount equal to the total income in society is spent on goods and services, then the value of production is realized in sales. In that case, profits remain high, and businessmen are willing to produce the same amount or more in the succeeding period.

Keynes called this a *circular flow:* Money flows from businesses to the public in the form of wages, salaries, rents, interest, and profits; this money then flows back to the businesses when the public buys goods and services from them. As long as businesses sell all they have produced and make satisfactory profits, the process continues.

But this does not happen automatically. When money flows from businesses to the public, some of it does not flow directly back to the businesses. The circular flow has leakages. To begin with, all people do not spend all their incomes. A percentage is saved, usually put into banks, and therefore withdrawn from the spending stream. This saving may be offset by other persons who borrow money from banks and spend more than their income. Keynes, however, pointed out that at the peak of prosperity, saving is usually greater than consumer borrowing; thus, there is usually net saving, or a net leakage, from circular income-expenditure flow.

Keynes also identified two other leakages. (1) People buy goods and services from foreign businesses, but the money spent on these imports cannot be spent on domestically produced goods. (2) The taxes people pay are also withdrawn from the income-expenditure flow.

These three leakages (saving, imports, and taxes) may be offset by three spending injections into the income-expenditure flow. (1) Imports can be offset by exports. They are exactly offset when foreigners buy goods produced in the United States in amounts equal to foreign imports purchased by Americans. (2) The government uses taxes to finance the purchase of goods and services. If it uses all taxes for this purpose and balances the budget, then government expenditures will exactly offset taxes in the spending stream. (3) If businessmen wish to expand their capital, they can finance investment in capital goods by borrowing the funds that were saved. Investment, then, may exactly offset the saving leakage.

If these three injections into the income-expenditure flow are just as large as the three leakages, then spending equals the value of production. Everything that has been produced can be sold, and prosperity reigns.

Keynes, however, believed that it was unlikely that the process could continue uninterrupted for very long. Investment, which is necessary to absorb savings, enlarges the capital stock and hence increases the economy's productive capacity. In order to utilize the new productive capacity fully, production and income must increase in the next period. But with the higher income, there will be more saving, which necessitates more investment, and this investment is by no means automatically forthcoming.

Keynes saw that those individuals with higher incomes saved a higher percentage of their incomes than those with low incomes. He concluded that this pattern would also hold for all society. As the aggregate income of society increases, the total savings increases more than proportionately. In other words, at each new higher level of income, a larger percentage of income is saved.

Thus, investment would have to increase at a faster rate than income if it were to continually offset saving. Only this rapid increase would permit businesses to sell everything they produced, but the faster investment grows, the more rapid is the increase in productive capacity. Because of this, the economy must invest even-greater amounts (both absolutely and relatively) in each successive period if the balance is to be maintained. In any mature private-enterprise economy, however, according to Keynes, the number of profitable investment outlets is limited. Hence, as the process of economic growth continues, the difficulty of finding sufficient investment outlets becomes more and more acute.

If it becomes impossible to find enough investment outlets, then investment falls short of saving, and the total expenditures for goods and services fall short of the value of those produced. Businesses, unable to sell all they have produced, find that their inventories of unsold goods are increasing. Each business sees only its own problem: that it has produced more than it can sell. It, therefore, reduces production in the next period. Most businesses, being in the same situation, do the same thing. The results are a large reduction of production, a decrease in employment, and a decline in income. With the decline in income, however, even less will be spent on goods and services in the next period. So businessmen again find that even at the lower level of production, they are unable to sell all they have produced. They again cut back production, and the down-ward spiral continues.

Under these circumstances, businesses have little or no incentive to expand their capital goods (because excess capacity already exists), and therefore investment falls drastically. Expenditures of all types plummet. As income declines, saving declines more than proportionately. This process continues until the declines in income have reduced saving to the point where it no longer exceeds the reduced level of investment. At this low level of income, equilibrium is restored. Leakages from the income-expenditure flow are again equal to the injections into it. The economy is stabilized, but at a level where high unemployment and considerable unused productive capacity exist.

Keynes' analysis was not, in its essentials, drastically different from those offered by Marx (Chapter 6) and Hobson (Chapter 9). The principal cause of a depression was, in the opinion of all three thinkers, the inability of capitalists to find sufficient investment opportunities to offset the increasing levels of saving generated by economic growth. Keynes' unique contribution was to show how the relation of saving to income could lead to a stable but depressed level of income, with widespread unemployment.

Marx (and Lenin) had believed the disease to be incurable. Hobson had prescribed measures to equalize the distribution of income and thereby reduce saving as a cure. Could Hobson's prescription work? This probably is not a very meaningful question. In most industrial capitalist countries, wealth and economic power determine political power, and those who wield power have never been willing to sacrifice it to save the economic system.

In the United States, for example, out of 300,000 nonfinancial corporations existing in 1925, the largest 200 made considerably more profit than the other 299,800 combined. The wealthiest 5 percent of the population owned virtually all the stocks and bonds and received in excess of 30 percent of the income. Needless to say, this 5 percent dominated American politics. In these circumstances, speculating about what would happen if the income and wealth were radically redistributed amounts to mere fanciful daydreaming.

Keynes' answer to the problem was more realistic. Government could step in when saving exceeded investment, borrow the excess saving, then spend the money on socially useful projects. They would be chosen in order not to increase the economy's productive capacity or decrease the investment opportunities of the future. This government spending would increase the injections into the spending stream and create a full-employment equilibrium. In doing so, it would not add to the capital stock. Therefore, unlike investment spending, it would not make a full-employment level of production more difficult to attain in the next period. Keynes summarized his position thus:

> Ancient Egypt was doubly fortunate, and doubtless owed to this
> its fabled wealth, in that it possessed *two* activities, namely,
> pyramid-building as well as the search for precious metals, the
> fruits of which, since they could not serve the needs of man by
> being consumed, did not stale with abundance. The Middle
> Ages built cathedrals and sang dirges. Two pyramids, two
> masses for the dead, are twice as good as one; but not so
> two railways from London to York.[8]

What type of expenditures ought the government to make? Keynes
himself had a predilection toward useful public works such as the
construction of schools, hospitals, parks, and other public conveniences. He realized, however, that this would probably benefit
middle- and lower-income recipients much more than the wealthy.
And because the wealthy have the political power, they would
probably insist on policies that would not redistribute income away
from them. He saw that it might be politically necessary to channel
this spending into the hands of the large corporations, even though
little that was beneficial to society would be accomplished directly.
He wrote:

> If the Treasury were to fill old bottles with banknotes, bury them
> at suitable depths in disused coal-mines which are then filled
> up to the surface with town rubbish, and leave it to private
> enterprise on well-tried principles of laissez faire to dig the
> notes up again . . . there need be no more unemployment. . . .
> It would indeed be more sensible to build houses and the like;
> but if there are political and practical difficulties in the way
> of this, the above would be better than nothing.[9]

The depression of the 1930s dragged on until the outbreak of
World War II. From 1936 (the year Keynes' *General Theory* was
published) to 1940, economists hotly debated the merits of his theory
and policy prescriptions. When the various governments began to
increase armament production rapidly, however, unemployment
began to melt away. During the war years, under the stimulus of
enormous government expenditures, conditions in most capitalist
economies were rapidly transformed from situations of severe
unemployment to acute shortages of labor.

The American armed forces mobilized 14 million people who had
to be armed, quartered, and fed. Between 1939 and 1944, the output
of the manufacturing, mining, and construction industries doubled,
and productive capacity increased by 50 percent. The American

[8] J. M. Keynes, *The General Theory of Employment, Interest and Money* (New York:
Harcourt Brace Jovanovich, 1936), p. 131.

[9] Ibid., p. 129.

economy produced 296,000 planes, 5,400 cargo ships, 6,500 naval vessels, 64,500 landing craft, 86,000 tanks, and 2,500,000 trucks.[10] During the war period, the most pressing problem was a *shortage* of labor, as contrasted with the 19 percent unemployment that existed as late as the beginning of 1939.

keynesian economics and ideology

Most economists believed that this wartime experience had proven the basic correctness of Keynes' ideas. Capitalism could be saved, they proclaimed, by the wise use of the government's powers to tax, borrow, and spend money. Capitalism was, again, a viable social and economic system.

But viability alone was insufficient as an ideology for capitalism. Russia had not experienced unemployment in the 1930s, and its spectacular rate of growth during this period had proven the viability of the soviet economic system. This challenge elicited a resurgence of the older neoclassical economic ideology. Older theories were cast in an esoteric and highly elaborate mathematical framework. Typical of these new economists was Paul A. Samuelson, whose book *The Foundations of Economic Analysis* is among the technically most formidable treatments of economics.[11] In 1947, The American Economic Association awarded him the first John Bates Clark Medal for the most outstanding contribution to economics made by an economist under forty years of age. The book was also instrumental in securing the Nobel Prize in economics for Samuelson in 1970.

Samuelson has made an even more significant contribution in terms of his influence on the dominant economic ideology of capitalism in the last 25 years. His introductory text, *Economics,* which has undergone eight editions, has been translated into almost every major language, and has sold millions of copies.[12] The first edition set out mainly to explain and simplify Keynes' ideas. Each subsequent edition has tended to bring in more of the traditional neoclassical ideology of capitalism. In 1955, Samuelson offered his "grand neoclassical synthesis," an integration of Keynesian with neoclassical economics. The Keynesian theory would provide the knowledge necessary to maintain a full-employment economy, and the market system could operate within this Keynesian framework to

10 All figures taken from Hacker, op. cit., p. 325.

11 Paul A. Samuelson, *The Foundations of Economic Analysis* (Cambridge, Mass.: Harvard University Press, 1947).

12 Paul A. Samuelson, *Economics* (New York: McGraw-Hill, 1948).

allocate resources according to the time-honored principles of the neoclassical ideology.

Almost every student of economics for the last 25 years has learned his elementary economics from Samuelson's text, or from one of the many others that have attempted to copy his approach and content.

the efficacy of keynesian economic policies

After 1945, Keynesian economics became orthodoxy for both economists and the majority of politicians. Almost 3 million veterans were demobilized in that year. In 1946, another 11 million joined the civilian labor force. Congress and many economists feared a new depression and immediately took steps to apply the new Keynesian ideas. Passage of the Employment Act of 1946 legally obligated the government to use its taxing, borrowing, and spending powers to maintain full employment. The act declared that "It is the continuing policy and responsibility of the Federal government to use all practicable means . . . for the purpose of creating and maintaining . . . conditions under which there will be afforded useful employment opportunities, including self-employment, for those able, willing, and seeking to work, and to promote maximum employment, production and purchasing power."

Have Keynesian economic policies worked? The answer to this question is very complex. Since World War II, there have been no major depressions in the United States, but there have been five "recessions" (the modern euphemism for a mild depression). In 1948–1949, a recession lasted for 11 months; in 1953–1954, for 13 months; in 1957–1958, for 9 months; and in 1960–1961, for 9 months. As of this writing, the 1969–1971 recession has been going on for over two years.

Because of recessions, the economy's performance in the 1950s left much to be desired. The real rate of growth of GNP was 2.9 percent, which does not compare very favorably with the 4.7 percent for 1920–1929 or the 3.7 percent for 1879–1919. The brightest spot in the American economy's performance has been the growth rate in the 1960s, which averaged around 5 percent.

Unemployment for the 1950s and early 1960s averaged 4.6 percent, although it dipped to 3.5 percent in the mid-1960s. Moreover, inflation has been a persistent problem since World War II. From 1945 through 1968, the average annual increase in wholesale prices was 3.8 percent (most of which occurred in the late 1940s); the rate of increase from 1968 to 1970 was nearly 5 percent. The 1969–1971 inflation was accompanied by an economic recession in which unemployment soared to rates of over 6 percent. The simultaneous occurrence of both high unemployment and a high rate of inflation led to President Nixon's attempt to freeze wages and prices in late 1971, followed by the "phase II" plan for government control over increases in wages and prices.

On balance, Keynesian policies appear to have worked with moderate success. Before judging this performance, however, it is necessary to see what the American government substituted for the pyramids of Egypt and the cathedrals of the Middle Ages. In 1960, one observer wrote: "A central aspect of our growth experience of the past two decades is one which few spokesmen for the future candidly discuss. This is the fact that our great boom did not begin until the onset of World War II, and that its continuance since then has consistently been tied to a military rather than to a purely civilian economic demand."[13]

the warfare economy

In 1940, military and military-related expenditures were $3.2 billion, or 3.2 percent of GNP. By 1947, they were still only $9.1 billion, or 3.9 percent of GNP. From that time onward, the amount spent on militarism grew steadily and rapidly. By 1960, military expenditures were 8.9 percent of GNP. During the rapid growth of the 1960s, military expenditures grew at approximately the same rate as GNP. If other expenses that are related to militarism but not included in the "defense" budget are taken into account, the total has been close to 15 percent in recent years.[14] The United States has spent and continues to spend more on militarism than any other country—more in absolute terms, relative terms, and per capita.

The result of these enormous expenditures has been the growth of the *military-industrial complex* as a necessary adjunct to economic prosperity. Its essential features have been described as follows:

> The warfare state we have constructed over the last two generations has a large clientele. At the top of the pyramid is the so-called military–industrial complex. It comprises, first, the Defense Department of the Federal Government, along with such satellites as the CIA and NASA. The admirals and generals, the

13 Robert Heilbroner, *The Future as History* (New York: Harper & Row, 1960), p. 133.

14 See, for example, Daniel R. Fusfeld, "Fascist Democracy in the United States," *Conference Papers of the Union for Radical Economics* (December 1968), pp. 11 and 34–35.

space scientists and the intelligence men, like all government
bureaucrats, are busily engaged in strengthening their influence.
To this end they cultivate congressmen and senators, locate
military establishments in politically strategic districts, and
provide legislators with special favors. Former military men are
drawn into the net of influence through the Army and Navy
associations and through veterans' organizations.
The military are supported by the industrial side of the complex.
These are the large corporations on whom the military depend
for the hardware of modern war. Some sell the bulk of their
output to the military, like North American Aviation, Lockheed
Aircraft, General Dynamics, McDonnell-Douglas, and Thiokol
Chemical. Others are important military suppliers but make the
bulk of their sales in civilian markets, such as Western Electric,
Sperry Rand, General Electric, or IBM. Others, such as Dupont
and General Motors, are only occasionally military contractors.[15]

The extent to which military production dominates the American
economy is indicated by a recent survey which showed that five key
military-related industries accounted for 7.9 percent of all employment in New York, 12.3 percent in New Jersey, 13 percent in Texas,
14.6 percent in Massachusetts, 15.7 percent in Maryland, 20.9 percent
in Florida, 23.4 percent in Connecticut, 30 percent in Kansas, 31.4
percent in California, and 34.8 percent in Washington.[16]

Military expenditures operate in exactly the way Keynes believed
pyramid-building operated in the ancient Egyptian economy. For
generals and most politicians, a tenfold overkill potential is twice as
good as a fivefold overkill; two ABM (antiballistic missile) systems are
twice as good as one, but only half as good as four. And if the public
cannot be easily convinced of this, the immense amount of research
financed by the military-industrial complex comes to the fore.
Weapons and delivery systems are rapidly superseded by new
models. Horror stories convince the public that a further escalation
of the arms race is necessary and that "obsolete" (and often unused)
models must be scrapped.

Military spending keeps the capital-goods industry operating at
near full capacity without raising the economy's productive capacity
as rapidly as would be the case if they provided capital goods for
industry. Demand does not tend to drop below supply as persistently
as it formerly did; military spending increases demand without
increasing productivity.

The neglect of these effects of the Keynesian military-induced
prosperity is perhaps "the most important abdication of any by the

15 Ibid., p. 13.
16 Ibid., p. 15.

economists."[17] This type of economic theory has led to "an
ahistorical, a technical or mechanical, a nonpolitical view of what
the economy is and how it works."[18]

Very few Keynesian economists have been willing to come to grips
with the implication of militarism as a tool of economic policy.

> The arms economy has been the major Keynesian instrument
> of our times. But its use has been cloaked as "national interest,"
> its effects have been largely undermined, its international conse-
> quences largely deleterious and destabilizing, its importance
> making for uncritical acceptance and dependence by large
> segments of the society, its long-run effects hardly glanced at.
> The arms economy has done much more than distort the use of
> scarce creative scientific and engineering talent. . . . It has
> forced us to neglect a whole range of urgent social priorities,
> the consequences of which threaten the fabric of our society.[19]

summary

The severity of the Great Depression of the 1930s caused many
economists to become dissatisfied with the orthodox neoclassical
economists' view that unemployment was merely a short-run,
ephemeral "adjustment" to a temporary disequilibrium situation.
Keynes' new ideas were rapidly accepted by most important
economists. World War II proved that massive government intervention in the market economy could create full employment, indeed,
Hitler's Germany had already established this in the 1930s.

Since the war, the United States has not had a major depression.
Most economists agree that massive government spending is largely
responsible for this improved performance of American capitalism.
Critics have argued, however, that the social price of this prolonged
prosperity has been the creation of a military-industrial complex that
currently threatens the entire fabric of American society.

If this view is correct, then it is possible to conclude that Keynes'
theories did enable the neoclassical ideology to come to grips with
the most important economic problem of the 1930s but have obscured
if not worsened other problems. Some of these problems and some
contemporary ideologies of capitalism will be examined in Chapter 11.

[17] Sumner M. Rosen, "Keynes Without Gadflies," in T. Roszak, ed., *The Dissenting
Academy* (New York: Random House, Vintage Books, 1968), p. 83.

[18] Ibid., p. 85.

[19] Ibid., pp. 86–87.

chapter 11
contemporary american capitalism and its defenders

Since World War II, the American economy has experienced five mild recessions, albeit its growth has been fairly satisfactory by historical standards. Gross national product, in constant (1958) dollars, grew from $355 billion in 1950 to $727 billion in 1969. Disposable personal income, again in constant (1958) dollars, grew from $250 billion to $512 billion over the same period.[1] Judged by historical standards, this has certainly been a creditable performance.

The technological advances of American capitalism have been particularly impressive. For several decades prior to World War I, the increases in output per man-hour in American industry had been about 22 percent per decade. After World War II, output per man-hour increased by 35–40 percent per decade.[2] This growth has been made possible by huge expenditures on research and development, which increased from $3.4 billion in 1950 to $12 billion in 1960; fully one-half of these funds came from the federal government.

With these improvements in technology and increases in produc-

---

[1] Figures taken from the *Federal Reserve Bulletin* (August 1970), pp. A68–A69.

[2] Louis M. Hacker, *The Course of American Economic Growth and Development* (New York: Wiley, 1970), p. 326. The increases in productivity in the 1920s had been even more impressive, however.

tion has come a greater concentration of economic power in the hands of a very small number of corporations. In 1929, the 100 largest manufacturing corporations had legal control (actual control being far greater) of 44 percent of the net capital assets of all manufacturing corporations. By 1962, this figure had increased to 58 percent.[3]

In 1962, there were 420,000 manufacturing enterprises. But a mere 5 of these enterprises owned 12.3 percent of all manufacturing assets; 20 owned 25 percent of the total. The total assets of the 20 largest firms were approximately as large as those of the 419,000 smallest companies combined. These 20 giants took a whopping 38 percent of all after-tax profits, leaving the smallest 419,980 to divide 62 percent. Furthermore, of the 180,000 *corporations* involved in manufacturing, the net profits of the 5 largest were nearly twice as large as those of the 178,000 smallest corporations.[4]

The rate of concentration has quickened. In every year since 1959, there have been more than 60 mergers a year involving the acquisition of companies having over $10 million in assets. The number of mergers has increased throughout the sixties. Table 11.1 illustrates this trend.[5] From 1968 to 1970, the evidence points to an ever-faster rate of acquisition. The process of increasing economic concentration, which began about 100 years ago, continues unabated today.

TABLE
11.1

large mergers and acquisitions, 1966–1968

	1966	1967	1968
Total number of acquisitions	1,746	2,384	4,003
Number of acquired manufacturing and mining companies with more than $10 million assets	101	169	192
Value of assets of acquired companies with more than $10 million assets (in billions)	$4.1	$8.2	$12.6
Number of acquisitions made by 200 largest companies	33	67	74
Value of assets of companies acquired by 200 largest companies (in billions)	$2.4	$5.4	$6.9

[3] Gardiner C. Means, "Economic Concentration," in *Hearings before the Subcommittee on Antitrust and Monopoly of the Committee on the Judiciary, United States Senate* (Washington, D.C.: U.S. Government Printing Office, July 1964), pp. 9–19.

[4] Willard F. Mueller, "Economic Concentration," *Hearings,* op. cit., pp. 111–129.

[5] Table constructed from data of the Federal Trade Commission, derived by Paul Sweezy and Harry Magdoff, "The Merger Movement: A Study in Power," *The Monthly Review* (June 1969), pp. 1–5.

The post–World War II prosperity has not reduced the extremes of inequality in the United States. In the most complete study of the distribution of ownership of wealth ever undertaken,[6] it has been shown that the wealthiest 1.6 percent of the population owns over 80 percent of all corporate stock and virtually all state and local government bonds. Furthermore, the concentration of ownership of these income-yielding assets has steadily increased since the early 1920s.

The distribution of income reflects the same extreme inequality. Despite the economy's impressive growth over the past three decades—and the much-publicized war on poverty of the early 1960s, which proved to be a half-hearted minor skirmish—poverty has remained an acute problem in the United States. In 1970, for example, 25.5 million Americans lived in families that had an annual income of less than $3,900, the officially designated "poverty level."[7] The U.S. Bureau of Labor Statistics (BLS) reported that with the high prices that prevailed in 1970, it would require about $7,100 for a family of four to live with "a sense of self-respect and social participation."[8] Thus, most of these 25.5 million persons lived on less than one-half the amount necessary to generate "self-respect." Tens of millions more lived on less than $7,100.

In stark contrast to this widespread poverty, the wealthiest 5 percent of the American population received over 20 percent of all income. At the top of this 5 percent was the elite 1.6 percent that owns most of the income-yielding stocks and bonds in the United States. The richest of the elite had incomes estimated to be between $50 million and $100 million per year (the latter income is about $275,000 per day).

Furthermore, taxes do little, if anything, to reduce the inequities in the distribution of income. It is commonly supposed that the U.S. tax system reduces inequality by taking a higher percentage of the income of the wealthy than is taken from the poor. The personal income tax does tend to reduce income inequalities, but the effect is much smaller than most people imagine. When economists analyze the total tax burden, however, they find that taxes actually increase inequality in the distribution of income because sales taxes, excise taxes, property taxes, and social security taxes all take a much-larger percentage of the poor man's income than of the rich man's.

One economist, a recognized authority on taxes, has analyzed the

---

[6] Robert J. Lampman, *The Share of Top Wealth-holders in National Wealth, 1922–1956* (Princeton, N.J.: Princeton University Press, 1962).

[7] *Los Angeles Times,* May 8, 1971, part I, p. 1.

[8] Ibid., December 21, 1970, part I, p. 18.

total tax burden on incomes along the entire distribution spectrum. He found that families with incomes below $2,000 per year—certainly a level of abject poverty—paid out one-third of their incomes in taxes. As incomes got higher, people paid a lower percentage of their incomes in taxes. For example, families making between $10,000 and $15,000 paid a proportion of their income that was nearly one-third lower than that paid by families with incomes below $2,000. Only among the wealthiest 5 percent of families did the total tax bite exceed that exacted from the poorest. The wealthy elite actually paid out, on the average, 36.3 percent of their income for taxes, a mere 3 percent higher than the poorest segment of society paid.[9]

Thus, it appears that on the one hand, American capitalism in the last three decades has proven fairly successful if judged solely by the criteria of economic growth and productivity (although there has been persistent unemployment and inflation). On the other hand, the extreme inequalities in the distribution of wealth and income have continued and even grown worse. It is not surprising, therefore, that these decades have seen numerous ideological defenses of American capitalism as well as socialist and radical critiques of the U.S. economy.

contemporary classical liberal ideology

Neoclassical economics was the principal purveyor of the classical liberal ideology of capitalism during the late nineteenth and early twentieth centuries. Since the 1930s, neoclassical economics has become more and more complex mathematically, which has enabled modern economists to gain many new theoretical and scientific insights. Its most important assumptions, however, those on which the entire theory rests, are still metaphysical in character. They have not been established on a scientific basis, either empirically or theoretically.

The finest summary of contemporary neoclassical economics is C. E. Ferguson's *The Neoclassical Theory of Production and Distribution*.[10] The mathematical reasoning in this book is so complex that very few people other than professional economists who are thoroughly competent in higher mathematics can understand it. Professor Ferguson is aware, however, of the tenuous nature of many of the assumptions of this ideology, which, like the medieval religious

[9] B. A. Musgrave, "Estimating the Distribution of the Tax Burden," In *Income and Wealth*, Series 10 (Cambridge, England: Bowes & Bowes, 1964), p. 192.

[10] C. E. Ferguson, *The Neoclassical Theory of Production and Distribution* (London: Cambridge University Press, 1969).

ideology of feudalism, ultimately must be accepted on faith alone. He admits this and asserts his personal faith: ". . . placing reliance upon neoclassical economic theory is a matter of faith. I personally have the faith; but at present the best I can do to convince others is to invoke the weight of Samuelson's authority. . . ."[11]

When the thrust toward esoterica removed classical liberal ideology from the level at which it could be widely understood, however, it also substantially reduced its effectiveness as a popular ideology of capitalism. To promote the widespread popular accept-ance of the ideology has been the task of numerous organizations. The best-known American organizations, which propagate a simplified, more popular version of the classical ideology, are the National Association of Manufacturers (NAM), the Foundation for Economic Education, the Committee for Constitutional Government, the United States Chamber of Commerce, and the American Enterprise Association.

A congressional committee found that of $33.4 million spent "to influence legislation," $32.1 million was spent by large corporations. And of this $32.1 million, about $27 million went to such organizations as those mentioned in the previous paragraph.[12] The NAM uses this money to publish a large amount of probusiness propaganda, including "an educational literature series, labor and industrial relations bulletins, news bulletins, a magazine of American affairs, and numerous studies on legislation, education, anti-trust laws, tariffs and unions."[13]

The Foundation for Economic Education reviews and distributes books that reflect the classical liberal ideology of capitalism and publishes and distributes, free of charge, a monthly journal, *The Freeman*, which propagates this ideology. The other organizations engage in numerous publishing and promotional activities designed to inculcate the same ideology as widely as possible.

The popularized statement of the classical ideology lays principal stress on the benefits of the free market. It is argued that the forces of supply and demand in a free market will always lead to results that are preferable to anything that could be achieved by the

---

[11] Ibid., pp. xvii–xviii. Professor Ferguson's candid admission was prompted by a rather esoteric debate among academic economists. They were debating what they called the "reswitching of productive techniques." The debate proved conclusively that some of the most fundamental tenets of neoclassical orthodoxy were untenable. For a summary of the conclusions of the debate, see E. K. Hunt, "Religious Parable Versus Economic Logic: An Analysis of the Recent Controversy in Value, Capital and Distribution Theory," *Inter-Mountain Economic Review* (Fall 1971), also see section III of E. K. Hunt and Jesse Schwartz, *Critique of Economic Theory* (London: Penguin, 1972).

[12] R. Joseph Monsen, Jr., *Modern American Capitalism* (Boston: Houghton Mifflin, 1963), p. 19.

[13] Ibid.

government or a central planning agency. The NAM, for example, asserts that the proper function of the government is to strengthen and "make more effective the regulation by competition."[14] Almost none of its literature, however, suggests much concern with the concentration of corporate power. Rather, the main economic problems are the powers of big labor unions and the "socialistic" welfare measures of the government.

In essence, most of this literature uses a drastically simplified version of some of the classical and neoclassical economists' analyses. It supports the view that any conceivable threat to the operation of the free market, whether real or potential, is an evil to be avoided at any cost. These organizations have had considerable success in propagating this point of view, particularly among small businessmen. (Big business, however, generally continues to look with favor on government intervention—because it usually benefits from such actions.)

contemporary variants of the classical liberal ideology

Most critics of the classical liberal ideology emphasize its failure to come to grips with the realities of the concentration of immense power in the hands of considerably less than 1 percent of the corporations. Several attempts have been made to construct an ideology that retains the competitive, private-enterprise flavor of classical liberalism while recognizing the existence of concentrated corporate power. Two of these will be discussed: the *countervailing power* ideology, associated primarily with the economist John Kenneth Galbraith, and the *people's capitalism* ideology, associated primarily with Professor Massimo Salvadori.

In his famous book *American Capitalism, the Concept of Countervailing Power,* Professor Galbraith recognized the existence of large, special-interest power blocks in the American economy, but argued then that they should not be of much concern because "private economic power begets the countervailing power of those who are subject to it."[15] The result of this newly created countervailing power is "the neutralization of one position of power by another."[16]

[14] National Association of Manufacturers, Economic Principles Commission, *The American Individual Enterprise System, Its Nature and Future* (New York: McGraw-Hill, 1946), p. 57.

[15] John Kenneth Galbraith, *American Capitalism, the Concept of Countervailing Power* (Boston: Houghton Mifflin, 1956), p. 4.

[16] Ibid., p. 1.

Thus, strong unions neutralize strong business firms in the field of labor relations, and strong buyers' associations neutralize the monopolistic or oligopolistic powers of strong sellers. The result, then, is a kind of market equilibrium or invisible hand that harmonizes the interests of all. The harmonious whole is now simply made up of a few neutralized giants rather than numerous, atomistically competitive small firms.[17]

Another influential attempt to show the innocuous (or even beneficial) nature of corporate concentration was made by Professor Salvadori, who used the slogan "people's capitalism" to characterize what he believed to be the most essential feature of contemporary American capitalism: the diffusion of ownership. The widespread diffusion of ownership of corporate stock, as well as other types of assets, means, to Salvadori, that capitalism is no longer a system where a tiny minority reaps most of the privileges, but one in which the majority are rapidly becoming capitalists and getting a share of the privileges.[18] Salvadori has conveniently summarized his people's capitalism ideology:

> At present in the United States there are nearly half a million corporations; stockholders total about ten million (1959). Their numbers have increased rapidly in the post-war period. Standard Oil of New Jersey, for instance, had about 160,000 stockholders in 1946; twelve years later there were three times as many, close to half a million. As a rule, the larger the corporation the more widely spread the ownership. Large corporations in which a majority of shares are owned by an individual or by a family are fewer and fewer. It is already exceptional for a single individual to own more than four or five per cent of the stock of a given corporation. Unincorporated non-farm businesses number about four million; they belong to one or more individuals and this means millions of "capitalists." Nearly four million farmers (three-fourths of the total) are full owners or part owners of the farms they cultivate. Even considering that there is a good deal of overlapping among the three groups (shareholders, individual non-farm owners, farmers) one can say that at least one-fourth to one-third of all American families share the ownership of natural and artificial capital. There are also half a million independent professional

[17] It should be mentioned that Professor Galbraith has published several books since *American Capitalism, the Concept of Countervailing Powers* appeared. Even a cursory reading of these books shows that he has altered his opinions fundamentally. Nevertheless, because the countervailing power of ideology has been very influential, and because most of this influence flows from his book, we are justified in associating this ideology with his name.

[18] This is curiously similar to socialist Eduard Bernstein's idea, discussed in Chapter 9.

people—lawyers, doctors, architects, engineers, accountants, etc.—whose other means of production are not only equipment of one kind or another but also skill and training, and whose income is related to the capital invested in acquiring professional efficiency; they are "capitalists" just as much as owners of natural and artificial capital. Most other families own durable consumer goods (houses, summer cottages, furniture, cars, electrical appliances, etc.), federal, state, and municipal bonds, insurance policies and savings to the extent that they can consider themselves "capitalists."[19]

Thus, bigness of corporations does not, for Salvadori, appear to be an issue. Ownership is becoming more equitably distributed because most people are becoming "capitalists," and hence, by implication, none is powerful enough to exploit another. Disciples point out that by 1970, there were approximately 30 million stockholders. In this view, the United States is becoming a nation where the majority are capitalists.

Even many defenders of capitalism concede that Salvadori's analysis serves only to obscure the nature of the concentration of economic power in the United States and that it neither eliminates nor justifies this concentration. A. A. Berle, Jr., a distinguished scholar of American capitalism as well as a corporation executive, has written:

In terms of power, without regard to asset positions, not only do 500 corporations control two-thirds of the non-farm economy, but within each of that 500 a still smaller group has the ultimate decision-making power. That is, I think, the highest concentration of economic power in recorded history. . . . Since the United States carries on not quite half of the manufacturing production of the entire world today, these 500 groupings—each with its own little dominating pyramid within it—represents a concentration of power over economies which makes the medieval feudal system look like a Sunday school party.[20]

Contrary to the tone of this quotation, Berle is not a critic of American capitalism, but one of the most important developers of a contemporary corporate, or collective, ideology of capitalism.

[19] Massimo Salvadori, *The Economics of Freedom* (Garden City, N.Y.: Doubleday 1959), pp. 70–71.

[20] A. A. Berle, Jr., "Economic Power and the Free Society," in Andrew Hacker, ed., *The Corporation Take-Over* (Garden City, N.Y.: Doubleday, 1965), p. 97.

the contemporary corporate ethic
and capitalist ideology

The tactics of the late nineteenth-century robber barons led most people to reject the corporate ideology (discussed in Chapter 8). Their destructive competition and financial wheeling and dealing hardly supported the conclusion that they were becoming socialized stewards of the public welfare. And yet the classical liberal ideology had no real defense for the existing concentration of economic and political power. The Christian corporate ethic, with its emphasis on the paternalistic benevolence of the powerful, was still the only successful ideological defense of great inequalities of wealth and power.

It was simply not credible to cast the nineteenth-century capitalist in a kindly, paternalistic role. But some twentieth-century ideologists of capitalism have argued that capitalism has changed so drastically that capitalists have lost their importance in the system and have been replaced by a new class of professional managers. These theories envision this "new man," the professional manager, as the paternalistic steward of public welfare.

In 1932, A. A. Berle and G. C. Means published an important and influential book, *The Modern Corporation and Private Property.*[21] In it, they argued that ownership of most of the colossal corporate giants had become so widely diffused that the owners of stock had lost or were rapidly losing control of these corporations. With no single owner holding more than 1 or 2 percent of the stock and with no effective ways of colluding, the owners were left with only the formal voting function when selecting the boards of directors. Candidates for whom they could vote were selected by the existing boards of directors. Thus, the boards chose their own replacements and were, essentially, a self-perpetuating oligarchy. They wielded power but had no necessary connection with the owners of stock. They were not capitalists in the usual sense of the term.

In 1955, Berle wrote another book, *The Twentieth Century Capitalist Revolution,* in which he argued that corporations had developed a quasipolitical status. Managers were primarily motivated by the desire to promote the general public interests in their decision-making, and any who were not so motivated would be forced by public opinion and the threat of government intervention so to act.

21 A. A. Berle and G. C. Means, *The Modern Corporation and Private Property* (New York: Macmillan, 1932).

This view has been widely accepted. Another economist, for
example, wrote:

> No longer the agent of proprietorship seeking to maximize
> return on investment, management sees itself as responsible to
> stockholders, employees, customers, the general public, and, perhaps
> most important, the firm as an institution. . . . There is no display
> of greed or graspingness; there is no attempt to push off onto
> workers or the community at large part of the social costs of the
> enterprise. The modern corporation is a soulful corporation.[22]

The corporation was "soulful," of course, because, in this economist's
opinion, its managers were conscientious, paternalistic stewards of
society's welfare.

The managerial ideology was spelled out in some detail in a
series of lectures delivered by prominent corporation managers at
Columbia University in 1956. According to the chairman of General
Electric, the lectures were intended "to coax us businessmen out of
our offices and into the arena of public thought where our managerial
philosophies can be put to the test of examination by men trained in
other disciplines."[23]

One of the dominant themes in these lectures was that because
American capitalism is "new," the complaints men once may have
had against capitalism are no longer justified. Thus, the chairman of
Sears-Roebuck asserted: "The historic complaint that big business,
as the producing arm of capitalism, exploited the many for the profit
of the few and deprived the workers of the products of their own
labor had a valid basis in the facts of European capitalism, but lacks
substance when applied to American capitalism today."[24]

Another theme was the justification of bigness on the grounds of
better efficiency and higher quality. "The American public," asserted
the chairman of United States Steel, "has gradually become
accustomed to larger and larger groups and has become convinced
that big production groups are outstanding in reliability and in the
quality of their products and services and are necessary to perform
America's larger production tasks in research, in production, and
in the procurement of raw materials."[25]

Finally, the businessmen all saw managers as "professional" men
who are as much concerned with "customers, share owners,

[22] Carl Kaysen, "The Social Significance of the Modern Corporation," *American
Economic Review* (May 1957), pp. 313–314.

[23] Quoted in Robert L. Heilbroner, *The Limits of American Capitalism* (New York:
Harper & Row, 1966), p. 30.

[24] Ibid., pp. 31–32.

[25] Ibid., p. 32.

employees, suppliers, educational institutions, charitable activities, government and the general public" as they are with sales and profits. They believed that managers "all know that special power imposes special responsibilities on those who hold it." Most managers, they asserted, fully accept "their responsibilities for the broader public welfare."[26]

Since 1942, this corporate managerial ideology has been assiduously disseminated by the Committee for Economic Development (CED). The CED readily accepted big business and also "the fact that government was big and was constantly growing bigger and that there was no returning to a simpler, happier past in this respect. It believed that the question was not *how much* government should do, but *what* it should do."[27] Government should not only accept all the duties assigned to it by the classical liberal ideology but also follow Keynesian policies to ensure stable full employment. Further, government should cooperate with corporate management in resolving conflicts and maintaining the tranquil, stable atmosphere within which management can effectively perform its public-spirited, paternalistic functions of promoting the public welfare.[28]

Big business and big government are accepted by this ideology as not only inevitable but also necessary for maximum efficiency. Big labor unions are also accepted as long as they recognize that most of their legitimate interests are in harmony with the interests of business and management.

Another important propagator of the managerial ideology has been the United States Information Agency (USIA), the official government agency charged with the worldwide propagandizing of the "American point of view." The USIA operates on a grand scale. Its Voice of America broadcasts are heard around the world daily in scores of languages, and it publishes dozens of newspapers and magazines, maintains libraries, shows motion pictures, and engages in countless other propaganda operations.

Arthur Larson, who "was a semi-official ideologist to the Eisenhower Administration and a former head of the United States Information Agency,"[29] published a book, *What We Are For*,[30] in which he explained the philosophy of USIA propaganda. In the modern capitalist economy, Larson argued, the government should do only what "needs to be done" and cannot be done "as well" by

[26] Quotations in this paragraph are all from ibid., pp. 32–33.

[27] Karl Schriftgiesser, *Business Comes of Age* (New York: Harper & Row, 1960), p. 224.

[28] See Monsen, op. cit., pp. 25–29.

[29] Ibid., p. 42.

[30] Arthur Larson, *What We Are For* (New York: Harper & Row, 1959).

private businesses.[31] Modern capitalism has a plurality of powerful interest groups such as big business, big unions, big government, and so forth, which have no major or basic conflicts. Rather, their interests harmonize, and they mutually support each other. Larson assumed both that business managers are motivated primarily by the desire to promote social welfare to meet the "basic political and economic needs of all people,"[32] and that businesses operate more efficiently than government. There is, therefore, a built-in preference for a minimal role for government in the economy.[33]

criticisms of contemporary capitalist ideologies

Criticisms of capitalism have often gone hand in hand with criticisms of capitalist ideologies. In the remaining part of this chapter, criticisms of the ideologies of capitalism will be examined. Some of the principal criticisms of contemporary American capitalism will be discussed in Chapter 12.

CRITICISMS OF NEOCLASSICAL IDEOLOGY

Neoclassical economics completely dominated orthodox academic economics in the late nineteenth and early twentieth centuries. From the 1930s onward, however, it increasingly came under attack. In 1938, Oscar Lange and Fred M. Taylor published their significant book *On the Economic Theory of Socialism*.[34] Lange and Taylor accepted the neoclassical argument that a "purely" and "perfectly" competitive economy will lead to an "optimum allocation of resources," but they also showed that such an economy need not be a capitalist economy. They demonstrated that a socialist economy, in which the means of production were collectively owned, could also operate (through perfect planning or through decentralized decision-making) in a state of "optimal economic efficiency." Private ownership had absolutely no formal or theoretical importance in the neoclassical theory. Furthermore, under socialist ownership, they argued, the inequities of income distribution under a capitalist system would disappear.

[31] Ibid., pp. 16–17.

[32] Monsen, op. cit., p. 45.

[33] Larson, op. cit., p. 17.

[34] Oscar Lange and Fred M. Taylor, *On the Economic Theory of Socialism* (Minneapolis, Minn.: University of Minnesota Press, 1938). Lange had published his essay two years earlier in *Review of Economic Studies* (October 1936), pp. 53–71, and (February 1937), pp. 123–142.

The conclusion that many people drew from this book was that the neoclassical liberal ideology could be used equally as well (if not better) as an ideology of socialism. This was, indeed, a radical undermining of neoclassical economics as an ideology defending capitalism.

The classical liberal ideology was rejected by many persons, however, because it seemed to present a severely distorted picture of the realities of twentieth-century capitalism. Its basic assumption of pure competition, that no buyers or sellers were large enough to affect prices, was patently ridiculous. Furthermore, it had little or nothing to say about the important problem of pollution of the environment. Economists also established that the simple counter-cyclical policies in the "neoclassical-Keynesian synthesis" were insufficient to obviate the problems of capitalism's cyclical instability.[35]

Finally, the coup de grace came in J. De V. Graaff's tightly reasoned *Theoretical Welfare Economics*.[36] Graaff showed that economists had not really appreciated the long and restrictive list of assumptions necessary for the optimally efficient allocation of resources envisioned in the model of a competitive, free-market capitalism to be realized. He cited 17 such assumptions,[37] many of which were so restrictive and unrealistic that Graaff concluded that "the measure of acceptance . . . [this theory] has won among professional economists would be astonishing were not its pedigree so long and respectable."[38]

A few of Graaff's 17 conditions will suffice to illustrate his point. Neoclassical ideology requires (1) that any individual's welfare is identical with his preference-ordering, that is, that children, dope addicts, fiends, criminals, and lunatics, as well as all other persons, always prefer that which is best for them; (2) that neither risk nor uncertainty is ever present; (3) that productivity is totally unaffected by the existing distribution of wealth; and (4) that all capital goods, as well as consumer goods, are infinitely divisible. In the opinion of many, this book completely destroyed the basis for the economic analysis upon which the classical liberal ideology was constructed.

---

[35] On this last point, see Milton Friedman, "The Effects of a Full Employment Policy on Economic Stability: A Formal Analysis," in *Essays in Positive Economics* (Chicago: University of Chicago Press, 1953); and William J. Baumol, "Pitfalls in Counter-Cyclical Policies: Some Tools and Results," *The Review of Economics and Statistics* (February 1961), pp. 21–26.

[36] J. De V. Graaff, *Theoretical Welfare Economics* (London: Cambridge University Press, 1967).

[37] Ibid., pp. 142–154.

[38] Ibid., p. 142.

CRITICISMS OF THE MANAGERIAL IDEOLOGY

The managerial ideology has also come under extensive criticism. Many economists (including several in the neoclassical tradition) argue that bigness on the scale of American big business cannot be shown to be related to efficiency or better service. Giant corporations are presently much larger than maximum productive efficiency would dictate. These economists contend that a drastic reduction in the size of many corporate giants would greatly increase productive efficiency.[39] Examples such as the electric power industry's competition with the Tennessee Valley Authority (TVA), the oligopolistic airlines' struggle with small, unscheduled competitors, and the challenge to the American steel industry from foreign competition are used to point out that private profits and monopoly power, not social welfare or social efficiency, are the prime motivations of big business.[40]

Critics also argue that managers have exactly the same motives as owner-capitalists. They cite an extensive study of the behavior of "management-controlled" and "owner-controlled" giant corporations, which showed that managers were as profit-oriented as owner-capitalists. The author of the study concluded that "it would appear that the proponents of theories of managerial discretion have expended considerable time and effort in describing a phenomenon of relatively minor importance. The large management-controlled corporations seem to be just about as profit-oriented as the large owner-controlled corporations."[41]

Many critics assert that modern managers have no more social conscience or "soul" than the nineteenth-century robber barons. The late Professor Edwin H. Sutherland, once known as the "dean of American criminologists" and former president of the American Sociological Association, conducted a thorough and scholarly investigation of the extent to which corporate executives were involved in criminal behavior. He took the 70 largest nonfinancial corporations, made only a few additions and deletions (due to special circumstances), and traced their criminal histories through official records.[42] There were 980 court decisions against these corporations. One corporation had 50 decisions against it, and the average per

---

[39] See, for example, Walter Adams, "Competition, Monopoly, and Planning," in M. Zeitlin. ed., *American Society, Inc.* (Chicago: Markham, 1970), pp. 240–248.

[40] Ibid.

[41] Robert J. Larner, "The Effect of Management-Control on the Profits of Larger Corporations," in Zeitlin, op. cit., p. 258.

[42] Edwin H. Sutherland, *White Collar Crime* (New York: Holt, Rinehart & Winston, 1961).

corporation was 14. Sixty of the corporations had been found guilty of restraining trade; 53, of infringements; 44, of unfair labor practices; 28, of misrepresentation in advertising; 26, of giving illegal rebates; and 43, of a variety of other offenses. There were a total of 307 individual cases of illegal restraint of trade, 97 of illegal misrepresentation, 222 of infringement, 158 of unfair labor practices, 66 of illegal rebates, and 130 of other offenses.[43] Not all those cases were explicit criminal cases. But 60 percent of the corporations had been found guilty of criminal offenses an average of four times each.

From May 10, 1950, to May 1, 1951, a United States Senate Special Committee to Investigate Crime in Interstate Commerce, under the chairmanship of Senator Estes Kefauver, probed the connections of business and organized crime. Senator Kefauver, Democratic vice-presidential candidate in 1956, later wrote a book based on those hearings. Although he emphasized the fact that there was no evidence to link most big corporations with organized crime, he was nevertheless greatly alarmed at the extent of such connections:

> I cannot overemphasize the danger that can lie in the muscling into legitimate fields by hoodlums . . . there was too much evidence before us of unreformed hoodlums gaining control of a legitimate business; then utilizing all his old mob tricks—strong-arm methods, bombs, even murder—to secure advantages over legitimate competition. All too often such competition either ruins legitimate businessmen or drives them into emulating or merging with the gangsters.
> The hoodlums are also clever at concealing ownership of their investments in legitimate fields—sometimes . . . through "trustees" and sometimes by bamboozling respectable businessmen into "fronting" for them.[44]

In 1960, Robert Kennedy, who later became Attorney General of the United States, published *The Enemy Within.* He gathered the material for this book while serving as chief counsel of the United States Senate Select Committee on Improper Activities in the Labor or Management Field. Kennedy, like Kefauver, stressed the fact that he was not condemning all or even most businessmen. He wrote that:

> we found that with the present-day emphasis on money and material goods many businessmen were willing to make corrupt "deals" with dishonest union officials in order to gain competitive advantage or to make a few extra dollars. . . . We came across

[43] These data are summarized by F. Lundberg in *The Rich and The Super Rich* (New York: Bantam, 1968), pp. 131–132.

[44] Estes Kefauver, *Crime in America* (Garden City, N.Y.: Doubleday, 1951), pp. 139–140.

more than fifty companies and corporations that had acted improperly—and in many cases illegally—in dealings with labor unions . . . in the companies and corporations to which I am referring the improprieties and illegalities were occasioned solely by a desire for monetary gain. Furthermore we found that we could expect very little assistance from management groups. Disturbing as it may sound, more often the business people with whom we came in contact—and this includes some representatives of our largest corporations—were uncooperative.[45]

Kennedy's list of the names of offending companies included many of the largest and most powerful corporations in the United States.

Ferdinand Lundberg has described the extent to which corporate leaders and management receive either very light punishment or no punishment at all when they become involved in improprieties or illegalities. Among the many cases he cites is

the case of the bribe of $750,000 by four insurance companies that sent Boss Pendergast of Missouri to jail, later to be pardoned by President Truman. . . . It was almost ten years before the insurance companies were convicted. Then they were only fined; no insurance executives went to jail.

There was, too, the case of Federal Judge Martin Manton who was convicted of accepting a bribe of $250,000 from agents of the defendant when he presided over a case charging exorbitant salaries were improperly paid to officers of the American Tobacco Company. While the attorney for the company was disbarred from federal courts, the assistant to the company president (who made the arrangements) was soon thereafter promoted to vice president: a good boy.[46]

Critics of the managerial ideology do not cite such studies and examples to show businessmen to be criminals. Obviously, most of them are not. The point they wish to make is that the power of monetary incentives and the quest for profits are no less pronounced among managers than among owner-capitalists. In fact, the pressure to acquire ever-increasing profits is so strong on many businessmen and managers that some persistently resort to illegal or improper means. With such pressures, the critics argue, society can ill afford to turn to the managerial class for paternal stewardship of the social and economic welfare.

[45] Robert Kennedy, *The Enemy Within* (New York: Harper & Row, 1960), p. 216.
[46] Lundberg, op. cit., p. 135.

summary

Since World War II, the concentration of corporate power has become more extreme, and inequalities of income distribution have been reduced very little, if at all. Despite these facts, many contemporary ideologies continue to rely on the classical liberal defense of capitalism. Other ideologists continue to place the corporate ethic at the base of their defense of capitalism. This latter group stresses the "efficient, far-sighted policies" of the large corporations, and the "professionalism," as well as "broad, humanistic concerns," of corporate managers. Critics of this point of view argue that the corporate managers are motivated by the same force that moved nineteenth-century capitalists: the quest for maximum profits.

chapter 12
contemporary american capitalism and its radical critics

Radical criticism of American capitalism was widespread during the depression of the 1930s. During the late forties and early fifties, however, pervasive repression of dissent, combined with a relatively prosperous economy, effectively stifled most radical criticism.[1]

All this changed abruptly in the 1960s and early 1970s. The two most important galvanizers of this resurgence of radical criticism were the civil rights movement and the war in Vietnam.

the civil rights movement

The struggle for equality for blacks in America really began in 1619 when the first black slaves were brought to the colonies. Since that time, the struggle has been nearly continuous. In the 1950s, however, the blacks' quest for their basic human rights entered a new phase.

On May 17, 1954, in the case of *Brown* v. *Board of Education of Topeka,* the U.S. Supreme Court unanimously concluded "that in the field of public education the doctrine of 'separate but equal' has no place!" and declared that "separate educational facilities are inherently unequal."

---

[1] For a thorough description of the repression of this period, see Fred J. Cook, *The Nightmare Decade: The Life and Times of Senator Joe McCarthy* (New York: Random House, 1971).

In 1954 and 1955, the few black individuals who applied for admission to white schools were rebuffed and very often suffered severe reprisals. It began to appear that the court decision would have little effect on the patterns of segregation that then existed. In December 1955, however, a black woman in Montgomery, Alabama, refused to give up her bus seat to a white man. She was immediately arrested. Within days, the blacks of Montgomery had organized a boycott of the bus company.

After one year of intense and bitter conflict, the protest ended in victory. The 50,000 blacks of Montgomery succeeded in getting the local bus segregation law nullified. This victory had a symbolic significance that was far greater than the particular issue of bus segregation. Blacks everywhere vicariously shared a new sense of dignity, freedom, and power. They began to organize actively to fight white racism.

Their attempts met with fanatical resistance. In the fall of 1957, Arkansas Governor Orville Faubus used armed troops to bar the entrance of nine black students into Central High School in Little Rock. The federal government interpreted this as a blatant challenge to its authority and sent in paratroopers to enforce the federal court orders. Many southern communities chose to close their public schools rather than allow them to be integrated.

In 1957 and 1960, Congress passed civil rights acts designed to extend voting rights to blacks. The Kennedy Administration urged young people, black and white, to concentrate on a massive registration drive to get southern blacks on the voting lists. Attracting both radical critics of capitalism and liberal young people who generally did not seriously question the basic social and economic system of capitalism, the civil rights movement was nationwide. In the early 1960s, the liberals dominated the movement numerically. They believed that a massive protest against racism would open the public's eyes and that an aroused population would demand new laws which would improve, if not completely cure, the situation.

During this period, civil rights activists organized sit-ins at segregated lunch counters and bus depots, pray-ins at segregated churches, and wade-ins at segregated beaches. Massive, nonviolent demonstrations, or nonviolent civil disobedience, they hoped, would reach the consciences of enough people to achieve integration.

Despite some successes in terms of new civil rights legislation, disillusionment began to affect large numbers of blacks as well as white civil rights workers. They began to realize that political franchisement had little effect on the vast economic inequalities that blacks suffered. Of what use was the vote if a black man could not secure a job, or if he was paid a salary that kept his family in a condition of poverty and degradation? Whereas in 1950, the average

salary earned by a black was 61 percent of that earned by a white,
by 1962, it had fallen to 55 percent. In the face of a massive civil
rights movement, the relative economic position of the blacks had
actually deteriorated. Furthermore, whereas in 1950, the rate of
unemployment among blacks had been slightly less than twice as
high as that for whites, by 1964, it was significantly greater than
twice as high. In 1947, blacks constituted 18 percent of the poorest
class in America; by 1962, they comprised 22 percent of this class.

Many civil rights advocates became convinced that the most
significant barriers to black equality were economic. They turned
their attention to a critical analysis of American capitalism as a
means of understanding the perpetuation, and indeed the worsening,
of the inequities suffered by blacks.

the war in vietnam

The other major force that helped spark the resurgence of radical
criticism was the war in Vietnam. Throughout the 1950s, the United
States government consistently fought against fundamental social
and political change in underdeveloped countries. Under the guise of
"protecting the world from communism," the United States had
intervened in the internal affairs of at least a score of countries.
In some, such as Guatemala and Iran, U.S. agents actually engineered
the overthrow of the legitimate governments and replaced them
with regimes more to American liking.[2]

Most criticism was muted by the political repression of McCarthy-
ism. The college students of the 1950s, the "silent generation,"
generally acquiesced in the national mood of anticommunism that
provided the justification for political repression at home and
extensive intervention in other nations' internal affairs. During the
1950s, American intervention in Vietnam attracted little special
attention. It was merely one of many countries that were being
"saved from communism." In the 1960s, however, all this was to
change drastically. The Vietnam War then became a powerful force
in regenerating radical criticism of American capitalism. For this
reason, a brief examination of the origins of the Vietnam War is
needed here.

During the World War II occupation of Vietnam, the French colonial
regime collaborated with the Japanese. Toward the end of the war,
the Japanese locked up the colonial administrators and established

2 For a popular account of these interventions, see David Wise and Thomas B. Ross,
The Invisible Government (New York: Random House, 1964).

a puppet regime under the Annamite Emperor Bao Dai. Throughout this period, the Americans (and, indeed, all the Allies) had supported a resistance movement (the Vietminh) headed by Ho Chi Minh. When Japan surrendered, there was a peaceful transfer of political power to the Vietminh.

The French did not want to lose this part of their colonial empire but realized that they were too weak to inflict a quick military defeat on the new government. On March 6, 1946, they signed an agreement with the Ho Chi Minh government that read in part: "The government of France recognizes the Republic of Vietnam as a free state having its government and its parliament, its army and its finances, forming part of the Indo-Chinese federation and of the French Union."[3] This agreement clearly intended that the Ho Chi Minh government would enjoy a status similar to the governments of the members of the British Commonwealth. It legally established Ho Chi Minh's regime as the legitimate government of *all* Vietnam. Nothing that subsequently occurred changed this essential fact.

The French were confident, however, that they could make a subservient puppet of Ho Chi Minh. They failed completely in this task. Unable to reduce Ho Chi Minh to this role, they brought back Emperor Bao Dai, even though he had voluntarily abdicated his throne, changed his name, and retired to Hong Kong. They "installed" him as "chief of state" and declared the Vietminh to be outlaws. There followed six years of intensive, bitter warfare. Finally, in 1954, the Vietminh decisively defeated the French. The Geneva Accords (July 1954), which arranged for the French surrender, called for a cease-fire and a *temporary* separating of opposing forces. Ho Chi Minh's followers were to move north of the seventeenth parallel and Emperor Bao Dai's were to move to the south. This arrangement was to end within two years with a national election to choose the leader of all Vietnam. Shortly after these negotiations, American-backed Ngo Dinh Diem ousted Bao Dai, proclaimed the existence of a "Republic of Vietnam," and appointed himself as its first president.

There were no elections. The Americans and Diem simply asserted that now there were two Vietnams. The reason for refusing to have the election was candidly admitted by President Eisenhower in his book *Mandate for Change.*

I am convinced that the French could not win the war because the internal political situation in Vietnam, weak and confused, badly weakened their military position. I have never talked or corresponded with a person knowledgeable in Indochinese affairs who did not agree that had elections been held as of the time of the fighting, possibly 80

3 Quoted in Leo Huberman and Paul M. Sweezy, "The Road to Ruin," *Monthly Review* (April 1965), p. 787.

percent of the population would have voted for Communist Ho Chi Minh as their leader rather than chief of state, Bao Dai.[4]

Obviously, the substitution of Diem for Bao Dai did not change the situation.

This American-imposed solution was rejected not only by Ho Chi Minh and his followers in the North but also by people in the South. So the war of national liberation, which had been fought against the Japanese and the French, was continued against the United States.

Americans were repeatedly told that their government was fighting a war to protect the South Vietnamese from the armed aggression of North Vietnam. The North Vietnamese were pictured as violators of the Geneva agreements, determined to enslave the South Vietnamese.

Critics of American policy challenged this official version of the nature of the war. Their assessment of what was happening in Vietnam received widespread support in academic circles, and college campuses became centers of antiwar sentiment. From the early 1960s through about 1966, most opposition to the war was largely confined to the campuses. During the last years of the decade, however, persons from all segments of society actively opposed the war. The antiwar movement had become a mass movement.

Finally, in 1968, U.S. Secretary of Defense Robert S. McNamara, himself becoming disillusioned with the official rationale for the war, ordered the U.S. Department of Defense to prepare an in-depth account of how the United States became involved. In early 1971, the report was completed. The 7,000-page document was obtained by the *New York Times* which paid researchers to determine whether new facts had been brought to light. The Defense Department admitted that (1) the Eisenhower Administration had played a "direct role in the ultimate breakdown of the Geneva settlement;"[5] (2) from 1954 onward, the United States had engaged in "acts of sabotage and terror warfare against North Vietnam;"[6] (3) the United States "encouraged and abetted the overthrow of President Ngo Dinh Diem" when he was no longer considered to be of use; (4) for many years prior to 1965, the United States government undertook "the careful preparation of public opinion for the years of open warfare that were to follow."[7]

American involvement increased steadily until by 1968, the United States had an army of over 500,000 men on Vietnamese soil and were spending nearly $3 billion per month ($100 million per day!)

---

4 Quoted in ibid., p. 789.

5 Quoted in Neil Sheehan, "The Story Behind the Vietnam War, Based on a Pentagon Study," *New York Times News Service,* June 13, 1971.

6 Ibid.

7 Ibid.

attempting to impose a "suitable political solution" on the Vietnamese.[8]

As American battle casualties rose (hundreds of thousands of Americans have been wounded and well over 50,000 Americans have been killed), young people everywhere began to question the morality of the war. Beginning in 1964, teach-ins protesting the war were mounted on college campuses around the United States. Most organizers and participants were convinced that American involvement in the war was a tragic mistake that would be rectified if the public could be made aware of the true facts of the situation.

The antiwar movement grew rapidly. President Johnson's landslide victory in 1964, as well as his decision not to seek another term in 1968, are often attributed in part at least to the powerful, widespread opposition to the war. After a few years of debate, however, antiwar critics were convinced that most Americans did know the basic facts of Vietnam and wanted a hasty end to the war. Yet the American government, without giving any convincing reasons for its actions, continued to seek military victory.

Critics began to ask whether there was not some deeper motive than simple anticommunist sentiment propelling the American government. In particular, they began to search for an economic motive or an economic rationale for the war. They began seriously to reexamine the older radical theories of capitalist imperialism.

contemporary critiques of american capitalism

The frustrations of the civil rights movement and the antiwar movement led to a burgeoning literature critical of the basic institutions of American capitalism. As had earlier critiques, this literature censured the grossly unequal distribution of income, wealth, and power in the United States. These critics, as did the left-Keynesians, deplored the extent to which post–World War II economic stability had been purchased at a cost of thoroughgoing militarism (discussed in Chapters 10 and 11).

On these points, radical and liberal critics have been in agreement. Liberal critics believe that political reform and electoral politics are sufficient to correct these perversions of the American economy. Radical critics, however, believe that inequality and militarism are inherent to a capitalist economy, and that it also necessarily involves

[8] As of this writing (December 1971), there is no end in sight in the Vietnam War, despite the fact that the American army has succeeded in training more Vietnamese to do the fighting, and hence has been able to reduce American troop strength. The destruction of Vietnam through air attacks has, in fact, intensified.

(1) imperialistic exploitation of underdeveloped countries as a means of maintaining high output and large profits in the United States, (2) endemic discrimination against minority groups and women, (3) inability to control pollution and exhaustion of resources and (4) a degrading commercialism and social alienation. In the remainder of this chapter, some of the literature in these four general areas will be described.

american imperialism

One of the first and most influential of these critics was Paul A. Baran. His book *The Political Economy of Growth*,[9] first published in 1957, has undergone two editions, has been translated into several languages, and has sold very well in the United States and even better in most underdeveloped countries. Baran argued that before an underdeveloped country could industrialize, it would have to mobilize its *economic surplus,* or the difference between what is produced and what has to be consumed in order to maintain the economy's productivity. It is the source of investment capital with which the country can industrialize. Under present institutional arrangements, most underdeveloped countries either waste their surpluses or lose them to imperialistic capitalist countries.

"Far from serving as an engine of economic expansion, of technological progress and of social change, the capitalist order in . . . [underdeveloped] countries has represented a framework for economic stagnation, for archaic technology, and for social backwardness."[10] The peasant agriculture usually produces a sufficiently large surplus in these countries. In fact, Baran pointed out the surplus is frequently as high as 50 percent of the total amount produced. "The subsistence peasants' obligations on account of rent, taxes, and interest in all underdeveloped countries are very high. They frequently absorb more than half of his meager net product."[11]

The problem is in the disposition of this surplus. Part goes to middlemen, speculators, moneylenders, and merchants—petty capitalists who have neither the interest nor the wherewithal to finance industrialization. A much larger part goes to the landowning ruling class which uses its "share" to purchase luxury consumption goods, usually imported from capitalist countries, and the extensive military establishments needed to maintain their internal power.

[9] Paul A. Baran, *The Political Economy of Growth* (New York: Monthly Review Press, 1962).

[10] Ibid., pp. 163–164.

[11] Ibid., p. 165.

Importing luxuries and military hardware necessitates sending exports to the industrialized countries. Exports usually consist of one or two primary agricultural products or mineral resources. The capitalist countries with which they trade have such monopsonistic buying power that the terms of trade are very unfavorable to the underdeveloped countries. The large, multinational corporations that purchase the raw materials are not interested in the industrialization of these countries. Thus, foreign capitalist investment is limited to that which is necessary for the profitable extraction of resources.

An alliance between the reactionary land owning class and foreign capitalists protects both their interests by suppressing dissidence and keeping the masses at a subsistence standard of living. Thus, landowners can maintain their position and capitalists are guaranteed cheap labor and large profits.

Small wonder that under such circumstances Western big business heavily engaged in raw materials exploitation leaves no stone unturned to obstruct the evolution of social and political conditions in underdeveloped countries that might be conducive to their economic development. It uses its tremendous power to prop up the backward areas' comprador administrations, to disrupt and corrupt the social and political movements that oppose them, and to overthrow whatever progressive governments may rise to power and refuse to do the bidding of their imperialistic overlords.[12]

Baran believed that the American government works hand in hand with American big business. Most U.S. economic and military aid provided underdeveloped countries is given, in his opinion, in order to prop up client governments.

Often such governments are not strong enough to survive on their own, even with this aid. Under these circumstances, the United States intervenes, either clandestinely (through CIA sabotage and intrigue) or directly (through the use of military force).

Baran and like-minded critics see the interventions in Guatemala, Iran, Korea, Cuba, the Dominican Republic, Vietnam, and Cambodia as examples of American endeavors to protect business interests, both current and potential, against threats from more progressive social and political movements. They point to 53 different "U.S. defense commitments and assurances" that commit the United States to the use of military force to maintain existing governments, very often against their own people.[13]

The dependence of underdeveloped countries upon a small number of export commodities is documented in a study based on

12 Ibid., p. 198.

13 See Harry Magdoff, *The Age of Imperialism, The Economics of U.S. Foreign Policy* (New York: Monthly Review Press, Modern Reader Paperbacks, 1969), pp. 203–206.

International Monetary Fund data. Each of the 37 countries considered earns 58 to 99 percent of its export receipts from 1 to 6 commodities.[14] Furthermore, the United States depends upon imports as the principal source for most of the 62 types of materials the Defense Department classifies as "strategic and critical." For 38 of these, 80 to 100 percent of the new supplies are imported; for 14 more, 40 to 79 percent are imported.[15]

A large and increasing percentage of U.S. corporate sales and profits results from exports and sales of foreign subsidiaries (many of which, of course, are in underdeveloped countries).[16] Furthermore, detailed examination reveals that the foreign trade of the underdeveloped countries is very lopsided. Raw materials and metals in their first state of smelting constitute 85 percent of exports; manufactured goods (mostly textiles), only 10 percent. But about 60 percent of their imports are manufactured goods.[17] Because most manufactured imports are consumer goods, such a pattern of trade cannot lead to development, but only to continued economic dependence.

Critics of this point of view (i.e., defenders of American economic foreign policy) argue that although foreign trade and foreign investments are important to American corporations, they also benefit the underdeveloped countries. The orthodox argument is expressed in a widely used textbook:

> In general, a restrained optimism as to the future prospects for underdeveloped countries in their trading relations with the developed countries seems to be warranted. The most encouraging sign is the growing recognition on the part of developed countries that opening their markets to the export products of underdeveloped areas is an essential part of their accepted program to assist underdeveloped countries to grow.[18]

But this position does not deal directly with radical critiques of American economic foreign policy. It simply assumes that all the underdeveloped countries need is *more* trade. Another orthodox scholar who studied the problem more thoroughly admits that "increasing the flow of private capital to underdeveloped countries will probably require a *recasting of economic policies* in both underdeveloped and advanced countries."[19] He does not go on to

---

[14] Magdoff, op. cit., pp. 99–100.

[15] Percy W. Bidwell, *Raw Materials* (New York: Harper & Row, 1958), p. 12.

[16] Magdoff, op. cit., p. 57.

[17] Pierre Jalee, *The Pillage of the Third World* (New York: Monthly Review Press, 1965), p. 8.

[18] Delbert A. Snider, *Introduction to International Economics* (Homewood, Ill.: Irwin, 1963), p. 548.

[19] Benjamin Higgins, *Economic Development* (New York: Norton, 1959), p. 593; italics added.

analyze what obstacles prevent this "recasting of economic policies."

Conservative defenders of American policies grant that developed capitalist countries have had immense economic, political, and military power which they have used to influence and control peoples around the world. They deny, however, that this "imperialism" is basically economic in nature. Thus, the widely respected economic historian Professor David S. Landes writes:

> It seems to me that one has to look at imperialism as a multifarious response to a common opportunity that consists simply in disparity of power. Whenever and wherever such disparity has existed, people and groups have been ready to take advantage of it. It is, one notes with regret, in the nature of the human beast to push other people around—or to save their souls or "civilize" them as the case may be.[20]

One radical critic has answered this assertion by noting that the modern capitalist drive to save people's souls from communism and to civilize them is perfectly compatible with economic motives. He cites the following quotation from an officer of General Electric Company: "Thus, our search for profits places us squarely in line with the national policy of stepping up international trade as a means of strengthening the free world in the Cold War confrontation with Communism." The critic, Harry Magdoff, summarizes his position: "Just as the fight against Communism helps the search for profits, so the search for profits helps the fight against Communism. What more perfect harmony of interests could be imagined?"[21]

Many books written in the 1960s attempted to explain contemporary American foreign policy—and the cold war between the United States and the Soviet Union—in terms of American economic imperialism.[22]

racism and sexism

Radical critics also point to the pervasive effects of discrimination based upon race and sex that exist in capitalist countries, particularly in the United States. Virtually everyone agrees that racism and sexism create severe discrimination. Defenders of American capitalism explain this discrimination in one of two ways.

---

[20] David S. Landes, "The Nature of Economic Imperialism," *The Journal of Economic History* (December 1961), p. 510.

[21] Magdoff, op. cit., pp. 200–201.

[22] See Magdoff, op. cit., D. F. Fleming, *The Cold War and Its Origins* (Garden City, N.Y.: Doubleday, 1961); Gar Alperowitz, *Atomic Diplomacy: Hiroshima and Potsdam* (New York: Simon & Schuster, 1965); David Horowitz, ed., *Corporations and the Cold War* (New York: Monthly Review Press, 1969); and David Horowitz, *Empire and Revolution* (New York: Random House, 1969).

The more reactionary is to argue that job discrimination merely reflects the innate inferiority of women and blacks. Few, if any, intellectuals embrace this position, but it apparently is accepted by a large minority in the United States. The other contention is that racism and sexism are products of a fairly universal human bigotry and are not related to capitalism or any other economic system.

Critics of capitalism point out that the wages of blacks and women make up a significant part of capitalists' wage costs. In 1969, for example, the wages of American women averaged only about 60 percent of the wages of men doing the same jobs. On that basis, it would appear that approximately 23 percent of all manufacturing profits are attributable to the lower wages paid to women. Profits made as a result of racial discrimination would certainly be smaller, but they would still be significant.

In one of the most influential socialist critiques, Paul A. Baran and Paul M. Sweezy have argued that it is necessary to

Consider first the private interests which benefit from the existence of a Negro subproletariat. (a) Employers benefit from divisions in the labor force which enable them to play one group off against another, thus weakening all. . . . (b) Owners of ghetto real estate are able to overcrowd and overcharge. (c) Middle and upper income groups benefit from having at their disposal a large supply of cheap domestic labor. (d) Many small marginal businesses, especially in the service trades, can operate profitably only if cheap labor is available to them. (e) White workers benefit by being protected from Negro competition for the more desirable and higher paying jobs.[23]

They also assert that in addition to increasing profits, discrimination increases social stability in a capitalist economy. The class structure of capitalism, they hold, leads to a situation in which

each status group has a deep-rooted psychological need to compensate for feelings of inferiority and envy toward those above by feelings of superiority and contempt for those below. It thus happens that a special pariah group at the bottom acts as a kind of lightening rod for the frustrations and hostilities of all the higher groups, the more so the nearer they are to the bottom. It may even be said that the very existence of the pariah group is a kind of harmonizer and stabilizer of the social structure.[24]

Although Baran and Sweezy's assertions pertain to racism, many critics argue that sexism performs much the same function in a

[23] Paul A. Baran and Paul M. Sweezy, *Monopoly Capital* (New York: Monthly Review Press, 1966), pp. 263–264.

[24] Ibid., pp. 265–266.

capitalist society. These critics generally do not believe that capitalism is the original creator of racism and sexism, but rather that capitalism perpetuates and intensifies racism and sexism because they serve valuable functions.

Today, transferring the locus of whites' perceptions of the source of many of their problems from capitalism and toward blacks, racism continues to serve the needs of the capitalist system. Although an individual employer might gain by refusing to discriminate and agreeing to hire blacks at above the going black wage rate, it is not true that the capitalist class as a whole would profit if racism were eliminated and labor were more efficiently allocated without regard to skin color. . . . The divisiveness of racism weakens workers' strength when bargaining with employers; the economic consequences of racism are not only lower incomes for blacks but also higher incomes for the capitalist class coupled with lower incomes for white workers. Although capitalists may not have conspired consciously to create racism, and although capitalists may not be its principal perpetuators, nevertheless racism does support the continued well-being of the American capitalist system.[25]

alienation

Many contemporary radical critics have refined and elaborated upon Marx's theory of the human alienation inherent in the capitalist economic system.[26] Baran and Sweezy, for example, maintain that total alienation pervades and dominates contemporary American capitalism:

Disorientation, apathy, and often despair, haunting Americans in all walks of life, have assumed in our time the dimensions of a prolonged crisis. This crisis affects every aspect of national life, and ravages both its socio-political and its individual spheres— everyman's everyday existence. A heavy strangulating sense of the emptiness and futility of life permeates the country's moral and intellectual climate. High level committees are entrusted with the discovery and specification of "national goals" while gloom pervades the printed matter (fiction and non-fiction, alike) appearing daily in the literary market place. The malaise deprives work of meaning and purpose; turns leisure into joyless, debilitating laziness; fatally

[25] Michael Reich, "The Economics of Racism," in David M. Gordon, ed., *Problems in Political Economy: An Urban Perspective* (Lexington, Mass.: Raytheon/Heath, 1971), pp. 109–110.

[26] See Chapter 6.

impairs the education system and the conditions of healthy growth
in the young; transforms religion and church into commercialized
vehicles of "togetherness"; and destroys the very foundation of
burgeois society, the family.[27]

The fact of alienation, like the facts of racism and sexism, is
explained by many defenders of capitalism as an unfortunate but
inevitable by-product of industrial civilization. An industrialized
socialist economy would, they assert, create the same type of
alienation. Few people, regardless of political and economic views,
would be willing to forego the advantages of industrialization in order
to combat alienation. And even if people did want to return to
preindustrial society, there is simply no practical way of turning back
time to some imagined golden age.

Socialist critics reply that although some amount of alienation will
surely exist in any industrialized society, capitalism significantly
intensifies alienation and makes it more pervasive. Erich Fromm, the
famous psychoanalyst, social philosopher, and author, argues that
the most important single cause of alienation is the fact that the
individual feels no sense of participation in the forces that determine
social policy. He sees these forces as anonymous and totally beyond
the sphere of any individual's influence. "The anonymity of the social
forces," writes Fromm, "is inherent in the structure of the capitalist
mode of production."[28]

Fromm identifies several types of alienation created by the
capitalist mode of production. Conditions of employment alienate
workers. Their livelihoods depend upon whether capitalists and
managers are able to make a profit by hiring them, and thus they are
viewed as means only, never as ends. The individual worker is "an
economic atom that dances to the tune of atomistic management."
Managers "strip the worker of his right to think and move freely. Life
is being denied; need to control, creativeness, curiosity, and
independent thought are being balked, and the result, the inevitable
result, is flight or fight on the part of the worker, apathy or
destructiveness, psychic regression.[29]

And yet Fromm argues that the "role of the manager is also one
of alienation," for he too is coerced by the ineluctable forces of
capitalism and has very little freedom. He must deal "with impersonal
giants; with the giant competitive enterprise; with giant impersonal
markets; with giant unions, and the giant government."[30] His position,

[27] Baran and Sweezy, op. cit., p. 281.

[28] Erich Fromm, *The Sane Society* (New York: Fawcett World Library, Premier Books,
1965), p. 125.

[29] Quoted in ibid., p. 115.

[30] Ibid., pp. 115–116.

his status, his income, in short, his very social existence, all depend upon making ever-increasing amounts of profits. Yet he must do this in a world in which he has little personal influence upon the giants with whom he deals.

Fromm also maintains that the process of consumption in a capitalist society "is as alienated as the process of production." The truly human way of acquiring commodities, according to Fromm, would be through need and the desire to use: "The acquisition of bread and clothing [should] depend on no other premise than that of being alive; the acquisition of books and paintings on my effort to understand them and my ability to use them."[31] But in capitalist societies, the income with which to purchase these commodities can only come through sales in the impersonal market.

As a consequence, those who have money are subjected to a constant barrage of propaganda designed to create consuming automata. Capitalist socialization processes make consumption-hungry, irrational, compulsive buying machines of us all. The acts of buying and consuming have become ends in themselves, with little or no relation to the uses or pleasures derived from the commodities.

Man today is fascinated by the possibility of buying more, better, and especially, new things. He is consumption-hungry. The act of buying and consuming has become a compulsive, irrational aim, because it is an end in itself, with little relation to the use of or pleasure in the things bought and consumed. To buy the latest gadget, the latest model of anything that is on the market, is the dream of everybody in comparison to which the real pleasure in use is quite secondary. Modern man, if he dared to be articulate about his concept of heaven, would describe a vision which would look like the biggest department store in the world, showing new things and gadgets, and himself having plenty of money with which to buy them. He would wander around open-mouthed in his heaven of gadgets and commodities, provided only that there were ever more and newer things to buy, and perhaps that his neighbors were just a little less privileged than he.[32]

Finally, the most severe alienation is the alienation of a man from his "self." A person's "worth" in a capitalist market economy is determined in the same way as the "worth" of anything else: by sales in the marketplace. In this situation,

man experiences himself as a thing to be employed successfully on the market. He does not experience himself as an active agent, as the bearer of human powers. He is alienated from these powers. His

---

31 Ibid., p. 120.
32 Ibid., p. 123.

aim is to sell himself successfully on the market. His sense of self does not stem from his activity as a loving and thinking individual, but from his socio-economic role. . . . If you ask a man "Who are you?", he answers "I am a manufacturer," "I am a clerk," "I am a doctor." . . . That is the way he experiences himself, not as a man, with love, fear, convictions, doubts, but as that abstraction, alienated from his real nature, which fulfills a certain function in the social system. His sense of value depends on his success: on whether he can sell himself favorably, whether he can make more of himself than he started out with, whether he is a success. His body, his mind and his soul are his capital, and his task in life is to invest it favorably, to make a *profit* of himself. Human qualities like friendliness, courtesy, kindness, are transformed into commodities, into assets of the "personality package," conducive to a higher price on the personality market. If the individual fails in a profitable investment of himself, *he* feels that he is a failure; if he succeeds, he is a success. Clearly, his sense of his own value always depends on factors extraneous to himself, on the fickle judgment of the market, which decides about his value as it decides about the value of commodities. He, like all commodities that cannot be sold profitably on the market, is worthless as far as his exchange value is concerned, even though his use value may be considerable.[33]

Thus, socialist critics argue that the impersonal nexus of the capitalist market mediates all human relationships. It makes profit and loss the ultimate and pervasive evaluative criteria of human worth. This means that human alienation must inevitably be extremely severe in a capitalist market economy.

environmental destruction

Capitalism must either experience economic growth or suffer depression, unemployment, stagnation, and all the attendant social problems (see Chapter 10 for a discussion of the reasons). But economic growth can also create situations in which the pursuit of profits comes into direct conflict with the public welfare. Critics of capitalism have argued that corporate profit-seeking is generally accompanied by very little concern for conservation or for a clean, livable environment.

Pollution is of concern to defenders of capitalism as well as to critics. Defenders argue that it is a problem common to all industrialized economies. Critics assert that the problem is worse in

[33] Ibid., pp. 129–130.

a capitalist economy. Furthermore, they maintain that it would be virtually impossible to control pollution effectively in a capitalist system. This is so, they argue, because the basic economic cause of pollution in a capitalist economy is that business firms do not have to pay for *all* the costs incurred in the production process. They pay for labor, raw materials, and capital used up in production. But they use the land, air, and water for the disposal of waste products that are created in the process of production. Generally, they pay little or nothing for the use of the environment as a garbage disposal.

It has been estimated[34] that each year businesses are responsible for over 25 billion tons of pollutants being spewed in the air and dumped into the water and on the land. This is about 125 tons of waste per year for every man, woman, and child in the United States. Included in this figure are about 150 million tons of smoke and fumes that blacken the skies and poison the air, 22 million tons of waste paper products, 3 million tons of milltailings, and 50 trillion gallons of heated and polluted liquids that are dumped into streams, rivers, and lakes each year.

Critics argue that it is extremely difficult if not impossible for a capitalist economy to deal with these problems because those who receive the profits from production do not pay these social costs, and those who do pay the social costs have little or no voice in the operation of the businesses.

In response to the widespread public demand for control of pollution and polluters, the government has given contracts to many corporations to devise new methods of combating pollution. In effect, the government is asking private corporations to act as the controllers of other private corporations. Radical critics are convinced that this corporate integration of polluters and controllers will never lead to any substantial improvement. Most of the important pollution-control companies have become subsidiaries of the giant corporations that do most of the polluting.

One radical critic has analyzed the effects of this corporate control.

It is the chemical industry . . . that best illustrates the consequences of the incest between the pollution control business and the industrial polluters. First, the chemical industry is in the enviable position of reaping sizable profits by attempting to clean up rivers and lakes (at public expense) which they have profitably polluted in the first place. To facilitate this practically every major chemical company in the U.S. has established a pollution abatement division or is in the process of doing so. . . .

[34] These estimates are taken from an important and impressive study on pollution: R. C. d'Arge, A. V. Kneese, and R. V. Ayres, *Economics of the Environment: A Materials Balance Approach* (Baltimore: Johns Hopkins, 1970).

A second consequence of placing the "control" of pollution in the hands of big business is that the official abatement levels will inevitably be set low enough to protect industry's power to pollute and therefore its ability to keep costs down and revenues high. According to a recent study by the FWPCA (Federal Water Pollution Control Administration) if the chemical industry were to reduce its pollution of water to zero, the costs involved would amount to almost $2.7 billion per year. This would cut profits almost by half.[35]

Under such circumstances, the critics do not expect much progress in cleaning up the environment unless fundamental social, political, and economic changes occur first.

liberal versus radical critiques of capitalism

The glaringly unequal distribution of wealth, income, and political power and the facts of militarism, imperialism, vicious discrimination, social alienation, and environmental destruction are all recognized and decried by both liberal and radical critics of capitalism. There is, however, an immensely important difference between the positions of liberals and radicals.

Liberals tend to see each of these social and economic problems as separate and distinct. The problems, they believe, are the results of past mistakes, inabilities, and ineptitudes or the results of random cases of individual perversity. Liberals also tend to consider the government as detached, disinterested, and motivated by a desire to maximize the welfare of all its citizens. Hence, liberals generally favor government-sponsored reforms designed to mitigate the many evils of capitalism. These reforms never threaten the two most important features of capitalism: private ownership of the means of production and the free market.

Radicals, however, see each of the social and economic problems we have discussed as the *direct consequence* of private ownership of capital and the process of social decision-making within the impersonal cash nexus of the market. The problems cannot be solved until their underlying causes are eliminated, but this means a fundamental, radical economic reorganization. If private ownership of capital is eliminated, and if significant restrictions are placed on the areas in which the market determines social decisions, the resulting system would no longer be a capitalist economic system. It would, of necessity, be some type of socialist society.

[35] Martin Gellen, "The Making of a Pollution-Industrial Complex," in Gordon, op. cit., pp. 469–470.

summary

From the late 1950s to the early 1970s, the civil rights movement
and the antiwar movement generated a resurgence of radical
criticism of American capitalism. The radicals argue that inequality,
discrimination, alienation, environmental destruction, militarism, and
imperialism are integral parts of a capitalist economy. Unlike liberals,
who believe that these evils are accidental and that the system can be
reformed, radicals contend that these evils cannot be overcome
unless the basic structure of capitalism is fundamentally changed.

The principal obstacle to the achievement of such reforms is the
fact that political power is derived from economic power. Radicals
see capitalist governments as plutocracies hidden behind phony
façades of democracy. Both political parties, they point out, spend
many millions of dollars on each election. As a consequence, both
political parties are almost completely controlled by the wealthiest
2 percent of the population that owns most of the income-producing
capital.[36] In this situation, one would not expect the wealthy elite
to support any government that threatened to destroy the basis of
their wealth, privileges, and power. Therefore, fundamental reform
seems unlikely unless a reformist movement can establish a base of
power that is independent of wealth. This explains the popularity at
radical gatherings of the slogan, "Power to the People!"

[36] For detailed evidence for this point of view, see G. William Domhoff, *Who Rules
America* (Englewood Cliffs, N.J.: Prentice-Hall, 1967), and Domhoff, *The Higher
Circles: The Governing Class in America* (New York: Random House, 1970).

part two

prices and poverty: a radical introduction to microeconomics

part
two

chapter 13
market allocation of resources:
efficiency versus fairness

Part I of this book sketched some of the highlights in the history of economic thought and in the evolution of the private-enterprise, or capitalist, system. In Parts II and III, the actual working of the capitalist system is discussed. Part II will concentrate on *microeconomics,* the economics of individual enterprises and individual workers and consumers; Part III will deal with *macroeconomics,* the operation of the economy as a whole. Thus, in Part II, we shall discuss, among other things, how enterprises set prices and make profits under competition and monopoly, how workers' wages are determined, how the government affects the distribution of income, and the economics of racial and sexual discrimination.

A private-enterprise economy is one in which the factories, the tools, and the stocks of goods with which production is carried on are owned by private individuals. Individual ownership includes, of course, the corporate form of ownership. In the corporation, individuals own the whole capital, but each person's ownership is specified in the form of the stock or shares that he holds.

Most modern private-enterprise economies are distinguished by socially and technologically complex methods of production and distribution. It is possible to imagine an economy of small farmers and artisan-producers in which each individual owns his own means of production and is a fairly independent producer. In the reality of the modern private-enterprise economy, however, this type of individual independence is completely impossible. The factory system, which the industrial revolution ushered in, has made individual producers completely dependent. A worker in an automobile factory, for example, owns no tools of production. He cannot, by himself, produce anything. He depends, for his continued existence, upon being able to sell his labor time to a company that employs hundreds of thousands of persons just like him. His work generally consists of one small, insignificant, and tedious operation (such as screwing a particular nut on a particular bolt) that he repeats endlessly for eight hours.

In the American economy, about 1.8 percent of the population owns 80 percent of all corporate stock. Most of the remaining 98.2 percent own little or no capital and depend on the *market* for their labor services to earn a living. When a worker succeeds in selling his labor services, he is paid a wage that is then spent in the market for goods and services. By purchasing these goods and services, he is playing a small (usually a *very* small) role in creating the demand that provides jobs for the other workers who produce these goods and services. In fact, in the U.S. economy, the continued employment of any individual may depend on the actions and behavior of hundreds of thousands or even millions of other persons. All these persons are related to this individual through only one social institution: the market. It is therefore vitally important to understand how the market functions.

In a private-enterprise economy, the market determines what is to be produced, how it is to be produced, and for whom it is to be produced. Capitalists, or their hired managers, are motivated primarily by their drive to maximize profits. They go to the market to hire labor and buy raw materials which they combine with the factories, machinery, and tools they own in order to produce an output. (Many capitalists are strictly middlemen and financiers and are not directly connected with productive output, but for our present purposes we shall ignore them.) They then sell their output in the market.

Their objective is to maximize the difference between their sales proceeds and their money expenses incurred in buying raw materials, hiring labor, and replacing used-up capital. This difference is, of course, profits. They constantly search for commodities that can be produced and sold profitably.

The capitalists' costs of production represent income to laborers and the owners of raw materials. Profit is the income that accrues to the capitalist. The recipients of these incomes spend them in the market for the goods produced by the capitalists' business firms. Thus, money circulates from the business firms to the general public in the form of incomes generated in the production process. The money then returns to the business firms when the public purchases the goods and services these firms sell in the market.

There is thus an amazingly complex circulation of money from hundreds of thousands of business firms to hundreds of millions of people and back into the hands of the business firms. At all points, the guiding force is the capitalists' constant search for profits. The decisions concerning what goods to produce (or even whether to produce), what inputs to buy, what wages to pay, and so forth are all determined by the criterion of profitability. All economic relations between people are mediated by the institution of the market. The market is obviously one of the most important social institutions in a private-enterprise economy. In this and the several following chapters, we shall attempt to achieve a clearer understanding of what markets are and how they function.

It is important to begin by distinguishing a particular market and the market system (or, as it is often referred to, *the* market). Historically, a market was an area, usually near the center of a village or town, where producers and traders would meet and exchange goods. Later, any place where a merchant habitually sold his wares was a market. Today we sometimes refer to a grocery store as a market, but the word *market* is more generally used as an abstract concept. It refers, in general, to the negotiating of exchange transactions that generally involve *money* and the determining of the prices at which these exchanges are transacted.

We speak of the stock market, the labor market, or the automobile market when we are referring to the buying and selling of stocks, labor services, or automobiles. We speak of the market or the *market system* when we wish to refer to monetary exchange and price determination in general. It is obvious that any market system that successfully facilitates price determination and exchange must contain complex systems of customs and traditions, laws, and agencies of law enforcement as well as the physical buildings in which business is transacted.

In this part of the book, physical settings of markets and many of the customs and laws that enable markets to function will be ignored. We shall concentrate on exchange (buying and selling) and the determination of price.

A market is basically a two-sided phenomenon with buyers facing sellers. Buyers have money they wish to exchange for goods, and sellers have goods they wish to exchange for money. The amount of a good that buyers would like to purchase at any given time is referred to as the *demand* for that good. Similarly, the amount of the good that sellers would like to sell is referred to as the *supply* of the good.

It should be stressed that demand is not necessarily related to need or desire. A penniless child longingly gazing through the window of the candy store adds nothing to the market demand for candy. Similarly, in the Great Depression of the 1930s, millions of persons went hungry while tons and tons of wheat and thousands of cattle and sheep were destroyed and wasted due to *lack* of any market demand for them. The problem, of course, was that like the child at the candy store, the unemployed millions had no money to exchange for food.

demand and supply

Restated more formally, the definitions of demand and supply are as follows: *Demand for a good refers to the amount of that good that buyers would like to purchase during a given time period and at a given price.* Obviously, demand must be expressed in terms of a given time period if it is to have any meaning. The number of auto-mobiles people wish to purchase is certainly very different over the course of a week as opposed to a year. Similarly, a given price must be specified. Clearly, the number of Ford cars people would like to buy will be very different if the price is $500 or $5,000. An important point is that a demand for $100 worth of a good is simultaneously a willingness to supply $100 in money.

The definition of supply is very similar to the definition of demand. *Supply of a good refers to the quantity of that good that sellers would like to sell during a given period and at a given price.* The supply of $100 worth of a good is simultaneously a demand for $100 in money.

If the reactions of buyers and sellers at different prices are con-sidered, it becomes possible to define a demand schedule and supply schedule. A *demand schedule* relates *various prices* of that good with *amounts* of that good that people would like to buy at each of the various prices. If the people of the United States were polled to

number of Ford Pintos demanded at various prices		TABLE
PRICE	QUANTITY DEMANDED PER YEAR (in 100,000s)	13.1
$1,000	10	
1,500	8	
2,000	6	
2,500	4	

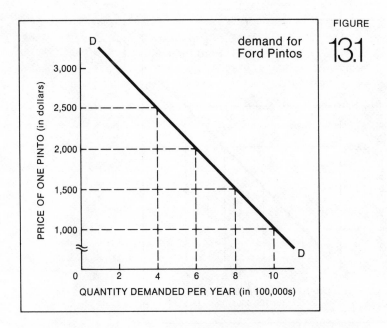

FIGURE 13.1

demand for Ford Pintos

determine the number of Ford Pintos they would like to buy at various prices, the results might be similar to those given in Table 13.1.

The information contained in this demand schedule can be shown on a graph as a demand curve (see Figure 13.1). A *demand curve,* like a demand schedule, relates prices to quantities demanded. The *DD* curve makes it possible to select any price and ascertain the quantity buyers would like to purchase at that price.

In a similar manner, it is possible to find the number of Ford Pintos the Ford Motor Company would desire to sell at various prices. Table 13.2 summarizes this hypothetical information. In Figure 13.2, this same information is expressed in the form of a supply curve, demonstrating the quantities sellers would like to sell at various prices.

TABLE 13.2

number of Ford Pintos supplied at various prices	
PRICE	QUANTITY SUPPLIED PER YEAR (in 100,000s)
$1,000	2
1,500	4
2,000	6
2,500	8

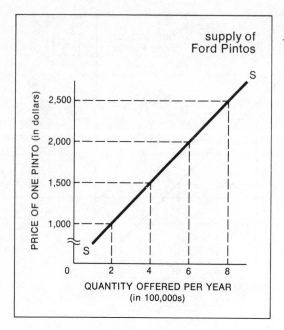

FIGURE

13.2

supply of
Ford Pintos

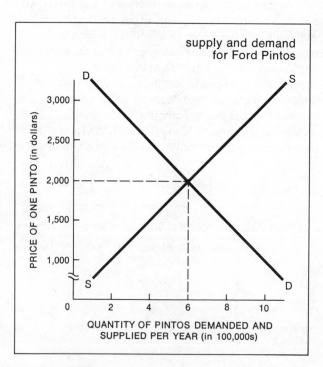

FIGURE

13.3

supply and demand
for Ford Pintos

Market prices are determined by the forces of supply and demand. Sellers wish to exchange products for money, and buyers wish to exchange money for products. When a particular price is established, a specific quantity will be offered for sale and a specific quantity will be demanded. If these two quantities are equal, both sellers and buyers are able to conduct transactions in the desired quantities. For example, in Figure 13.3, the demand curve for Ford Pintos (from Figure 13.1) is superimposed on the supply curve (from Figure 13.2). If a price of $2,000 is established, the point at which the curves intersect indicates that buyers and sellers want to buy and sell 600,000 cars.

When the desires of buyers and sellers are consistent and both are able to conduct their desired exchanges, the market is said to be in *equilibrium.* The notion of an equilibrium is central to most economic theory. It generally means that supply and demand are equal and that the exchange desires of buyers and sellers are mutually consistent. At equilibrium prices, everyone is able to buy or sell all that he chooses to buy or sell within his budget.

If a price that is higher than the equilibrium price is established, then supply will exceed demand. This is called a situation of *excess supply.* In Figure 13.4, if the price of Pintos is set at $2,500, an excess supply exists. The Ford Motor Company would like to sell 800,000 Pintos at that price, but buyers would like to buy only 400,000. There is an excess supply of 400,000.

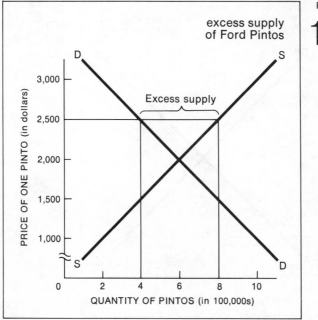

excess supply
of Ford Pintos

FIGURE

13.4

In many markets, there is a *tendency* for the forces of supply and demand to cause price changes that will eliminate excess supply and equilibrate the market. In the situation illustrated in Figure 13.4, thousands of Pinto dealers will find that at the established price of $2,500, they are unable to sell the quantity of cars they had antici-pated. As unwanted inventories of unsold cars accumulate, the dealers cut back or eliminate entirely their orders with the Ford Motor Company. With production geared for the 800,000 cars that the manufacturer had hoped to sell, it is not long before large unwanted inventories pile up at the factory.

In order to reduce these inventories and stimulate sales, the manufacturer *may* reduce the price, which definitely would improve the imbalance between supply and demand. As long as the price remains above $2,000, however, the excess supply will persist, and the motive to cut the price further will continue to exist. Only at the equilibrium price of $2,000 will excess supply disappear and the market be cleared.

At a price below $2,000, demand would exceed supply (Figure 13.5). Dealers would find long lines waiting to buy the few available cars. Orders sent to the Ford Motor Company would go largely unfilled because these orders would far exceed the numbers of Pintos that were being produced. Figure 13.5 shows that at the low price of $1,000, Ford will offer to supply only 200,000 cars, but

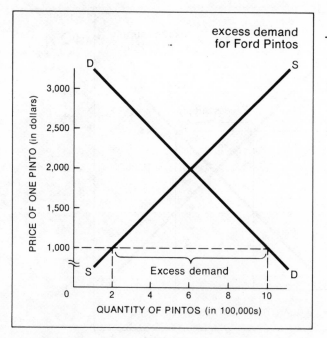

FIGURE

13.5

excess demand
for Ford Pintos

consumers wish to buy 1,000,000 cars. There is, therefore, an excess demand of 800,000 cars.

Under these conditions, it would be obvious to the dealers and the manufacturer that more cars could be sold at higher prices. The search for higher profits would dictate that the price be raised. As the price is raised, the amount of excess demand declines. But at any price below $2,000, there will continue to be some excess demand. There will, therefore, continue to be an upward pressure on the price until it reaches the equilibrium level of $2,000.

The rate at which price changes bring the market into equilibrium varies greatly from market to market. In some markets, sellers are very sensitive to unwanted changes in inventories, so that adjustments in price occur very quickly. The New York Stock Exchange is highly sensitive to hour-by-hour fluctuations in supply and demand. Frequent price changes serve to keep the market very near equilibrium at all times.

At the other extreme, what is for most people the most important of all markets—the labor market—may go for years in a situation of disequilibrium. With only a few exceptions (mostly in time of war), this market has had a persistent excess supply, which means, of course, involuntary unemployment of people. This is a subject that will receive considerable attention in Part III.

There are also many cases in which control of supply or demand gives an individual or group of individuals the power to *fix prices.* In this case, excess supply or demand *may* not lead to price changes if those changes are not in the best interests of the price-fixer. We shall examine this fact and its implications in several later chapters (16, 17, and 18) on imperfect competition, *oligopoly* (when a few firms control supply), and *monopoly* (when one firm controls supply).

changes in demand

Ideally, an examination of demand theory would consider everything that could affect demand, but this would make the theory impossibly complex. Instead, the discussion will concentrate on the one factor that seems most generally to exert the strongest influence on demand: the price of the commodity. How do changes in the price of a commodity affect the demand for the commodity? The only way this can be determined is by assuming that all other factors that influence demand *remain constant* as the price changes. In reality, during the period in which the price is changing, many of these other influences may also be changing.

In Figure 13.6, an ordinary demand curve (solid line D_1D_1) is constructed on the assumption that all other influences on demand

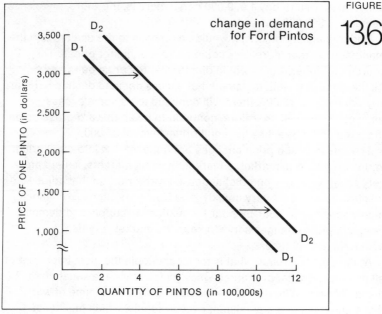

FIGURE

13.6

change in demand
for Ford Pintos

remain constant while the price changes. Along demand curve D_1D_1, any change in the quantity demanded is caused only by a change in the price.

Now consider another influence on demand. Suppose there was a general increase in the incomes of all persons consuming this good. With the new higher incomes, individuals will now probably buy *more* of the commodity at *every* possible price. The new, higher incomes cause a *shift* in the demand curve. This produces a *new demand curve* (broken line D_2D_2). *At any price,* the new demand curve shows that people wish to buy more at that price than they formerly did (when solid line D_1D_1 was the demand curve).

This increased demand is the result of the increase in income. In general, whenever there is a change in any of the factors (other than price) that affect demand, this change will be shown as a *shift* in the demand curve.

A bit of terminology here will make you sound like a sophisticated economist—and may save you some confusion later on. Whenever an economist says flatly "demand has changed," he means that the *whole demand curve has shifted.* An increase in demand means a shift of the curve outward (to the right, from D_1D_1 to D_2D_2); it means that *more* Pintos are demanded at any given price. A decrease in demand means a shift of the curve inward (to the left, from D_2D_2 to D_1D_1); it means that *fewer* Pintos are demanded at any given price.

When everything else stays the same (i.e., the curve does *not* shift) and only the price changes, the economist will *not* say "demand has changed." He will just say there has been *"movement along* the demand curve," or a change in quantity demanded. He will say, "at a higher price, less quantity was demanded" or "at a lower price, more quantity was demanded," but with no change or shift in the demand curve as a whole. In other words, with no shift in demand, Ford could sell more Pintos only by lowering the price (and if Ford raises the prices, they will sell fewer Pintos).

Of course, in reality, both things often happen at once: (1) prices of Pintos change, and (2) income and other factors affecting demand change. As a result of both (1) and (2), the quantity of Pintos demanded has changed. But it is impossible to be sure how much of the demand change was a result of the price change (movement along the demand curve) and how much was a result of changes in income and other factors (shift in demand curve). In other words, reality does not draw curves; only economists draw curves to try to analyze what is going on.

changes in supply

The explanation of shifts in demand and movements along demand curves may be repeated for changes in supply. The student should work this through himself in Figure 13.7. Consider, for example, the way in which higher or lower prices per car would cause Ford to

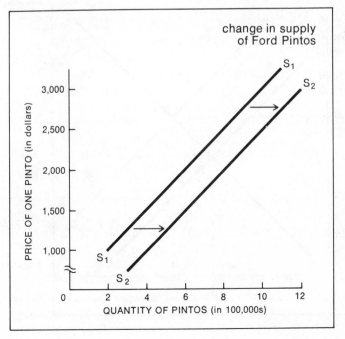

FIGURE 13.7

change in supply of Ford Pintos

move along the supply curve (S_1S_1), offering more or fewer Pintos to the consumer market at different prices. But also consider the way in which lower costs per car (such as a lower price of steel per ton) might motivate Ford to offer more Pintos at each given price that consumers would pay (i.e., a shift from supply curve S_1S_1 to S_2S_2).

changes in supply and demand

Finally, by putting the changes in supply and demand together it is possible to explain how prices are forced to change. The effect on the price of Pintos of an increase or decrease in demand (with supply conditions remaining unchanged) is shown in Figure 13.8.

An increase in demand for Pintos can be explained as a *shift* up from curve D_1D_1 to D_2D_2, or as a movement along the supply curve *SS* up and to the right. Either description is correct. Either way, the fact is that Ford can sell *more* Pintos at a *higher price*. The quantity sold went from 600,000 to 800,000; the price went from $2,000 to $2,500. Of course, there is nothing mysterious about that delightful

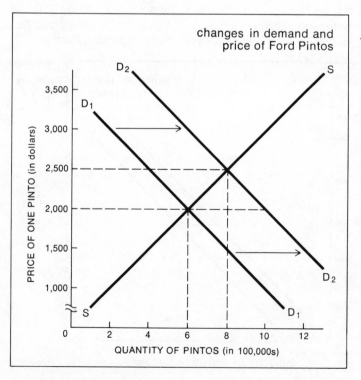

FIGURE

changes in demand and
price of Ford Pintos

13.8

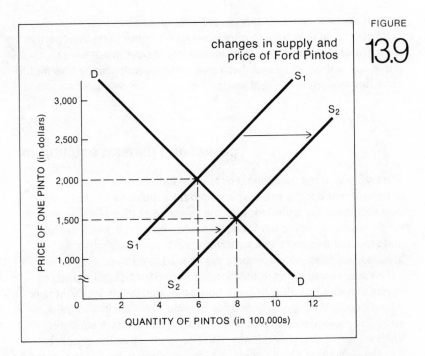

FIGURE

13.9

changes in supply and
price of Ford Pintos

result for Ford. It happened because it was assumed that demand
shifted to Pintos (from Chevrolets or Volkswagens, perhaps). In the
example in which Ford could sell more Pintos only at a lower price,
it was assumed that there was *no* shift in demand to Pintos.

Similarly, in Figure 13.8, a decrease in demand for Pintos means a
shift down from curve D_2D_2 back to D_1D_1. Suppose that consumers
shift demand from Pintos to Volkswagens. Then Ford will sell *fewer*
Pintos at a *lower* price per car, assuming the supply curve remains
as drawn.

Now, on the other side, consider the changes in the supply of
Pintos while the demand for Pintos remains the same.

An increase in supply means a shift over from curve S_1S_1 to S_2S_2.
For some reason, perhaps lower costs per car or competition from
Volkswagen, Ford is offering to supply more Pintos at every price at
which consumers might demand them. There is an outward *shift* in
the supply curve; or, there is a *movement* out *along* the demand
curve. With demand unchanged, Ford is selling more Pintos by
lowering their price. Whereas they previously sold 600,000 Pintos at
$2,000 each, they now sell 800,000 at only $1,500 each.

A decrease in supply means shifting back from S_2S_2 to S_1S_1.
Suppose, for example, that Ford's production costs rise for some
reason. They may then charge higher prices *and* sell fewer cars. The
supply curve has shifted, moving back along the demand curve, so

that prices have gone up and fewer Pintos are being sold.

Of course, in reality, *both* curves may shift in the same time period. Because of that possibility, it is usually impossible to tell which curve has shifted and which has remained stationary (or by how much each has moved) in the real world.

partial and general equilibrium

The analysis of the adjustment of supply and demand to some equilibrium price (the price where amount supplied and amount demanded are the same) for a single commodity (Ford Pintos) in a single market is called *partial equilibrium* analysis. It was a useful first step, but it is important to understand that the adjustment processes in the whole economy are related to each other.

The supply and demand for Pintos do not depend on the price of Pintos alone. It has already been noted that the demand for Pintos is influenced by changes in consumer income. Demand is also influenced by changes in the prices charged by competitors such as Volkswagen or Chevrolet. It has also been noted that the supply of Pintos is influenced by its costs, for example, the prices of the steel and rubber used in its construction and also the wages of Ford workers. Thus, adjustments in all markets must mesh together. The analysis of these related adjustments is called *general equilibrium* analysis.

One of the central findings of such an analysis is the extreme difficulty of achieving a general economic equilibrium, in which there is no excess demand or supply for any good. Assume, for example, that all goods except two are in equilibrium (i.e., have no excess supply or demand). Of the two in disequilibrium, one has an excess supply and the other has an equivalent excess demand. Now, as the excess demand forces the one price up and the excess supply forces the other price down, *many, many* other goods that were formerly in equilibrium will be forced into disequilibrium. This is because the supply and demand for many of them will be affected by the price changes of the two goods that were in disequilibrium initially. Prices of goods affected by the two original price changes will all begin to change. But each of these prices affects the supply and demand for other goods. The prices of these latter goods will begin to change.

Thus, an initial disequilibrium in only two particular markets may spread rapidly to hundreds and thousands of markets. It is now easy to see that the self-equilibrating tendencies of the market system, which appeared to be quite simple and direct when only one particular market was considered, are extremely complex when the

interactions of all markets are taken into account. When the
secondary and tertiary effects of a few price changes are examined,
it is easy to understand why the history of the private-enterprise
market system has generally been characterized by extensive
disequilibriums in many markets. (The implications of these disequilibriums for aggregate unemployment and inflation in a private-
enterprise economy are analyzed in Part III.)

the market as an allocative device

One of the central problems with which economics deals is the
allocation of scarce resources. Perhaps the most universal of social
and economic problems faced by all societies is the fact that no
society's capacity to produce or secure goods has yet been sufficient
to satisfy all the wants, needs, and desires that people have for these
goods. Any good is considered by economists to be a *scarce good*
when demand would exceed supply *if the good were to be given
away freely in any desired quantity with no price charged for it.* It is
obvious that most objects people need and desire are scarce goods.

Any society must devise a method of dividing up or allocating
scarce goods among its citizens. In a slave economy, the slaves, like
productive domesticated animals, are given enough to keep them
fairly healthy so that they can work and reproduce themselves; the
rest of the economy's output goes to their masters. In the feudal
economy (described in Chapters 1 and 2), conditions of land tenure
largely determined the distribution and allocation of goods. The
feudal serf, like the slave, got a minimal subsistence income; whereas
the feudal lord, like the slave's master, received a much larger share
in the fruits of production.

In a private-enterprise economy, the market allocates scarce
resources and goods. If the needs and desires for a particular good
far exceed the available supply (as is the case with most goods), then
the good goes to those who are willing and able to pay the highest
price for it in the market.

It may be the case that many people desperately need a car like
the Pinto but cannot afford its present price, although they could
afford to pay a lower price. Now suppose the government fixes the
price by law below the point at which supply and demand meet.
There would still be two groups of people excluded from the consumption of Pintos. (1) Those who could not afford to pay even the
lower price would again be excluded. (2) Those who did not get their
places in line before the supply of Pintos was exhausted would be
excluded, in spite of the fact that they would have been willing and

able to pay even the higher price. This kind of shortage may become a common situation in America if the wage-price controls begun in late 1971 are continued for a long period. In some socialist countries, such as the Soviet Union, price-fixing of this type is fairly common. This explains the frequent reports of "shortages" and long queues in these countries.

Obviously, to the extent that markets tend to be self-equilibrating in a private-enterprise economy and that there is no government price-fixing, there will be a tendency for these shortages to be eliminated. It must be emphasized, though, that economists use the term *shortage* in a way that has no necessary relation to the abundance or lack of abundance of a good relative to people's need for it. The shortage is only relative to the demand *in money terms* by paying customers.

For example, imagine two economies, one in which an efficiently self-equilibrating market exists and the other in which goods are all given away free on a first-come, first-served basis. In the first economy, there may be an extreme paucity of provision, with only a tiny elite minority receiving most of the meager supply of available goods. If the markets are all in equilibrium, there are no shortages in the economists' sense despite the fact that many may be dying of starvation. In the second economy, there may be an abundance of goods that are given away at no charge. Even though virtually everyone might be very well off relative to even the richest citizens in the first economy, if some people want more than is available to them, there will be economic shortage.

It is important to understand clearly the economist's meaning of the word *shortage* because the assertion that a market economy has fewer shortages than a nonmarket, or planned, economy is often misconstrued to imply that the material welfare of people in a market economy must be higher than that of people in a nonmarket economy. This welfare may or may not be higher, but it has nothing to do with the existence or nonexistence of economic shortages. In fact, in economies where the decision has been made *not* to use the market as the primary device to allocate scarce resources, the people have chosen to divide the produce of society by some nonmonetary means. They will no longer exclude those who cannot afford to pay the market price for a scarce good, but must use some other principle of distribution.

How can the market versus nonmarket means of allocating scarce goods be evaluated? Such an evaluation would require the weighing of many diverse considerations. The market tends to allocate scarce goods with a minimum of inconvenience and bureaucratic red tape. The whole process is generally quite efficient and impersonal. By contrast, look at two widely used nonmarket allocative mechanisms. First, there are rationing coupons such as those used by America

during World War II, which limit the amount of a scarce good any
individual can purchase, regardless of the amount of money he has.
Second, there is the technique of first-come, first-served, where those
at the end of the queue are automatically eliminated when the supply
of the good in question is exhausted.

The first of these nonmarket allocative mechanisms involves a high
cost of extensive record-keeping and some inevitable bureaucratic
inefficiencies in the control and distribution of the coupons. The
second method causes much wasted time as people wait in queues.
It often leads to bitterness and resentment, because persons who can
afford to buy the scarce commodity wait in line for long periods of
time, only to find the supply is exhausted when they finally work
their way to the head of the line.

Thus, it can be said in terms of convenience and efficiency,
the market is probably superior to these two nonmarket allocative
mechanisms (the superior efficiency relates only to the allocative
process and implies nothing about technological efficiency in the
production of goods and services in private-enterprise versus
nonmarket economies).

The market is frequently criticized, however, on the grounds
that the resultant allocation of scarce goods is inequitable,
unfair, and unjust. It is argued that in a private-enterprise economy
such as the United States, where a few people receive the overwhelming bulk of all profits generated by the economy, an unjustly
lopsided concentration of income and purchasing power is created.
Many economists feel that as a consequence of this concentration of
purchasing power the private-enterprise economy concentrates on
producing primarily for the wealthy. In allocating scarce medical
care, for example, the private-enterprise system places more importance on psychiatric care for the neurotic pets of the wealthy than it
does on the provision of minimal health services for the children of
the poor.

To illustrate this last point, imagine a hypothetical island economy
that is periodically struck with an epidemic of a disease that affects
only children. From past experiences, the islanders have found that
when the disease strikes, it randomly affects 80 percent of the
children. They have also discovered a preventative antidote that
reduces the chances of death if it is taken before the disease strikes.
A child who has taken no doses of the antidote has a 90 percent
chance of dying when he contracts the disease. With one dose of the
antidote, the chance of death is reduced to 10 percent. Two doses
reduce the chance to 8 percent; three doses reduce the chance to
6 percent; four doses reduce the chance to 5 percent. Beyond four
doses, the antidote has no further effect, and the chances of death
remain at 5 percent.

Suppose that the island has 1,000 children and that at the first sign of a new outbreak of the dreaded disease, the people have produced and accumulated 1,000 doses of the antidote. The antidote must be used immediately if the children's lives are to be saved. What system of allocation *ought* the people to use to distribute this extremely important scarce good? If the government on the island issues rationing coupons so that each child gets one dose of the antidote, then the following results could be expected: 800 children will get the disease, but since each has had one dose of the antidote, only 80 children will die; 920 children will survive the epidemic.

On the other hand, suppose the relative distribution of income and wealth on the island reflects perfectly the relative distribution of income and wealth that exists in the United States today. According to this income distribution, the islanders leave the allocation problem to the private-enterprise, free market system, with the following results: the 250 children who have the wealthiest parents will each take four doses of the antidote; of these 250, about 200 will get the disease and about 10 will die; of the remaining 750 children, 600 will get the disease and about 540 of them will die.

Using a nonmarket allocative mechanism, the islanders were able to save 920 children while 80 died. Given the unequal distribution of income and wealth that exists in the private-enterprise market allocation, they saved 450 children while 550 died. This is admittedly a farfetched example with hypothetical percentages chosen to illustrate our point dramatically. But the point is there, and perhaps exaggeration is the most effective method of illustrating it. The student is urged to read *Don't Get Sick in America*,[1] a frightening but scholarly study which shows that this example is by no means as distorted as it might appear at first glance.

In ending this discussion on market allocation, it should be noted that one's view of the desirability of the market system depends upon whether one is more impressed with the efficacy and impersonality of this allocation mechanism or with its lopsided results. Thus, one defender of capitalism writes: "The case for capitalism is at its strongest on the simple thesis that the market knows best how to allocate and use the scarce resource of capital."[2] A critic of capitalism sees it differently: "The main reason that freedom of contract has never been as free as advertised—and it is a painfully obvious reason—is that sellers and buyers are not equal in bargaining power. So the terms of sale will simply reflect the power, or lack of it, that each party brings to the market place. So a market is also a financial slaughterhouse, where the strong chop up the weak."[3]

[1] D. Schorr, *Don't Get Sick in America* (Nashville, Tenn.: Aurora Publishers, 1970).

[2] Simon Webley, "The Utilization of Capital," in M. Ivens and R. Dunstan, eds., *The Case for Capitalism* (London: Michael Joseph, 1967), p. 41.

[3] D. T. Bazelon, *The Paper Economy* (New York: Random House, Vintage Books, 1963), p. 52.

Even the "efficiency" of the capitalist market has been criticized as a very narrowly limited concept. As will be seen in Chapters 16, 17, and 18, such efficient allocation of resources would operate only under pure competition; America, however, is characterized by a high degree of monopoly power. In Chapter 20, we explore the fact that if there is discrimination, the market will reflect it and may reinforce it. In examining the aggregate economy in Part III, it is demonstrated that "efficient" use of resources applies only to employed resources, but that the market system may leave many resources, both machines and human beings, unemployed. In Part III, we also note that private efficiency may ignore social costs such as pollution. This list of qualifications to market "efficiency" will be lengthened still further in Part III, particularly when we consider the international market mechanism that includes the underdeveloped two-thirds of the world.

summary

In a competitive market economy, prices are determined by the conditions of supply and demand. Demand is based on consumers' desires and consumers' incomes. No cash, no sale. *If* there is pure competition, the market mechanism will allocate resources to each industry according to the cash demand for its product. Supply is based on the firm's costs of production. Thus, as costs go up, higher prices are required in order to induce the firm to supply more. However, as the price goes up, consumers will demand less. The equilibrium price will be the point at which supply and demand just balance. Its defenders claim that this system of production for private profit is efficient, even if it is not humane (but even its efficiency is very narrowly defined).

chapter 14
price determination:
utility versus labor cost

In Chapter 13, we examined the ways in which competition in the
market allocates all resources under private-enterprise capitalism.
We explored the mechanics of price determination by supply and
demand. Now it is necessary to make a careful examination of the
ways in which market supply and market demand are themselves
determined by other forces. This will involve looking at consumer
behavior in the market and then at enterprise behavior in the market.
Finally, we will demonstrate the relationships between this understanding and the theories of value and price described in Part I.

utility and demand

It has been demonstrated that the competitive market tends to
allocate resources to produce things according to the pattern of
consumer demand (with each customer's desires weighted according
to how much money he has to spend). The heart of neoclassical
economics, from early theorists like Stanley Jevons to most present-
day textbook writers, is the notion that consumer demand, in turn, is
determined by the utility of each commodity to the consumer. *Utility*
is defined as the pleasure or satisfaction one receives from consuming a good. Most textbooks state that utility alone determines how
much people will be willing to pay for the good or how much of the

good people will buy at various prices. However, several qualifications to this statement of the importance of utility must be made.

First, consumers often are persuaded by false and misleading advertising that they will receive a great deal more pleasure from a commodity than is attainable. On this basis, they purchase the commodity, only to be disappointed and receive little or no satisfaction from it. Second, many actions are guided not by a search for pleasure, satisfaction, or utility, but by habit, caprice, impulse, or any one of dozens of motives psychologists could list. Third, and most generally, a market society tends to inculcate a "buying mentality" in many consumers. The objective in making purchases sometimes becomes simply the *spending* of money, per se, rather than the satisfying of real needs or desires for the things purchased. This finding has been particularly emphasized in recent work in psychology concerning the feelings of emptiness and alienation.[1]

For these reasons, we believe that the pattern of consumer demand is forced into a particular form by many things other than the actual pleasure or satisfaction derived directly from consumption of each commodity. But because the term *utility* is almost always used to explain demand, it will be retained, but redefined for our purposes. We conceive of utility as synonymous with desire. If we say that a particular good possesses utility for a particular person, we simply mean that that person *desires to buy* the good in question. The desire may be the result of any number of motives. It may be a healthy desire that will, if satisfied, increase the person's well-being, or it may be a perverted or morbid desire that will, if satisfied, lead to pernicious or harmful results. In other words, the satisfaction of any particular desire cannot be said, a priori, to be either morally good or morally bad until there is sufficient information available to make an independent moral judgment.

diminishing marginal utility

Our examination of the theory of demand begins with the principle of *diminishing marginal utility*. The marginal utility of a good is defined as the strength of the consumer's desire to purchase *one additional unit* of the good. The principle of diminishing marginal utility states that *as more and more of a good is acquired, the marginal utility of the good diminishes.*

On a hot summer day, for example, a person may desire a malted milk very intensely. But if he has one malted milk, the intensity of his

---

1 See the discussion by Erich Fromm in Chapter 12.

desire for another diminishes. If he has two malted milks, the intensity of his desire for a third will be very low (he may have no desire at all for a third). Another way of stating this is to say that the marginal utility of malted milks diminishes as one more is bought.

how consumers maximize utility

When consumers spend their income, they strive to maximize their utility. Suppose their income permits them to purchase a large number of different groups, or *bundles,* of commodities. They will try to choose the bundle that satisfies their strongest or most urgent desires; that is, they will attempt to maximize their utility.

Suppose next that a person can spend his income on only three commodities: apples, bread, and cake. It is then possible to determine the quantities of each that he will buy in order to maximize his utility. Utility will be maximized if he buys those quantities of apples, bread, and cake that will leave the marginal utilities of each at a level at which the following condition holds:

$$\frac{\text{Marginal utility of apples}}{\text{Price of apples}} = \frac{\text{marginal utility of bread}}{\text{price of bread}} = \frac{\text{marginal utility of cake}}{\text{price of cake}}$$

The equality of these three ratios means that utility is maximized when the last dollar spent on apples yields the same utility as the last dollars spent on bread and on cake. A numerical example will help explain this principle.

Table 14.1 shows amounts of apples, bread and cake ranging from 1 pound to 6 pounds. The number of units of marginal utility for each good and the number of units of marginal utility per dollar for each

QUANTITY (in pounds)	MARGINAL UTILITY OF APPLES (in units of utility)	MARGINAL UTILITY OF APPLES PER DOLLAR (price: $1.00)	MARGINAL UTILITY OF BREAD (in units of utility)
1	12	12	24
2	11	11	22
3	10	10	20
4	9	9	18
5	8	8	16
6	7	7	14

quantity of each good can be determined by reading across the table. Of course, in reality, it is not so clear that each consumer exactly measures or knows how many units of subjective utility he gets from each additional commodity. (Could you measure *exactly* the relative desire or utility to you of one more apple versus one more loaf of bread?)

Still, the theory does help to elucidate consumer behavior in a rough sort of way. Now imagine that a consumer with an income of $24 dollars buys 6 pounds of cake for $18, 2 pounds of bread for $4, and 2 pounds of apples for $2. He has spent his entire $24 income, but he has not maximized his utility. The ratios of marginal utility to price are not the same for the three commodities. The ratios are as follows:

for apples $\dfrac{11 \text{ units of utility}}{\$1}$ = 11 units of utility for last dollar

for bread $\dfrac{22 \text{ units of utility}}{\$2}$ = 11 units of utility for last dollar

for cake $\dfrac{15 \text{ units of utility}}{\$3}$ = 5 units of utility for last dollar

The utility he received from the last dollar spent on cake (5 units of utility) was considerably smaller than the utility of the last dollars spent on apples and bread (11 units each). Obviously, this individual's utility could be increased if he shifted some of his purchases from cake to apples and bread.

If he gives up 3 pounds of cake, he will lose 54 units of utility but gain $9 to be spent on apples and bread. With this $9, the consumer purchases 3 more pounds of apples (thereby gaining 27 units of utility) and 3 more pounds of bread (thereby gaining 54 units of

MARGINAL UTILITY OF BREAD PER DOLLAR (price: $2.00)	MARGINAL UTILITY OF CAKE (in units of utility)	MARGINAL UTILITY OF CAKE PER DOLLAR (price: $3.00)
12	30	10
11	27	9
10	24	8
9	21	7
8	18	6
7	15	5

TABLE 14.1

utility). Thus, by shifting $9 worth of purchases, the consumer gives up 54 units of utility and gains 81 units.

Obviously, the second bundle of goods has more utility than the first. If the units of utility in the first bundle are added, they total 204 (6 units from cake = 135; 2 units from bread = 46; and 2 units from apples = 23). The total number of units of utility in the second bundle is 231 (3 units from cake = 81; 5 units from bread = 100; and 5 units from apples = 50). The ratios of marginal utility to price for the three goods in the second bundle are as follows:

for apples $\dfrac{8 \text{ units of utility}}{\$1}$ =   8 units of utility for last dollar

for bread $\dfrac{16 \text{ units of utility}}{\$2}$ =   8 units of utility for last dollar

for cake $\dfrac{24 \text{ units of utility}}{\$3}$ =   8 units of utility for last dollar

Thus, the maximizing condition holds, that is,

$$\frac{8}{\$1} = \frac{16}{\$2} = \frac{24}{\$3}$$

Purchases cannot be shifted among the commodities any further without losing some utility. The reader should experiment with such shifts in order to convince himself that this is a maximum.

With this information, it is now possible to demonstrate why demand curves slope downward and to the right—that is, why the quantity demanded *increases* as the price *decreases* (see Chapter 13). Imagine an initial position at which all consumers are maximizing their utility—that is, they have equated the ratios of their marginal utilities and prices for all the goods. It is then possible to trace the effects of a decrease in price.

If the price of one good, say apples, were to decrease, consumers would find that the utility received for the last dollar spent on apples would be higher than the utility received for the last dollar spent on other goods. Consumers would immediately shift some of their purchases from other goods to apples. Thus, the initial result of a decline in the price of apples is an increased quantity of apples demanded.

But what determines exactly how much demand will shift to apples? Exactly how much will the demand for them increase when the price declines? That depends on their marginal utility (the desire for an additional apple) relative to the marginal utility of other goods (the desire for more bread and cake). As consumers buy more and more apples, their desire for an additional one declines (this is just one illustration of the law of diminishing marginal utility). At the same time, consumers are buying less of all other goods (less bread and less cake). So the *marginal* utility of other goods rises; at the margin, their desire for an additional piece of bread or cake is now increased. The process of shifting demand from bread and cake to apples stops when an additional dollar spent for more apples (even at the new lower price) yields just the same marginal utility as that spent for bread or cake (even at their old, unchanged prices).

elasticity of demand

Economists have developed concepts to describe demand curves in terms of how much the amount demanded reacts to a price change. If a small price change up or down causes a very big change in quantity demanded, the demand is said to be very *elastic.* But if a significant price change causes almost no change in quantity demanded for the commodity, the demand is said to be very *inelastic.*

What kind of commodities have elastic demands (big reactions to price changes)? Mostly luxuries, such as movies or cake or Cadillacs. If the price is low enough, a consumer will be happy to buy a piece of cake or go to a movie or buy a new car. But if the price of one of these luxuries goes up while his income stays the same, the consumer will have to cut back on the luxury to buy things he needs more. Demand for luxuries is very sensitive to prices; it is elastic.

The demand curve for cake might look like the one in Figure 14.1. The demand is elastic because when price declines, the rise in quantity is more than proportionate, so the total expenditure (or revenue to the seller) actually rises. Thus, at $3, only 100 cakes are

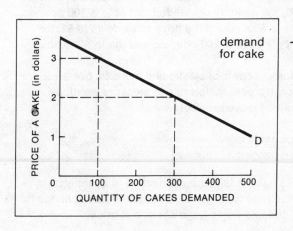

FIGURE
14.1

demand for cake

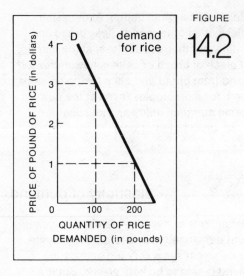

FIGURE

14.2

demand for rice

sold, and the total revenue is $300. But if the price goes down to $2, then 300 cakes are sold, and the total revenue rises to $600.

What kind of commodities have inelastic demands (small reactions to price changes)? Mostly necessities, such as medicine or basic foods. If you are diabetic and need insulin to stay alive, then you will still buy almost the same amount even if its price doubles. If you live in China and your main food is rice, then if the price rises considerably, you will reluctantly look for a substitute, but you may still demand quite a bit. If the price of rice falls, you may demand more, but if it was already 80 percent of your diet, you will not demand much more.

The demand curve for rice in China might look like the one in Figure 14.2. The demand is inelastic because when price declines, the rise in quantity is *less than proportionate,* so the total revenue declines. Thus, at $3, the quantity demanded and sold is 100 pounds, and the total revenue is $300. But if the price goes down to $1, the quantity demanded only goes to 200 pounds, and the total revenue *declines* to $200.

These, then, are the concepts of elastic and inelastic demand. Some readers may wish a general formula to measure elasticity. Elasticity may be defined more precisely as

$$\text{Elasticity} = \frac{\text{percentage rise in quantity demanded}}{\text{percentage cut in price}}$$

Of course, it is just as easy to talk about a decline in quantity demanded due to a price rise; or, in general, the percentage *change* in quantity demanded due to a percentage *change* in price.

For those who prefer symbols to words, call elasticity E, call quantity demanded Q, call price P, and let Δ mean "the change in." Then

$$E = \frac{\Delta Q/Q}{\Delta P/P}$$

The reader should not worry about the details of calculation.[2]

The elasticity of demand for cake (shown in Figure 14.1) works out this way. Rise in quantity demanded is $300 - 100 = 200$. Average quantity, on which the percentage is based, is $(300 + 100) \div 2 = 200$. Fall in price is $\$3 - \$2 = \$1$. Average price is $(\$3 + \$2) \div 2 = \$2.5$. Therefore

$$E_{cake} = \frac{200/200}{1/2.5} = \frac{1}{0.4} = \frac{100\%}{40\%} = 2.5$$

The percentage change in demand (100 percent) is much greater than the percentage change in price (40 percent); therefore, the demand is elastic. More precisely, demand is elastic if E is greater than 1, and here E is 2.5.

Similarly, the elasticity of demand for rice (shown in Figure 14.2) works out this way. Rise in quantity demanded is $200 - 100 = 100$. Average quantity is $(200 + 100) \div 2 = 150$. Fall in price is $\$3 - \$1 = \$2$. Average price is $(\$3 + \$1) \div 2 = \$2$. Therefore

$$E_{rice} = \frac{100/150}{2/2} = \frac{0.67}{1} = \frac{67\%}{100\%} = 0.67$$

Here the percentage change in demand (67 percent) is less than the percentage change in price (100 percent); therefore, the demand is inelastic. Or, if you wish, it is inelastic because E is 0.67, which is less than 1.

To complete the concept, economists say that the demand curve is of *unitary elasticity* when E is 1. In this intermediate case, the percentage change in demand is just the same as the percentage change in price.

At one extreme, a *perfectly inelastic* demand curve is shown by a vertical straight line. There is *no* change in demand when price changes. Thus, E equals zero when demand is perfectly inelastic.

---

2 For those who like calculations, the details: Assume a move down the demand curve from some point 1 to point 2. The change in quantity demanded is $\Delta Q = Q_1 - Q_2$. The change in price is $\Delta P = P_2 - P_1$ because the price went down while quantity went up. The base for figuring the percentage could be either Q_1 or Q_2, with somewhat different results. As a convention, economists always use the average, so $Q = Q_1 + Q_2/2$. Similarly, by convention, $P = P_1 + P_2/2$.

However a *perfectly elastic* demand curve is shown by a horizontal straight line. When demand is perfectly elastic, E equals infinity. The firm can sell an infinite quantity of goods at the present price. Although these extreme cases are unrealistic, the concepts will be helpful later.

supply and marginal cost

Consumer behavior and demand have been examined in great detail. In order to complete the picture, it is necessary to examine the behavior of business enterprises in supplying goods, but only in enough detail to supply the information necessary for an understanding of price determination in the competitive market. The details of business price and output behavior are very different for pure competition and for various degrees of monopoly power; these details will be discussed in the chapters on competition and monopoly.

A firm's decision regarding the quantity of its product that it wishes to supply at various prices depends on many things. The most important factor, though, is usually its costs of producing different quantities of its product. Just as neoclassical economics emphasizes marginal utility in determining consumer demand, it emphasizes marginal cost in determining business supply to the market.

Marginal cost is the additional cost of producing one more unit of output. Suppose a firm owns a single factory with 100 machines. It can increase its output only by adding more raw materials and more workers. Here, however, there is a law of increasing marginal cost for firms that is similar to the law of diminishing marginal utility for consumers.

Assume a given factory and machines (and no time to add more or to improve technology). Then the lowest cost per unit is reached at some particular flow of raw materials and some *given number* of workers. To make it simple, assume raw material flow is always adjusted to the number of workers. As the number of workers is increased, the cost changes. If there are too few workers, they will not be able to handle the whole factory efficiently. But as the number of workers increases beyond some point, they add less and less to the product; or, the marginal cost of one more unit of output rises. For example, if there are only 100 machines and each machine needs only 1 man, what can more than 100 workers contribute? Certainly, some are needed to bring in raw materials and to take them away, clean up, and repair. At some point, however, whether it is 125 or 150 or even 200, an additional worker could only add less than the previously hired worker.

Within these rigid assumptions, it is hard to quarrel with this law. On its basis, it is possible to picture marginal costs rising with output (after some minimal cost point is passed). Entrepreneurs will obviously not supply additional goods to the market at a price below their additional cost. Therefore, as the marginal cost of production rises for additional output, the prices at which additional supply will be offered must also rise.

In a perfectly competitive market, the firm's supply curve is identical to its marginal-cost curve (see Chapter 16). The reason that firms will supply goods at "cost" is that the traditional neoclassical definition of cost includes a "normal" profit. (The implications of this peculiar neoclassical definition will be examined in Chapter 16.) With imperfect competition or monopoly, the amount a firm will supply is not solely determined by its costs. (This will be discussed in Chapters 16 and 17.) In the present context, however, it is sufficient to know that the firm's marginal cost is important in determining how much it will supply to the market.

the price and output of an industry

Based on an understanding of the ways in which consumer desires (and income levels) determine demand and the ways in which enterprise costs determine supply to the market, it is possible to sum up the action of supply and demand for a whole industry. The mechanics of it were studied in Chapter 13. Here, the main point is recapitulated in this new context.

Figure 14.3 shows the usual supply and demand curves (based on Figure 13.3). Supply *SS* is based on marginal cost; demand *DD* is based on marginal utility.

The point at which supply and demand meet determines both the price of the car and the number of cars produced. At any lower price level, there is excess demand, and therefore the industry can produce more cars *and* raise their price, hence making more profit. At any higher price level, there is excess supply, and therefore the industry is forced to produce fewer cars and lower its prices.

The demand behavior is based on the marginal utility of a Pinto to the consumer. The supply behavior is based on the marginal cost (always including a "normal" profit) of a Pinto to the Ford Motor Company.

This is a much-oversimplified statement of the current view of

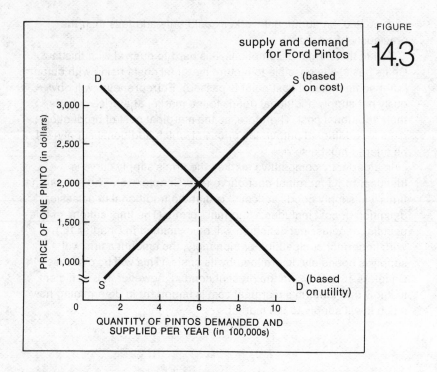

FIGURE

14.3

supply and demand
for Ford Pintos

price determination. Before it can be further refined and compared with earlier theories, one more tool is required: the elasticity of supply.

elasticity of supply

It is not necessary to become involved in a detailed discussion of the elasticity of supply because the concept is exactly analogous to the elasticity of demand. Supply is elastic if it responds more than proportionately to a price change, and it is inelastic if it responds less than proportionately to a price change. More precisely

$$\text{Elasticity of supply} = \frac{\text{percentage rise in quantity supplied}}{\text{percentage rise in price}}$$

Unlike demand, the quantity supplied moves in the same direction as price because a higher price means a higher profit (costs remaining the same), which induces a business to produce and sell more.

Inelastic supply reaction is most often found with perishable goods. Ripe tomatoes *must* be sold quickly, regardless of the price that can be obtained in the market. But durable goods such as furniture may show an elastic (sensitive) supply reaction to price changes. If the price of furniture falls, it can simply be stored away and not offered for sale.

momentary supply and price equilibrium

Even in the preceding examples, the length of time considered is clearly important. Besides tomatoes already in the market, what about the longer-run reaction of tomato growers? If the price falls for a long-enough time, the number of tomatoes grown *will* decline considerably.

In the 1890s, Alfred Marshall used this notion to clarify the concept of price determination. He distinguished the supply reaction to a price or demand change in three time periods: momentary, short run, and long run. The momentary period is so short (an hour, day, or week, depending on the product) that the amount of supply in the market cannot be varied at all. The short-run period is long enough for a factory to produce more or less for the market within its capacity but too short for any new factories to be built or put into use. The long-run period is long enough for as many new factories to be built as are necessary to bring the supply up to the demand.

How does this time factor affect elasticity of supply (and thus indirectly affect prices)? Assume that at a given moment, Ford dealers have a certain supply of Pintos on hand. No matter what sudden change there is in demand, they cannot sell more until they receive more: Momentary supply is perfectly inelastic.

Assume now that the one Ford dealer in a town usually sells ten Pintos a week and that the factory delivers ten Pintos each Monday. One week, he sells six Pintos up through Thursday. So on Friday, he has four Pintos to sell. But on Friday, eight customers want to buy Pintos immediately (and are not willing to wait until Monday).

In this case, the supply is fixed (at four), so the dealer will raise the price to take advantage of the higher demand. Suppose the list price is $2,000, but he has been giving a $200 discount, thus selling at $1,800. Because he cannot sell eight at $1,800, he may try to sell the four he has at $2,000 (see Figure 14.4).

The Ford dealer was ready for the usual demand D_1D_1, but the demand shifted that day to D_2D_2. Still, the supply is perfectly inelastic for that day; he simply cannot get more cars to sell in that period. So the higher demand reaches equilibrium with the fixed supply at a higher price.

Most of the early utility theorists (from the crude J. B. Say to the

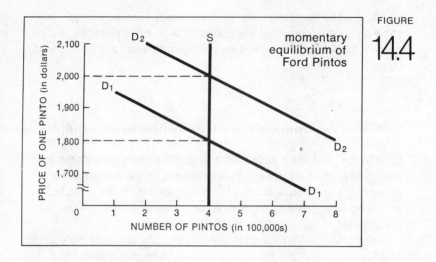

FIGURE

14.4

momentary
equilibrium of
Ford Pintos

very sophisticated Léon Walras) concentrated on market exchange
and gave little consideration to changes in supply conditions.
Consequently, it seems that this given momentary supply is the only
case they considered. They stated (and it is true in this case) that
marginal utility determines demand, and that demand changes largely
determine price changes. These theorists used this case to attack
the older theory (of Marx and the classicals—Ricardo and Smith)
that labor cost determines supply, which ultimately determines price.
Certainly, *in this case,* where supply is perfectly inelastic, supply
cannot change and, therefore, cannot explain changes in price.

short-run supply and price equilibrium

What price will bring an equilibrium of supply and demand in the
short run? Or how do supply and demand changes affect price in the
short run? These are the questions emphasized by Alfred Marshall
and in every neoclassical beginning text to the present day.

Briefly, in the short run, marginal cost tends to rise when a firm
tries to produce additional units of output beyond some point
because the short run is, by definition, a period in which the firm has
a *given* factory and machinery and no time to expand it. Technology
requires some particular number of workers to run the plant at
capacity (or at the cheapest cost per unit). When the firm tries to
produce more than the capacity for which the factory is designed by
adding more workers, the product per additional worker naturally
declines; or, the marginal cost rises.

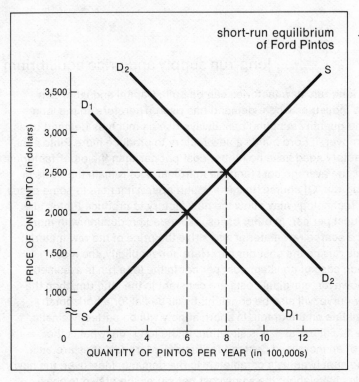

FIGURE

14.5

short-run equilibrium
of Ford Pintos

Because supply will never be below marginal cost, the supply
curve naturally rises (up and to the right, as in Figure 14.3) as output
expands. In other words, with rising costs, the firm will supply more
goods only at higher prices; or, the supply curve is more or less
elastic, depending on the product, but it is certainly no longer
perfectly inelastic.

A shift upward in demand will raise prices, as in the previous case,
but now the new equilibrium price is clearly also affected by the
movement along the supply curve.

Figure 14.5 shows that an increase in demand for Pintos raises
both the price (from $2,000 to $2,500) and the quantity (from 600,000
to 800,000). The quantity rises because the supply curve is somewhat
elastic. This reflects the fact that existing Ford plants have the
capacity to turn out more Pintos, although at rising costs per car.
It is clear in this case that *both* the quantities supplied and demanded
change and so together determine the new price equilibrum.

Alfred Marshall thus emphasized that supply and demand operate
like the two blades of the scissors. Supply behavior is based on
marginal costs. Demand behavior is based on marginal utility.
It follows in the modern neoclassical view that both utility and cost
together determine prices or values.

long-run supply and price equilibrium

In the long run, new factories can be built. Capital and labor can
shift to industries where demand has risen. Therefore, in the long
run, the quantity supplied can always rise as much as demand does.

Moreover, if Ford builds a new factory to produce more Pintos, the
new factory need have no higher cost per car than the older factories.
Hence, the average cost (and the marginal, too) remain the same in
the long run. Of course, this is a rough approximation. In some cases,
better technology may allow the new factory to produce Pintos at a
lower cost per car. In other cases, expanded production with more
use of a scarce raw material may drive the price of the raw material
up, thus raising the cost per car. Here, for simplicity, the most
common case of constant cost per car in the long run is assumed.

If, however, marginal costs are constant in the long run, then the
supply curve will also be constant. It will be flat, or a horizontal
straight line on the graph. In short, supply will be perfectly elastic.
Figure 14.6 illustrates this situation. In the long run, what is the
effect of an increased demand for Pintos? More factories are built,
and the supply adjusts completely to the demand. Moreover, the new
factories have about the same cost per car as the previous ones

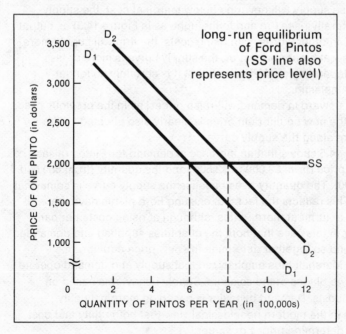

FIGURE

14.6

long-run equilibrium
of Ford Pintos
(SS line also
represents price level)

(assuming additional cost from greater use of resources is about canceled out by better technology).

In the long-run case, therefore, it can be asserted that the sole effect of an increase in demand is an equal increase in quantity produced. But the rise in demand has *no* effect on the price level. Of course, at the initial moment of rise in demand, prices rose. However, that called forth more supply from existing factories in the short run, and therefore prices dropped a bit. In the long run, the entire rise in demand was met by an equal increase in supply from new factories (at the same cost per car as before), and hence the price dropped back to its old level.

Therefore, in the long run, *demand determines the amount of production* (or the allocation of resources), *but supply alone determines the price level.* It can be said that the relative marginal utilities of different commodities determine the demand for them and the proportionate amounts of each produced. The long-run price level, however, is solely determined by the level of costs per unit (i.e., the supply conditions).

This is the case that the classicals and Marx emphasized. They were not so much interested in momentary or short-run market exchange and demand as in the long-run price or value of commodities. This they found to be determined solely by cost of human effort or, as Marx put it, the total amount of human labor embodied in the product (including the labor involved in mining the raw materials and building the factories and machines used up in that production).

Marshall and the modern neoclassicals would agree that in this particular case of long-run supply and constant costs, a change in marginal utility *does not* affect the price, but a change in the cost per unit *does* affect the price. The argument comes over the exact meaning of *cost.* The neoclassicals maintain that capitalists as well as workers put out an effort of some kind (though the "effort" may be a purely subjective "sacrifice" of immediate higher consumption for a later return on capital invested), but Marx insisted that it is only the workers' objective expenditure of labor that determines long-run price or value.

This dispute arises, of course, because these economists are concerned not only with the mechanics of price determination but also with the how and why and the equitableness of income distribution. How the contributions to production of labor and capital (the different components of cost) are viewed obviously has much to do with how the distribution of income is viewed. Should Ford workers or owners of Ford stock receive the income from sales of the Pinto? This question of income distribution is discussed in Chapter 15.

summary

Demand for a good is based on its utility, or the desires of the consumer plus the consumer's income. Supply is based on the cost of production. At any given moment when supply is fixed, the changing demand (based on utility) sets the price. In a short run just long enough so that a factory may produce more or less, both supply and demand change and affect the price. In a long run long enough to build new factories, the demand will still determine how much is to be produced (the allocation of resources to different industries). In the long run, however, any quantity that is demanded can be produced, so the price level will simply be determined by the cost (including a normal profit). In other words, in the long run, twice as much demand will mean twice as much production of the commodity; but if cost per unit stays constant, then the price will also stay constant.

chapter 15
distribution of income: marginal productivity versus exploitation

Different theories of the distribution of income lead to very different ideological positions vis à vis the evaluation of capitalism. Highly controversial issues are in question—for example, how capitalists make profits, and whether workers are "exploited." Before these problems in theory are probed, it will be helpful to state the present factual situation to which they are relevant.

poverty

Everyone knows that much of the world lives in poverty, but it is more surprising to learn of the vast amount of poverty in the richest country in the world. In 1966, in absolute figures, 14 percent of all American families had less than $3,000 income, 46 percent had less than $7,000, and 59 percent had less than $9,000.[1] What do these figures mean in human terms?

According to the definition of the Social Security Administration, an urban family of four persons was below the poverty line in 1966 if it had an income below $3,150. This definition, however, is much too narrow in its view of minimum needs. It is based on an "economy

[1] U.S. Bureau of the Census, Department of Commerce, *Statistical Abstract of the United States: 1968* (Washington, D.C.: U.S. Government Printing Office, 1968), p. 326.

diet . . . meant for emergency or temporary use when funds are low
—in other words a diet which over long periods of time does not
meet minimum nutritional requirements."[2] Yet more than 24,836,000
Americans were below that poverty line.[3] This means that most of
them had not enough to eat of nutritional foods, lived in rat-infested
slums, and obviously could not afford to give their children a good
higher education.

The Bureau of Labor Statistics (BLS) calculates a "moderate but
adequate city worker's family budget." It is certainly not extravagant:
It assumes that clothes are replaced only after three years and that
the worker has a used car or uses public transport. Furthermore, it
allows a movie only every two or three weeks, books and materials
only as school expenses, nothing for college, and no saving for
emergencies.[4] Because of inflation, even this limited budget was
calculated as $9,100 for 1966, which meant that 59.4 percent of
American families fell below that line.

inequality

When contrasted with these absolute low-income levels, the relative
inequality of income distribution is even more striking. Table 15.1
presents data compiled by the Bureau of the Census.

On one side are the very poor, the lowest 20 percent of families
with only 5 percent of all family income (and the lowest 20 percent of
unrelated individuals with only 3 percent of all individual income).
On the other side are the rich, the top 5 percent of families with
almost 15 percent of all family income (and the top 5 percent of
unrelated individuals with almost 22 percent of all individual income).
Then there are the elite, the very rich; these are the top 2 percent
whose incomes are above $25,000 per family. Finally, there are the
very, very rich; those were the mere 0.08 percent (less than one-
tenth of one percent) of all taxpayers whose incomes exceeded
$200,000 in 1966.

Because income is highly concentrated, saving is also. A small
number of individuals and firms do most of the saving and investing
of capital. In 1965, personal savings by individuals was only $25
billion, whereas saving by businesses and corporations was
$83 billion. Even within the category of personal savings, households
in the lower two-thirds of the income range did no saving at all. On

2 Donald Light, "Income Distribution," *Occasional Papers of the Union for Radical
Political Economics* (December 1969), p. 2.

3 U.S. Bureau of the Census, op. cit., p. 330.

4 Light, op. cit., p. 3.

	PERCENTAGE OF INCOME RECEIVED BY EACH FIFTH (20%) FAMILY	PERCENTAGE OF INDIVIDUAL INCOME RECEIVED BY EACH FIFTH (20%) UN-RELATED INDIVIDUAL
Lowest	5.4%	2.9%
Second	12.4	7.6
Middle	17.7	13.3
Fourth	23.8	24.2
Highest	40.7	52.0
TOTAL	100.0	100.0
Top 5%	14.8	21.8

TABLE 15.1

inequality of income distribution, United States, 1966

Source: U.S. Bureau of the Census, *Statistical Abstract of the United States: 1968* (Washington, D.C.: U.S. Government Printing Office, 1968), p. 324.

the contrary, most of this two-thirds consumed more than their total income. More than half of all the personal savings available for investment was supplied by those in the upper 5 percent income bracket.

types of income

Income is not randomly distributed among all individuals. On the contrary, distribution is closely related to the type of income. Does most of a person's income come from labor (wages) or does it come from property (rent, interest, or profits)? If this fact is known, a good guess can be made about his income bracket.

Almost all the bottom 59.4 percent of families in 1966, those with less than the "moderate but adequate" budget, were working-class families, and most of their income came from wages and salaries earned by their labor. But most of the income of the top 2 percent came from ownership of property in the form of rent, interest, or profit—in short, the income of the capitalist class. Moreover, the very, very rich elite in 1966 (those few taxpayers whose incomes exceeded $200,000) collected 23 percent of all dividends and 37 percent of all capital gains. Fully 90 percent of the income in that top tax bracket was from property, and only 10 percent was from wages and salaries.[5]

[5] U.S. Internal Revenue Service, *Statistics of Income, 1966: Individual Income Tax Returns* (Washington, D.C.: U.S. Government Printing Office, 1968).

Privately held wealth (the total that someone owns at a given time) is even more concentrated than current income. In 1953, three American academic economists estimated that only 0.2 percent of "spending units" (i.e., 1 in 500 individuals or families reporting to the Internal Revenue Service) owned 65 to 71 percent of all publicly held stock.[6] In 1956, according to another conservatively calculated estimate, one-fourth of all U.S. privately held wealth was owned by only 0.5 percent of all Americans, and just 1.6 percent of the people held 32 percent of the wealth, including 82 percent of all stock.[7]

Notice the cumulative and self-reinforcing nature of the concentration of wealth and income. High concentration of stock ownership leads to a high concentration of income from profits. This income is so concentrated that its recipients are in the highest income brackets. But it is only these highest income brackets that are willing and able to save significant amounts. Therefore, they are the ones who make large investments, thus increasing their stock ownership. In other words, large ownership of stock leads to high income in the form of profits, but high income leads to more stock ownership.

The process of wealth and income concentration is self-reinforcing in other ways. For example, one vital prerequisite of upward mobility is education. But many careful studies have revealed that in a large percentage of cases, "the father's income rather than the boy's brains determines who shall be college trained."[8] If you are poor, it is hard to support yourself through college even if you are of average intelligence. If you are rich but not bright enough to get into top universities, you can always find some private university willing to accept you for enough money.

Even with an education, though, the poor man can attempt to work his way up in business only from the point at which he is hired. The rich heir to a business may have little education and less intelligence, but may still step into his father's shoes if he controls enough stock in the corporation. "It is very difficult to climb to the top. . . . It is easier and much safer to be born there."[9] In fact, many of the wealthy today merely inherited a great deal of stock. From 1900 to 1950, some 70 percent of the fathers of the very rich were big businessmen.[10] It is true that most of the very rich have "worked" as big business-

[6] Keith Butters, Lawrence Thompson, and Lynn Bollinger, *Effect of Taxation on Investments by Individuals* (Cambridge, Mass.: The Riverside Press, 1953), p. 400.

[7] Robert Lampman, *The Share of Top Wealth-Holders in National Wealth* (Princeton, N.J.: Princeton University Press, 1962), p. 24.

[8] C. Wright Mills, *White Collar* (New York: Oxford University Press, 1956), p. 257. For precise data, see chapter 19.

[9] C. Wright Mills, *The Power Elite* (New York: Oxford University Press, 1959), p. 115.

[10] Ibid., p. 105.

men; nevertheless, completely at-leisure coupon clippers increased from 14 percent of the very rich in 1900 to 26 percent by 1950.[11]

There has also been a long-run trend toward less self-employment, with more people simply employees of businessmen. In 1800, perhaps 80 percent of the occupied population were self-employed entrepreneurs.[12] By 1870, the figure had fallen to 33 percent, and by 1940, to 20 percent. This self-employed category includes all businessmen (big and small), all farmers (big and small), and all independent professionals. The percentage of those whose incomes came mostly from work for others thus rose from about 20 percent of the occupied population in 1800, to 67 percent in 1870, to 80 percent in 1940. This trend has continued in recent years.

theories of income distribution

Adam Smith talked about *rent* going to the owners of land, *wages* going to labor, and *profits* going to the owners of capital. What determines the share of each of these types of income in the net national income? Economists' answers to this fundamental question differ greatly according to their basic world views. In fact, there are really two closely related questions: (1) What determines the share of each type of income? (2) Is the present distribution of income among different types good or bad?

To simplify the question, in this chapter we shall ignore the rent of land. In the modern United States and most industrialized economies, it is a very small category and thus not essential to the argument. That leaves two of Smith's categories: wages and profits. We define *wages* to mean all labor income, including time and piece wages, monthly salaries, commissions, bonuses, and managerial salaries. We define *profits* to mean all the return on capital. For the purposes of this argument, profits are included both as the return on the entrepreneur's own capital (*dividends*), and the return on borrowed capital (*interest*). For other purposes in later chapters, it will be necessary to distinguish these two forms of profits. *Capital* is the factories, machinery, raw materials, and money with which production and commerce are conducted.

In discussing how income is distributed between wages and profits, economists have advanced two distinct and opposing views. The conservative view has generally dominated and is still taught as

[11] Ibid., p. 108.

[12] For this estimate and other facts in this paragraph, see Mills, *White Collar,* op. cit., pp. 63–64.

gospel in most American textbooks. According to it, (1) profits result from the sacrifices and productivity of capitalists (as wages result from the labor of workers), and (2) therefore the present distribution of income, in which many high incomes are made from profits, is just and equitable. The radical view has been advocated for at least 150 years, but it is just now gaining prominence in the United States. According to it, (1) capitalists are unproductive and extract their profits from the product of labor, and (2) therefore we need a new economic system in which private profit is eliminated.

THE CONSERVATIVE THEORY

The concept of profit as the reward to a capitalist for abstaining from immediate consumption was developed in the early nineteenth - century by the economists W. Senior and J. B. Say. Each argued that provision of capital for production is a subjective cost, or disutility. The capitalist practices abstinence from consumption in order to invest capital and therefore is morally justified in making a profit from his investment. Similarly, wages result from subjective unpleasantness, or disutility, in providing labor.

In the 1870s, Alfred Marshall[13] substituted the word *waiting* for *abstinence.* He argued that when the capitalist invests his capital in production, he must *wait* to get the return from it until a future date. And the fact that he must wait to use all his wealth for consumption justifies his making a profit. Indeed, because he will not invest otherwise, a normal profit is simply a necessary cost of production.

The modern conservative theory of marginal productivity first appeared in full detail in John Bates Clark's *The Distribution of Wealth,* published in 1899.[14] It is dedicated to the propositions that workers and capitalists each receive in income exactly what they contribute as their marginal product and that this is an ethically just system. In other words, a worker's wage will just equal the additional (or marginal) product he adds to output. Likewise, the capitalist's profit will just equal the additional (or marginal) amount of product added by the piece of capital he adds to the productive process. This theory is "gospel" in all conservative textbooks, among them Paul Samuelson's famous work.[15]

The theory of marginal productivity is basically a very simple argument. Assume that there is a fixed amount of capital—that is, a particular factory and machinery. How many workers should be added by the rational capitalist to maximize his profits? Assume

[13] See Alfred Marshall, *Principles of Economics* (New York: Macmillan, 1953 [first ed., 1890]).

[14] John Bates Clark, *The Distribution of Wealth* (New York: Augustus Kelley, 1966 [first published in 1899]).

[15] Paul Samuelson, *Economics* (8th ed.; New York: McGraw-Hill, 1970 [first published in 1948]).

TABLE 15.2

NUMBER OF MACHINES	NUMBER OF WORKERS	TOTAL PRODUCT PER WEEK	MARGINAL PRODUCT PER WEEK
5	10	$1,000	$90
5	11	1,090	80
5	12	1,170	70
5	13	1,240	

next that each additional worker adds something to the product, but that each additional worker adds less than the one before him. This is the case because there is a fixed number of machines for them to use; therefore, workers can add very little beyond the optimum capacity of the given factory. Suppose that there are five machines and ten workers and that most efficient functioning requires two workers per machine. Table 15.2 demonstrates the contribution to the marginal product of additional workers in this hypothetical factory.

The capitalist should continue to add workers until he finds that the last worker's product just equals his cost, or wage. If the wage rate is $70 a week, he should hire only 13 workers (or just 12). Because the thirteenth worker makes no additional profit for the capitalist he should hire no more workers. The wage will just equal the additional (or marginal) product of the last worker.

Notice that what this theory has arrived at is a rule for capitalists to follow if they wish to maximize profits. If they do act this way (and they usually do), then the assertion that the wage is the same as the marginal product is at best a platitude: Workers are not hired if they produce a lower marginal product. This is simply because by hiring additional workers profits would be reduced. But some conservatives believe that they have thereby proven that this is a just and ethical distribution of income.

The conservative theory does exactly the same thing for profits. Assume that the capitalist employs a fixed number of workers. How much new machinery should he add? Suppose that each machine adds less than the one before it. This is the case because there is a fixed number of workers; therefore, additional machines cannot be used efficiently. Even if the capitalist could enforce a speed-up, 100 workers could not handle 1,000 machines. Stated with these rigid assumptions, the theory of diminishing marginal productivity is likewise a truism. But in the real world, the capitalist adds both workers and machines and new technology to boot, so there may be no diminishing productivity.

In this simple example, however, each additional machine adds less to the product than the previous machine (because workers and perhaps factory space are limited). Thus, the capitalist should add machines until the additional product of one more machine will just equal its cost. Beyond that point, more machines give no more profit, so no more machines should be bought. Therefore, the cost of providing an additional machine (whether out of the capitalist's own capital or from borrowed capital) will just equal the value of its additional (or marginal) product. Conservatives conclude that what is paid to capital is *its own* marginal product and that profits are a necessary cost of production and may be ethically justified.

Of course, this argument applies only under pure competition. Even Samuelson's conservative text agrees that *extra profits* (beyond the marginal product of capital) *are made under monopoly* to the degree that monopoly power controls the market. (This point is emphasized in Chapters 16, 17, and 18.)

RADICAL CRITIQUE OF
MARGINAL-PRODUCTIVITY THEORY

It is important to give the devil his due. Samuelson's conservative argument does show that marginal-productivity theory provides a general notion of how to allocate resources. It tells the capitalist to keep hiring workers (or adding machines) as long as they produce extra profit. When the additional profit approaches zero (because the additional product drops down to the cost level), then the capitalist should stop adding workers (or machines).

Samuelson also shows that these are useful rules even for socialist planners to follow in allocating resources among investment projects. They must "introduce first those investment projects with the higher net productivity,"[16] and use every additional worker and every additional machine in each project up to the point at which an additional unit would cost more than it adds to the product. In relation to the allocation of capital (factories and machines), this means that socialist planners must use something like a profit or interest rate to calculate which projects will bring the most return to society and which have returns too low to invest in.

Finally, Samuelson quietly adds a point about interest, or profits, under socialist planning that should be loudly and repeatedly stressed: "But, of course, no one necessarily receives interest income from them."[17] In other words, a planned socialist economy would have to calculate rates of return on different uses of capital to decide where to allocate it, *but it would not have to distribute any of these returns as income to any individual.*

[16] Samuelson, op. cit., p. 580.
[17] Ibid.

We are concerned here, however, with the issue of how a capitalist system distributes income to individuals and groups. In relation to income distribution, radicals have attacked the marginal-productivity theory on several levels. They claim (1) that it is a tautology, (2) that it cannot really be measured, and (3) that it confuses the productivity of capital and the productivity of the capitalist.

On the first level, it was indicated earlier that, given its assumptions, the analytic conclusions of marginal productivity follow practically by definition (but not its political–ethical conclusions). If it is assumed that the capitalist always acts to maximize profit, then he will never hire an additional worker who would cost more than he produces. He will only keep hiring workers who produce a surplus above their wages. If the product of the last worker hired is defined to be the marginal product, then it follows that his wage must be equal to that, neither more nor less. Similarly, a unit of capital will be utilized only if the additional product from its use equals the additional cost of its use. Given the assumption of profit maximization, these are tautologies in the sense that the conclusions are hidden in the definitions. But, of course, such tautologies tell us little or nothing of the real world and do not automatically lead to *any* policy conclusions.

Certainly, in any society, it may be correct to allocate machines so that the return, or profit from adding one more machine to production equals its cost. But this useful rule does not prove that it is necessary to have a society in which private capitalists provide the money to buy the machines. Nor does it prove that the capitalist's profit is justified even if it equals the marginal product of capital. This theory provides a particular description of the process of allocation of capital, but it represents no advance beyond older ethical justifications of profit income in terms of the capitalist's abstinence or waiting. (Incidentally, these older theories have long been ridiculed by radicals on the grounds that the capitalist makes very little sacrifice in abstaining from consuming his whole income or waiting for his profit return. Should we sympathize with the sacrifice of a fellow who sits on his yacht and decides to invest 50 percent of his $1-million income rather than consume it all?)

The second radical criticism is that the marginal-productivity theory is unrealistic because it does not refer to anything measurable. What is meant by a *unit of capital*? If it means a particular machine, of what relevance is theorizing about transferring it to a more productive use? Particular machines are designed to do particular jobs. If we find that a marginal product is less than its cost in an industry, how can the machine be moved to another industry? It is not designed for other work. Furthermore, the theory assumes that small units of capital can be added or subtracted at the margin. But most machines represent very considerable investments; they are not infinitely divisible.

Third, even admitting that the theory offers insights about how capitalists should invest and that it has some roughly definable meaning, still it pertains only to the production contributions of labor and physical *capital*. It says nothing about the capitalist's contribution. This is probably the most important point of criticism. Radicals admit that a machine may increase production, that workers need them, and that they increase the worker's productivity. In that sense, Samuelson is right to say that "capital" has a "net productivity." But it is the physical capital that is productive (jointly with the worker), *not* the capitalist. The capitalist owns the capital, but he is not himself the machine. The machine does the work (with the worker); the capitalist gets the profit.

Radicals agree that machines are a necessary, or "productive," part of the physical productive process; they would even agree to the importance of managerial labor. Radicals argue, however, that this productivity of physical capital goods (created by another labor process in the past) is significantly different from the capitalist owners' ability to capture a certain portion of the product as interest or profit. "It is, of course, true that materials and machinery can be said to be physically productive in the sense that labor working with them can turn out a larger product than labor working without them, but physical productivity in this sense must under no circumstances be confused with value productivity."[18] In other words, "Under capitalism 'the productiveness of labor is made to ripen, as if in a hothouse.' Whether we choose to say that capital is productive, or that capital is necessary to make labor productive, is not a matter of much importance. . . . What is important is to say that owning capital is not a productive activity."[19] This is clear in the case of a mere coupon clipper (as most stockholders are today). The fact that some capitalists may otherwise perform productive labor through their own managerial work is not in contradiction to the fact that they also make money by mere ownership of capital.

THE RADICAL THEORY

Inspired intially by Karl Marx's views, the radical analysis of income distribution argues first that the labor of humanity operating on nature is the ultimate source of all production. And radical interpretations of profit and wages emphasize the sociological facts that *the capitalist*

[18] Paul Sweezy, *The Theory of Capitalist Development* (New York: Oxford University Press, 1943), p 61.

[19] Joan Robinson, *An Essay on Marxian Economics* (New York: St. Martin's Press, 1960), p. 18.

class owns all of the productive facilities and resources, while the working class owns only its own labor power. Assuming these institutional conditions, the capitalists *must* be paid a profit or they will not invest their capital. Because the capitalists own the resources and productive facilities, they receive a large share of national income while putting forth no effort (or, as Marx phrased it, under these conditions, they are able to extract, or "exploit," this profit from the workers' product).

This theory is not a quantitative economic theory of prices and wages, but primarily a historical statement of the political-economic relationships of capitalism. Profit is traced not to a single "cause," but to the functioning of the capitalist economy as a whole within the given class and institutional framework. Profits are viewed as the residual product after wages are paid.

It is a fact that the average worker produces far more in a day than he is paid in wages and that the rest of the net product goes to the capitalist. The practical problem is to explain why long-run wages remain at a level that does not eat up the profits of capital. In empirical terms, there was an amazing degree of agreement concerning the wage level among nineteenth-century economists. It is Marshall, not Marx, who stated: "If the economic conditions of the country remain stationary sufficiently long, . . . human beings would earn generally an amount that corresponded fairly well with their cost of rearing and training, conventional necessaries as well as those things which are strictly necessary being reckoned for."[20] In other words, the long-run price of labor power is the cost of "producing" the worker (with given traditions and under present cultural conditions).

Some evidence that wages in the United States are still set at or below the cost of subsistence of the workers is the fact that the one-third of family units with the lowest incomes go into debt in an average year. For wage workers as a whole, it may be claimed that the debts of some just about equal the savings of others. As noted previously, most workers' families earn less than the BLS "modest but adequate" budget. Thus, it is true that in the long run, 95 to 100 percent of wages ordinarily must be devoted to consumption spending.[21] To this extent, Marx's theory of wages at "subsistence according to the cultural standard of the country" is proven. Admittedly, however, the "cultural standard" is always rising, so that the average American wage is not what the rest of the world would normally consider a "subsistence" wage.

20 Marshall, op. cit., p. 577.

21 See Milton Friedman, *A Theory of the Consumption Function* (Princeton, N.J.: Princeton University Press, 1957), pp. 69–79.

Modern radical criticism is concerned, not with physical subsistence theories, but with the fact that workers' wages *are* less than the total product they produce. Radicals do not deny that as workers' productivity and total product have risen, wages have risen very significantly over the last 100 years. (Whether the *share* of wages in national income has remained constant or fallen is a controversial point among economic statisticians.) But profits have risen spectacularly and still grab a large part of the product. Compared with the very high incomes of profit recipients, workers' wages are low. (And, of necessity, workers still consume most or all of their income and save very little.)

Disagreement among economists has centered on the question of *why* the long-run wage level remains this low. Why do wages not rise to the point at which workers have the entire net product and there are no profits? To answer this question we must examine the factors of supply and demand on either side of the labor market.

On the supply side, the number of workers available at the going wage depends on the amount of population, on the laws (such as those about child labor and retirement benefits), and on sociological attitudes (such as those toward women working). Laws and basic attitudes about work change very slowly, so it may be assumed they are constant. The classical economists, such as Malthus, emphasized the effects of population on wages. High wages would lead to more births and more survivals, and as population increased so would the supply of workers, which would hold down wages. Radicals have, for the most part, rejected population as a factor of prime importance in wage determination because (1) human beings do not react so directly to changes in income (at least, above the starvation level), and (2) population levels change slowly, whereas wage rates change fairly often and rapidly.

On the demand side, the marginal-productivity theory correctly concludes that demand for labor is much affected by technological change which may substitute machines for workers. But technology also changes fairly slowly, and thus this factor does not exert a significant effect on wages. The theory may, to some extent, help explain long-run changes in wages, but it is of no help at all in understanding, for example, why wages decline in a depression.

Many radical economists believe that it is most important to examine the overall demand for goods in the economy because that is the main determinant of the demand for labor. Workers are hired only while the capitalist expects to sell the goods they produce. When the overall, or aggregate, demand for goods is less than the supply in the market, production declines and workers are unemployed. Unemployment means that capitalists can set lower wages because workers compete for jobs. *Unemployment is the strongest factor holding down wages.*

The unemployment may be traced to lack of aggregate demand for goods (although it may be aggravated in the long run by a shift to machinery in the production of the goods). The reasons for lack of demand are very complex and will be discussed in the chapters concerned with depressions and unemployment. It should be noted here, however, that this theory means both that aggregate demand largely determines wages and that wages (or the distribution of income) help determine aggregate demand. It is a circular process in which (1) workers are unemployed because there is not enough demand for the goods they produce, but (2) there is not enough demand for goods partly because many workers are unemployed. In other words, demand itself is dependent partly on total income and partly on the distribution of income (because the poor must spend a much larger percentage of their income than the rich just to stay at minimum consumption levels).

Beyond the aggregate factors that determine the demand for workers, radicals emphasize that this is a world of monopoly, not pure competition. It will be seen that within the broad limits allowed by aggregate supply and demand, the wage rate represents a bargain, between labor and capital, which is directly influenced by their relative power. On the one side stands the enormous economic and political power of the largest corporations. On the other side stand the vast numbers of workers, some unorganized and powerless, some organized into unions with a small amount of power. In Chapter 16, we begin the analysis of monopoly, eventually returning to its effects on wages. The immense impact of the government on the struggle over income distribution will be considered in Chapter 19.

tentative conclusions

Of course, many of these factors are recognized to a small extent by neoclassical economists, and many more are recognized by the liberal wing of Keynesian economists. Thus, all economists share in a slight measure of agreement on *how* wages are determined, at least about broad analytic outlines, but they disagree, often violently, over the importance of different factors. When it comes to an interpretation of the facts, the conservatives still believe that profits are justified. They talk about the productivity of capital, and they claim that capitalists must be paid profits or else they will not *abstain* from consumption and will not *wait* for their returns from investment. This position is, of course, supported by all capitalists and their sympathizers.

The political or ethical view of the radicals is that profits are unjustified. They argue that capitalists merely own capital, but that they themselves produce nothing. They use their monopoly of capital to *exploit* the workers by taking some of the workers' product as profits. In this view, *any* profits are bad. This stand is endorsed by many workers and by those radicals who sympathize with the workers' view.

It could be said that both sides are "merely" emphasizing different aspects of the same reality—or those aspects of reality consonant with their own conclusions. And it could be said that to some degree most choose according to their own interests. Even among economists, those who most loudly claim to be objective usually turn out to be the most partisan advocates when their masks are removed.

summary

There still exists a great deal of poverty in America. Moreover, distribution of U.S. income is very unequal. Most of the income of the rich is profit income; most of the income of the vast majority of the nonrich and poor is wage income.

According to marginal-productivity theory, workers receive the marginal product of labor and capitalists receive the marginal product of capital. This conservative theory tries to justify the present distribution of income. Critics admit that it says something about allocating labor and capital to different industries. But they claim that in relation to income distribution, it explains nothing, is unrealistic and refers to nothing measurable, and confuses the product of capital with the product of the capitalist.

According to radical theory, workers produce the whole product, but capitalists expropriate part of it in profits (by means of their control of all the resources and productive facilities). Radicals argue that private profits should be abolished and that resources and productive facilities should be taken from the small minority of capitalists and placed under the democratic control of the whole public.

chapter 16
pure competition and monopoly

In this chapter, we wish to explore in detail how a firm maximizes its profit. Profit is the difference between revenue (or sales proceeds) and costs. The revenue a firm gets in a given supply-and-demand situation depends on how much competition it faces in its industry.

An *industry* is the total of all firms selling a particular product. Thus, when we speak of the steel industry or the automobile industry, we are referring to all the individual business firms producing steel or automobiles. Industries fall within one of four categories: pure competition, monopolistic competition, oligopoly, and monopoly.

market structures and the degree of competition

A *purely competitive industry* is one in which four essential conditions are present. (1) The industry is made up of a very large number of firms, and there are also a large number of buyers of the product they sell. (2) Each seller supplies so small a percentage of the market that its actions have virtually no effect on the price at which the industry sells the product, and each buyer demands so small a percentage of output that his purchases alone also have virtually no effect on the price at which the industry sells the product. (3) It is very easy for new firms to get into the industry or for old firms to leave it. (4) Each firm produces a product that is so nearly identical to the product of the other firms that consumers are largely indifferent about which firm within the industry produced the product they buy.

A *monopoly* exists when there is only one seller of a product that has no close substitutes. In a monopolistic industry, one firm *is* the industry. If the monopolist's position is to be maintained, he must erect barriers that prevent competitors from entering the industry. If he is successful in doing this, the payoff is generally very large. Because he has complete control over the price of his product (within the limits set by the demand schedule), he can set the price at the level that will maximize profits.

Between the extremes of pure competition and monopoly, economists make two further classifications. Closer to pure competition is *monopolistic competition.* A monopolistically competitive industry has a large number of small sellers who engage in some slight amount of *product differentiation* (perhaps a seller packages his product more attractively or gives friendlier service), so that some consumers prefer one or another particular seller's product. For this reason, firms have a small degree of control over price, and a firm cannot enter the industry as easily as it can enter a purely competitive industry.

Closer to a monopoly (and often tantamount to monopoly) is an *oligopoly.* An oligopolistic industry has a few giant sellers each of whom controls a significant share of the market. Entry into an oligopolistic industry is very difficult, often as difficult as into a monopolistic industry. There is generally, but not always, some product differentiation. The most significant feature of an oligopoly is the fact that, because of their interdependence, no firm can make significant changes in price without reckoning with the reactions of its competitors.

In this chapter, we discuss the profit-maximizing behavior of a firm in a purely competitive industry and a firm under conditions of monopoly. Profit-maximizing behavior of monopolistically competitive firms and oligopolistic firms will be examined in Chapter 17.

demand and price for a purely competitive firm

For a whole industry, a larger amount can be sold *only* at a lower price (or lower average revenue). This is *not* the case for a single competitive firm. *In a purely competitive industry, each firm is so small that whatever quantity it chooses to sell will have a negligible*

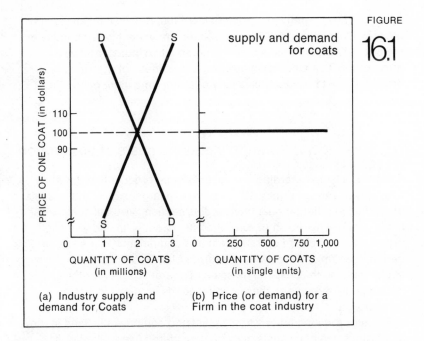

FIGURE

16.1

supply and demand for coats

(a) Industry supply and demand for Coats

(b) Price (or demand) for a Firm in the coat industry

effect on the supply for the entire industry. Therefore it can sell all that it wishes at the going price.

The situation for both a purely competitive industry and one firm within that industry is demonstrated graphically in Figure 16.1. Figure 16.1(a) shows the supply and demand for coats, *which is assumed to be a purely competitive industry.* Figure 16.1(b) shows the price (or demand curve, since they are the same in this case) for the individual coat-making firm.

The price of a coat ($100) is determined in the industrywide market for coats by the intersection of the industry supply and demand curves. The graph shows that *at this price, the individual firm can sell any quantity it wishes.* Because it has been assumed that the individual firm cannot affect supply for the entire industry, and because the market demand is equal to the industry's supply at the prevailing price ($100), the firm never experiences any problem in selling all it wishes to sell at this price.

Therefore, the demand curve for the individual firm's output is a horizontal line at the industry-determined price. The firm sells any quantity it chooses at this price. Assume that it decides to raise its price in order to increase its revenue. Because the firms in a purely competitive industry all produce an identical product, no consumer will pay more than $100 for one firm's product when he can buy an identical product from a competitor for $100. Similarly, the firm will never sell any quantity at a price below $100. Because it can sell any quantity it chooses at $100 there would be no incentive for it to lower the price. Thus, the firm in a purely competitive industry faces a given price; it cannot vary it upward, and it does not wish to vary it downward (but the situation is very different for a monopoly).

supply and the costs of production

A firm's decision regarding the quantity of its product that it wishes to supply at various prices will depend, to a large extent, on the costs of producing different quantities. In this section, we shall analyze the firm's cost during the short run, when its output is limited to the productive capacity of current plant and equipment. Over a longer period, the firm could construct a larger plant and install new equipment and thus expand its scale of operations, but for the shorter period considered here, these capital goods are fixed in size and number.

Because the amount of a firm's plant and equipment is fixed in the short run, some of its costs must be considered fixed, whether it produces nothing or operates at capacity. *Fixed costs* include the costs of maintaining plant and equipment, rent, and costs of watchmen and guards, and others. Obviously, if the firm produces more goods, then the *average* fixed cost will decline because the same cost is spread over, or divided by, more units.

The average cost of production per unit (total cost divided by the quantity produced) does *not* continuously decline, however, but rises after some point. To understand this relationship, we must examine other kinds of costs. Even during the short run, some costs—notably, the costs of labor and material—are variable. The firm can produce more or less of its product by hiring more or fewer workers and using more or less raw materials.

The *average* variable cost for a unit of output is obtained by taking the total costs of labor and raw materials and dividing it by the quantity produced. If one laborer combined with a given amount of raw materials produced ten coats, and if each additional laborer combined with the same amount of raw materials continued to produce ten coats, then the average variable cost per unit produced would remain the same regardless of the amount the firm produced. The average variable cost curve would be a straight horizontal line showing that the quantity of coats produced had no effect on its magnitude.

This situation does not obtain in most types of productive processes. Generally, the firm's plant and equipment have been designed and constructed to operate most effectively at a particular level of output. The production of a single commodity usually involves numerous productive processes, which occur at different rates and are difficult to coordinate. For maximum efficiency, no single process should be halted or stopped because it is outstripping the other processes; nor should other processes be stopped because this process cannot keep pace.

After engineers have calculated the various rates at which different productive processes will take place, the plant is constructed and equipped in such a way that there is some *optimal* level of production at which all productive processes can be effectively coordinated. Average variable costs are lowest at the optimum level of production, but are higher below *and* above that level. Because average fixed costs fall continuously, the total result is that cost per unit (average cost, *including variable and fixed costs*) may fall rapidly at first and continue to fall until the optimal point is achieved; then average cost may slowly rise. This usual short-run behavior of average costs (a U-shaped curve) is illustrated in Figure 16.2.

According to Figure 16.2, the quantity of 1,000 coats is the production level at which all production processes are most effectively coordinated and plant and equipment are most efficiently utilized (the cost is only $75 per coat). At smaller quantities, bottlenecks occur and some equipment is *underutilized,* and consequently, average costs are higher. At larger quantities, plant and equipment are being *overutilized* and various bottlenecks and inefficiencies are encountered, and consequently, average costs are higher. The farther a firm gets from the optimally efficient quantity

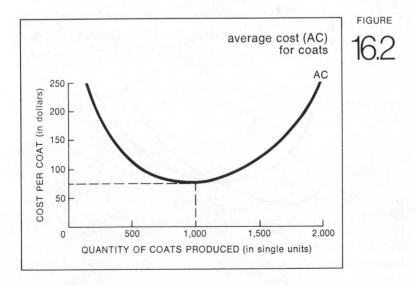

FIGURE

16.2

average cost (AC) for coats

(1,000 coats in this case), the higher its average costs are. This is true whether the firm produces quantities smaller or larger than the optimal amount.

Because it is the basis of the supply curve, marginal cost is even more important than the average cost. *Marginal cost* is defined as follows:

$$\text{Marginal cost} = \frac{\text{increase in total cost}}{\text{increase in quantity}}$$

Because we may speak of decrease as well as increase, we may substitute the word *change* for *increase* in the definition to make it more general.

In the example of Figure 16.3, marginal cost represents the increase in total costs of production attributable to an increase in output of one additional coat. If the change in cost attributable to producing one more coat is *lower* than the average cost of producing the product, then it may be said that the lower marginal cost is pulling the average variable cost downward. This is similar to the case of a person taking several tests. The last test score pulls the average score up or down depending on whether it is higher or lower than the average. Thus, it is possible to conclude that as long as the average cost is declining, the marginal cost must be below it. When the average cost is rising, the marginal cost must be above it, pulling it upward. These relations between the average and marginal cost are illustrated in Figure 16.3.

Notice that at low production levels, those at which each additional

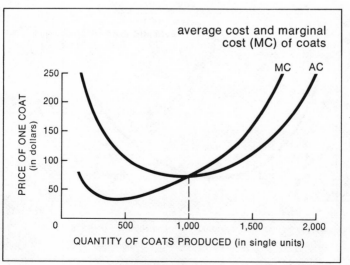

average cost and marginal cost (MC) of coats

FIGURE

16.3

coat is produced at less cost, marginal cost is very low (only $25 at 500 coats) and is well below the average. But at production beyond the optimal capacity, when the average cost of producing coats is rising, marginal cost rises rapidly to a high level ($150 at 1,500 coats), and goes farther and farther above the average.

These mechanical relations may be summarized as follows: (1) Average cost is at its minimum point when it is equal to marginal cost. (2) When marginal cost is below average cost, it is pulling average cost downward. (3) When marginal cost is above average cost, it is pulling average cost up.

clarifying the meaning of costs

Two more points relating to the traditional (neoclassical) economist's treatment of costs must be clarified. The economist's concept of costs differs from the accountant's definition of the term. For the accountant, a cost must involve a monetary outlay. In other words, he records costs only when money changes hands. Economists include two types of costs in their analyses: explicit costs and implicit, or imputed, costs. *Explicit costs* are the accountant's costs; *Implicit costs* include those that the company's owner would have to pay *if* he owned no capital and did none of the work himself. Thus, a normal (or socially defined average) rate of return on the owner's capital and a normal wage for the labor he performs are counted among implicit costs.

Assume, for example, that a man saves $20,000 and opens a service station. During the first year, his accountant calculates that his total revenue was $32,000 and his costs were $22,000. The accountant informs him that he has made a profit of $10,000. A traditional economist would assess his costs differently. Suppose the owner worked 60 hours every week, and that it would have cost him $3 per hour to hire a man to do this work. In addition to this, if the owner had invested his money in safe bonds he could have earned 6 percent on these bonds. The economist would add the imputed wage of $9,360 and the imputed foregone interest on bonds of $1,200, and inform the owner that he had registered a loss of $560 rather than a profit of $10,000.

For neoclassical economists *profits* means only excess profits— that is, they are excess over all explicit *and* implicit costs, *including* a normal or average profit. Although this definition is useful in one way, it has a very conservative bias in another sense.

It is useful in that the capitalist *does* require the bribe of an average rate of profit to get him to use his capital in production. He usually

considers normal and necessary the rate that has been the average
for the last few years. Thus, only if an average profit is included with
costs can it be said that supply behavior is completely determined
by costs. This definition is employed here because it is convenient to
be able to say, in agreement with all current economics books, that
in pure competition the supply curve is identical with the marginal
cost curve—this point is examined on p. 240.

The neoclassical definition of costs sneaks in the idea that the
capitalist *deserves* to receive an average profit as a cost of providing
capital for production. It is true that physical capital goods are
necessary for production, that in any society limited capital goods
must be allocated to maximize returns, and that allocation is a social
cost because it means other areas cannot use those capital goods. It
is also true that *given a private-enterprise system,* the capitalist
entrepreneur must be bribed with the average profit to get him to
furnish his capital. It was shown in Chapter 15, however, that the
productivity of capital goods implies neither that the capitalist is
productive nor that he deserves his profit. In other words, a socialist
society would provide capital to itself out of public funds; it would
consider provision of capital a cost of production; and it would
calculate rates of profit in each industry to decide where to allocate
capital (see Chapter 34). But a socialist society would not pay the
profits to any private individual.

There is only one other point essential to make in this discussion
of costs. Total cost can be shown quite easily on the graph of per-unit
costs. Because the average cost is the total cost divided by the
quantity produced, it follows that total cost is given by the product of
average cost multiplied by the quantity produced. In Figure 16.4, total

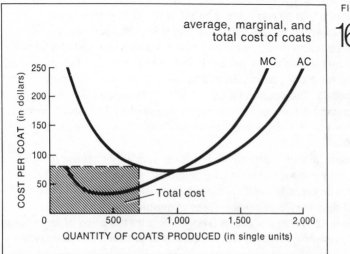

FIGURE

16.4

average, marginal, and
total cost of coats

cost is shown as a shaded rectangle. Taking any quantity (for
example, 700 coats in Figure 16.4), we go up to the average cost
curve and then over to the cost axis of the graph. Here, the average
cost per unit required to produce 700 coats is found: $80. We know
that the total cost will equal 700 × $80. But because line 0-to-700 and
line $0-to-$80 are adjacent sides of a rectangle, their product is equal
to the area of the rectangle. Therefore, the shaded rectangle in
Figure 16.4 represents the total cost of producing 700 coats: 700 ×
$80 = $56,000.

maximum profit under competition

In an earlier section, it was shown that once the price of the industry's
product is determined, then the individual competitive firm faces a
demand curve (or a given price) that is a straight horizontal line. It
also is assumed that each firm has the U-shaped average cost curve
described above. In Figure 16.5 the demand curve has been
superimposed on the cost curves in order to present the whole
picture for the competitive firm.
    In order to understand the firm's reaction to the market price ($100),
it is necessary to ascertain what motivates the firm's owners (or
managers). The answer provided by the vast majority of economists,
from Adam Smith to the present, is that the one overriding objective
of all capitalists, or their managers, is to maximize their profits. We
accept this answer provisionally and treat each firm as a profit
maximizer.

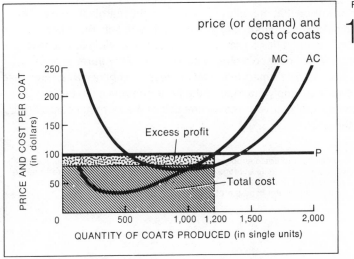

FIGURE

16.5

price (or demand) and
cost of coats

The manager whose cost and revenue curves are pictured in Figure 16.5 will maximize his profits by producing and selling 1,200 coats. At this quantity, the firm's marginal cost is equal to its price. The rule for maximizing profit under competition is to produce the quantity *that equates marginal cost and price.* There are two shaded rectangles in Figure 16.5. The combined area of the rectangles is equal to the firm's total income from sales or revenue (because it represents the price times the quantity that the firm sells). The area of the lower rectangle is equal to the firm's total cost (because it is the product of the firm's average cost times the quantity it produces). The area of the upper rectangle is equal to the firm's profit (because it represents total revenue minus total costs, which is, by definition, profit).

In order to understand why 1,200 coats in Figure 16.5 is the quantity that maximizes the firm's profit, imagine that the firm produces and sells a smaller quantity of the product. For any quantity below 1,200, the firm's price per unit is higher than its marginal cost. Consequently, if the firm produces and sells an additional coat, this last coat will add more to the firm's total revenue than it adds to the total cost. The last coat, therefore, adds to the firm's profit. As long as the firm is producing fewer than 1,200 coats, it can add to its profit by producing and selling more coats.

However, imagine that the firm is producing more than 1,200 coats. For any quantity above 1,200, the firm's marginal cost exceeds its price per unit. If the firm were to produce and sell one less coat, the reduction in its costs would exceed the reduction in its revenue. Its profit would therefore increase. As long as the firm continues to sell more than 1,200 coats, it can add to its profit by producing and selling less. It is now easy to see why the competitive firm maximizes its profit by equating its marginal cost and its price.

For any price that prevails in the market, the marginal-cost curve will indicate what quantity the firm would like to sell. But a line showing the quantities a firm would like to sell at various prices is exactly what we defined a supply curve to be. *Therefore, in pure competition, a firm's marginal-cost curve is its supply curve.*[1] Because the industry is simply the total of the firms comprising it, the industry's supply curve is the summation of the marginal cost curves of all these firms.

[1] Strictly speaking, the firm's supply curve would be only that portion of its marginal-cost curve that lies above its average-variable-cost curve. If the price were to go so low that it would not cover the firm's variable costs of production, then, it is assumed, the firm would not produce at all.

equilibrium for the firm and
the industry in pure competition

In the purely competitive industry, price is determined by the intersection of the industry supply and demand curves. The individual firm adjusts its quantity in order to maximize profit. Figure 16.6(b) shows an individual firm's cost and revenue curves.

In Figure 16.6, the firm and industry are in short-run, but not long-run, equilibrium. The industry is in short-run equilibrium because supply equals demand. The firm is in short-run equilibrium because it is producing at the point where its price and marginal cost are equal. But neither the industry nor the firm is in long-run equilibrium because the firm is making excess profit.

Two points should be made about the firm's excess profit. (1) It is assumed that all firms have access both to the same technology that this firm is using and to inputs of comparable quality. It can be concluded, therefore, that the cost curves of virtually all firms in the industry are nearly identical to those of the firm pictured in Figure 16.6(b). (2) It must be remembered that the firm's cost curves include an imputed cost covering an average return on the owner's capital; thus, normal, or average, profit is included in the cost.

It must be concluded, therefore, that the firms in this industry are making excess profits, or profits above an average return to capital. Because it is easy to enter a purely competitive industry, capitalists who are making only an average profit in other industries will be attracted to this industry by the lure of excess profits.

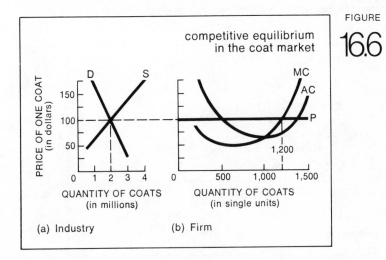

FIGURE
16.6

competitive equilibrium
in the coat market

(a) Industry   (b) Firm

An industry is said to be in long-run equilibrium when there is no tendency for firms either to enter or to leave it. The industry pictured in Figure 16.6 is not in long-run equilibrium because it is earning excess profits and, therefore, new firms will be entering it.

As new firms enter, their additional outputs must be added in order to derive the industry's new supply curve. This means the supply curve will shift to the right. Figure 16.7 illustrates the original situation depicted in Figure 16.6, but also shows what happens as the supply curve shifts to the right (from the original position, S_1, to a new position, S_2). When the supply curve shifts, it must ultimately shift to S_2. If it stops short of S_2, excess profits will continue and more firms will be attracted, shifting the curve farther to the right until it reaches S_2.

With the greater supply provided by the new firms entering the industry, all excess profits have been eliminated. At the new lower price of $75, the firm reduces its output from 1,200 to 1,000 coats in order to equate its marginal cost with the new price. This lower output maximizes the firm's profits in the new conditions. At that point, however, it is also true that the firm's average cost is just equal to its price per unit. The decline in price from $100 to $75 has eliminated the firm's excess profits (because its average cost is also $75).

With no excess profits, there is no longer any incentive for new firms to enter the industry. The firms within the industry are receiving a normal, or average, rate of return on their capital and labor. Therefore, there is no tendency for firms to leave the industry. It can now be said that when the new supply curve results in the establishment of a new price equal to the long-run average cost of each firm, then the industry is in long-run equilibrium because the number of firms within the industry has been stabilized.

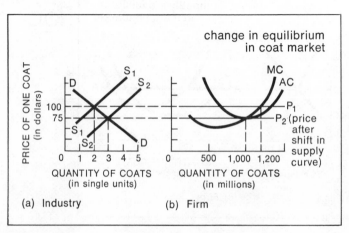

FIGURE

16.7

change in equilibrium in coat market

(a) Industry

(b) Firm

Thus, when both the individual firms and the purely competitive industry are in long-run equilibrium, the following equality holds for each firm:

Price = marginal cost = average cost

The fact that price equals marginal cost indicates that the firm is satisfied that its current level of output is the most profitable for it. The fact that price equals average cost indicates that there will be no tendency for firms either to enter or to leave the industry (because the average cost includes just an average rate of profit).

relevance of the competitive model

The reader has probably wondered which industries in the contemporary American economy are purely competitive. Only one or two industries (out of many thousands) in the entire American economy present a factual resemblance to the model just worked through.

The most obvious choice of a purely competitive industry might be from agriculture. Traditionally, in the wheat industry, for example, each farmer produced a homogeneous product and no farmer produced enough to affect the price significantly. Each would take as given the price determined in the market. Whether he sold all or none of his crop at this price was virtually irrelevant to the determination of price.

Over the past several decades, however, two important changes have occurred in agricultural markets. (1) The government has extensively intervened in the market through various schemes of subsidies and production controls. (2) The agricultural industry increasingly has been coming under the control of giant corporations which in no way resemble the small, relatively powerless firms pictured in the theory. These two developments have so fundamentally altered the agricultural market that the model of pure competition definitely does not explain or describe it.

Are there any purely competitive industries in the American economy? One or two mineral-resources industries (e.g., the bituminous coal) resemble the model closely enough that the theory may facilitate analysis of the operations of these industries.

If only one or two industries even resemble the model, then a second question must be asked: What is the relevance of this analysis to the American economy of the 1970s? The answer is that such analysis reveals more about the thinking of many economists than it does about the functioning of the economy.

The model of pure competition is the basis of the neoclassical economists' claim that the unencumbered private-enterprise market system results in a situation of optimum production and distributional efficiency (see Chapter 7 for a more complete discussion of neoclassical economics). From the above analysis it can be seen that in pure competition, each firm, in equilibrium, produces the quantity at which its costs are minimized and its production is most efficient. The firm receives only the socially defined normal rate of profit. No excess profits exist. The consumer gets the product at the lowest-possible price. The theory also claims that every factor of production gets the value of what it contributes to production (although the theory says nothing about the inequitable ownership of factors of production that prevails).

Such is the economic ideal for the neoclassical, laissez faire economists: a beautiful, well-ordered, just world. But examination of the contemporary American economy reveals that theirs is a totally illusory world.

A tiny minority of the neoclassical economists have honestly admitted the degree to which reality differs from their ideal.[2] But most persist in arguing that what exists bears a reasonably close resemblance to their model. Thus, the neoclassical analysis generally is used to show that the free-enterprise market economy is the best and most just of all possible worlds. Therefore, the theory of pure competition is studied here primarily to understand the basis of a very important conservative ideology supporting capitalism. (The model of pure competition, in its simplest form, also does provide analytic tools that can be used to study more realistic cases.)

demand and revenue for a monopoly

A *monopoly* exists when a single firm constitutes the entire industry. The firm sells a product for which there are no close substitutes, and potential competitors are prevented by one way or another from entering the industry.

Under competition, the demand curve for a whole industry slopes down and to the right (because the quantity sold increases only when the price falls). The demand curve for a competitive firm, however, is a horizontal straight line (because the firm's output is so small it can sell as much more as it wishes at the same price). A monopoly firm, by definition, is the only seller of a commodity; it *is* the whole industry. Therefore, *the demand curve for a monopoly firm is exactly like the demand curve for a whole competitive industry:* It slopes down and to the right. The monopoly-demand curve shows that unlike the owner of a competitive firm, who faces a given price, the monopolist can *choose* to sell more goods at a lower price or fewer goods at a higher price (he is not a price taker, but a price fixer).

Thus, a market-demand curve shows the maximum revenue per unit of the commodity that a monopolist will receive at any particular level of sales he may choose. When they view it from this seller's standpoint, economists call the demand curve an *average-revenue curve.* It shows the average revenue per unit of the commodity sold for any level of sales.

Figure 16.8 shows a demand curve for a monopolized commodity, say, aluminum [for many years the Aluminum Company of America (ALCOA) had a pure monopoly of aluminum]. It can be labeled a demand curve *or* an average-revenue curve. The curve in Figure 16.8 is labeled "demand = average revenue" to underscore this equivalence. At $1,000 a ton, consumers wish to purchase 10 million tons. Alternatively, if the monopolist wishes to sell 10 million tons, then $1,000 is the maximum price he can charge.

When ALCOA (assumed here to be a pure monopoly) decreases the price of aluminum and, hence, increases its sales of aluminum, two separate effects result in change in its total revenue: (1) the *quantity effect,* and (2) the *price effect.* More aluminum can be sold only by lowering the price of aluminum. The decline in the price of aluminum multiplied by the quantity of aluminum sold at the old price is an amount of revenue that the firm loses in order to expand sales. Thus, when the quantity sold is *increased* by a *lower* price, the quantity effect always increases total revenue while the price effect decreases

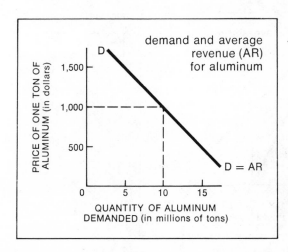

FIGURE

16.8

demand and average revenue (AR) for aluminum

D = AR

PRICE OF ONE TON OF ALUMINUM (in dollars)

1,500
1,000
500

0   5   10   15

QUANTITY OF ALUMINUM DEMANDED (in millions of tons)

total revenue. The net change in total revenue may be positive or negative, depending upon whether the quantity effect or the price effect is larger.

Assume that ALCOA (or any monopoly) wishes to know how much *total revenue* will be increased if sales are increased by one ton. The information ALCOA is looking for is what economists call the *marginal revenue,* which may be defined as the change in the total revenue the firm will receive as a result of a sale of one additional unit, in this case, one more ton of aluminum. Marginal revenue is defined as follows:

$$\text{Marginal revenue} = \frac{\text{change in total revenue}}{\text{change in quantity sold}}$$

The average and marginal revenue of a monopoly are illustrated in Figure 16.9.

Notice that at any quantity of aluminum, the marginal revenue is lower than the average revenue in the figure. Whenever the average revenue is decreasing, the marginal revenue must be lower than the average revenue. Again, this is similar to the case of a person taking a series of tests (see p. 236). If the average score declines as more tests are taken, it must mean that the marginal score (or the score on the last test taken) is below the average. In fact, it is the lower marginal score that pulls the average score down. Similarly, if the average revenue is decreasing, the marginal revenue must be below it and pulling it down.

When 10 million tons of aluminum are sold, marginal revenue is zero, or total revenue can be increased no further with the given demand: The quantity effect just offsets the price effect.

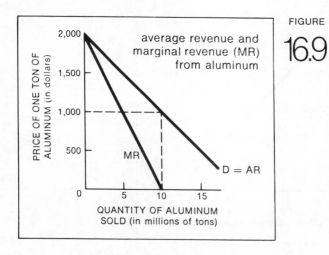

FIGURE

16.9

average revenue and marginal revenue (MR) from aluminum

At quantities below (to the left of 10 million), the quantity effect is more significant than the price effect, and therefore the marginal revenue is positive. As the quantity of aluminum sold increases, the price effect becomes more important and the quantity effect becomes less important, until at 10 million they are equal. At higher quantities of aluminum (to the right of 10 million), the price effect is more important, and therefore the marginal revenue is negative. It is possible to conclude from this that a monopolist would always sell a smaller quantity than 10 million tons because if he expands sales to 10 million, the increase in revenue as a result of the last unit sold is zero. If he sold a greater quantity, he would actually lose revenue because marginal revenue is negative at quantities above 10 million.

equilibrium for the monopoly

In order to see the equilibrium price a monopolist will charge and the quantity he will sell, the monopolist's revenue curves must be super-imposed on his cost curves. From the discussion in the previous section, it is known the average-revenue curve will slope downward and to the right and that the marginal-revenue curve will be below it and have a steeper slope. These curves are pictured in Figure 16.10. The profit-maximizing position is reached when the monopolist produces and sells that quantity (6 million tons) at which *his marginal revenue equals his marginal cost.* The reason for this is easy to comprehend. Below this level, one additional ton of aluminum brings in more revenue than its additional (or marginal) cost. Above this point, one additional ton of aluminum costs more than the revenue it brings in to ALCOA. Notice how the monopoly rule differs from the competitive rule that price should equal marginal cost. Because the monopolist has the entire market, his demand curve slopes down-ward, and therefore his marginal revenue is below the average revenue. In the competitive case, the firm is so small that the demand curve appears purely elastic in relation to it. Therefore, the competitive price or average revenue *equals* its marginal revenue. Because the monopolist's marginal revenue is lower (and the more general rule is marginal cost equals marginal revenue), the monopo-list chooses to supply less output to the market than would be the case in a competitive industry with similar cost and demand curves.

The average-revenue curve in Figure 16.10 indicates that $1,500 is the maximum price at which 6 million tons can be sold. The shaded area shows the excess profits received at that price. For a monopoly, unlike a purely competitive firm, the making of excess profits is the usual and expected case. Nothing in the short run or the long run

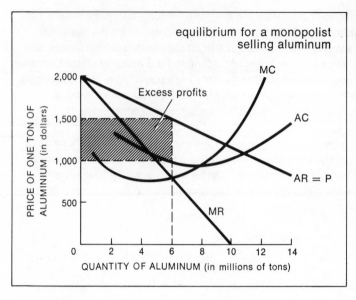

FIGURE 16.10

equilibrium for a monopolist selling aluminum

tends to reduce these excess profits (except for changes in the general business conditions as the economy undergoes cyclic fluctuations, a topic that will be examined in Part III).

In addition to the high price that the monopolist charges and the excess profits he makes, he almost never produces at the most efficient level of production. As shown in Figure 16.10, the monopolist stops producing before the point at which his average costs are minimized is reached. He does this, of course, because he is interested in maximum profits, not in maximum efficiency. If he had produced the quantity that minimized his costs, he would have been forced to sell his product at a much lower price, and this would have reduced his excess profits. The reader can now easily see what is meant by the age-old charge that monopolies restrict output and sales in order to increase their excess profits. The reader can also see why from the very beginning of the capitalist, private enterprise economic system, most businessmen have tenaciously fought to acquire monopoly powers.

modification of monopoly analyses

In the discussion of the market equilibrium for a monopolist, it was assumed both that the monopolist took his revenue and cost curves as *given,* and that he maximized his profits by equating marginal cost and marginal revenue *within the fixed constraints* of externally determined revenue and cost curves. These assumptions enabled us to examine only one aspect of the monopolist's ceaseless drive for more excess profits. The monopolist also can increase his excess profits by shifting his cost curves downward and by shifting his revenue curves upward.

Shifts in the revenue curves can be effected in several ways. The first and most obvious method is through advertising. If the monopolist can persuade more consumers that they want–need his product, then he will be able to sell more of it at all prices along the demand curve—that is, the demand curve will shift upward and to the right. Thus, we are literally bombarded with advertising. In a thousand and one ways at least, businessmen endlessly attempt to convince us to consume ever-increasing amounts of their products.

Another way that monopolists can increase the demand for their products is by convincing the government that it should erect and maintain protective tariffs to eliminate foreign competition. Although a firm or a group of firms often manages to achieve a monopoly within national boundaries, only very infrequently can a worldwide monopoly be achieved (however, many American-based multinational firms are working feverishly in that direction). To the extent that consumers buy a close foreign-made substitute for a monopolist's product, the demand for his product is reduced. Protective tariffs can eliminate foreign competition, and thereby increase demand for the monopolist's product. Over the past several centuries, businessmen have—generally with considerable success—sought the aid of governments in creating and protecting their firms' domestic monopolies by enacting protective tariffs. Such tariffs increase monopoly revenues at the expense of the consumer, who is forced to pay a higher price for "protected products." They are much like a tax levied by the government against all consumers, part of the proceeds of which is turned over to the monopolist to augment his excess profits.

Many large business firms also are able to increase the demand for their products through massive sales to the government. The bulk of these sales are connected with military procurement. For many of the largest U.S. corporations, these sales represent from 5 to 100 percent of their total sales. This topic is pursued in greater depth in Part III of this book.

There also are many ways in which business firms can shift their cost curves downward. They can press for government legislation that weakens labor unions; the Taft–Hartley Act of 1947 is an example of very restrictive legislation. They can also work to elevate "cooperative" and "reasonable" men to positions of leadership in unions, men who will not press very hard for wage increases that would disturb the status quo in the wage and profit distribution. They can also get President Nixon to appoint business-leaning "public" men to the wage and price control boards. These measures enable large firms to keep their wage costs to a minimum.

Monopolies also seek to achieve a monopsonistic position. A *monopsony* exists when a firm is the *only buyer* of a particular resource or intermediate product. A monopsonist can offer a very low price for the resource he is purchasing, and the seller must accept the offer or not sell his resource. Thus, resource costs can be decreased if the firm can achieve monopsonistic buying power, which is no less actively sought than monopolistic selling power.

The immense political power that stems from their economic power permits giant corporations to reduce costs in other ways. The government often is persuaded to allow them to use government-owned facilities for production connected with the armaments they are selling to the government. These facilities are generally used *free of charge.* And when the government has charged rent, it has reimbursed the corporations and given them extra profits *on this* rent; this is the so-called cost-plus contract. In other words, the government has actually paid the giant corporations to use government-owned facilities free of charge. Such a case was described by a U.S. Senate Committee report on pyramiding missile profits:

> Much of Western Electric's Nike production was done at two government surplus plants, which under the ordinary method of doing business with the government would have been supplied to Western Electric without cost. However, Western Electric instead of having the plants supplied free, rented them from the Government. Western Electric included the rentals as part of its overall costs and then charged the government a profit on these costs. The total rentals paid to the government by Western Electric for these plants amounted to over $3,000,000. When added to Western Electric's costs, the rentals generated additional profits to the company of $209,000. In such a situation, there could be little resistance on the part of Western Electric to having the government raise the rent, because as the rent went up, so did Western Electric's profit, since the complete amount of the rent was repaid by the landlord back to the tenant together with a profit.[3]

These are only a few of the ways in which large monopolistic corporations are constantly striving to use their economic and political power to maximize profits.

[3] U.S. Senate, Government Operations Subcommittee, *Pyramiding of Profits and Costs in the Missile Procurement Programs,* Senate Report No. 970 (Washington, D.C.: U.S. Government Printing Office, 1964).

who are the monopolists?

Most introductory economics texts identify pure competition and monopoly as the extreme cases along the spectrum of industrial organization. They argue (and we agree) that there are almost no purely competitive industries. Most monopolies, they assert, are either local or regional in scope, ranging from the single grocery store in the small village to the single giant real-estate developer in a large city. They maintain that national monopolies are as rare as purely competitive industries. According to these texts, monopoly theory is primarily of intellectual interest as an extreme case with little actual or practical applicability at a national level in the American economy.

This view, we believe, is in error because it adheres strictly to the definition of monopoly as existing when there is only one seller. It interprets one seller to mean one firm. Admittedly, there are very few national markets where a single business firm is the only seller. Most important nationwide markets are dominated by a few giant corporations, or are oligopolies. In Chapter 17, however, we shall see that despite some distinct differences between oligopolies (a few firms) and monopolies (a single firm), most oligopolies act *as if* they were monopolies. We shall argue that our analysis of monopolies applies generally to oligopolies on questions of pricing, output, and the shifting revenue and cost curves. If our analysis is correct, so that we can redefine monopolies to include industries that behave *as if* they were a single seller, then monopolies totally dominate almost all important national markets in the United States.

natural monopolies and government regulation

There are some industries that economists call *natural monopolies.* The technology used in these industries creates a cost curve on which the minimum average cost is not reached until a firm is producing a very large quantity. Generally, before the minimum average cost is reached, a single firm can supply the entire market with the commodity in question. If two firms divided the sales between them, each would produce such a small quantity that its average cost would be much higher than that of a single firm supplying the

entire market. In this circumstance, a free market will always lead to
one firm's acquiring a monopoly position.

The most common examples of natural monopolies are public
utilities such as electric and telephone companies. Because each of
these companies supplies a commodity that is a vital necessity for
most individuals and most other business firms, they are almost
always regulated by the government. This regulation generally takes
the form of an imposed price ceiling (although the regulating
agencies are often controlled by the monopolies, so the price ceiling
is usually high enough to allow considerable excess profits).

The governing agency can reduce the monopolist's excess profits
by lowering the price he will charge the public and/or increasing the
quantity of the product he will sell. If the government wishes to
increase the public welfare and still allow the monopolist to choose
a profit-maximizing quantity to sell, it will generally attempt to set the
price at the level at which the monopolist's marginal cost is equal to
his average revenue. This type of a price ceiling is illustrated in
Figure 16.11.

For those quantities at which the price ceiling is below the firm's
average-revenue curve, that ceiling becomes, in effect, an average
revenue and marginal revenue for the firm. The reasoning is
analogous to that for a firm in pure competition whose price is
determined independently of its actions. The monopolist, unlike the
purely competitive firm, however, cannot sell any quantity he wishes
at that price. For those quantities at which his original average-

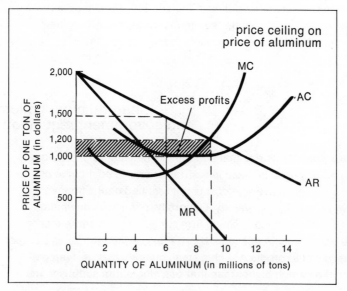

FIGURE

16.11

price ceiling on
price of aluminum

revenue curve falls below the price ceiling, the maximum price he can charge is determined by his average-revenue curve. In Figure 16.11, for quantities up to 9 million tons, the price ceiling serves as an average-revenue and marginal-revenue curve. At quantities larger than 9 million tons, the firm reverts back to its original revenue curves. If the firm is not regulated, it will charge $1,500 and sell 6 million tons. The price ceiling is imposed at that price ($1,200) that will equate the firm's average revenue and its marginal cost (as under competition). The firm then treats the price ceiling as a marginal-revenue curve up to the quantity 9 million tons. The monopolist will maximize profits by producing 9 million tons (where the price ceiling equals the average revenue and the marginal cost). He is then selling more at a lower price and receiving less profit.

Although the general public (and other business firms) are obviously better off after the price ceiling has been imposed, it is obvious that the monopolist is still making large excess profits (i.e., his average-cost curve is still below his average-revenue curve). But as long as the monopolist is left free to choose the quantity he wishes to sell, there is no price that will both clear the market (i.e., equate supply and demand) and in any way result in better service for the public. For example, if the price ceiling were set at a lower level, the quantity the firm wishes to sell would fall short of the quantity the public wishes to buy, so a market disequilibrium will result. If the price ceiling were set at a higher level, the government would merely be returning the monopolist nearer to his original profit-maximizing position at the expense of the general public's and other business firms' welfare. This happens frequently because of the monopolists' control of the regulatory agencies.

summary

In this chapter, we defined four types of market structures: pure competition, monopolistic competition, oligopoly, and monopoly. Pure competition and monopoly were analyzed in depth. Purely competitive industries are almost nonexistent. They are studied because the analysis of pure competition is the foundation of the classical liberal, laissez faire policy prescription. Because a purely competitive firm will tend to produce at its most efficient, low-cost level of output, the level at which the firm earns no excess profits, pure competition is also sometimes used as a theoretical *norm* against which to evaluate and compare existing industries.

Monopolistic firms, however, almost never produce at the most efficient, low-cost level of output. Furthermore, they generally receive large excess profits because of their control over the price that they charge consumers. Even if the government were to attempt to control a monopolist in order to mitigate the exploitation of the general public, the monopolist would probably continue making excess profits.

chapter 17
monopolistic competition and oligopoly

In the United States today, there are about 12 million business firms (of which nearly 14 percent are corporations). If agriculture is excluded as a special case not clearly fitting into any market structure, well over 99 percent of the remaining firms fit into the category we called monopolistic competition. Judged in terms of numbers of firms, it is by far the most important category of industrial organization.

The overwhelming majority of business firms are, however, minute firms in the fields of retailing, wholesaling, and the service industries (e.g., small drugstores, hot dog stands, barber shops, and so forth). In a very important sense, the more basic industries (e.g., mining, agriculture, banking, transportation, manufacturing, and communications) are the foundation upon which the prosperity of the nation depends. Those who control these industries dominate the entire economy. Almost all the basic or fundamental industries are completely controlled by giant oligopolistic corporations. Therefore, judged in terms of economic power, oligopoly is by far the most important category of industrial organization. Of the approximately 180,000 U.S. manufacturing corporations, for example, a mere 100 (0.0006 percent) own 58 percent of the net capital assets.

If we were to describe America's industrial landscape, we would begin with a vast plain of millions of tiny pebbles, representing all the economically powerless, monopolistically competitive business firms. At the center of this enormous plain would rise a few hundred

colossal towers, representing the important oligopolistic corporations. These few hundred towers would be so large that they would
dwarf into insignificance the entire plain below them.

equilibrium for a
monopolistically competitive firm

Monopolistic competition exists in an industry made up of many
small firms each producing a slightly differentiated product. The
differentiation may be merely in the packaging, the location of a retail
store, or the service offered, but in any case, it creates a certain
amount of consumer loyalty which creates demand curves that slope
downward and to the right. If a firm raises its price, it will lose only
a portion of its customers to competitors. Many will continue to buy
the product at higher prices. But if a firm lowers its price, it will
attract a few of its competitors' customers.

The monopolistically competitive firm maximizes its profits when
it equates marginal cost and marginal revenue. In many cases, if the
firm recently has substantially differentiated its product, it may make
large, monopolistic, excess profits. Such a situation is shown in
Figure 17.1(a).

A monopolistically competitive industry, however, has no significant barriers preventing the entry of new firms. New firms, seeing
the excess profits, will begin producing and selling highly similar
products and will drain the demand away from the firm pictured in
Figure 17.1(a). As a consequence, the original firm's average-revenue
curve will shift downward and to the left. As long as excess profits

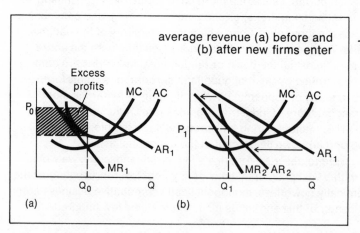

FIGURE

17.1

average revenue (a) before and
(b) after new firms enter

remain, new firms will continue to enter and the average-revenue curve will continue to shift downward and to the left. Therefore, the downward shift will come to a halt only after the average-revenue curve just touches, but does not cross, the average-cost curve.

This situation is pictured in Figure 17.1(b). The average-revenue curve just touches, but does not cross, the average-cost curve. At that quantity, the firm's marginal cost is equal to its marginal revenue; to maximize its profits, it produces at this point. It also is the quantity at which the firm's average revenue is equal to its average cost.[1] All the excess profits have been squeezed out by the entry of new competitors.

Notice, however, that the new equilibrium is always above the *minimum* point of the firm's average-cost curve. In Figure 17.1(b) the new demand curve, because it is still not flat as in pure competition, meets the average-cost curve above the minimum point. The price is above the minimum cost level, but there are no excess profits because at the actual production level costs are also higher than the minimum. In other words, the firm in monopolistic competition produces less output at a higher price and at a higher cost than the purely competitive firm in long-run equilibrium. We can therefore say that in equilibrium, monopolistically competitive firms incur waste by never producing at their most efficient level (in fact, it is only a purely competitive firm that can be shown to produce efficiently in a private-enterprise economy).

The only way in which the firm can hope to regain some of its lost excess profits is to convince the public, usually through advertising, that its product has been more substantially differentiated from the products of its competitors. But when one firm advertises and attracts new customers, its competitors generally retaliate by competitively advertising their own products. The net result often is that things are brought back to the point at which they were before the first firm began to advertise. Now, however, no firm is willing to curtail its advertising for fear of losing its customers to its competitors who continue advertising.

Advertising becomes almost a pure waste that is locked into the system. We say "almost" a pure waste because we grant that advertising may occasionally impart useful information. Most advertising, however, is so notorious for its use of half-truths, emotional appeals, brainwashing, and psychological appeals to people's most basic frustrations that few people can tell when any genuinely useful information is being offered. Most of us consciously dismiss advertising as a totally unreliable source of information, even though we

---

[1] It might seem to the reader that this result is attributable to the way in which we arbitrarily drew the curves in Figure 17.1. This is not so, but to prove it involves some knowledge of calculus, so we leave the proof to more advanced books.

may unconsciously be affected by the constant barrage of advertising aggressively hurled at each of our senses.

Thus, we have sketched the picture of monopolistic competition, a picture that fairly adequately describes the overwhelming majority of small businesses in a private-enterprise economy. Millions of tiny, nearly powerless businessmen work feverishly to create or protect some amount of monopolistic excess profits. Millions of competitors try equally hard to take away those excess profits. No competitor is able to sustain the acquisition of excess profits for a very long period, but each perpetually struggles, worries, competes, connives, and battles in a never-ending war in which there are no victors. Millions of firms almost never produce at the most efficient, lowest-cost level of production; billions of dollars are wasted on the aggressive propagation of inane, mind-dulling, and obnoxious advertising.

oligopoly

An *oligopoly* exists when a few business firms dominate an industry. Unlike any of the industrial categories discussed up to this point, an oligopolistic firm does *not* face a definite, unambiguous demand curve for its product. The amount that the oligopolist can sell at any price can be substantially affected by his rivals' actions. Furthermore, because his actions similarly affect his rivals, any time he changes his price, he must assume that competitors will react in some way to this change. His rivals' reactions will, in turn, affect the customers' response to his initial price change. He must be prepared to respond to any unexpected moves by his competitors. Thus, the fact of *interconnectedness* and *mutual dependence* of oligopolistic firms is the outstanding feature of an oligopolistic industry.

How can the effects of competitors' reactions be analyzed? First, their reactions to a price increase and a price decrease can be differentiated. If a firm raises its price, it will automatically *lose* many of its customers to its rivals who sell a highly similar product. Consequently, its action is not likely to provoke a reaction from its rivals. They are happy to acquire new customers.

However, if the firm lowers its price, it will *attract* its rivals' customers if they do nothing to retaliate. Rather than lose their customers, they are likely to lower their prices by the same amount. It might seem that these price changes would cancel each other out, leaving each firm selling the same quantity at a lower price. This is not the case, however. When all the firms lower their prices,

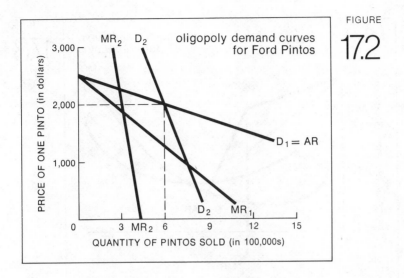

FIGURE 17.2

oligopoly demand curves for Ford Pintos

they attract new customers. Furthermore, old customers may buy more of the product sold by the industry.

Figure 17.2 provides two demand curves for an oligopolistic firm in an oligopolistic industry: the Ford Motor Company (and our old friend the Pinto). Demand curve D_1D_1 is constructed on the assumption that rivals ignore price changes made by Ford. Demand curve D_2D_2 is constructed on the assumption that rivals follow suit and change their prices by the same amount. For demand curve D_1D_1, marginal-revenue curve MR_1 is constructed. For demand-curve D_2D_2, marginal-revenue curve MR_2 is constructed. Demand curves D_1D_1 and D_2D_2 intersect at the price and quantity that prevailed before the price change.

From the discussion of oligopoly behavior, it is assumed here that beginning at $2,000, Ford's rivals will not react if it raises its price. Therefore, for all prices above $2,000 (and quantities below 600,000 Pintos) the curves D_1D_1 and MR_1 are Ford's actual demand- and marginal-revenue curves. If Ford lowers its price below $2,000, the rivals will lower their prices accordingly. Therefore, for prices below $2,000 (and quantities greater than 600,000 Pintos), the curves D_2D_2 and MR_2 are the firm's actual demand and marginal revenue.

By eliminating the irrelevant sections of the two demand curves, it is possible to construct the firm's actual demand and marginal-revenue curves. In Figure 17.3, these curves are constructed and the firm's cost curves are superimposed upon them. Two things should be carefully noted. The average-revenue or demand curve is kinked (where the demand curve abruptly turns down), and the

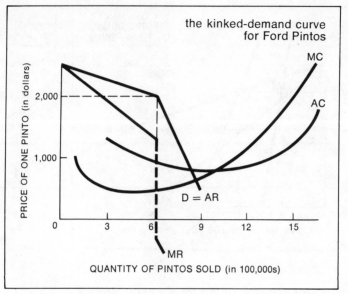

FIGURE

17.3

the kinked-demand curve
for Ford Pintos

marginal revenue (at 600,000 cars) suddenly falls off into the negative
quadrant of the graph.

It is clear from the graph that Ford will lose profits if it changes its
price either upward or downward from the initial price of $2,000.
It is also clear that it would be highly unlikely that the revenue
curves could ever shift so far downward and to the left that Ford
would ever lower the price it charged. An increase in costs or an
increase in the revenue curves would have to be fairly substantial
for the firm to raise its price, unless business conditions led rival
firms to raise their prices as well.

This analysis helps to explain the historically observed fact that
prices in oligopolistic industries are very stable in the face of short-
run small variations in demand. It also helps to explain why, over the
longer run, oligopolistic prices almost never fall. Rather, they show
a persistent tendency to rise during periods of inflation and remain
stable during periods of recession or deflation.

OLIGOPOLY PRICES

The analysis does not show, however, how the price charged by
oligopolists is arrived at. Whatever price is established, a kink will
develop at that price. But how is the price established in the first
place?

Most textbooks develop elaborate models of oligopolistic behavior
based upon the assumption that regardless of how many times the

actions of rivals upset their expectations, the rivals never learn that they are mutually dependent.[2] The German economist H. von Stackelberg developed a sophisticated analytic model of oligopolistic behavior which proved that oligopolistic rivalry will never result in the establishment of a stable price unless all the firms accept a single firm as a *leader* and all other firms accept positions as followers.[3] In other words, stability requires that a single firm (or any other single decision-making body) make the decisions in the oligopoly and that the remaining firms accept the decisions made by the leader.

What type of decisions will be made by the oligopolistic leader in a private-enterprise economy? The answer to this question is simple once the absurd assumption that oligopolistic firms do not recognize their mutual dependence is rejected. "If we assume that they recognize it [their mutual dependence], then they will set industry price at the monopoly price. The number of firms in the industry does not matter so long as they realize their interdependence."[4]

In other words, the large corporations prevent price competition although they do compete through alleged quality differences and advertising. With no price competition, the sellers of a given commodity have an interest in seeing that the price or prices established are such as to maximize the profits of the group as a whole, so that each product is priced *as if* it were sold by a single monopoly corporation. This is the decisive fact in determining the price policies and strategies of the typical large corporation. And it means that the appropriate price theory of an economy dominated by such corporations is *not* competitive price theory, but monopoly price theory. What nineteenth-century economists treated as a special case is now the general situation!

It is true that there is little open collusion in the United States because of the antitrust laws. Yet some kind of tacit collusion probably exists to a large degree in most industries, reaching its most developed form in what is known as *price leadership.* It is a mutual security pact in which no formal communication is necessary.

In this situation, when one firm raises or lowers the price, all the others will follow. When collusion is forbidden, the price leader calculates the share of the total market demand which his rivals will supply at various prices. He then chooses that price where the remaining demand (after the rivals have chosen their appropriate supply quantities) will maximize his profits. For the industry as a

2 For a good, brief discussion of three such models see Richard A. Bilas, *Microeconomic Theory* (New York: McGraw-Hill, 1967), pp. 213–219.

3 H. von Stackelberg, *The Theory of the Market Economy,* trans. A. T. Peacock (New York: Oxford University Press, 1952), pp. 194–204.

4 Bilas, op. cit., p. 219.

whole, this solution approximates the pure monopoly solution. So long as all firms accept this solution, which is really nothing else but a corollary of the ban on price competition, it becomes easy for the group as a whole to feel its way toward the price that maximizes the industry's profit. In the Appendix to this chapter we examine the exact mechanism of price leadership and other mechanisms by which oligopolies set a monopoly-like price.

There is the qualification that oligopoly prices do not, in fact, move upward or downward with equal ease, as they would in a pure monopoly. If one seller raises his price, this cannot possibly be interpreted as an aggressive move. The worst that can happen to him is that the others will stand pat and he will have to rescind (or accept a smaller share of the market). In the case of a price cut, however, there is always the possibility that aggression is intended, that the cutter is trying to increase his share of the market by violating the taboo on price competition. If rivals interpret the initial move in this way, the result may be a price war with losses to all. Hence, everyone is more likely to be careful about lowering prices than about raising them. Under the present situation of oligopoly, in other words, prices tend to be stickier on the downward side than on the upward side, and this fact introduces a significant upward bias into the general price level in a capitalistic economy dominated by oligopolies.

oligopoly or monopoly?

In Chapter 16, four general classifications of market structures (pure competition, monopolistic competition, oligopoly, and monopoly) were described. We found that there were almost no purely competitive industries. In this chapter, it has been argued that in their decisions regarding pricing, output, and sales, there is very little difference between oligopolies and monopolies.

Are there other differences of sufficient importance to make the category oligopoly a useful analytical tool? Or would it be better to drop oligopoly and simply refer to all industries that are dominated by a few giant corporations as monopolies?

The principal difference between oligopolistic and monopolistic firms is the rivalry that exists among the former. Although they have found by experience that this rivalry is mutually disastrous when it is extended to competitive pricing, they remain rivals. Their competition is generally confined to advertising, sales promotion, and cost-reduction campaigns, and their actions do not differ substantially from the monopolist's behavior, particularly in ways in which the monopolist attempts to shift his revenue curves upward and his cost curves downward.

It seems, therefore, that only when the passage of time results in a substantial shift of relative power within an oligopolistic industry are there important differences between a monopoly and oligopoly. During such a situation, a struggle for the industry's price leadership might develop. Such a struggle might result, temporarily, in destructive price competition (or worse). But once a new leader emerged, the industry would generally return to the types of policies that make it hardly distinguishable from a monopoly.

Thus, the category oligopoly is useful for analyzing temporary situations during which destructive competition takes place. It might also be useful to differentiate between monopolies and oligopolies in analyzing difference between advertising and sales-promotion techniques for firms that sell commodities for which there are close substitutes (oligopolistic firms) and for firms that sell products for which there are no close substitutes (monopolistic firms).

In almost any other situation or context, the differences between monopolistic and oligopolistic firms are insignificant. In most discussions, it is quite appropriate to refer to all giant corporations as monopolistic firms, as is generally done in ordinary conversation. The economist's narrower definition of monopoly, although sometimes helpful, is so restrictive that it eliminates almost all existing business firms. Yet the formal analysis of a monopolist's pricing and output decisions form the basis for understanding the behavior of most giant corporations. In Chapter 18, we shall use the term *monopoly* in its more general sense, to denote any large, powerful corporation.

summary

Most American business firms fit into the market structure of monopolistic competition. Our analysis has shown that although these firms do not generally receive excess profits, they incur waste by never producing at their most efficient level and by wasting enormous amounts of resources on competitive advertising.

Comparatively few powerful oligopolistic giants dominate the industrial landscape of American business. Oligopolies generally set prices as if they were monopolies (this point is developed further in the appendix which follows). Large excess profits and inefficiency characterize their operations. The performance of oligopolies and monopolies will be more closely examined in Chapter 18.

appendix to chapter 17

PRICE DETERMINATION IN AN OLIGOPOLY

The simplest and most direct method of oligopoly pricing occurs when the oligopolistic firms form a formal cartel. A *cartel* is an association that acts as a monopoly. Within a cartel, each firm is treated as if it were merely a separate plant owned by the monopoly.

Figure 17.A1 shows that a cartel's price determination is identical to that of a monopoly. The monopolist has a single marginal-cost curve; the cartel's marginal-cost curve is determined by adding together the various individual oligopolists' marginal-cost curves. The industry price is set at $2,000, and 3,000,000 compact cars is the quantity sold by the industry. Each firm produces that quantity at which its own marginal cost is equal to the industry's marginal cost (and the marginal revenue).

Cartels, as such, are illegal in the United States. But many oligopolistic industries have found several ways of engaging in covert collusion that enables them to cooperate in such a manner that their pricing and output decisions become almost tantamount to a formal cartel.

When this type of collusion is not possible, many oligopolistic industries rely upon the *price leadership* of the dominant firm within the industry. The dominant firm may be either the largest or the most

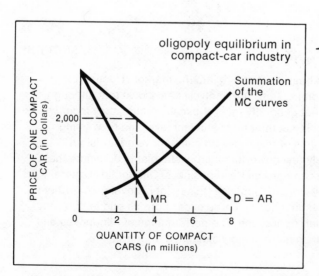

FIGURE

17.A1

oligopoly equilibrium in compact-car industry

PRICE OF ONE COMPACT CAR (in dollars)

Summation of the MC curves

2,000

MR

D = AR

0   2   4   6   8

QUANTITY OF COMPACT CARS (in millions)

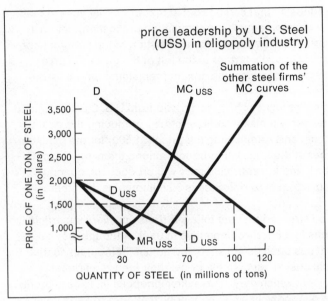

FIGURE

17.A2

price leadership by U.S. Steel (USS) in oligopoly industry)

efficient; sometimes it is both. In this situation the dominant firm sets the price. The other firms take that price as given, in the same way that a purely competitive firm accepts the industry price as given. They produce up to the point at which their marginal cost is equal to that price (which they take as their marginal revenue).

In order for the dominant firm to maximize its profits, it must know approximately what the marginal costs are for the other firms. For some time, U.S. Steel was the price leader in its industry. Figure 17.A2 illustrates how price is determined in such an industry. *DD* is the industry-demand curve; the demand curve for U.S. Steel is labeled $D_{uss}D_{uss}$. The summation of the marginal-cost curves for all firms other than the price leader is also shown.

The demand curve for the price leader (D_{uss}) is computed in the following manner: Whatever price the leader (U.S. Steel) selects, it knows the other firms will produce up to the point at which their marginal cost equals that price. U.S. Steel knows, therefore, that the other firms, taken collectively, will produce that quantity (in Figure 17.A2, 70 million tons) at which the summation of their marginal-cost curves equals the price it establishes. The demand for the leader's output will be the total market demand at that price minus the quantity the other firms sell. In other words, the leader's demand curve at any price will be equal to the difference between the market-demand curve and the summation of the other firms' marginal-cost curves.

For example, if the leader establishes a price of $2,000, the other firms will produce all that can be sold at that price (because at that point, market demand equals the summation of the marginal-cost curves). At prices below $2,000, the summation of the marginal-cost curves falls successively farther to the left of the demand curve. Therefore, as price declines, the demand remaining for the leader increases.

The marginal revenue (MR_{uss}) is derived from U.S. Steel's demand curve. The leader will maximize its profit by producing the quantity (30 million tons) and establishing the price ($1,500) for the industry. The remainder of the firms will produce, among them, the quantity 70 million tons, and the entire industry will produce the quantity 100 million tons (equal to U.S. Steel's 30 million plus the others' 70 million).

It should be stressed that the follower firms only very superficially resemble firms in a purely competitive market. Although they take the price that has been established and adjust their output so that their marginal cost is equal to the price, their long-run normal position is one in which they also make monopolistic, excess profits. Because the oligopoly, like the monopoly, manages to keep new firms out of the industry, there are no market forces that would tend to erode profits.

A third method of establishing a monopoly price is through the creation of a government regulatory agency to supervise the industry. Although these agencies ostensibly exist to protect the general public's interests, very often they function as means of coordinating the industry and establishing a monopoly price (this was discussed in Chapter 8).

chapter 18
monopoly power: increasing or decreasing?

The world of numerous, small competitive capitalist enterprises, which Adam Smith thought would produce the best result for all concerned, is gone forever. Since the period of the 1890s and early 1900s, western Europe and the United States have been characterized by the domination of relatively few giant firms. This new stage of monopoly has not ended capitalism, but it has intensified many old qualities and has added some entirely new (and unpleasant) features.

In the monopoly stage of capitalism, the setting of prices and outputs is quite different than under pure competition, and the profit result is equally different (these points were discussed in theory in Chapters 16 and 17; here we look at the concrete factual picture). The amount of waste, manipulation of the consumer, limitation of the worker's wages, and conflict between profit-seeking and social needs (such as the need for a decent environment) exist on entirely new scales. If Adam Smith's harmony-of-interests theory ever had a grain of truth, it is surely not applicable to the monopoly stage of capitalism.

the trend of concentration

In a purely competitive economy, each competing business unit would be so small that its actions taken alone could not appreciably influence the quantity of goods or the price in the market. Such, more or less, was the U.S. economy during the early nineteenth century.

Small farms and small businesses produced most of the output, and there were no giant corporations dominating an entire industry (though there were many local monopolies). As late as 1860, in many of the major urban industrial centers, there were still no incorporated business firms. Since that time, the picture has changed drastically.

In Chapters 7 and 8, the rise of big corporations in the post–Civil War period was discussed. By 1900, the share of manufacturing output produced by corporations had grown to two-thirds. Some of the big corporations developed by virtue of rapid internal growth; others arose by the merger of formerly independent firms.

Mergers have come in waves. The first massive movement, which lasted from the early 1890s to the outbreak of World War I, was characterized by *horizontal* mergers in which a big corporation absorbs other corporations who were its direct competitors. The results of such mergers are, of course, industries dominated by fewer and much larger corporations.

The second "wave" came in the 1920s. It was characterized by *vertical* mergers which take place between firms producing goods in sequence, as when a giant corporation absorbs its suppliers or absorbs the firms to which it sells its output.

The 1960s witnessed a third and unique wave. Most of these mergers were of the *conglomerate* variety, in which the giant corporations absorb other corporations that have no relation to it. The aim is simply to establish a colossal corporate empire that will give its controllers immense economic and political power.

From 1950 through 1959, there were an average of 540 corporate mergers a year. From 1960 through 1967, the average was 1,100 a year. In 1968, there were 2,655 mergers. More and more of these are conglomerate mergers between two giants in different industries. From 1948 through 1953, conglomerate mergers comprised 59 percent of the total. From 1960 through 1965, they comprised 72 percent of the total. In 1968, conglomerate mergers accounted for 84 percent of all mergers.[1]

Today, there still are millions of very small industrial enterprises, but a few hundred corporate giants hold most of the wealth and do most of the producing (see Table 18.1).

Table 18.1 reveals the extremely high concentration of corporate assets in comparatively few firms. At the bottom, a large number of small corporations (906,458, or 59 percent of the total) held a miniscule portion of corporate assets ($31 billion, or 1.5 percent). At the top, a few giant corporations (958, or just 0.06 percent) held a majority of all assets ($1,070 billion, or 53.2 percent). That some

---

[1] All data in this paragraph from the Federal Trade Commission and were cited in Federal Reserve Bank of Cleveland, *Economic Commentary* (May 12, 1969), p. 3.

TABLE
18.1

distribution of corporate assets
(all U.S. corporations, 1967)

SIZE (lower limit)	CORPORATIONS	ASSETS OWNED
$ 0	59.00%	1%
100,000	29.00	5
500,000	10.00	10
5,000,000	1.94	31
250,000,000	0.06	53
TOTAL	100.00%	100%

Source: U.S. Internal Revenue Service, Statistics of Income, Corporation Income Tax Returns (Washington, D.C.: U.S. Government Printing Office, 1967).

900 U.S. corporations would hold more than $1 trillion of assets is incredible; that is more than the total value of all western European assets. Among those 958 corporations, there is still a great concentration within just the top 200 or 300 corporations.

The figures for all corporations average out differences in various sectors. For example, in the important sector of banking alone, there are approximately 13,775 commercial banks, but a mere 14 of them hold 25 percent of all deposits, and the 100 largest banks hold 46 percent of all deposits.[2]

Another function of banks is to hold assets in *trust* for individuals and corporations. Banks exercise the voting power for these stocks, which gives them immense power without having legal ownership. Less than 2 percent hold 61 percent of all the trust assets in national banks. Only 49 of the largest banks hold over 5 percent of the common stock in 147 of the 500 largest industrial corporations in the United States. They also hold at least 5 percent of the common stock in 17 of the largest companies in the fields of merchandising and transportation. These banks are represented in the boards of directors in the majority of the largest corporations in the fields of manufacturing, merchandising, utilities, transportation, and insurance.

Finally, let us turn to the decisive sector of manufacturing taken alone. In the general category of manufacturing enterprises, there were 180,000 corporations and 240,000 unincorporated businesses

2 The figures on the concentration in banking are taken from the Patman Committee Staff Report for the Domestic Finance Subcommittee of the House Committee on Banking and Currency, Commercial Banks and Their Trust Activities; Emerging Influence on the American Economy (Washington, D.C.: U.S. Government Printing Office, July 1968).

in 1962.[3] Ninety-eight percent of all manufacturing assets were owned by the corporations. Of the 420,000 manufacturing firms, the 20 largest (not 20,000, but 20!) owned 25 percent of all assets of all manufacturing firms. The largest 50 firms owned 36 percent of all assets, and the largest 200 owned 56 percent. If adjustment is made for giant firms that are owned by even larger giants (i.e., if their ownership is added together), we arrive at a much higher percentage of control. The fact is that after adjustment for ownership of subsidiaries, a mere 100 firms owned 58 percent of the net capital assets of all the hundreds of thousands of manufacturing corporations. Another index of the imbalance of economic power is the fact that the largest 20 manufacturing firms owned a larger share of the assets than the smallest 419,000 firms combined.

When profits earned are examined, the contrast is even more striking. The *net* profits of the 5 largest corporations were about *twice as large* as those of the 178,000 smallest corporations combined.

Between 1950 and 1962, the share of all manufacturing assets held by the largest 200 firms increased by 17 percent. Between 1962 and 1970, the rate of increase was even more rapid. Since 1959, big business has been absorbing other business firms that have $10 million or more in assets at a rate exceeding 60 a year, every year. Since 1950, 1 out of every 5 of the 1,000 largest manufacturing companies has been swallowed by an even larger giant. In 1966, 101 companies, each with assets of more than $10 million, were absorbed by other companies; in 1967, the number was 169; in 1968, it was 192. Obviously, oligopolistic business giants are far from satisfied with the immense size and power they already have. There is nothing to lead us to believe that these mushrooming industrial empires are about to discontinue merging.

Furthermore, these few large firms control most research and thus will continue to grow more rapidly. A 1960 survey showed that just 4 firms accounted for 22 percent and just 384 firms accounted for 85 percent of all industrial research and development.[4]

If the individual industries, which are the arenas of most direct competition, are examined, the picture of economic concentration may be even more sharply drawn. Let an *industry* be defined so that there is easy substitution among the products of all firms within it, and very little possible substitution with products of outside firms.

[3] The data that follows are taken from Willard F. Mueller, "Economic Concentration," in hearings before the Subcommittee on Antitrust and Monopoly of the Committee on the Judiciary, United States Senate, 88th Congress, 2nd Session, pursuant to S. Res. 262, *Part I: Overall and Conglomerate Aspects* (Washington, D.C.: U.S. Government Printing Office, July 1964), pp. 111–129.

[4] See John K. Galbraith, *The New Industrial State* (Boston: Houghton Mifflin, 1967), p. 23 and sources cited therein.

Three or four giant oligopolistic corporations control most of the production of most industries. Many small firms also exist in most industries, but altogether they produce a small percentage of the total output.

The economy of the United States has thus changed from a predominantly competitive to a predominantly oligopolistic production situation. In Chapter 17, it was seen that the few oligopolistic firms in each industry tend to act like a single monopoly, and in this chapter, the huge number of conglomerate mergers of the giants from different industries has been described. As a consequence, the apparent degree of concentration may not change in each industry, but the same conglomerate may now control a large firm in each of many industries. Thus, the data on particular industries, which indicate that the shares of the 3 or 4 largest have not increased much for several years, severely understate the trend toward concentration of power in the 100 largest firms in all manufacturing.

the reasons for monopoly

The fundamental cause of the emergence of the giant corporation is the economy of scale that can be derived from large-size production units which turn out cheaper goods by using more specialized machinery, more specialized workers, and mass-production assembly lines. Small firms are driven out of business by the cheap goods produced through large-scale applications of technology. The large firm gains a monopoly by selling at a lower price while making more profit.

In addition to improved technology based on the economies of scale, there are other reasons for the greater profitability of huge firms such as General Motors. These firms grow internally or by merger far beyond the technologically necessary minimum because they wish to exercise monopoly power over the market. With small competitors eliminated or dominated, the few remaining giant firms can restrict output and set higher prices to make higher profit rates. Moreover, they can plan with more certainty over a longer period of time with less risk.

This elimination of risk and uncertainty entails not only controlling their own industry's output but also (1) buying out raw material suppliers, (2) buying out dealers and outlets for the finished product, (3) vast nationwide advertising, and (4) linking up with banks and other financial sources. With these motivations, there is no clear upper limit to desirable size. The motto seems to be *the bigger the better.*

prices and profit maximization

What is the effect of monopoly on the price structure? The essence of the monopolist's position is his ability to keep competitors out of the market by greater efficiency, by control of natural or financial resources, by control of patents, or by any other legal or illegal methods. Thus, he can charge what the market will bear, and there is no competitive mechanism to bring his higher profit back down to the average rate of profit in all industry.

Although the monopolist can make a higher than average rate of profit, he cannot make profit out of thin air. Total profit still remains within the limits of the total value of output above costs. To some extent, monopoly does not affect aggregate prices or aggregate profits but only redistributes the aggregate profits. From a given amount of aggregate profits, monopolists may take away part of the profits of small businessmen and small farmers by their competition for the consumer dollar. They may also increase their share of profits by their power to buy raw materials and food at low prices and sell finished goods at high prices to these small entrepreneurs. However, monopolists may also increase total profits by using their power to raise prices or to restrict money wages in order to lower the workers' real wages.

As was seen in Chapter 16, monopoly price and quantity of production are set by the monopolist as he sees fit. In order to maximize his profits, however, he can only set the quantity at the point of greatest difference between total revenue (determined by demand) and total cost (determined by the cost of labor plus material costs). Once the quantity is set, even a monopoly can only sell at a price determined by the demand at that point. The difference between this and the competitive situation is that under monopoly *the quantity supplied is set lower so that the price is higher.* Therefore, the short-run rate of profit is higher than the average under competition. The long-run rate of profit *remains* higher because capital cannot freely enter the industry.

Contrary to this view, many economists claim that modern businessmen do not always attempt to maximize profits. It is hard to see what they are arguing, except that the case is not simple. The capitalist today is not the individual businessman, but the corporation. Whether the businessman is rational and calculating in his private life is essentially irrelevant to the functioning of the system. In his company life, there can be no doubt that the making and accumulating of profit hold as dominant a position today as they ever did. As was the individual enterprise of an earlier period, the giant corporation is an engine for maximizing profits, but it is used not merely as an enlarged version of the personal capitalist. There are two differences: (1) The corporation has a much longer time horizon, and (2) it is a much more rational calculator.[5]

Having said that much, it is important to avoid a dogmatic notion that every corporate decision is made in terms of immediate dollars-and-cents returns. Certainly, corporate management may sacrifice short-run profits to ensure the security of their market control, to spur company growth, and even to act as dictated by the somewhat vague concept of prestige. Thus, prices are *not* always set as high as the market will bear. It could be said that management maximizes a multiple set of objectives. Equally well (because the difference is only semantic), it could be emphasized that each of the other objectives is merely a rational way to achieve maximum long-run profits which are the real sole objective.

who controls the corporation?

Liberals agree that monopoly is an evil aspect of capitalism, but they believe a remedy short of doing away with capitalism is possible. Some rely on stricter enforcement of antitrust laws. Others admit that these laws have clearly proven to be inadequate and advocate stricter laws. Still others claim that a process of internal change in giant corporation is automatically eliminating most of its negative qualities. Professor Galbraith is the leading spokesman of this latter view.

Galbraith[6] maintains there is a great contradiction between the notion that the modern corporation is mostly controlled by the management and that it nevertheless ruthlessly tries to maximize profits for the stockholders. Furthermore, he argues that the most important factor of production is no longer capital, but the specialized talent of scientists and technologists and that real power passes from stockholders and top management to the members of the *techno-structure* (i.e., the technical personnel, including scientists and technicians). According to Galbraith, the members of the technostructure do not get the profits that they are supposed to maximize. Because the technostructure supplies talent, not capital, why should they worry about the return to capital? He says that the modern corporation has the capacity to shape society, but its resources are used, as might be expected, to serve the deeper

[5] In this respect see James Earley, "The Impact of Some New Developments in Economic Theory: Discussion," *American Economic Review*, Proceedings, (May 1957), pp. 333–335.

[6] Galbraith, op. cit., chaps. 5, 6, 7, and 8.

interests or goals of the technostructure, which possesses the
real power.

Galbraith agrees that a few hundred giant corporations control the
market, regulate output and prices, and exercise enormous political
control. Yet by a wave of his hand, he eliminates the corporate
executive and puts the control of the corporation in the hands of all
scientists and technically skilled workers. He then finds that the
technostructure really manages the corporation and that, for their
own reasons, they manage it in the best interests of all society. In
other words, Galbraith is very critical of capitalism, especially of the
tremendous centralization of the means of production, but
nevertheless is apologetic in the sense that he concludes that the
industrial system has actually solved (or is solving) its problem.

The radical view is that Galbraith ignores the real position of
modern corporate management. In the first place, the fact that so
many top executives hold stock means their motivations cannot
possibly be inconsistent with profit-making. For example, in early
1957, 25 officers of General Motors owned an average of 11,500
shares each.[7] They might not be able to affect policy even with that
amount of stock in General Motors, yet each owned roughly $500,000
in the company, and it is improbable that any was indifferent to
profits. Further, among stockholders there are both more managers
than representatives of any other group and a larger proportion of
managers than in any other group.

Galbraith, of course, argues that it is not the motivation of the
managers but the motivation of the technostructure that is decisive.
Radicals counter that the goals of the technostructure would be the
same as those of the managers: survival of the firm, growth, independence from outside control. All these demand profit-making.
More important, it flies in the face of reality to believe that the
technicians control the corporations. The managers hire and fire the
technicians, not vice versa. In the end, it is the boss rather than his
hired hand, who makes the decisions (and will use expert advice only
to make more profitable decisions).

monopoly profit rates
(and income distribution)

The monopoly structure of American capitalism has been examined,
and the price-setting behavior of its management has been investigated. How do structure and behavior affect the performance of
American capitalism? In this section, the effect on profit rates is

---

7 See Gabriel Kolko, *Wealth and Power in America* (New York: Praeger, 1962), p. 13.

reviewed. First, the sources, in theory, of monopoly profit are briefly recapitulated, then the facts of monopoly profit are presented.

The whole point of monopoly (or oligopoly) control of markets is, of course, to restrict output and charge higher prices. All consumers are hurt by higher monopoly prices. Workers' real wages are lowered. Purchasers of producer goods also suffer, so the profits of small businesses and farmers are lowered. Some large firms have extra market power as large buyers of commodities (technically, oligopsony power). This fact may allow the large firm to shift some profit to itself by buying at a lower price from small businesses and farmers.

Some giant firms have extra market power as large buyers of labor (again, oligopsony power). Thus, the large firm may also add to its profits by buying labor at a rate lower than the average wage. This factor may, of course, be somewhat offset by trade-union action. In the modern world of monopoly, wages are not determined simply by automatic market supply and demand. Wages are determined by the bargaining strength of capital and labor, with monopoly capital usually in the stronger position.

Additional monopoly profits come from lucrative government military contracts, which are financed from the workers' tax money, thus again increasing total profits (though the particular workers engaged in military production do make higher-than-average wages). Extra-high returns from foreign investments abroad also add to monopoly profits; that is, profits are extracted from workers in foreign countries (see Chapter 32).

long-run profit rate, by corporate size (all U.S. corporations, 1931–1961, excluding the war years 1940–1947)		TABLE 18.2
	PROFIT RATE (profit before taxes divided by stockholders' capital)	
$ 0–$ 50,000	−7.1%	
50,000– 100,000	4.1	
100,000– 250,000	5.9	
250,000– 500,000	7.4	
500,000– 1,000,000	8.3	
1,000,000– 5,000,000	9.3	
5,000,000– 10,000,000	9.7	
10,000,000– 50,000,000	10.4	
Over $50,000,000	10.4	

Source: Reprinted by permission from Howard Sherman, *Profit Rates in the United States* (Ithaca, N.Y.: Cornell University Press, 1968), p. 41.

Turning to the facts, we may investigate first how the profit rates of an enterprise are affected by its absolute size. The size of a business is indicated by the total amount of its assets, and the profit rate is the total profit divided by the capital investment of all the stockholders. Profit rates by asset size for all corporations since 1931 are given in Table 18.2.

In an economy of pure and perfect competition, all profit rates should be equalized in the long run. As Table 18.2 demonstrates, in the U.S. economy, the long-run profit rate is *not* the same for all corporations. On the contrary, the smallest corporations have low or even negative profit rates, and the profit rate rises with the scale of the corporation, although the differences are quite small among the largest-size groups. This is a proof of the existence of monopoly power and imperfect competition.

Economic concentration, however, has another important aspect. The indicator of market power is a firm's relative size and importance

INDUSTRY GROUP	CONCENTRATION RATIO (percent of sales by eight largest sellers)
Motor vehicles and parts	98.1%
Tobacco	91.5
Transportation equipment, except motor vehicles	75.6
Rubber	74.2
Primary metals	70.8
Chemicals	63.3
Electrical machinery	60.8
Petroleum and coal	57.7
Instruments	56.1
Stone, clay, glass	55.0
Food and beverages	45.7
Machinery, except electrical	44.4
Fabricated metal	40.3
Paper	39.4
Textile mill	37.1
Leather	33.7
Furniture	23.8
Printing and publishing	21.5
Apparel	20.5
Lumber	15.5

Source: Reprinted by permission from Howard Sherman, *Profit Rates in the United States* (Ithaca, N.Y.: Cornell University Press, 1968), p. 85.

in its own industry. A *concentration ratio* in each industry may be defined as the percentage of sales controlled by the eight largest corporations in the industry. Several studies have found a definite relationship between an industry's concentration ratio and its profit rates. Some evidence is presented in Table 18.3.

The very high concentration of production that exists in many industry groups reflects the fact that in the majority of U.S. industries, the bulk of production is concentrated in a few giant corporations, with hundreds of smaller companies producing very little. Moreover, inspection of the table reveals a considerable rise of profit rates as the degree of concentration rises (the few noticeable exceptions are easy to explain from special cases). Thus, in the ten industry groups over the 50 percent concentration level, the average rate of profit is 20 percent; it is only 12.8 percent in the ten industry groups under the 50 percent concentration level.

This analysis may be extended to the trend of aggregate profits

	TABLE
profit rates and concentration ratios, by industry group (all U.S. manufacturing corporations in 1954)	18.3

	PROFIT RATE (profit before taxes divided by stockholders' capital)
	27.1%
	20.3
	29.8
	17.8
	13.0
	19.9
	20.7
	7.7
	23.9
	19.9
	14.4
	16.2
	15.6
	17.3
	5.1
	11.4
	12.8
	15.1
	7.6
	12.2

under capitalism. It appears that the giant corporations have steadily reduced production costs per unit and that there have been powerful impulses to innovation. Yet monopoly cannot be considered a rational and progressive system because although it reduces costs, it continues to set extremely high prices. Moreover, its increased productivity does not benefit everyone, but only a few. Profit rates increase and the share of profit in national income rises. Contrary to the nineteenth-century economist's vision of falling rates of profit, under monopoly the rate tends to rise.

monopoly and waste

During the period since the U.S. economy has changed to a predominantly monopolistic structure, the rate of economic growth appears to have declined. Thus, the GNP (in constant prices) grew by 4.31 percent per year in 1839–1879, by 3.72 percent a year in 1879–1919, and by 2.97 percent a year in 1919–1959.[8] It is impossible to say to what extent, if any, this decline is related to the high level of oligopoly power because so many other factors have been operative.

We do know that production cannot reach optimum efficiency below a certain point, or quantity. Thus, the fact that large firms account for most U.S. output means that most of the economy has the ability to produce at lower costs than ever before. Studies of cost data reveal the possibility of high efficiency at a fairly constant level beyond the necessary minimum scale of production.[9] Of course, because the very large firms also have disproportionately larger research facilities and control a very large percentage of all unexpired patents, they have the most potential for increasing efficiency. Moreover, many investment projects require resources beyond the means of small firms.

But the large, entrenched firm stands to lose most from the obsolescence of present machinery and from product improvements that reduce the number of units the customer need buy, for example, a longer-lasting light bulb. Therefore, if the large firm has an oligopoly position and faces no serious competitive pressure for improvement, it may develop, patent, and not use important inventions. Monopoly power has paradoxical effects on innovation. Giant firms have a rapid rate of technological progress, but they retain a large amount of technologically obsolete equipment.

[8] Joint Economic Committee, Congress of the United States, *Staff Report on Employment, Growth, and Price Levels* (Washington, D.C.: U.S. Government Printing Office, 1961), p. 34.

[9] See J. S. Bain, "Price and Production Policies," in Howard S. Ellis, ed., *A Survey of Contemporary Economics* (New York: McGraw-Hill, 1948), p. 140.

Oligopoly power may also be used to restrict supply in order to maintain prices. Thus, as will be seen in later chapters, *oligopoly power is one of the principal causes of inflation.* Oligopolies will expand production as rapidly as possible only in extraordinary periods of unlimited demand. This usually occurs only when government demand skyrockets, as in World War II. In wartime, oligopolies can cease restricting output but still charge prices as high as the government will allow.

Moreover, as also will be seen in Chapter 28, the existence of economic concentration may have increased the severity and, possibly, the number of depressions because of its destabilizing effects on remaining small businesses. Unless such concentration has had a fully offsetting effect of increasing growth during prosperity, it would seem that this is another reason why the net effect of oligopoly may be to lower the rate of economic growth. This is not to say, of course, that breaking up large firms into smaller units would increase economic growth. Reducing the American economy to small firms would certainly cause a major decrease in economic efficiency and most likely would have negative effects on investment.

The rate of growth (and waste) under monopoly is also affected by the fact that the sales effort has greatly expanded. Once a relatively unimportant feature of the system, sales effort has become one of its decisive nerve centers. The impact of advertising and related expenditures on the economy is outranked only by militarism. In all other aspects of social existence, the influence of advertising is second to none. In an economic system in which competition is fierce and relentless, but in which the small number of rivals rules out price-cutting, advertising becomes to an ever-increasing extent the principal weapon of the competitive struggle. There is little room under atomistic competition for advertising; in monopoly, it is the most important factor in the firm's survival.

Relatively large firms are in a position to exercise a powerful influence upon the market for their output by establishing and maintaining a pronounced difference between their products and those of their competitors. This differentiation is sought chiefly by means of advertising, trademarks, brand names, distinctive packaging, and product variation. If successful, it leads to a condition in which the consumers believe that the differentiated products can no longer serve as close substitutes for each other.

Several studies have demonstrated that advertising involves a massive waste of resources, a continual drain on the consumer's income, and a systematic destruction of the consumer's freedom of choice between genuine alternatives.[10] Furthermore, advertising in all its aspects cannot be meaningfully dealt with as some undesirable

---

10 See, e.g., Galbraith, op. cit., *passim.*

excrescence on the economic system that could be removed if we would only make up our minds to get rid of it. Advertising is the very offspring of the monopoly form of capitalism, the inevitable by-product of the decline of price competition; it constitutes as much an integral part of the system as the giant corporation itself. The economic importance of advertising lies partly in its causing a reallocation of consumers' expenditures among different commodities. Even more important, however, is its effect on the magniutde of aggregate effective demand and thus on the level of income and employment. In other words, it generates useless expenditures, both by capitalists and by consumers, which soak up part of its "overproduction" by getting consumers to spend money beyond their direct needs.

Advertising affects profits in two ways. The first effect is the fact that part of advertising and other selling expenses are paid for through an increase in the prices of consumer goods bought by productive workers. Their real wages are reduced by this amount, whereas total profit is maintained by the higher prices.

The other, more complicated, effect is that the profits and wages some capitalists and workers make from the business of advertising constitute an expense for other capitalists. This component of the outlays on advertising and sales effort does not constitute an increase in total profit but does cause its redistribution. Some individuals living off profit are deprived of a fraction of their incomes in order to support other individuals living off profit, namely those who derive their incomes from advertising itself.

Furthermore, in making it possible to create the demand for a product, advertising encourages investment in plant and equipment that otherwise would not take place. The effect of advertising on the division of total income between consumption and saving is not measurable, but is clear in direction and probably very large. The function of advertising, perhaps its dominant function today, is to wage a relentless war on behalf of the producers and sellers of consumer goods against saving and in favor of consumption.

Actually, much of the newness with which the consumer is systematically bombarded is either fraudulent or related trivially, and in many cases even negatively, to the function and serviceability of the product. Moreover, other products are introduced that are indeed new in design and appearance but that serve essentially the same purposes as old products they are intended to replace. The extent of the difference can vary all the way from a simple modification in packaging to the far-reaching and enormously expensive annual changes in automobile models.

In addition, most research and development programs, which constitute a multibillion-dollar effort in the United States, are more closely related to the production of salable goods than to their much-touted mission of advancing science and technology. For example, if monopoly profit and dealers' markups are excluded, then the real cost of production of the 1949 automobile, built with the technology of 1960, would have been less than $700 in 1960 and far less in 1970. According to this calculation, useless automobile model changes alone amounted to about 2.5 percent of GNP by 1960. Thus, the total amount of waste from all the time and effort devoted directly and indirectly to *selling* products under monopoly must considerably lower the rate of economic growth.

Not only does monopoly greatly increase the waste of capitalism, but it also raises pollution and environmental destruction to a new level. In the competitive model, apologists could claim that consumer preference dictated what was produced and therefore that pollution was merely an unfortunate by-product of the demands of the public. The apologists argue that these unfortunate by-products of public preferences could be handled by some minor public action in beautifying the environment. Under monopoly, such apologetics are no longer possible; it is clear that consumer preference is manipulated and directed toward whatever products are most profitable to produce, and therefore "environmental damage becomes a normal consequence of the conflict between the goals of the producing firm and those of the public."[11]

So far, only the unemployment, inflation, civilian wastes, and peace-time pollution caused by monopoly have been considered. Its full effect cannot be appreciated until its political power and militarist trend, international spread, and social effects are analyzed.

summary

In several waves of mergers since the late 1890s, the American economy has been converted from one of numerous small competitive industrial enterprises to one dominated by giant corporations. In each industry, three or four corporations together make the decisive output, investment, and pricing decisions. All small businesses together produce a small percentage of total output and receive an even smaller percentage of profits. The high degree of concentration increases instability and unemployment in at least two ways:
(1) Driven to the wall, small businesses reduce employment (and sometimes set off depressions); many go bankrupt (thus worsening

11 John K. Galbraith, "Economics as a System of Belief," *American Economic Review* (May 1970), p. 477.

depressions). (2) The giant corporations keep their own prices and output high by restricting the supply of output and further reducing employment.

Giant firms increase their prices rapidly during prosperity, causing inflation by pushing profits up through the use of monopoly power over the market. Since the 1950s, they have even had the power to continue raising prices during recessions (though more slowly than during expansions). The giant firms also mount giant advertising campaigns, wasting vast resources on the false claims that their products are better than others. Finally, the giant firms contribute giant pollution to the air, land, and sea; it is just not *profitable* to spend their money on purifying devices for their industrial processes or for their consumer products, such as cars.

chapter 19
government and inequality

In Chapter 15, we examined the distribution of income in the United States and found a small number of very rich (mostly recipients of profit income from capital) and a very large number of poor and low-income people (mostly wage workers or unemployed workers). In Chapter 18, we found that even in the corporate world, there are a few very big fish and millions of small ones. Clearly, economic power lies in the hands of a few thousand owners and executives of the major corporations.

In this chapter, the relationship of economic power to political power will be examined. First, we shall explore the degree to which their vast economic power gives disproportionate political power to that same relatively small number of top corporate owners and executives. Then we shall see how the resulting government affects economic inequality via taxation, welfare, farm subsidies, antitrust laws, and education. In Chapter 27, government policies, particularly military spending, will be considered in relation to unemployment and inflation.

how economic inequality
produces political inequality

In spite of our formal political democracy, money talks in politics as elsewhere. Thus, it is no surprise that many writers, not all radical, have alleged that those with economic power are dominant in U.S. politics. While he was President of the United States, Woodrow Wilson wrote: "Suppose you go to Washington and try to get at your Government. You will always find that while you are politely listened to, the men really consulted are the men who have the biggest stake —the big bankers, the big manufacturers, the big masters of commerce, the heads of railroad corporations and of steamship corporations. . . . The masters of the Government of the United States are the combined capitalists and manufacturers of the United States."[1]

How far can Wilson's hypothesis be substantiated by the facts? Do the large number of low-income workers or the few high-income, upper-class capitalists dominate U.S. politics? The economics of class structure has been examined; now we must ask about consciousness of class background because this will affect political behavior. A careful study conducted in 1964 found, contrary to the myth of an all-middle-class America, that 56 percent of all Americans said they thought of themselves as "working class." Some 39 percent considered themselves "middle class." (It is true, though, that 35 percent of all those questioned said they had never thought of their class identification before that moment.) One percent said they were "upper class," and only 2 percent rejected the whole idea of class.[2]

An individual's political behavior is strongly influenced by class background. But that leads to a puzzle. If a majority identify with the working class, and everyone has one vote, why do parties favorable to the working class not win every election? Why do government policies usually further, not working-class interests, but (as Woodrow Wilson asserted) those of the wealthy capitalist class? More precisely, given formal democracy and capitalism, exactly how does our extreme economic inequality tend to be translated into inequality of political power?

[1] Woodrow Wilson, *The New Freedom* (New York: Doubleday, 1914), p. 83.

[2] This study is reported in Marian Irish and James Prothro, *The Politics of American Democracy* (Englewood Cliffs, N.J.: Prentice-Hall, 1965), p. 38. To avoid the imputation of a radical bias, we have taken all of the data in this section from their widely used traditional text. In turn, all of their footnotes refer to well-known conventional political scientists.

In the first place, there is the simple fact that the degree of political participation tends to vary with class background. "The average citizen has little interest in public affairs, and he expends his energy on the daily round of life—eating, working, family talk, looking at the comics (today, TV), sex, sleeping."[3] More exactly, 86 percent of those identified in another 1964 study as middle class voted, but only 72 percent of the working class voted. Similarly, 40 percent of the middle class had talked to others about voting for a party or candidate, but only 24 percent in the working class had talked about it. Among the middle-class people interviewed, 16 percent gave money to a political cause, 14 percent attended political meetings, and 8 percent worked for a party or candidate; in the working class, figures on the same activities were only 4 percent, 5 percent, and 3 percent, respectively.[4]

Thus, political participation of all kinds increases with income. Some of the reasons are obvious. Lower-income workers have less leisure time, less money above minimum needs, more exhausting jobs. Furthermore, detailed studies show that because workers have less education and less access to information they have less knowledge of the importance of various issues, which accounts, in part, for their lower participation. The same studies show more cross-pressures on workers—for example, the racial antagonisms that conveniently divide and weaken their working-class outlook.[5]

Unequal political power is also achieved by control of the news media. Even if the average worker "had an interest in politics, he would have great difficulty getting accurate information; since the events of politics unfold at a great distance, he cannot observe them directly, and the press offers a partial and distorted picture."[6] Even the quantity of news is limited. Although 80 percent of Americans read newspapers and 88 percent have television sets, only 2.8 percent of total newspaper space and even less television time is devoted to political news.[7]

If the quantity of political news is deplorable, its quality is abysmal, or worse. The first problem is that only one view is available to most people because of increasing concentration of newspaper ownership. In 1910, some 57 percent of American cities had competing daily papers; but in 1960, only 4 percent had competing dailies. Furthermore, news media tend to have a conservative bias because (1) they do not want to offend any powerful interests; (2) they especially do

3 Ibid., p. 165.
4 Ibid., p. 38.
5 Ibid., p. 193.
6 Ibid., p. 165.
7 Ibid., p. 183.

not want to offend major advertisers, all of which are big businesses; and (3) most important, "Since the media of communication are big businesses, too, the men who control them quite naturally share the convictions of other businessmen."[8]

Economic power also worsens the substantial inequality of political power available to different pressure groups. Thus, the standard political text quoted extensively here points to *status* as the most important factor in determining the influence of a pressure group. After listing other sources of status, it concludes: "Finally, since status is so closely tied to money in the United States, the group with greater status will almost automatically be able to command greater financial resources. And it costs money to engage in pressure politics. . . ."[9]

The fact of economic power weighs all the more heavily because advertising is now a vital component of politics. ". . . pressure groups . . . are now spending millions of dollars every year on *mass propaganda*. Not only broad groups like the National Association of Manufacturers, but even individual companies maintain elaborate bureaucracies to sell 'correct' ideas on general policy questions along with favorable attitudes to the company."[10]

The vast amount of business advertising reinforces the general ethos of capitalism. What is its message? Ours is a lovely country; material luxuries represent the summum bonum; everyone can have these material luxuries. A certain percentage of business advertising is devoted to specifically political issues. Yet, the government permits *all* business advertising to be counted as a cost, that can be deducted from income when taxes are computed. Of course, labor unions are not allowed this tax deduction for political advertising.

Specifically, the unequal distribution of economic power means a very unequal distribution of the power to control political parties and their choice of candidates, as well as to influence elections. Thus, in America, upper-income classes have a very disproportionate effect on campaigns. Two conservative writers state that "because campaigns are exceedingly costly, the wealthier a person is, the more strategic his position for bringing pressure to bear on politicians."[11]

In the 1950s a candidate for Congress spent $15,000–$25,000; in 1970 many spent over $100,000. In the 1950s a Senate campaign ran up to a half million dollars per candidate; in 1970 the three candidates in New York spent about $5 million altogether. Sums

8 Ibid., p. 184.
9 Ibid., p. 245.
10 Ibid., p. 249.
11 Robert Dahl and Charles Lindblom, *Politics, Economics, and Welfare* (New York: Harper & Row, 1953), p. 313.

spent for the presidential elections are astronomical; in 1972 Edmund Muskie expects to spend about $12 million *in the primaries alone*. It is estimated that President Nixon spent $29 million in the 1968 campaign and will spend $40 million in the 1972 campaign. Total spending for the two main American capitalist parties at all levels has been rising rapidly: the best estimates are $140 million in 1952, $155 in 1956, $175 in 1960, $200 in 1964, and $300 million in 1968.[12]

The influence of money on elections has become still more obvious as politicians hire professional public relations firms to conduct their campaigns. Who can be hired and how much they will do depends on how much money the candidates are willing—and able—to spend.[13]

Another line of control of considerable importance is the private foundations, which spend money to support education and research. Naturally, the big businessmen who establish them have some influence on how their money is spent. Moreover, many of these foundations get direct help from the government, at least in their beginnings, and many are closely connected with the espionage and intelligence network.

Finally, the fact that upper-income groups exercise disproportionate political power naturally allows them to use the government itself to increase their power further. These political feedback effects on political behavior and the economic structure will be examined in a later section. They include such areas as the educational system; the police, army, and intelligence services; and even the pronouncements of the President. Also not to be overlooked is the effect exerted on people's political behavior by the control over their jobs, both private and public.

economic background of political leaders

Upper-income members of the capitalist class hold a disproportionate percentage of the top political positions. From 1789 to 1932, fathers of U.S. Presidents and Vice-Presidents were 38 percent professionals, 20 percent proprietors and officials, 38 percent farm owners, and only 4 percent wage earners or salaried workers. Similarly, from 1947 to 1951, fathers of U.S. senators were 22 percent professionals, 33 percent proprietors and officials, 40 percent farm owners, and only 4 percent wage earners or salaried workers. Finally, from 1941

[12] Data presented and discussed in Milton Cummings and David Wise *Democracy Under Pressure* (New York: Harcourt Brace Jovanovich, 1971), pp. 304–305.

[13] See Irish and Prothro, op. cit., pp. 257–266.

to 1943, fathers of U.S. representatives were 31 percent professionals, 31 percent proprietors and officials, 29 percent farm owners, and only 9 percent wage earners or salaried workers.[14]

Data for 1970 show that 266 of the 435 members of the House of Representatives (about three-fifths) had outside financial interests providing over $5,000 income a year beyond their congressional salaries.[15] This figure may be an underestimation because income of wives and children was not listed (nor was income under $5,000 listed). To make $5,000 a year from stocks and bonds requires at least $70,000 or $80,000 in holdings. The congressmen were not required to reveal the extent of their holdings. Some voluntarily disclosed this information. Very wealthy men, with fortunes ranging from many tens of thousands of dollars up to the slightly under $3,000,000 listed for Representative Pierre Du Pont, sit in Congress.

What are the sources of their wealth? A total of 102 congressmen held stock or well-paying executive positions in banks or other financial institutions; 81 received regular income from law firms that generally represented big businesses. Sixty-three got their income from stock in the top defense contractors; 45, in the giant (federally regulated) oil and gas industries; 22, in radio and television companies; 11, in commercial airlines; and 9, in railroads. Ninety-eight congressmen were involved in numerous capital-gains transactions; each of them netted a profit of over $5,000 (and some as high as $35,000).

In the executive branch (with the exception of the President and Vice-President), upper-income, business-oriented individuals have had a majority of all the important positions throughout U.S. history. This includes the members of the cabinet, their assistants and department heads, and heads of most regulatory agencies. They quite naturally, with no conspiracy, tend to consult big businessmen and groups as experts (such as the Committee for Economic Development or the Council on Foreign Relations). Wealthy families have also contributed a majority of federal judges, top military men, and top leaders of intelligence agencies. Finally, it should be noted that there is much crossing over at the top: Ex-generals often become corporate executives, and corporate executives often get to be cabinet members.

Of course, no serious radical would state the thesis of big-business control of government quite as strongly as President Wilson did in his anger at the moment he wrote. There are many qualifications. For example, although there are many men of means in Congress, the influence of wealth is much, much less than in the cabinet and

14 Ibid., p. 39.

15 All of these data were taken from statements filed with the House Committee on Standards of Official Conduct in April 1971; they were discussed in an article in the *Los Angeles Times* (May 24, 1971), Part I, p. 12.

other executive offices. Similarly, in state and local governments, the influence of the wealthy is very strong, but certainly they do not have exclusive control. Moreover, even among the members of the capitalist class in high positions, there are many differences of opinion, mistakes in perceiving their own interests, and conflicts of interest between different business groups. Thus, the rule of the captalist class is by no means monolithic; it rules through the forms of shifting coalitions and liberal or conservative styles, as reflected in the Democratic and Republican parties. Finally, the working class (including farmers, industrial workers, intellectual and professional workers, the poor and unemployed, and workers from minority groups) can sometimes organize sufficiently to overcome the power of money by pure weight of numbers and exert pressure, elect representatives, and sometimes even prevail on particular issues.

effects of government on economic inequality

Although everyone knows that there is extreme inequality in the United States, liberals argue that the inequality is much reduced by higher tax rates on the rich, welfare payments to the poor worker, subsidies to the poor farmer, public education for the poor, and antitrust laws, which decrease the concentration of income and power. Many radical critics, however, do not believe that any one of these is effective in the way that liberals argue. Each will be considered in detail.

HIGHER TAX RATES ON THE RICH

It is certainly true that income-tax rates rise as income rises, so that in theory individuals in the higher income brackets not only must pay more taxes, but also must pay a higher percentage of their incomes in taxes. Indeed, the theoretical tax rate today seems to take most of an individual's income, once that income exceeds $1 million.

In practice, rich taxpayers find many loopholes that allow them to pay much lower tax rates. Thus, in 1932, the highest tax rate was 54 percent, but only 47 percent was collected from the richest taxpayers.[16] In 1957, the highest tax rate had risen to an apparently confiscatory 91 percent, yet that category of taxpayers paid only 52 percent to the government.

One kind of loophole for the rich is *capital gains.* These are the income derived from sale of a piece of property at a higher price

[16] For this and much of the following information, see Gabriel Kolko, *Wealth and Power in America* (New York: Praeger, 1962), chap. 2.

than the price at which it was bought. The increase in value of property (held more than six months), or capital gain, is taxed at a maximum tax rate of 25 percent, which is considerably less than 91 percent. In 1957, 20 percent of incomes above $100,000 a year was in capital gains. But it should be noted that this loophole does not save money for the poor. For taxpayers in the $3,500–$4,000 income bracket, capital gains comprised only 0.3 percent of income.

Another large loophole is tax-free bonds. The interest on federal bonds cannot be taxed by states, and the interest on municipal bonds cannot be taxed by states or by the federal government. Of course, to make a significant amount of money from bonds, a very large investment is necessary; and bonds are typically sold in large lots that only the rich can afford.

As a result of these loopholes, some startling statistics have appeared. In 1965, a taxpayer had an income of $20 million but paid no taxes! In 1959, 5 Americans had incomes above $5 million but paid no taxes. In 1961, 17 Americans had incomes above $1 million but paid no taxes. One fellow has had an income of over $2 million a year since 1949 but has paid no taxes. And the number of millionaires paying no taxes has been steadily increasing in recent years. It has been estimated that the total loss of government revenue from all loopholes in the income-tax laws is about *$40 billion* a year.

Whereas the rich, with their income from property, can find many tax loopholes, there are none for the average worker with wage income. Consequently, there is in fact only the slightest redistribution of income as a result of the federal income tax. The data for 1962 indicate that the richest fifth (or top 20 percent) of the population had 45.5 percent of all income before taxes.[17] After taxes, their percentage of national income had decreased by only 1.8 percent! The poorest 20 percent had increased their share by only 0.3 percent; the second fifth, by only 0.6 percent; and the third fifth, by only 0.5 percent. Thus, *after taxes* the richest 20 percent still had far more income than the poorest 60 percent combined.

Even more important is the fact that the federal income tax amounts to only 40 percent of all taxes and is the only one that is progressive to even a slight extent (*progressive* means that the tax falls more heavily on the upper-income groups). The other 60 percent of taxes are mainly "regressive" according to most observers, in that they fall more heavily on the lower-income groups. "We might tentatively conclude that taxes other than individual income taxes do not reduce, and probably increase, income inequality."[18]

[17] These data come from Edward C. Budd, *Inequality and Poverty* (New York: Norton, 1967), pp. xiii and xvi.

[18] F. Ackerman, H. Birnbaum, J. Wetzler, and A. Zimbalist, "Income Distribution in the United States," *Review of Radical Political Economy* (Summer 1971), p. 24.

What are these other taxes? A little less than 30 percent are corporate income taxes. But corporations do not really pay these taxes out of their profits. On the contrary, corporations consider them a necessary cost and pass most of them on to the consumer in the form of higher prices. There is a great deal of controversy over exactly how much of the corporate income taxes are passed on to consumers. But it is striking that big changes in the tax rate do *not* seem to affect profit rates after taxes very much, if at all.

A little more than 30 percent of all taxes are state and local, such as the sales tax and the property tax. These fall much more heavily percentagewise on lower and middle incomes than on the rich. For example, a tax on gasoline or telephone service is spread quite equally among the population; therefore these taxes take a much higher percentage of a poor person's income. Thus, in 1958, the lowest income class ($0–$2,000) paid 11.3 percent of their income in state and local taxes. But each higher income group paid a smaller and smaller percentage: 9.4 percent ($2,000–$4,000 group), 8.5 percent ($4,000–$6,000 group), 7.7 percent ($6,000–$8,000 group), 7.2 percent ($8,000–$10,000 group), and 6.5 percent ($10,000–$15,000 group); 5.9 percent (over $15,000 group).[19] Thus, the higher the income group, the lower its state and local tax rates.

It also is thought that wealth is redistributed by inheritance taxes. But inheritance-tax rates are not very high, and federal and state laws are notable for their immense loopholes. Thus, large gifts can be given during the individual's lifetime, of which a considerable amount is free of any tax and the rest is taxed at a very low rate. Moreover, inheritances can be put into trusts so that one's descendants get the income immediately but direct control of the principal amount only after a fixed time. It is estimated that trusts can save up to 70 percent of inheritance taxes.

Finally, significant taxes are paid in the form of compulsory contributions by workers to social security. These taxes are highly regressive. In conclusion, the whole tax system redistributes very little, if any, income from rich to poor. It certainly does virtually nothing to mitigate poverty or reduce inequality.

WELFARE

Liberals assert that absolute poverty is the only income problem left, ignoring the fact that extreme inequality of income creates a relative, or social, poverty as well. They argue that because a growing number of people are getting larger welfare payments, the poverty problem will be solved. But poverty is not simply defined as an

[19] All data from Kolko, loc. cit.

absolute income level of less than $3,000; it is *relative* to the society in which a person lives. The people in India live on a median income of $100. There, a person earning $3,000 per year might be considered wealthy. But there can be no doubt that an American family living on that income could afford neither the cultural nor the physical necessities of life. So even if one earns $3,000 in a society as affluent as the United States, he still lives in relative poverty. Therefore, "brutalizing and degrading poverty will exist as long as extreme income inequality exists."[20]

Because taxation does not redistribute income, the question is whether welfare programs have a significant effect in that direction. In the first place, expenditures for welfare have been fairly small. In 1968, welfare spending under all federal, state, and local programs was only $26.9 billion. This included public aid, unemployment payments, workmen's compensation, health and medical programs, public housing, and educational aid to low-income students. These payments do help the poor somewhat, but the effect is small; it has virtually no effect in altering the relative positions of the poorest or the richest segments of society.

This $26.9 billion was only 3.82 percent of all personal income in 1968. Therefore, although it could make a few people better off, it could not change things very much.

What has been the historical trend of welfare payments? In 1938, welfare payments were 6.7 percent of personal income; in 1950, welfare was down to 3.86 percent; in 1960, it was down a little more, to 3.31 percent. Thus, the 3.82 percent level in 1968 was back to the 1950 level, and still just about half the 1938 level. Not only is welfare a small percentage of personal income but also it has actually decreased as a percentage in 30 years of much-touted new programs. Furthermore, there are qualifications. Some of that 3.82 percent does not go to the poorest groups. Welfare money spent on school lunches or university scholarships benefits middle-class children as well.

Moreover, the poor help pay for welfare, so the net amount received is even less. It is estimated that in 1968, the poorest 40 percent of the population (those with incomes below $7,500) paid in taxes about $6 billion of the money budgeted for welfare. This estimate assumes that taxes fell equally on the entire population and were not regressive, as the total tax burden may well be. Thus, net welfare to the poor (assuming all the welfare payments went to the poorest 40 percent) was not $26.9 billion, but $26.9 minus $6, or $20.9 billion. The percentage of income paid in net welfare is even

[20] Richard Edwards, "Who Fares Well in the Welfare State," in R. Edwards, M. Reich, and T. Weisskopf, eds. *The Capitalist System* (New York: Prentice-Hall, 1972), p. 244.

smaller than it looks at first. It is no wonder, then, that our tax and welfare systems have not resulted in any significant redistribution of income.

Interestingly, this same pattern of small effects and no significant reduction in income inequality over many decades also holds true for the capitalist countries of western Europe. Even in Denmark and Sweden, where taxation and welfare programs are supposed to be very, very progressive, recent studies have shown little change in income distribution (after taxes and welfare) for several decades. A U.N. report reveals that for all western Europe, "the general pattern of income distribution, by size of income, for the great majority of households, is only slightly affected by government action."[21]

The problem is that the social and economic conditions of a private-enterprise economy lead to a psychology in which one works only if one has to work. Thus, only by offering extremely unequal incomes for differing amounts of work done can work incentives be maintained under this system. It would take very different institutions with very different education and propaganda to change this psychology. Thus, U.S. welfare programs are very carefully designed to go to those who do not work: children, the old, the blind. No welfare income goes to those who work hard but are paid very low wages (who constitute about half of the poverty group) because that might lower their "incentives." A few programs give the low-paid worker minimum health and education so that he is able to work, but very carefully do not provide any food, clothing, or shelter. This philosophy of welfare leads to extreme degradation of welfare recipients. In order to galvanize the working poor to ever greater effort, welfare recipients are kept in such a pitiful, dehumanized condition, that anyone would rather work, even at the most disagreeable jobs and at the lowest pay.

The dole a welfare recipient receives is grossly insufficient for even the barest subsistence livelihood. Moreover, in return for this paltry sum, the individual loses many basic civil rights supposedly guaranteed to everyone. The single woman supporting a family on welfare, for example, must permit welfare workers to search her house and subject her to a demeaning grilling to ascertain if her personal sexual conduct is proper and fitting. This is only one of many ways welfare recipients are degraded and dehumanized. It is quite absurd to argue that programs such as these will ever eliminate poverty.

21 U.N. Economic Commission of Europe, *Incomes in Postwar Europe: A Study of Policies, Growth, and Distribution* (Geneva: United Nations, 1957), pp. 1–15.

farm subsidies

The rural poor have suffered the most pathetic poverty. For most of the twentieth century, the incomes of small-farm owners and farm workers have lagged far behind other U.S. incomes. For that reason, liberals have persuaded Congress to pass various bills aiding farmers with subsidies. What has been the practical effect of these subsidies?

First, the high economic concentration among the business firms engaged in farming should be noted. At present, the richest 10 percent of farms produce over 50 percent of all agricultural output. The poorest 50 percent of all farms produce only 5 percent of farm output.

Second, the farm-support programs benefit mainly the richest farmers and give very little support to the poorest farmers. In the years 1963–1965, the poorest 20 percent of farms received only 1 percent of the farm subsidies given in sugar cane, rice, and feed grains; 2 percent, in cotton; 3 percent, in wheat, 4 percent, in peanuts and tobacco; and 5 percent, in sugar beets. At the same time, the richest 20 percent of farms (with the highest incomes before subsidies) received 83 percent of the farm subsidies given in sugar cane; 69 percent, in cotton; 65 percent, in rice; 62 percent, in wheat; 56 percent, in feed grains; 57 percent, in peanuts; 53 percent, in tobacco; and 51 percent, in sugar beets.[22]

Third, it appears, in fact, that the net result of the farm program is to increase the percentage of total farm income going to the richest farmers and to decrease the percentage of total farm income going to the poorest farmers. Roughly, this can be seen from the fact that in 1963, the poorest 20 percent of farmers and farm managers received 3.2 percent of farm income, whereas the richest 20 percent received 50.5 percent of farm income. Yet the data cited on subsidies showed that many of the farm programs gave less than 3.2 percent of the benefits to the poorest farmers, and more than 50.5 percent of the benefits to the richest farmers. Thus, not only do most of the benefits go to the richest farmers, but their share of the subsidies is *higher* than their share of the presubsidy income, so the disproportionate subsidies make farm income more extremely unequal than it would be without them. Clearly, income inequality in farming is actually *increased* by the farm programs. In other words, it appears to be a regressive program, although we cannot say just how

---

[22] All data from James Bonnen, "The Effect of Taxes and Government Spending on Inequality," in *The Capitalist System,* pp. 235–243.

regressive: "the net effect of these programs may be less regressive than the data suggest—or possibly more regressive—but the pattern is clear."[23]

The discussion to this point shows the effects of the farm programs on farmers who own their own farms. There is a fourth factor: what are the effects on farm workers who own nothing but their power to labor? The answer is very simple. The two main farm programs provide farm owners, mainly on the largest, richest farms, price supports to maintain prices at a certain level above costs, and payments to keep some land out of production in order to reduce the supply of farm goods. No money from these programs goes to farm workers. In fact, the programs may hurt farm workers to the extent that the programs pay to keep land out of production, thereby increasing unemployment. "The State pays the owners of farm property not to produce, but pays virtually nothing to farm workers who become unemployed as a result of this dole to property owners."[24]

Finally, the net result of this program—to help farm workers not at all, to help poor farmers slightly, and to help rich farmers very much —is not at all surprising. Indeed, it represents a continuation of a consistent pattern in U.S. history. Large corporations have always been the ones helped by government subsidies. In the nineteenth century, for example, three-fourths of all railroad construction was paid for by the government and huge amounts of land were given to the railroads.

EDUCATION AND INEQUALITY

Government-subsidized education is often thought to decrease the inequality of incomes. "The government gives free education to all," goes the argument, "so anyone can improve his station in life by going to school for a longer period."

Clearly, there is a significant positive correlation between amount of education and level of income. Thus, in 1968, those with only eight years schooling had a median income of only $6,600.[25] The median income for high-school graduates was $8,300, and that for college graduates was $11,800. In part, more schooling is the cause of better jobs and better pay for the individual. In part, however, better schooling is the effect of having a high income (and to some extent individuals from high-income families may get high-income

23 Ibid., p. 242.

24 Howard Wachtel, "Looking at Poverty from a Radical Perspective," Review of Radical Political Economics (Summer, 1971), p. 12.

25 All data in this paragraph are from F. Ackerman, H. Birnbaum, J. Wetzler, and A. Zimbalist, "Income Distribution in the United States," op. cit.

jobs merely because their fathers own the businesses in which they work).

It is a fact that individuals from high-income families are able to get more schooling in the United States than individuals from low-income families. This may be seen in the following data from a survey that classified students graduating from high school in 1966 according to their family's income in 1965.[26] Of those in the under $3,000 income group, only 20 percent started college by February 1967. In the same period, 32 percent in the $3,000–4,000 group started college, 37 percent in the $4,000–6,000 group, 41 percent in the $6,000–7,000 group, 51 percent in the $7,000–10,000 group, and 61 percent in the $10,000–$15,000 group. Fully 87 percent of those with family incomes over $15,000 started college. Thus, the higher one's family's income, the greater his chance of going to college.

Children of richer parents get more schooling mainly because they can afford to keep their children in school longer than can poor parents. They can pay high tuitions in private schools that admit students even with low grade averages. Even in the public universities, where the tuition may be much lower or nonexistent, there are still living expenses. Many students must drop out of college or not enroll simply because they have no money on which to live while in school.

Furthermore, children of richer families have a better chance to do well in school and learn more. Opportunities and encouragement provided in the home and community are much more likely to produce highly motivated children who know how to study. Cultural background is very important in performance on IQ tests and college entrance record examinations. These examinations, which purport to test general ability, in reality are designed to conform to middle-class, white, urban experience. A student from a poor or black or rural background will lack the necessary cultural references to understand the questions or have any intuition of the answers. This has been proven over and over again, but the tests are still used. They determine which "track" (discussed below) an elementary student is put into, and they determine who enters college. Thus, it is no surprise that only 7 percent of college students come from the poorest 25 percent of families.

Another condition that hurts students from poor families and helps those from richer families is the fact that schools in different areas get very different amounts of money. Central-city slum schools often receive less money per student and almost always attract less competent teachers. Suburban township schools are apt to receive more money per student and attract better teachers.

26 Ibid.

Students in elementary and high schools are put into different *tracks*.[27] One track is vocational training, which prepares the poor for manual labor. Another track, college preparation, equips students from upper-middle-class and richer families for college, in order to get high-income jobs (so that their children can go to college, and so forth). In elementary schools, it is often called *ability grouping* of the bright and the stupid. But the degree of ability is determined by IQ tests that do not assess innate intelligence, but, as noted previously, do discriminate on the basis of class background.

The tracking system exists both within high schools, and between high schools. Within some high schools, counselors push the poor and the minority groups into vocational training and the rich into college preparation. Within others, such pushing is hardly necessary because of the vast differences among schools. Schools in the black slums provide only basic, or vocational, training. Schools in the richest areas give only college preparation. These different tracks are enforced both formally by the tests given and informally by counselors and teachers. One investigation in New York showed that middle-class white children were usually offered voluntary classes in how to pass college examinations, but that in Harlem, even seeing the old tests was "against the rules."[28]

We may conclude with certainty that our educational system does not reduce inequality from generation to generation. On the contrary, the richer students have more opportunities to get a good elementary and high-school education, to get into college, to remain in college, and therefore to get a high-income job after college—and then to send their children to college. Thus, the educational system seems to transmit inequality from one generation to the next.

GOVERNMENT AND BUSINESS

In the United States, the industrial revolution commenced after the Civil War. In the more than a century of American industrial capitalism, the relationship between government and big business is seen by some observers as having been desultory and often contradictory. This is because many government programs and legislative acts were designed to promote big business, whereas some laws, particularly antitrust legislation, were ostensibly designed to curb the size and power of big business.

Thurman Arnold, former "trust-busting" head of the federal government's antitrust division, believes that these contradictory policies

---

[27] The best description of 'tracking" is in Florence Howe and Paul Lautner, "How the School System Is Rigged," in *The Capitalist System*, pp. 229–235.

[28] Ibid., p. 234.

and laws have stemmed from "a continuous conflict between opposing ideals in American economic thinking."[29] The power of "economic
thinking," taken alone, explains very little, however. A more realistic
explanation of these seeming contradictions would be based on the
two broadest objectives of government in its dealings with big
business.

First, the government has been committed to the maintenance of
the capitalist system and the promotion of the interests of big
business. This commitment has generally dominated the relationship
between government and business. The interests of various capitalists
and business firms, however, are not always mutually compatible.
Many conflicts are so intense that if left unresolved, they could
eventually threaten the very existence of the capitalist system.
Government's second objective, therefore, is to act as the arbiter in
these rivalries and to resolve the difficulties before they become so
extremely serious.

The antitrust laws have given the federal government a measure
of power to enforce its function as arbiter. When interpreted in this
way, the government's policy toward business has not been contradictory. Nor has this policy been designed, as many liberals believe,
to curb the immense power of giant corporations. Rather, it has
always attempted to promote the *general interests* of *all capitalists*
and *all businesses*. Sometimes the individual interests of capitalists
have coincided, as, for example, in the late nineteenth-century
attempt to crush labor unions. But, in instances of industrial or
commercial rivalry between two giant corporate empires, the interests
have been in conflict. In such cases, the general interests of all
capitalists would depend upon at least partial restriction of one or
both of the rivals.

American industrialization was aided significantly by the intimate
association of government and business. Big business was supported
by protective tariffs, which began with the Morrill Tariff of 1861 and
were expanded significantly in 1890, 1894, and 1897. Thus, large
corporations were protected from foreign competition and could use
fully their domestic monopoly powers to charge high prices.

Banking and treasury policies resulted in prolonged price declines.
This generally helped bankers and creditors because the money they
received in payment was worth more than that they loaned out.

The due process clause of the Fourteenth Amendment had been
intended to give equal rights to blacks. In the late nineteenth century,
it was not used to help blacks at all. Rather, it was interpreted to
prohibit state regulation of corporations (who were held to be legal

---

[29] Thurman Arnold, "Economic Reform and the Sherman Anti-trust Act," in J. A.
Garraty, ed., *Historical Viewpoints: Volume Two, Since 1865* (New York: Harper &
Row, 1969), p. 151.

"persons"). The courts denied state governments the right to interfere in any way with even the most abusive, malicious, and socially deleterious corporate behavior.

The railroad magnates were among the most important entrepreneurs in the American industrial revolution. Through bribery, chicanery, and fraud, they amassed great personal fortunes. Building railroads was never more than the vehicle from which they launched their financial schemes. The federal government responded by generously giving federal lands to the railroads. Between 1850 and 1871, the railroads were handed 130 million acres of land, an area as large as all the New England States plus Pennsylvania and New York. During the same period, state governments gave the railroads another 49 million acres. All this, and yet some economic historians still refer to the second half of the nineteenth century as an age where government stayed out of business affairs!

Toward the end of the nineteenth century, the relationship between the federal government and big business became a symbiosis in which the government governed in ways that big business wanted it to govern; and big business furnished the money, organization, and power structure through which politicians could come to power in the federal government. When progressive elements of the Democratic party saw that Democratic President Cleveland's relationship with big business was hardly distinguishable from the Republican–big business relationship, they captured control of the party and nominated William Jennings Bryan, a champion of the workers and farmers. William McKinley, the big-business Republican candidate, raised campaign funds estimated to total as much as $15 million, 50 times more than Bryan's $300,000. From that time onward, the Democratic party has been more careful about picking a candidate of whom at least a large segment of big business approves.

In Chapter 8, it was seen that many government regulatory agencies have been established since the creation, in the late nineteenth century, of the ICC. These commissions are commonly thought to be watchdogs of the public interests, but in general they are merely a more effective way to achieve monopoly powers for an oligopoly. The commissions look after the interests of those they are supposed to regulate, not the interests of the general public.

ANTITRUST LAWS

There have been four major laws designed ostensibly to decrease the monopoly power of big business and to extend the federal government's power over big business. The first was the Sherman Antitrust Act of 1890, which forbade any contract, combination, or conspiracy to restrain trade.[30] In fact, it forbade any agreement not to compete, regardless of how the agreement was achieved. It also forbade monopolies or attempts to monopolize.

The Clayton Act of 1914 forbade corporations to engage in price discrimination or to enter into exclusive or tying contracts. It also prohibited *interlocking directorates* where this would lead to a substantial lessening of competition.

The Federal Trade Commission Act of 1914 outlawed *unfair* methods of competition and established the FTC to investigate the methods of competition used by business firms. Finally, The Celler-Kefauver Act of 1950 forbade the purchasing of either the stock of a competing corporation (which had already been illegal) or the assets of competing corporations (which had been a big loophole in the laws).

The most interesting feature of the antitrust laws is that they were designed to limit the concentration of economic power among corporations. Yet, as one observer has written, "the fact that after the passage of the Sherman Act the country witnessed a spectacular merger movement, another wave after the passage of the Clayton Act (1914), and again after the Celler-Kefauver Act, indicates that the laws have been ineffective in 'limiting the concentration of control.' "[31]

For the first two decades after the passage of the Sherman Act, the antitrust laws were used almost exclusively to break the power of labor unions to strike against employers. Although there have been periodic convictions of business firms throughout the twentieth century, most observers agree that virtually all the important oligopolistic corporations are constantly violating most of the antitrust-law sanctions. There is almost no price competition among the giants. There are many, many instances of interlocking director-ates, and almost no one doubts the pervasive existence of illegal collusion among giant corporations.

Why then are a few corporations occasionally singled out for conviction for violations of which virtually all corporations are guilty? We believe that in these cases the government uses the antitrust laws to act as arbiter in the irreconcilable conflicts between various corporations. Antitrust convictions are generally mildly punitive government actions, taken when the government decides which group of corporations should be supported in a particular conflict of interest. This was most apparent recently when the U.S. government acted against certain conglomerate mergers in which "young newcomers" tried to take over old established corporations.

[30] For a more detailed historical account of the Sherman act and its early enforcement, see Chapter 8.

[31] Douglas F. Dowd, *Modern Economic Problems in Historical Perspective* (Boston: Raytheon/Heath 1965), p. 49.

The government does not really attempt to eliminate the pervasive illegal policies of corporations. Throughout American history, the government has done everything it could to create and promote the interests of monopolistic businesses. For the good of all, a few must occasionally be slapped on the wrists. Antitrust laws make this possible. They therefore operate to blunt some of traditional anti-monopoly sentiment and to resolve some conflicts between different corporate interests.

summary

The economic power of a comparatively few corporations and individuals, which was examined in previous chapters, was shown here to result in a disproportionate degree of political power for this same group. This is not an accident, but a perfectly natural result of their control over the press, television and radio, advertising, financing for political campaigns and for lobbying, of foundations, and many other avenues of control open to those with wealth.

Because of this natural influence (and not any conspiracy), government policies do not decrease inequality in the American economy. In fact, after considering only those policies that are supposed to reduce inequality (such as taxation, farm subsidies, and education), we can conclude that many of them actually increase the degree of inequality. If we had considered all government policies, the net effect would undoubtedly have been to substantially increase inequality. Given the present sources of political power, it appears very doubtful whether the government will ever take actions that would substantially reduce poverty and inequality.

chapter 20
economics of discrimination: eternal facts or capitalism?

Most elementary economics books ignore racial and sexual
discrimination as social phenomena external to economics. These
phenomena, however, have political–economic roots and, in turn,
affect the economy in important ways.

racial discrimination

In the United States, racism involves prejudice and discrimination
against many minorities. The most common form is use of an ideology
claiming that another race is inferior, in order to justify profit-making
and discrimination against them. For example, the white colonists in
America declared that the Indians were inferior and then stole their
land and almost eliminated them physically.

Ironically, each succeeding wave of white settlers was met by a
form of racism called *nationalist* prejudice, which was directed at
them by those who were already here. Thus, all eastern Europeans
were held to be backward in culture; Italians were all lazy; Irish were

This chapter largely reproduces the ideas developed at greater length in Chapter 11
of Howard J. Sherman, *Radical Political Economy: Capitalism and Socialism from a
Marxist-Humanist Perspective* (New York: Basic Books, 1972).

all loud and uncouth. Against Chinese and Japanese immigrants, there was a combination of nationalist and racist prejudice. During World War II, all Americans of Japanese ancestry on the West Coast were confined to concentration camps (German-Americans never were). Finally, nationalist and racist prejudice also combines to support discrimination against Americans of Mexican and Puerto Rican origin (both were incorporated into the United States through imperialist expansion, one group in the war against Mexico, and the other in the war against Spain).

Religious bigotry is another form of discrimination closely related to national chauvinism and racial prejudice; indeed, all are similar both in causes and in effects. In Europe, Protestants and Catholics killed each other for centuries; and in America, the Catholic minority is still subjected to a certain amount of prejudice and discrimination. Much worse, of course, was the many-centuries-long oppression of the Jews, forcibly converted, limited to certain occupations, often taxed to bankruptcy, periodically massacred. Yet in the late nineteenth and early twentieth centuries, it appeared that anti-Jewish sentiment was dying away; and it has never been as severe in America as in some other countries, although it certainly exists. But just as the Jews began to feel secure, Hitler's fascism unleashed the worst racist atrocity in the history of the world. More than 6 million Jewish men, women, and children were tortured, gassed, and burned to death. It is surely one of the great ironies of history that some of the few survivors, now the leaders of Israel, themselves preach and practice discrimination, not only against the Arabs but also against their "inferior" fellow Jews from Asia and Africa.

Another racist atrocity was the enslavement of black Africans throughout three centuries and their shipment under horrifying, inhuman conditions to various places of prison and work, especially the American South. This enslavement was not done in the name of Aryan domination, as was Hitler's killing of the Jews and other "inferior" peoples, but in the gentle name of Christianity, it being the white man's burden to bring civilization and the true faith to the black man. One result of this enslavement is that blacks today constitute the largest single minority in the United States, and one of the most oppressed.

When blacks were slaves doing simple agricultural work in the South, racism played its usual function of explaining that blacks were inferior to whites, that slavery was their natural condition, that such simple labor was all they could do, and that they were very happy in this condition. Now that blacks are a large part or a majority in many American cities and do all the complex tasks required to run American industry and urban life, the prejudices have changed somewhat, but the discrimination is as fierce as ever.

The current data[1] show that (in 1968) the per capita income of American whites was $2,616, but that of blacks was only $1,348. Only 8 percent of white families but 29 percent of black families were below the official poverty level (understated at $3,553 for an urban family of four). According to the Bureau of Labor Statistics, a "modest but adequate" family budget was $9,100 (computed at the much-lower prices of 1966). Only 20 percent of whites but 47 percent of blacks earned below $5,000 in family income. Some 42 percent of whites, but fully 71 percent of blacks earned below $8,000 in family income. At the other extreme, 2.8 percent of white families but only 0.4 percent of black families had incomes over $25,000.

The same dreary picture exists for unemployment statistics. In February 1970, when white unemployment was officially at the very low figure of 3.8 percent, nonwhite (92 percent black) unemployment was almost double that figure, 7.0 percent. Similarly, among married men, white unemployment was a negligible 1.4 percent, whereas nonwhite unemployment was 2.5 percent. Among teenagers, white unemployment jumped to 11.7 percent whereas nonwhite unemployment was an incredible 25.3 percent. Imagine the plight of black youth when average white unemployment goes up to a 6 percent level (the level of unemployment for all workers in California as this is written is 7 percent).

Discrimination shows up in every aspect of American life. Even the very conservative *Time* magazine concluded that "Black Americans pay more than whites for comparable housing, and are four times more likely to live in substandard housing."[2] In fact, 25 percent of blacks reported leaky ceilings; 26 percent, overcrowding; 29 percent, rats; 32 percent, faulty plumbing; 38 percent, cockroaches.

Time's survey (same issue) found that in 1969, there were only 9 black representatives, and 1 black senator in the U.S. Congress. Of 24,000 architects, only 450 were black. Of 6,338 American radio stations, blacks owned 11. Of 690 television channels, blacks owned none. Of 300,000 American lawyers, only 3,000 were black. Only 5 percent of all reporters and photographers were black. Thirty-eight percent of the Atlanta population were black, but only 10 percent of the city's police force; 39 percent of the Detroit population but only 5 percent of their police force; and 63 percent of the Washington, D.C., population, but only 21 percent of the police force are black. Of 459 federal judges, only 22 were black. Of 12,000 city and state judges, only 178 were black. Blacks are arrested three to four times more often than whites, and of those arrested, a larger proportion are jailed, convicted, and get stiff sentences. As of April 1970, more than

---

[1] United States Department of Commerce, various publications.
[2] *Time* (April 6, 1970), p. 53.

50 percent of those condemned to death and awaiting execution were black.

Consider health next.[3] Blacks constitute almost one-half of all American drug addicts. The suicide rate of the black ghetto is about twice the white rate. In 1967, per 100,000 Americans, there were 15.3 cases of tuberculosis among whites and 65.1 cases among nonwhites. The death rate from tuberculosis was 2.8 per 100,000 whites and 8.4 per 100,000 nonwhites. At birth, the maternal death rate per 100,000 for whites was 19.7 but 37.5 for nonwhites. The death rate for infants in the first 28 days was 15 for whites but 25 for nonwhites. The infant death rate for 1 to 11 months was 4.7 for whites but 12.5 for nonwhites. Life expectancy for whites was 71.3 years; for nonwhites, 64.6 years.

In education,[4] 73 percent of whites complete eighth grade, but only 58 percent of blacks. And in mid-1970, three-fourths of blacks in the South still attended elementary schools that were at least 95 percent black; whereas one-half of all blacks in the North attended elementary schools that were at least 95 percent black. High school is completed by 62 percent of whites but by only 40 percent of blacks. Only 6.4 percent of college students are black, and half of these are in all-black colleges in the South. Blacks constitute only 1 percent of all doctoral candidates, 3 percent of all law students, 3 percent of all medical students, and less than 1 percent of the faculty at 80 public universities. Moreover, even if blacks surmount all the barriers and get an equal education, they still face job and salary discrimination. Thus, whites graduating from eighth grade have higher incomes than blacks graduating from high school. And whites graduating from high school have higher incomes than blacks graduating from college.

Finally, recent trends show the situation worsening rather than improving in several aspects.[5] The differences between black and white incomes and between black and white unemployment rates have been increasing in the last decade. Moreover, blacks constitute a growing percentage of workers in "declining job categories"—that is, unskilled jobs and industries with no employment growth. Blacks also constitute an increasing percentage (now over 25 percent) of all the long-term, or permanently, unemployed. Furthermore, "Patterns of residential segregation between Negro and white . . . are more pronounced than they were a decade ago."[6]

---

[3] Data from U.S. Department of Health, Education, and Welfare.

[4] *Time*, loc. cit.

[5] See data and analysis in Louis Ferman, Joyce Kornbluh, and J. Miller, eds., *Negroes and Jobs* (Ann Arbor: University of Michigan Press, 1968).

[6] Ibid., p. 194.

It is not necessary to detail the comparative facts for other minorities in America because they are quite similar. The degree of oppression is particularly intense in relation to the second-largest minority group, the Americans of Mexican and Puerto Rican descent. Actually, although there might be some controversy over recent trends, every writer on the subject, conservative or liberal as well as radical, seems largely to agree on the present extent of discrimination. The argument comes over the causes and the solutions.

The most conservative view is now, as always, that there are inherited biological differences, making the blacks (and Mexicans, Indians, Jews, Catholics, ad infinitum) intellectually and physically inferior. The inferiority is the cause of lower income, less educational achievement, and so forth. Moreover, they are lazy and like to live in squalor. Because these arguments are not backed by any scientific evidence, and because refutations do not lessen the prejudice one bit, we may leave this view without further comment. (Races, are, of course, defined by their superficial physical differences, but there are *no* important biological differences among the races of humankind, much less any inherited intellectual differences.)

Liberal analysts tend to see the problem as a vicious circle: The environment causes inferior performance, which leads to more prejudice, which leads to less achievement, with the result that the victims cannot leave their poor environment. For example, the problem is said to be that blacks have "distinctive values" which isolate them culturally and hinder them economically. They have "a set of beliefs that favor a social dependency role for the Negro rather than one of independence; . . . female role dominance as against males; and low aspiration patterns that set limited achievement goals."[7] Although not necessarily asserting that the problem is inherited inferiority, this "liberal" view still locates the problem in the mind of the black. In this sense, the approach is related to the conservative racist view of inherent inferiority.

In the radical view, the problem cannot be that blacks want dependency or have "low aspiration patterns." On the contrary, discrimination is imposed on the black by white society in every aspect of life, even against the minute few who struggle against the barriers to the highest levels of educational achievement. The real causes of racist discrimination do not lie in inherent black inferiority (because that is nonexistent), nor even in inherent white racism (because that has changed at different times and can be changed further in the future). The real causes are the institutional relationships that give racism a useful function for ruling political and economic interests.

7 Ibid., p. 108.

Radicals maintain that in the pre–Civil War South, racism was a useful apologia for slavery. It meant that the slaveowners would have no guilty consciences, the slaves might accept their lot more easily, and the northerners would not interfere. Racism declared that slavery was divinely ordained by God as a benefit to the inferior black. Thus, its first function is to justify economic exploitation.

Radicals maintain that the second function of racism is to find a scapegoat for all problems. For example, the white is told that the dirt and violence of the modern city is all due to the black. Similarly, Hitler told German workers that unemployment was all due to Jewish bankers, and the middle class was told that all the agitation was due to Jewish Communists.

The third function of racism, according to radicals, is to divide the oppressed so that the elite can rule. For example, no one is more oppressed or poverty-stricken than the white southern sharecropper. But he has always fought against his natural allies, the blacks. Instead, the poor white has given political support to the wealthy white southerners who not only monopolize southern state and local politics but also wield disproportionate influence in Congress because they succeed to and hold key committee chairmanships and leadership positions by virtue of seniority. In another example, the white worker is set against the black worker, so that unionization is prevented altogether in many southern areas, and each can be used as a strikebreaker against the others. The same kind of divide-and-rule tactic is used in northern cities.

Radicals also claim that racism is a particularly handy tool of imperialism. England especially has long used the strategy of divide and rule: Hindu against Moslem, Jew against Arab, Protestant against Catholic, Biafran against Nigerian, black against Hindu in Guyana. And America is quite willing to use the same tactic: Vietnamese against Cambodian, Thai against Laotian. Moreover, "inferiority" (inherited or acquired) is still being given as a reason for lack of development—where imperialism is the real reason. Finally, national chauvinism, or patriotism, always asserts that aggression comes from the other, evil people, and "our" own pure motives should not be questioned.

Radicals assert that blacks are exploited within the United States, both as an internal colony and as workers. Blacks today constitute about one-third of the entire industrial labor force and an even larger percentage of unskilled manual laborers. Racial discrimination keeps them "in their place" as a large pool of unskilled and often unemployed workers, to be used to hold down wages in times of high demand for labor; racial prejudice justifies that place. Thus, racism is in this respect only one more added apologia for considerable extra profits extracted at the expense of the lowest-paid part of the American working class.

Because that exploitation is at the heart of the system, legal reforms cannot give much help to most blacks. Radicals claim that

> the system has two poles; wealth, privilege, power at one; poverty, deprivation, powerlessness at the other. It has always been that way, but in earlier times whole groups could rise because expansion made room above, and there were others ready to take their place at the bottom. Today, Negroes are at the bottom, and there is neither room above nor anyone ready to take their place. Thus only individuals can move up, not the group as such: reforms help the few, not the many. For the many, nothing short of a complete change in the system—the abolition of both poles and the substitution of a society in which wealth and power are shared by all—can transform their condition.[8]

sexual discrimination

Sexism, or the theory of male supremacy, is an ideology that serves to justify discrimination against the majority of Americans (women comprise about 51 percent of the U.S. population). Although sexism is similar in the pattern of discrimination and in ideology to racism, in most aspects, but not all, racist discrimination is worse. Yet sexism is more pervasive, more deeply ingrained, and harder to combat. Clearly the black woman is held to be doubly "inferior" and suffers the most discrimination.

The facts bear out these generalities. In 1966, only 5 percent of all four-person U.S. families headed by white males were below the official poverty line. Of families headed by black males, 20 percent were below the poverty line. Of families headed by white females, 37 percent were below the poverty line. And of families headed by black females, 62 percent were below the poverty line.[9]

The problem is no longer that women are not allowed to work outside the house. In 1968, women constituted 37 percent of the whole civilian labor force. In fact, in 1969, some 48 percent of all women age 20 to 64 were in the labor force.[10] These figures could be higher, but that is not the main problem. The point is that over 90 percent of

[8] Paul Sweezy and Paul Baran, *Monopoly Capital* (New York: Monthly Review Press, 1966), p. 279.

[9] U.S. Bureau of the Census, *Extent of Poverty in the United States 1959 to 1966*, Current Population Reports Series p-60, no. 54 (May 1968).

[10] Department of Labor data.

these women work not by desire, but by economic necessity; and they face discrimination on the job.

Thus, in 1968, the average woman employed full time earned only 58 percent of the average male's salary. This, in fact, was a decline from the 64 percent of ten years earlier. Specifically, the median salary of full-time workers was $7,870 for white men, $5,314 for black men, $4,584 for white women, and only $3,487 for black women. Furthermore, women who surmount the barriers to their getting an education discover that an equal education *does not* give them equal jobs or equal pay. Women with college degrees make just a little more than men with eighth-grade educations! Among women with four years of college, 17 percent take jobs as unskilled or semiskilled workers. Even among women with five years or more of college, 6 percent take unskilled or semiskilled jobs.

Moreover, in 1968, women constituted only 9 percent of all the professions: 7 percent of the doctors, 3 percent of the lawyers, and 1 percent of the engineers. Women are only 5 percent of all individuals with incomes over $10,000, only 2 percent of business executives listed in *Standard and Poor's Directory,* less than 4 percent of all federal civil servants in the six highest grades, 1 percent of federal judges, and 1 percent of the U.S. Senate.[11] In 1968, California women with four years or more of college earned on the average only $4,151 a year; California men with the same education averaged $8,108 a year. In fact, a 1961 poll of the National Office Managers' Association found that one-third of the members admitted that they systematically paid women less than men for the same jobs.

Furthermore, more working women are unemployed. Typically, if white men are 5 percent unemployed, white women will average 10 to 15 percent unemployment, black men will average 10 percent, and black women will average 20 percent. It might be added that discrimination against youth also is reflected in the unemployment figures. Among teenage black women looking for jobs, unemployment will run 40 percent. It should also be said that women face discrimination even in getting unemployment benefits; for example, in 37 states, a woman fired because she is pregnant does *not* get the benefit of unemployment insurance.

Discrimination against women workers means a significant amount of extra profits to employers. In 1969, women's wages averaged about 40 percent less than men's wages for the same job. On that basis, it can be calculated that the extra profits from employing women at lower rates amounted to about 23 percent of all corporate manufacturing profits.

The ideologies of racism and sexism are similar in many ways.

11 See Caroline Bind, *Born Female: The High Cost of Keeping Women Down* (New York: Pocket Books, 1969), p. 82 ff. This book gives an excellent factual survey, including most of the material cited here.

Both are based on the supposed inferiority of some groups of human beings to others: "all discrimination is eventually the same thing—Anti-Humanism."[12] Women have long been alleged to be inferior both in intelligence and in physical ability to do hard work. Even in the present "enlightened" age, the ideology of sexism continues in unabated fury. Thus, the conservative view still justifies lower pay for women: "If a woman were more like a man, she'd be treated as such."[13] This view ignores the main point: that millions of women get less pay for doing the same work as men.

A more "liberal" statement of sexism comes from Dr. Edgar Benson, member of the Democratic party's Committee of National Priorities (and a close friend of former Vice-President Hubert Humphrey), who says "that physical factors, particularly the menstrual cycle and menopause, disqualifies women for key executive jobs."[14] Is it not fortunate that instead of nervous females, who might get us into wars, we have had our destiny in the hands of a series of calm, masculine politicians?

All tests show that men and women are equal in intelligence, although they usually progress at different rates in childhood learning, with women leading in the early years.

Radicals certainly admit that there are physical differences between men and women. With respect to working ability, however, it is by no means clear that the differences make women inferior. Many modern tests indicate that women have more stamina as well as more patience, at least in Western society, and in some primitive societies, where women normally carry heavier loads than men. The question is one of training and expectations. Listen to the lot of the slave woman of the American South as stated by the great black abolitionist Sojourner Truth: "Look at my arm! I have ploughed and planted and gathered into barns, and no man could head me—and ain't I a woman? I have borne thirteen children, and seen most of 'em sold into slavery, and when I cried out with my mother's grief, none but Jesus heard me—and ain't I a woman?"[15]

Even in social and sexual matters, in the radical view, it is not a given eternal fact that man must always dominate. In some primitive societies, men and women appear to have about equal social and sexual roles (perhaps especially societies in which the economic roles of the two are roughly equal in importance, as when women

12 Congresswoman Shirley Chisholm, "Racism and Anti-Feminism," *The Black Scholar* (January–February 1970), p. 45.

13 Angus Black, *A Radical's Guide to Economic Reality* (New York: Holt, Rinehart & Winston, 1970), p. 37.

14 Quoted in the *San Francisco Chronicle* (July 27, 1970), p. 9.

15 Quoted in Bind, op. cit., p. 25.

gather wild food and men hunt). In other primitive societies, women appear to play the dominant role. If nothing else can be said without controversy, at least modern anthropology makes clear that there are many types of family organization (including various kinds of group marriages), not just one.

Only with the coming of civilization (meaning economic stratification and the possession of property in land, cattle, slaves, or serfs) does the woman also become a piece of property. In fact, for purposes of clear inheritance of property, the woman of the upper classes in ancient civilizations was very well-guarded; only the male could freely violate the theoretical monogamy (the beginning of the double standard).

In the radical view, the particular attitudes of American men and women are carefully inculcated, not inherited. "Women are taught from the time they are children to play a serving role, to be docile and submissive. . . ."[16] Women are taught to be ornamental, and Americans thought of cosmetics as solely for women until very recently. Yet the French noblemen before the Revolution used plentiful cosmetics. And except for prostitutes, women in the West did not use cosmetics before the nineteenth century.

What are the causes for the ideology of sexism and the discrimination against women? In the radical view, some of its functions are similar to those of racism. First, it is an excuse for extra profit-making at the expense of women workers. Second, the division between male and female workers makes it possible to keep all workers weaker and ruled. Third, it is a means to ensure family stability, which is considered to be an important basis for the stability of capitalism.

Furthermore, advertising has associated the number of gadgets in the household with the welfare of the family, so the family unit provides a powerful boost to the spirit of unlimited competition. Thus, the women's magazines find the perfect heroine in the woman who says she is thankful for having a "wonderful husband, handsome sons . . . big comfortable house . . . my good health and faith in God and such material possessions as two cars, two TVs and two fireplaces."[17] Of course, working-class women do not have these material possessions, but they can have faith in God.

It has often been said that the position of women in a society usually mirrors the general condition of human rights in a society. Even in the nineteenth century, the connection was pointed out to those radicals who wished to ignore it: "Every socialist recognized

[16] Marilyn Goldberg, "The Economic Exploitation of Women," *The Review of Radical Political Economics,* (Spring 1970), p. 35.

[17] Ibid., p. 64.

the dependence of the workmen on the capitalist . . . but the same socialist often does not recognize the dependence of women on men because the question touches his own dear self more or less clearly."[18] In the twentieth century, the ideology of women's inferiority reached its high point in Nazi Germany. The Nazi directive to women was to be with "children, kitchen, and church." The glorification of housework can also be profitable. In the words of one male advertiser: "Properly manipulated . . . American housewives can be given the sense of identity, purpose, creativity, the self-realization, even the sexual joy they lack—by the buying of things."[19]

So what if the usual middle-class housewife has a narrow world and no chance to realize her human potentialities? So what if this means an empty relationship with her husband, ending in divorce in a high percentage of cases? So what if she tends to overprotect her children and not allow them to grow up? She has her gadgets, and they shall make her happy—or do they? Of course, there are women who enjoy the role of housewife and make it genuinely creative. Most of these, however, also have a lively, independent life, ranging from the arts to political activity.

We have seen, though, that half of all working-age American women are forced to work, whether they wish to or not. The problem for the working-class woman, and especially for the black working woman, is discrimination at work, low pay, last hired and first fired and never promoted. And on top of that, she is often expected to do all the housework when she gets home.

There are many reforms on which all those fighting against sexism can agree. For example, we need free child-care centers, equal pay for equal work, equal access to all education, equal access to equal kinds of jobs, free birth-control information and devices so that women can determine when they wish to have children, and as a last resort, free and legal abortions when necessary.

The problem is that it is unlikely that these reforms will change basic attitudes, nor is it clear that all these reforms can actually be achieved under capitalism. It is a fact that the lower wages of women are a source of additional profit. Perhaps even more important, it is a fact that the submissive attitude of women, encouraged by church and television alike, serves as an important prop to the status quo. There are thus strong and vested interests in favor of maintaining the ideology of male supremacy and the practice of sexual discrimination.

---

[18] Statement in the 1890s by August Bebel, in *Women and Socialism* (Berlin, 1892), quoted in *Monthly Review* (September 1969), p. 27.

[19] Quoted in Betty Friedan, *The Feminine Mystique* (New York: Dell, 1963), p. 199.

summary

National, religious, and racial discrimination exist in America against blacks, Mexican and Puerto Rican Americans, all foreign-born, American Indians, Japanese and Chinese Americans, Catholics, and Jews. The well-documented oppression against blacks is very severe in housing, education, jobs, health, and every other area of life (even in death; there are segregated cemeteries). The racist ideology against blacks originated as an apology for slavery, but it continues as an apology for low wages, high ghetto rents, exclusion of blacks from the political process in the South and elsewhere, and many other profitable reasons for maintaining racist myths.

Myths and discrimination against women are much older, having been present in many previous societies. American women continue to suffer from fewer educational opportunities, fewer job opportunities, lower pay for the same jobs, and a sexist ideology that says they are inferior. The ideology and discriminatory patterns continue to be supported, in part, because some important interests find them very profitable.

part three

unemployment and waste:
a radical introduction
to macroeconomics

chapter 21
aggregate problems: unemployment, inflation, pollution, and underdevelopment

In this part, issues involved in aggregate, or macroeconomics, the working of the economy as a whole, are examined. First, the historical evolution of the institutions of the private enterprise system and the theory of aggregate income determination are reviewed. The analysis turns then to why the economy continues to be subject to periods of substantial unemployment and why it continues to have those noticeable fluctuations of output and employment called *business cycles*. Next, the problem of inflation is considered, and the impact of monopoly power and of vast military spending on unemployment and inflation is investigated. Then the causes of retarded economic growth, as well as the human costs of economic growth, such as pollution, are discussed. Finally, the international relationships between the advanced and underdeveloped countries, and the barriers to growth in the underdeveloped countries (including imperialism) are examined.

the problem of economic growth

The foremost economic problem confronting the world is that of achieving the most rapid growth of income per person. Surely, for the three-quarters of the world population with incomes at the bare subsistence level (and sometimes not even that), it is *the* economic problem. Upon its solution rests the decision for revolution or evolution, socialism or capitalism, democracy or dictatorship, and ultimately for peace or war.

Most of this part, however, focuses on the United States, where, some argue, the problem of economic growth is less critical. It is said that America already has achieved the affluent society and that other issues are therefore more important than mere growth of output. It is true, the average U.S. income level is far above levels in the underdeveloped countries. But there are enough Americans with very low incomes that the federal government found it necessary to mount a war on poverty in the early 1960s. Another war intervened. Vietnam commanded a higher priority in the competition for government funds: The poverty continues. In 1966, the U.S. Department of Labor estimated that, on the average, it would take $9,100 for a city worker to provide a family of four with a "modest but adequate" standard of living. Such a budget would contain only the goods and services necessary for a healthful, self-respecting mode of life, adequate care of children, and some participation in community life.[1] In that year, *nearly three-fifths of the nation's families* got by on less than this "modest but adequate budget."

The problem of economic growth is closely linked with that of full employment. In the advanced capitalistic countries one cause of low economic growth is frequent periods of insufficient demand for goods, during which significant numbers of men and machinery are idle. Not only can full employment increase economic growth, but also a high rate of growth means more demand for products, which leads to more employment.

the problem of unemployment

There are many reasons for unemployment. The most important in the United States in the twentieth century has been the persistence of the *business cycle,* which is the economic term for alternating periods of prosperity and depression in business activity. We shall concentrate on the cyclical unemployment that results from the depression phase of the business cycle, although the United States has recently also been plagued by some amount of chronic, or long-run, unemployment.

In the early 1920s, a thorough study was made, from every available source, of the business history of 17 countries.[2] It was determined that in none of these countries had periods of

---

[1] Clair Wilcox, *Toward Social Welfare* (Homewood, Ill.: Irwin, 1967), pp. 25–30.
[2] W. C. Mitchell and W. L. Thorp, *Business Annals* (New York: National Bureau of Economic Research, 1926).

prosperity continued for more than five or six years, and that periods of prosperity had always alternated with periods of depressed business activity. In the United States, from 1899 to 1959, there were recessions or depressions in 24 of the 60 years.[3] From 1945 to 1959 alone, Americans experienced economic recession during about 23 percent of those months. Many economists believe that only the Vietnam War prevented a recession from 1965 through 1968. Starting in late 1969 and continuing in 1970 and 1971, however, a new recession brought high levels of unemployment.

The problem, then, is to discover why the economies of so many countries are subjected to recurring cycles of depression and prosperity, or why growth occurs in spurts and not at a fairly steady rate. Periods of prosperity are marked by rising production, relatively high rates of profit, high wages, high prices, and comparatively full employment. Periods of depression are characterized by slower rises or actual declines in production, business losses, bankruptcies, relatively low wages, low prices, and large amounts of unemployment.

These phenomena are not random; they exhibit a certain measurable regularity in the recurrence of the prosperous and depressed phases of business activity, and may therefore be called a business cycle. The content of the cycle, the repetition of expansion and contraction, is similar in most times and places where it is found. The form, however, including the duration of its phases, the apparent importance of different factors, the rapidity of its spread, and so forth, all differ very greatly from cycle to cycle.[4]

What is found in the usual business cycle is the recurrence of four phases, each of which lasts a certain amount of time, ranging from a few months to some years. The cycle almost always includes each of these phases, but it is impossible to predict how long each will last. The phase of expansion of production is called *prosperity,* though it may be only relative prosperity. Then there is an upper turning point area in the cycle, usually called the *peak.* The peak period of the business cycle leads into the phase of contraction, which is called the *depression.* Finally, there is a lower turning point, called the *trough,* at which the bottom is reached and recovery begins.

Figure 21.1 indicates the usual phases of trough, prosperity (or expansion), peak, and depression (or contraction). Because the peak, or upper turning point, is often a period of violent change from an expanding to a contracting economy, it used to be called the *crisis* by many writers. Others called it the period of *panic* because it was usually a time when banks failed and businesses went bankrupt. Still

---

3 See U.S. Congress, Joint Economic Committee, Staff Report, *Employment, Growth, and Price Levels* (Washington, D.C.: U.S. Government Printing Office, 1959), p. xxiii.

4 Concerning the similarity and differences amongst business cycles, see Mitchell and Thorp, op. cit., pp. 33–37.

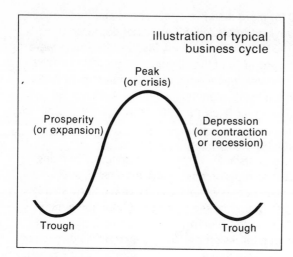

FIGURE

21.1

illustration of typical business cycle

Peak
(or crisis)

Prosperity
(or expansion)

Depression
(or contraction
or recession)

Trough   Trough

looser terminology was used when people referred to the whole depression period as a crisis or panic.

In reality, the occurrence of the business cycle (defined as the periodic rise and fall of general business activity) has been very different from the very simple picture we have drawn. First, each and every business cycle is different from any other in duration as well as intensity. Second, the index of production or price of any particular commodity may fluctuate widely at any time in a different direction from the general movement of business activity. It is only in some of the more general indexes of all business activity that we observe a given direction of movement over a significant length of time.

Figure 21.2 provides the index of U.S. industrial production in the "normal" peacetime period between the two world wars, from 1919 to 1939. This period has been studied intensively, and most modern business-cycle theories are strongly influenced by the facts of these years. Here we see the minor depressions of the 1920s and the Great Depression of the 1930s. Notice that even in this so-called normal period, the pattern is not so clear as the simple picture of four clear-cut phases would indicate.

After 1939, production rose swiftly to meet the wartime needs of the government. Since the war, the U.S. government has continued to play a major role in the economy. For this and other reasons, the business cycle has been more moderate and has shown very different characteristics.

The postwar performance of the American economy is treated in detail in the discussion of government policy in Chapters 19, 27, and 28. It is sufficient to note here that there have been no major depressions since World War II. Nevertheless, there have been

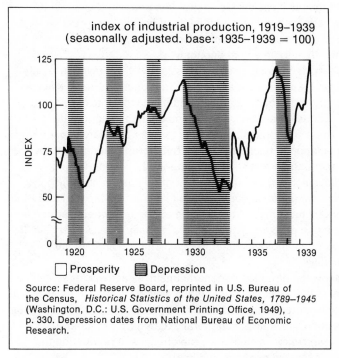

FIGURE

21.2

index of industrial production, 1919–1939
(seasonally adjusted. base: 1935–1939 = 100)

☐ Prosperity   ▤ Depression

Source: Federal Reserve Board, reprinted in U.S. Bureau of
the Census, *Historical Statistics of the United States, 1789–1945*
(Washington, D.C.: U.S. Government Printing Office, 1949),
p. 330. Depression dates from National Bureau of Economic
Research.

several minor depressions, which are defined as small declines in
business activity on the order of 5 or 10 percent. It is now fashionable
to call a minor depression a *recession* (*depression* has become a
nasty word). Some authorities prefer even more euphemistic terms
such as *rolling readjustment.* Even in minor depressions, millions of
human beings are unemployed and suffer extreme deprivation (e.g.,
cases of malnutrition have recently been found among the families
of those long unemployed).

The most comprehensive description of business cycles is to be
found in the work of Wesley Mitchell.[5] Mitchell's analysis of 794
different economic series (up to 1939) revealed that a very large
percentage always move in the same direction as general business
activity, though a few move contrary to it. Even some of those that
always move in the opposite direction can easily be shown to be
governed by the cycle; for example, it is not surprising to find the
indexes of business failures moving contrary to the cycle. About 89
percent of Mitchell's economic series are dominated by the business
cycle, and only 11 percent move irregularly with reference to it.[6] It

[5] Wesley C. Mitchell, *What Happens During Business Cycles* (New York: National
Bureau of Economic Research, Inc., 1950).

[6] Ibid., p. 77.

seems that the business cycle is a problem presented by real life and not by fancy, although the difficulty of having "too great" a supply of all goods does seem more appropriate to Alice in Wonderland than to an actual economy.

Even a very general index of business activity will reveal not only gradual ups and downs, but also small, frictional disturbances every day. *Frictional disturbances* are caused by movements of demand from one product to another, but with no change in aggregate demand. These frictional disturbances form a necessary background to the explanation of business cycles, but mere frictional disturbance is not an adequate explanation of the general and long-lasting cyclical movements found in the economy. Thus we shall largely ignore *frictional unemployment,* which is defined as the period during which workers must move from one job to another, whenever demand moves from one product to another. Statistically, this is a very small percentage of unemployment, although it still is painful to the workers involved.

If we follow the direction of general business activity for some time, we shall also find *seasonal fluctuations* which are caused by seasonal changes in weather conditions. Because these are not the main focus of our attention, we shall also generally disregard *seasonal unemployment* which is caused by the changes of production that accompany seasonal changes in climate.

There will still remain in any general index of business conditions a recurring cycle of prosperity, peak, depression, and trough. Minor depressions, which may not be noticed by many but which still cause extreme hardship for some people, are observable every two or three years in the United States. Major depressions, of the sort that shake up the entire economy, occurred every 7 to 13 years between 1854 and 1939. In the postwar period, there has been no major depression, although we have continued to witness minor depressions and a significant amount of chronic unemployment.

The importance of the problem of business cycles is quite apparent from both the social and the individual point of view. For the society as a whole, it means periods of unused resources, lower output and employment, and a much slower long-run rate of growth. Many attempts have been made to calculate the amount of loss to society from just one major depression. An official estimate put the total loss for the years 1930–1938 at 43,435,000 man-years (valued at $293 billion in 1929 dollars).[7] A *man-year* is the amount of work that one

[7] Isador Lubin, then Commissioner of Labor Statistics, U.S. Department of Labor, quoted in U.S. Temporary National Economic Committee, *The Concentration of Economic Power,* Hearings, Part I (Washington, D.C.: U.S. Government Printing Office, 1939), pp. 12 and 159.

unemployed person could produce in a year. For comparison, it should be remembered that initially, in 1929, there were only 49,440,000 Americans working and that the gross national product was only $104 billion (in 1929 dollars). If these calculations were extended back to cover all the depressions in U.S. economic history, the total loss would be very considerable.

Depressions and economic instability have other effects, however, which cannot be calculated in economic terms. There are sociological effects as reflected in population growth, divorce rates, crime, physical and mental health, and even suicide rates.[8] If few resort to suicide, the total effect is, nonetheless, incalculably great on all who lose jobs, small businesses, or farms; who wander about on an enforced vacation with meager subsistence provided by private or public charities; who find all of their previous plans destroyed as if by a flick of a magic wand. Unemployment certainly amounts to a vast social wastefulness as well as an individual tragedy. Moreover, unemployment is not evenly spread, but is highest among such economic groups as the migrant farm worker and the untrained youth and among such minority groups as blacks, generally the first fired and the last hired.[9]

When a newspaper casually mentions that 5 million Americans want work but cannot find it, these are not just 5 million statistics, but 5 million afflicted individuals. If a large firm closes down or moves to a new location, it leaves behind engineers and executives suddenly reduced from a useful job at $400 a week to unemployment compensation at $40 a week, as well as a large number of unskilled workers with no future prospects. At times, whole mining towns seem to lose animation, and hundreds of miners' wives line up at soup kitchens and welfare departments for food allotments. In the "prosperous" year of 1959, a 38-year-old unemployed auto worker represented millions of others when he said: "I've been looking for work all over but I just can't get a job. I hate being on welfare. It's enough to make a man jump into the river."[10] When the majority of the people are working for good wages, very few men really want to subsist as a useless stick of wood on a handout of a few dollars a week.

---

[8] For the Great Depression of the 1930s, there is an immense literature on each area; for an overall study of the effects of earlier business cycles, see D. C. Thomas, *Social Aspects of the Business Cycle* (New York: Knopf, 1927).

[9] See Gunnar Myrdal, *An American Dilemma* (New York: Harper & Row, 1944), pp. 297–303.

[10] Reported in an excellent survey by A. H. Raskin, "People Behind Statistics: A Study of the Unemployed," *New York Times* (March 16, 1959), p. 1.

the problem of inflation

Inflation is defined as a rise in the general price level of all goods. A rise in one price offset by a fall in another is not inflation; this is constantly occurring as a result of shifting demand (e.g., from butter to margarine). There are many varieties of the disease known as inflation. *Aggregate* inflation occurs when there is too much spending in the whole economy or when aggregate demand is greater than the present supply of goods. *Partial* inflation occurs when prices rise only in certain sectors, pushed up by monopoly power rather than pulled up by aggregate demand. *Short-run* aggregate inflation results from temporary factors such as a rapid rise in demand at the peak of prosperity or the unlimited demand for munitions by government in wartime. *Long-run* aggregate inflation may result when a country is continually trying to develop faster than is actually possible. For example, the government of an underdeveloped country may bid against private enterprise for scarce capital goods or raw materials, thus driving their prices steadily upward.

Furthermore, we must distinguish the effects of a slow and gradual inflation from those of a very rapid, or galloping, inflation. If inflation results in the rise of prices by a few percent per year, then it is only a social irritant. It does work a great injustice on those who possess savings, who have made loans, who must live on a fixed income, or whose wages lag behind prices, because these groups find the value of their dollars steadily declining. This decline of real wages and real savings may exacerbate many economic and political conflicts. For a country as a whole, gradual inflation of domestic prices may reduce the volume of goods sold abroad, and for goods that face stiff competition, entire overseas markets may be lost.

The situation is much more serious, however, when the rate of price inflation reaches some hundreds of percent per year, as happened in Germany in the early 1920s. Rampant inflation brings such a rapid decline in the value of money that ultimately there can be complete dislocation and collapse of the economy, with correspondingly violent political reactions. At such times, money and the market system fail completely. Productive effort is paralyzed and exchange retrogresses to barter. In recent years, there have been several underdeveloped countries, such as Brazil and South Vietnam, in which galloping inflation does threaten to disrupt all normal economic processes.

Even in the United States, the magnitude of inflation is indicated by the fact that the consumer-price level quadrupled between 1900

and 1958, and doubled between 1938 and 1958, alone.[11] During the
six years from 1945 to 1950, wholesale prices rose 52.6 percent and
consumer prices rose 33.7 percent. Nevertheless, inflation in the
United States was in the very gradual category of 1 or 2 percent
a year in most years from 1951 to 1965. After the escalation of the
war in Vietnam in 1965, however, inflation became progressively
worse. It has been one of the major economic issues of the 1968 and
1972 presidential elections.

Since 1969, we have experienced persistent inflation combined
with rates of unemployment in excess of 5 percent. The economist in
the United States and western Europe today must often meet the
problem of reconciling the need for full employment with the need
for price stability. Both inflation and unemployment have many
harmful effects, and we wish to eliminate both. Unfortunately, some
of the strongest policy weapons for full employment tend to produce
inflation, and powerful measures to combat inflation sometimes tend
to produce unemployment.

pollution and waste

No one who opens his eyes in Los Angeles can be unaware of air
pollution—it is that lovely yellow-brown smog in the air that makes
you cry and rub your eyes. No one who swims in the lake near
Chicago or Gary can be unaware of water pollution—it gives you that
delightful blackish oil and metal film on your skin. Anyone who sees
our vast acres of garbage, old car dumps, or open-face mines will
understand the beauties of land pollution. Moreover, this is one of
the advantages of U.S. culture that industrialization is rapidly
spreading around the world (you will cry as easily in Tokyo as in
Los Angeles).

Many industrial products not only are harmful to the environment,
some are useless as well. The widespread existence of useless
production is primarily the result of advertising. For every bit of
useful information in small print, there tend to be 999 neon signs
filled with exhortations and lies. We shall also find that the effort to
sell goods penetrates into production, so that engineers spend
millions of valuable hours putting tails on cars or even designing
products with only limited durability, thus forcing the consumer to
buy new ones.

The greatest waste, however, comes from military spending. An

11 See Willard L. Thorp and Richard F. Quandt, *The New Inflation* (New York:
McGraw-Hill, 1959), p. 1.

atomic bomb or a battleship does nothing constructive. A large portion of this part of the book will investigate the impact of the huge military waste on the economy, for example, how it may stimulate inflation, and moreover, who profits from it.

underdevelopment and imperialism

The human face of underdevelopment is the child with a bloated belly, suffering from various kinds of malnutrition. Over a billion people in underdeveloped countries are on the margin of starvation. Hundreds of millions have dread diseases. Housing is little and poor or even nonexistent. Clothing consists of rags. Why?

Why in a world of tremendous productive powers is this still the lot of the majority? Part of the answer is that all of these countries suffered from two or three centuries of imperialism. The old colonial regimes first plundered these countries of all that was movable, such as the gold and silver of Mexico and Peru. Then they set up an unequal trade exchange, taking out raw materials at low prices, selling back finished goods at high prices. In every area, they exploited the abundance of cheap labor at the point of a bayonet. In Africa, they enslaved millions for labor elsewhere.

Why are these countries still making little or no progress? Part of the answer lies in the present low level of capital there, the present low level of human skills, and the overpopulation relative to their meagre resources. Clearly, these present evils again stem in part from past colonialism. Yet another part of the answer is even more damning. It appears that the advanced capitalist countries continue to keep the underdeveloped ones in a state of neo-colonialism. Like the older colonial type of imperialism, the new neocolonialism involves dependent patterns of trade, removal of much plunder (in the form of high profits on investment), and continued political domination (as in the "free elections" of October 1971 in Vietnam, in which the American-backed President Theiu was the only candidate).

summary

This chapter is the introduction to Part III. It briefly presents the main issues to be discussed: (1) how unemployment and inflation may occur in a capitalist economy; (2) the role of government, particularly the vast impact of its military spending; (3) the flow of wasteful and even harmful products, as well as the cost of growth in terms of environmental destruction; (4) growth in the underdeveloped countries, with particular attention to the damage done these countries by Western colonization and imperialism.

To lay a systematic foundation for understanding these macro-economic problems, we must begin (in Chapter 22) by tracing the operation of the institutions of the U.S. economy. Historically, to what extent have the basic institutions of capitalism allowed us to achieve stable economic growth without inflation or unemployment?

chapter 22
the institutional setting

Our economy experiences periods of prosperity and depression, or boom and bust. Sometimes, therefore, the total supply of produced goods is either too small or too great in terms of the total demand for goods. Certainly, if total supply and demand were always equal, there could be no such periodic phenomena as overproduction and underproduction.

The first question to be asked is simple but basic. In what kind of an economy must total supply and demand always be equal? Under what economic institutions is it possible for demand to be greater or less than supply? Before an analysis of the historical facts can be undertaken, an obstacle must be removed from the path. That obstacle is the traditional theory of classical economics known as Say's law, named after the economist J. B. Say.

say's law

In its most rigid form, Say's law states that aggregate demand must always equal aggregate supply at any level of supply including the full-employment level. This denies the possibility of either a deficiency or an excess of aggregate demand and therefore denies the possibility of depressions or inflations in general business activity. Say's law does *not* state that aggregate supply and aggregate demand are "identical" or are equal by definition: ". . . though Say's law is not an identity, his blundering exposition has led a long series of writers to believe that it is one—and this in no less than four different senses."[1] Rather, it says that an increase of supply, through various automatic processes, calls forth an equal amount of demand.

Aside from a few dissenters, whole generations of economists refused to accept the possibility that there could be involuntary unemployment or an excessive supply of goods. Furthermore, they never challenged the assumption that all commodities could always be sold at prices equal to their full, long-run costs. They admitted only the possibility of temporary, accidental maladjustments in one or a few industries. Such maladjustments were sure to be corrected as soon as competition could force capital to switch from one industry to another. In a typical statement, Ricardo argued: "Too much of a particular commodity may be produced, of which there may be said to be such a glut in the market as not to repay the capital expended on it; but this cannot be the case with all commodities."[2]

The kernel of truth in Say's law is the platitude that every purchase constitutes a sale, and every sale means some money income to someone, which again may, and ordinarily will, be used for more purchases. Ricardo phrased the case for Say's law in this way: "No man produces but with a view to consume or sell, and he never sells but with an intention to purchase some other commodity which may be useful to him or which may contribute to future production. By purchasing them, he necessarily becomes either the consumer of his own goods, or the purchaser and consumer of the goods of some other person."[3]

This argument *must* be wrong as applied to modern private-enterprise economies because observation reveals that such economies have never been without periodic depressions within the last century or more. Say's law is, indeed, true for certain earlier types of economies; the mistake was in taking these simpler economies as a model and then applying the conclusions to the modern private-enterprise economy without considering the fact that entirely new institutions have evolved since the medieval period.

---

1 Joseph A. Schumpeter, *History of Economic Analysis* (New York: Oxford University Press, 1954), p. 618.

2 David Ricardo, *The Principles of Political Economy and Taxation* (London: Gonner, Bell, & Sons, 1891 [reprinted from 1821 edition]), p. 276.

3 Ibid., p. 273.

production for the market

It is characteristic of the private-enterprise economy, which was fully developed in England by the end of the eighteenth century, that most production was directed solely toward its sale on the market. This was hardly ever true of earlier societies. In the most primitive societies, almost all productive activity is directed at production of food by gathering or hunting. These activities are necessarily carried out by the collective unit of all the males and/or females of the tribe. Generally, almost all of the produce is distributed according to some fixed scheme among the tribe's membership.

Even at a somewhat higher economic stage, production is still for use, and not for sale. None of the Indian tribes of the Americas, not even the Aztecs, bought or sold land or produced crops to sell for a profit to others. In fact, "For the red man soil existed only in order to meet the necessities of life, and production, not profit, was the basis of his economy. . . . Unemployment was certainly never a problem in the Indian communities of early America."[4] Because there was little division of labor within the tribe, there was little if any trade among its members. Furthermore, very little commerce was transacted between the most primitive tribes, and that "was virtually restricted to materials small in bulk and precious for their decorative or magical qualities."[5] We find that all over the world for thousands of years almost all economic systems, whether tribal or feudal, were based on relatively self-sufficient agricultural units.

In the Roman Empire, there was a great deal of trade, but most of it was in luxury goods.[6] This trade, therefore, did not affect the self-sufficiency of the basic agricultural unit, the slave-run plantation, although a lack of surplus food could bring starvation to large numbers of city dwellers. As one author says, ". . . notwithstanding the phenomenal expansion of trade and industry, the vast masses inside the Empire still continued to win their livelihood from the soil. Agriculture remained throughout antiquity the most usual and most typical economic activity, and land the most important form of wealth."[7]

The same was true of feudal England, where the primitive level of

4 John A. Crow, *The Epic of Latin America* (Garden City, N.Y.: Doubleday, 1948), p. 54.

5 Grahame Clark, *From Savagery to Civilization* (London: Cobbett Press, 1946), p. 96.

6 See, for example, the brief account in F. W. Walbank, *The Decline of the Roman Empire in the West* (London: Cobbett Press, 1956), pp. 11–13.

7 Ibid., p. 18.

technology made impossible the supply of large urban populations and even greatly restricted trade between the villages. As a result, in the England of that day, "Towns developed slowly; each group of burgesses solved their local problems on their own initiative and in their own time. Even in 1377 not much more than eight per cent of the population were townsmen, and only a minority of these had independent dealings with continental markets."[8]

Of course, in the later medieval period there were areas of more highly developed industrial production, such as Flanders and northern Italy; and even relatively backward England carried on a systematic wool trade with Flanders. Yet these were exceptions to the general rule of the feudal economy and may be considered early signs pointing to the beginning of the end of that economy.

If there happened to be a surplus from the slave or feudal estate, then it might be marketed in return for foreign luxury items to be used by the lord of the estate. Finding a market, however, was not a matter of life and death for the economic unit. If the surplus found no market, the manor was still supplied with its necessities for that year, and could and would continue the process of production for the next year's needs. What could disturb such economically self-sufficient societies were only those catastrophes that were more or less external to the economy—natural disasters such as droughts, plagues, or floods, or political troubles such as government interference, war, or revolution. These phenomena could and did depress production in various randomly spaced intervals, as well as seasonally because of the special seasonal sensitivity of agriculture. This type of economy could not, however, conceivably face the problem of lack of effective demand for all commodities because the economic unit directly consumed most of the products of its own land and could do without trade altogether. Thus, in discussing the business cycle of depression and prosperity, Mitchell observes that ". . . the total number of past business cycles may well be less than a thousand. For business cycles are phenomena peculiar to a certain form of economic organization which has been dominant even in Western Europe for less than two centuries, and for briefer periods in other regions."[9]

In the transitional period, in the England of the sixteenth, seventeenth, and eighteenth centuries, the majority of the people still lived on the land and consumed their own products. As time went on, however, more and more products, both agricultural and industrial, were delivered to the marketplace. By the end of the eighteenth

8 Marion Gibbs, *Feudal Order* (London: Cobbett Press, 1949), pp. 7–8.

9 W. C. Mitchell, *Business Annals* (New York: National Bureau of Economic Research, 1926), p. 47.

century, the private-enterprise system of production for the market embraced most of economic activity. By the nineteenth century, one business entrepreneur might own a factory producing millions of shoes, though his whole family could consume only a few pair. The shoes had to be sold in order to buy other consumer goods for his family, to pay wages to his employees, and to replace and expand the plant and equipment of his business.

In the United States, the transformation to a market economy took place in the nineteenth century. In 1800, two-thirds of the U.S. population labored in agriculture, and most of the remainder were employed in commerce and shipping. Except for the foreign-trade sector, markets were small and local. Many families and communities were almost self-sufficient. Native industry, which had a foothold in 1800, spurted during the War of 1812, when imports from England were cut off, and by 1815, New England mills and factories were capable of supplying textiles and simple manufactures to the nation. Transportation networks were built to link communities and regions. This permitted farmers to specialize in commercial crops for cash income with which they purchased in the market the necessities of life. By 1840, a large national market for manufactures had been created. Families turned away from self-sufficiency and purchased cloth, flour, farm implements, and household items. Rapid industrialization followed. In 1860, the United States was producing more than one-fifth of the world manufacturing output, and by 1913, American production had risen to one-third of the world total.

The process of industrialization, starting first in England and spreading to the rest of western Europe and the United States, had changed the character of production and employment. Production required a greater number of stages, or steps, as materials and products became less simple. Labor grew more specialized, and labor's employment came to be linked with the expanded use of capital.

In the modern market economy, every man's productive effort is related to sales in the market and every man's income depends on the income of others. A man working in an automobile factory, for example, depends for his continued employment upon millions of persons buying cars each year. In turn, most of these car buyers depend upon millions buying the products they produce. If consumers are unable to buy their cars, the automobile worker immediately loses his job. The car manufacturer needs less steel, less rubber, less paint, and so on. Each of these industries, in turn, lays off workers. The process goes on and on because of the interconnectedness of the market economy. Each time more workers lose their jobs their income ceases. They can no longer buy the hundreds of goods and services they normally purchase, and the crisis widens and becomes more severe.

The sale in the market of privately produced goods and services generates all income. Decisions to purchase are made by thousands of small- and large-income receivers, and the total of these purchasing decisions makes up the total, or aggregate, demand. In previous economic systems, the self-sufficient economic unit—the craftsman producing a trickle of handmade items for known customers—could not possibly be troubled by lack of demand for his product. When almost all that was produced by the economic unit was consumed by it, Say's law had to be true. In the industrialized private-enterprise system, however, the businessman produces for the market and cannot continue production if there is no market demand for his products. This, then, is the first major institutional feature of the private-enterprise economy. Appearing in the eighteenth century and continuing to the present day, it is one of the factors that make business cycles possible.

regular use of money

Another institutional condition that is necessary before there can be a deficiency of aggregate demand is the regular use of money in exchange. The monetary system takes the place of the barter system of exchanging good for good. It was seen that production for the market makes cyclical unemployment possible. Use of money in the market exchange will be shown to be a second necessary condition for the emergence of business cycles.

THE USES OF MONEY

Money replaced the barter system because it is much more convenient to use. What precisely are its functions in the modern economy? Traditionally, money is said to have four functions:

1. Money is the *unit of accounting,* or the standard of value—that is, it is a measuring stick for everything else. All contracts are drawn up in money terms, with so much money to be paid for a certain product at a certain time. We think of a coat or a table as being worth so many dollars. The usual ease of money valuation is apparent if we contrast it with the difficulties encountered in international transactions, when different people are using different money measurements.

2. Money is the *medium of exchange,* or actual intermediary

between commodities (including services). Under barter, one commodity is exchanged for another commodity. In the monetary economy, a commodity is exchanged for money; then the money may be exchanged for another commodity.

3. Money is a *store of value*, or a device for hoarding. When money is received as an income, it need not be spent immediately. Instead, if it is in a nonperishable form such as gold, it may be buried or stored away and hoarded until the possessor chooses to use it. In the modern world, money is deposited in a bank account, which is completely nonperishable; the money may even grow by earning interest while it is on deposit.

4. Money is a *standard of deferred payment,* or a unit of accounting for future payments on debts. In other words, I may buy something from you now, but promise to pay for it later. My promise is always in terms of so many units of money, not, for example, in so many pairs of shoes. In the United States, paper money is a legal tender (or legally acceptable unit) for the payment of any debt.

Anything that is readily acceptable in payment within a society is "money," whether or not it is a produced commodity. In the United States, the traditional limitation of "money" to the commodities silver and gold has been ended. Our money today is (1) coin and paper currency in circulation plus (2) all demand deposits (checking accounts) in commercial banks. Neither is a commodity having any significant worth of its own. In fact, bank deposits are visible only when a bookkeeping entry is looked at. Both of these forms of money serve all the functions of money and so are "money."

Some other financial assets—for example, savings accounts and short-term government bonds (maturing within one year)—are readily convertible for spending, even while safely performing the store-of-value function of money. Therefore, such assets are called "near money." Only coins, paper currency, and demand deposits, however, are normally considered to be money. Before 1932, the United States also had a commodity money: gold. In the nineteenth century, notes of many banks circulated as money. Whatever form money takes, it must be plentiful enough to meet the needs of trade and exchange; yet it must also be scarce enough to fulfill its functions as a store of value and a standard of deferred payment. Should it fail on either count, economic activity is either disrupted or directed into perverse channels.

THE ABUSES OF MONEY

Money does not serve its four functions equally well under all conditions. Imagine that there is catastrophic inflation, with prices doubling every hour, which means that the value of money falls by half each hour. Money then functions badly as a *unit of accounting* because the same product sells at such rapidly changing prices that neither consumers nor sellers can keep track of them. With rapid inflation, money is also a poor *medium of exchange:* People may refuse to accept it at all because its buying power is so uncertain and may diminish further before it can be spent.

With rapid inflation, money is also a very bad *store of value* because money hoarded away now will buy so very much less in the future. Instead of keeping money, everyone rushes to buy goods or real property that will be worth more and more units of money as the inflation continues. Anyone with cash savings in paper money or bank accounts or government bonds is badly hurt, so it may happen that no one will put money in banks or buy government bonds at almost any interest rate. Finally, with rapid inflation money cannot function as a *standard of deferred payment* because the standard itself keeps changing. If someone lends $100 today, and if it is only worth $1 when it is paid back tomorrow, then the lender is very badly hurt. When people refuse to accept the medium of exchange because they have lost confidence in it, economic activity falls to that level that can be maintained by barter.

The use of money, even in ancient times, brought many new complications onto the economic scene. In the Roman Empire, for example, vast amounts of money were needed by the government to support wars of expansion, large standing armies, police and bureaucracy, and an unfavorable balance of trade (due to import of luxuries from the East). The emperors were eventually forced to the expedient of debasing their coins by "clipping" (decreasing the metalic content of coins) or by mixture with less valuable metals. As the government debased the coins and as production of goods declined in the later days of the empire, the amount that could be bought with the coins declined rapidly; in other words, a catastrophic inflation occurred.[10]

Despite their difficulties with it, the regular use of money did not lead to the modern type of depression because most of the Roman economy was still contained in self-sufficient agricultural units.[11] The luxury trade did suffer from the extreme inflation, but only as one more affliction in addition to colonial wars and slave revolts, the extreme inefficiency of employing slave labor, and the Roman citizens' attitude that any participation in the work process was degrading (because only slaves should work).

With the breakup of the Roman Empire, trade suffered a considerable decline. In early feudalism, the pattern was overwhelmingly that of the isolated, self-sufficient manor. Barter, therefore, grew in importance, and the use of money declined. On each manor, in

[10] See, for example, Walbank, op. cit., pp. 42–43 and 51–52.
[11] See ibid., p. 18.

return for the lord's protection, the serf provided all the services and consumer goods needed and required by the lord, his family, and his retinue. However, when technology began to improve, industry and commerce slowly began to revive in western Europe. The widespread trade of the later medieval period eventually led to the replacing of barter by a money economy; at the same time, following the pattern discussed in the previous section, production was increasingly designed for sale in the market rather than use at home.

The modern private-enterprise economy demands the continuous use of money as the go-between in market exchange by the entire population. In a barter economy, it *is* possible for one commodity to be brought to market in larger supply than there is demand for it; but it is impossible for "total supply" to exceed "total demand" because the two are identical; both are the same aggregate bunch of products brought to the market. The important point, however, is not the definitional identity of total supply and demand in a barter economy. It is that there may be a mismatch of particular supplies and demands, but no lack of *aggregate* demand. For example, those who bring cows to market may find more shoes and fewer coats produced than they desire; that is, they would rather "spend" their cows for fewer shoes and more coats than are available. The excess supply of shoes is balanced by the excess demand for coats. The result is only a temporary, or frictional, unemployment of shoe producers, which could be cured by a shift to coat production. It is true that in the actual medieval economy, rigid feudal restrictions did not allow many such shifts in production or occupation, but it was just these restrictions that the classical economists wished to abolish.

The mistake made by the classical adherents of Say's law was to apply the impossibility of general unemployment in a pure barter economy to a money economy. They extended the argument by means of the general observation that money is merely the means of exchanging two commodities, so that the operation of the money economy is "essentially" the same as that of the barter economy. Thus, we find Ricardo contending that "Productions are always bought by productions, or by services; money is only the medium by which the exchange is effected."[12] One function of money is to facilitate the exchange of commodities, but it has other uses as well. In the modern economy, the seller obtains only money for his commodities, which money he may or may not use immediately or later to buy other commodities. Thus, money functions as the means for the storage of value for future use. The wants of mankind may be infinite, but it is not always the case that all buyers have money to buy what

[12] Ricardo, op. cit., p. 275.

they want. There is, therefore, no inherent necessity in a money economy that sellers should find buyers for all commodities brought to market.

The problem is not an aggregate lack of money in the economy. While those who wish to buy may have no money, those who have money may be taking it out of circulation and not using it in any way, or *hoarding* it. The chain of circulation may then be broken at any point at which the flow of money is stopped or withdrawn from the system. In that case, the reduction of the flow of circulation, like the reduction of the volume of water flowing in a stream, causes a slow-down in the movement of products being circulated by this means. While it is basically true that products exchange for products even after the introduction of money, the mere necessity of the money bridge makes all the difference in the world. If the bridge is absent, finished commodities may pile up in warehouses, while potential consumers are unable to buy them. Only money can make a possible consumer into an actual buyer in the private-enterprise system.

An *excess* of supply in this economic system does not mean that everyone is fully satisfied. People's wants are elastic; we may have as much of a particular commodity as we want at one time, but there is always an infinity of other things that we desire, things that still have use-value or utility for us. Therefore, the problem is not overproduc-tion of the total commodities relative to what people want or desire. The problem is rather that there may be too many commodities on the market relative to the *effective demand,* which is limited by definition to those desires that are backed by money in the market-place.

credit money

In the United States at present, the largest part of the money supply, about four-fifths of the whole, is pure credit money. *Credit money* consists of demand, or checking, deposits at banks, which are dollar amounts owed by the banks to the holders of the accounts. Credit money is created whenever banks make loans to a customer and "credit" his checking account with the amount of the loan. Except for the legal constraints on the loaning of money, banks could go on creating money without limit as long as people had confidence in the acceptability of the money. Only the smallest portion of the money supply consists of coins and paper money issued by the U.S. Treasury. A somewhat larger portion is paper money issued by the Federal Reserve System (Fed). Technically, even these parts of the money supply are credits to the private sector because they are debts of government agencies which are payable on demand. Dollar bills, however, are no longer payable in gold, so a $10 bill presented to the Treasury or the Fed could be paid by any legal tender, say two $5 bills. Thus, the Treasury or Fed may create money simply by using the printing press. Although Congress does impose a legal limit, it often raises that limit.

The use of credit intensifies all money problems; not only may a person sell something and not immediately purchase something else, but also it is possible to sell something and not receive the proceeds of the sale for some time. If Brown owes Smith, and Smith owes Johnson, and Johnson owes Martin, a break anywhere along this chain of credit circulation will be disastrous for all of the later parties in the chain. Moreover, the credit chain in the modern private-enterprise economy is usually circular in nature, so that the reverberations reach the starting point and may begin to go around again. This does not, of course, explain why the chain should ever break in the first place.

It has been amply demonstrated that when money and credit institutions become the usual way of doing business, the business cycle of boom and bust becomes a possibility. Does this mean that these institutions are sufficient to explain the business cycle? We know that money and credit existed in ancient Rome and in the sixteenth to eighteenth centuries in western Europe, yet the financial disturbances of those times do not seem to have been the same phenomena as the modern type of business cycle. It is true that after the development of money and credit, every catastrophic natural happening or violent political event might be reflected in a financial panic. For example, when the English fleet was burnt by the Dutch in 1667, and also in 1672, when Charles II stopped payments from the Exchequer, there were sudden runs on the London banks. In the eighteenth century, financial crises resulted from the Jacobin conspiracy in 1708, the bursting of the South Sea stock speculation bubble in 1720, the fighting with the Pretender in 1745, the aftermath of the Seven Years' War in 1763, and the disturbances caused by the American Revolution.[13] These panics were unlike the modern business cycle, both in cause and effect, because they originated in external causes and resulted in only limited depressions in a few trades for brief and random periods. The first truly general industrial depression of the modern type appeared as late as 1793 in England.[14]

In summary, there is evidence of a long period of extensive use of money and credit with only temporary and externally caused financial panics. Conversely, in the nineteenth and twentieth centuries, there

[13] See discussion of all these events in W. C. Mitchell, *Business Cycles* (Berkeley, Cal.: University of California Press, 1913), pp. 583–584.
[14] Ibid.

have been depressions, as well as many minor recessions, that did not produce financial panics. There is no reason, all other things being equal, why money and credit should not flow steadily through the process of circulation, so long as business expectations remain optimistic. It may be tentatively concluded that the regular use of money and credit is a necessary prerequisite, but not a sufficient explanation, of business cycles.

production for private profit

We have examined two conditions—production for the market and the regular use of money—that must be present if business cycles in which demand fluctuates below the full-employment level of supply are to occur. But at least one more institutional condition is necessary before we can contend that total demand may not equal supply in this economy—that is, that Say's law does not hold true. It is the existence of private ownership of production facilities and production for private profit; this condition also seems to be implicitly assumed by those economists who emphasize only the regular use of money in attacking Say's law. Even in an economy characterized by exchange in the market through the medium of money, supply and demand can be kept in balance, or quickly brought back into balance, if both supply and demand are consciously planned by the same national agency.

A centrally planned socialist economy is one in which the government owns and plans the use of all means of production. Most business-cycle economists admit that industrialized socialist economies do not experience the business-cycle phenomena characteristic of industrialized private-enterprise economies. This is the case because a socialist economy can make one unified plan for growth without concern for private profit. Thus, all of the data on Soviet economic development indicates continuous full employment (except for retraining time or movement between jobs).

In a private-enterprise economy, each individual enterprise makes its own plans on the basis of its own estimate of whether it will obtain a private profit by production. In the national plan of a socialist economy, *the same agency decides both the aggregate supply and the aggregate demand.* It sets the aggregate consumer demand by setting wages, and it controls the aggregate investment demand directly through the government budget. Note that this may even apply to a socialist economy with completely decentralized production planning by workers' committees in individual enterprises, as in Yugoslavia, so long as the government continues to make its new investments (including reinvestment by individual enterprises) just equal to the gap between aggregate supply and consumer demand.

Of course, socialist planners may make many mistakes in allocation of resources and new investment, especially because there are changes in technology and other new conditions each year. They may allocate resources to uses that are not as productive as others, or even order the production of one thing, say, automobiles, but not order enough production of other things going into it, say, rubber tires. In such cases, there may be supply bottlenecks holding back production in some industries and temporary oversupply and unused capacity in others. Such mistakes may lower the rate of growth or even cause output to fall in one year (as in Czechoslovakia in 1963).

Moreover, much recent data on eastern Europe and the Soviet Union show a cyclical recurrence of slow growth periods. Each time the economy starts growing rapidly, the bureaucrats get overoptimistic. They push production more rapidly than is physically possible, leading to supply bottlenecks. If they order too many new factories to be built at once, the result is half-built factories and little or no increase in current output. Nevertheless, there remain very important distinctions from a private-enterprise economy. There need be no secondary effects, no cumulative collapse of production, because socialist investment is not based on private profit (and the economy does remain at a point of full employment).[15]

In an economy based on private ownership of individual competing units, the sum of decisions to produce may not equal the sum of decisions by other individuals and businesses to spend—that is, to consume and invest. If the sum of the outputs produced at present prices is greater than the sum of the monetary demand, then there is not enough revenue to cover the costs of production and also yield a profit for the private entrepreneur. This criterion is decisive because if the private entrepreneur can make no profit, he will not continue production, his machinery will stand idle, and all of his workers will be unemployed.

the u.s. economy

Alternating periods of expansion and decline of output and employment have occurred regularly in the United States for over 150 years. The very earliest cycles were clearly tied to events abroad, but

[15] Naturally, the fact that a socialist economy is not subject to cyclical unemployment does not prove by itself that it is better or worse than a private-enterprise economy. For that overall judgment, we would have to consider all the criteria for comparing economies, including full employment, efficiency, growth, distribution of income, and political and social effects.

internally generated instability was evident by the 1840s. In its infancy, the American economy depended heavily upon European trade. The country prospered with every quickening in the flow of ships and goods from Atlantic ports. When this flow was interrupted, distress in the coastal towns persisted until some new stimulus brought a return of strong demand for American shipping. Most profits came from commerce, and largely foreign commerce at that. It was in commerce and shipping that the most important capital investment was occurring. Therefore, between 1800 and 1815, a remarkably close correlation existed between demand for American exports and the health of the American economy as a whole.[16]

While any interruption of the export trade severely hurt American commerce by reducing foreign demand for U.S. goods, the same interruptions of trade would cut off imports and might thereby stimulate the economy to produce those (formerly imported) goods by itself, thus spurring domestic investment and industrial growth. A restriction of imports in 1808 and the cessation of trade with England throughout the period of the War of 1812 brought a sudden upsurge of manufacturing in New England and the direction of capital away from commerce and the carrying trades. The number of cotton mills mushroomed and cotton manufacture grew rapidly. New machinery and factories for the woolen, glass, and paper industries followed the lead of cotton. The transformation of the economy had begun.

Production of crops for marketing advanced after 1816, when European agricultural demand turned upward. In the meantime, English manufactured goods returned to compete with the higher-priced goods of the young American industries. Many mills were closed, and although information on this period is scanty, there is evidence of urban unemployment and widespread foreclosures and failures in the crisis of 1818–1819. Prices collapsed in the face of general overproduction. The depression was short-lived, however. In the ensuing prosperity, major canal-construction ventures opened western lands to immigration, which promised wider domestic markets. The canal-building boom, beginning with the Erie and Champlain canals in New York, reached a peak in 1840. Various regional markets were linked into larger market areas, and there was a rush to lay out new town sites. The profit prospects for canals attracted European investment funds, but many of the projects did not turn a profit, nor did town lots and farm acreage rise in price sufficiently to justify the speculation. In 1836, when European economic activity declined and the American expansion faltered,

16 See W. B. Smith and A. H. Cole, *Fluctuations in American Business, 1790–1860* (Cambridge, Mass.: Harvard University Press, 1935).

Europeans sold many of their holdings and withdrew their funds, intensifying the major depression that followed.

After 1840, foreign influence persisted, but the course of the economy was increasingly shaped by the domestic environment. By midcentury, American business cycles were more clearly internally generated; a pattern of fluctuation characteristic of modern capitalist economies had set in.

The somewhat regular pattern of fluctuations has been traced and dated by the National Bureau of Economic Research. Table 22.1 shows the timing and duration of the aggregate cycle since 1854 in the United States. The 26 cycles have averaged about 50 months in length, but this includes several periods of war. Wartime expansions,

STANDARD REFERENCE DATES

TROUGH	PEAK	TROUGH
Dec. 1854	June 1857	Dec. 1858
Dec. 1858	Oct. 1860	June 1861
June 1861	Apr. 1865	Dec. 1867
Dec. 1867	June 1869	Dec. 1870
Dec. 1870	Oct. 1873	Mar. 1879
Mar. 1879	Mar. 1882	May 1885
May 1885	Mar. 1887	Apr. 1888
Apr. 1888	July 1890	May 1891
May 1891	Jan. 1893	June 1894
June 1894	Dec. 1895	June 1897
June 1897	June 1899	Dec. 1900
Dec. 1900	Sept. 1902	Aug. 1904
Aug. 1904	May 1907	June 1908
June 1908	Jan. 1910	Jan. 1912
Jan. 1912	Jan. 1913	Dec. 1914
Dec. 1914	Aug. 1918	Mar. 1919
Mar. 1919	Jan. 1920	July 1921
July 1921	May 1923	July 1924
July 1924	Oct. 1926	Nov. 1927
Nov. 1927	Aug. 1929	Mar. 1933
Mar. 1933	May 1937	June 1938
June 1938	Feb. 1945	Oct. 1945
Oct. 1945	Nov. 1948	Oct. 1949
Oct. 1949	July 1953	Aug. 1954
Aug. 1954	July 1957	Apr. 1958
Apr. 1958	May 1960	Feb. 1961
Feb. 1961	Nov. 1969[a]	Jan. 1972[a]

[a] As of this writing (January 1972) the date of the last peak has not been agreed upon. There is also uncertainty about the date of the trough (or even whether it has been reached) of the current recession.

Source: National Bureau of Economic Research.

of course, tend to be longer than peaceful expansions; they last at least as long as the period of mobilization and fighting. The 45 months' average duration for the 22 peacetime cycles better describes the historical pattern. Leaving out the wartime cycles, we find 13 cycles in which the depression phase lasted longer than the ensuing prosperity. There were also two cycles in which there were as many months of contraction of output as there were months of expansion. Remembering that this is the record of a young, vigorous economy experiencing rapid technological change (and rapid spread into new frontier areas in the nineteenth century), these frequent and often protracted declines in output point to the presence of serious instability.

TABLE

22.1

timing and duration of business cycles in the
United States since 1854

DURATION (MONTHS)

EXPANSION (trough to peak)	CONTRACTION (peak to trough)	CYCLE (trough to trough)
30	18	48
22	8	30
46	32	78
18	18	36
34	65	99
36	38	74
22	13	35
27	10	37
20	17	37
18	18	36
24	18	42
21	23	44
33	13	46
19	24	43
12	23	35
44	7	51
10	18	28
22	14	36
27	13	40
21	43	64
50	13	63
80	8	88
37	11	48
45	13	58
35	9	44
25	9	34
105	15[a]	—

The decades after 1840 saw major changes in the economic environment. Great railroad systems were built, stimulating enterprise and extending the economy. In the 1840s, 7,000 miles of track were laid, and 20,000 miles were added in the 1850s. By 1860, the railroads were operating over 30,000 miles, and the volume of rail traffic equaled that of canal shipping. The rate of construction slowed during the Civil War, but track mileage doubled in the 1870s and doubled again in the 1880s. The practice of combining a large amount of capital under the corporate form of ownership started with the railroad ventures and extended rapidly to other industries after the 1870s.

The last 25 years of the nineteenth century and the first 20 years of the twentieth century was the turbulent period during which the American economy made the transition from the domination of agriculture to the preeminence of industry. Many of the nation's strategic industries (e.g., railroads, meat packing, large-city banking, steel, copper, aluminum) and important areas of manufacturing came under the control of a relatively small number of immensely powerful firms.

Prior to 1880, agriculture accounted for over one-half of U.S. national income; by 1900, it accounted for less than one-third. By the mid-1890s the United States had become the world's leading industrial power, and by 1913, the American economy produced over one-third of the world's industrial output, more than double that of its closest competitor, Germany.[17]

With the exception of the railroads, most industries in the immediate post–Civil War years were still relatively competitive by present-day standards. Although accurate statistics are not available for this early period, it has been estimated that the largest 200 non-financial enterprises would have controlled a very minor and inconsequential percentage of all business assets. By the end of the 1920s, however, the largest 200 controlled 33 percent of all assets.[18]

Accompanying this concentration of industry was an equally marked concentration of income received by a small percentage of the population. Despite the fact that there are no accurate statistics for the early part of the period under consideration, it seems reasonably certain that the degree of concentration of income increased substantially between the 1880s and 1920s. By 1929, 5 percent of the population received 34 percent of personal disposable income.[19] The degree of concentration had probably reached this extreme as early

17 Ross M. Robertson, *History of the American Economy* (2nd ed.; New York: Harcourt Brace Jovanovich, 1964), p. 331.

18 Joe S. Bain, *Industrial Organization* (New York: John Wiley, 1959), p. 192.

19 U.S. Department of Commerce, *Historical Statistics of the United States* (Washington, D.C.: U.S. Government Printing Office, 1963), p. 167.

as 1913.[20] By the end of the 1920s, the top 20 percent of "families and unattached individuals" were receiving in excess of 50 percent of all personal income.[21] During this period of American industrialization (1880s through 1920s), ". . . millions lived in abject poverty in densely packed slums. . . . They struggled merely to maintain their families above the level of brutal hunger and want for such little pay that their status was a tragic anomaly in light of the prosperity enjoyed by business and industry."[22]

Prosperity *was* enjoyed by business and industry. Output, productivity, and profits all climbed impressively. Yet the last decades of the nineteenth century saw frequent periods of distress and depression. From 1873 to 1879, thousands of small businesses failed, farms were lost to foreclosure, and the accumulated savings of thousands of families, caught by bank failure, disappeared. Estimates of unemployment during the long depression that began in 1873 range from 1 to 3 million. When recovery came in the 1880s, output expanded more rapidly than at any other time in U.S. history, and yet the decade was interrupted by three years of depression. Vigorous expansion did not return to the economy until late in the 1890s; the depression of the early 1890s is generally regarded as the most severe on record prior to the Great Depression. Over 4.5 million workers were unemployed in 1894, or almost 20 percent of the labor force, and unemployment remained high until 1899.[23]

The inadequacies and deficiencies of the banking community and of the monetary system operated to aggravate the mild as well as the severe cyclic disturbances not only in the nineteenth century but also well into the twentieth century. As the economy matured, the frequency of banking crises accelerated. Precipitous monetary failures occurred in 1873, 1884, 1890, 1893, and again in 1907.

At the start of the 1873 panic, failure of the investment banking house of Jay Cooke and Company led to panic selling of stocks. In 1890, failure of the British investment bank Baring Brothers caused a break in the U.S. bond and stock markets because Europeans sold U.S. bonds to retrieve funds from the American market. Stock prices recovered, but by mid-1893, when renewed European selling of both stocks and bonds coincided with rising U.S. business failures, the stock market again witnessed continued selling that did not abate. Within a month, demands for converting deposits into cash were mounting and banks in all parts of the country began to fail. Some

20 Ibid.

21 Ibid., p. 166.

22 Foster R. Dulles, quoted in Richard O. Boyar and Herbert Morais, *Labor's Untold Story* (New York: Marzani & Munsell, 1955), p. 34.

23 See Stanley Lebergott, *Manpower in Economic Growth: The American Record Since 1800* (New York: McGraw-Hill, 1964).

financial houses failed during recurring panics in the stock market in 1901 and 1903, but no generalized banking crises developed.

Then came the contraction of 1907. Industrial and agricultural output had both been rising in response to strong European and domestic demand; prices and profits had been moving upward; and the money supply had expanded with a recent upsurge in gold production. Although stock prices had fallen sharply early in the year, they had begun to recover. Suddenly, five months after the temporary upturn, New York banks began experiencing cash withdrawals that could not be met by the individual banks, and within a few days the large Knickerbocker Trust Company failed to meet its depositors' demands. The rush to withdraw funds spread to the outlying banks, and these in turn withdrew reserves from banks that were simultaneously being squeezed by their depositors.

What had appeared at first to be a mere suspension in the economy's upward movement became instead a swift and severe contraction. As the trough was reached, Congress passed the Aldrich-Vreeland Act which led to the creation, in 1914, of the Federal Reserve System (discussed in Chapter 29). It was felt that the monetary needs of expanding trade as well as the cash needs of the banking system would be met easily through the institutional device of central banking, and that, therefore, a remedy for crises, at least financial crises, had been prescribed.

World War I brought economic expansion. It was followed, however, by the severe depression of 1920–1921. The new Fed used all of its power to mitigate the severity of the economic decline, yet production fell by 20 percent and employment dropped 11 percent within a year. Furthermore, prices, which had been rising since the war years, fell to less than one-half their peak 1920 level.

The rebound out of the 1921 trough was a strong one, and the downturns of 1923–1924 and 1926–1927 notwithstanding, the 1920s were growth years. Major advances in productivity took place, employment was high, and prices were steady, or gently falling. Major new industries led the expansion. Automobile production tripled during the decade, making up one-eighth of the value of manufacturing by 1929. The automobile's stimulus to the construction, steel, glass, rubber, oil, retail trade, and service industries led to widespread increases in production. These were boom years for new construction of electric-power facilities and for new housing and business construction as well. Radio was a growth industry, while production of other consumer durables reached record levels. Agriculture, however, did not share proportionately in the prosperity.

Except for the rising volume of new loan money entering the stock market for speculative purposes, the final expansion period, which began in November 1927, had few signs of danger ahead. Durable-goods production had climbed 40 percent between the trough in

1927 and June 1929. Employment was at an all-time high, and consumer spending was strong. Wages were not rising, and prices showed no evidence of being pulled up by consumer demand. Residential construction had turned down sharply in 1927, bringing total construction into decline, but business and public construction were still strong. With little or no inflation, no break in corporate profits, and record employment, there appeared to be little cause for gloomy predictions.

In October 1929, the stock market collapsed. It would be difficult to support a view that the stock-market break was the basic cause of the depression of the 1930s. Manufacturing had begun to falter at least three months earlier and the construction industry had been depressed for almost two years. But the collapse of the stock market *was* spectacular. Buyers for securities vanished as everyone rushed to sell. Debts that could not be paid encompassed the lenders in the downward spiral of asset values. Moreover, the loss of wealth was being matched by the loss of income as prices, sales, and production continued to fall. There were signs that the debacle had ended in early 1931, but instead of recovery the downward momentum suddenly quickened. By 1933, at least 30 percent of the labor force was unemployed. The homeless, the hungry, and the desperate were never fully counted. The economy improved slightly until 1938, when it took another plunge downward. Full employment was restored only by the all-out war spending of World War II.

Since World War II, the American economy has been plagued by instability, although debacles approaching the seriousness of the Great Depression have been avoided. Several small recessions in the 1950s were followed by prolonged prosperity in the 1960s. After 1968, however, the problem became one of inflation as well as unemployment.

Before we can examine the very special conditions that must hold if there is to be full employment and balance in a private-enterprise economy, we must look at the system of national-income accounting. The national-income accounts discussed in the next chapter provide the basis for understanding the concepts economists call *aggregate demand* and *supply*. The notions of aggregate demand and supply help us understand more thoroughly the problem of economic stability.

summary

According to Say's law, aggregate demand will always automatically adjust to aggregate supply. This was roughly true of earlier societies in which production was for self-sufficient isolated units, and the little exchange that existed was by barter. It is also roughly true in socialist economies where production and investment are planned for social use. Say's law is *not* true for modern private-enterprise, capitalist economies in which production is for the market, exchange operates by means of money and credit, and the aim of production is private profit. Thus, despite its impressive long-run growth the American economy has been plagued by instability. The growth of large-scale, oligopolistic, corporate capitalism in the late nineteenth century only increased this instability. As a result, ever since the industrial revolution and the establishment of full-blown capitalist systems, western Europe and the United States have been subject to periodic depressions of "overproduction" in which output falls, factories are idle, and millions of workers are unemployed and on relief.

chapter 23
national income accounting

In order to examine the economy's overall performance and to study the forces that underlie its movements, we need consistent measures of the total and of each component part of the nation's economic activity. The national-income and national-product accounts provide these measures. Any system of accounts for an individual or a firm is a record of receipts and expenditures. Similarly, the national-income and national-product accounts record the nation's receipts of income from the production of goods and the provision of services. These production accounts are balanced by the record of spending for these goods and services by consumers, investors, and government.

gross national product

Gross national product (GNP) is defined as the total value of all the finished goods and final services produced by a nation in a year's time. Each good or service is valued at its market selling price. The market pricing system thus provides a yardstick by means of which totally different and otherwise unrelated items can be compared and aggregated. Besides the Gross National Product, there is an elaborate system of national accounts which has been devised by the U.S. Department of Commerce. Some of the concepts of our national accounting will be examined in detail because these terms are used every day in the newspapers, in congressional reports, and in reports by the President's Council of Economic Advisers. The same terms are used throughout this book; they reveal some of the framework of the U.S. economy as well as traditional economic thinking.

the circular flow

The national flow of production and income may be thought of as a circular flow of supply and demand between households and businesses. In this simplified picture of the economy, there is no foreign trade because, if it were included, the circle of supply and demand would be broken at that point. Because the volume of foreign trade is a small percentage of American GNP, most of our economic activity is represented accurately enough even when foreign trade is omitted from the picture. The government sector also is not included for the sake of simplicity. Understanding the circular flow in this uncomplicated economy is essential to understanding the concepts of aggregate supply and aggregate demand. These same concepts underlie the construction of the national income and product accounts.

In a capitalist economy, some households own property while others own only their power to work. Together, they supply certain amounts of labor, capital goods (e.g., factories and machinery), and natural resources (e.g., land and minerals) to business. At each given level of technology, this will enable business to supply households with a certain amount of consumer goods and new capital goods (e.g., new factories owned by individual stockholders).

Consumer goods keep the households alive and ready for labor, and the new capital goods are available for further business expansion. Of course, the services supplied by households to businesses as well as the products supplied by businesses to households are furnished for payment, not free of charge. In a primitive economy, services can be bartered directly for products, but a complex economy cannot be based on such a system of exchange. Payment must be made by means of money, which is the only type of effective demand in the U.S. economy.

In our simplified version of an economy (with no foreign trade and no government) the demand that calls forth the supply of business goods and services may be divided into two spending flows: private consumption and private investment. *Thus, aggregate demand for the national product is equal to private spending for consumption and for investment.*

The payment for the supply of services from households may be similarly divided into various income streams: wages, rent, interest, and profits. Wage income includes hourly wages, piecework wages, salaries, and commissions. Profit income includes profits of both corporate and unincorporated business. Rental income includes the rent from land as well as buildings. Interest income includes all returns on borrowed money. It is assumed at this point that all of these business incomes are actually paid out to households.

The circular flow of supply and demand is depicted in Figure 23.1, which indicates how (1) money spending flows from households to

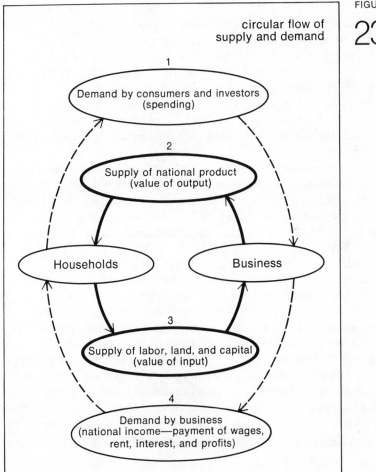

FIGURE
23.1

circular flow of
supply and demand

1
Demand by consumers and investors
(spending)

2
Supply of national product
(value of output)

Households

Business

3
Supply of labor, land, and capital
(value of input)

4
Demand by business
(national income—payment of wages,
rent, interest, and profits)

business in return for (2) the flow of products from business to households. At the same time, (3) the services and property of households flow to business, in return for (4) the flow of money income from business to households. Notice that money moves in one direction around the circuit, whereas goods and services meet it in their equal and opposite movement. If there is no hitch, the supply and demand will flow smoothly and just balance each other in both sets of transactions.

Gross national product may be calculated in two different ways, corresponding to the money flow from households to business or the equal money flow from business to households. In the first, the aggregate money demand for all products, or the *flow of money spending* on consumer goods and investment goods, is examined.

$$\$ \text{ GNP} = \$ \text{ spending} = \$ \text{ consumption} + \$ \text{ investment} \tag{1}$$

This flow of money spent for products must correspond, of course, to the equal and opposite flow of products to their final buyers. In the marketplace, the money flow from purchasers is precisely the measure of the value of the GNP sold by business. Thus, in Figure 23.1 the two upper loops, labeled (1) and (2), show the movement of money in one direction and the equal movement of goods and services in the other direction. The two are equal by definition because the exchange price has been agreed to by both buyers and sellers.

The second way of calculating GNP is to add up the money paid out by businesses for all of its costs of production. Most of these costs of production constitute *flows of money income* to households. These incomes include wages paid for the services of labor, rent for the use of land, interest for the use of borrowed capital, and profit for capital ownership. Thus, the two lower loops of Figure 23.1, labeled (3) and (4), depict the movement of goods and services to business in one direction and the equal movement of money as income to households in the other direction.

Actually, businesses have other costs which have not yet been discussed. These costs make the second way of calculating GNP a little more complicated than suggested by the simple diagram of Figure 23.1. One of these costs is *depreciation,* or the funds set aside to replace the machinery and factory buildings that are used up or eventually worn out in the process of production. These funds are paid out not to any individual but to other businesses when it is time to replace the worn-out instruments of production. So, when depreciation is added to the flows of money incomes, we get

$$\$ \text{ GNP} = \$ \text{ cost of production} = \$ \text{ wages} + \$ \text{ rent} + \$ \text{ interest}$$
$$+ \$ \text{ profits} + \$ \text{ depreciation} \tag{2}$$

The first method of calculating GNP takes into account all kinds
of spending to purchase final output; it reveals the *source* of all
business receipts. The second method takes into account all costs of
doing business (the expenditures of the business sector); it shows
all of the ways of disposing of business income (including profit
payments), or the *allocations* of GNP. By definition, this GNP must be
equal to the GNP arrived at by the first method. Indeed, the U.S.
Department of Commerce, which makes these calculations, always
does arrive at the same amount by either method (after allowing for
statistical mistakes).

gross national product,
net national product, and national income

We are now ready to bring government into the calculation of GNP,
and also to admit that goods are sold and bought abroad.
Government could be viewed as a giant household or business, but
because government output of services is not sold in the marketplace
there is no obvious way to value the services it provides. The U.S.
government is not to any appreciable extent an owner of any instruments of production; it receives its income by taxing the incomes of
labor and of privately owned instruments of production. Yet government spending in the private sector is a very significant part of
overall demand, and government employs about 18 percent of the
labor force.

For our purposes, the role of government in the economy will be
simplified by assuming it merely siphons money from the circular
flow by taxing, and injects it back into the spending stream by buying
goods and services from businesses. The types of goods and services
it buys and the uses to which it puts them will be considered in later
chapters. Gross national product, with government in the economy
and with foreign trade, when calculated from the expenditure side,
becomes

$$\text{\$ GNP} = \text{\$ spending} = \text{\$ consumption} + \text{\$ investment}$$
$$+ \text{\$ government} + \text{\$ net exports} \qquad (3)$$

Net exports are the difference between what is sold and what is
bought abroad. Exports bring a flow of dollars into the country in
exchange for goods produced at home but sold abroad. Imports
result in a flow of dollars out of the country for the purchase of goods
produced abroad. If more is exported than imported, the net figure
is an addition to the total amount of spending taking place for

domestically produced goods and services. Foreign trade is also discussed in greater detail in a later chapter.

With government in the picture, another cost of doing business must enter the calculation of production costs: the sales or excise taxes. These taxes include general sales taxes on all or most commodities, such as a 5 percent state tax on all sales. They also include special taxes, such as the tax on cigarettes, which affect only the purchasers of one commodity. In either case, the government extracts the money at the point of purchase before it can be considered as income by business. These are sometimes called indirect taxes because they are not a direct tax on the income of any individual or business. From the income or cost side, GNP is now calculated by adding the sales taxes as a cost of doing business. Thus

$$\text{\$-GNP} = \text{\$ cost of production} = \text{\$ all wages} + \text{\$ interest} + \text{\$ profit} + \text{\$ depreciation} + \text{\$ sales taxes} \qquad (4)$$

Net national product (NNP) differs from GNP in only one respect: NNP does *not* include the amount of depreciation that has occurred during the year. *Depreciation* is defined as the amount of capital used up in the production process. The NNP is very useful as a measure of what part of the economy's total production is actually available for use. Certainly, production that merely replaces machinery that has worn out and is no longer usable should not be considered as adding to the amount of capital available to the economy. Thus, to compare useful production of two countries, we would compare NNP not GNP because when we compare product actually available for use, we are not interested in the amount of depreciation or capital used up in producing the available product. To arrive at the figure for NNP, simply subtract depreciation from GNP.

$$\text{\$ NNP} = \text{\$ GNP} - \text{\$ depreciation} \qquad (5)$$

In the national accounts, depreciation is called *capital consumption allowance.* Unfortunately, the capital consumption allowance does not always reflect physical depreciation accurately because it involves many problems of estimation which are affected by the practices of accountants. These accountants must view not only the expected life of capital equipment but also the implications for tax liability. From the cost or income side, NNP can be calculated by eliminating depreciation (or the capital consumption allowance).

$$\text{\$ NNP} = \text{\$ wages} + \text{\$ rent} + \text{\$ interest} + \text{\$ profits} + \text{\$ sales taxes} \qquad (6)$$

If we were still excluding government, NNP and national income would be identical. *National income* is defined as the income of the nation in a year's time that is wholly derived from the production of final, usable goods and services. It is the income going to *all* the economic classes: wages to workers, rent to landlords, interest to lenders, and profit to capitalists. Sales taxes and all other indirect business taxes go to the government and do not become income to any class of citizens. When they are subtracted from NNP, the national income is simply

$ National income = $ wages + $ rent + $ interest + $ profits   (7)

or

$ National income = $ NNP − $ sales tax   (8)

At many places in the following chapters, the government's role will be ignored (as a first approximation for simplicity). In these instances, because indirect taxes are being left out it may be assumed that NNP and the national income add up to the same amount.

personal and disposable income

The government imposes various taxes on the national income but also adds to the income stream many kinds of welfare payments. Therefore, the total of payments to all classes in production (i.e., the national income) is not the amount of income that households actually have at their disposal. Households' income comes from production *plus* various welfare payments *minus* various taxes.

In order to proceed from national income to the income that actually goes to persons (i.e., the *personal income*), various additions and subtractions must be made. First, some corporate profits are kept by corporations and are not paid out to individual stockholders. These profits, called *retained corporate profits,* must be subtracted from national income in the process of determining the personal income actually going to individuals. Second, the government collects taxes from corporations according to the amount of their annual profits; these *corporate profit taxes* are also subtracted from national income. Third, individuals pay out of their wage income certain compulsory contributions for social insurance to the government (these are payments for what is usually called *social security*); these also must be subtracted from the national income.

On the positive side, the government pays *interest on the national debt* to individuals; this must be added to the national income because it does become personal income. Finally, the government makes many *transfer payments,* or transfers from all taxpayers to various individuals for reasons other than current services rendered to the government. Typical transfer payments are unemployment compensation, farm subsidies, veterans' benefits, and social security payments by government to individuals. All such payments must be added to national income if we wish to calculate the personal income. Totaling all the additions and subtractions from national income, the result is personal income. The procedure is indicated by the following unwieldy equation:

$ Personal income = $ national income
　　　　　　　　　− $ retained corporate profits
　　　　　　　　　− $ corporate income taxes
　　　　　　　　　− $ contributions for social insurance
　　　　　　　　　+ $ government transfer payments
　　　　　　　　　+ $ net interest paid by government　　　　(9)

Finally, there is *disposable personal income,* which is that amount of money actually at the disposal of individuals and households for spending on consumption or for personal saving. In order to find this quantity, *personal income taxes,* which are the taxes an individual or household must pay in proportion to its yearly income, must be deducted. The result is expressed as

Disposable personal income = personal income − personal income taxes (10)

Consumers may now spend and save out of disposable personal income. If consumption expenditures are subtracted, we arrive at personal saving.

A simplified listing of the accounts discussed is shown in Table 23.1.

national income accounts	TABLE 23.1

Gross National Product
　− Depreciation (or capital consumption)
= *Net National Product*
　− Indirect Business Taxes (mostly Sales Taxes)
= *National Income*
　− Retained Corporate Profits
　− Corporate Income Taxes
　− Contributions for Social Insurance
　+ Government Transfer Payments
　+ Net Interest Paid by Government
= *Personal Income*
　− Personal Income Taxes
= *Disposable Personal Income*
　− Consumption Expenditures
= *Personal Saving*

TABLE

23.2

national income accounts for 1969
(in billions of dollars)

Gross National Product		931.4
− Depreciation (or Capital Consumption)	78.9	
Net National Product		852.5
− Indirect Business Taxes (mostly Sales Tax)	83.0	
National Income		769.5
− Retained Corporate Profits and Corporate Income Taxes	61.1	
− Contributions for Social Insurance	53.6	
+ Transfer Payments	65.1	
+ Net Interest Paid by Government and Consumers	29.0	
Personal Income		748.9
− Personal Income Taxes	117.3	
Disposable Personal Income		631.6
− Consumption Expenditures	594.0	
Personal Saving		37.6

Source: Federal Reserve Bulletin, August, 1970. The item Consumption Expenditures includes $16.5 billion net interest paid by consumers.

An example of the actual figures in these accounts for one year is shown in Table 23.2.

saving and investment

Most of our national income is spent for *consumption*—that is, the aggregate purchase of consumer goods and services by all U.S. households. Whatever part of national income *is not spent for consumption* is defined as *saving.* Thus, the following definition may be written:

$ Saving = $ national income − $ consumption   (11)

Aside from the government, there are only three sources of saving in the economy. First, individuals and households do some personal saving. Second, businesses save by putting aside their depreciation funds. Third, businesses also retain some profits as another form of saving. These savings are the source of all the money being invested in the economy.

It is necessary to distinguish between the concepts of wealth, capital, and investment. *Wealth,* the broadest concept, is the total holding by everyone of all durable consumer goods (*plus* natural resources) *plus* the total holding of the entire stock of capital. Wealth is not measured in the national income and product accounts. A high level of production certainly means that a large stock of wealth exists in the form of productive capital. The national accounts, however, measure only the value of the flow of production, and hence income. They are not designed to measure the holding of wealth either in its form as *capital* or, for that matter, in the form of claims measured in money, which would be called *financial wealth. Capital* is defined as the total value of all existing buildings and factories, machines and equipment for production, and inventories. *Inventories* are defined as the existing stocks of raw materials, goods in process, and finished goods stockpiled.

Investment may then be defined simply as the *change* in capital, its increase or decrease within a year or some other period of time. This means that any individual investment that does not increase the amount of capital, such as the purchase of old shares of stock by one individual from another, does not count as net investment for the nation. Even if a corporation sells new stock, the proceeds do not become net investment in the economy until the corporation actually uses the money to purchase new factories, equipment, or inventories. In other words, the investment discussed here is not mere *financial* dealing or mere individual investment of money, but the *real,* or physical, expansion of the nation's economic capacity. More specifically, this year's investment consists of new construction, new producers' durable equipment, and the change in business inventories.

Only one more distinction in this area of analysis need be made. The total investment in the economy is called *gross investment.* It includes both *net investment,* or investment to expand productive capacity, and *replacement investment,* or investment needed merely to replace the depreciation of present productive capacities.

There is, of course, a close connection between net and gross investment and net and gross national product. The connection can be easily stated through the spending approach to national product. Leaving aside government spending and net export spending, we find that

$$\$ \text{ Gross national product} = \$ \text{ consumption} + \$ \text{ gross investment} \qquad (12)$$

In this equation, gross investment includes replacement investment, which is equal to depreciation. Similarly, without government or net exports, we find that

$ Net national product = $ consumption + $ net investment   (13)

By definition, saving and investment are *always* equal in the national accounts. Leaving out government and foreign trade, the two calculations of national income can be stated as follows:

$ National income = $ consumption + $ net investment   (14)

$ National income = $ wages + $ interest + $ profits + $ rent   (15)

Because national income is either spent or saved, we have the following identity:

$ National income = $ consumption + $ saving   (16)

Comparing this with the definition of national income from the expenditure side, we get:

$ Consumption + $ net investment = $ consumption + $ saving   (17)

The equality between saving and investment is an accounting identity. Both are equal to national income minus consumption, by definition. Had we started from GNP, depreciation funds would have been included on both sides, making gross investment equal to gross saving of businesses and individuals (the following equations will hold for net or gross amounts, so we do not distinguish).

With government included, the identity becomes

$ Consumption + $ investment + $ government
            = $ consumption + $ savings + $ taxes (18)

This is so because national product is now the sum both of the three spending flows and of the three allocations between consumption, saving, and the tax payments. The sum of investment spending and government spending is identical with the sum of private saving and taxation. If government spending and taxation are equal, the government budget in the national accounting framework is in balance. In practice, the difference between government spending and government taxation is called *government saving,* which may be positive if taxes exceed government spending, or negative if there is a budget deficit.

When foreign trade is added, the identity becomes

$ Consumption + $ investment + $ government + $ exports
            = $ consumption + $ saving + $ taxes + $ imports (19)

This identity can be understood as representing, on the left side, the expenditures for goods and services by the four spending sectors, and on the right side, the uses of national income. The difference between exports and imports is often called *net foreign investment.* If it is positive, it indicates that foreigners cannot pay for all of U.S. exports with the money spent on imports from them. They must make up the difference by giving Americans either debt or equity capital in their economy. Hence, Americans are said to be investing in foreign economies when U.S. exports exceed U.S. imports. By rearranging accounting terms and subtracting consumption from both sides, the overall identity between saving and investment can be written as follows:

$ Investment + ($ exports − $ imports) = $ saving
+ ($ taxes − $ government)   (20)

The sum of net domestic private investment and net foreign investment is identical to the sum of net private saving and governmental saving. Or, in brief, saving equals investment in the national accounts.

the value-added concept

The GNP of the United States includes only final products. It avoids counting the value of the same product more than once when this product appears at various intermediate stages of the production process. Suppose *both* the value of all the steel produced and the value of all the automobiles produced were counted in GNP. A great deal of steel is used in automobile production. Therefore, we would be counting the value of that steel twice, once by itself and once as a principal ingredient in automobiles.

The correct procedure is to include only the *value added* by capital and labor (and land) in each industry—that is, the increase in the worth of the product in the production process of that industry beyond the worth of the raw materials bought from other industries. Therefore, the value added by capital and labor (and land) to the raw material in the steel industry would be counted. Then the value added by capital and labor (and land) in making automobiles out of the steel would also be counted. But the value of the steel, or any other product from another industry, used by the auto industry would not be counted again. The whole calculation of gross product (using the cost of production, or income, approach) may be illustrated as follows:

Gross product in steel and auto industry
= steel (wages + profits + rent + interest + depreciation)
+ auto (wages + profits + rent + interest + depreciation) (21)

Notice that neither the cost of the iron or coal used in the steel industry, nor the cost of the steel or rubber tires used in the auto industry is included; both are values produced by other industries and not values added by this industry. The value added is thus less than the price in each industry by exactly the amount of goods and materials bought from other industries.

gross national product in real terms

To know whether a change in GNP reflects a change in national welfare, we must determine whether the change was due to a change in the economic measuring rod (prices) or a change in the *real* quantity of goods and services produced. If the national product doubles in money value, but the price level has also doubled, then the real product—the goods and services available to the nation—has remained the same. Or, if GNP in current prices has risen 5 percent, but the overall price level has risen 3 percent, physical output has increased by only 2 percent.

In calculating GNP, the government must use current prices. But to make comparisons between years when price changes have occurred, the money value of GNP can be deflated by dividing the current value by an index showing how much prices have changed:

$$\frac{\text{Prices} \times \text{quantity produced} = \$ \text{ GNP}}{\text{Price index}} = \text{real (or deflated) \$ GNP}$$

The Department of Commerce compiles price indexes for the many components of GNP. It also deflates each component by its index. Each index is constructed from the price changes that have occurred in the items that make up that component. By choosing a base year such as 1929 (1929 = 100), against which all price changes are measured, deflated GNP data can be made comparable over the years.

potential gross national product

Many times, a part of the nation's productive capacity goes unused. Factories may stand idle or only partially used while millions of unemployed workers search for jobs. During such periods, economists can calculate the approximate *potential* GNP that would obtain *if* the unemployed laborers could be put to work and *if* the factories not being utilized could be used to their full capacity. The difference between potential GNP and actual GNP is a widely used measure of the economic costs of recessions and depressions.

per capita gross national product

Last, interest may be focused not on the total national product but on the national product per person of the population. If China has the same national product as England, then the average Chinese is much worse off than the average Englishman because of the difference in population. Therefore, to measure the improvement in individual welfare, the increase in total national product must be deflated by the increase in population to find the increase in national product *per person* (or per capita).

summary

For the purposes of analysis, economists try to keep accounts measuring all of national output. Everything put together is called the *gross national product,* the demand for which comes from consumers, investors, government, and foreign buyers. Although it is an important measure, we should not be mesmerized by the size of GNP because it includes many wasteful or even harmful goods and services (advertising, cigarettes, military). A second concept is the *net national product,* which equals GNP *minus* depreciation. Third, *national income* equals NNP *minus* sales taxes (and a few similar taxes). Fourth, *personal income* is what actually winds up in the hands of individuals; so it equals national income earned in the usual ways *plus* welfare and subsidies and interest payments from the government *minus* profits kept by corporations and corporate taxes and employee's social security taxes paid to the government. Fifth, *disposable income* is equal to personal income *minus* personal income taxes. Finally, *savings* equals disposable income *minus* consumption. Because *investment* is also defined as all income or output minus consumption, saving and investment are equal by definition in the national-income accounts (but, as will be seen in the next chapter, what some people plan to save and others plan to invest may *not* be equal).

chapter 24
income determination

Economists use the idea of an equilibrium of the forces of aggregate supply and demand as their most important analytical tool for understanding the level of output and employment. *Aggregate supply* is defined as the total output, or NNP, which business produces and plans to sell.

Aggregate demand, a concept for which there is no direct statistical measure, is defined as the total dollar amount of final goods and services that consumers, businessmen, government, and foreigners *plan* or *desire* to buy from the business sector. Equilibrium exists when planned aggregate demand equals planned aggregate supply. The remainder of this chapter explains the nature and significance of aggregate economic equilibrium.

equilibrium of aggregate supply and demand

In the national-income accounts, it turns out that by definition the supply of NNP must exactly equal the demand for consumption goods plus net investment goods. Not only are aggregate supply and demand identical, but also it turns out that saving and investment are identical (because both are defined as equal to national income minus consumption). Why should this be so in the national-income accounts? Assume that more products are offered for sale at the present price level than purchasers are able or willing to buy. In this case, the statisticians consider the excess products, whether consumer or investment goods, to be an increase of inventories. But any increase of inventories is investment according to the statisticians' definition of the national-income accounts. For example, an increase of 1,000 bushels of ripe tomatoes on hand is investment. Therefore, total demand, which is composed of consumer spending plus investment spending, *including unintentional and unwanted increase of inventories,* always equals the supply of product according to the national-product accounts.

All of this, however, refers only to the *statistical* (or after-the-fact) spending and investment figures that appear in the national-income accounts. The situation is quite different if the demand that arises from *planned* (or intended) spending is examined. Planned spending is defined as all spending except the spending on unwanted increases in inventories. Planned supply and planned demand will be equal only when the economy is at equilibrium, meaning that buyers' and sellers' desires exactly agree at present prices. If, however, 1,000 bushels of ripe tomatoes go unsold, then the supply at present prices is greater than the planned demand. Similarly, only in equilibrium will planned consumption plus planned net investment (which does not include investment in unwanted inventories) equal planned NNP. Yet this condition does not hold true in the economy at most times. In other words, the two sides are equal only if there is equilibrium of aggregate supply and demand, but they are *not* equal as a general rule.

The problem may be explained still another way by saying that only in equilibrium are consumption plus planned investment (or aggregate spending) equal to consumption plus saving (or aggregate use of income). *Saving* is defined to be the difference between national product and planned consumption spending. Because income can be spent either for consumption or for investment, equilibrium is maintained only if saving out of income (what is left over after consumption) is just equal to planned investment spending. This is the famous Keynesian equilibrium condition that *planned saving must equal planned investment.* It is just another way of saying that aggregate income (or the money value of output supplied) must equal aggregate spending (or the money value of output demanded).

The problem of economic equilibrium is illustrated in its simplest form in Figure 24.1. Business pays the national income to households for services rendered. Then, if there is equilibrium, all of that income is spent by households to buy goods from business. In this case, all income that is not spent for consumption is *saved* in the form of investment spending.

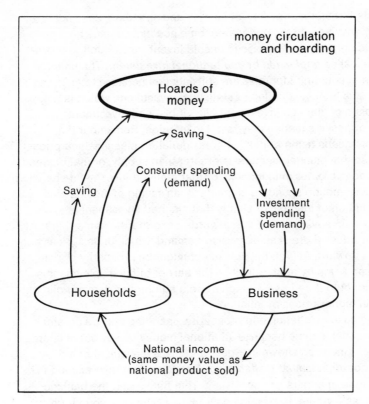

FIGURE

24.1

money circulation
and hoarding

Hoards of
money

Saving

Consumer spending
(demand)

Saving

Investment
spending
(demand)

Households

Business

National income
(same money value as
national product sold)

depression or inflation conditions

Disequilibrium may result in depression or inflation. Remember that
depression means declining output and unemployment (while
prosperity means rising output and employment). A depression
situation results when planned demand is less than supply, or
phrased differently, when planned spending is less than income. This
means that consumption plus planned investment is less than
consumption plus saving, or stated simply, planned investment
spending is less than the saving of income. In any case, the result is
that some goods cannot be sold at present prices. Then when
businessmen find that unwanted inventories are piling up, they may
lower output and employment or lower prices and take losses.

According to Figure 24.1, the national income from business may
be disposed of in three ways. It may be spent for consumption, spent
for investment, or *hoarded,* which means that it may be put aside in
some form of money and not spent at all. *Saving* is the name for all
nonconsumption use of income. Hoarding, which represents loss

from the circular money flow of income and spending, does not appear anywhere in the national-income accounts. It may be indicated only by an increase in unsold inventories, which, we have seen, is called *unplanned* or *unintentional investment*. The national-income accounting identities are still satisfied because total saving still equals total accounting or statistical investment, which is composed of planned investment plus unplanned investment.

The opposite situation may result in inflation. Remember that inflation means rising prices (whereas deflation means falling prices). Suppose that planned demand is greater than supply, or that planned spending is greater than income, or that planned investment spending plus consumption spending is greater than saving of income plus consumption of income, or simply that planned investment is greater than saving. All of these words describe the same thing: At present prices there is an excessive demand, which drives prices and outputs upward. At first, the only effect might be prosperity or rising output and employment. But when the barrier of full employment is reached, output can rise no higher, so a still higher demand can only result in higher prices or inflation.

In the case of inflation and prosperity, spending may be greater than national income because additional money moves out of hoards into investment, as shown in Figure 24.1. This movement of money out of hoards is called *dishoarding*. Spending can also exceed income if the spenders are borrowing from banks and the banking system, as a whole, is creating new money. The consequent unexpected sales, which may be greater than total production, result in unplanned reductions of inventories, which is called *unplanned disinvestment*. Of course, it is still true that in the national accounts the total statistical saving equals the total statistical investment because this is composed of the planned investment plus the unplanned disinvestment. In spite of the statistical equality in the accounts, inflation is another kind of disequilibrium, one in which planned spending is greater than planned production.

monetary equilibrium

In order to cast further light on the process of hoarding, the monetary framework must be examined. In referring to the total supply of money, it must be clearly understood that the whole stock of money in the society is being considered, and not merely the amount of money spent in a given time, such as investment during a particular period. The total demand for money may be divided into the stock of money used in circulation to facilitate transactions and the stock of money being hoarded. Assuming here that the total stock of money is constant, a decrease in the stock of money needed for transactions means an increase in the stock of money hoarded.

However, if the banking system increases the money supply, and the money needed for transactions remains constant, then the increase in the money supply is reflected by increased hoarding. This increase in the stock of money hoarded during a given period is by definition the amount of hoarding in that period. Thus, hoarding may be defined as a relative or percentage decrease in money in circulation for transactions and a movement of money into cash hoards. Dishoarding then means a movement out of cash hoards into circulation for use in transactions. It can be seen that either dishoarding or increases in the money supply can finance aggregate expenditures in excess of national income.

LONG-RUN AND SHORT-RUN EQUILIBRIUM

Finally, in connection with the analysis of economic equilibrium, the length of time involved also must be considered. In economics, the *short run* is defined as that time period short enough that new net investment does not yet lead to an actual increase in the capacity to produce. The *long run* is long enough that investment means an increased capacity for production. To this point, the analysis of equilibrium has been exclusively short run.

In the short run, there is equilibrium *if planned investment equals planned saving*. In the long run, something more is necessary because investment means the growth of capacity to produce. Any investment would lead to greater ability to produce, but a growth of production indicates a changing economy, not an equilibrium economy. Therefore, in the long run, there is an unchanging equilibrium only if net investment is exactly zero. In this case, all saving goes into replacement investment, which just equals depreciation. Furthermore, all of net produce would have to be in consumer goods, just equal to consumer spending.

In the short run, concern is limited to obtaining an equilibrium of demand with supply *at the full employment level* of output, which is that amount of output that could be produced if all workers were fully employed. Thus, using all of present capacity to produce is emphasized. In long-run analysis, attention is concentrated on how fast may be the *growth* of capacity to produce and on the equating of this growing supply of output with a growing demand. In this chapter, the short-run *possibility* that the economy may not have an equality of planned demand and supply at full employment is examined. In Chapter 28, why our economy seldom if ever has a short-run full-employment equilibrium is discussed. Later, the conditions necessary for a steady long-run rate of growth in the economy will be examined.

keynes and say's law

John Maynard Keynes is perhaps the most important economist of the first half of the twentieth century. His background does not appear to be that of a radical or an earthshaker. Born into a respected English family and educated in the best British schools, Keynes worked for His Majesty's Civil Service and the Bank of England, edited the *Economic Journal,* and wrote careful treatises on Indian finances and formal logic as well as the general problems of money. He was an active promoter of the fine arts and married a most beautiful ballet dancer. Keynes was always considered one of the Establishment in culture, government, and financial circles, yet he rocked the Establishment both in England and the United States by demolishing the myth of Say's law and automatic full employment.

Say's law had been attacked before by such unorthodox economists as Malthus and Marx. Keynes, however, attacked it in detail using the respectable academic tools of the classical and neoclassical economists. In his most famous book, written at the depths of the Great Depression he destroyed Say's law and proved that the equilibrium level of the economy might be either at a point of heavy unemployment or at over–full-employment and inflation.[1]

keynes and consumer behavior

Keynes begins by classifying the elements of aggregate demand for net product into two categories: consumer spending and net investment spending. He first considers the behavior of consumer spending, which he believes to be determined for the most part by the level of national income. His reasoning as to consumer behavior is based on certain broad psychological presumptions. (1) At a very low income level, the average individual still needs some minimum consumption and therefore he will spend all of his income on consumption and may even dip into savings or go into debt to spend more than his whole current income on consumption. (2) As his income rises, he needs a smaller percentage of it to cover his minimum needs, so at some break-even point he reaches an equality of income received and consumption spending. (3) As income rises to a very high level, consumption needs and desires may be filled through the use of a smaller proportion of income, so that an increasing percentage may be saved.

[1] John Maynard Keynes, *The General Theory of Employment, Interest, and Money* (New York: Harcourt Brace Jovanovich, 1936).

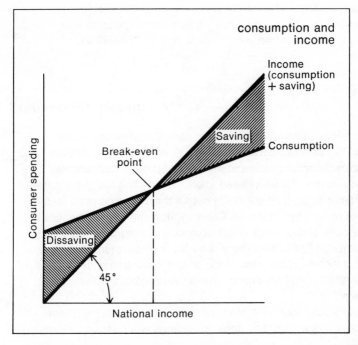

FIGURE

24.2

consumption and income

Income (consumption + saving)

Saving

Consumption

Break-even point

Dissaving

45°

Consumer spending

National income

This usual behavior of consumers is illustrated in Figure 24.2. The line labeled "Income (Consumption + Saving)" shows the total income at each point; it is equal by definition to the income spent for consumption plus the income saved. *If* income exactly equaled consumption at every income level, then that line (at 45°) would also show consumer spending. In reality, they are different. The line labeled "Consumption" shows how much consumer spending there actually is at each level of income. The space between these two lines obviously reflects the amount by which consumption differs from income. At low levels of income, the consumer spending by the poor is greater than their income, so there is *dissaving* (using up of reserves or going into debt) by these consumers. At high levels of income, the consumer spending by the rich is much less than their income, so there is saving by this group.

consumption and income

This schedule of aggregate consumer spending at different income levels is called the *consumption function*. It tells us that in the short run, consumption is not some constant proportion of income. Rather, as income rises, consumption rises, but saving rises too.

Therefore, *as income rises the percentage of income spent on consumption declines.* The relationship between income and consumption is explored more thoroughly in Chapter 25.

aggregate demand

Consumption spending is the largest component of aggregate demand. In a simple economy, with no government and foreign transactions, consumption and investment together constitute aggregate demand. As has been seen, the demand may be greater or less than the aggregate supply of output that could be produced if everyone were fully employed. Consumption spending is generally considered to be the most *stable* component of aggregate demand. If consumption really behaves in a stable fashion, then, given any level of investment, our knowledge of consumer behavior enables us to derive the level of equilibrium income associated with that level of investment.

Take any arbitrary level of investment. Assume that this level of investment is constant (i.e., does not change when income changes).

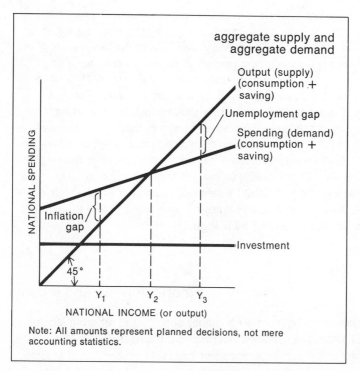

FIGURE

24.3

aggregate supply and aggregate demand

Output (supply) (consumption + saving)

Unemployment gap

Spending (demand) (consumption + saving)

Inflation gap

Investment

45°

Y_1 Y_2 Y_3

NATIONAL SPENDING

NATIONAL INCOME (or output)

Note: All amounts represent planned decisions, not mere accounting statistics.

This investment is combined with Keynes' view of consumer behavior (the consumption function) in Figure 24.3. The aggregate-demand, or spending, line is derived by adding the constant amount of investment to the consumption function (from Figure 24.2) at every level of income. The dollar amount of income is by definition equal to the dollar value of output.[2] This is why the supply of output is shown as rising at a 45° angle, always remaining exactly equal to income received.

Figure 24.3 illustrates the economic results at three levels of income or output. If there is a relatively small labor force available, then full employment can produce only Income 1, a relatively low level of output. If there is a larger labor force, then full employment can produce Income 2. With a relatively large labor force, full employment can produce Income 3, a relatively high level of output.

It is clear that there is only one level of income where aggregate demand (consumption plus investment) is equal to aggregate supply (output, or consumption plus saving): Income 2. This is called the *equilibrium level of income and output.* If full employment happens to produce this level, there is no problem.

Assume, on the contrary, that there is a large labor force, which at full employment produces Income 3. At this level, it is obvious that the total of planned spending (aggregate demand) is less than the level of output (aggregate supply). The difference, labeled "unemployment gap," represents goods and services produced that neither businesses nor consumers want to buy. These goods and services become unwanted inventories. Because this buildup of inventories shows up as investment in the national-income accounts, saving is again equal to investment in the accounts' classificatory scheme.

The difference between wanted and unwanted or unplanned investment is crucial, however, from the economist's point of view. In the next production period, businessmen will cut back on production to avoid the continued buildup of unwanted inventories. This decrease in production (and in the number of workers employed) must continue until output at Income 2 is reached. At that point, output is just equal to what will be voluntarily purchased. The expectations of both businessmen and consumers are consistent at Income 2. There are no longer forces at work that will lead to changes in output and income. This is why Income 2 is called the *equilibrium* level of income. But remember that all of the workers fully employed *could* produce output or Income 3, so at level 2 there is unemploy-

2 In the national-income accounts, the government somewhat arbitrarily deducts indirect business from national product to get national income. For our purposes, we ignore this accounting difference between output and income.

ment. It is an equilibrium *below* full employment. Only if all the unemployed workers died of a plague or were killed in a war would this be an equilibrium with full employment.

Now assume the opposite case. If we begin with a much smaller labor force that can only produce output or Income 1, aggregate demand will be higher than aggregate supply (see Figure 24.3). Businessmen will be able to sell more than they have produced. This can only be accomplished with an unplanned and unwanted reduction of inventories, or "disinvestment" to the national-income accountant. If inventories are reduced to zero, and no more can be produced (because full employment has already been attained), then how will the businessman react to the excess of demand over the supply of goods? Obviously, because he can produce no more goods he will raise prices! This is the inflation situation (considered further below).

If the businessman can find more workers (perhaps by importing foreign workers), he then will produce more in the next period. This process, again, must continue until Income 2, the equilibrium level of income, is reached. Thus, if the national income is initially above or below Income 2, the forces of supply and demand will push it toward Income 2. At Income 2, the income level will tend to stabilize until something causes an increase or a decrease in investment. What happens when investment changes will be discussed in Chapter 25.

There is no reason to suppose, in this example, that the equilibrium level of output and income is that level at which the entire work force is fully utilized. As has been demonstrated, the level of output that could be produced (if the work force were fully employed) could be higher or lower than that produced at Income 2.

If full employment of workers happens to produce output and national income at Income 3, then at full employment, the aggregate supply will be greater than the aggregate demand. In other words, in this case, at full employment, saving (plus consumption) is *greater* than investment (plus consumption). This implies that the excess of money saved is being hoarded. Then there may be price declines or unplanned and unwanted increases of inventories. Output and national income, therefore, begin to decline toward Income 2, where aggregate demand and supply come into equilibrium. At Income 2, the lower level of output implies a lower level of employment. In other words, the equilibrium level of output is below the full-employment level of output. Therefore, unemployment is the result of the gap between aggregate supply and demand at the full-employment income level.

If, in the opposite case, full employment of workers can only produce output and national income at Income 1, the aggregate supply available at that level is less than the aggregate demand. In other words, in that instance, saving (plus consumption) is *less* than investment (plus consumption). This implies that there is an excess of investment funds, which comes from dishoarding of previous savings or from an increased money supply. Then there may be unplanned declines in inventories and attempts to increase output beyond the full-employment level. Because output cannot rise beyond the full-employment level, *prices* must then begin to rise. Therefore, the result of the gap between demand for output and the smaller supply of it is price inflation. The inflationary tendency will continue until the *money* value of national output and national income approach the Income 2 equilibrium level (although *physical* output cannot go above the given full-employment level of Income 1).

a full-employment income level

Starting from a situation of large-scale unemployment, it can reasonably be assumed that any rise in aggregate demand will call forth a greater supply of output while prices remain essentially unchanged. In this situation of considerable unemployment, any price inflation can be ruled out. If aggregate demand exceeds supply when the economy has much unemployment, then the result is just more employment of workers and more output, with little or no change in prices.

Keynes wished to ask what changes would be necessary to bring an economy up to full employment from a lower level of output and income, where supply and demand are in balance, but there is considerable unemployment. This change could be represented in Figure 24.3 by a move from Income 2, which for the economy being considered represents an equilibrium level of output below full employment, up to Income 3, the full-employment level. If investment could be raised so that the schedule of total spending shifted up, the unemployment gap could be closed, and the full-employment level of output in this economy could also be an equilibrium level of output, where full employment of the labor force would be sustained.

If, however, Income 1 were the economy's full-employment level of output and income, a fall in investment spending would be in order. If investment continued at a lower level, the schedule of total demand would shift down and full employment could be sustained without inflation. Of course, this kind of description involves great over-simplifications because everything else is being held equal, assuming that nothing else changes, in order to focus on the heart of Keynes' theoretical model.

The same analysis can be seen in Figure 24.4, which is the simpler

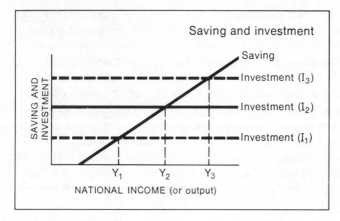

FIGURE

24.4

Saving and investment

Saving

Investment (I_3)

Investment (I_2)

Investment (I_1)

SAVING AND INVESTMENT

Y_1 Y_2 Y_3

NATIONAL INCOME (or output)

picture of income determination because it shows only the saving and investment schedules. The saving schedule is found by subtracting planned consumption from the 45° line (see the shaded area of Figure 24.2). Again, investment is assumed to be given in order to find the equilibrium level of income and output that corresponds to that amount of investment.

If investment is at the rate shown by the solid line (Investment 2) in Figure 24.4, then saving and investment plans are equal at the Income 2 level of income, and this is the equilibrium income. It may or may not be that output at which all of the labor force is fully employed. If Income 3 represents full-employment output and income, then this level can be reached and maintained only if investment spending is raised to the Investment 3. If investment spending falls to a rate as low as Investment 1, income can be sustained only at Income 1. However, if Income 1 happens to be the full-employment level, then Investment 1 and Income 1 are the levels of investment and output at which there will exist full employment without inflation.

The Keynesian analysis, in its simplest form, demonstrates how the nation's income is determined by the equilibrium between aggregate demand and aggregate supply. It shows that this level of income may be one that is well *below* the level that could be generated by producing with the labor force fully employed, so the equilibrium level of a capitalist economy may be such as to cause large-scale unemployment. On the other side, the Keynesian analysis shows that the level of income and spending may be *above* the production possible with the labor force fully employed, in which case the equilibrium level of a capitalist economy may be such as to cause considerable price inflation.

money and prices

This whole analysis may be approached in another way, concentrating more on money demand as a whole than on its consumption and investment components. The *money flow,* or spending for all purposes, may be represented as the total *money supply* multiplied by the *velocity of money,* where velocity is the number of times per year that an average piece of money changes hands. The money supply may be taken to include money in hoards as well as money actually in circulation—that is, to include all coins and paper money and all demand deposits at banks.

The aggregate supply of products sold may be represented as the average *price* level per unit multiplied by the number of *transactions,* or sales of units of products, by all business. Once again, as in the national-income accounts, only the final sales of products and not the intermediate transactions within industries may be counted as transactions. For example, all sales of automobiles are included, but not the sale of steel to auto makers. Similarly, in calculating the velocity of money its change of hands in intermediate transactions is not considered. In this case,

Supply of GNP = (prices) × (transactions with products)

and

Demand for GNP = (money) × (velocity of money)

It follows that in the statistics of national production it will always be found that

Money × velocity = prices × transactions

This famous formula is a platitude when interpreted in this way.

However, leaving aside the accounting or statistical sense of money demand (which includes the unplanned demand for inventories that unexpectedly pile up), then the *planned* money flow of demand may be more or less than the supply of products to the market. If the demand, or money multiplied by its velocity, is *less* than the supply, or present prices multiplied by transactions with products, then there are unsold goods and falling prices, a depression or deflation situation. But if the planned demand, or money multiplied by transactions with products is greater than the supply of goods at present prices, then there is pressure to increase production or raise prices, a prosperity or inflation situation. Tendencies in each condition will be examined in more detail using these new analytic tools.

Both money and its velocity tend to fall in depression. We have said that demand deposits in banks and credit money are the most important part of the money supply. In depression, credit rapidly disappears as lenders grow cautious, and the money supply contracts. Furthermore, the velocity or speed with which total money supply is spent must rapidly decline when people hoard as much as possible of their income, as they do at the beginning of a depression. If money flow (money multiplied by velocity) declines, then either prices or transactions with products or both must also decline. Generally, in a depression, the production and sales of goods do decline considerably. Usually, however, these transactions do not fall as much as the decline in the flow of money demand. Therefore, prices also usually decline.

Notice that this analysis shows that money demand cannot necessarily be increased to ease a depression merely by increasing the money supply. The money flow is money *multiplied by* its velocity, or rate of spending. Thus, increased money supply only leads to more flow of demand *if* its velocity stays constant. In a depression, however, it is likely that the increased money supply will all be hoarded because people expect that prices will drop still further. Therefore, the velocity of money may fall just as fast as its supply is increased.

This point is important because of the lingering influence of an earlier and cruder form of analysis called the *quantity theory of money*. This theory accepts the truism that money multiplied by its velocity equals price multiplied by transactions with products. It assumes, however, that the velocity of circulation of the money supply is always roughly constant. In that case, at any given level of transaction, the behavior of prices would be solely determined by the money supply. This erroneous assumption of fixed velocity led to the erroneous conclusion that prices (and demand for goods) could always be raised in a depression by manipulating the money supply.

Inflation of prices, in our more precise analysis, occurs when the total money flow, or money multiplied by its velocity, rises more rapidly than transactions with products. In the usual prosperity, the rising flow of money demand (i.e., greater money supply and faster spending) simply leads to more production and sales, with only gently rising prices. But if the ceiling of full employment is reached so that production can go no higher, while money flow is still rising, then prices must rise and inflation begins.

In a war, destruction or military needs may even lower the real transactions with consumer products in the face of rising money flow, resulting, of course, in rapid inflation. Sometimes, as in the consumer panic at the beginning of the Korean War, mere subjective expectations can lead to a greater velocity of money spending, thus causing inflation even though money supply and transactions with products are little changed. Thus, the analysis again emphasizes that price inflation may or *may not* be related to changes in money supply, depending on what is happening with the velocity of money spending and total products transactions. The reader should work out for himself each of the possible relationships causing price inflation within the analytic framework of

Money × velocity = price × transactions

Generally speaking, it is more fruitful to look at aggregate demand through its spending components (consumption, investment, government, foreign demand) because these spending flows can be more easily estimated statistically and the relationships between them can be empirically tested. However, the influences that determine changes in velocity are difficult to separate and quantify. Monetary analysis is further complicated by changes in the money supply that occur when business firms and consumers switch between checking accounts and the various liquid forms of financial assets. The upshot is that the explanation of aggregate demand and supply in strict money terms requires a better measure of hoarding than is now available. Nevertheless, the velocity approach is still used by many economists. Because this approach focuses more directly on money and monetary policy, it is sometimes thought to be more useful in investigating purely monetary issues.

summary

We have now shown how the equilibrium level of output may be higher or lower than the full-employment level of output. If aggregate demand is much less than the supply of output at full employment, depression and unemployment result. If aggregate demand is much greater than the supply of output at full employment, the result is price inflation (though, as will be seen in later chapters, there is actually an intermediate zone in which both unemployment and inflation can and do exist at the same time). In a simple economy with no government or foreign transactions, investment spending and consumption spending seem to be the keys to understanding the level of income and employment. In the next few chapters, we shall examine the consumption and investment components of aggregate demand. Then we shall ask how and why the economy actually moves far below full employment at periodic intervals.

appendix to chapter 24

KEYNES AND THE CLASSICAL ECONOMISTS

Keynes calls "classical" all of those economists from Adam Smith to Pigou who accept some form of Say's law. As has been seen, the most rigid form of Say's law, which denies the possibility of deficient (or excess) demand and assumes that hoarding is always zero, holds true only for a society quite different from the monetary private-enterprise economy. But until Keynes wrote in the 1930s, most economists *did* believe that a somewhat more flexible form of Say's law actually applied to the modern private-enterprise economy. They admitted that there might be a temporary lack of demand and temporary hoarding of money, but argued that the perfect working of the competitive price mechanism would quickly and automatically return the economy to equilibrium at the full-employment level of output if only the government would not interfere. In other words, if planned demand falls short of supply at present prices, prices will fall enough to bring back equilibrium at full employment.

The belief that the economy automatically reaches equilibrium at full employment, which may be called the classical viewpoint, implies some very particular assumptions about the markets for products, labor, and money, as well as about the relations between these three markets.

Classical economists argue that if demand in the product, or commodity, market falls short of supply, (1) competition among sellers will cause a drop in prices, then (2) demand will be stimulated to increase, and (3) supply will fall until equilibrium is reached. With regard to the money market, they maintain that if investment demand is less than the supply of saving, (1) competition among lenders will cause a drop in the interest rate (or price of borrowing money), then (2) investment will be stimulated to increase, and (3) saving will decline until equilibrium is reached. Finally, they argue that if the demand for workers in the labor market is less than their supply, (1) competition among workers will cause a drop in wages, then (2) demand for labor will be stimulated (although some workers may withdraw from the market) until (3) equilibrium is reached, at full employment of the workers still in the market.

Keynes and his followers challenged the basic classical assumptions about each market. First, even assuming the relationships to be as described by the classical economists, the Keynesians question whether commodity prices are at all flexible downward. Given a certain degree of monopoly power, prices may remain near constant while output and employment decline. Second, there may be a floor to the interest rate because there is a level below which savers will not make loans but would rather hold cash or other perfectly liquid assets. The reason is that lenders know that the future is not as certain as is assumed by the perfectly competitive model. Therefore, the interest rate may be stuck at a high level such that there is too much saving of liquid assets and not enough investment to reach equilibrium at full employment; this is Keynes' so-called liquidity trap. Third, Keynes pointed out that many institutional factors make wage rates very resistant to downward pressures.

The Keynesians not only have questioned the assumption of the flexibility of the prices of commodities, capital, and labor, but also have asserted that, even with pure and perfect competition and flexible prices, there may be more fundamental reasons why the equilibrium achieved by competitive adjustments may be far below the point of full employment. Keynes pointed out, for one thing, that the classical analysis is geared to individual industries and that it may not hold true at all in the aggregate. For example, lower wages might stimulate demand for labor by a single employer, but lower wages in the aggregate may lower the demand for goods and hence may lower the demand for workers to produce those goods.

OUTPUT AND EMPLOYMENT

Contrast the overall picture of market relationships seen by classical economists with that seen by the Keynesians. The essence of the classical picture, leaving aside the money market, is presented in Figure 24.A1. The most important market mechanism insuring full employment in the classical system, supply and demand in the labor market, is shown in Figure 24.A1(a). The supply of labor is said to be a function of the price of labor—that is, the real wage rate offered workers. The demand for labor also is supposed to be determined by the price of labor. If there is an excess of labor at the present wage, the consequent unemployment will cause a decline in the wage rate. The decline in the wage rate will mean a decrease in the supply of labor and an increased demand for labor until the economy again reaches equilibrium *at full employment.*

The key role of the labor market in the classical system arises from the fact that it determines the (equilibrium) level of employment. Then, with a given technology, capital, and resources, the level of employment determines the level of output, as in Figure 24.A1(b). Thus, the supply and demand in the labor market automatically produce not only full employment but also the full-employment level of production.

The essence of the Keynesian picture, aside from the money

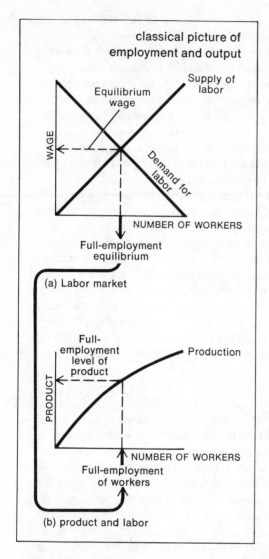

FIGURE

24.A1

classical picture of employment and output

(a) Labor market

(b) product and labor

market, is presented in Figure 24.A2. Keynes focuses on the product or commodity, market, as pictured in Figure 24.A2(a). He emphasizes that at the full-employment level of output and income there may be quite rational reasons why all of income is not spent on either consumption or investment. Consumption is primarily determined in the Keynesian scheme by the level of national income. Investment also is mainly determined by national income because it is the demand for goods that produces the expectation of a high profit. The behavior of consumer and investor demand together determine the equilibrium level of supply of national product.

With a given technology, capital, and resources, the production of

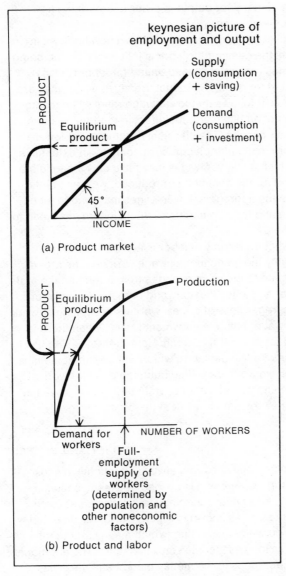

FIGURE

24.A2

keynesian picture of employment and output

(a) Product market

Supply (consumption + saving)

Demand (consumption + investment)

Equilibrium product

45°

PRODUCT

INCOME

(b) Product and labor

Production

Equilibrium product

PRODUCT

Demand for workers

NUMBER OF WORKERS

Full-employment supply of workers (determined by population and other noneconomic factors)

a certain supply of national product means that employers will demand a certain amount of labor. This demand for labor, derived from the demand for commodities, may or *may not* be equal to the number of workers available for work.

Figure 24.A2(b) illustrates a typical Keynesian picture, in which the demand for labor happens to be less than the full-employment level. Classical economists begin with an analysis of full employment of labor in order to determine how much product would be produced.

Keynes begins with demand for output in order to determine how many workers will be employed.

Keynes also looks at the labor market itself in a new light. As in the classical system, the demand for labor is influenced by the going wage rate. But Keynes recognizes that demand for labor is also influenced by demand for national product. Because wage rates are not the only influence, it follows that lower wage rates will *not* automatically mean greater employment; the effect in the total system may even be just the opposite. The classical argument that lower wages make for more demand for labor is true only to an extent in a single industry in which the lower wages may have only a negligible effect on the demand for the commodity produced. Keynes points out, however, that in the aggregate, lower wages may lead to much lower consumer demand for commodities, which, in turn, may lead to less demand for labor.

Keynes believes that the supply of labor is available up to full employment at roughly the going money wage. Workers, he argues, pay much less attention to the price changes that determine the real wage; they are under a "money illusion" and bargain primarily for money wages. Thus, regardless of prices, workers are willing to work at the going money wage; but unemployment results when there is insufficient demand for labor at that wage. Here the Keynesian has in mind a given amount of available labor, which will be subject to mass unemployment when workers are willing but unable to find work at the going wage. The unemployed are not voluntarily unemployed in any sense, nor are they refusing to work at the present wage.

MONEY AND INTEREST

In the classical scheme, total spending always adequately disposes of all income no matter how income is divided between consumer spending and saving. All saving is automatically invested at some equilibrium rate of interest, as shown in Figure 24.A3. Assume that there is a decline in consumer spending, which means that there will be more saving as long as income stays the same. The additional saving will supply more funds to the money market and thus will lower the rate of interest. At some low rate of interest, it becomes attractive for investors to borrow (and spend) all money offered. Thus, investment always takes up any gap in demand left by a drop in consumption.

In the Keynesian system, the supply of money is set by the banks or by the government. The demand for money is viewed in a more flexible fashion than in the classical view of the quantity theory of money. Whereas the quantity theory considers the velocity of money to be constant, Keynes considers that the speed of money turnover

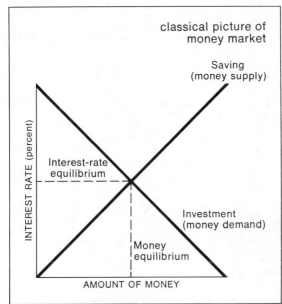

FIGURE

24.A3

classical picture of
money market

Saving
(money supply)

INTEREST RATE (percent)

Interest-rate
equilibrium

Investment
(money demand)

Money
equilibrium

AMOUNT OF MONEY

or the amount of hoarding continually varies with the state of business expectations. He does admit a *transactions* motive to holding money—namely, a need to use money as a go-between in exchanging commodities; and he admits that this need will increase in some relation to the money value of the national product. Keynes also distinguishes, however, two other and quite different motives for holding money instead of commodities: the *precautionary* motive and the *speculative* motive. Money is held for precautionary reasons such as emergencies or old age, and this amount of money probably increases somewhat as our income increases. Money is also held for speculative reasons such as the expectation of a higher rate of return on loans in the future, and this speculative holding will probably increase as interest rates fall to a low level because it is expected that they will some day rise back to whatever level is considered normal. Notice that the precautionary and speculative motives for holding money are not related to immediate exchange of commodities, but allow for the very nonclassical possibility of holding money outside of current circulation merely as a store of value for future use. Once the supply and demand for money is known, the price of money, that is, the interest rate, can be determined.

The Keynesian picture of the money market (Figure 24.A4) allows for some complications that may prevent an equilibrium of saving and investment. First, even with "normal" saving and investment behavior (Investment curve 1), it is possible that the equilibrium rate of interest

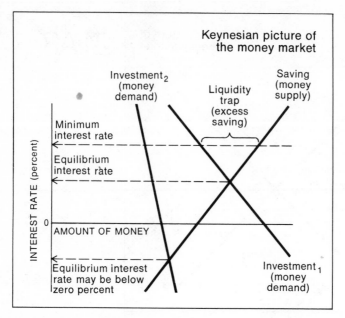

FIGURE

24.A4

Keynesian picture of the money market

is lower than some minimum point below which it cannot drop. In other words, there may be some minimum interest rate below which the risk and administrative expense prevent *any* lending and savers would rather hoard their money for precautionary and speculative reasons. This situation, in which the equilibrium level lies *below* a minimum floor, is the famous *liquidity trap,* in which an excess of saving is left unused for any investment.

Keynesians have also explored the possibility that investor demand for funds may be very inelastic, as in investment curve 2 in Figure 24.A4. "Inelastic" means that investment demand shows very little reaction to a change in interest rates. Indeed, in the Keynesian picture, investment is viewed as far more sensitive to profit expectations (derived from expected demand for products) than to the interest rate. Thus, if businessmen expect a negative profit rate, or losses, from further investment, it would take a negative interest rate (or *payment* by savers to investors) to induce them to borrow more funds for investment. Because an interest rate below zero is impossible, such an equilibrium of saving and investment would be impossible to reach.

CONCLUSIONS

The Keynesian argument concludes that demand may be either insufficient or excessive at the full-employment level, and that the equilibrium of supply and demand can be reached only far below the full-employment level, implying a depression, or far above the full-employment level, implying price inflation. This analysis appears to be far more realistic than that of the classical economists, which is built around Say's law. Nevertheless, the Keynesian analysis is static and does not explain the continuous movement of the economy over time. The Keynesian argument will not be pursued in further detail here. Most of the issues will be reexamined systematically in later chapters from the viewpoint of post-Keynesian theories of economic growth and business cycles.

Where Keynes shows that equilibrium of supply and demand may be reached only far below the full-employment level, a fully dynamic approach argues that the economy may not reach equilibrium at all. Once the economy begins moving downward, the relationship and time lags between reactions may be such that it continues downward in disequilibrium with supply remaining greater than demand. The economy reacts to downward pressures by moving farther down, and moves right through what would be the equilibrium point. Then, when supply is enough lower than demand, the economy begins a disequilibrium movement upward. It continues moving upward far beyond the point where supply and demand are equal, until final demand is so much lower than supply that the downslide commences once more. The result may be an endless repetition of prosperity and depression.

chapter 25
consumption

The pattern of consumer behavior plays an important role in aggregate economics. This chapter looks at some factors influencing the relationship between consumption and income, the so-called consumption function, and examines the way in which this relationship affects the size of changes in the level of national income.

psychological propensities and social facts

Keynesian economists use certain shorthand terms to describe the relationship between consumption and income. The *average propensity to consume* (APC) is the proportion of income spent for consumption, or the ratio of consumption to income at any particular level of income. Similarly, the *average propensity to save* (APS) is the ratio of saving to income at this particular level of income. (Remember that saving is defined as all income not consumed.)

Keynesian economists also speak of the *marginal propensity to consume* (MPC), which can be thought of as the proportion that will be spent out of any additional increment to income. It is defined as the ratio of the *change* in consumption to the *change* in income. Similarly, the *marginal propensity to save* (MPS) is the ratio of the change in saving to the change in income.

(Some of these relationships are further explored in the appendix to this chapter.)

The use of the word *propensity* to describe consumer behavior seems to imply that consumers follow some purely innate psychological laws. On the contrary, consumer behavior is determined not by any natural drives but by social conditioning. We are not born with a desire for television sets. Nor is there any innate compulsion to consume exactly 90 percent of our income and save 10 percent. Our desires for television sets, as well as our decisions on the ratios of consumption and saving to income, are determined by society's attitudes, ideologies, and institutions. Certainly, family background has a significant influence on consumption habits, as do secular and religious educational systems. And last, but not least, the vast volume of advertising in the U.S. economy affects the pattern and even aggregate amount of consumption.

Thus, consumer psychology is largely socially determined. Even more important than consumer psychology, or desires, however, are the objective social facts of how income is distributed. Even if they have the very same psychological attitudes, an unemployed worker with a tiny income will not be able to save anything (and may dissave, or go into debt), whereas a businessman with a million dollar income may only consume 10 percent of his income (and still have a damned high consumption standard). Thus, the data show that groups with very low incomes spend all (or more than all) their incomes on consumption. Groups with very high incomes spend only a small percentage (but more dollars) on consumption; the rest they save, either in the form of hoards or investments.

Obviously, a change in the distribution of income will affect the percentage of income spent on consumption. Hence, if society taxes the rich and gives to the poor, the percentage of income spent on consumption (the propensity to consume) will usually rise. But if society taxes the poor and gives to the rich, the percentage of income spent on consumption will usually fall.

Propensity to consume, therefore, depends mainly on just two factors (although it is influenced by many others): (1) consumer psychology as determined by social conditioning and (2) how society distributes income. In this context, the term *propensity to consume* is perhaps misleading. A more neutral term, perhaps *consumption ratio,* might more easily include behavior based on both psychological desires and income distribution. Because most economic literature does use propensity to consume, we bow in this text to tradition, always remembering that it refers not to innate drives but to socially conditioned psychology and the objective facts of income distribution.

the distribution of income

Comparative studies of family budgets show that families with the higher disposable incomes save a much larger proportion of their incomes than do lower-income families. And families in the very lowest income brackets are so poor that, as a group, they dissave. Of course, some families in the high brackets dissave, and many in the lower brackets save, but, overall, the propensity to consume is lower for higher-income families.[1] Thus, as was noted previously, any change in distribution of income toward higher- or lower-income families will affect the propensity to consume.

It is, therefore, instructive to examine the distribution of income in the United States. Until recently, a majority even of Americans thought of the United States as an affluent society in which most people live in a nice, suburban home, have two cars, a color television plus one or two black and white televisions in bedrooms, washers, dryers, dishwashers and the thousand and one other conveniences of modern life. Many, including experts and other authorities, were surprised if not shocked to learn that a vast amount of poverty exists in the richest country in the world. In 1966, the reader will recall from Chapter 15, 14 percent of all American families had incomes below $3,000 (officially considered a "poverty" income); 46 percent had incomes below $7,000; and 59.4 percent had incomes below $9,100 (officially considered a "modest but adequate" income).[2]

Striking inequalities of income distribution also were described in Chapter 15 (see Table 15.1). At one extreme, are those who live in abject poverty, the lowest 20 percent of families with only 5.4 percent of all family income (and the lowest 20 percent of unrelated individuals with only 2.9 percent of all individual income). At the other extreme, are the wealthy, the top 5 percent of all families with almost 15 percent of all family income (and 5 percent of unrelated individuals with almost 22 percent of all individual income). Among the wealthy are the elite, the richest 2 percent whose incomes range from $25,000 to an estimated $100,000,000 per year.

Because these estimates are based upon income-tax returns, many economists argue that the statistics severely *underestimate* the extent of the inequality in the distribution of income. They maintain

[1] Simon S. Kuznets, *Shares of Upper Income Groups in Income and Savings* (New York: National Bureau of Economic Research, 1953).

[2] U.S. Department of Commerce, Bureau of the Census, *Statistical Abstract of the United States: 1968* (Washington, D.C.: U.S. Government Printing Office, 1968), p. 326.

that the number of very poor people is underestimated. Furthermore, these data do not include income from expense accounts and fringe benefits of various types, both of which accrue primarily to the upper middle class and wealthy because of their connections with the large corporations. Specific tax allowances, for example, the notorious oil depletion allowance, increase the money received but not reported by the wealthy. Moreover, underreporting of income is most serious on income from dividends, interest, and rent—the primary sources of income for the rich—and least significant on income from wages and salaries—the source of income for middle- and low-income families. Taking all of these qualifications into account, income is unquestionably more unequally distributed than the statistics indicate.[3]

Furthermore, taxes do little, if anything, to reduce this inequality (this issue was more fully discussed in Chapter 19). It is commonly supposed that the U.S. tax system takes a higher percentage of the income of the wealthy than of the poor. The income tax does tend to reduce income inequalities, although the effect is much smaller than most people imagine. However, analysis of the *total tax burden* reveals that taxes actually *increase inequality* in the distribution of income because sales taxes, excise taxes, property taxes, and social security taxes all take a much larger percentage of the poor man's than of the rich man's income.

B. A. Musgrave, a recognized authority on taxes, has analyzed the total tax burden on incomes along the entire distributional spectrum. He found that families with incomes below $2,000 per year, certainly a level of abject poverty, paid out one-third of their incomes in taxes. And as incomes got higher, people paid a lower percentage in taxes. For example, families in the $10,000–$15,000 bracket paid a proportion of their income that was nearly one-third lower than that paid by families with incomes below $2,000. Only for the wealthiest 5 percent of families did the total tax bite exceed that which the poorest were paying: The wealthy elite actually paid 36.3 percent of their income in taxes, a mere 3 percent more than that paid by the poorest segment of society.[4]

What accounts for these extremes of inequality? The answer is fairly simple. In the private-enterprise system, the vast majority of people work for wages and salaries. The poorest 20 percent of the population is made up primarily of people who are disadvantaged in the competition to secure good jobs, or any job at all. They include

3 For sophisticated arguments supporting these points, see Selma F. Goldsmith, "Changes in the Size Distribution of Income," *American Economic Review* (May 1957), pp. 504–518; and Victor Perlo, "A Review of 'Shares of Upper Income Groups in Income and Savings,' " *Science and Society* (Spring 1954), pp. 168–173.

4 B. A. Musgrave, "Estimating the Distribution of the Tax Burden," in *Income and Wealth*, Series X (Cambridge, England: Bowes & Bowes, 1964), p. 192.

the aged, the disabled, the fatherless families whose mothers must care for their children and get whatever money they can, the teen-agers, the blacks, the Puerto Ricans, the Chicanos, and other groups that face discrimination in the labor market.

At the other extreme, the wealthiest 2 percent derive very little of their incomes from wages and salaries, and when they do work it is often in sinecures obtained through family connections. Most of this group's income comes from ownership of assets, from profits, divi-dends, interest, and rent. In the most complete study of the distribu-tion of ownership of wealth ever undertaken, it was shown that in 1956, the wealthiest 1.6 percent of the population owned at least 80 percent of all corporate stock and virtually all of the state and local government bonds. Furthermore, the concentration of ownership of these income-yielding assets has steadily increased since the early 1920s.[5]

Thus, it can be said that the extreme inequalities of income distri-bution are not attributable to differences in rates of wages and salaries, although there are large inequalities here, to be sure. The very poor are largely those who cannot, for various social, political, and personal reasons, compete in the job market; and the very rich are largely those whose incomes derive principally from ownership.

Because the distribution of wealth changes very slowly, if at all, and the problems of the poor persist decade after decade, it is not surprising that the relative distribution of income remains quite stable over long periods of time. It has been pointed out that studies that show a narrowing of the distribution of income contain errors both of omission and commission. Recent investigators conclude that it is narrowing extremely slowly, if at all.[6] In fact, in the 1960s the degree of inequality actually increased.

As noted earlier in this chapter, an income shift from the rich to the poor will tend to raise the propensity to consume (because the poor have to consume all of their income), and an income shift from the poor to the rich will tend to lower the propensity to consume (because the rich consume a much lower percentage of their income). Further, most of the income of the rich comes from ownership of property (profits, rent, interest, and dividends), and most of those whose income comes almost solely from wages and salaries fall into that 59 percent of American who have less than the "moderate but adequate" income defined by the BLS. Thus, the effects of shifts between property income and wage income are similar to those of shifts between rich and poor: If less goes to property owners and

[5] Robert J. Lampman, *The Share of Top Wealth-holders in National Wealth, 1922–1956* (Princeton, N.J.: Princeton University Press, 1962).

[6] Goldsmith, op. cit., and Perlo, op. cit.

more to wage workers, the result is a *higher* propensity to consume
because wage workers consume almost all their income, whereas
if less goes to wage workers and more to property owners, the result
is a *lower* propensity to consume because property owners consume
a small percentage and save a very large percentage of their
incomes.

empirical data on consumption behavior

The changes in consumption and saving at different levels of income,
as postulated in the consumption function, may be illustrated by
actual data. In 1929, at the peak of prosperity, the level of consumer
expenditure reached its highest point of the decade, as did national
income. Personal saving was also at record levels of $4,168 million.[7]
By 1933, in the depths of the depression, aggregate income had
fallen by one-half. Consumption had fallen swiftly, but not quite as
disastrously, because people were spending on consumption *more*
than their aggregate income by dipping into their stock of assets
accumulated in previous years and by going into debt. As a result,
personal saving was actually negative in 1933, at *—$648* million
(dissaving).

   Empirical studies of consumption and income levels in other
decades confirm as fact that total consumer spending rises when
national income rises and falls when income falls. Consumption,
however, neither rises nor falls as rapidly as income. Thus, in prosperity, a sizable proportion of high incomes is usually saved whereas
in a depression when income suddenly falls, all or more than all
income is often spent on consumption. In other words, when national
income rises in prosperity, the average propensity to consume (the
ratio of consumption to income) generally falls, but when national
income declines in a depression, the average propensity to consume
generally rises.

   There is, in fact, a great deal of evidence that indicates ". . . that
as income falls in the business cycle, consumption will fall proportionately *less* than income; and again when income rises
cyclically consumption will rise proportionately less than income."[8]
Furthermore, this relationship is consistent with the fact that the
marginal propensity to consume (the ratio of change in consumption
to change in income) is far less than 1. Using the statistics of 1947 to

7 All data here are from U.S. Department of Commerce, Bureau of the Census,
Statistical Abstract of the United States: 1964 (Washington, D.C.: U.S. Government
Printing Office, 1964).

8 Alvin Hansen, *A Guide to Keynes* (New York: McGraw-Hill, 1953), p. 76.

1958, it has been calculated that 88 percent of additional disposable income is spent for consumption, and 58 percent of additional GNP is spent for consumption.[9]

Empirical estimates for much longer periods also are available. One careful study estimated the average ratio of consumption to NNP by overlapping decades from 1869 to 1928.[10] Average consumer spending varied only between 84 percent and 89 percent of NNP, and the average saving ratio, consequently, varied only between 16 percent and 11 percent of national product. Thus, the propensity to consume out of national income did not change much, even though the average family income level *rose tenfold* in that period.

At first glance it may seem somewhat strange that the propensity to save did not rise over so long a period during which income was rising. Did Keynes not teach that it tends to rise at higher income levels? It is true that *at any given time,* higher-income groups save a larger proportion of their income. For example, in 1948–1950, business owners (with relatively high incomes) saved 23 percent of their income, farmers saved only 12 percent, and nonfarm wage workers (with relatively low incomes) saved a mere 4 percent.[11]

The answer to the riddle of a constant or even falling propensity to save lies in the fact that what constitutes a basic, adequate standard of living is determined by social mores, not by biological necessities. The average man learns that in the long run, everyone's income, including Mr. Jones next door, rises by the same percentage. Therefore, the average man, in the long run, raises his own percentage of consumption to keep his standard of living up with that of the Joneses. In other words, if all income classes raise their income proportionally, then the propensities to consume and save stay about the same after a period of adjustment to new standards.

It would appear, then, that a person's position in the overall distribution of income is more important in explaining his consumption behavior than is the absolute level of his income.

relative income

If consumption were determined by the absolute level of income alone, a doubling of all family incomes should result in a fall in the ratio of consumption to income. If, however, relative position on the income scale strongly influences the family's consumption decisions,

[9] See Bert G. Hickman, *Growth and Stability of the Postwar Economy* (Washington, D.C.: Brookings Institution, 1960), p. 224.

[10] Simon S. Kuznets, *National Product Since 1869* (New York: National Bureau of Economic Research, 1946), p. 119.

[11] See Milton Friedman, *A Theory of the Consumption Function* (Princeton, N.J.: Princeton University Press, 1957), pp. 69–79.

a doubling of the incomes of all families would leave the ratio unchanged because there would be no change in the relative living standards. Thus, the comparative constancy over long periods of the propensity to consume can be explained in terms of (1) the extent to which minimal subsistence standards of living are socially determined, (2) the desire to emulate the patterns of those in higher-income groups affecting consumer behavior, and (3) the fact that the relative standings of different income classes have changed very little in the last 100 years.

The relative-income hypothesis also helps to explain why the propensity to consume falls in prosperity and rises in depressions. In the short run, when there are fairly sudden changes in national income, each individual sets his consumption in terms of his own previous level until he adjusts to the new national standards.[12] Thus, if his income suddenly is higher, he can keep to the old average standard of consumption and save a higher percentage. If his income suddenly drops in a depression, however, he tries desperately to maintain his own previous peak consumption, or standard of living, and therefore the percentage of his income that is saved drops rapidly. It is for this reason that the average propensity to consume rises in a depression, but slowly reverts to the long-run percentage as income climbs back toward the previous peak.

In the short run (over a period of a few years or so), the Keynesian consumption function, in which it is assumed that the average propensity to consume falls as income rises, is a reasonably accurate reflection of the relationship between consumption and income. Over longer periods, however, both theory and empirical evidence suggest that consumption remains, on the average, a fairly constant percentage of income.

the multiplier

Some economists believe that Keynes' most important conceptual contribution to macroeconomics is the consumption function, and that the most important analytic tool to come out of the Keynesian dissection of consumption is the multiplier. The *multiplier* expresses the relation between an initial increase (or decrease) in one of the components of aggregate demand and the total increase (or decrease) in national income caused by it. The initial spending change may come from any one of the components of aggregate demand, but investment spending is the most volatile. Investment spending characteristically rises sharply or falls drastically during cyclical

[12] See James S. Duesenberry, *Income, Saving, and the Theory of Consumer Behavior* (Cambridge, Mass.: Harvard University Press, 1949).

fluctuations. Its fluctuations are usually of much greater amplitude than those of consumption.

Obviously, it is vital that government policy-makers know how any change in spending, whether in direct government spending or in private investment encouraged by government spending, will affect national income. This question first received considerable attention during the 1930s when New Deal politicians debated ways of combating the depression.

We leave government spending for a later chapter and concentrate here, as Keynes did, on the effects of changes in investment spending. In precise terms, the *investment multiplier* may be defined as the ratio of change in national income to a change in investment. This is more than a definition; there is a causal relationship running from a change in investment spending to a change in income. A change in investment usually causes a *larger* change in income and output because some of the money spent on investment will be *respent* by its recipients for additional consumption.

Assume that during a period with some unemployment a firm decides to construct a large new factory. This sudden increase in

1 Suppose an increase in investment of $1,000

2 Also suppose a marginal propensity to consume of 4/5, or 80 percent

NUMBER OF ROUNDS OF SPENDING	INCREASE IN INVESTMENT	INCREASE IN CONSUMPTION
0	$1,000	
1	0	$ 800
2	0	640
3	0	512
4	0	410
5	0	328
6	0	262
—	0	—
—	—	—
—	—	—
—	—	—
—	—	—

INFINITE NUMBER OF ROUNDS OF SPENDING	TOTAL INCREASE IN INVESTMENT	TOTAL INCREASE IN CONSUMPTION
	$1,000	$4,000

investment spending will increase the incomes of the contractors who supply the necessary machinery and materials and provide jobs for previously unemployed workers. Now assume that the initial increase in spending and income is $1,000. The recipients of this income will immediately respend most of it for consumer goods, which will result in new income for businessmen and workers in the consumer-goods industries. These income recipients will, in turn, spend much of their new income on more consumer goods. Exactly how much additional spending occurs on each round will depend on the marginal propensity to consume of the income recipients. But it is already clear that any additional consumer spending must mean that the total income generated will be more than the original $1,000 of investment spending.

The easiest way to see how the multiplier is supposed to work is to study a numerical example. In the example in Table 25.1, only some initial change in investment and a certain marginal propensity to consume need be assumed. One thousand dollars of investment becomes $1,000 of income when it is spent. It is assumed that 80 percent, or $800, of that income is respent for consumption, which

TABLE

how the multiplier works

25.1

	INCREASE IN NATIONAL INCOME	INCREASE IN SAVING
	$1,000	
	800	$ 200
	640	160
	512	128
	410	102
	328	82
	—	66
	—	—
	—	—
	—	—
	—	—
	—	—
	TOTAL INCREASE IN NATIONAL INCOME	TOTAL INCREASE IN SAVING
	$5,000	$1,000

means another $800 of national income going to other individuals. They will then spend 80 percent, or $640, of *that* income, and so it goes. In the first round, 20 percent, or $200, leaks out into saving, and in the second round, 20 percent of the remaining income, or $160, leaks out into saving. The process ends only when the last $1 of the increased income is saved. At that point, the whole $1,000 of investment has been saved, but there already have been many rounds of consumption spending in between. In this example, the total of all the rounds of consumption spending (or responding) will eventually approach $4,000, and national income will approach a level that is $5,000 higher than before.

If investment returns to its old level after completion of the factory, the entire process will then work in reverse. Therefore, when the multiplier is used as an analytical tool, it is necessary to distinguish between a one-time injection of new investment spending and a rise in the level of new investment spending which is sustained over a long period of time.

If the $1,000 increase in investment is considered as a one-time injection of new spending, then the totals at the bottom of Table 25.1 represent only temporary additions to consumption, saving, and national income. After these one-time increases are realized, however, total spending will eventually return to its original level. But if the $1,000 increase is a new stepped-up rate of investment spending that continues through several subsequent time periods, the totals represent the rise from the old lower levels to the new higher levels of spending flows, which will persist in each future period.

From this description of how the multiplier works, it should be clear that if less is saved out of each increment to income, then each increment to consumption spending will be larger. In other words, if the marginal propensity to save declines, the subsequent increases in consumption and income will be larger.

The multiplier formula is just a shortcut for finding where the process of Table 25.1 ends without repeating the calculation a great many times. Because the formula works equally well for an initial increase *or* decrease of investment, we shall speak generally of *changes* rather than increases or decreases. By definition:

$$\text{Multiplier} = \frac{\text{change in income}}{\text{change in investment}} \tag{1}$$

However, movement from one to another equilibrium position is assumed; therefore, at the end, the change in saving must equal the change in investment. Substituting saving for investment, we get

$$\text{Multiplier} = \frac{\text{change in income}}{\text{change in saving}} \tag{2}$$

or, by simple mathematical manipulation,

$$\text{Multiplier} = \frac{1}{\dfrac{\text{change in saving}}{\text{change in income}}} \tag{3}$$

Lo and behold! The denominator of this fraction is nothing but the marginal propensity to save. So the formula to remember is just

$$\text{Multiplier} = \frac{1}{\text{MPS}} \quad \text{or} \quad \frac{1}{1 - \text{MPC,}} \tag{4}$$

because the marginal propensities to save and consume always add up to exactly 1.0.

Look again at the example in Table 25.1. It has been established that *total increase in income = increase in investment × the multiplier*. In this example, the increase in investment is \$1,000. What is the multiplier? The MPC is ⅘, so the MPS is ⅕. The multiplier must equal 1 divided by ⅕, which is 5. So we may write

Total increase in income = \$1,000 × 5 = \$5,000

This demonstrates how the multiplier is used to find the end result of investment spending.

Notice that if the multiplier is reduced, then the investment spending has less effect. At one extreme, if the multiplier is just 1, the change in income is just equal to the change in investment. At the other extreme, if the multiplier approaches infinity, any small change in investment will cause an infinite change in income.

Of course, the value of the multiplier is controlled by the MPC or MPS. If MPC falls, so does the multiplier (because less is respent out of each increase in income). A multiplier of only 2 means an MPC of only ½. A multiplier of only 1 means that everything is saved and the MPC is zero. But a multiplier of infinity means that all income is immediately respent for consumption, the MPC is 1, and the MPS is zero.

There are some obvious weaknesses or, at least, qualifications that must be kept in mind when the multiplier theory is used. First, so far the *time element* has been ignored; it takes a certain amount of time before income received is respent for consumption, and still more time before the second and the third and later rounds of respending may occur. If the time lag happens to be very long or varying, a much more complicated multiplier will be needed to get a realistic answer to the change in income for one year.

Second, it has been assumed that MPC remains constant until the process is completed. In reality, MPC often changes and is affected by many psychological and institutional factors. For example, the accumulated savings of World War II greatly increased the propensity to consume in the immediate postwar years.

Moreover, saving is not the only leakage from the income stream. Higher or lower taxes also will change MPC out of national income. Furthermore, if purchases of imports (e.g., Volkswagens) increase, there will be a leakage from domestic consumer spending. Thus, the domestic MPC may change too often to permit accurate prediction of the multiplier for more than a few months in the future.

Third, the multiplier formula assumes that investment will remain the same while consumption and national income are expanding rapidly. Obviously, the simple multiplier theory cannot be used if further changes in investment are to be considered.

For all of these reasons, we conclude that while the multiplier is a helpful explanatory device, it cannot be relied on for an exact estimate.

summary

Consumer behavior is determined by both social conditioning and by income distribution. Income is distributed very unequally, a few rich families having very high incomes, a large number of poor having very low incomes. The poor (mostly wage earners) consume a very high percentage of their income. The rich (mostly profit and interest receivers) consume a small percentage of their income. For the most part, people make consumption decisions on the basis of their perceptions of the general standard of living.

The investment multiplier measures the change in national income that results from a change in investment. The formula for estimating this multiplier is roughly 1 divided by the MPS. This formula is far from exact because it neglects (1) time lags, (2) leakages from increased saving, taxes, and foreign imports, and (3) further changes in investment.

appendix to chapter 25

SOME MYSTERIES OF THE CONSUMPTION FUNCTION

The APC was defined as the ratio of consumption to income at any particular level of income. Similarly, MPC was defined as the ratio of change in consumption to change in income. Figure 25.A1 illustrates the consumption function and gives some definitions and identities.

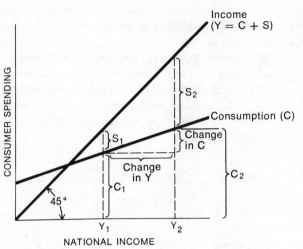

propensities to consume
and save

Income
(Y = C + S)

S_2

Consumption (C)

S_1

Change
in C

Change
in Y

C_2

C_1

45°

Y_1 Y_2

NATIONAL INCOME

CONSUMER SPENDING

Average propensity to consume (APC) $= \dfrac{C}{Y}$

Average propensity to save (APS) $= \dfrac{S}{Y}$

Marginal propensity to consume (MPC) $= \dfrac{\text{Change in C}}{\text{Change in Y}} = \dfrac{C_2 - C_1}{Y_2 - Y_1}$

Marginal propensity to save (MPS) $= \dfrac{\text{Change in S}}{\text{Change in Y}} = \dfrac{S_2 - S_1}{Y_2 - Y_1}$

IDENTITIES:

1. $Y = C + S$

2. $Y_2 - Y_1 = (C_2 - C_1) + (S_2 - S_1)$
   or change in Y = (change in C + change in S)

3. $\dfrac{C_1}{Y_1} + \dfrac{S_1}{Y_1} = 1$ or APC + APS = 1

4. $\dfrac{C_2 - C_1}{Y_2 - Y_1} + \dfrac{S_2 - S_1}{Y_2 - Y_1} = 1$ or MPC + MPS = 1

The reader should review them thoroughly to make sure that he
understands all the terms and concepts Keynesian economists use to
describe the consumption function.

In Figure 25.A1, as the level of income rises, APC falls; that is, the
ratio of C_2 to Y_2 is less than the ratio of C_1 to Y_1. Notice that the MPC
is simply the slope of the consumption function. It is assumed for
simplicity that MPC is constant, which means that equal additions to

income will result in equal additions to consumption. In reality, though, MPC probably declines somewhat as income rises.

As the level of income rises, APS rises; that is, the ratio of S_2 to Y_2 is greater than the ratio of S_1 to Y_1. Because MPC is assumed to be constant, MPS also stays constant; that is, equal additions to income produce equal additions to saving.

Four simple identities result from these definitions. First, consumption plus saving (or dissaving) must always equal income. Second, the change in consumption plus the change in saving (or dissaving) must always equal the change in income. Third, because consumption plus saving equal income, APC plus APS must always equal 1. Fourth, MPC plus MPS must always equal 1.

ASSUMPTIONS		
INCOME (Y)	CONSUMPTION (C)	PERIODS
$ 0	$2,000	1
$ 2,000	$3,000	2
$ 4,000	$4,000	3
$ 6,000	$5,000	4
$ 8,000	$6,000	5
$10,000	$7,000	6

A numerical example may more clearly fix these definitions. Assuming that consumption for each level of income is known, then all the other quantities may be calculated according to their definitions. This procedure is illustrated in Table 25.A1.

In this table the simplest possible assumption is used: Consumption rises by \$1,000 with each \$2,000 rise in income. This is a constant MPC (and a constant MPS). Nevertheless, because it was assumed that consumption began above income(because some minimum consumption is necessary even at very low income levels), the table also reveals a falling APC with a rising APS.

TABLE
25.A1

income and consumption relationships

CALCULATIONS

SAVING (S) = Y − C	AVERAGE PROPENSITY TO CONSUME = C/Y	AVERAGE PROPENSITY TO SAVE = S/Y
− \$2,000	$\frac{2}{0}$ (or + infinity)	$-\frac{2}{0}$ (or − infinity)
− \$1,000	$\frac{3}{2}$ (or 1.50)	$-\frac{1}{2}$ (or − 0.50)
\$ 0	$\frac{4}{4}$ (or 1.00)	$\frac{0}{4}$ (or 0.00)
\$1,000	$\frac{5}{6}$ (or 0.83)	$\frac{1}{6}$ (or 0.17)
\$2,000	$\frac{6}{8}$ (or 0.75)	$\frac{2}{8}$ (or 0.25)
\$3,000	$\frac{7}{10}$ (or 0.70)	$\frac{3}{10}$ (or 0.30)

chapter 26
investment

The classic study of the behavior of aggregate demand covers the four business cycles between 1921 and 1938.[1] During this period, consumer spending averaged 82.3 percent and investment spending averaged only 17.7 percent of GNP. In terms of percent, government and foreign-trade effects were small and need not be separately investigated. Because consumption is so much larger than investment, its absolute changes are also larger. Thus, during these four cycles, 59.6 percent of the prosperity expansion in GNP was in consumer goods, whereas 51.9 percent of the depression contraction in GNP was in consumer goods.

At the same time, changes in investment spending constituted only 40.4 percent of the expansion and 48.1 percent of the contraction in GNP. Yet it is striking that with investment averaging less than one-fifth of GNP, it still managed to represent close to one-half the change in GNP. Obviously, this means that in percentage terms, the fluctuations of investment are pretty violent. In fact, as a percentage of its own average value for the whole period, investment rose 55.4 percent in expansions and fell 49.3 percent in contractions. Consumption, however, rose by only 15 percent and fell by only 9.9 percent of its average value. These facts are exactly what we would have expected from the theory developed in the last two chapters. They are illustrated in Figure 26.1.

[1] All data in this section are from Wesley C. Mitchell, *What Happens in Business Cycles?* (New York: National Bureau of Economic Research, 1951), pp. 154–155.

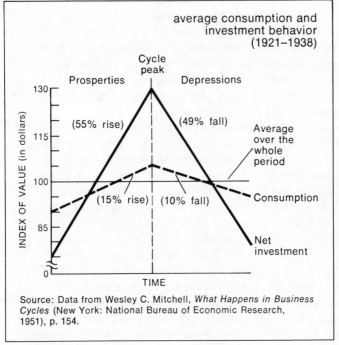

FIGURE

26.1

average consumption and
investment behavior
(1921–1938)

Source: Data from Wesley C. Mitchell, *What Happens in Business Cycles* (New York: National Bureau of Economic Research, 1951), p. 154.

The multiplier, which accounts for the magnified effect of fluctuations in investment on national income, was examined in Chapter 25. Analysis turns now to the characteristically violent fluctuation of investment spending itself. Attempts to explain investment behavior constitute the heart of many business-cycle theories. Economists have long realized, from the standpoint of understanding business fluctuations, that investment spending is the most important component of aggregate demand. Yet it is also the most difficult to explain and accurately predict.

gross and net investment

In Chapter 23, *net investment* was defined as simply the change in capital within a time period. Obviously, the stock of capital is steadily diminished through use, wear and tear, and obsolescence. However, the stock of capital grows as new capital goods are produced and purchased. *Gross investment* was defined as the total of all capital goods produced in a year. To determine *net investment,* the amount by which the capital stock has depreciated is subtracted from gross investment.

For example, in the crucial year 1929, $8.7 billion were invested in new construction and $5.8 billion in new producers' durable equipment, and there was a $1.7 billion increase in business inventories, or a total of $16.2 billion gross investment. Because allowances for depreciation or capital consumption were $8.6 billion in that year, it can be assumed that $8.6 billion of the gross investment was for replacement. By definition, the net investment must have been at the level of $7.6 billion.

Assume that the total amount of capital in the United States on January 1, 1929, was exactly $100 billion. According to the figures given above, there was an $8.6 billion depreciation during the year, just balanced by an $8.6 billion replacement investment. In addition, however, there was a net investment or addition to capital capacity of $7.6 billion during the year. It follows that on January 1, 1930, the amount of capital would have risen to $107.6 billion.

Although it was assumed that the amount of replacement investment can be measured by the estimated depreciation, the decision to replace depreciated capital goods is not automatic. In 1933, gross investment (and gross saving of all persons and businesses) was only $1.4 billion, but depreciation was still $7.2 billion. Therefore, net investment (and net saving of all persons and businesses) was actually at the negative level of −$5.8 billion. The capital stock and hence the economy's productive capacity was rapidly diminishing. Gross investment could never be negative, for at worst, no new capital goods would be produced. In that event net investment would be negative and equal to depreciation.

In an investigation of aggregate demand, it is gross investment that is important. *Any* investment spending is a part of the demand for currently produced capital goods. If growth of productive capacity is being considered, however, then net investment indicates by how much the capital stock has increased, and thereby permits an estimation of the increase in the economy's capacity to produce.

decision to invest

The businessman contemplating the order and purchase of a new plant or equipment will not decide to make the purchase unless the value of the profits he expects to receive from this investment is greater than, or at least equal to, the purchase price of the capital goods. Otherwise, of course, the purchase would involve a net loss to him. If it is assumed that he knows what the proposed investment will return to him during each year of its life, then the *present value* of the expected income, or return, is the total of that money income after it has been discounted by the rate of interest. This is because $100 received a year from now is worth less than $100 now, and $100 five years from now has a present value that is much less than $100 now.

The discounting process is easily illustrated. Assume (1) that the businessman expects an investment to return $100 above operating costs each year for three consecutive years and (2) that the market rate of interest is 5 percent. Then the present value of the proposed investment can be calculated as follows:

$$\text{Present value} = \frac{\$100}{1 + .05} + \frac{\$100}{(1 + .05)^2} + \frac{\$100}{(1 + .05)^3}$$

or

$$\$95.24 + \$90.90 + \$86.21 = \$272.35$$

If the price of the capital good were higher than $272, the purchase would not be made. In other words, the present value of the expected future income from a proposed investment is compared to the initial cost, or outlay that must be made. If the outlay, which in this example is the price of the capital good, were anything less than $272, the investment could profitably be made. If the price of the capital good were greater than $272, the businessman would receive more profits by simply loaning his money to someone willing to pay the 5 percent interest on it. Of course, if the rate of interest were lower, the present value of the expected income from the capital good would be higher.

Another way to approach the same calculation is to estimate the *percentage rate of return* that the capital investment will yield. Assume that an investment of $250 now will yield $100 yearly above operating costs for three years. Then the percentage rate of return on the capital invested (which Keynes called the *marginal efficiency of capital*) can be found as follows:

$$\$250 = \frac{\$100}{1 + \text{rate}} + \frac{\$100}{(1 + \text{rate})^2} + \frac{\$100}{(1 + \text{rate})^3}$$

The calculation is based on the formula used to find the present value of the three annual $100 returns, but by this method we are solving for the rate of profit in order to determine what percentage rate of return this $250 investment represents. The percentage yield, or rate of profit on capital, is about 10 percent. If, however, the cost of the capital good were $272 (as before) then the rate of return on capital would be only 5 percent. This probable rate of profit, so calculated, is then compared to the market rate of interest. If the percentage rate of return from the investment project is equal to the market rate of interest, or below, then the businessman could do as well or better by merely collecting interest on his money.

There are thus two methods of investment decision making. In one, the present value of the expected returns from the investment is determined and compared with the cost of the investment. In the other, the percentage rate of profit on capital is determined and compared with the market rate of interest. In either case, an answer to the question, "Will the investment yield a *profit?*" has only been simulated. Without the expectation of future profits, capital accumulation comes to a halt in a capitalist system.

It was assumed that the businessman could project with some confidence that the investment would make a net return of $100 each year for three years. In reality, he must project output and sales into the future, while allowing for all probable costs of producing this additional output. A large amount of guesswork is involved in projecting future sales, prices, and costs. These uncertainties are the usual business risks, and there are additional risks unique to the project or purchase which is being contemplated. Businessmen will not invest if they do not receive a remuneration for risking their money. This remuneration must be in addition to the profits already discussed. When business risks are taken into consideration, the return on the capital asset (i.e., the return the businessman can assume with some certainty that he will get) will be not $100, but, say, $90 in the first year and less each succeeding year.

In this view, the businessman may decide not to purchase the capital good unless the percentage rate of return he expects with certainty (above all costs, including the cost of assuming risks) exceeds the market rate of interest. Alternatively, the businessman may use a rule of thumb that the investment will not be made unless the percentage rate of return exceeds a certain norm, which is the usual, or warranted, rate on capital investment in his industry, or which he considers necessary to compensate for uncertainty and risk undertaken.

Obviously, profits are exceedingly important in determining the level of investment, and hence output, income, and employment, in the U.S. economy. Indeed, the prime motivation for investment in a private-enterprise economy is the expectation of future profit on the new investment. But because future profits cannot be known with certainty it is mainly on the basis of the present level of profits and the changes in profits that businessmen form their expectations. Accordingly, at least in competitive situations, high or rising profits will lead to optimistic expectations and new investment, whereas low or falling profits will lead to pessimistic expectations and a decline in new investment.

The other and quite distinct reason for the importance of profits is the fact that more profits add to the liquidity of the firm and provide the funds for investment. If there are no profits, the firm may lack funds to invest even if it wishes to do so. Although the capital funds can sometimes be borrowed, more profits make it easier for the firm or its stockholders to obtain credit. Moreover, most firms are quicker to invest from internal sources, and in practice, most expansion is financed with retained profits. It is imperative, therefore, to inquire into the nature of profits in the American economy.

profits in the united states

One of the most important determinants of profits in any industry is the extent to which the industry is competitive, or the extent to which economic power is concentrated in the hands of a few firms within the industry. Many discussions of investment behavior (and hence of business cycles and of economic growth) have assumed or implied an economy of pure or perfect competition. That would be an economy composed of individual business units competing with each other, where each is so small that its actions taken alone could not appreciably influence the quantity of goods or the price in the market. This more or less adequately describes the U.S. economy of most of the nineteenth century, when small farms and small businesses produced most of the output, and there were no giant corporations dominating an entire industry (although there were many local monopolies). Since the 1890s or early 1900s, this picture has mirrored not reality but a theory that in its basic assumptions is thus irrelevant.

Today, U.S. industry still has millions of very small enterprises, but a few hundred corporate giants hold most of the wealth and account for most of the production. In Chapter 7, we traced the early development of monopoly power. In Chapter 8 we showed the vicious tactics used by the giant firms to eliminate competitors. In Chapter 16, we saw why theory predicts that the giant oligopolies will restrict output, and have higher prices, and higher rates of profit. In Chapter 18, we examined the present results of incredibly high levels of economic concentration.

At the bottom, a large number of small corporations (906,458, or 59 percent of the total) held a tiny portion of corporate assets ($31 billion, or 1.5 percent) in 1967. At the top, a few giant corporations (958, or just 0.06 percent) held a majority of all assets ($1,070 billion, or 53.2 percent). That fewer than 1,000 U.S. corporations should hold more than a trillion dollars of assets is incredible; that is more than the value of all west European assets and in the same range as the value of all Soviet assets! Among those 958 corporations, there are

200 or 300 giant giants. In the decisive sphere of manufacturing alone, the top 200 firms held 59 percent of all manufacturing assets in 1967.[2]

In most individual industries (with *industry* so defined that there is easy substitution among the products of all firms within it and very little possible substitution with products of outside firms), three or four giant corporations control most of its production. This domination of an industry by a few large firms is called an *oligopoly.* Many small firms also exist in most industries, but altogether they produce a small percentage of the total output. The economy of the United States has thus changed from a predominantly competitive to a predominantly oligopolistic production situation.[3]

It also was demonstrated in Chapter 18 that monopoly (or oligopoly) finds many ways to make above average rates of profit on investment. These are briefly reviewed here. First, the whole point of monopoly (or oligopoly) control of markets is, of course, to restrict output and charge higher prices which squeezes extra profits out of all consumers. Second, higher monopoly prices hurt all the farmers and small businesses that purchase producer goods; they must accept lower profits. Third, if a large firm has extra market power as a buyer of commodities (technically, *oligopsony* power), it may also gain extra profits by buying at a lower price from small business and farmers.

Fourth, if a giant firm has extra market power as a large buyer of labor (again, oligopsony power), it may also add to its profits by buying labor at a lower rate than the average wage. Fifth, additional monopoly profits come from lucrative government military contracts (this will be discussed in Chapter 27). Sixth, additional monopoly profits come from concentrated ownership of investments abroad. In many cases, foreign-based subsidiaries enjoy the same monopolistic advantages in the host countries. Furthermore, as was established in Chapter 18, the smallest corporations have low or even negative profit rates. Profit rates rise with the scale of the corporation.[4]

Another important aspect of economic concentration was discussed in Chapter 18. The indicator of market power is the relative size and importance of a firm in its own industry. The *concentration ratio* in each industry is the percentage of sales controlled by the

[2] Federal Trade Commission data cited in Federal Reserve Bank of Cleveland, *Economic Commentary* (May 12, 1969), p. 2.

[3] For convenience, the terms *monopoly* and *monopoly power* are used in this chapter to include (a) concentration of a large part of all U.S. corporate assets in 200 or 300 giant firms, and (b) oligopoly control of most individual markets. The meanings are differentiated where necessary.

[4] See Howard J. Sherman, *Profit Rates in the United States* (Ithaca, N.Y.: Cornell University Press, 1968), pp. 40–50.

, eight largest corporations in the industry. Several studies have found a definite relationship between an industry's concentration ratio and its profit rates.[5] When all industries were divided into twenty groups, a considerable rise of profit rates as the degree of concentration rises was found. Thus, the average rate of profit on capital in the ten industry groups over the 50 percent concentration level was 20 percent in 1954. In the same year, the rate of profit on capital was only 12.8 percent in the ten industry groups below the 50 percent concentration level.[6]

monopoly power and
cyclical investment behavior

How does economic concentration affect the amount of change in business performance from prosperity to depression? There is considerable evidence that cyclical performance, as indicated by profit rates, is significantly different for big business and small business. Specifically, annual data on the profit rates of all corporations from 1931 through 1961 reveal the larger corporations had much more stable profit rates than smaller ones. The smaller the corporation, the greater was the amplitude of rise and fall in its profit rate.[7]

Quarterly data on profit margins in U.S. manufacturing industries from 1947 through 1963 indicate that the industries with the lowest degree of concentration have the greatest cyclical changes in profit margins.[8] For example, apparel and lumber, two very competitive industries, have the highest cyclical changes in profit margins both in prosperity and in depression. But tobacco, one of the more concentrated industries, has the lowest cyclical changes in its profit margin both in expansion and contraction.

Investment behavior is closely related to profit rates and, thus, to monopoly power. It is known that profit rates of small and competitive businesses are the first to turn at the peak of the business cycle. Similarly, there is some (weak) evidence that new capital appropriations and actual investment expenditures on new plant and equipment

[5] See, for example, J. S. Bain, "The Relation of Profit Rate to Industrial Concentration, American Manufacturing, 1936–1940," *Quarterly Journal of Economics* (August 1951), pp. 292–324.

[6] Such a difference is statistically significant—that is, it could occur by chance far less than one percent of the time.

[7] Sherman, op. cit., pp. 156–166.

[8] Ibid., Table 7–8, p. 171.

begin to decline at the cycle peak significantly earlier in the more competitive industries.

The evidence is much stronger that the amplitude of fluctuation in investment is affected by corporate size and degree of concentration (in the same way as profit rates are affected). Thus, one careful study found that small firms (assets below $4.9 million) had more rapid rates of capital growth during periods of expansion but much higher rates of decline during recessions.[9] It also appears (on the small amount of available evidence) that investment tends to be more stable in industries with a high degree of concentration than in the more competitive industries. In other words, small businesses are hurt the most by recessions, and their investments decline the most (partly because their profits are taken away by the monopolies).

psychological attitudes

Because investment decisions are based on projections of sales and returns into the future, it would be easy to say that fluctuations in aggregate investment are caused by changes in investors' confidence about economic conditions. Although it points to a vital aspect of economic behavior, such a "formula" actually explains nothing. There can be no denying the sensational effects of changes in expectations upon real economic conditions in the private-enterprise system. Between 1929 and 1932, children did not have enough to eat, men jumped from tall buildings, women pawned their fur coats. What caused the trouble? Pessimism?

To say that waves of optimism or pessimism strongly affect the economy is to make a very incomplete statement. What causes the optimism or pessimism? In 1929, most indexes of production, new investment, and profits turned down in the summer, but the stock-market crash and the collapse of expectations did not occur until autumn. For example, the industrial peak was June 1929, but prices of stocks did not peak until October 1929.[10] In a competitive, private-enterprise economy, especially as it increases in complexity and interrelatedness, the single enterprise cannot accurately predict its future costs and receipts; therefore, it tends to keep an optimistic outlook until it encounters obstacles. In fact, it appears to be the usual order of events in depressions that, first, production and financial indexes decline despite the most extreme optimism. It is

9 John R. Meyer and Edwin Kuh, *The Investment Decision* (Cambridge, Mass.: Harvard University Press, 1957), pp. 163–167.

10 See U.S. Department of Commerce, *Historical Statistics of the United States, 1789–1945* (Washington, D.C.: U.S. Government Printing Office, 1949), p. 345.

only then, because of the change in economic conditions, that the optimism changes to pessimism, which reinforces the depression and may postpone the recovery. The reverse process seems to occur in economic expansions when rises in production and profits are followed by a shift from pessimism to optimism.

Of course, optimistic business expectations have a powerful uplifting effect, especially on new investment, which will be carried to much higher levels than it would otherwise have reached. Similarly, pessimistic business expectations cause a much greater decline in investment and even in consumption than the objective situation warrants. But the ultimate cause of pessimism in businessmen's attitudes is the fact that disequilibria in the market system lead to widespread adverse consequences which impede the search for profits.

inventions and innovations

Innovation is defined as the putting to use of inventions in the economy. It may lower costs on a given output or create more output with the same cost or improve the quality of old products or create new products. Many argue that inventions and innovations act as random stimuli; by making investment more profitable, they prolong prosperity or bring an economy out of a depression.

Entrepreneurial expectations may vary widely as a *result* of economic prosperity or depression. Wesley Mitchell argues that in a depression every effort is made to find ways (inventions) to reduce costs, but that firms hesitate to make major new investments to innovate: "It is the season when alterations are planned; revival is the season when they are executed on the largest scale."[11] Thus, the rate of innovation may be expected to decline drastically in depression both because the rate of invention may decline somewhat and because business expectations usually become very pessimistic. In prosperity, however, innovation is greatly increased both by business optimism and, probably to a lesser extent, by more new invention.

By lowering cost per unit, innovations may improve profit expectations and thereby increase investment. By improving products or making new products, output demanded may be stimulated. Depression, however, is intensified not only by the drop in the rate of innovation, but by the fact that innovation may not be as stimulating in a generally pessimistic situation.

11 Wesley C. Mitchell, *Business Cycles and Their Causes* (Berkeley: University of California Press, 1959 printing, 1927 ed.), p. 190.

A cost-cutting innovation may also cause old machinery to become obsolete more rapidly, thereby tending to cause a temporary increase in replacement investment if business conditions make replacement desirable. If the innovation is in the quality of a product or in a new product, then it may lead to a net increase of investment demand, although the innovating firm's final output of improved or new consumer goods must still compete for the consumer's dollar with the output of other industries. Of course, the total effect cannot be precisely predicted because it depends on just how demand reacts in the different industries, the speed of the demand reaction, and the effects on price of the changes in demand in the different industries.

the accelerator

The basis for the explanation of investment behavior in many business-cycle theories is the concept of the accelerator. Although it includes the impact of expected sales on the investment decision, the accelerator theory is based on an unrealistic assumption that businessmen's behavior conforms to a rigid mechanistic pattern (several more realistic qualifications are discussed below). Nevertheless, the accelerator does help explain why the cyclical fluctuations of investment are so much more violent than those of consumption.

In accelerator theory, investment is supposed to equal the change in output multiplied by an accelerator coefficient. The *accelerator* is defined as the ratio of investment (or a change in capital) to a change in output. What is the reasoning that links investment to the change in output?

With a given technology, a factory needs a certain amount of capital equipment to produce a certain output. Assume that there is an increase in demand for his products, so that the factory owner wishes to increase its output beyond the present capacity. If the technology stays the same, he must increase his capital equipment in proportion to the increase in output demanded. Therefore, his demand for new capital (net investment) bears a precise relation to the increase in output.

This reasoning may be extended to the determination of net investment in the whole economy. At a given level of technology, aggregate output can be increased only with a certain aggregate increase in capital (net investment). Therefore, the *demand* for an increase in capital is in some ratio (the *accelerator*) to the decision to increase output. Thus, in general, we may say that

Change in capital = accelerator × change in output

By definition, *capital* means the value of productive facilities. But the expenditure to increase productive facilities is, by definition, *net investment*. Because net investment is precisely the change in capital, we may write:

Investment = accelerator × change in output

We may simply note the definition that

$$\text{Accelerator} = \frac{\text{investment}}{\text{change in output}}$$

and remember that this theory claims that the accelerator ratio is some precise and roughly constant number.

In the United States, yearly output runs about one-third of the value of all capital. Therefore, it may be assumed that roughly 3 units of new capital are required to add 1 unit to national product. The accelerator coefficient thus may be thought of as relating about 3 units of net investment to each added unit of output.

As an example, the output of shoes may be related to the investment in new shoe machinery. More demand for shoes means more investment in equipment. But if demand for shoes stays the same, there should be no further investment in shoe machinery. Finally, if demands for shoes declines, then the accelerator causes disinvestment. Disinvestment here means that some shoe machinery is allowed to wear out and is not replaced.

If the value of the accelerator is known, then what will happen to net investment for any movements of output can be predicted exactly. Table 26.1 picks some arbitrary changes in the output of shoes to see what will happen to investment in shoe machinery (given an accelerator set at 3).

The movements of shoe production are given arbitrarily; the rest of the table follows by assumption and definition. Thus, from period 1 to period 2 output rises by $10, but because $3 of capital are required to produce $1 of output, capital must rise by $30. In other words, under this assumption, a change in output of $10 causes net investment of $30. Similarly, in the next interval, a $20 rise in output causes $60 of investment. A *smaller* $5 *rise* of output from period 3 to period 4, causes a *decline* in investment to only $15, and in the next interval, output does not change, so net investment, or the change in capital, must be zero.

From period 5 to period 6, output declines slightly, but investment must decline by three times as much. Next, a larger decline in output means a much larger decline in investment, and then a smaller decline in output causes a rise in investment to a less negative level. When output stops declining for a period, investment rises to zero. Finally, a small $10 rise in output again leads to $30 of investment. Throughout, the level of net investment, or the change in capital, is related to the *change* in output. The desired new investment will always be the excess of desired capital over actual capital.

To illustrate the most important features of this process, the movements of output (shoe production) and net investment (increase or decrease of shoe machinery) may be graphed. The data in Table 26.1 are used as the basis for the graph in Figure 26.2.

Notice that in Figure 26.2, the movements of net investment in shoe machinery do not resemble the movements in the output of shoes; investment moves earlier and more sharply. However, the movements of investment in shoe machinery are exactly similar to the movements of the *change* in the output of shoes (multiplied by 3).

Several studies have indicated that in the long run, when productive capacity must grow if output is to grow, there is a roughly stable relationship between net investment and the change in output. In any short-run period, however, concern is focused on investment as an immediate psychological reaction to prospective changes in the amount of output demanded. It is easy to see that in the short run, the rigid relationship between investment and change in output posited by the accelerator theory must be qualified in many ways.

TIME PERIOD	SHOE PRODUCTION (output)	SHOE MACHINERY (capital)
1	$100	$300
2	110	330
3	130	390
4	135	405
5	135	405
6	130	390
7	110	330
8	100	300
9	100	300
10	110	330

First, even if the accelerator holds true for a ten-year period, does investment react exactly in that ratio to a change in demand in a one-month period or even in a whole year? In reality, the time lag between changed demand and net investment varies from industry to industry and even from phase to phase of the business cycle. A long and complicated process takes place before investment spending actually results. If demand improves, the corporate directors must come to *expect* increased future demand. But entrepreneurial expectations may also be affected by any noneconomic, psychological, or political factor. Then the directors must appropriate funds for investment purposes and perhaps arrange outside financing. Next, engineers must design new factories or new machines. Even after the construction actually begins, it is sometime before all of the investment funds are fully spent.[12]

Second, the accelerator assumes that each industry faced with higher demand is already running at full capacity. That is not true, however, in a depression or in the early stages of recovery from a depression. During a depression there is much idle machinery, and there are many empty, unused factories. Therefore, in such periods

[12] The timing of investment spending is discussed in detail in Howard Sherman and Thomas Stanback, "Cyclical Behavior of Profits, Appropriations, and Expenditures," *Proceedings of the American Statistical Association* (September 1962), pp. 274–285.

TABLE

26.1

the accelerator in shoe production (assuming $3 more of capital are necessary to produce $1 more of output.)

CHANGE IN OUTPUT	CHANGE IN CAPITAL (or net investment)
$10	$30
20	60
5	15
0	0
−5	−15
−20	−60
−10	−30
0	0
10	30

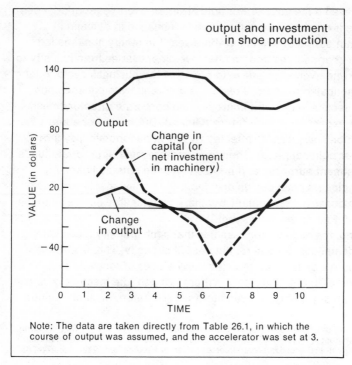

output and investment in shoe production

FIGURE 26.2

Note: The data are taken directly from Table 26.1, in which the course of output was assumed, and the accelerator was set at 3.

any new demand can be met easily *without net investment.* Thus, the accelerator ratio is notably weaker whenever there is much unused capacity to produce.

Third, the accelerator ignores the physical limitations on the amount of investment or disinvestment in any given period. No matter how much the demand increases at the peak of prosperity, the investment-goods industries can produce only so much in a given time. Therefore, it must be assumed that *these* industries have just enough excess capacity to produce the investment goods called forth. Moreover, falling demand in a depression may indicate much disinvestment. But the whole economy can only disinvest (or reduce its capital stock) in one year to the extent of the depreciation of capital in that year. In other words, capital can be reduced in the economy as a whole only as fast as it wears out or becomes obsolete.

Fourth, the simple accelerator ignores the effects of changes in the relative levels of prices and costs. At the peak of prosperity, the great demand on the capacity of the capital-goods industries may raise the *cost* of capital goods and thus weaken investment incentives (this will be discussed in detail in Chapter 28). It might also be expected that a fall in the cost of labor relative to the cost of capital goods would impel entrepreneurs to substitute labor for capital in new projects; but there is little evidence that this occurs over short periods.[13] Finally, it might be imagined that at the peak of business activity, the large demand for capital funds would cause interest rates to rise and choke off investment. However, if profits are high, and rising, this effect may be felt primarily in new, large construction projects. Empirical studies indicate that interest costs may not actually be of much quantitative importance in making investment decisions.[14]

Of course, because the change in profits and the change in the value of output will usually behave in the same way the investment accelerator could be based on either one. Only if costs per unit move differently from prices will profits move differently from the value of output. The effects of a changing cost-to-price ratio according to overinvestment theories will be investigated in Chapter 28.

In conclusion, the accelerator principle says that net investment is related in a definite ratio to the change in output during the business cycle. Although this is roughly true, several factors indicate that there is no reliable single fixed figure for the accelerator ratio. First, there is a long and varying time lag from the first indication of increased demand for output to the actual investment expenditure. Second, in a depression, when there is plenty of idle capacity to meet increased demand, the accelerator is greatly weakened. Third, investment cannot make as extreme swings as predicted because there is an upper limit given by the capacity of the capital-goods industries, and a lower limit given by the amount of depreciation. Fourth, the simple accelerator is modified by changes in the relation of prices and costs because these changes affect profits and, consequently, investments. There is no space here for a discussion of other modifications, such as the fact that the accelerator may work only in the aggregate and not at all in many individual industries. For all of that, the accelerator does embody a large grain of truth, and does emphasize the basic fact that new capital goods are built to meet new demand. In Chapter 28, we shall combine the multiplier with the accelerator to explain a simple business-cycle theory.

summary

Investment shows violent fluctuations over the cycle, whereas, in terms of percent, consumption changes much less. Investment depends on profit expectations. Profit expectations depend on expected revenues from sales and expected costs of production.

13 See Meyer and Kuh, op. cit., pp. 181–189.
14 Ibid., pp. 25–2€ ınd 189.

Larger corporations and highly concentrated industries make higher profit rates than smaller corporations in more competitive industries. The giant corporations and concentrated industries also have more stable prices, profit rates, and investments; small business is badly hurt and reacts strongly to even the slightest recession (many go bankrupt). Business investments rise and fall even more than the objective increases and declines in profit rates would indicate because of irrational and exaggerated psychological reactions ("confidence" or "lack of confidence").

The accelerator measures the reaction of investment to a change in output demanded. The theory tries to explain why small percentage changes in consumer demand usually result in huge changes in investment (net investment may become negative in a depression, and rise very, very rapidly in a recovery).

chapter 27
government:
welfare or warfare?

In American society, the economy is powerfully influenced by the government, though the government is shaped to a large extent by the economy. The U.S. government has always affected the economy in many ways, from the inflationary spending of the Revolutionary War period through the deficit financing of the 1930s. An essentially new relationship has emerged, however, in recent years. Since 1941, the government has become far and away the largest single source of income flow. The newly emerged economic structure is dominated not only by large private firms but also by pervasive governmental activity, mostly centered around military production. It follows that the actions of the U.S. government now form an integral part of the American economy. The following sections present a very brief introduction to each of the areas in which the governmental activity has affected economic growth and stability. (Earlier, in Chapter 19, we discussed the role of government in relation to the distribution of income.)

government and the early economy

The history of U.S. government activity is a record of the conflicts between the interests of sectors, regions, and groups, and most often these interests have been economic. As Madison said:

> But the most common and the most durable source of faction has been the various and unequal distribution of property. Those

> who hold and those who are without property have ever formed
> distinct interests in society. Those who are creditors, and those
> who are debtors, fall under a like discrimination. A landed
> interest, a manufacturing interest, a mercantile interest, a
> moneyed interest, with many lesser interests, grow up of
> necessity in civilized nations, and divide them into different
> classes, actuated by different sentiments and views. The
> regulation of these various and interfering interests forms
> the task of modern legislation. . . .[1]

From the Revolutionary War through the nineteenth century, the
government was concerned primarily with the protection of property,
the promotion of business, and the establishment of the necessary
institutional framework for a commercial, industrial economy.

One of the earliest demands on the national government was for
tariff protection. American shipping and young, inefficient manufacturing industries wanted protection from European competition.
From the very first, U.S. tariff policy was generally designed to serve
American business interests and to ensure high profits by reducing
foreign competition. Even when businessmen held the doctrine of
laissez faire in the very highest esteem, they continued, as a group,
to advocate tariffs. Allowing for a few brief, exceptional periods, the
government gave them their tariffs and protected their internal
monopolistic powers.

Just as important to the economy was a sound currency. The
government actively pursued a policy of providing a stable and
adequate money supply, and eventually central control over the
monetary system, called for in the Constitution, was realized. The
proper amount of money was a matter of considerable dispute
throughout the nineteenth century. Many interests argued for more
abundant, or easy, money; others argued for restricted, or tight,
money.

Many sophisticated arguments were given in defense of easy and
tight money. These arguments, however, often only thinly veiled the
pleading of special interests. The advocates of easy money were the
farmers and small businessmen, particularly along the frontier, who
needed credit to buy and develop land. The eastern capitalists, who
were generally creditors, did not enjoy the prospect of lower interest
rates or plentiful dollars. Usually, the federal government was
accused of aligning with the eastern money interests. This widespread view helped Jackson kill the second United States Bank,
which would have established a uniform banking and monetary
system.

The conflict became particularly intense in the last third of the

1 James Madison, *The Federalist*, No. 10.

nineteenth century, when the average price level fell continuously. This was very damaging to debtors who borrowed money when it was worth less and paid it back when it was worth more. Farmers, in particular, became a disgruntled class. With the advent of mechanized agriculture, they had gone deeply into debt. Agricultural prices fell precipitously, but freight rates failed to decline substantially. As money became worth more and more, they were continuously and ruthlessly squeezed. During this period, agricultural and labor interests united to demand currency reform and the abolition of the gold standard. This cry for easy money was one of the unifying forces in the Populist political movement.

Another important function of the government in the eighteenth and nineteenth centuries was the creation of efficient transportation networks, a primary prerequisite for the growth of a commercial, private-enterprise system. The importance of a stable currency and efficient transportation can be seen by examining the projects state governments financed through borrowing. Table 27.1 gives a breakdown of the nearly $171 million of state government debts in 1838.

Although the market was potentially national in size, a huge investment in transportation was necessary before regional markets could be united. Between 1815 and 1860, federal and state governments made 73 percent of the total investment in canal development, and governments were large suppliers of capital funds for railway construction before the Civil War.

After the Civil War, the railroad boom became even more important to the American economy. Between 1865 and 1914, railroad mileage increased from about 37,000 to almost 253,000 miles. During this period, the federal government became a major source of railroad financing. Earlier, between 1850 and 1871, the U.S. Congress had given away 175,350,000 acres of choice public lands to the railroads, a gift to private enterprise of taxpayers' property worth about

state governments' uses of borrowed money in 1838		TABLE 27.1
Banking	$ 52,640,000
Canals	60,201,551
Railroads	42,871,084
Turnpikes	6,618,868
Miscellaneous	8,474,684
TOTAL	$170,806,187

Source: Tenth Census of the United States, Vol. VII (Washington, D.C.: U.S. Government Printing Office), p. 526.

$489,000,000.[2] In addition, in that same period, the government had granted the railroads $65,000,000 in special low-cost credit.

Thus, throughout the period during which American capitalism was developing into an industrial giant, the government was instrumental in providing the institutional and economic framework in which profitable business could be conducted. Private enterprise profited handsomely as taxpayers subsidized many of the business and industrial ventures which helped provide these necessities.

fiscal policy

The economic role of government that most directly influences the level of output, income, and employment is its taxing and spending of money, or fiscal policy. During most of American history, the federal government has based its taxing and spending decisions upon the political value of the project on which the money was to be spent. The effects of fiscal policy on output, income, and employment were ignored until the depression of the 1930s.

The prevailing economic philosophy was that taxes should be used only to finance necessary government expenditures. It was thought to be an unsound financial practice for governments to borrow money. If a balanced budget, in which expenditures equaled taxes, could not be achieved, it was thought to be preferable to have taxes exceed expenditures so that any debts incurred in the past could be retired. Only the Great Depression and the World War II experience forced a change in this policy. The trend since that time has been for government spending to rise much more rapidly than taxes.

Federal government spending in the United States in 1929 was only 9.8 percent of GNP. By 1939, as the New Deal responded to the depression, it had jumped to 19 percent of GNP. With World War II, federal government spending rose to the incredible height of 41 percent of GNP in 1943 and 1944. After the war, in 1946 and 1947, it fell to prewar levels. By 1949, it had again risen to 23 percent of national product; in 1959, it was 27 percent; and in 1968, it was back to 23 percent.[3]

2 G. C. Fite and J. E. Reese, *An Economic History of the United States* (2d ed.; Boston: Houghton Mifflin, 1965), p. 330.

3 Data for 1929–1959 in Council of Economic Advisers, *1962 Supplement to Economic Indicators* (Washington, D.C.: U.S. Government Printing Office, 1962), p. 3. Data for 1968 from U.S. Department of Commerce, Bureau of the Census, *Statistical Abstract of the United States, 1969* (Washington, D.C.: U.S. Government Printing Office, 1969), p. 312.

government expenditures
and aggregate demand

In the income-determination model discussed in Chapter 24, an
economy in which there was no government was assumed. We now
move a step closer to reality by considering government spending
and taxes.

Taxes, like saving, are a leakage from the income stream. Government expenditures, like investment, are an injection into the spending
stream. Aggregate supply is now the total of consumption, saving, and
taxes. Aggregate demand is the total of consumption, investment
spending and *government spending.* The equilibrium of aggregate
supply and demand is depicted in Figure 27.1.

Figure 27.1 is exactly like Figure 24.3 (p. 370) except that government expenditures and taxes have been added. Income 2 is the
equilibrium level of income. If Income 3 is the full-employment level
of income, there is an unemployment gap. Now, however, increases
in *either* investment or government spending can move the aggregate

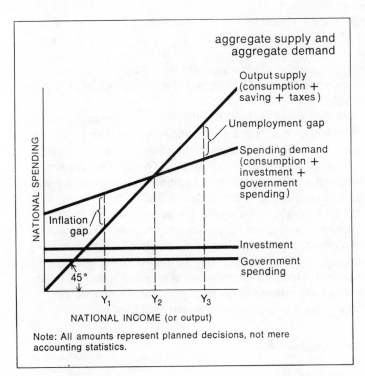

FIGURE

27.1

aggregate supply and
aggregate demand

Output supply
(consumption +
saving + taxes)

Unemployment gap

Spending demand
(consumption +
investment +
government
spending)

Investment

Government
spending

Inflation
gap

45°

NATIONAL SPENDING

Y_1 Y_2 Y_3

NATIONAL INCOME (or output)

Note: All amounts represent planned decisions, not mere
accounting statistics.

demand line up until the equilibrium level of income coincides with the full-employment level of income. A decrease in taxes can result in an increase or upward shift in the consumption function. This will also move the aggregate demand line up and push the equilibrium level of income closer to the full-employment level of income.

Similarly, if Income 1 is the full-employment level of income, decreases in *either* investment or government spending will lower the aggregate demand line and eliminate the inflation gap. An increase in taxes, by lowering the consumption function, will accomplish the same thing.

the government multiplier

The obvious objectives of governmental fiscal policy are to *increase the net flow of demand during depressions* by increasing spending and lowering taxes and to *reduce the net flow of demand during inflation* by reducing spending and raising taxes. Not only the direct effects but also the secondary effects of these policies are important. For example, in a depression it is hoped that increases in government spending will mean more income to businesses or individuals, and that this, in turn, will lead to further increases in private consumption and investment.

The secondary effects of a government expenditure may be quantified in terms of the government multiplier. The *government multiplier* is the ratio of increase in national income to an increase in government spending. (The reader will recall that the investment multiplier was defined as the ratio of an increase in national income to an increase in private investment.)

Take the very simple assumption that investment remains constant while consumption reacts in a given ratio to an increase in income. This means that every increase in income automatically leads to a certain increase in consumption spending. This spending means a further, though smaller, increase in income, some of which will be spent for a second round of consumption, and so forth.

The formal apparatus for studying the *government* multiplier is exactly the same as that for the *investment* multiplier. It may help to review a numerical example in which we assume (1) a certain increase in government spending with a given marginal propensity to consume and (2) that the increase in government spending takes place without any change in tax receipts. Under these simple assumptions, the formula for government multiplier is

$$\text{Government multiplier} = \frac{1}{\text{MPS}}$$

or

$$\text{Government multiplier} = \frac{1}{1 - MPC}$$

Remember that MPS stands for marginal propensity to save and MPC stands for marginal propensity to consume. Also remember that MPS is just 1 − MPC. And MPC is defined as the ratio of an increase in consumption to an increase in income. Thus, in Table 27.2, the government multiplier is 5, and the national income increases by $5,000.

Suppose, in different economic conditions, that only one-half of additional income is always consumed and fully one-half is saved. Then only one-half of new government spending will be respent for consumption. But one-half of that amount, as it becomes income, will be spent in a second round of consumption. Then one-half of the second round of consumption will be spent for a third round of consumption, and so forth. The end result is that if MPC is just ½, the multiplier approaches 2. That is, the total additional consumption will just equal the additional government spending, so the total increase of income is just twice the initial increase of income received from the government. Thus, if the government spends an extra $1 billion, a multiplier of 2 says that a total increase of $2 billion in national income will be generated, of which $1 billion will be the initial government spending and $1 billion will be the secondary consumer spending.

For similar reasons, if MPC rises to ⅔, the government multiplier rises to 3. If, however, the marginal propensity to consume is zero, then the multiplier is 1. In this case, there are no secondary effects because all of the first round of spending is saved. In the other extreme case, if MPC moves toward 1, the multiplier moves toward infinity—that is, the secondary effects are infinite because all income is immediately respent for consumption.

Of course, the government multiplier ratio is an artificial concept because it does not take into account all the changing factors and complications involved. The first qualification is the fact that the second, third, and fourth rounds of spending do not occur instantaneously; it takes time before income is respent for consumption. Long or varying time lags make it much more difficult to speak of an exact multiplier. Second, the multiplier explained above assumes that investment is a given constant and is not affected by changes in income. As has been seen in earlier chapters, however, there is probably a close connection between investment and the change in income. If this is so, changes in government spending, as well as the secondary changes in consumer spending, may directly affect

TABLE

27.2

how the government multiplier works

1   Suppose government increases is spending by $1,000 (while private investment does not change)

2   Also suppose a marginal propensity to consume of 4/5, or 80 percent.

INCREASE IN GOVERNMENT SPENDING	INCREASE IN CONSUMPTION	INCREASE IN NATIONAL INCOME	INCREASE IN SAVING
$1,000 ⟶		$1,000	
0	$ 800	$ 800	$ 200
0	$ 640	$ 640	$ 160
0	$ 512	$ 512	$ 128
0	$ 410	$ 410	$ 102
0	$ 328	$ 328	$ 82
—	—	—	—
—	—	—	—
—	—	—	—

TOTAL INCREASE IN GOVERNMENT SPENDING	TOTAL INCREASE IN CONSUMPTION	TOTAL INCREASE IN NATIONAL INCOME	TOTAL INCREASE IN SAVING
$1,000	$4,000	$5,000	$1,000

investment. However, government spending may have negative psychological effects on investment if it is thought to take away funds by taxation or to compete by means of cheaper products. At any rate, government spending is likely to have some direct or indirect effect on investment, and as a result investment may *not* legitimately be considered a constant in this regard.

The third major set of qualifications to the government multiplier arises from the fact that MPC does not remain constant, yet it is the very rock on which the multiplier theory is founded. It does not remain constant because, for one thing, consumption is actually influenced by many factors other than income. The marginal consumption ratio also varies because there are different leakages from the process at different times. For example, the effect of an increase in government spending on national income may be partly siphoned off by the levy of higher taxes or merely by automatic movements into higher tax brackets. Furthermore, it may happen that increased spending for imports removes some proportion of income from the domestic multiplier process. For all of these reasons, MPC may change too often for any accurate prediction of the multiplier beyond a short period of only one or two rounds of the process.

The fourth and last qualification has to do with how the government spending is financed. If the government takes back through taxation the same amount that it spends, then there is no net addition to consumer spending, only the initial government spending is added to the economy, and the multiplier will be only 1. The national income will increase by the amount of the increase in government spending.

If increased government spending is financed by the sale of government bonds, or by *deficit spending,* the effect on the private economy depends on how the bondholders would have used the money had they not lent it to the government. If they had used it all for consumption or investment anyway, then there would be no net stimulation to the private economy. If they had used only a small percentage of it for consumption or investment (which is often the case), then the government spending would have a very powerful net effect on the private economy.

Finally, the most inflationary method of financing government spending is to print new money because this withdraws nothing from the private sector either by taxation or borrowing. In a deep depression, a government may finance expenditures by printing money; at full employment, it will attempt to use only taxation; and with a small degree of unemployment, it may use borrowing.

automatic stabilizers

Excessive or deficient demand can be combated in two ways: with *automatic* fiscal devices and *discretionary* fiscal policies. Automatic fiscal policy is built into the present structure of governmental taxing and spending to react automatically to inflation or depression. Discretionary fiscal policies are changes in the fiscal structure made by current and conscious government decisions. Since World War II, the government has placed more reliance on automatic than on discretionary fiscal measures. The fiscal structure is supposed automatically to expand net government demand in depressions and to decrease net government demand in inflations.

To understand the working of the automatic stabilizers, we must glance back at the circular flow of income and spending. The circular flow, with the addition of government income and spending, is illustrated in Figure 27.2. Note that some government money flows *to* business (demand for goods and services) and *to* households (welfare payments). The government receipts flow *from* business (sales taxes, corporate profit taxes, and social security taxes) and *from* households (personal income taxes). An automatic stabilizer is a government device built into the fiscal system that automatically

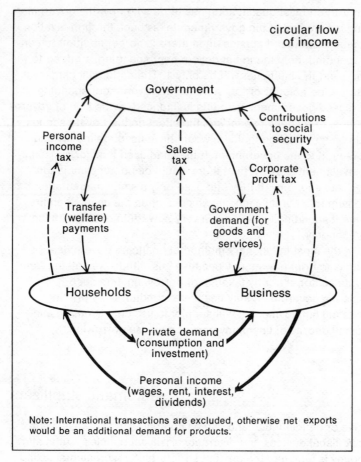

FIGURE

27.2

circular flow
of income

Note: International transactions are excluded, otherwise net exports
would be an additional demand for products.

increases or decreases government flows to or from the rest of the
economy in response to changes in economic conditions.

In a depression, when GNP tends to drop, the stabilizers should
automatically increase government money flows to businesses and
households and/or decrease money flows from businesses and
households to the government. This will prevent disposable personal
income from dropping as rapidly as otherwise, and thus investment
and consumption expenditures can be maintained at a higher level.
Similarly, in an inflation, the automatic stabilizers are supposed to
decrease the amount given and increase the amount taken away from
businesses and households, thus decreasing the total amount of
consumer and investor spending. In either case, the net changes in
government flows should have a multiple effect.

Now what are the magic devices by which the government is
supposed to keep the economy automatically stable? First, there are

government taxes that automatically fall and rise faster than national income. The most important of these is the personal income tax. Most property taxes, sales taxes, and corporate taxes do *not* fall or rise faster than national income. But the personal income taxes paid to the federal government and to many states are a *progressive* tax system, which means that tax rates are higher in higher income brackets and lower in lower income brackets. Therefore, as national product falls in a depression, personal income taxes fall faster because income falls into lower tax brackets. As a result, consumer and investor spending may fall less rapidly than they would otherwise. However, as the money value of national income rises in an inflation, the average tax bracket moves upward, and personal income taxes rise faster than national income, thus restricting the amount of private spending.

At the same time, on the spending side of the ledger, the government makes many types of welfare payments that automatically increase in depression and automatically decrease in inflation. For example, as full employment is approached, there will be very little unemployment compensation; but in a depression, with growing unemployment, this may become a significant source of buying power. Furthermore, many other kinds of relief to children or unwed mothers may have to be greatly increased in a depression, but may become much less necessary in prosperity. Of course, the individuals receiving unemployment compensation or relief benefits will have very high propensities to consume, and thus the spending multiplier from these payments will be very high. Finally, because farm prices usually drop much faster than other prices, the farm subsidies necessary to maintain parity prices are a major automatic source of spending power in depressions.

As a result of the automatic stabilizers, in a depression, total government spending will automatically rise while taxes fall *if* discretionary spending and tax rates remain unchanged. In an inflation, total government spending will automatically decline while taxes rise *if* discretionary spending and tax rates remain unchanged. In this way, some of the lack of demand in a depression may be automatically taken up by the rise in net government spending. Inflation may be automatically restricted by less net government demand and should be characterized by accumulation of tax surpluses. In other words, the desired effect of the automatic stabilizers is to increase greatly the ratio of consumer spending to national product in a depression and to reduce the ratio of consumer spending to national product in an inflation. Because this means that the change in demand is much less than the change in national product it should also mean that investment will react less strongly to a change in national product. As a result, there should be a higher

amount of investment in depression and a smaller amount of investment in inflation than would otherwise be the case. Obviously, the
effect of these changes would be to moderate the business-cycle
fluctuations.

The effects of the automatic adjustments are, however, conceded
to be limited even by their staunchest supporters. They may have
mitigated the postwar recessions, but recessions still do occur on a
significant scale, one after the other. The simple fact is that the
magnitude of the spending flows induced by the automatic stabilizers
does not approach the level required to close the unemployment gap
in most peacetime situations. The periodic deficiency in aggregate
demand requires massive discretionary government expenditures if
unemployment is to be kept at a satisfactorily low level. Furthermore,
it is clear analytically that if a longer and more severe depression
should occur, the effect of the automatic compensatory devices
would be greatly reduced. For example, tax rates can only fall to
their minimum; then they must level off. Furthermore, unemployment
compensation is limited not only in amount but also in length of time
that it may be received.

Another problem lies in the fact that the automatic anticyclical
devices may have worked all too well in choking off the upswings of
the economy in the postwar period. Even if they do not set off a
depression, they may be partly responsible for the economy's
slowed rate of long-run growth and for the chronic unemployment,
which has run at an official 5–6 percent in recent years, even in
prosperity. For the automatic devices do not begin to work only when
the economy reaches full employment and heads for inflation; rather
these devices begin automatically to retard demand the minute that
income begins to recover from a depression. In other words, by
restricting the amount of new investment in each period of expansion,
they may reduce the rate of creation of new capital and thereby hold
down the long-run of economic growth. For these reasons we can
conclude that the automatic stabilizers probably result in as much
economic harm as benefit.

discretionary fiscal policies
and social priorities

Because the automatic devices have failed to fully stabilize the
economy or to help it grow, liberal Keynesian economists maintain
that discretionary fiscal measures are necessary both to eliminate
depression and inflation and to foster a higher rate of long-run
growth. They contend that the legislature merely needs to increase

spending and lower taxes in depression, and lower spending and increase taxes in inflation. These measures also are not free from political and economic complications.

There are three different policy views of what government discretionary fiscal policy ought to be. The most conservative economists, such as Adam Smith or the contemporary American Milton Friedman, argue that *no* discretionary fiscal measures are needed. The government should stay out of the economy. Friedman agrees with Adam Smith that the less government the better. He attributes many of our economic problems to too much government interference with private enterprise, which would otherwise automatically adjust to all situations in a near-perfect manner. To the extent that he admits any need for government policy, he says that only monetary measures are necessary (such policies are discussed in Chapter 30). Conservatives favor measures affecting the money supply (via interest rates, for example) rather than any fiscal measures of spending or taxation because they feel that monetary measures do not directly interfere with business. They view an adequate money supply merely as one of the prerequisites for a private-enterprise economy. Other prerequisites, which they believe government should provide, include police and armies to maintain "law and order," primarily to protect private property from its domestic and foreign enemies.

The second, the liberal, view is that of such economists as John M. Keynes or the contemporary American Paul Samuelson. Liberals admit that capitalism has real problems, such as general unemployment and inflation. Keynesians argue that adequate government measures of increased or decreased spending or increased or decreased taxation are necessary to correct these problems. Finally, they maintain that such measures can always successfully bring about full employment with stable prices, although some of them now define *full* employment as "only" 4 percent or 5 percent unemployment and *stable* prices as "only" 2 percent or 3 percent inflation per year.[4]

The radical view is expressed by Karl Marx or the contemporary American Paul Sweezy. Radicals argue that problems such as periodic unemployment are deeply rooted in the capitalist system and cannot be cured by any amount of monetary or fiscal measures. They contend that the U.S. economy has reached full employment only during major wars. In normal peacetime years, they believe, unemployment and/or inflation is the usual state of capitalism. They argue that the necessary drastic fiscal measures cannot be taken by capitalist governments because powerful vested interests oppose each such step, aside from military spending.

4 See, for example, James Tobin and Leonard Ross, "Living with Inflation," *New York Review of Books* (May 6, 1971).

All economists know and agree that government intervention can theoretically prevent large-scale unemployment or runaway inflation. The basic fiscal formula (to which may be added certain monetary measures) is to (1) raise taxes and lower spending during inflation and (2) lower taxes and raise spending during depression. Moreover, corporate executives and congressmen alike are by now well aware of and receptive to these techniques. But that by no means settles the issue.

The problem remains to find suitable ways of spending the amounts of money necessary to maintain full employment. Many outlets which would be socially beneficial conflict with the vested interests of large corporations or wealthy individuals. Larger welfare payments tend to raise the wage level; government investment in industrial ventures or in public utilities tends to erode monopolistic privileges.

In the years immediately after World War II, the problem was to spend $15 to $20 billion annually. This might have been a very agonizing social and political issue except for the advent of the Cold War.

Dollars for Cold War armaments did not violate any vested interests. Such expenditures had the same short-run effect on employment and profits as would have expenditures on more socially useful projects. The long-run effect was even more favorable because no new productive equipment was created to compete with existing facilities. During the last 25 years, the main change has been that the necessary addition to the income stream has risen to at least $70 to $80 billion a year. If it were politically possible, the whole amount could be spent on public commodities, such as housing or health or education, rather than on military waste. So the problem with stability under American capitalism is primarily in the political sphere, rather than in any lack of economic analysis.

One popular cure for depression is reduction of taxes to allow more money to flow into private spending. Given the composition of the U.S. government, however, tax cuts always end up in benefiting mainly the rich and the corporations. Even in the liberal Kennedy Administration, taxes of the poor were reduced very little and of the rich very much, resulting in redistribution of income to the deserving members of the wealthy class. Especially in a depression, however, the wealthy will not spend their increased income. The consumption of the wealthy remains at adequate levels even in a depression; and they have no desire to invest in the face of probable losses. Hence, the political restriction as to *who* gets the tax cuts makes this policy economically ineffective.

Similarly, all economists (and even most businessmen) may see a need for more and more vast government spending under capitalism. The prime political question, however, is spending on what, for it is here that vested interests come into play. Thus, even small vital expenditures on medical care have sometimes been defeated by the American Medical Association. Powerful vested interests oppose almost every item in the civilian budget as soon as expansion proceeds beyond the necessary minimum. What kind of interests must be defeated to have the necessary spending to fill a $70 to $80 billion deficiency in demand? Constructive projects such as the Missouri Valley Authority could develop dams, irrigation, and cheap power, but these have been fought tooth and nail by the private power interests (and indeed, might lower private investment by direct competition). There could be large-scale public housing, but private contractors have long kept such programs to a minimum.

There might be other welfare spending, for example, on hospitals and schools. The rich, however, see these as subsidies to the poor for things that the rich can buy for themselves out of their own pockets. Proposals to increase unemployment compensation or lower taxes paid by the poor encounter even greater resistance because they would transfer income from the rich to the poor. Likewise, billions could usefully be spent in aid and loans to the underdeveloped world, where poverty and human suffering is so widespread. That, however, could be passed on a massive scale only over the bodies of hundreds of congressmen, who represent well the wishes of their self-interested constituents, and have no concept of the long-run gain to world trade and world peace. If any of these measures are to some extent allowed, it is only after a long political fight, certainly not promptly enough to head off a developing depression.

We could list, one by one, all the areas in which powerful vested interests stand in opposition to the satisfaction of some of the nation's most basic social needs. These interests will not tolerate government competition with private enterprise, measures that undermine the privileges of the wealthy, or policies that significantly alter the relative distribution of income. The only major exception to this generalization is government spending on highways, which is actively promoted by the largest and most lucrative single industry after defense, the automobile producers.

the military economy

From the viewpoint of many industries, military expenditures are the best method of combating unemployment. But as the national product gets larger and larger, and the relative deficiency in buying power increases, military spending not only must remain high, but also must continuously increase if it is to fill the widening gap between effective consumer demand and potential supply. Bigger and costlier Vietnams are a very high price to pay for American economic stability. (Such imperialist wars in other countries, which constitute a main reason for high military spending, are fully discussed in Chapter 33.)

Of course, military expenditure does *not* increase the amount of productive facilities available. Therefore, an economy at full employment with 10 percent to 15 percent of the workers employed in military production will have a much lower rate of growth than an economy at full employment with no military production (assuming the same composition of civilian goods). There *was* a high growth rate in the 1960s because of full employment, but it would have been much, much higher without military spending, if investment spending had taken up the slack in aggregate demand. When military spending is used to create more aggregate demand, more munitions and military hardware often are accumulated wastefully far beyond any conceivable military need. For example, America already has enough missiles to destroy the entire Soviet Union at least 50 times, but the supply is still being rapidly expanded.[5]

The political nature of the problem has become even more apparent in the inflationary situation of the last twenty years. The Korean and Vietnam wars caused so much government demand for military supplies that inflation resulted (prices rising, especially in 1950–1953 and in 1967–1970). To cure inflation, the simple Keynesian prescription is to increase taxes and reduce spending.

But whose taxes, which spending? Major increases in taxes on the wealthy are not easily passed by our government. And there is not that much room for further taxes on the poor and the middle class without provoking rising discontent. So it is easier to reduce government spending. But not military spending; politicians and spokesmen for industry and the military continue to convince the nation that these are absolutely necessary. Thus, welfare spending is cut. Already a tiny percentage of the American government budget, welfare was nevertheless cut further as a tool to fight inflation. Hence, the burden of inflation fell on the common man in the forms of rising prices, rising taxes, and falling welfare spending all at the same time.

At different times since World War II, perhaps most notably in the late 1960s and early 1970s, the American economy experienced a "first" in the nation's history: concomitant unemployment and inflation (this is explored in greater detail in Chapter 30). This situation appears impossible according to elementary Keynesian analysis

[5] See Seymour Melman, *Our Depleted Society* (New York: Holt, Rinehart & Winston, 1965), p. 19. Also see Ralph E. Lapp, *The Weapons Culture* (New York: Norton, 1968), *passim.*

because inflation implies an excess of demand over supply, while unemployment implies an excess of supply over demand. The answer to the riddle lies in the monopoly power of American capitalism. In spite of a certain amount of unemployment, the largest corporations actually still have the power to continue to raise their prices, which might be called *profit-push* inflation.

No aggregate fiscal policy can remedy or prevent *both* inflation and unemployment in these circumstances. To end unemployment by increasing aggregate demand sufficiently to affect output in all sectors means to allow the monoply sector to set off another inflation spiral. To end inflation by reducing aggregate demand sufficiently to affect monopoly prices means to cause considerable unemployment in the whole economy. The capitalist governments of America (and England) have generally chosen to combat inflation at the expense of more unemployment of workers.

The question of social and political priorities often boils down to a conflict between the genuine needs of the majority versus the desires of the tiny minority which possesses immense economic and political power. Government spending cannot be put to use in clearing slums, providing adequate housing and medical care, fighting disease, combating pollution, in meeting any of the other pressing social needs, unless some form of arms reduction and a drastic scaling down of defense spending is accepted. But given the present economic structure, any sudden move in that direction could be disastrous.

To measure the extent of the potential disaster, we must recall that the U.S. Defense Department is the largest planned economy in the world today outside the USSR. It spends more than the net income of all U.S. corporations. By 1969, it had 470 major and 6,000 lesser installations, owned 39 million acres of land, spent over $80 billion a year, used 22,000 prime contractors and 100,000 subcontractors— thus directly employing in the armed forces and military production about 10 percent of the U.S. labor force.[6] Some key areas of the economy are especially effected. As early as 1963, before U.S. entry into the Vietnam War, studies show that 36 percent of the output of producers' durable goods were purchased directly or indirectly by the federal government (mostly for military use).

Recent studies quantify the impact of disarmament more precisely. In 1969, there were 3.7 million persons unemployed. Another 8.3 million were employed directly as a result of military programs. These 12 million comprised 14.3 percent of the labor force. In addi-

6 These data come from U.S. Defense Department documents, which are reported and analyzed thoroughly in Seymour Melman, *Pentagon Capitalism: The Political Economy of War* (New York: McGraw-Hill, 1970). Melman's work was reviewed by Robert Heilbroner in *New York Review of Books* (July 23, 1970)

tion, through expenditure of incomes attributable to military expenditures (the so-called multiplier effect), the Defense Department indirectly stimulated another 10 percent of employment.[7] Therefore, all other things remaining the same, the effect of total disarmament in that year would have been 24.3 percent unemployment. Yet unemployment in 1932, the worst year of the Great Depression, was only 24.9 percent.

It should be emphasized that military spending not only benefits the capitalist system as a whole (by finding an outlet for surplus goods), but also is crucial for the profits of the largest oligopoly corporations. Thus, between 1950 and 1967, according to U.S. Defense Department reports, the 100 largest contractors received two-thirds of the value of all military contracts, and just 10 firms received almost one-third![8] Furthermore, the giant firms require a stable market and a long period in which to develop new products, especially because of the rate of expansion of modern technology. These important benefits to the large firms are provided by, and only by, government military (and space) spending.[9]

summary

The apparent rigidity of our military expenditures not only precludes the possibility of meaningful attacks on pressing social problems, but also destroys the flexibility the government must have in order to use discretionary fiscal policies effectively. It must be emphasized, however, that while it has caused inflation and waste of resources, military spending has undoubtedly been very convenient in preventing large-scale unemployment. Military spending took the United States out of the Great Depression and has prevented a major depression ever since. At full employment, we can convict militarism of wasting about 10 percent of annual output.

In the next chapter, we shall ask why cyclical unemployment is a basic feature of the capitalist system and why this system periodically cannot dispose of all the goods it can produce (even though people may be going hungry) except through military spending.

---

[7] Ibid., p. 241.

[8] John K. Galbraith, *New Industrial State* (New York: New American Library, a Signet Book, 1968), p. 74; and Melman, *Pentagon Capitalism,* op. cit.

[9] "That weaponry in the higher megaton ranges of destruction power has an organic relation to the performance of the economic system leads to unpleasant introspection," Galbraith, op. cit., p. 229.

chapter 28
business cycles
and unemployment

The main cause of unemployment is the *business cycle,* which may be defined as the movement of the economy between alternating periods of depression and prosperity. In *depression,* aggregate effective demand falls and production of total goods and services declines; the result is large-scale unemployment. In *prosperity,* aggregate effective demand rises and production of total goods and services rises, the economy more or less approaches full employment of men and full use of capacity (though in some so-called prosperities there is still a significant amount of unemployment and unused capacity). We begin with a brief outline of various theories. Then some of the more important theories are presented in detail, beginning with the simplest.

the variety of theories

Until the 1930s, the main body of neoclassical economic theory did not try to explain, but rather tried to explain away, the business cycle. First, it was argued that the amount of general unemployment was exaggerated and that there were only partial and frictional fluctuations of production. Second, each depression was said to be the last. Indeed, in the 1920s, they were said to be gone forever, after more than 100 years of business-cycle phenomena.

These attitudes are traceable, in the main, to the general social outlook of that period, but, in part, they may have resulted from the lack of much theory about or interest in the movements of aggregate demand. Neoclassical economists dealt mainly with demand for particular products based on the subjective utility to individual consumers. Individual desire, however, must obviously be limited and must begin to decline after some given quantity is consumed. Thus, Robertson asserts: ". . . it is natural . . . that after the brisk demand of the Indian ryot [peasant] for braziers in 1910, or of the American public for motor cars in 1922–23, the intensity of the desire for these articles should fall away."[1] This approach leads naturally to thinking of the problem as one of absolute overproduction, of *too much* production. When, however, the entire economy is examined, not just each individual product, it becomes clear that the problem in a major depression is *not* that more is produced than people subjectively desire to consume. On the contrary, there is not nearly enough produced to fulfill the desires or even the minimum health needs of the population; there is *too much* only relative to the objective circumstances of the lack of effective purchasing power.

As long as most economists accepted Say's law, which insists that there cannot be a general deficiency of effective demand relative to supply, there were only a few logically possible explanations for the fluctuations of aggregate output. One such explanation is that external, or noneconomic, shocks to the economy may limit supply or bring sudden demands. For example, sunspots may cause bad weather, and bad weather leads to bad harvests; unions may go on strike; governments may foolishly interfere with production activities; wars may stop the flow of raw materials or bring sudden demands for military production; and so forth. Thus, Duesenberry declares: "Major depressions have been produced by a variety of different types of 'shocks,' not by a regular cycle-producing mechanism."[2] Certainly, such shocks as wars and bad weather do affect the economy; but their happenings do not always coincide with the major swings in the economy, some of which occur in the absence of an apparent outside shock. Furthermore, economies operating with other than private-enterprise institutions have reacted quite differently to outside shocks. Therefore, we may at least ask what mechanisms in the American economy give rise to cyclical movements as a result of these random shocks. In fact, in this chapter, we shall first try to understand how the self-working of the economy

---

[1] D. H. Robertson, *Banking Policy and the Price Level* (New York: Augustus M. Kelley, 1949), p. 10. Perhaps it should be mentioned that Robertson is one of the most careful and competent pioneers of business-cycle analysis.

[2] James S. Duesenberry, *Business Cycles and Economic Growth* (New York: McGraw-Hill, 1958), p. 11.

might produce a business cycle even on the assumption of no external shocks.

One type of explanation emphasizes that accidental dislocations may lead to too much supply in one area and too little in another. Proponents of this view usually begin with the fact that the U.S. industrial economy is very complex and interrelated and, therefore, that a partial dislocation may spread over the whole economy. For example, a shift in demand from one industry to another may cause unusual profits in one and losses in the other. Eventually, adjustment will be made by a shift of capital and labor from the losing to the gaining industry, but in the meantime there may be considerable unemployment. These theories, however, would seem to account only for temporary and partial fluctuations in given industries, not for a general lack of demand in all industries lasting a considerable time.

The psychological type of theory also reaffirms Say's law to the extent of contending that aggregate demand cannot be deficient for very long. It is argued that hoarding money is never rational; if money is not used for consumption, it is always most profitable to lend it at interest for further investment. Yet there may be temporary panics during which money is hoarded and credit is withheld. Typical of these explanations is the statement that "The chief cause of the evil is a want of confidence."[3] The defect of these theories lies in the fact that no one has ever demonstrated cycles of optimism and pessimism in businessmen independent of the economic cycle. In fact, the height of optimism is always reached, as in 1929, at the peak of the business cycle. Only *after* economic conditions have objectively worsened are there irrationally large reactions by businessmen, which intensify the economic downturn. Similarly, irrational optimism may intensify an economic expansion after conditions have objectively improved.

Closely related to the kind of theory described above is the notion that the main fault of the system lies in the banking structure, which irrationally brings any industrial expansion to an end. According to this view, the boom is brought about by the expansion of bank credit, but the bankers cannot or will not continue to expand credit indefinitely at the necessary rate.[4] Certainly, speculative expansion followed by excessive restriction of credit may magnify a disturbance, but banks have generally continued to increase credit rapidly until *after* profit expectations begin to fall. What must be explained is why these profit expectations change.

Wesley C. Mitchell, in 1913, was one of the first important and

---

3 A. and M. P. Marshall, *The Economics of Industry* (London: Macmillan, 1881), Book III, p. 155.

4 See, for example, R. G. Hawtrey, "The Trade Cycle," in Gottfried Haberler, ed., *Readings in Business Cycle Theory* (New York: McGraw-Hill, 1944), pp. 330–350.

relatively orthodox economists to view business-cycle phenomena as other than accidental or external to the economy.[5] The thrust of all Mitchell's work is to demonstrate that the business cycle is a self-generating series of normal phases of business, each leading into the next under the conditions given by present economic institutions. Thus, a depression is the direct result of the preceding prosperity, but it, in turn, generates the next prosperity. Although Mitchell never formulated the comprehensive theory at which he was aiming, his immense empirical research forms the basis for all further scientific investigation of this field.

Until the 1930s, however, few economists paid more than lip service to the facts presented by Mitchell. Those who mentioned these facts at all contended that they represented a special problem beyond the confines of the proper area of economics, which was to describe the process by which individual firms and individual consumers made minor adjustments in a basically stable economy. In the Great Depression, that complacency was forever shaken, although it raises its head anew in every expansion period.

The economist whose name is connected with the theoretical revolution of the 1930s is John Maynard Keynes (discussed in Chapters 10 and 24). As has been seen, Keynes' contribution was the demolition of Say's law, which he accomplished from a sophisticated theoretical viewpoint acceptable to neoclassical economists. He recognized the possibility that the economy as a whole may be in equilibrium at other than full employment, that is, that more or less may be demanded than is supplied at full employment at the present price level. Most of his theory is to be found in some form in the work of earlier, but less orthodox, economists such as Marx (see Chapter 6) or Hobson (see Chapter 9). Furthermore, one of his most prominent followers comments that "Keynesian economics, in spite of all that it has done for our understanding of business fluctuations, has beyond doubt left at least one major thing unexplained; and that thing is nothing less than the business cycle itself."[6] Keynes' popularity perhaps is attributable to his having said, in a striking manner, the right thing at the right time, for he not only explained the possibility of depressions and inflations, but also laid down possible solutions for these problems within the bounds of the private-enterprise economic system.

Keynes focused attention on the fact that all income derives from either consumers' purchases or purchases for investment purposes. The two principal modern cycle theories are phrased in terms of the

[5] Mitchell's first work on cycles was published in 1913. His last work, which argued the same basic position, was Wesley Mitchell, *What Happens During Business Cycles?* (New York: National Bureau of Economic Research, 1951).

[6] J. R. Hicks, *The Trade Cycle* (Oxford: Clarendon Press, 1950), p. 1.

reasons for an upturn or downturn in these two categories of purchases. According to the theories of *underconsumption,* consumption turns downward to cause the end of prosperity because income is so concentrated among a few that there is little purchasing power available to most of the population. Investment declines because the lack of consumer demand causes manufacturers to reduce their own demand for investment goods. This theory is often interpreted, mainly by trade unionists, to mean that higher wages are the cure-all for depressions.

According to the theories of *overinvestment,* excessive investment precipitates the crisis. Too much investment has been attempted on the basis of the available resources, with a resulting excess demand for labor, machinery, and credit. The problem, it is alleged, is that both producer-goods industries and consumer-goods industries are attempting to expand at the same time. The latter is trying to bid factors of production away from the former, and, consequently, wages, prices of machinery, and interest rates are rising in all industries. When costs rise far enough, the rate of profit is lowered and, as a result, investment declines. The recovery begins when production costs have fallen far enough to again raise the rate of profit. These theories are often interpreted, mainly by managerial personnel, to mean that lower wages are a cure-all for depressions (not to speak of inflations).

Post-Keynesian economics has generally recognized that the random shock theories, as well as the underconsumption and overinvestment theories, possess an element of validity. Therefore, most modern writing has attempted to synthesize these elements in more general frameworks. Here, we begin with a very simple and crude theory, then slowly add the elements of reality appearing in the more sophisticated theories.

the simplest theory

The simplest theory of the business cycle provides only a bare sketch of reality, but it is an excellent means of illustrating the analytical framework upon which more realistic theories may be built.[7] The theory, sometimes called the *multiplier-accelerator theory,* consists of just three relationships. First, aggregate demand (or income) is composed of consumption spending plus investment. Of course, this does *not* mean that all national income of one period is automatically spent in the next period for further consumption and investment.

[7] See Paul Samuelson, "Interactions Between the Multiplier Analysis and the Principle of Acceleration," *Review of Economic Statistics* (May 1939), pp. 75–78.

On the contrary, some money income may be hoarded, in which case (assuming a constant money supply) the spending flow of the next period will be less than it was in the current period.

How much income is spent for consumption depends on the second relationship: Consumption is determined by some given propensity to spend out of last year's income. Third, investment is determined by the change in income during the previous year. If these three statements are accepted as reasonable approximations of reality, what kind of cyclical behavior results?

Assume that national income is expanding in the prosperity phase of the business cycle. The increase in income causes (according to the accelerator, discussed in Chapter 26) an even greater demand for new capital goods, or net investment. But an initial increase in investment spending causes (according to the multiplier, discussed in Chapter 25) a multiple increase in consumer spending and in national income. Then the process continues because the increase in income leads to more investment, which leads to more consumption and income, causing still more investment, and so forth. The multiplier and accelerator together thus spell out a cumulative process: An initial expansion in the economy leads to continuing expansion.

Assume now that national income is contracting in the depression phase of the business cycle. The decrease in income causes (according to the accelerator) a much larger disinvestment of capital. The vast decrease in investment spending means much less income and (according to the multiplier) many times less consumption and income. The further decrease in income leads to further disinvestment, which causes a multiplied lowering of consumption, and so forth. Thus, the combination of multiplier and accelerator also explains the cumulative process of contraction in the depression: An initial decline leads to continuing decline.

What is more difficult to understand is why the economy ever passes from the continuous expansion of prosperity to the continuous contraction of depression, or, for that matter, how we move from depression back to prosperity. The multiplier and accelerator theory can also explain these turning points, although not as persuasively as it explains cumulative expansion or contraction.

It is true that at the peak of prosperity, income, consumption, and investment are all expanding. Yet the careful observer can begin to discern strains and even cracks in the impressive façade of prosperity. Consumption increases, but the propensity to consume begins to decline as the proportion of income saved increases. As a result, the aggregate demand out of national income rises more and more slowly. But a *smaller* increase in national income means, according to the accelerator, an absolute decline in net investment. A decline in net investment, however, means a multiplied fall in consumer spending and national income. Thus begins the process of contraction into depression.

Similarly, at the lowest point in a depression (the trough), it is true that income, consumption, and investment are all contracting. Yet as total consumption declines, the propensity to consume rises. As a result, the aggregate demand out of national incomes falls more and more slowly. But a *smaller* decline in national income means, according to the accelerator, an absolute rise in the level of investment (or at least less disinvestment). This causes a rise, no matter how small, in aggregate spending. Then the rise in spending means more income and a multiplied rise in consumption. Thus begins the process of recovery and expansion into prosperity.

Some readers may gain understanding from an arithmetic example of the whole process of prosperity, downturn, depression, upturn,

TABLE

28.1

arithmetic example of simplest business cycle theory[a]

(Assumes that consumption is always $9.6 billion plus 90 percent of the previous period's income, and that net investment is always equal to the change in income to one period ago from two periods ago. Also assumes national income is expanding from $99.6 billion in first period to $100 billion in second period. All figures in billions of dollars.)

TIME PERIOD	CONSUMPTION	NATIONAL INCOME	NET INVESTMENT
1		$ 99.6	
2		100.0	
3	$99.6	100.0	$ 0.4
4	99.6	99.6	0.0
5	99.2	98.8	−0.4
6	98.5	97.7	−0.8
7	97.5	96.5	−1.1
8	96.4	95.2	−1.2
9	95.3	94.0	−1.3
10	94.2	93.0	−1.2
11	93.3	92.3	−1.0
12	92.7	92.0	−0.7
13	92.8	92.5	−0.3
14	92.8	93.3	0.5
15	93.6	94.4	0.8
16	94.5	95.6	1.1
17	95.7	96.9	1.2
18	96.9	98.2	1.3
19	97.8	99.1	1.3
20	98.7	99.6	0.9
21	99.5	100.0	0.5
22	99.6	100.0	0.4
23	99.6	99.6	0.0
24	99.2	98.8	−0.4

[a] *Note:* Some of the numbers are not exact because of rounding.

and again prosperity. Such an example can be constructed from the simple assumptions about consumption and investment behavior. Assume that net investment always equals the preceding change in income (that is, the accelerator is exactly 1). Also assume that the marginal propensity to consume is 0.90, or 90 percent of the previous period's income, to which we always must add some arbitrary minimum consumption, say, $9.6 billion. The resulting cyclical process of expansion and contraction is shown in Table 28.1.

The time periods here may be taken as two or three months. Notice that after the initial rise, the national income falls for ten periods (from $100 billion to $92 billion), then rises for ten periods (from $92 billion to $100 billion), and then begins to fall again. This same fluctuation will continue forever, or as long as we keep the same assumptions. Consumption is always determined by the preceding national income and net investment is always determined by the difference between the two preceding national incomes. National income itself is always the sum of the consumption plus the net investment of the same period. Thus does the simplest (or multiplier-accelerator) theory give a consistent picture of how the economy produces depression out of prosperity and prosperity out of depression in a continuing business cycle.

an underconsumptionist theory of the cycle

From the many theories grouped under the general label *underconsumption,* we shall try to extract one systematic outlook. We shall, first, briefly review some of the history of this theory, then examine the facts of the main relationships considered valid by underconsumptionists, and finally, try to present the workings of the theory as a whole.

REMARKS ON PREVIOUS UNDERCONSUMPTION THEORIES

Several of the earliest socialists argued quite simply that workers' wages are limited to the subsistence level.[8] Therefore, as production expands, the workers' share in national income declines. As a result, they argued, consumer demand does not rise as rapidly as output, and a crisis of overproduction ensues. Some went even further and spoke of a continuing absolute decline in workers' income and in consumer demand. These early theories were soon criticized on several grounds, primarily because they neglect both investment demand and consumer demand by nonworkers, and because they

[8] See, for example, Karl Rodbertus, *Overproduction and Crisis* (New York: Scribner's, 1898)

do not explain recovery (if a depression is caused by a continuing absolute or relative decline in workers' wages and standards of living, it is not clear how it would ever come to an end).

Even Marx, whose own theory contains elements of underconsumption, criticized the early socialists for understating the considerable rise of both wages and consumer demand in the expansion phase of the cycle.[9] Marx did not provide a complete theory of his own to explain the business cycle, but he did offer a good many hints in the direction of the underconsumption theory (as well as some other theories). Influenced by these hints, many socialist writers produced various underconsumptionist explanations of the business cycle.

There also has been a long series of underconsumption theories formulated by nonsocialists from Thomas Robert Malthus to the prolific John Hobson. The theory presented here is generally based on the arguments of Hobson and a few other modern underconsumptionists, which are considerably stronger, both factually and theoretically, than the simple notions of the early socialists.

FRAMEWORK OF THE ECONOMY

The more sophisticated underconsumptionist theory can be formulated in five basic relationships between five national aggregates: income, consumption, net investment, wages, and profits. (1) Consumption spending and investment spending compose the total income in a given period. (2) Total income is divided by definition into just two parts: wages and profits. These two relationships spell out the grain of truth in Say's law concerning the structure of the economy. For every product produced and sold, there is an equal amount of income received, either as wages or as profits. This does *not* imply, however, that the circle of money flow is closed and complete, or that all income received is spent on consumption or investment in the next period. Tomorrow's total spending may be less than today's income if there is hoarding, or greater if there is dishoarding. The other three relationships are discussed in the following sections: (3) how consumption is determined by income, (4) how income distribution behaves over the cycle, and (5) how investment is determined by changes in income and demand.

CONSUMPTION BEHAVIOR

Consumption behavior, according to the underconsumptionists, is quite different from that described in Keynesian theory. They claim that because aggregate consumption is determined by (1) the level of aggregate income of the previous period and (2) the distribution of

9 See Karl Marx, *Capital* (Chicago: Charles H. Kerr, 1933 [first published in 1894]), vol. II, pp. 475–476.

that income between wages and profits, the propensity to consume from wage income must be considered separately from the propensity to consume from profit income. Many underconsumptionists believe that the propensity to consume from wage income is just about 1. In other words, they believe that all of wage income is spent for consumption; none is invested or hoarded. This assumption does *not* necessarily mean acceptance of the rigid classical or Marxist doctrine of a subsistence wage. The real wage may, in fact, be rising both in the short-run cyclical upswing and in the long-run trend. This assumption merely states that, on the average, wage income is just sufficient to meet the wage workers' presently necessary standard of living (including physical and psychological needs). Moreover, this assumption does *not* mean that no individual saves any wage income; it just states that the *aggregate* wage income equals the *aggregate* consumption spending out of wages. The argument is based on the facts that a large percentage of wage earners in the lowest income brackets go into debt each year, that another large group in the middle-income brackets just balance their consumption by their income, but that some of the highest-paid workers save part of their income. The aggregate propensity to consume out of wage income will be 1 as long as the saving of the highest-paid workers is balanced by the increase of debt (dissaving) of the lowest-paid workers.

The strict assumption that the propensity to consume out of wage income is 1 is not necessary for the underconsumptionist argument. It is only necessary that the marginal propensity to consume (MPC) out of wages is significantly higher than MPC out of profits. And for this less extreme assumption there is considerable evidence. A semi-official model of the Dutch economy for the period 1947–1954 found that MPC out of disposable wage income was 0.85, while MPC out of disposable nonwage income was only 0.40.[10] Similar results were obtained in a model of the British economy for the period 1947–1956, and in a model of the U.S. economy for 1929–1952.[11]

The difference in the propensities to consume would be even greater if retained corporate profit were considered part of profit income. The disposal of profit income is decided in two steps: (1) The business decides how much profit to retain for its own future use and how much to pay out as dividends; (2) the dividend receiver decides what percentage of his dividends will be used for consumption. Dividend payments are determined not only by present profits but also by the previous pattern of dividend payments because there is some attempt to maintain a fairly steady payment of dividends per

[10] Reported in Lawrence R. Klein, *An Introduction in Econometrics* (Englewood Cliffs, N.J.: Prentice-Hall, 1962), p. 228.

[11] See Lawrence R. Klein and A. S. Goldberger, *An Econometric Model of the United States, 1939–1952* (Amsterdam: North Holland Publishing Co., 1955).

share of stock. As a result, the ratio of retained profits to total profits rises rapidly in prosperity and declines in depression. If retained profits are considered as saving out of total profits, it follows that the propensity to consume out of total profits over the cycle is even lower than the propensity to consume out of disposable profit income.

It is important to note that in this theory, aggregate consumption is related not only to aggregate income but also to the distribution of income between wages and profits. Before the implications of this consumption behavior are discussed, we shall examine the cyclical changes that occur in the distribution of income between wages and profits.

INCOME DISTRIBUTION BEHAVIOR

The underconsumptionist theory assumes that wages rise and fall proportionately less than aggregate income, and there is much empirical evidence to support this assumption. Many have noted that wages and salaries fluctuate less and profits fluctuate more than the total national income. One conservative economist says: "Thus in a time of great activity, wages and salaries constitute a smaller fraction of increased national income than in a time of depression."[12] The aggregate data demonstrate that the ratio of wages to national income falls in prosperity but rises in depression. During the four business cycles from 1921 through 1938, wages (or aggregate employees' compensation) rose on the average in prosperity, or expansion periods, by only 19.8 percent of their average value over the whole period. At the same time, the nonwage part of national income (profits, rent, and interest) rose by 23.3 percent. In these same four cycles, wage income fell on the average in depressions, or contraction periods, by only 13 percent of its average value, whereas nonwage income fell by 26.4 percent.[13] The differences, although small in percentages, are very significant in billions of dollars. These facts of income distribution are illustrated in Figure 28.1.

Furthermore, one of the single most important sources of saving today is corporate profits, either directly through corporate reinvestment or indirectly through dividend income. In the years 1921–1938, the average net profit of all corporations rose in expansions by an astounding 168.8 percent and declined in contractions by an equally startling 174.6 percent of their average value for the whole period.[14]

12 John Maurice Clark, *Strategic Factors in Business Cycles* (New York: National Bureau of Economic Research, 1935), p. 79.

13 Data derived from Wesley C. Mitchell, *What Happens in Business Cycles?* (New York: National Bureau of Economic Research, 1951), p. 155.

14 Ibid., pp. 154–155 and 324.

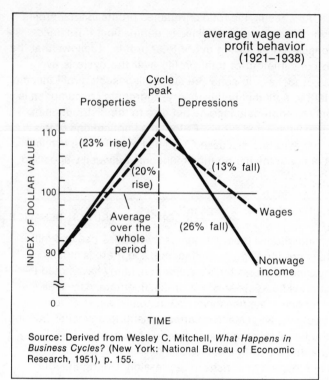

FIGURE

28.1

average wage and
profit behavior
(1921–1938)

Source: Derived from Wesley C. Mitchell, *What Happens in Business Cycles?* (New York: National Bureau of Economic Research, 1951), p. 155.

The underconsumptionists attribute the fact that wages rise and decline more slowly than national income to several factors. (1) The recovery phase of the cycle begins with large numbers of unemployed, and wages cannot rise appreciably until near the full-employment level. (2) Because the pressure of demand during expansion is met, in part, by a technological shift from labor to machinery, the derived demand for labor does not rise as rapidly as the demand for output. (3) In a world of unions and monopolies, the bargaining power of unions is greater in maintaining the status quo of wages against downward pressures than in raising wages to catch up to productivity increases. (4) It may be that workers have a money illusion, as alleged by Keynes, and therefore bargain for money wages rather than real wages. In that case, a rise in the price level during prosperity would cause money wages to fall as a proportion of the money value of output. But a falling price level in depression would cause a rise in the proportion of money wages to money national output.

INTERACTION OF INCOME DISTRIBUTION
AND CONSUMPTION BEHAVIOR

Combining the assumptions about consumer behavior and income distribution yields interesting possibilities. Assume, as is probably true, that profits rise and fall more rapidly than wages. Furthermore, assume throughout that the propensity to consume out of wages is higher than the propensity to consume out of profits. Now in this case, *both* the psychological influence of previous peak consumer spending *and* the shift in income distribution may help explain the fluctuations in the propensity to consume. During a depression, the propensity to consume out of wages and the propensity to consume out of profits may both rise because of the attempt to maintain previous peak consumption. In addition, however, the shift from profits to wages in depression means a shift in income to a group with a higher propensity to consume. Similarly, in prosperity, the propensity to consume begins to decline again both because aggregate income approaches or passes its previous peak level and because of the shift in income from wages to profits.

Figure 28.2 illustrates the typical behavior of consumption and

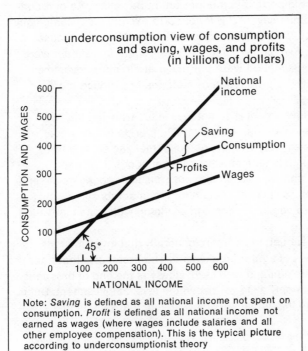

FIGURE
28.2

underconsumption view of consumption
and saving, wages, and profits
(in billions of dollars)

Note: *Saving* is defined as all national income not spent on consumption. *Profit* is defined as all national income not earned as wages (where wages include salaries and all other employee compensation). This is the typical picture according to underconsumptionist theory saving as well as wages and profits according to the underconsumptionist view of the business cycle. *Saving* is defined as all national income not spent on consumption, and *profit* is defined as all national income not earned as wages (where wages include salaries and all other employee compensation). As the national income rises, the profit percentage increases because of the pressures holding down wages. Because of the shift to profits and because of the psychological propensities of both profit receivers and wage earners, consumption is also held to a much slower rise than national income. Therefore, the percentage saved also rises in times of expansion. The reader should spell out for himself the reverse process, which takes place when national income contracts in a depression (wages decline more slowly than national income, therefore . . .).

INVESTMENT BEHAVIOR

While some of the cruder underconsumption theories speak as if a declining propensity to consume were sufficient to explain a downturn, this is clearly not the case. Demand is based on both consumption and investment spending, and there could never be an aggregate decline if planned investment always equaled the value of the output left over after subtraction of consumer spending. This, in fact, is the most important kernel of truth in Say's law. As one conservative economist says: *"It will not do to explain the insufficiency of investment by the insufficiency of effective demand because effective demand would be sufficient if aggregate investment were."*[15] Of course, if consumption were not rising at all, more investment could only mean the production of factories to produce more factories.

It is true that investment is sometimes made with no idea of meeting any immediate demand. Over a longer period, however, businessmen invest only with the object of meeting some part of aggregate demand. In fact, most investment goods (e.g., shoe machinery) can only be used to turn out consumer goods as the end result. Nevertheless, it is not enough for the underconsumptionist merely to point to consumer demand as the only ultimate motive for investment.

It is not even enough to say more generally that investment depends on the level of aggregate demand. The problem is that if the level of aggregate demand rose more slowly at the end of prosperity, this could explain only a slower rise in the level of investment. But it could not explain the actual fall of investment that sets off the

[15] William Fellner, "The Capital-Output Ratio in Dynamic Economics," in *Money, Trade, and Economic Growth; Essays in Honor of John Henry Williams* (New York: Macmillan, 1951), p. 121.

depression. A fall in investment can be explained only as a result of a slowing up of the increase in aggregate demand *if* investment is related to the *change* in demand rather than to its level.

Underconsumptionists are, therefore, very receptive to the *acceleration* principle, which argues that the level of total output is determined by the level of demand, but that expansion of output and net investment are determined by the *change* in demand. At first, the acceleration principle referred only to changes in consumer demand. But this narrow formulation was attacked on the grounds that increased demand in the investment industries themselves also serves to increase the total demand for investment goods. It is possible, however, to maintain the underconsumptionist argument even if it is admitted that investment is determined by the change in the whole of aggregate demand (including both consumer and investor demands). A slower rise of consumer demand may still cause a decline in the total increase of demand, thereby causing a decline in investment. For the moment, then, we accept the acceleration principle with all of its weaknesses (which were outlined in Chapter 26) as the investment behavior in the underconsumptionist business-cycle theory.

HOW THE THEORY WORKS

Any description of the cycle must fail to some extent because so many events are happening simultaneously and in an endless chain. Begin arbitrarily with the recovery period. When aggregate consumption is rising, there is a strong impetus to investment, which rises more rapidly at this time than any other. As both consumption and investment are rising, total income increases rapidly, but wages rise more slowly, and therefore the proportion of profits to income begins to rise. In the prosperity phase, the increasing proportion of profits in aggregate income means a shift of income to those with lower propensities to consume. Therefore, though consumption continues to rise, the propensity to consume begins to decline. When there is a decline in the rate of increase of demand, there is less desire for new capital and hence a trimming down of investment. The declining investment and slowed or declining consumption mean a drop in both wage income and profit income; the depression has begun.

In the depression phase, the drop in income means a decline in consumption, which leads to a rapid decline of investment. Income continues to fall as the depression deepens, but at a reduced pace as the forces of adjustment assert themselves. Wage income is prevented by various institutional rigidities from falling as rapidly as national output. The lag in the decline of wages causes a shift in the proportion of national income from profit to wage income. The result is a higher propensity to consume and a gradual slowing of the rate of decline of consumption (also brought about by the attempt of all income recipients to maintain their previous peak consumption). Because consumption, and hence total income, declines more slowly, this raises the level of investment from its lowest point. An increase in investment leads to an increase in both wage and profit income, which must eventually cause a rise in the level of consumption, and the recovery has begun.

the overinvestment theory of the cycle

The *overinvestment* theory of the business cycle is quite different in approach and emphasizes quite different aspects of the economy. It has as long and complex a history as the underconsumption theory, to which it has always been contrasted. Ricardo and Marx both spoke of a declining ratio of profit caused by *too much* capital investment. The idea that the economy runs into trouble when it is saturated with investment has continued to fascinate economists.[16]

We begin, as usual, in the Keynesian framework by stating that in any given time period consumption plus planned net investment spending exactly determines the net national income. Of course, it is *not* necessarily the case that all income of this period will be spent as consumption or investment in the next period.

CONSUMPTION BEHAVIOR

According to overinvestment theory, investment is the primary cause of depressions. Thus, a very simple consumption behavior may be assumed. Let the level of consumption rise or fall in direct proportion to increases and decreases in the level of income, so that the propensity to consume remains constant. With a constant propensity to consume over the cycle, we may concentrate on fluctuations in investment to explain fluctuations in the level of economic activity.

INVESTMENT BEHAVIOR

The basic proposition here is that investment is some function of profit. This is a reasonable assumption. In fact, a great many researchers have documented a close relationship between investment decisions and profits. One such study, utilizing quarterly data for

[16] See, for example, Frederick Hayek, *Profits, Interest, and Investment* (London: Routledge & Kegan Paul, 1939).

each of fifteen manufacturing industry groups, discloses a significant correlation between total profits and investment decisions in almost every industry (as shown in new capital appropriations).[17] Various other studies have found a positive correlation between profits and investment, whether the measurement is of profits before taxes *or* profits after taxes, the level of profits *or* the change in profits, total profits *or* the profit margin per dollar of sales, present profits *or* previous profits of one or two periods ago. For simplicity, in this discussion we assume that it is the change in aggregate profits (ignoring taxes for the moment) that is perhaps most closely related to aggregate investment.

Finally, we must ask how long it takes for the change in profits to affect investment. It must be emphasized that while there is evidence of a loose relationship, the speed of reaction is extremely different in different industries, in different cycles, and at different phases of the average business cycle. As much as two to three quarters before the decline in general business activity, the decline of the change in profits is followed by an absolute decline in total profits. On an average of about a month and a half later, the new capital appropriations decline, evidencing a *decision* to restrict new investment. This is quite different from the actual decline of investment *spending,* which takes place much later, often at about the same time as the general decline begins. Thus, if we speak of the effect of changes in aggregate profits on investment expenditures with any fixed time lag, this is the loosest sort of approximation to reality.

PRICE-COST RELATIONS AND INFLATION

To this point, only real variables have been considered, but profit depends on total revenue minus total cost (or price per unit multiplied by total output *minus* cost per unit multiplied by total output). We have spoken as if prices and costs per unit were constant, but in actuality, prices do not stand still over the business cycle. For many decades prior to World War II, prices varied systematically over the business cycle, almost always rising in prosperity and declining in depression. The best index of wholesale prices in the United States reveals that in 23 of the 26 cyclical expansions and contractions between 1890 and 1938, prices moved in the same direction as business activity and production.[18] Thus, part of the rise in demand during expansion is taken up by higher output, but part is taken up by higher prices. Similarly, part of the decline in demand during

17 See Howard J. Sherman and Thomas M. Stanback, Jr., "Cyclical Behavior of Profits, Appropriations, and Expenditures: Some Aspects of the Investment Process," *Proceedings of the American Statistical Association* (September 1962), pp. 274–286.

18 Mitchell, op. cit., pp. 170–171.

contraction is met by lower output, but part is met by lower prices.

The greater volume of effective demand in prosperity is financed both by a greater *volume* of money, as banks increase credit, and by a greater *velocity* of money, as optimistic expectations speed up spending and reduce the percentage of money hoarded. Similarly, the volume of spending in depression is reduced by restriction of new credit, liquidation of many old loans, and increased hoarding. Prices, however, are not isolated from costs; the price of one commodity may be part of the cost of another commodity. Higher prices mean higher costs, which, in turn, cause higher prices; the process is cumulative. This cumulative expansion of prices, pushed up by higher costs and pulled up by more credit and faster spending, may be called the *normal inflation* of the average prosperity period.

Now costs may be divided into two main categories: (1) the cost of labor and (2) the cost of capital goods, including used-up raw materials, machines, and factories. The underconsumptionist theory given earlier assumes that the total cost of labor rises *less* rapidly than the total revenue from output. Here, in order to concentrate on capital costs, we make the neutral assumption that the cost of labor rises as fast as but not faster than price.

The essence of many overinvestment theories may be stated in the assumption that costs of capital goods rise faster than prices in prosperity and decline faster in depression. The argument rests basically on the acceleration principle, which states that the demand for capital rises as the demand for output rises. In prosperity, the increase of demand for output causes a high level of investment demand, which outruns the supply of capital goods and thereby causes a rapid rise in the price of capital goods. Moreover, demand for finished capital goods is transmitted to earlier stages of production in a further accelerated manner, so that the prices of raw materials rise even more rapidly.

The theory of accelerated price increases in the earlier stages of production is borne out in a careful study of price behavior by Frederick Mills, which includes data for many years (up to 1938) on prices of 22 consumer goods, 48 producers' goods (or capital goods except raw materials), and 32 raw materials.[19] Mills found that in the average prosperity period, consumer-goods prices rise by only 12 percent of their average value, but producer-goods prices rise by 21 percent and raw-materials prices rise by 23 percent. Similarly, in the average depression, consumer-goods prices fall only 18 percent, but producers-goods prices fall by 25 percent and raw-materials prices fall by 26 percent. Some of these movements are illustrated in Figure 28.3.

In general, consumer-goods prices rise and fall the least, producer-

[19] Frederick C. Mills, *Price-Quantity Interactions in Business Cycles* (New York: National Bureau of Economic Research, 1946), pp. 132–133.

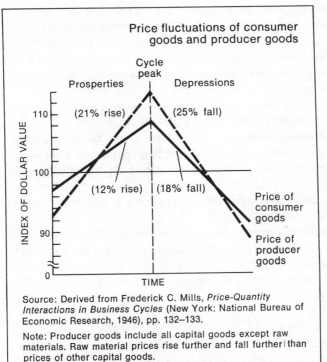

FIGURE

28.3

Price fluctuations of consumer goods and producer goods

Source: Derived from Frederick C. Mills, *Price-Quantity Interactions in Business Cycles* (New York: National Bureau of Economic Research, 1946), pp. 132–133.

Note: Producer goods include all capital goods except raw materials. Raw material prices rise further and fall further than prices of other capital goods.

goods prices rise and fall considerably more, raw-materials prices rise and fall the furthest over the average business cycle. In the purely aggregate approach, fashionable since Keynes, the full significance of these cyclical changes in prices and costs is sometimes ignored. Obviously, as the peak of prosperity is approached the profit margin in consumer goods may fall, while the profit margin in producer goods (and raw materials) may be still rising. But what does it matter if some industries make more profits while others make fewer profits, as long as the aggregate profit is unaffected?

The overinvestment theorist points out that it may make a great deal of difference if profits fall in one whole *stage of production*. The stage of production is a very useful concept in economics, which emphasizes that one group of industries must logically produce their products before another group can operate at all. Thus, production of raw materials may be considered the first (or earliest or lowest) stage of production. The second stage would be production of producer goods such as machines and factories. The third and last stage would be the production of consumer goods.

We have been saying that prices in the third (consumption) stage rise and fall much less than those of the earlier stages. But prices of goods in the earlier stages (producer goods and raw materials) are costs of producing consumer goods. Thus, as prosperity continues, prices are not rising as rapidly as costs in this whole range of consumer industry (which is by far the largest part of all industry). Therefore, profit margins begin to fall in all of the consumer-goods industries. Not only does this slow up consumer-goods production, but also it must (by the accelerator) result in a great decline of demand for all investment goods. Thus, the squeeze on profit margins in conumer goods not only causes less production in the whole final stage of production of consumer goods, but also reaches back to cause a decline in production of producer goods and raw materials. The point is that these earlier stages of production only exist for the ultimate purpose of providing the means of producing consumer goods. The decline of profit margins in consumer goods is enough to set off the depression.

The opposite process takes place in depression. Consumer prices fall more slowly than the costs of producer goods and raw materials. The improvement of profit margins in consumer goods leads to more investment, and thus begins the recovery into prosperity.

HOW THE OVERINVESTMENT THEORY WORKS

To summarize the overinvestment theory: In prosperity, rapidly rising demand for investment goods (overinvestment) causes a rapid rise in the cost of these goods to investors. The prices of consumer goods rise more slowly, squeezing profit margins in that sector, and as a result the increase of total profits proceeds more slowly. Because investment is determined by the increase of profits, less increase in profits causes less investment. Less investment causes less income, which causes less consumption, which causes less investment, and so forth until the depression is well under way.

In depression, rapidly falling demand for investment goods causes a rapid fall in the cost of these goods to investors. The prices of consumer goods fall more slowly, so profit margins in that sector show improvement, and as a result the decrease of total profits proceeds more slowly. This causes more income and more consumption, which causes more investment, and so forth until prosperity comes into full blossom.

a general theory of the business cycle

Although the underconsumption and overinvestment theories appear superficially opposed, it is possible to treat them as two different aspects of a more general process. At the peak of prosperity, the limited consumer demand *and* the rising cost per unit act together to squeeze profits and choke off economic circulation. At the trough of the depression, the end of decline in consumer demand *and* the falling costs per unit increase profits and stimulate economic activity.

Both theories may be stated here, very briefly, within the same general framework. Demand for output is composed of consumption plus investment. Cost of output is composed of wages plus plant, equipment, and materials used up. Total profit is the difference between the value of output demanded and the cost of output produced.

We assume the underconsumptionist version of consumer behavior. Consumption is a function of wage income and profit income. There is a high propensity to consume out of wage income and a lower propensity to consume out of profit income. Furthermore, we may assume with the underconsumptionists that wages rise (and fall) more slowly than national income. Thus, as income rises in prosperity, the proportion of income spent for consumption *must decline* because there is a shift of income from the wage earners, who have a high propensity to consume, to the profit takers, who have a significantly lower propensity to consume.

On the overinvestment side of the picture, we may assume that unit costs of capital goods rise faster than general prices, thereby reflecting the excessive demand for capital goods caused by overinvestment. (Wages are important because they are the largest single element of cost. But wages do *not* rise as rapidly as prices.) Costs of capital goods *do* rise more rapidly than prices, and it may be that this element by itself causes total unit costs to rise more rapidly than prices at the peak of prosperity. Thus, we may admit that total wages are rising absolutely in prosperity, but still argue (as do the modern underconsumptionists) that the wage share has been a declining *percentage* of national income in most past cyclical prosperities. To complete the picture, we need only add that it is consistent with both theories and with the facts to assume that aggregate investment is determined by the change in aggregate profits.

According to our assumptions, the synthesized business cycle will appear phase by phase as follows: In the prosperity period, national income and profits are rapidly rising. As income rises, wages and capital costs must also rise. As wages and profits are both increasing, aggregate consumption must increase. But the shift from wages to profits means a lower propensity to consume, which means that eventually aggregate consumption rises more slowly than aggregate income. For a while, however, investment increases quickly enough to fill the gap between aggregate output and consumption.

At the height of prosperity, the maturation of these very tendencies causes the economy to reverse direction. Wages lag further and further behind aggregate income and the propensity to consume continues to decline, and therefore consumer demand lags behind output. At the same time, profit rates are squeezed from the other side by rising costs of capital. As demand for output rises more slowly, and costs rise faster than prices, the profit margin stops rising and may actually decline in many industries. With profits no longer rising rapidly, investment cannot stay at a high level, let alone rise sufficiently to fill the gap between output and consumption. As total demand falls short of supply, the depression commences.

In the first stages of depression, aggregate output, consumption, investment, wages, and profits all fall rapidly. Eventually, as wages fall less than profits, consumption falls less than national income, and demand is relatively improved. On the other side, costs per unit decline more than prices until profits stop falling so rapidly (and actually begin to rise in some industries). With both the demand and cost picture looking less gloomy, investment picks up again. Rising investment means more employment, more wages, more profits, and a stimulus to consumption. Thus the recovery begins, and we arrive back in the prosperity period, where we start the cycle over again.

THE CYCLICAL IMPLICATIONS
OF ECONOMIC CONCENTRATION

In the 1890s, the United States passed finally from an economy comprised mostly of small competitive units with some local monopolies to a situation of oligopoly in most industries. What effect did this important structural change in industrial production have upon the business cycle? Clearly, the business cycle of prosperity and depression persists, yet there are basic changes in its operation.

Of course, if all competition were eliminated and there were only one big firm in each industry, then the business cycle might disappear; it would at least have an entirely different manifestation from that known today. This, however, has never happened. In most industries, a few large firms have most of the assets and sales, but a very large number of small firms continue in business. There is still violent competition between (1) small firms and large firms within the same industry, (2) large firms with products that are substitutes, and (3) all firms for the consumer's dollar. It can hardly be said that a situation of long-run industrial planning has replaced competition even if a few large firms do such planning for themselves. In this environment, it is easy to understand why the prediction that the advent of trusts and oligopolies would completely eliminate the business cycle has proven false.

What about the opposite prediction, that the oligopolistic structure of industry would increase instability and intensify the business cycle? Because there is so little concrete evidence concerning the earlier business cycles, it is very difficult to make a before-and-after comparison. About the most that can be said directly is that the 1929 depression was perhaps the worst on record and that the depression of the 1890s was one of the worst. It is true that no serious depression has yet been seen in the post–World War II period, but the period since 1940 really represents a still further structural stage in which large-scale governmental action has again basically altered the economic environment.

At any rate, certain characteristics of the modern business cycle are clearly related to the predominance of oligopoly in the economy. Our explanation of the cycle should take into account the fact that in most industries the few large oligopolistic firms have a more stable and protected profit position than the average, while thousands of small firms have very unstable profit margins.

The smaller and more competitive firms are the first to be affected by the profit squeeze in prosperity because of (1) the increasing numbers of inefficient firms in their ranks, (2) their greater sensitivity to credit restriction, and (3) their lesser ability to maintain prices. The fact of their earlier decline in profit margins (as indicated in the evidence presented in Chapter 26) strongly implies that *it is these smaller firms that precipitate the depression* because the decline in their profit margins is soon followed by a decline in their investment decisions and expenditures. The fact that the large oligopolistic firms often maintain their own investment expenditures for some time, even after the cycle turning point, is not sufficient to stop the depression that is already under way and spreading to all areas of industry.

We also have seen that in depressions the profit margins of the small and competitive firms drop enormously, many turning into losses even in minor recessions. Moreover, their large declines in profits are translated into very sharp declines in investment expenditures, which must considerably intensify the depression. Are these losses and declines in investment in the competitive sectors offset by the comparative stability of profits and investment among the large oligopoly firms? This question is difficult to answer in quantitative terms. And we must also consider whether the investment decline of the more unstable competitive group causes unfavorable expectations in the other oligopoly group, in which case even the observed behavior of the large oligopoly firms may be less stable than it otherwise would have been. Other feedback mechanisms, such as the effect of rigid oligopoly prices on the costs of small firms that must buy supplies at these high prices, have been mentioned. Although the net effect cannot be precisely estimated, the fact that the economy consists of a few relatively stable oligopolies and millions of unstable small firms certainly must contribute to the frictions and disproportions of the depression.

realistic modifications of cycle history

In our neat and relatively simple theory, we have assumed away the *fact* of long-run economic growth. During each depression there are, in fact, increases in both the labor supply and the available capital capacity, not to speak of continual improvements in technology. These increases in potential economic output cannot find expression in a depression because there is not sufficient demand for the output already available. When, however, the economy moves into the prosperity period and demand is expanding very rapidly, these growth factors contribute to the extremely rapid growth of supply. Each prosperity period sees the expansion of output carried to a much higher peak than in the previous prosperity.

But this whole theory of growth and cycles does not include a consideration of many other factors. Some are external to our theory, but are themselves affected and influenced by the state of the economy—things such as inventions and innovations, depreciation and replacement processes, and policies of financial institutions. These factors act to intensify both depression downswings and prosperity upswings. Then there is a range of factors such as psychological attitudes, weather conditions, unions and strikes, colonization and decolonization, and even the modern phenomena of hot and cold wars that are external to the theory. Many of these are external to the economy as a whole and act as random shocks that affect its functioning.

EXPECTATIONS

There may be random changes in expectations unrelated to the phase of the cycle. In 1950, for example, at the outbreak of the Korean War, the expectation of scarcity persuaded consumers to hoard, which resulted in temporary shortages and increased prices. But changes in expectations are also part of the phenomena of business cycles. It appears to be the usual order of events in depressions that, first, production and financial indexes decline in spite of the most extreme optimism. Then, because of the change in economic conditions, the optimism changes to extreme pessimism and the extreme pessimism reinforces the depression and may postpone the recovery. The reverse process occurs in economic expansions when rises in production and profits are *followed* by a shift from pessimism to optimism. These psychological expectations of economic conditions are not random. Specifically, *after* prosperity begins, optimism greatly intensifies the expansion. And *after* depression sets in, pessimism greatly intensifies the business contraction.

WEATHER

Obviously, because they pursue a systematic seasonal pattern, many economic activities are affected by the weather. Most industries can shelter themselves to a very large extent from changes in weather. But agricultural production often is drastically affected, and this does have some small random effects on the rest of the economy. To the extent that agricultural output is of diminishing importance to aggregate economic output this factor is of decreasing importance.

LABOR UNIONS

Labor unions and labor strikes can also influence economic activity. If wage rates rise with no initial change in employment, then the overinvestment theory would emphasize the increase of costs. Higher costs per unit would mean lower profit margins, thereby lowering investment in depression further or helping to cause its downturn at the cycle peak. Underconsumptionists, however, would emphasize the rise in consumer demand caused by the shift in income from profit makers to wage earners. Both effects are possible in our more general theory; the crucial question is the quantitative importance and speed of reaction of the two contrary effects. Of course, the final result is also strongly affected by the effects of wage changes on the expectations of consumers and businessmen.

FOREIGN INVESTMENT

Obtaining new colonies or new major areas of investment abroad, or the loss of colonies or confiscation of investment abroad, are random shocks that are apt to affect the level of economic activity. Like other random factors, they cannot account for the systematic fluctuation between long periods of expansion and long periods of contraction. For a small country, the loss of a colony might be a major disruption. But for the United States, even the loss of all investments in Cuba had little aggregate effect (although it affected several individual corporations quite adversely). There is little evidence to indicate any direct and systematic causal connection between investment abroad and domestic business cycles. This is not to say that foreign investments are unimportant to American corporations. On the contrary, they appear to be increasing in importance, as will be seen in Chapter 33.

INVENTIONS AND INNOVATIONS

To this point, the state of technology has been taken as given, but the causes and economic effects of technological changes must be considered. Present inventions are certainly based on the mass of previous inventions and scientific discoveries and on the problems set by present-day use of technology. If, as seems to be the case, these factors are cumulative, not fluctuating, a constant rate of increase in the aggregate of inventions can be expected, although any particular invention may appear to be unrelated to previous technical progress.

There is no apparent reason to assume that the whole mass of inventors should have ideas in clumps.[20] Of course, one major invention is likely to lead to many others in that or in closely related fields, but unusual inventive activity in one area may be canceled *on the average* by unusual lack of activity in some other area. There would still be some random variation in the rate of invention; but it would be within moderate limits around the given rate, certainly not enough by itself to set off a major depression or recovery.

However, the rate of invention may be influenced by the state of the economy. In a period of prosperity, increased demand for output means increased desire for better technology with which to expand output rapidly. And more funds may be available for research. Yet the evidence indicates that even in the face of minor recessions, private research expenditures remain constant, although they did drop in the severe depression of 1929–1933.

In any event, inventions do not directly influence the economy until they become *innovations,* which are defined as the putting to use of inventions in the economy. Although the rate of innovation has its random movements, the only movements great enough to cause significant intensification of the business cycle are the declines in innovation registered *after* depressions have begun and the rise in innovations registered *after* expansions have begun. It thus appears that changes in the rate of innovation are mostly *determined by* changes in business conditions; they are *not* an outside factor that causes business cycles (although in the long-run innovations are an important factor leading to economic growth).

[20] For the opposite argument, that inventions and innovations inevitably tend to appear in waves and that business cycles "are due to the intermittent action of the 'force' of innovation," see Joseph A. Schumpeter, *Business Cycles* (New York: McGraw-Hill, 1939), p. 175 and *passim*.

DEPRECIATION AND REPLACEMENT

Because depreciation averages 50 percent or more of gross investment, we must consider what happens to replacement investment over the cycle. A careful study found that replacement of depreciated capital goods was 63 percent of gross expenditures on construction and producers' durables between 1919 and 1928,[21] which clearly indicates the importance of depreciation.

If depreciation saving is greater than replacement spending, demand will decline at the time, if the funds are not invested elsewhere. Vice versa, if replacement is greater than depreciation, total demand will increase, if other investment spending stays the same. It also must be recognized that in practice it is difficult to distinguish between replacement and net investment. Much investment takes the guise of replacement of old capital by new innovations, which may lead to net investment as well as replacement. Moreover, the new capital may be hurried into place long before the old has fully depreciated.

Furthermore, most changes in the difference between replacement and depreciation are not random with respect to the business cycle. During a depression, when there is no desire to maintain a high level of output, many necessary replacements may be postponed. Yet depreciation continues, and thus this source of saving may be far greater than the replacement investment during such a period. In fact, because depreciation is related to aggregate capital accumulated in many previous years, it declines only very slightly except in very long depressions. For example, in the four business cycles from 1921 to 1938, depreciation of all business capital fell an average of only 0.5 percent of its cycle average during each of the depressions.[22]

Because most new investment is made during the height of prosperity, the average machine will wear out by some fixed time after that date. Assume that prosperity lasts five years and that the depression lasts another five years. If the average machine is bought in the third year of prosperity and lasts ten years, then the spending for its replacement will not take place until the next boom period. On these assumptions, we may even have a somewhat independent reason for the business cycle, with replacement spending exceeding depreciation saving in each expansion and depreciation saving exceeding replacement spending in each contraction. Keynes observed that the duration of the depression may depend to some extent on the lifetime

---

[21] See Simon S. Kuznets' data, discussed in R. A. Gordon, "Investment Opportunities in the United States," in Business Cycles in the Post-War World (New York: Oxford University Press, 1952), p. 293.

[22] See Mitchell, op. cit., p. 142.

of machinery because when it begins to wear out, some of the corporation's idle funds may begin to be used for replacement investment.[23]

There are, however, many reasons why replacement needs may be far from a mechanical function of previous investment. In addition to all the technical factors, there is the fact that firms are as strongly influenced by their expectations when making replacements as when making net investments. Even such apparently technical factors as the lifespan of the machinery become quite flexible when the very standard of scrapping is influenced by business expectations.

The economic lifetime of a machine is a function not only of its physical wear and tear, but also of rates of obsolescence and available replacements, scrap values, operating and maintenance costs, and rates of interest. Moreover, both the present and *expected* values of each of these factors are important, and each factor is systematically influenced by the changing business expectations over the cycle.

Replacement expenditures are often postponed as not "needed" during depressions. But when a period of prosperity seems to be certain, then firms may spend for replacement much sooner than necessary. Differences between depreciation and replacement by particular firms may at any time give rise to small random shocks to the economy. Furthermore, once a new piece of capital is installed, there *may* be some replacement called forth at the end of its lifespan, regardless of other business conditions, and this may be some help in starting a new cyclical expansion. Far more important, however, is the tendency to an induced and systematic excess of depreciation saving over replacement investment during depressions, when replacement is postponed. Similarly, there is an excess of replacement spending over depreciation in prosperity, when the latest innovations are made as "replacements" long before the old machinery has finished its useful life.

POLICIES OF FINANCIAL INSTITUTIONS

Examination of the policies of financial institutions over the business cycle reveals that the amount of credit being issued is highest at the cycle peak and turns down after recession has begun. Also, interest rates, which rise in the later stages of prosperity, continue to rise for some time after the depression begins because demand for credit remains greater than supply. It appears better to hold money than goods when prices are falling; therefore, individuals and firms

---

[23] John M. Keynes, *General Theory of Employment, Interest, and Money* (New York: Harcourt Brace Jovanovich, 1936), p. 317.

borrow for speculative reasons, as well as to finish construction already begun and to meet old obligations. At the same time, the pessimistic outlook for repayment drastically reduces the available supply of credit.

Similarly, interest rates not only fall for most of the depression, but also continue to fall after recovery has begun.[24] Restriction of credit and high interest rates may be important in bringing on a depression, and they usually intensify the depression after it begins. However, easing of credit and low interest rates do not seem to have an important role in initiating prosperity, although after the prosperity is under way, they may give somewhat more power to the expansion.

REALISTIC MODIFICATIONS (CONCLUSIONS)

After prosperity has begun, investors become very optimistic about future profits, bankers become very willing to extend credit on easy terms, businessmen decide to replace even more equipment than is technically necessary, funds are available to stimulate research, and large-scale industrial innovation appears very attractive. Thus, these secondary factors can help explain how the beginnings of a weak recovery can be transformed into a roaring boom. However, *after* depression has begun, investors become pessimistic about future profits, bankers become unwilling to extend credit on any terms, businessmen postpone even necessary replacement spending, fewer funds are available for research, and it appears too risky to try any new inventions in industry. Hence, these secondary factors can explain how a mild downturn can become an awful depression.

summary

Our basic business-cycle theory has been modified to a considerable degree. The rigid multiplier and accelerator mechanisms, basic to all the theories of the cycle examined in this chapter, are not by any means the full explanations of the history of economic expansions and contractions. We saw in the underconsumptionist theory that it is not enough to consider how consumption is determined by the level of all income. Income must be separated into wages and profits, and the shift to profits in prosperity, with a return toward a long-run ratio in depression, must be considered. There is a higher propensity to consume out of wages, so a shift to profits means a lower propensity to consume.

24 See Avram Kisselgoff, *Factors Affecting the Demand for Consumer Installment Sales Credit* (New York: National Bureau of Economic Research, 1952).

We also examined overinvestment theories, which stress changes in costs of capital goods and raw materials, and their effects on profit margins. Then we looked at the impact of monopoly, noting that rigid monopoly prices make adjustments to depression more difficult, raise unemployment, and cause low profits and bankruptcies among small businesses. Finally, we found that both booms and busts are intensified by many secondary factors, including psychological reactions, the credit mechanism, and postponements (or speedups) of replacements and innovations.

appendix to chapter 28

INVENTORY BEHAVIOR

Our study of the external and random shocks to the economy's cyclical growth is now completed. The neatness of the model must be further disturbed, however, by recognition of the fact that the discussion so far has been built on the behavior of investment *as if* all investment were solely in equipment and factory construction. Aggregate net investment is actually composed of the increase in plant construction, the increase in equipment, *and* the increase in inventories.

The statistics of national investment also include residential construction, although this is probably better classified as a consumer good. Construction appears to follow a business cycle of much longer duration than most commodities. Many writers claim that our most severe depressions may be explained by the fact that the downturn in the long cycle of construction (about every twenty years) happened to coincide with the downturn of a regular business cycle. The long cycle of construction has been discussed in many complex books and articles and cannot be pursued here.[25]

Changes in inventory investment play a very important role in most business cycles. For example, in the five business cycles from 1919 through 1938, the average change in inventory investment accounted for 23.3 percent of the average rise in GNP in expansions and 47.5 percent of the decline in GNP in contractions. In the same period, changes in construction and producers' durable equipment together accounted for an average of only 20.5 percent of the rises and

[25] See, for example, Manuel Gottlieb, "Long Swings in Urban Building Activity," *43rd Annual Report of the National Bureau of Economic Research* (New York: National Bureau of Economic Research, 1963).

37 percent of the declines.[26] This finding was confirmed for the post-war period when changes in inventories again constituted very large percentages of the cyclical changes in GNP.[27]

If the longer and more severe, or major, depressions or expansions are examined, it appears that much of the decline or rise is in investment in plant and equipment. Examination of the shorter, less severe, minor recessions or expansions reveals, however, that most of the decline or rise is in inventory investment. During the contraction or expansion phases of short cycles lasting eight months to one year (in the 1919–1938 period), the change in inventory investment was 96 percent of the change in GNP. For cycle phases lasting 1.50 to 2.25 years, the change in inventory investment was 47 percent of the change in GNP. For cycle phases lasting 3.75 to 4.17 years, the change in inventory investment was only 19 percent of the change in GNP. It seems that the adjustment of inventories to cyclical changes in production is carried out more rapidly than that of plant and equipment, although the latter must make a very large adjustment if the phase lasts long enough.

What is the cyclical behavior of inventories? In most of the prosperity phase, both inventory stocks and inventory investment (which is the increase in stocks) are rising, and they continue to rise up to the cycle peak. In this period, demand is greater than supply; consequently, production and sales increase. Inventory investment then rises in order to reach the desired ratio of inventory to sales. This is a kind of acceleration principle; that is, if the stock of inventory is determined by the level of sales, then investment in inventory is determined by changes in sales. Suppose, for example, that a firm wishes to keep its inventories at 50 percent of its sales. If sales increase from 80 to 100, then inventories must increase from 40 to 50, an inventory investment of 10 units. If sales then increase, but more slowly, to 110, inventories must rise to 55, but this means an actual decline of inventory investment to only 5 units.

Of course, inventory investment must not be thought of as determined by a purely mechanical relationship to the change in sales. For one thing, prices are rising in this phase of the cycle; as a result, holding inventories provides the possibility of more profit by selling the goods at an enhanced value. Therefore, some inventories will be acquired on a purely speculative basis. There is also a time lag

26 See Moses Abramowitz, *Inventories and Business Cycles* (New York: National Bureau of Economic Research, 1950), p. 5.

27 See Thomas M. Stanback, Jr., *Post-war Cycles in Manufacturers' Inventories* (New York: National Bureau of Economic Research, 1962), p. 6. The data used in this appendix come from either Stanback's book or Abramowitz's book (cited in the previous footnote).

between the change in sales and the acquisition of inventories. Consequently, inventory investment continues approximately up to the peak of the cycle.

What occurs with inventories at the crucial period right after the peak of the cycle? At this point, supply has risen above demand, and there is little if any further planned inventory investment. Inventory investment does continue, however, because there is an unplanned increase of inventories of unsold goods. It appears that inventory investment declines after the peak, but does not reach zero for some months. Annual data for the period 1919–1938 indicate that inventories continued to accumulate after the cycle peak for from six to twelve months; quarterly data for the period since 1945 indicate that inventory stocks continue to rise for one to eight months after the cycle peak.

Some argue that overstocked inventories at the end of expansion are an independent factor causing part of the decline, and that in minor cycles they may be the sole factor causing decline.[28] The theory implies that inventories are becoming excessive at the cycle peak relative to sales—that is, that inventory investment must decline because the increase in sales declines. This theory, however, meets one great difficulty in the fact that the ratio of inventories to sales drops during the whole expansion and reaches its lowest point at the cycle peak. Inventories are still trying to catch up to the desired ratio to sales at the peak, and even some of the inventory investment after the peak may be desired rather than purely unplanned.

Because investments both in inventories and in plant and equipment show a significant decline at about the same time, although inventory investment has led by a little in a few cycles, many of the same factors may cause the decline of both categories of investment. To some extent, inventory investment, like other investment, may be affected at the peak of prosperity by the profit squeeze, which is caused by rising costs and less rapidly rising demand.

Fewer profits mean both fewer funds with which to purchase inventories and fewer optimistic expectations for the sale of inventories. To some extent also, the decline in the increase of sales will eventually affect inventory investment, although there is a very considerable time lag before increased production allows the increasing inventories to approach the desired ratio to sales. Furthermore, the beginnings of price decline after the peak will cause a collapse of the speculative motive for holding inventories. Finally, when sales do begin an absolute decline, planned inventory investment may be pushed downward until it is quite negative.

[28] See, for example, Lloyd A. Metzler, "Nature and Stability of Inventory Cycles," *Review of Economics and Statistics* (August 1941), pp. 113–129.

In reality, as we have said, inventory investment does decline when depression starts, but does not become negative until some months later. Insofar as inventory investment at the beginning of depression is unplanned and undesired, the accumulation of such goods naturally has a depressing effect. Nevertheless, there is some generation of income for the people who produce the inventories, although this effect is of quite secondary importance. The net effect of unplanned inventory investment in the depression must be to intensify the depression further.

Eventually, during the depression, supply of output begins to drop more rapidly than demand, so unplanned inventory investment ceases. But demand, or sales, is so low by then that inventories are definitely above the desired ratio to sales (and the desired ratio itself may decline in the pessimism of the depression) and planned disinvestment of inventories occurs. In fact, inventory investment generally reaches its most negative point at just about the depression trough. In spite of the continued reduction of inventories, the ratio of inventory stocks to sales generally reaches its highest point at the depression trough. Keynes argues that the length of time necessary to reduce inventories to their desired level is an important factor in determining the duration of the depression.[29] Yet this does not necessarily mean that inventory investment plays an independent role in causing the recovery, as is implied in some modern theories.[30] Rather, the fact that the ratio of inventories to sales is at its highest point at the depression trough leads us to doubt strongly that there is a desire to increase inventories at that time.

After the trough in the early expansion, inventory investment does begin to rise, but for some months remains negative; that is, inventories are still being reduced, but more slowly. Inventory stocks continue to decline for six to twelve months after the trough in the annual prewar data and decline for one to eight months after the trough in the postwar quarterly data. The fact that inventories continue to fall in early cyclical expansion is probably an unplanned phenomenon caused by supply rising more slowly than demand. Supply rises most rapidly in recovery but is still physically limited. Demand for both output and inventories is greatly stimulated for many reasons. Because profits and profit rates are rising there are more funds available, as well as more incentive to invest. Sales are rising, the ratio of inventory to sales begins to drop, and this makes more inventory desirable. Furthermore, the outlook is for prices to rise, which encourages speculation in inventories. For all these reasons, enterprises plan more inventory investment, and the con-

29 Keynes, op. cit., p. 317.
30 See, for example, Metzler, loc. cit.

tinued reduction of inventories for some months is simply an unplanned result of the rapid rise in sales. Of course, this further reduction of inventories in the face of rising demand becomes an additional urgent reason for more inventory investment.

We have now followed the role of inventories throughout the cycle. There is little evidence of inventory investment as an independent factor causing cycle turns. It seems better to consider inventory investment as reacting to most of the same factors as plant and equipment investment, with the actual role of inventories being greater the shorter the cycle, and the role of plant and equipment being greater the longer the cycle. Of course, all fluctuations, and especially the shorter, would be much less severe if there were no inventory fluctuations.

chapter 29
money and banking

Aggregate demand is the total planned spending of money in exchange for the economy's current output of goods and services. In order to isolate what determines the level of this demand, we assumed that the money supply remained constant when we examined changes in investment or consumption spending. Using this approach, any fall in total demand implies a rising flow of money into hoards, and any rise in total demand, as would occur when planned investment exceeds the flow of saving, implies that dishoarding is occurring. Therefore, in equilibrium, there is neither hoarding nor dishoarding, planned investment equals planned saving, and the total money supply is being used recurringly in exchange for goods and services. In this case, a constant sum is being held in money balances. More realistically, when total demand is rising, the money supply may also be rising because new money may be created by the commercial banking system. Conversely, when total demand falls, the money supply may shrink because new credit money is not created and loans are repaid to banks. Our purpose in this chapter is to examine the money supply and to investigate the money-creation powers of commercial banks.

The present money supply consists of coins and paper currency outside of commercial banks and checking accounts (demand deposits) in commercial banks. In November, 1971, the total U.S. money supply was $227.1 billion, $52.1 billion in currency and $175.0 billion in demand deposits. The recent growth of the money supply and its component parts is shown in Table 29.1.

DATE	TOTAL MONEY SUPPLY	CURRENCY	DEMAND DEPOSITS
December 1947	$110.5	$26.1	$ 84.4
December 1950	114.6	24.6	90.0
December 1957	135.9	28.3	107.6
December 1960	141.1	28.9	112.1
December 1966	170.4	38.3	132.1
December 1968	199.6	42.6	157.0
December 1970	208.6	47.8	160.8
November 1971	227.1	52.1	175.0

the money supply and its component parts (billions of dollars)

TABLE 29.1

Source: Federal Reserve *Bulletin* (November, 1971), p. A17

Demand deposits, which have comprised a fairly constant percentage of the money supply (76.4 percent in 1947, and 77.1 percent in 1971), are the debts of commercial banks. To say that banks create money refers to the fact that banks have the ability to create demand deposits. After considering a conjectural history of money, we shall investigate a conjectural evolution of this money-creation power. (It is conjectural in that it is not an exact history of one place, but what we believe to have been the logical and approximate development in most places.)

a conjectural history of money

Money is defined as any widely accepted medium of exchange. A commodity that is used as money does not necessarily have any intrinsic value aside from its general acceptability in exchange and for the settlement of debt. If the law requires that it be accepted in the settlement of debt, it is also *legal tender.*

Among the most primitive tribes, exchange was conducted by the barter system. *Barter* means that one commodity is directly traded for another in the market, without the use of money. For example, we may find trade in this form:

1 coat = 2 hats

If this exchange ratio persists for some time, people may come to think of one coat as *worth* two hats, or they may think of one hat as worth half a coat.

The second evolutionary step was to the crudest kind of money, a stage in which some particular commodity was used as money. Any convenient or often-used commodity might eventually attain the status of money if it were relatively scarce, and therefore desired. For example, in a community in which the number of cows owned was a status symbol, we might find that cows played the role of money. Thus:

2 coats = 1 cow   1 cow = 4 hats

People in this society would calculate all of their production and wealth in terms of cows. They might also actually sell or trade coats for cows and then use the "cow money" to buy hats, or vice versa.

Cows, however, are not a very convenient money commodity. They are perishable and not easily divisible, problems that could be solved by using precious metals or stones. The need to have large numbers of pieces of money that are of equal value led to the third step of the evolution, the development of *metallic money.* Precious metals have several virtues as a medium of exchange: (1) They are valuable; one need only carry a small amount to buy other commodities. (2) They are easily divisible. Uniform coins of various values can be made by melting and thus the exact amount necessary for any purchase can be used. (3) They are nonperishable and hence can be stored indefinitely.

The durability and portability of metallic money means that it may be used not only for calculating value ratios but also in every exchange. Thus, trade takes this form:

1 coat = 1 oz. gold   1 oz. gold = 2 hats

Any commodity (e.g., a coat) may be sold for metallic money. Then the metallic money is put away until its holder wishes to buy another commodity (e.g., a hat).

The next step in the evolution came when paper claims were substituted for metallic money such as gold; but they still were claims that were payable in gold. These claims were originally issued by goldsmiths, private bankers, and merchants. Governments soon followed suit, issuing their own paper money, which consisted of IOUs, or promises by the government to pay in gold on demand. Of course, it was possible to issue more paper money than gold because not everyone demanded gold at the same time.

The modern issue of *inconvertible paper money* is the fifth step in the evolution of money. Paper money looks the same as before, but a government declares that it will no longer convert, or pay its paper IOUs in gold on demand. This method of money creation financed the American and French revolutions and the U.S. Civil War. Almost all governments had recourse to this expedient in the monetary chaos following World War I and during the Great Depression. At the same time, they usually prohibited private institutions from issuing paper

money. One way governments made their paper money more acceptable to the populace was to accept it themselves for tax payments
and to declare it legal tender. Of course, the value of inconvertible
paper money today has no direct connection with gold reserves.

The most recently evolved form of money is the checking account.
Sums of money in checking accounts are bookkeeping entries which
are called *deposits*. They are actually promises to pay—that is, they
are debts of the bank. Checks written against these accounts are
orders to transfer deposit funds to others' accounts or to convert
some of the deposit account into currency. The owner of such an
account may have brought currency to the bank or may have
deposited a check. He may have signed a note and borrowed the
money. In such a case, the bank and the individual merely exchange
IOUs. But the bank's IOU, the demand deposit, serves all the functions of money. Checks drawn against the balance make payment
without the use of currency or coin. Although a check is not legal
tender, the deposit is convertible into legal tender, and the deposit
account is money. It is apparent that the distinguishing characteristic
of a bank is that, unlike any other private enterprise, the evidence of
its debt to an individual is accepted as money.

a conjectural evolution of modern banking

Perhaps we can illustrate the role of the modern banker by returning
to conjectural history. Centuries ago, when the market system was
evolving, goldsmiths had large quantities of precious metals. To
protect them, secure storage facilities had to be constructed. Other
individuals sought the same security for their money but did not have
enough money to justify the expense of constructing such facilities.
The local goldsmith began to accept their coin (the sole form of
money at this time) and precious metals. As evidence of these
deposits, he provided the depositor with a receipt. The goldsmith
earned income by demanding payment from the individual depositor
for the safekeeping function he performed.

In time, goldsmiths who had developed reputations for honesty
found that these deposit receipts began to circulate and could be
used by the individuals holding them in payment of debt. For example, merchants, instead of carrying coin on business trips, would
deposit it with a reputable and renowned goldsmith. The receipt
could then be used to settle his accounts in distant lands. Hence, as
long as the goldsmith was willing and able to redeem these deposit
receipts, or paper claims, on demand for coin, they performed the
function of money. Here we see the initial stages in the development
of both the banking system and of paper claims as money. The

validity of the paper claims as money was premised on their general
acceptability as money, which depended on the confidence that the
public had in the goldsmith's ability to convert the paper claims into
coin on demand.

Thus far, however, the goldsmith has not performed the prime
distinguishing function of a banker, the money-creation function.
All he has done is to match his metallic assets with paper claims.
His balance sheet probably would resemble this:

Assets		Liabilities	
Coin in vault	$1,000	Deposits	$1,000
Total assets	$1,000	Total liabilities	$1,000

Sooner or later, the goldsmith realizes that he can create debt
(demand deposits and notes payable on demand) in excess of the
coin he holds in his vault. Why can he do this? First, because the
people have confidence in his ability to redeem their paper claims
into coin on demand. Second, this confidence leads other people to
accept the paper claims in settlement of their debts. Therefore, at
any given time, *only a small proportion of the paper claims need to
be converted into coin.*

As long as the goldsmith-banker can readily meet this small proportion of claims for coin, he is in a position to increase his total
liabilities beyond the actual amount of coin he has in his vault.
In other words, he is able to create money. And the total of coin,
bank notes, and deposit receipts now in circulation exceeds the
amount of coin that has been minted by the governmental authority.
The bank notes (issued by the goldsmith-banker to those who borrow
from him) and the deposit receipts are *money,* in the same manner
that coin is money, because people are willing to accept them in
payment for any debt. If an individual receives payment in the form
of either coin or a bank note or a deposit receipt, it makes no
difference to him at all, as long as he can use these equally for
making his own payments.

The goldsmith (who is now a banker because he creates money)
will then keep in his vault an amount of coin large enough to meet
the demands for coin that will be made upon him. Of course, he can
roughly estimate these demands from his experience. The banker-
goldsmith's balance sheet probably would resemble this:

Assets		Liabilities	
Coin in vault	$ 800	Notes payable	$ 600
Loans	800	Deposits	1,000
Total assets	$1,600	Total liabilities	$1,600

The banker's liabilities in this example clearly exceed the coin in his vault. What he has done is lend money to individuals, of which $200 has had to be paid out in the form of coin (reducing his coin from $1,000 to $800). However, people are willing to hold the other $600 of loans in the form of bank notes. Thus, the banker has created new liabilities while holding only one-half of his total liabilities ($800) in the form of coin. He now has an additional form of income: the interest he earns from the loans he makes. The banker has created money in excess of the coin in his vault to the amount of $800.

The banker's ability to create money is limited by the proportion of notes and deposits he is forced to hold in the form of coin because of institutional or other considerations. In this case, because he has to hold 50 percent of his deposit and note liabilities in the form of coin, he can expand the money supply by only twice the amount of coin in his vault.

Here we see the development, in its initial stages, of the modern banking system. The banker now creates debts that circulate freely as money and that slowly come to form an increasing part of the total money supply. He has succeeded in converting his idle coin, which earns no interest, into loans for which he charges a rate of interest. The borrowing-lending function, which was formerly performed by the moneylender, is now performed by the banker. The uniqueness of the banker, however, lies in the fact that, unlike the moneylender, he can make loans in excess of the actual coin in his vault.

operation of modern commercial banks

The banker's business consists of taking the money deposited with him, on some of which he pays interest, and lending it out at higher rates of interest. Money deposited in time or savings accounts pays interest to the depositor, but it must stay frozen, or on deposit, for some definite time before the interest is paid (thus, it is counted only as *near-money*). Money deposited in checking accounts available on demand (and therefore counted as part of the *money supply*), pays no interest. In order to pay the interest on savings accounts, the banker must get higher interest rates on the money he lends to others.

The banker is torn between two objectives. On the one hand, he wants to make as much profit as possible by lending out as much as he can (and the riskiest loans pay the highest interest rates). But on the other hand, he wants safety; he wants to be able to pay off easily any depositor who demands his money. Technically, the banker is said to seek *liquidity.* The most liquid assets are those most easily available in cash to pay off depositors. Thus, the most liquid asset is money in paper currency and coins (or even gold), which pay no interest to the banker. The next most liquid assets are government notes and bonds, sometimes called near-money, which pay low interest but can be cashed immediately (although at variable prices if cashed before maturity). Least liquid are risky private loans, which may pay high interest but cannot be cashed for a long time and may never be paid back if the individual goes bankrupt. The precise way in which the entire American banking system holds its assets is indicated in Table 29.2.

Bank liabilities consist mainly of deposits, or the amount that is owed to their depositors. The assets of the whole banking system include gold (held only by the government's Federal Reserve Bank), currency (a very small item), and U.S. government bonds. By far their largest assets, however, are the loans that banks will some day collect back from individuals and businesses. For purposes of analysis, we shall often classify all assets merely as *reserves* of money and near-money or as *loans* to businesses, individuals, and governments. We shall soon discover that modern banks are required by the government to keep a certain ratio of their deposits in the form of reserves, which limits their power to make loans.

federal reserve system

On December 23, 1913, President Woodrow Wilson signed the Federal Reserve Act establishing the Federal Reserve System (Fed). It was the government's answer to the banking failures and monetary panics of the early 1900s. The Fed is the central bank of the United States, corresponding to the Bank of England or the Bank of France. Its original purposes were to give the country a currency flexible enough to meet its needs and to improve the supervision of banking. Today, however, these form only a part of broader and more important objectives, which include maintaining price stability, fostering a high rate of economic growth, and promoting a high level of employment.

Federal Reserve functions are carried out through 12 Federal Reserve banks and their 24 branches, but there is also a central coordination by the Board of Governors in Washington. The Board of Governors consists of seven members appointed by the President and confirmed by the Senate. One of the Board's duties is to supervise all Fed operations. The Board participates in all of the principal monetary actions of the Fed. It has full authority over changes in the

ASSETS
(in millions)

Gold Certificates (held by Federal Reserve)	$ 10,500
Treasury currency	7,600
Loans	489,300
U.S. government bonds	133,800
Total assets	$641,200

Source: Federal Reserve Bulletin (November, 1971), p. A19

legal reserve requirements of banks (within the limits prescribed by Congress). The Board "reviews and determines" interest rates of the individual Federal Reserve banks. And the members of the Board constitute a majority of the Federal Open Market Committee, which buys and sells government bonds in the open market. In addition, it is responsible for the regulation of stock market credit, and it has the authority to establish the maximum rates of interest that member banks may pay on savings and other time deposits.

The Fed controls the money supply in order to achieve its purposes. The real bases of the value of the nation's money supply are the goods produced and confidence in the government. Until recently, however, the money supply of the United States had at its legal base the country's gold stock, which stood at $11.8 billion on August 26, 1970. Congress had required the Federal Reserve to hold an amount equal to 25 percent of its liabilities in the form of gold, but this was purely a congressional whim. The requirement was removed in 1968, with no significant effect on the efficiency with which money has performed its functions.

Although the Federal Reserve Banks still hold gold certificates, this is merely one of several types of assets. Gold certificates need bear no necessary relationship to Federal Reserve's liabilities (i.e. they bear no necessary connection to the U.S. money supply). The other principal types of assets are government securities and loans to the member banks. The principal liabilities are Federal Reserve note currency, which constitute most of the paper currency held by the public, and member bank reserves, which, as will be seen, form the basis for the creation of credit money by the banking system.

The Fed specifies exactly how much reserves each member bank must hold in relation to its deposits. Recently required ratios are given in Table 29.3. Bank reserves of money or "checking accounts at the Fed" may be kept either in the bank vault or in the nearest

TABLE

29.2

consolidated balance sheet for the banking system
of the united states on october 27, 1971

LIABILITIES AND CAPITAL (in millions)	
Total deposits	$571,000
Capital owned by stockholders	70,200
Total liabilities and capital	$641,200

Federal Reserve Bank. If it is kept as a deposit in a Federal Reserve Bank, the member bank may even earn a small interest on its money reserves. Country banks are given a lower required reserve ratio, apparently on the theory that they may also fall back on loans from the larger city banks.

The first purpose of the reserve system is, of course, to ensure that the bank has sufficient funds to meet its depositors' withdrawals. Yet in the Great Depression, thousands of banks failed because runs on the banks by depositors exhausted their reserves. This purpose is now more fully met by the Federal Deposit Insurance Corporation (FDIC), which guarantees all deposits up to $10,000. The more important purpose that the Fed now serves is to control the money supply as a tool of general economic control. This purpose will be discussed in Chapter 30.

how banks multiply money

Exactly how much money can banks create with a given amount of new deposits? Obviously, this depends in large part on what reserve ratio the Federal Reserve requires them to hold. Part of each new deposit must be held in reserve, part may be lent out. For convenience, assume that the Federal Reserve ratio is set at 20 percent for all kinds of deposits in all kinds of banks. Then if a bank receives a $1,000 deposit, it deposits the $1,000 at the Federal Reserve Bank, thus increasing its reserves by $1,000. The reader may imagine that this would permit the bank to make new loans totaling $4,000 and thereby created $4,000 in new money. Its new reserves of $1,000 would be 20 percent of the original $1,000 deposit and the $4,000 in new deposits created by the loans. It might thus appear that a single

TABLE

29.3

reserve requirements of member banks
(reserves as percentage of deposits)

DATE	DEMAND DEPOSITS (checking accounts in)		TIME DEPOSITS (saving accounts in)
	CITY BANKS	COUNTRY BANKS	ALL CITY AND COUNTRY BANKS
Dec. 31, 1948	22.0%	16.0%	7.5%
Sept. 1, 1949	18.0	12.0	5.0
Jan. 25, 1951	20.0	14.0	6.0
July 1, 1953	19.0	13.0	6.0
July 29, 1954	18.0	12.0	6.0
Apr. 24, 1958	16.5	11.0	5.0
Dec. 1, 1960	16.5	12.0	5.0
Oct. 25, 1962	16.5	12.0	4.0
Mar. 16, 1967	16.5	12.0	3.0
Jan. 11, 1968	16.5–17[a]	12–12.5[a]	3.0
Apr. 17, 1969	17–17.5[a]	12.5–13[a]	3.0
Aug. 31, 1970	17–17.5[a]	12.5–13[a]	3.0

LIMITS SET BY CONGRESS WITHIN WHICH THE FEDERAL RESERVE MAY SET THE REQUIREMENTS:

Minimum	10%	7%	3%
Maximum	22	14	10

[a] The first figure is for amounts under $5 million and the second is for amounts over $5 million.

Source: Federal Reserve *Bulletin* (September 1970).

bank could expand the money supply by a multiple of a new deposit it receives.

This is not the case, however. Something called *adverse clearing balances* prevents this. Assume that recipients of the $4,000 in new loans write checks, totaling $4,000, drawn on their newly created demand deposits. Now, assume (for simplicity of analysis) that these checks are all deposited with another bank. This second bank will immediately deposit these checks in the account it maintains at the Federal Reserve Bank, which increases the reserves of the second bank by $4,000, but simultaneously charges these checks against the reserve account of the original bank. This reduces the original bank's reserves by $4,000.

The Federal Reserve Bank then sends the checks back to the original bank on which they are drawn. The bank reduces by $4,000 the demand deposits of the writers of the checks. Thus, the bank finds its reserves reduced by $4,000 and its demand deposits reduced by $4,000. Because it had reserves equal to 20 percent of its demand deposits and because it is required to maintain this ratio of reserves to demand deposits, it can afford to lose only 20 percent as much in reserves as it loses in demand deposits.

When the bank lost $4,000 in demand deposits this permitted it to lose only $800 (20 percent of $4,000) in reserves. Thus, it has lost $3,200 in reserves which it could not afford to lose. Obviously, it overextended its loans by $3,200. If the bank had loaned only $800 instead of $4,000, it would not have experienced this difficulty.

To avoid these adverse clearing balances with the Federal Reserve Bank, a bank must restrict its loans to its *excess reserves.* When the bank received its new deposit of $1,000 it was required to hold only $200 of it in reserves. This means it had excess reserves of $800 (the original $1,000 it received minus the $200 it must hold as reserves). Thus, it can be concluded that if a single bank received a new $1,000 deposit, it must keep $200 in reserve, but it could lend out $800. It lends money by giving its customers a new demand deposit of $800, thus creating money.

Yet a single bank may reasonably claim it adds nothing to the money supply. When the customer actually uses the loan, he draws his deposit down to zero, while the bank merely pays out the $800 in cash. *It is when the whole banking system is considered that a new*

FIGURE

29.1

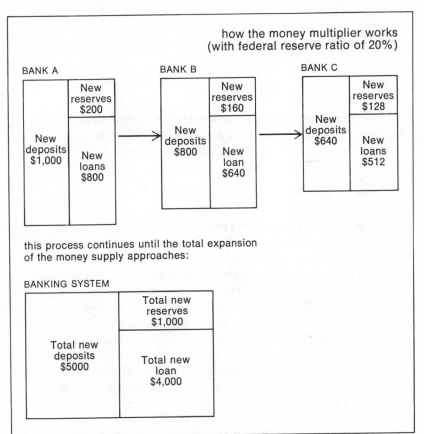

how the money multiplier works
(with federal reserve ratio of 20%)

BANK A

| | New reserves $200 |
| New deposits $1,000 | New loans $800 |

BANK B

| | New reserves $160 |
| New deposits $800 | New loan $640 |

BANK C

| | New reserves $128 |
| New deposits $640 | New loans $512 |

this process continues until the total expansion of the money supply approaches:

BANKING SYSTEM

| | Total new reserves $1,000 |
| Total new deposits $5000 | Total new loan $4,000 |

deposit will generally lead to a multiple expansion of the money supply. How this expansion works can be seen in Figure 29.1 and in Table 29.4.

When the $800 loan from Bank A (in Figure 29.1) is spent, it becomes new deposits in Bank B, which are the basis for new reserves of $160 and new loans of $640. In the case of the whole banking system, the process will continue until all of the original new deposit ($1,000) becomes required reserves in various banks. Because the new required reserves are then $1,000 (or 20 percent of all new deposits), the new loans are $4,000 (or 80 percent of all new deposits). Based on an initial new deposit of $1,000 in money, the banking system has thus created a total increase in deposits of $5,000 (assumed to be demand deposits and therefore counted as money).

For our analysis we use the concept of the money multiplier, which is analogous to, but not to be confused with, the investment multiplier of income determination. The *money multiplier* may be defined as follows:

$$\text{Money multiplier} = \frac{\text{total increase in deposits}}{\text{initial new deposit}}$$

A simple formula for deriving the money multiplier is

$$\text{Multiplier} = \frac{1}{\text{required Federal Reserve ratio}}$$

Assuming that each banker has to keep 20 percent of his deposit liabilities in the form of cash, the money supply can be expanded to five times the amount of cash that the banking system holds:

$$\text{Multiplier} = \frac{1}{0.20} = 5$$

Thus, the initial new deposit of $1,000 is multiplied by 5 to get $5,000 total increase in deposits (or in the money supply).

The analysis does not yet take into account several kinds of leakages that may occur in varying degrees over time. The assumption that banks are always fully loaned up is not consistent with the facts. There are often some excess reserves—that is, reserves in excess of the legal requirement. Therefore, the volume of expansion of deposits does depend on the degree to which bankers decide to make the maximum loans on their reserves. It also depends on the degree to which businessmen wish to accept these loans. Finally, the whole process takes time, and only a certain amount of the predicted expansion will occur in any given period.

It is, nevertheless, generally true that banks lend in some multiple of their reserves and that total expansion of the money supply will be

TABLE

29.4

		how the money multiplier works	

1 Assume an initial increase in deposits of $1,000

2 Assume a required Federal Reserve ratio of 20 percent

3 Assume that banks are always fully loaned out

BANK	INCREASE IN LOANS	INCREASE IN DEPOSITS (or money supply)	INCREASE IN RESERVES (required)
Bank A	$ 800	$1,000	$ 200
Bank B	$ 640	$ 800	$ 160
Bank C	$ 512	$ 640	$ 128
Bank D	$ 410	$ 512	$ 102
Bank E	$ 328	$ 410	$ 82
Bank F	$ 262	$ 328	$ 66
Bank G	•	$ 262	•
•	•	•	•
•	•	•	•
•	•	•	•
•	•	•	•

ALL BANKS	TOTAL INCREASE IN LOANS	TOTAL INCREASE IN DEPOSITS (or money supply)	TOTAL INCREASE IN RESERVES (required)
	$4,000	$5,000	$1,000

greater the smaller is the required Federal Reserve ratio. In the next chapter, we shall consider how the Federal Reserve uses the required reserve ratio and other tools to control the money supply. The relationship between money supply and price inflation also will be considered.

summary

In this chapter, we examined the money supply and its probable evolution from barter to paper money to credit. We saw that today the most important component of the money supply is the demand, or checking, deposits and credits granted by the banks. We noted too that the Federal Reserve System was established to control the banks so that they cannot go into an orgy of speculative lending which would end in monetary collapse. Finally, we examined how, within these limits, the banking system can still expand the money supply several times by giving credit to the allowed extent. This information will help us understand the problem of inflation and the monetary policies pursued by government.

chapter 30
inflation and monetary policy

Several varieties of price inflation have been discussed in previous chapters. Here, it is time to summarize our knowledge of the theory and facts concerning the money supply and price movements. We begin by recalling the general monetary framework of the economy and then briefly recapitulating the problems of inflation within that framework. Then some of the tools the Federal Reserve can use to control the money supply will be examined.

In Chapter 24, we explored the famous monetary equation:

Money supply × velocity of money = price level × transactions with products

Money supply is defined as the sum of coins and paper currency outside banks and demand deposits at banks (which form the largest part of the money supply). The *velocity of money* is defined as the speed (or number of times) with which money changes hands in a given period, and the *price level* is the general index of the average of all prices in the economy. The transactions discussed here are simply the physical volume of sales of the NNP.

normal inflation in prosperity

In Chapter 28, it was demonstrated that the price level has generally risen in prosperity and fallen in depression. The reasons may be stated in terms of the monetary equation. In prosperity, transactions or sales of the national product rise considerably, but the flow of money (money multiplied by its velocity) rises even faster. Because the equation tells us that the price level equals the money flow divided by the products sold, in this case, prices must rise.

Why does the flow of money rise so rapidly in prosperity? On the one hand, the money supply expands because banks give credit (in the form of demand deposits). Businesses want to borrow in order to take advantage of profitable opportunities, and banks want to lend because it appears that businesses can easily repay the loans with interest. The money multiplier process then assures that the money supply will increase several times.

On the other hand, the velocity of money increases as consumers and businesses both spend more rapidly. Consumers wish to get bargains before prices rise further and also because they feel assured of future income. Businesses likewise dig into their hoarded savings to make the investments that appear attractive. In prosperity, everyone wishes to spend in order to buy goods rather than to hoard money.

In depression, on the contrary, the money flow usually decreases even faster than the transactions with the national product. Banks call in their loans, and businesses do not want to make new loans; therefore, the money multiplier works in reverse to diminish the money supply several fold. Furthermore, individuals and businesses hoard their savings for the rainy days ahead, especially because there are no attractive opportunities for investment. As a result, the velocity of money circulation also falls considerably in depression. For these reasons, depression is normally a time of price deflation.

monetary policy

One of the long-standing methods for government to influence the economy has been through the use of policies designed to expand or diminish the flow of money and credit. The main idea is that in a depression an increased flow of money and credit will combat unemployment by increasing the purchase of both consumer and investment goods. In prosperity, restriction of money and credit will reduce inflationary pressures by reducing the flow of demand. Monetary policy works mainly through its effects on the price for renting the commodity called money—that is, the rate of interest on loans. If the government can increase or reduce the supply of money while the demand for it remains constant, then interest rates may be lowered or raised. And if spending plans are financed by borrowed funds and if these plans react in any way to changes in the rate of interest, it follows that changes in the supply of money for loans will have some effect on total spending.

In an inflationary situation, exactly how should monetary policy be applied and how effective is it? The supply of money and credit may be restricted by monetary policy through three major controls: (1) raising the required Federal Reserve ratio, (2) raising the interest rate the Federal Reserve charges banks, and (3) the sale of government bonds by the Federal Reserve. Let us see how each of these controls is supposed to work.

First, the Federal Reserve may raise the ratio of reserves banks are required to hold against their deposits in order to restrict credit. Furthermore, as soon as one bank decreases its loans, the effect on all banks may be several-fold by virtue of the money multiplier. Thus, in theory, the raising of the Federal Reserve ratio from 10 to 20 percent would lower the multiplication of money by banks from tenfold to only fivefold. If all banks were fully loaned out, this would cause a great decrease of loans. A reduction in the volume of loans may then mean less money available for consumer and investor spending, thus reducing inflationary pressures.

Second, the Federal Reserve also may raise the interest rate banks must pay if they wish to borrow from the Federal Reserve Banks. Then a bank will either have to charge higher interest rates on loans to its customers or reduce the amount it lends in order to avoid borrowing reserves from the Fed. Either way, less money may be available for further consumption and investment spending, which may reduce demand and thus lead to a lower rate of price inflation.

Finally, the Federal Reserve may sell more government bonds to banks or to rich individuals. The money to pay for the bonds must come from bank reserves or from individual bank deposits. In either case, the ability of banks to make loans is reduced (manyfold according to the money multiplier). Thus again, consumer and investment spending may be decreased and inflationary pressures lessened.

These methods of reducing money spending in an inflation may encounter certain obstacles. First, each assumes that banks had already made loans up to their maximum ratio of deposits to reserves. But banks often keep extra reserves above even the highest possible required reserve ratio and thus can keep lending until these reserves are exhausted. Second, these monetary controls assume that corporations must borrow from banks all of the money they need for new investments. But corporations often keep their own internal savings, which they may decide to use regardless of bank policies. Third, in cases where the government succeeds only in getting banks to raise their interest rates (by lowering money supply), there may be little effect on demand. If expected profit rates are rising even faster than interest rates, corporations may still be willing to borrow and invest more rapidly. In all of these cases, the government may be able to restrict the money supply, but the velocity, or speed, of spending the present money supply may increase even more rapidly.

Despite these weaknesses, monetary policy, if applied strongly enough (and rapidly enough because time is required for it to take effect), can choke off a general inflation. Of course, too severe a remedy may cause instability in the bond and stock markets, loss of confidence by domestic and foreign investors, and eventually a business downturn. Finally, it should be noted that general monetary tools are of little help in an inflation caused by monopolistic price-setting in particular industries. Monetary deflationary policies may even lower aggregate economic activity and increase unemployment if the inflation in particular industries occurs together with some amount of general unemployment (as appeared to be the case throughout the 1960s in the United States).

In a depression, exactly the opposite monetary policy may be applied. The supply of money and credit may be expanded through (1) lowering the required Federal Reserve ratio, (2) lowering the interest rate the Federal Reserve charges banks, or (3) the purchase by the Federal Reserve of government bonds in the open market to put more cash into the hands of individuals and banks. These measures are designed to increase the volume of borrowing and thus increase the volume of spending by increasing the supply of money for loans and lowering interest rates.

Obstacles to monetary policies intended to combat depression include most of those met by counterinflationary policies and a few that are different and more difficult to surmount. First, the interest rate cannot go below zero, and in actual practice, lenders will not go below a floor that is somewhat above a zero rate (during a depression it may require a zero or even negative interest rate to stimulate borrowing). Second, neither consumers nor most investors seem much stimulated to borrow by slightly lower interest rates. Business-men apparently consider the pessimistic outlook for smaller profits or even losses to be quantitatively much more important in invest-ment decisions. Moreover, most businesses prefer to invest from internal funds; when their profits fall drastically in a depression, they are not much attracted by any kind of loan.

You can lead a businessman to the river of loans, but you cannot force him to drink. In terms of the money equation, the government may increase the banks' supply of money, but consumers and businesses may reduce the velocity of their borrowing and spending even more rapidly. In short, monetary policies may have some effect in minor recessions, but when pessimistic expectations become general in a depression, monetary policy may be able to do little or nothing to expand the volume of spending.

inflation in wartime

The usual inflation experienced during peacetime prosperity has been very slow and very slight compared with the rapid and spectacular inflation stimulated by wartime spending. Just how closely price inflation is correlated with war may be seen in Figure 30.1. Very rapid price inflation accompanied the Revolutionary War, the War of 1812, the Civil War, and World War I.

During wartime there is little production of consumer goods or private producer goods in terms of the monetary equation. Thus, the transactions included within the private portion of the national product decline (or at least are prevented from rising). At the same time, there is full employment, with high wages and profits. The government finances the war production largely by increasing the money supply, either directly by printing money or indirectly by increasing the national debt (because more government bonds are used for credit expansion in these circumstances). Furthermore, as prices begin to rise rapidly, people rush to buy goods before prices rise further, thus increasing the velocity of money.

cost-push inflation

Turning to the modern period, we find all the varieties of inflation in developed countries well represented in U.S. price movements (see Table 30.1 and Figure 30.2).

Figure 30.2 records an initial large drop of prices during the Great Depression (1929–1933). Then, with the recovery of demand, there was a rise until 1937. The recession of 1938 caused a price drop, which was followed by the slow rise of prices during World War II (when price control held down inflationary pressures). Immediately following World War II, the vast demand for consumer and investment goods burst the dam and flooded the market with purchasing power, resulting in the rapid price rises of 1946 to 1948. A recession lowered prices in 1949, and then the Korean War caused a second major round of inflation in 1950–1951. Another recession lowered prices at the end of the Korean War, after which they rose steadily until 1959. Prices remained fairly stable in the early 1960s, but rose sharply from 1965 to 1971 because of the Vietnam War.

The surprising point is that the price index rose rather than declined in the recessions of 1958 and 1969–1971. During these

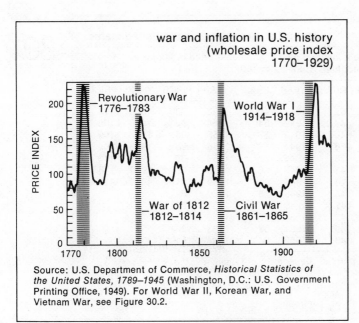

FIGURE

30.1

war and inflation in U.S. history
(wholesale price index
1770–1929)

Source: U.S. Department of Commerce, *Historical Statistics of the United States, 1789–1945* (Washington, D.C.: U.S. Government Printing Office, 1949). For World War II, Korean War, and Vietnam War, see Figure 30.2.

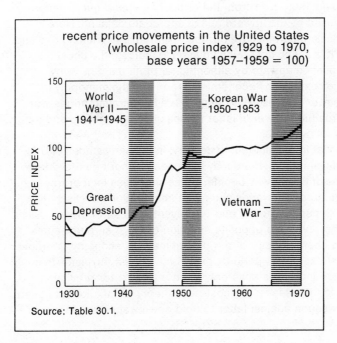

FIGURE

30.2

recent price movements in the United States
(wholesale price index 1929 to 1970,
base years 1957–1959 = 100)

Source: Table 30.1.

TABLE

30.1

recent price movements in the united states

(Price is defined as the wholesale price index for all commodities, 1957–59 = 100)

YEAR	PRICE	YEAR	PRICE	YEAR	PRICE	YEAR	PRICE
1929	52	1941	48	1953	93	1965	103
1930	47	1942	54	1954	93	1966	106
1931	40	1943	57	1955	93	1967	106
1932	36	1944	57	1956	96	1968	109
1933	36	1945	58	1957	99	1969	113
1934	41	1946	66	1958	100	1970	118
1935	44	1947	81	1959	101	1971	122
1936	44	1948	88	1960	101		
1937	47	1949	84	1961	100		
1938	43	1950	87	1962	101		
1939	42	1951	97	1963	100		
1940	43	1952	94	1964	101		

Source: U.S. Department of Commerce, *U.S. Statistical Abstract for 1964* (Washington, D.C.: U.S. Government Printing Office, 1964), p. 351, and Federal Reserve *Bulletin* (November 1971), p. A68.

recessions, the prices of industries with monopolistic power actually *rose* in the face of declining aggregate demand.

It is such evidence that forces us to distinguish the inflations of the late 1950s and 1969–1971 from the ordinary *demand-pull* inflation which is caused by the upward pull of aggregate demand. Here, instead, prices apparently are pushed upward by individual firms and industries. It is called *cost-push* inflation to indicate the belief that prices are pushed upward by either higher profit margins or by higher wage costs. Many economists argue that the monopoly or oligopoly power of firms is not responsible for spiraling prices, but that the bargaining power of labor unions pushes wages up and that prices only follow wages.

It is true that in the nineteenth century, in the early stages of U.S. industrial development, there may have been a shortage of workers during some of the railway booms. These shortages temporarily caused an increase in wages and made immigration necessary to keep up with capital growth and to prevent wages from rising. Since that time, however, the opposite situation of labor surplus seems much more characteristic of the peacetime U.S. economy. Moreover, in all recent expansion periods, profits have risen far faster than wages. Wage increases have only been a pretext for previously decided price increases; the cost-push theory of inflation has been used as a weapon against labor to hold down wages and increase profits.

Since World War II the United States has experienced long periods of prosperity but also a number of short-term recessions. It is, of course, normal during cyclical recovery to find prices rising as the demand for goods temporarily outdistances supply. The important point to note is that price rises take place long *before* full employment is reached. In fact, in the period since 1953, even during the prosperous periods there have been chronic excess capacity and chronic unemployment of at least 5 or 6 percent of the labor force according to official statistics. Thus the stage has been set for inflation by a fairly high level of demand. Demand, however, has still been below the full-employment level, therefore, it is not true that inflation has been caused by any real deficiency of labor supply relative to the demand.

The relationship of unemployment to inflation was first graphed by A. W. Phillips, and is therefore called the *Phillips curve.* He used the actual statistics from history. For simplicity we present here in Figure 30.3 a curve of the same variety, based on imaginary data (of roughly the same order as the real data).

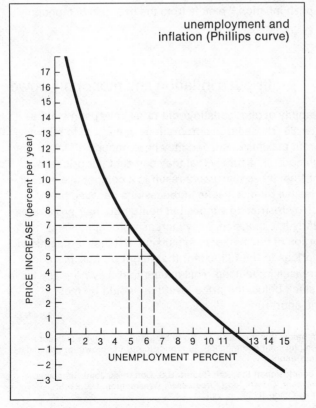

FIGURE

30.3

unemployment and inflation (Phillips curve)

This graph is merely a description of reality. The Phillips curve says that unemployment and inflation can and do exist together in the U.S. economy. It says that as unemployment decreases, inflation increases—or as unemployment increases, inflation decreases. That is generally true, since high unemployment means lack of demand, which makes it more difficult for businessmen to raise prices. At full employment, there is generally ample aggregate demand, and price increases are much easier for businessmen to impose.[1]

So far we have ony stated the fact that considerable unemployment (as high as 6 percent) may exist in our economy at the same time as considerable inflation (as high as 5 percent). Now we come to the difficult question: how and why is this possible?

This strange and socially very costly phenomenon of unemployment *and* inflation is obviously not covered by the standard Keynesian analysis of inflation caused by the pull of excess demand. Yet the *wage-push* theory (wages rising faster than prices) is factually untrue. Only one explanation remains to be considered. Oligopolistic freedom of price-fixing causes prices to rise in certain industries in the face of declining demand, *with prices rising even during recessions in recent years.* This phenomenon, which should be called "profit-push inflation," results from the exercise of monopoly power.[2]

profit-push inflation and monopoly power

The relative stability of oligopolistic profit rates have been emphasized in Chapter 26. These large corporations can afford to take a long view of profit maximization, and they have enough effect on the market through control of supply that they can set their prices at levels different from those that would result in a competitive market. Their profit rates fall relatively little in recessions because they maintain prices by restricting supply, but neither do their profit rates rise spectacularly in expansion. They increase production and retain their portion of the market in expansion, but they are cautious about raising prices to the full extent that might be feasible due to temporary increases in demand. This means that they normally leave considerable slack below the price level that would be most profitable in the short run.

[1] We shall explain below that the curve seems to be gradually shifting outward (more of both unemployment *and* inflation) in proportion to the growth of economic concentration in our economy.

[2] See the similar conclusion in the Staff Report, U.S. Congress, Joint Economic Committee, *Employment, Growth, and Price Levels* (Washington, D.C.: U.S. Government Printing Office, 1959), p. xxii.

As expansion continues, all firms are faced by rising costs both for labor and capital goods. The small firm whose price is set by competition can only watch its profit margin decline because the demand for its product is also limited. Not so the large oligopoly firm. Because it had intentionally set its prices below what the market would bear, it may now use up part of the slack to raise its prices, utilizing previous wage increases as an excuse. Higher wages may be part of the inflationary spiral, being themselves a response to earlier increases in price and profit. Higher wage costs, however, would have very little direct effect on prices if it were not for the oligopolistic structure of industry which allows freedom of price-fixing within wide limits.

The market power of oligopolies to influence prices has been documented in several investigations. In the 1930s, a famous study of price rigidity compared the lowering of prices by industries during the Great Depression with the ratio of concentration of production by the four largest firms in each industry. It was found that the prices of the more concentrated industries fell much less than competitive prices.[3] The evidence from expansions in the 1920s and 1930s is less clear, with more equal price rises in competitive and oligopolistic sectors, or even a slightly greater rise in the competitive sector (so that the advantage merely seesawed to some extent cyclically, with only a very slow rise of oligopoly power).

Empirical data for the period since World War II clearly document the pervasive effects of the exercise of monopoly power (reflecting the accelerated trend toward concentration as well as the lucrative military contracts going to the giant corporations). During the 1948 recession, prices in the nine most competitive industrial groups fell by 7.8 percent, but prices in the seven most concentrated industrial groups fell only 1.9 percent.[4] In the recessions of 1953 and 1957, even the more competitive prices fell only slightly, but the prices in the more concentrated industries actually continued to *rise* during the recessions. Of course, this greater resistance of oligopoly prices to a decline in demand is a major cause of their more stable profit margins during depressions.

The expansions since World War II give even stronger evidence of the increase of monopoly power. From the trough of October 1947, to the peak of July 1953, the prices of the seven most concentrated groups rose 23.3 percent, whereas prices in the nine most competitive

[3] Gardiner C. Means, writing for the U.S. National Resources Committee, *Structure of the American Economy* (Washington, D.C.: U.S. Government Printing Office, 1939), vol. I, p. 142. Also see John M. Blair, "Means, Throp, and Neal on Price Inflexibility," *Review of Economics and Statistics* (November 1956), pp. 427–435.

[4] The data given here are all adapted from a table by Robert K. Lanzillotti, in *Employment, Growth, and Price Levels*, op. cit., p. 2238.

rose only 12.4 percent. Similarly, from the trough of August 1954, to the peak of July 1957, prices of the seven most concentrated groups rose by 16 percent, whereas prices in the nine most competitive rose only 4.5 percent. Thus, the cyclical pattern seems to have been changed (or exaggerated) by a long-run movement toward higher relative prices in the more concentrated industrial groups. This long-run change seems to be responsible for a persistent outward shift of the Phillips curve (Figure 30.3), in which the same level of unemployment is accompanied by increased rates of inflation, or alternatively, where the same rate of inflation is associated with higher rates of unemployment.

What are the immediate policy implications for the U.S. government of the fact of profit-push inflation in the midst of unemployment? The Keynesian solution for unemployment is to increase aggregate demand (by spending more or lowering taxes), and the solution for inflation is to reduce aggregate demand (by spending less or raising taxes). These approaches are now clearly inadequate. A small increase in demand (usually by military production) does not necessarily stimulate output and employment, but is used by the dominant large corporations to raise prices even more and thus extract higher profits. A small decrease in demand (usually by cutting welfare spending or raising taxes) does not reduce most prices, but only leads to more unemployment.

wage-price controls

In August 1971 President Nixon began a policy of direct controls through a wage-price freeze, with the prospect of continued controls for a long time. Since we have shown why monetary and fiscal measures are inadequate at this period, it would seem that the Nixon program is just what the doctor ordered. If the government stimulates full employment by fiscal measures (such as lower taxes) and stops inflation by direct price controls, isn't this the best of all possible worlds?

On the contrary—conservative, liberal, and radical economists have all made severe criticisms of the program, and some argue that it is the worst of all possible worlds. The conservatives, such as Milton Friedman, are horrified at the violation of the First Commandment of laissez-faire economics: thou shalt not interfere with the market process of setting wages and prices.[5] They have always argued that resources, including labor and capital, cannot be

[5] Milton Friedman, *Newsweek* (August 30, 1971).

efficiently allocated if prices are not set by competition in the market. If government arbitrarily sets prices, then how can a businessman rationally calculate what to produce or what technology to use? More precisely, if a businessman does follow the arbitrary prices set by government, he will not produce what consumers desire nor will he produce it in the cheapest possible way (in terms of the real scarcity of resources). Thus, wage-price controls doom a capitalist economy to inefficiency (plus an enormous inefficient, and possibly repressive bureaucracy).

Strangely enough, liberal economists, such as Paul Samuelson, tend to cheer Nixon's wage-price controls.[6] They have long advocated the general idea that the economy needs an extension of governmental powers, and it was with their help that Congress passed the act allowing Nixon to extend those powers. Nevertheless, they also have strong criticisms. In the first place, we have seen that the heart of the problem is to curb monopoly power over prices and profits. But the Nixon administration has done the opposite. At the time of this writing, wages are more or less strictly controlled, but prices are controlled only lightly (and there are many loopholes in these controls), and profits and interest are uncontrolled. Obviously, some vague controls on profits and interest will accompany any long-lasting wage-price control, but the loopholes will be more important than the rules. As long as the capitalist government is dominated by monopoly capitalists and capitalist thinking (discussed in Chapters 19 and 27), this is a foregone conclusion.

Moreover, many liberals have pointed to another probusiness flaw in the program. The liberals assumed that equitable control of inflation would be accompanied by a powerful stimulus to full employment. Instead, the controls have been mainly on wages with much less control of prices and inflation, *and* there has been little stimulus to full employment. The encouragement by tax credits to business investment has been partially offset by attempts to *cut* government spending (on welfare programs, naturally). Thus, this program is not likely to reduce the unemployment of millions of workers, particularly the unemployment of blacks and women.

Some economists have also argued that the whole emphasis on inflation *versus* unemployment is false to some extent. They find evidence that the inflation rate does not change when unemployment moves from 4 to 6 percent, nor would it change if unemployment moved back down to 4 percent (in other words, the Phillips curve is constant in that range). Therefore, they argue that unemployment could be reduced to that extent *without* more inflation.

Finally, radicals agree with both conservative and liberal criticisms

6 Paul Samuelson, *Newsweek* (August 30, 1971).

of wage-price controls. First, as long as capitalism is maintained these controls will mean inefficiency and greater bureaucracy. Second, as long as capitalists control capitalist governments, the price controls will benefit business more than labor: the controls will hold down wages, but will allow profits to inch upward; and little will be done to reach full employment of labor. In addition, radicals have their own criticism. These controls over business and labor (besides being inefficient and inequitable) continue an economy based on private profit. This means that motivation continues to be moneygrubbing; and, in fact, is made still lower in reality by the reforms. As Milton Friedman shows[7] the businessmen will find loopholes that will raise prices surreptitiously. In a predictable length of time, controls will produce a black market, leaving even less supplies at legal prices. Moreover, prices and profits will also be increased by bribes and pressures on the bureaucratic controllers.

Opposed to this economy of moneygrubbing and extreme inequality, radicals consider wage-price controls a very bad halfway house, not an adequate road to full employment and price stability. The radical solution, of course, is direct ownership of the monopoly corporations by the public. Such public corporations could fully employ all workers and could set reasonable wages and prices. The profits of publicly owned corporations (after needed wage increases and necessary reinvestment) could be used for a wide expansion of social services. The details of operation of public or social ownership are discussed in Part IV of this book.

summary

The U.S. government uses the Federal Reserve to attempt to control inflation by (1) raising required bank reserve ratios, (2) raising interest rates on loans to banks, and (3) selling government bonds. All three of these monetary policies are intended to soak up money and thus reduce the amount in circulation. (Monetary policy is supposed to do the opposite during a depression.) Such policies may help somewhat to restrict mild price inflations, they may even help reduce somewhat the strong inflation caused by excess aggregate demand in wartime (which results from unlimited government demand for war supplies). Inflations caused by excess demand may also be met by fiscal policy, higher taxes or less government spending.

The present inflation, in the era of limited wars, is obviously very different because it is accompanied by significant unemployment.

---

7 Friedman, op. cit.

Since full employment does not exist, the inflation is *not* caused by excess aggregate demand. Instead, it is a profit-push inflation caused by the ability of the monopolies to raise prices even without excess demand (but certainly aided by the strong demand in the military sector). Obviously, control of this kind of inflation cannot be eliminated by traditional monetary policy—nor by traditional fiscal policy.

The Nixon administration tried direct price-wage controls to restrict cost-push inflation. Problems are: (1) inefficiency as prices no longer reflect demand and supply conditions, (2) probusiness bias allows for reduction of real wages through price loopholes and little attention to unemployment, and (3) continued monopoly profits based on old moneygrubbing, new loopholes, and new black markets.

chapter 31
economic growth and waste

This chapter does not attempt to present a complete theory of how an economy grows over time. It has the more modest purpose of examining some of the older theories, setting up a very general framework in which the question may be analyzed, and introducing some of the more complex problems of economic growth.

For the sake of simplicity, it is assumed in this section that aggregate effective demand rises as rapidly as aggregate supply, that Say's law holds, and that there are no depressions caused by lack of demand. Here, we ask, How fast is it technically possible for the economy to grow? What is the maximum *potential* rate of growth of output obtainable by the economy? Because all problems of demand are assumed away, the remaining problem may be resolved into two questions. (1) How much of each input (land, labor, capital) can be procured under existing circumstances for use in production? (2) How much output can be obtained from these inputs in the production process?

production is determined by labor, capital, natural resources, and technology

Many different physical inputs constitute an economy's production base. For convenience, these may be grouped into the three categories of capital, labor, and natural resources. *Capital* includes inventories of raw materials and goods in process as well as all plant and equipment. *Labor* means the number of man-hours available as well as the degree of skill of the available labor force. *Natural resources* include all useful materials (including land) known to be in the territory of the economy. Resources may be depleted by use or by natural erosion, but may be increased by new geological discoveries. *Technology* is the knowledge that determines how much output can be produced by a given combination of inputs. Therefore, the level of potential output is a function of the presently available technology, natural resources, capital, and labor. A thorough analysis of the growth potential of any existing economy should consider each of these inputs in turn as well as the interrelations between them.

The actual long-run economic growth of the United States is summarized in a recent government report as follows:

> It has been estimated that real gross national product grew 4.3 percent per year from 1839 to 1879; 3.7 percent per year from 1879 to 1919; and 3 percent from 1919 to 1959. . . . The growth of the labor force and of the capital stock partly explains our economic growth. In addition, more than half the growth is accounted for by improvement in the factors of production and technology.[1]

No one would deny the importance of improvements in technology or the quality of labor or capital; therefore, no one denies the urgent need for such things as research, education, and public-health measures. Recent studies, however, have shown that it is very difficult to get exact quantitative estimates of just how important have been the respective contributions resulting from the growth in the different factors of technology.[2]

Here we may leave aside the intricate factual questions involved in separating out the behavior and influence of each of the components of growth. The level of potential output may always be considered to be determined solely by the amount of any one factor (e.g., labor) and by the amount of output produced by a given level of that input (e.g., output per worker). Of course, the amount produced by any one factor is influenced by the levels of all the others and by improvements in technology.

[1] U.S. Congress, Joint Economic Committee, 86th Cong., 1st sess., *Employment, Growth, and Price Levels* (Washington, D.C.: U.S. Government Printing Office, 1959), p. xxiii.

[2] See, for example, E. D. Domar, "On the Measurement of Technological Change," *Economic Journal* (December 1961), pp. 709–729; also R. M. Solow, "Technical Progress, Capital Formation, and Economic Growth," *American Economic Review* (May 1962), pp. 76–86.

full-employment growth

In this section, the labor force is assumed to be always fully employed. Potential growth of output is then determined by the growth of the labor force and by the amount produced per unit of labor.

The law of diminishing returns states that each additional worker adds less output than the worker hired before him. It holds true *only if* capital, natural resources, and technology remain unchanged and *if* some minimum scale of employment is reached. Given these assumptions, the law of diminishing returns is a truism; it cannot be other than true. All other things remaining the same, it is obvious that if enough workers are crowded onto a single plot of land or even the entire world, the crowding alone will eventually cause the product of an additional worker to decline. But many of the classical economists, Malthus, for example, went much further than the truism embodied in the law of diminishing returns. They predicted that diminishing returns per worker in the economy as a whole *would* come about in actual fact. The Reverend Malthus reached this dismal conclusion on the grounds that population increase would be very rapid and would far outweigh the slow increase of capital, technology, and natural resources.

The gloomy long-run prediction based on this interpretation of the law of diminishing returns has not been borne out by the facts of historical progress. First, it is not even clear that the world population is at the minimum level at which further additions to the working force would bring diminishing returns, even if natural resources, capital, and technology were to remain constant. Second, labor itself improves in quality as scientific and technical education advance, although this may properly be classed as an aspect of technological improvement. Third, it was usual to argue that the earth is only so large and that its natural resources are slowly being depleted. The supply of *known* natural resources, however, is steadily expanding due to continuous geological discoveries of new reserves. Furthermore, there have been important discoveries of new uses for previously neglected materials—for example, coal was once merely a hard black stone of no use for fuel or heating purposes. Moreover, better ways have been found to use available resources—for example, power production by atomic fission or fusion, or food production by hydroponic farming. Of course, the last two means of resource expansion are again aspects of technological improvement.

Another reason why there have not been diminishing returns per worker in the economy as a whole is the increasing use of capital per worker, which allows a single worker to produce far more than previously. The final and most important reason for the defeat of diminishing returns is that development of technology in the last century has meant a much more efficient use of the available capital, natural resources, and labor. At the early date when Malthus wrote, it was still possible largely to ignore technological progress. Today, even the blindest economist is forced to consider the startling advances continually made in productive knowhow.

Empirically, the evidence shows that the population in the developed countries has not outraced technology, natural resources, and capital, but that, on the contrary, product per person has grown enormously. In U.S. agriculture, increase of output has far outrun increase of employment. In fact, between 1870 and 1940, employment in agriculture rose by only 34 percent, while output rose by 279 percent.[3] The United States thus has no problem of lack of food, but rather has a surplus relative to effective cash demand.

It may be concluded that in the industrialized private-enterprise economies slowed progress or retrogression is caused, not by natural and technical problems, but by man-made economic institutions that give rise to recurrent economic catastrophes. The advent of atomic energy makes it especially clear that the natural sciences have given us ample power to obtain in the future fantastic levels of abundance or to blow to pieces the entire world.

INCREASE OF LABOR

The increase of the labor force is primarily determined by population growth, but it is also governed by changes in the age composition of the population and by those sociological attitudes and labor laws that determine the ages of beginning and retiring from work as well as the maximum hours of work. Many Malthusian-minded persons mechanically project the present world rate of population growth into the near future and easily arrive at quite astronomical figures for total population. It was demonstrated above that, to date at least, capital and technology have had no trouble keeping ahead of population growth; they probably could keep pace with even massive population growth in the coming years.

The mechanical prognostications of vast population growth, however, do not seem to have taken into account the best present knowledge of population-growth patterns. Malthus described people breeding like animals and population exploding with only a few kinds

[3] See Arthur Burns, *Frontiers of Economic Knowledge* (Princeton, N.J.: Princeton University Press, 1954), p. 4.

of checks to its expansion. He spoke of "preventative checks" as those that cause lower birthrates. He recognized only abstention from sex or vice and sexual deviation and did not consider voluntary birth control through family planning and contraceptive methods. When preventative checks fail, according to Malthus, the result will be "positive checks" to population, where "positive" means a higher death rate! Thus, positive checks include wars, famine, and disease.

It is true that in many primitive economies at a low level of productivity, we often find very high birthrates. At this stage, however, population may be constant for centuries because it is held in check by equally high death rates, caused indeed by wars, disease, and starvation. A second stage of rapid population growth usually follows the beginnings of industrialization and the introduction of modern methods of public-health sanitation. With better control of disease and enough food production, death rates decline. As long as birthrates remain high, the population soars. (This problem is examined in Chapter 33.)

At the third stage, however, as the economy matures, we find culture and education spreading to all the population. There is also spread a knowledge of contraceptive devices for birth control as well as a desire to use these means in order to keep the family to a manageable size. Thus, all of the more industralized countries have shown some tendency toward lower and lower birthrates during the last 100 years, although there have been some upward spurts in the rate for short periods.

full-capacity growth

So far we have concentrated on the increase of the labor force and output per worker. It is more convenient for our purposes, however, to estimate the potential growth of output in relation to the increase of capital and the output per unit of capital. Of course, the output per unit of capital will reflect changes in technology, natural resources, and the labor supply.[4]

We may state a very simple relationship between output and capital at any given moment. The national product, or output, *must equal the output per unit of capital times the amount of capital in use.* Thus, a simple formula may be written:

$$\text{Output} = \frac{\text{output}}{\text{capital}} \times \text{capital}$$

[4] This approach is detailed in E. D. Domar, "Expansion and Employment," *American Economic Review* (March 1947), pp. 34–35.

Of course, this formula is always true by definition, and the only question is whether it is fruitful to think in these terms.

In the United States, about $3 of capital goods are in use for each $1 of annual national product. So the ratio of output to capital is about 1:3. Therefore, when the value of capital stock, including all machines and factories, was about $1,500 billion, the economy produced annually an output of about $500 billion.

Now we may extend this analysis to a growing economy. The rate of growth of output is determined by the growth of capital and the changes in output per unit of capital. More precisely, the rate of *growth* of output is equal to the *increase* in output per *increase* in capital multiplied by the ratio of the *increase* in capital to output. Thus, we may write the equation of growth:

$$\frac{\text{Increase in output}}{\text{Output}} = \frac{\text{increase in output}}{\text{increase in capital}} \times \frac{\text{increase in capital}}{\text{output}}$$

This equation is true by definition, so it is always true. Notice that the formula is true not only for increases but also for decreases in output; we could substitute the word *change* for the word *increase* to obtain a more general formula.

The change (increase or decrease) in output as a ratio to present output is how we define the *rate of growth* of output. For example, if we produced $100 last year, and we now produce $103, then the rate of growth is 3/100, or 3 percent a year.

The change in output as a ratio to the change in capital is defined as the *marginal* output/capital ratio. For example, if we invest $9 in additional capital and this results in a $3 increase in our output of national product, then we may say that the marginal output/capital ratio is 1:3. Finally, recall that an increase in capital is our definition of *investment*. Moreover, in this chapter, it is assumed (for the sake of simplicity) that the amount of investment is just equal to the amount of saving. Therefore, we may say that the *increase in capital* means the same thing as *investment,* or that it means the same thing as *saving.* Then the ratio of increase in capital to output might be written as investment to output or saving to output. Of course, the ratio of saving to output (taking output at its dollar value as equal to national income) is none other than our old friend the average propensity to save. For example, if the value of output or income is $100 (or $100 billion) and if saving is $9 (or $9 billion), then the average propensity to save is 0.09, or 9 percent. Here, we assume that all saving is invested and that all investment results in increase of capital.

If the equation of growth is put into these new terms, it may be written:

Rate of growth of output = marginal ouput/capital ratio × APS

This may be the easiest form in which to remember the formula. However, it is easier to make use of the growth equation in the form of ratios:

$$\text{Rate of growth} = \frac{\text{change in output}}{\text{change in capital}} \times \frac{\text{saving}}{\text{output}}$$

We are merely affirming that how fast the economy grows depends on how much is saved and invested *and* how much is produced by new investments.

Consider an example of the use of this equation of growth. If the average propensity to save is 9 percent and if the marginal output/capital ratio is 1:3, then we find that

Rate of growth = ⅓ × 0.09 = 0.03, or 3 percent a year

This has been approximately the performance of the U.S. economy over a long period of time.

The mechanics of the growth process may also be examined year by year. Table 31.1 assumes the same proportions as in the example just given of U.S. economic growth.

In Table 31.1, we have illustrated the arithmetic of a growing economy for a few years' time. The table begins at an arbitrary level of $100 for convenience in calculation. The table is not completed so that the reader may finish it. Start with output of the latest year. First, divide this output into saving and consumption according to a propensity to save of 9 percent, or a propensity to consume of 91 percent. Second, having found the amount saved or invested (the

(assume $\dfrac{\text{increase in output}}{\text{increase in capital}} = \dfrac{1}{3}$ and $\dfrac{\text{saving}}{\text{output}} = 0.09$)		
YEAR	CONSUMPTION = OUTPUT − SAVING	OUTPUT (or national product)
1	$91 ◄———————	$100 ◄————————
2	$93.70 ◄———————	$103 ◄————
3	$96.55 ◄———————	$106.10 ◄———
4	—	$109.28 ◄—
5	—	—
6	—	—
7	—	—
8	—	—
9	—	—
10	—	—

increase of capital), we can then find the increase of output for the next year by applying a marginal output/capital ratio of 1:3. For example, because saving or increase of capital was $9 in Year 1, the increase of output in Year 2 is one-third of that, or $3. The table is completed by merely repeating these two steps year after year. As long as the propensity to save and the marginal output/capital ratio remain unchanged, this economy will continue to grow at a steady 3 percent a year.

It is important to emphasize, as many recent studies have done, that the most important factors in determining how much output will be produced by a given capital investment are the level of technology and the level of education of the labor force. It has been shown repeatedly that *the most profitable social use of resources* is in education—or in production of *human capital,* as some cold fishes call it. Education not only raises the skills of workers in using physical capital, but also leads to more research and creates higher levels of technology. Those countries with a high degree of resources in education have grown most rapidly.

american growth experience

What has been the actual long-run trend of the output/capital ratio in U.S. history? According to estimates by Kuznets, it has fluctuated around the level of $1 of annual national product to every $3 of the stock of capital.[5] There was a declining trend of product per unit of

[5] Fully discussed in Nicholas Kaldor, *Essays on Economic Stability and Growth* (New York: Free Press, 1960), p. 260.

---

example of economic growth

TABLE

31.1

SAVING = INVESTMENT = INCREASE IN CAPITAL	INCREASE IN OUTPUT
$9	$3
$9.30	$3.10
$9.55	$3.18
—	—
—	—
—	—
—	—
—	—
—	—

capital from the 1880s to World War I, but this was just about balanced by a rising trend in productivity from then until the 1940s. Other conflicting studies have shown as much as a one-third rise in capital productivity since the 1880s.[6] Because the data are very poor and there are very difficult problems of definition of *output* and *capital,* the recorded changes may not be very significant; therefore, it does make some sense to treat the marginal output per unit of capital as roughly constant in the simplest approximation to a long-run projection.

At first glance, this seems a strange result because we might expect the product per unit of capital to rise as a result of great technological advances. However, that is not at all necessary because output per unit of capital is determined by two opposed trends. On the one hand, vast technological improvement has meant rapid growth in the output *per worker.* On the other hand, U.S. technology has been embodied in huge amounts of machinery per worker, and thus the growth of capital has been almost as rapid as the growth of output. Of course, it must be remembered that even if the ratio of output to capital in the U.S. economy has stayed roughly constant over a very long period, there are very wide differences among industries, and also very wide differences between prosperity and depression, when much capital may remain unused.

What has been the actual course of saving (and investment) behavior in the United States? We saw in Chapter 25 that the ratio of saving to NNP has remained remarkably stable over a very long period. Thus, in the United States, the long-run propensity to save remains roughly between 9 and 11 percent.[7] Furthermore, the evidence indicates that the marginal output/capital ratio has fluctuated in about the neighborhood of 1:3. Assuming that these two ratios hold for the future, we may predict growth according to the growth formula. Taking one-third of 9 percent, we have a 3 percent rate of growth. This is approximately the rate of growth that American GNP has achieved over a long period of time.

saving and growth

There are two quite distinct points of view about saving. The classical economists, concerned as they were about economic

[6] See, for example, Moses Abromowitz, "Resources and Output Trends in the U.S. Since 1870," *American Economic Review* (May 1956), p. 8.

[7] See Simon S. Kuznets, *National Product Since 1869* (New York: National Bureau of Economic Research, 1946), p. 119.

growth, called for as much thriftiness and saving as possible. In early nineteenth-century England, they observed that the savings of businessmen were being used to build more capital and drew the moral that more thrift and saving lead to more rapid increase of capital and, consequently, to a more rapid economic growth.

Keynes pointed out that this conclusion is true only if we assume full employment and the rule of Say's law, that demand is always enough for any supply of goods and that all saving is automatically invested. Indeed, we made this simplifying assumption when we asked how fast the economy could grow *if* there were always enough demand and *if* all saving were always invested. This assumption, however, is not true. During the Great Depression, it was painfully obvious to Keynesians that there was not full employment and that most saving was *not* being invested (except in the statistical sense of investment in unplanned and unwanted inventory pile-ups).

Keynes showed that, with unemployment and lack of investment opportunities, more saving may actually lead to *less* production rather than any economic growth. This finding constitutes the Alice-in-Wonderland theme of the *paradox of thrift,* which says that greater thrift and saving may sometimes lead to less investment, not

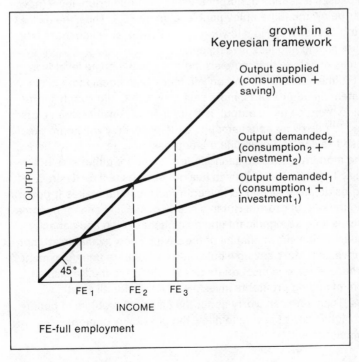

FIGURE

31.1

growth in a Keynesian framework

Output supplied (consumption + saving)

Output demanded$_2$ (consumption$_2$ + investment$_2$)

Output demanded$_1$ (consumption$_1$ + investment$_1$)

OUTPUT

45°

FE$_1$ FE$_2$ FE$_3$

INCOME

FE-full employment

more. If the economy is faced with a lack of money demand, then a higher propensity to save may simply lower consumer demand still further. The lower consumer demand may then lead to still less output and income, and therefore less aggregate saving and investment than there was before individuals tried to save more of their income. Thrift may always be an individual virtue, as Ben Franklin preached, but is not always a social virtue when there is a lack of paying customers in a private-enterprise economy.

The Keynesian point may be made more obvious by means of a diagram. In Figure 31.1, we see growth represented as higher and higher levels of full-employment output. Assume that there is an increase in the labor force, or that there is an improvement in the product per worker, which allows the same workers to produce more at full employment. If the growth of supply from FE_1 to FE_2 is met by an equal growth of demand from Demand$_1$ to Demand $_2$, then all is well. We return to an equilibrium at a higher level of full employment with greater saving and greater investment.

Assume, however, that output and income grow further from FE_2 to FE_3, but that there is no further growth of demand. This means that at FE_3 the saving (plus consumption) is greater than the planned investment (plus consumption). Therefore, at that level, we may speak of *too much* saving, which causes a lack of demand for output, which causes a decline of output back to the equilibrium level (now FE_2) far below the full-employment level (now FE_3). Thus, the excess of saving causes a fall to a lower level of output, at which there is both less saving and less investment.

We may conclude that more saving at a given income level is a benefit to the economy if, and only if, there is an equal increase in investment. In other words, more saving, which could supply more capital to produce more output, is helpful only if businessmen expect demand to rise by an equal amount. Otherwise, they will hoard the increased saving and precipitate a depression.

In the modern world, we cannot afford to ignore either side of the problem. The U.S. rate of growth has not been as fast as desired. Setting aside more saving to invest in more capital makes it *possible* to raise the rate of growth. But this happy possibility cannot become a reality as long as significant unemployment of men and capacity continues, which shows that all of the savings now available are not being invested. More saving would only cause more unemployment in this case. First, one must guarantee a solution to the Keynesian problem of finding profitable investment outlets for all existing savings. Then, one can worry about the classical problem of generating a higher rate of saving to allow the possibility of more investment.

militarism and growth

During the period since the U.S. economy has changed to a predominantly oligopolistic structure (and now with a large military sector), the rate of economic growth appears to have declined. Thus, GNP in constant prices grew by 4.31 percent per year in 1839–1879, by 3.72 percent a year in 1879–1919, and by only 2.97 percent a year in 1919–1959. From 1950 to 1970, the rate was 3.4 percent.[8] The increase in this period was, in large part, due to the stimulus of the Vietnam War. Many economists believe that after the boom period in the early 1960s only the escalation of the Vietnam War, from 1965 to 1968, prevented a serious recession. During these years, GNP, in constant prices, grew at a rate of 4.7 percent.

To some degree, military spending does lower the rate of growth by diverting men and resources from productive activity to military waste. In recent years in the United States, military waste has been in the neighborhood of 10 percent. But military spending has an additional multiplier effect on employment. So it provides not only the direct 10 percent, but another indirect 15 percent of employment, making a total amount of 25 percent of all U.S. employment. No one can say exactly what the effect of eliminating military employment would be. Assume, as some writers have claimed, that it has prevented a major depression (such as in the 1930s, when unemployment did reach 25 percent). Then we might say that its total effect on the rate of growth is positive because it wastes 10 percent of the product but may have raised employment and total product by 25 percent. If, however, you believe that unemployment would be increased less than 10 percent without military production, then you would conclude that its net effect on the growth rate is negative.

monopoly and growth

At any rate, except for the 1960s, the longer-run trend has been a declining rate of growth. To what extent, if any, this decline is related to the high level of oligopoly power is impossible to say because so many other factors have been operative.

We do know that production does not reach optimum efficiency

---

[8] U.S. Congress, *Employment, Growth, and Price Levels*, op. cit., p. 34; and Federal Reserve *Bulletin* (September 1970).

below some crucial size. Thus, the increase in importance of large firms does mean that most of the economy has the ability to produce at lower costs than ever before. The data on both costs and profit rates reveal the possibility of high efficiency at a fairly constant level beyond the minimum-size firm.[9] Of course, the very large firms also have disproportionately larger research facilities and hold a very large proportion of all unexpired patents. Therefore, they have the most potential for efficiency improvement. Moreover, many investment projects are simply too large for small firms.

But the large, entrenched firm stands to lose most by the obsolescence of present machinery. It also loses most from product improvements that will reduce the number of units the customer needs to buy, for example, a longer-lasting light bulb. Therefore, if the large firm has an oligopoly position and faces no serious competitive pressure for improvement, it *may* hide away and not use many important new inventions. Oligopoly power may also be used to restrict supply in order to maintain prices. Oligopolies will expand production as rapidly as possible only in the unusual periods of unlimited demand, such as World War II.

Finally, we have seen that the existence of economic concentration may have increased the severity and possibly the number of depressions because of its destabilizing effects on the remaining small businesses. If this is so, then unless it has had a fully offsetting effect in increasing growth during prosperity, it would seem that this is another reason why the net effect of oligopoly may be to lower the rate of economic growth. This is not to say, of course, that breaking up large firms into smaller units would increase economic growth; this would certainly cause a major decrease of economic efficiency in addition to probable negative effects on investment.

growth and social welfare

In the 1950s, the United States grew at a much slower rate than the Soviet Union. In the Cold War atmosphere of those years, this difference in growth rates was seen, in the United States, as a challenge of paramount significance. Economists and politicians both emphasized rapid growth as the nation's single most important economic goal.

Economic growth *is* important. With the widespread existence of poverty, no one can deny that a larger output of goods and services is needed. Yet excessive concern with growth for its own sake has

[9] See J. S. Bain, "Price and Production Policies," in Howard S. Ellis, ed., *A Survey of Contemporary Economics* (New York: McGraw-Hill, 1948), p. 140.

often obscured many significant economic and social problems. By looking exclusively at economic growth as the only answer to the problems of poverty, we tend to ignore the questions of how equitably the income is distributed (see Chapter 15).

We also tend to overlook the *composition* of the national product. Is more always better regardless of what the increment to output is? Much of what we produce adds little or nothing to people's present consumption and nothing to future growth.

The social costs of military spending, for example, can be seen in the fact that for each TFX airplane the United States has constructed, the nation gave up 13 elementary schools, or 570 dwelling units in low-rent public-housing projects, or 278 hospital beds. Similarly, each Polaris submarine "costs" 331 elementary schools, or 6,811 hospital beds, or 13,723 dwelling units in low-rent public housing.[10]

Military spending, however, is by no means the only type of expenditure from which the public welfare derives little or no benefit. Billions of dollars, for example, are spent yearly trying to convince consumers that one of two identical products is better. Costly model changes occur yearly to induce people to "junk" older but still useful products. Thousands of engineers are employed to design products that will not work after a short time so more new products can be sold. A study covering the period of the late 1950s estimated that 2.5 percent of GNP was wasted on the production of useless automobile model changes.[11] If we had similar information for all industries, the figure would be truly staggering.

Another consideration in evaluating growth performance is the misallocation of resources due to oligopolistic and monopolistic industrial organization of the United States. Economists have long realized that this type of industrial structure leads to distorted prices and inefficient allocation of resources. It also often leads to the holding back of new inventions and innovations to get longer use of present machinery. There is also waste that results from unnecessary duplication such as the existence of four competitive gas stations at a single intersection.

Even more important are the cases in which the pursuit of profits comes into direct conflict with the public welfare. In particular, profit-seeking generally results in little concern for conservation. One writer recently protested that "America was once a paradise of timberland and streams but it is dying because of the greed and money lust of a thousand little kings who slashed the timber all to

10 Seymour Melman, *Our Depleted Society* (New York: Delta Books, 1966), p. 37.

11 "The Costs of Automobile Model Changes Since 1949," *Journal of Political Economy* (October 1962). An abstract, omitting details of estimating procedures, was presented at the 1961 annual meeting of the American Economic Association and appears in the *American Economic Review* (May 1962), beginning at p. 259.

hell and would not be controlled."[12] Anyone who has seen the thousands of acres of once beautiful countryside that have been completely devastated by strip-mining can also attest to this tragic social cost of unrestrained profit-seeking.

Another cost of economic growth has been the pollution of our physical environment. Professor Galbraith, testifying before a congressional committee, has stated: "I am not quite sure what the advantage is in having a few more dollars to spend if the air is too dirty to breathe, the water too polluted to drink, the commuters are losing out in the struggle to get in and out of the city, the streets are filthy, and the schools so bad that the young perhaps wisely stay away, and hoodlums roll citizens for some of the dollars they saved in tax."[13]

The basic economic cause of pollution in a private-enterprise economy is that business firms do not have to pay for *all* the costs incurred in the production process. They pay for labor, raw materials and capital used up in production. They use the land, air, and water, however, for the disposal of waste products that are created in the process of production. Generally, they pay little or nothing for the use of the environment as a garbage disposal.

This use of the environment, however, does involve costs to other persons who usually do not reap any direct benefit from the operation of the business doing the polluting. Some of the costs are paid in money. When polluted air causes increases in laundry bills and doctor bills, or when taxes are raised to pay for more expensive water treatment to neutralize industrial waste in the water, thousands, and sometimes millions, of persons pay part of the money costs of production. But these people have no voice in the production decisions and receive none of the profits in a private-enterprise economy.

Even more important than these money costs, however, are the social costs which businesses inflict on the general public, but which have no price tag attached to them. The discomfort and pain of breathing polluted air, drinking polluted water, and listening to the constant, screeching cacophony of industrial noises are important nonmonetary costs which millions of people pay for industrial growth. The ugliness of a countryside devastated by strip-mining, of trees dying from pollutants in the air, of the constant, drab, gray haze that perpetually hangs over most cities, are also nonmonetary costs. Millions of us pay these costs; yet those firms that make profits from more production (and more pollution) pay not a penny of these costs.

[12] Garrett De Bell, ed., *The Environmental Handbook* (New York: Ballantine, 1970), p. 3.

[13] Quoted in Michael Harrington, "Reactionary Keynesianism," *Encounter* (March 1966), p. 51.

It has been estimated that each year businesses are responsible for over 25 billion tons of pollutants being spewed in the air and dumped into the water and on the land.[14] This is about 125 tons of waste per year for every man, woman, and child in the United States. Included in this figure are about 150 million tons of smoke and fumes that blacken the skies and poison the air, 22 million tons of waste paper products, 3 million tons of mill tailings and 50 trillion gallons of heated and polluted liquids that are dumped in our streams, rivers, and lakes each year.

Many of the chemical wastes such as DDT, and most common household detergents, do not decompose, or do so very slowly. Their adverse effects increase cumulatively over time, and many scientists are warning us of the inevitably dire consequences of this. The ultimate effects of many pollutants are unknown. For example, many scientists fear that the increased concentrations of carbon dioxide in the air may inhibit the dissipation of the earth's heat. This could conceivably make the world uninhabitable for human beings at some future time.

It is extremely difficult for a capitalistic private-enterprise economy to deal with these problems because those who receive the profits from production do not pay these social costs. Those who do pay the social costs have little or no voice in the operation of the businesses.

When one looks at these social costs and wastes involved in increasing the national product, the conclusion seems inescapable that economic growth cannot be judged apart from other social values. Certainly, there are private and public needs that are very pressing and that will require considerable economic growth if they are to be satisfied. But, if economic growth merely means we get dirtier air, more polluted water, and a generally deteriorating physical and social atmosphere, while production includes an increasing number of unneeded gadgets and trinkets, then we should question the social utility of growth.

summary

This chapter began by discussing what determines the quantity (and rate of growth) of output. The quantity of output is determined by the known natural resources, by the amount of capital available, even more by the level of technology, and most of all by the labor force and its level of education (because education level determines

14 The following estimates are taken from R. C. d'Arge, A. V. Kneese, and R. V. Ayers, *Economics of the Environment: A Materials Balance Approach* (Baltimore: Johns Hopkins, 1970).

the skill in use of capital and the creation of new technology).

It is clear from the discussion of this chapter, however, that the *quality* of economic growth (the amount of waste and pollution) is at least as important as the *quantity*. Let us repeat that growth *is* necessary if many social ills are to be solved. Furthermore, with a growing population, the economy must at least keep pace with the rate of population growth if we are to avoid the social ills of widespread unemployment.

We can conclude that economic growth is of the utmost importance, but there are other social problems attendant to this growth that are no less important. The economic challenge is constantly to increase productivity while using this enlarged capacity to meet society's real social and individual needs.

chapter 32
international trade and finance

Throughout most of Parts II and III, we have discussed the American economy as though it existed in isolation. In this chapter, we shall consider some of the economic and financial relationships between different countries. Market transactions over national boundaries are similar in some respects to transactions within a single country. Goods and services are purchased from foreigners, investments are made in foreign countries, and profits are made in these countries and then repatriated in much the same way as they would be between two states within the United States.

There are also important differences between foreign market transactions and domestic transactions. The most obvious is that when international boundaries are crossed different currencies must be used to make payments. A second and even more important difference is that various governments are involved, either directly or indirectly, in international transactions.

international economic relations

In market transactions, property rights are exchanged. We have already seen that it is through the system of property rights that the economically powerful derive and use their power. The essential feature of property rights is that there must be a government with the power to enforce these rights.

Within a single country, a fairly consistent set of property rights is protected by a single government. In the United States, about 1.5 percent of the population own most of the income-producing assets. Ownership gives this small minority the ultimate control of most of the political processes. It is through this control that they maintain governments that give the highest priority to the protection of the property rights upon which the economic power of the wealthy elite rests.[1]

Across national boundaries, however, there are often widely different property systems with different governments enforcing the property rights. Very little international trade would take place if there were not some commonly recognized core of property rights with some government or governments having the power to enforce them.

At present, international transactions are concentrated in two large groups of countries, the socialist countries and the capitalist countries. Within each group, there are generally fairly common sets of property relations and fairly definite power hierarchies. Although some trade does take place between capitalist and socialist countries (many of them are geographically adjacent to each other and have long histories of economic interaction), this trade is generally much smaller in volume than the trade with other economies within a country's own ideological and social sphere.

The power hierarchies within each of these two blocks assure a sufficient degree of stability and consistency in the enforcement of property rights so as to make extensive economic interaction possible. A given country finds its powers as well as its restrictions defined by its place within the hierarchy. Within the capitalist group, for example, the United States stands at the top of the power hierarchy. Canada, Japan, and the countries of western Europe are on the second level of the pyramid. At the bottom of the pyramid are the underdeveloped countries of Latin America, Asia, and Africa.

The relationships between pairs of countries on different levels of the hierarchy are various and complex. Most of the countries are nominally sovereign, independent states. Their particular position in the world hierarchy of capitalist countries, however, modifies and constrains this sovereignty and independence in a multiplicity of ways. A country in the middle level of the pyramid may find control being exerted on it from above, while at the same time it benefits and profits by exerting control on countries which are at a lower level. We can briefly examine Canada's position in order to illustrate the constraints that exist for a country in the middle-level of the hierarchy. (Canada is, perhaps, an extreme case because American control there has advanced beyond that which exists in any of the western European countries.)

[1] Evidence for this statement was presented in Chapters 19 and 27.

the case of canadian–american
economic relations

Canada invests hundreds of millions of dollars annually in under-developed countries. With these investment dollars goes a large measure of Canadian economic power within many of these countries. However, a Canadian government report in 1968 showed that foreigners owned $33 billion of Canadian assets. The principal owners of these assets were the United States (approximately 80 percent) and the United Kingdom (approximately 12 percent). The bulk of this foreign ownership was direct or equity ownership (about 60 percent).[2]

The composition of this foreign ownership conformed perfectly with the time-honored explanation of economic expansionism: the securing of sources of raw materials and markets for manufactured goods. Fifty-four percent of all Canadian manufacturing industries were owned by foreigners, and 60 percent were controlled by foreigners. Foreign ownership of mining and smelting stood at 62 percent. The petroleum and natural gas industry was 64 percent foreign owned and 74 percent foreign controlled.

Within the manufacturing sector, those industries that were oligopolistically organized were almost completely foreign owned. These figures are 97 percent of the automobile industry, 97 percent of the rubber industry, 78 percent in chemicals, and 77 percent in electrical apparatus. These industries were controlled almost exclusively by U.S. interests.

This control of oligopolistic industries was reflected in the fact that of the 414 corporations with assets above $25 million, 53 percent of these assets were in firms that were more than 50 percent owned by nonresidents: the figure for firms with assets below $25 million was 32 percent.

The immense profitability of American subsidiaries in Canada is grossly underestimated if one simply looks at the more than $1 billion a year in interest and dividends received from Canadian firms. Payments for management fees, royalties, franchises, advertising, rent, professional services, and so forth probably amount to nearly $500 million a year, although accurate statistics on these do not exist.

Very possibly an even larger source of profits (for which no statistics would be available) lies in the buying-and-selling policies of parents and subsidiaries. Thus, an American company controlling

2 *Canadian Privy Council Report of the Task Force on the Structure of Canadian Industry* (Ottawa: Queen's Printer, January 1968). These data and those that follow were taken from various pages of the report.

Canadian natural resources can pay a high price for these resources and show a large profit on the books of the subsidiary—or it may pay a low price and show the profits on its own books. Similarly, an American manufacturing firm that requires its Canadian subsidiary to purchase manufactured components from the parent company can follow pricing policies that can make the profits appear on either side of the border. This permits the company to use an optimum combination of tax loopholes in both countries.

It appears probable, however, that the greatest pressures exist for American corporate managers to maximize the parent company's profits. It is generally the profits of the parent upon which these managers' personal careers depend. Thus, a study of the National Industrial Conference Board showed that while manufactured component parts represented 35 percent of material costs for Canadian industries, they represented only 23 percent of material costs for American industries.

The results of this economic takeover have manifested themselves in the decreasing degree of independence both externally and internally in Canada's economic and political policies. Over the past ten years, Canada has been under constant pressure to follow the U.S. "line" on Vietnam more closely. U.S. subsidiaries have openly refused employment to U.S. immigrants who appear to be draft dodgers; Canada has not refused American nuclear weapons; U.S. subsidiaries, by taking orders from the parent company, follow U.S. State Department guidelines and partially subvert the Canadian government's attempts to increase trade with certain communist states.

Moreover, American control of the composition of Canadian investment results in a far less than optimally arranged industrial structure. American firms have literally made a "little America" of Canada's economy. The result in many industries is a large number of units each producing at a smaller than optimum scale. Canada, with a population roughly 10 percent that of the United States, gives its consumers an array of brand names that is virtually identical to that faced by the American consumer.

Perhaps in the long run, the worst evil of American ownership will be the complete elimination of the possibility for Canadians to achieve a more equitable distribution of wealth. Within a capitalist society, the primary means of redistributing wealth (at least in theory, if not in deed) have been the use or potential use of death duties, inheritance taxes, taxes on gifts and bequests, and capital-gains taxes. Because almost all Canadian assets owned by foreigners are owned by foreign corporations, and because the foreign corporations almost never die or divest themselves of their Canadian holdings, these methods can never substantially redistribute wealth.

Thus, an understanding of international economic transactions must be based on a knowledge of the relative power positions of the countries involved. A country's economic objectives and national policies will always be significantly influenced by its position in the international hierarchy of capitalist countries. (Socalist countries are discussed in Part IV.)

financing foreign transactions

In terms of volume, a country's most important kinds of foreign economic transactions are importing (the purchasing of commodities from foreigners) and exporting (the selling of commodities to foreigners). Imports and exports involve the exchange of different currencies and are, therefore, more complex than ordinary economic transactions. If an American business firm decides to import German beer, it faces a problem. The importer sells the beer in the United States for American dollars, but the German exporter must be paid in German deutschemarks (DMs).

Similarly, assume that the American Coca-Cola Company exports Coca-Cola to Germany. The German importer sells the Coca-Cola to Germans for DMs and with the proceeds pays its bill to the Coca-Cola Company. It pays in DMs, but the Coca-Cola Company wants to collect in dollars.

Now assume that the importing of beer and the exporting of Coca-Cola were the only economic transactions jointly involving Germans and Americans, and that Americans buy DM4,000 worth of beer and Germans buy $1,000 worth of Coca-Cola. If the rate at which DMs exchange for dollars were DM4 = $1, then all of the transactions could be easily facilitated. We shall trace through these simple transactions to show how foreign sales and purchases are financed.

The American beer importer will take a $1,000 check to his bank, say, the Bank of America, and exchange it for DM4,000 (because we have assumed that $1 exchanges for DM4). With the DM4,000, the importer can pay his debt to the German beer exporter.

Meanwhile, the German importer will take a check for DM4,000 to the Bank of America's German branch and exchange it for $1,000, with which he pays his debt to the Coca-Cola Company.

The Bank of America has engaged in two transactions. First it gave up DM4,000 in exchange for $1,000; then it gave up $1,000 in exchange for DM4,000. Thus, the two transactions cancel each other and the Bank of America is left with the same amount of both dollars and DMs. (In this simple example, we have ignored the fact that in each transaction the Bank of America will charge a fee for making the exchange, and will thereby add to its profits.) No dollars actually left the United States; nor did DMs actually leave Germany. It worked out exactly as though the American beer importer had paid the Coca-Cola Company and the German Coca-Cola importer had paid the beer exporter.

There are two reasons why our example worked out so neatly. First, the demand for *foreign exchange* (which is generally what foreign currencies are called) was exactly equal to the supply of foreign exchange. The demand for foreign exchange, it should be noted, arose from the import of foreign goods, while the supply of foreign exchange arose from the export of domestic goods. Second, the supply of and demand for foreign exchange were equal because the *exchange rate* at which dollars could be converted was $1 = DM4. There are then two important considerations in the financing of foreign transactions: (1) the number and magnitude of transactions giving rise to a demand for and supply of foreign exchange and (2) the rate at which dollars can be converted to foreign exchange, or the exchange rate between American dollars and the various foreign currencies. We shall consider each of these in turn.

the balance of payments and the demand for and supply of foreign exchange

We begin by taking the exchange rate as given and examining the international transactions that give rise to a demand for and supply of foreign exchange.

Our previous example gives us two very important types of transactions that create a demand for and a supply of foreign exchange. The export of Coca-Cola created a supply of foreign exchange, supplied by the German importer. The import of beer created a demand for foreign exchange, with which the German exporter could be paid.

There are many other types of transactions that perform the same functions. The *balance of payments* is a systematic accounting of all such transactions for one country for a given period of time, usually one year. Transactions are aggregated into different categories. The *current account* records all sales and purchases of goods and services between Americans and foreigners.

Table 32.1 summarizes the current account for 1970. All items on the left side of the table are transactions that created a supply of foreign exchange. The transactions listed on the right side created a demand for foreign exchange.

From the current-account transactions in 1970, the United States

TABLE

32.1

current account of u.s. balance of payments for 1970 (in billions of dollars)

TRANSACTIONS THAT CREATED A SUPPLY OF FOREIGN EXCHANGE		TRANSACTIONS THAT CREATED A DEMAND FOR FOREIGN EXCHANGE	
U.S. exports of merchandise	$42.0	U.S. imports of merchandise	$39.9
Foreign purchases of U.S. transportation, insurance and other private services	9.8	U.S. purchases of foreign transportation, insurance and other private services	9.5
U.S. income from private foreign investments	9.6	Foreign income from private investments in the U.S.	5.1
TOTAL	$61.4		$54.5
Net balance	$ 6.9		

Source: Federal Reserve *Bulletin* (April, 1971), p. 270.

earned $6.9 billion more foreign exchange than she spent. Other transactions were involved in the overall balance of payments, however. These are summarized in Table 32.2.

The most important of these other types of balance-of-payments entries are military spending (and sales) and federal government grants and investments in foreign countries on the one hand, and American private investment in foreign countries on the other. Because our worldwide military expenditures far exceed our sales of military equipment, and American capitalists always invest much more in foreign countries than foreigners invest in the United States, it is clear that these entries will create a net demand for foreign exchange. Since the early 1950s, these items have created a *larger* net demand for foreign exchange than the net supply of foreign exchange generated in the current account. As a consequence, the United States has had a deficit in its balance of payments. Strictly speaking, the balance of payments always "balances." This is because the net deficit generated in Tables 32.1 and 32.2 must be financed somehow. It has been financed by either (1) using up America's gold stock or (2) borrowing from foreigners (of which we shall say more in the following pages). If we had included the transactions that depleted the United States' gold reserves, and the transactions in which foreigners lent us enough to cover our deficit, then the balance of payments would have balanced. (The balance in this overall sense is merely a result of double-entry accounting. It should not confuse the reader. By saying that the balance of payments is in deficit, economists merely mean that the United States

TABLE
32.2

remainder of u.s. balance of payments for 1970
(in billions of dollars)

TRANSACTIONS THAT CREATED A SUPPLY OF FOREIGN EXCHANGE		TRANSACTIONS THAT CREATED A DEMAND FOR FOREIGN EXCHANGE	
Net balance carried forward from current account	$ 6.9	Remittances and pensions (net)	$ 1.4
Military sales	1.5	Military purchases abroad	4.8
Foreign investment in U.S.	4.4	U.S. government grants and investments abroad	3.5
		U.S. private investments abroad	6.4
		Change in U.S. liabilities to commercial banks abroad	6.5
		Errors and omissions	.9
Totals	$12.8		$23.5
Net balance			$10.7

Source: Federal Reserve Bulletin (April 1971), p. 270.

must use its gold or borrow from foreigners to finance its international transactions.)

From Table 32.2, we see that the $6.9 billion in foreign exchange earned in the current account was more than used up in these other types of transactions. In fact, in 1970, the United States incurred a deficit of $10.7 billion in her balance of payments. The deficit, considering only the transactions that were not part of the current account, was $17.6 billion. Of this sum, $6.5 billion was due to foreign commercial banks drawing down their balances in American banks. Military purchases abroad and U.S. government grants to foreigners accounted for $8.3 billion dollars, and American businessmen invested $6.4 billion abroad (which increased the value of American-owned foreign assets and investments to $166 billion).[3] To finance the $10.7 billion deficit, the United States gave up $3.3 billion in reserve assets (gold and claims on other currencies) and foreigners accepted $7.3 billion in American short-term IOUs.

Since 1945, the United States has nearly always exported more than she has imported, and therefore has had a favorable balance of trade (we have earned foreign exchange in the current account). This foreign exchange has been used to finance worldwide military ventures and corporate investments in other countries. But the

[3] Federal Reserve Bulletin (April 1971), p. 280.

financing of these transactions has used more foreign exchange than has been earned in current-account surpluses. Thus, Americans have had to come up with more money to finance military expenditures and foreign investments. The year 1970 was typical of what has happened nearly every year since 1950. The United States built up a foreign-exchange balance in current transactions, but militarism and foreign investment used much more foreign exchange than this balance would finance. The remainder was made up in two ways: the U.S. paid out gold, and foreigners were forced to extend low-cost loans to Americans. We shall examine each of these separately.

The drain on the U.S. gold stock is simple and easy to understand. When U.S. corporations and the government spend more than is earned from the export balance, some of the difference is paid out in gold. In 1957, the U.S. Treasury had $22.8 billion in gold stock. By 1969, this figure had fallen to $10.4 billion. In the 12 years between 1957 and 1969, about $12.4 billion of U.S. foreign investment was financed by exporting gold.[4]

The second source for financing excess foreign investments has been cheap foreign loans. To understand why foreigners *must* make these loans, we must discuss the role of the American dollar in the financing of international transactions.

the american dollar in international finance

With every country having a different currency, and some of the currencies having unstable values, it is necessary to have a currency with which to conduct international business. The American dollar is used far more extensively than any other country's currency for this purpose. The American dollar is, then, the currency of which other countries must keep a balance in order to facilitate their foreign financial transactions, just as the individual must keep a small balance of currency to finance his day-to-day transactions.

But the worldwide volume of international transactions has grown rapidly and continuously since World War II. This means that other countries have been forced continuously to build up their American dollar bank balances.

We have already seen, in Chapter 29, how the U.S. banking system can expand the money supply without cost. American businessmen take these dollars and send them to other countries in payment for their foreign investments. If U.S. currency were *not* the international medium of exchange, foreigners would immediately demand that the

---

[4] Figures taken from Federal Reserve *Bulletin* (September 1970), p. A75.

dollars be taken back in exchange for more U.S. exports or for gold. These commodity exports or gold exports would represent the *real* payment for the foreign resources U.S. corporations have taken over.

But because foreign countries must continuously build up American dollar balances if they are to continue to engage in international transactions, they are forced to keep them. This means they get *no real payment* for the resources they hand over to U.S. corporations. They are, in effect, extending low-cost loans which need never be repaid as long as the American dollar is the international medium of exchange. If the American dollar were not an important currency in international transactions, there would be no desire to hold American dollars and the costs to American businessmen of borrowing abroad would be substantially higher.

Between January 1950, and June 1970, the increase in the American "liquid liabilities to foreigners" was $37.3 billion dollars.[5] A large amount of this represents foreign investment for which no real payment (in exports or gold) was made. Although many other types of transactions are also included in this total, nevertheless, we estimate that over $30 billion was definitely in the category of *forced* foreign credit with which American corporations—almost without cost—financed foreign investments. In other words, America's role as world banker secured over $30 billions of loans for American foreign investment for which no payments in gold or commodity exports were ever made. Not only were there no net payments of these loans, but only the lowest, nominal interest charges were paid. It is obvious that being the world's banker has been lucrative for the United States.

the determination of exchange rates

We began our discussion of the balance of payments by assuming that the rate at which American dollars are exchanged for other currencies is given and fixed. We turn now to an examination of how this rate is determined.

If there were a free market for all currencies and the value of any currency were free to fluctuate, then the foreign-exchange rate would depend upon the demand for and supply of foreign exchange. The value of an American dollar, in relation to other currencies, would increase when the foreign demand for dollars exceeded the supply of dollars available to foreigners. Similarly, the value of a dollar would decrease if the foreign demand were less than the supply of

5 Data for 1950 to 1960 were taken from S. E. Harris, ed., *The Dollar in Crisis* (New York: Harcourt Brace Jovanovich, 1961), pp. 308–309; data for 1961 to 1970, were taken from Federal Reserve *Bulletin* (September 1970), p. A76.

dollars in international finance. The exchange rate would be in equilibrium when the demand for and supply of dollars to be exchanged for other currencies was equal, or when there was neither a surplus nor a deficit in the balance of payments.

To illustrate this, imagine that exports and imports are the only transactions that enter into the balance of payments. Assume, for example, that in our original illustration of the United States and Germany trading Coca-Cola and beer, that the exchange rate had been DM5 = $1. When the German importer of Coca-Cola purchased DM4,000 worth of Coca-Cola it would have bought him only $800 worth of Coca-Cola. However, had the American beer importer purchased $1,000 worth of beer he would have received DM5,000 worth of beer. The American demand for foreign exchange (DM5,000) would have exceeded the supply of foreign exchange (DM4,000). The same thing can be stated in terms of dollars: The foreign demand for dollars ($800) would have been less than the supply of dollars to foreigners ($1,000). The German balance of payments would show a surplus of DM1,000 while the American balance of payments would show a deficit of $200.

If nothing happens to alter demand or supply in either Germany or the United States, then the deficit can be eliminated only if the value of a dollar (in terms of DMs) declines. Conversely, the value of the deutschemark in terms of dollars would have to increase. This change in the exchange rate would tend to create an international balance for both countries. If, for example, the rate went to $1 = DM4, the German Coca-Cola importer would find that $1 worth of Coca-Cola now costs him DM4 rather than DM5, and he is likely to increase his purchases of it. The American importer of beer will find that DM1 worth of beer now costs him 25 cents rather than 20 cents, and he is likely to buy less beer. If these changes in quantities demanded (in both countries) are sufficiently large, the American deficit and the German surplus will both be eliminated.

Many economists have expressed the faith that if there were freely fluctuating exchange rates, then changes in exchange rates would induce large changes in exports and imports. These changes would automatically eliminate surpluses or deficits in the balance of payments. However, historically, the exchange rates for most currencies have not been free to fluctuate. The governments of most countries have fixed their exchange rates and, as a rule, have changed them only infrequently. Proponents of fixed exchange rates argue that flexible exchange rates would result in day-to-day fluctuations in currency values, which would make international commerce very uncertain. For example, the Coca-Cola company might export $1,000 worth of its product today when $1 = DM4, but next week, when the German importer pays the bill, the rate could be $1 = DM8. If this happened the German importer would become very reluctant to purchase more Coca-Cola in the future (because he had been forced to pay twice as much as he had anticipated paying).

With fixed exchange rates, a country cannot count on exchange-rate changes to eliminate surpluses or deficits in its balance of payments. Therefore, when a country experiences a surplus, it must accumulate large quantities of foreign exchange. But when it incurs a deficit, it must pay out large quantities of foreign exchange. Such fluctuations in foreign-exchange holdings necessitate large reserves of foreign exchange. Large reserves have been the only way for a country to be certain that it will be able to finance any deficits that might occur in its balance of payments.

Most of these exchange reserves in recent decades have been held in American dollars. We have already seen the advantage this bestows upon the American economy and American businessmen. It is, therefore, not surprising that American bankers have always favored fixed exchange rates.

recent international monetary crises

We have seen how the use of American dollars as the international medium of exchange has required that foreigners constantly increase their holdings of U.S. dollars to accommodate a constantly increasing volume of world trade. This has permitted the U.S. government to make enormous military expenditures in foreign countries and U.S. businessmen to purchase businesses and resources around the world in far greater quantities than could have been financed from current-account surpluses alone.

Once the processes of worldwide militarism and worldwide economic domination were set in motion, however, they had a momentum of their own. Neither the government nor the businessmen have attempted to limit these expenditures to an amount that could be financed out of current-account surpluses plus the increase in foreigners' desired holdings of dollars. Cold War propaganda and the lure of larger profits from foreign investments have propelled the government and the businessmen consistently to spend more dollars than foreigners have wished to hold.

In 1968, and again in early 1971, attempts by foreigners to convert their dollar holdings into gold or into other currencies created minor crises. Throughout the 1960s and early 1970s, it had been obvious that the size of the recurring American balance-of-payments deficit was too large. This meant that U.S. currency was *overvalued;* that is, in order to make the deficit manageable the value of the U.S. dollar should be decreased (or the value of undervalued currencies such as the German DM or the Japanese yen should be increased).

The problem was that in 1970 foreigners held $43.3 billion in American dollars.[6] If the value of the American dollar were decreased by 10 percent, these foreigners would suddenly lose the equivalent of about $4,330 million dollars. This large amount of wealth would simply evaporate. Consequently, if foreigners received the slightest hint that the American dollar was about to be devalued, they immediately sought to exchange their dollars for gold or other currencies before the devaluation could take place.

In the 1968 and early 1971 crises, the governments of the United States and the western European countries succeeded in convincing dollar holders that the exchange value of the dollar would be maintained. This averted a major crisis. But the problem remained. If the United States continued to spend lavishly on a worldwide military empire, and continued profligately to attempt to extend its worldwide economic hegemony, then the pressure of foreigners attempting to convert unwanted dollar balances into gold or other currencies would constantly present the threat of a worldwide run on the dollar any time the fear of devaluation became widespread. Most economists agreed that if such a "run" on American dollars were to develop, the international monetary structure would collapse. If this were to occur, foreign trade would undoubtedly be drastically reduced as it was after the international financial crisis of the early 1930s.

In the face of these dangers, President Nixon took drastic action on August 15, 1971. The fact that America's exports were substantially less than her imports for the first time in many years precipitated extreme policy measures. In order to end America's persistent balance-of-payments deficit the President did three things. First, he imposed a 10 percent tariff surcharge. In order to reduce demand for imports, Americans were forced to pay 10 percent more for all imported foreign goods. Second, the President announced a 90-day wage-price freeze (with wages frozen but leaving profits free to increase). This was designed mainly for domestic effects, but its foreign effect was to make American exports more competitive in foreign markets.

The third and most extreme measure taken by the President was to sever the direct link between the American dollar and gold. The American dollar had maintained a fixed exchange rate with other currencies by maintaining a fixed price of gold. As the value of gold in terms of other currencies was also fixed, this fixed the exchange rates between any two currencies. For example, if gold costs 35

6 Federal Reserve _Bulletin_ (April 1971), p. 270.

American dollars per ounce and also 15 British pounds per ounce, then the price (in American dollars) of one British pound would be fixed at $2.33.

When the President cut the tie between gold and the American dollar, the United States ceased having a fixed exchange rate. The value of the dollar in relation to other currencies was allowed to fluctuate according to supply and demand. It soon became apparent, however, that the central banks of various countries were prepared to step in and influence demand and supply, through their purchases and sales, in order to prevent sudden and drastic changes in the value of the dollar.

As of this writing (late 1971) the value of the American dollar has fallen nearly 10 percent in relation to many of the more important currencies. This means, of course, that holders of American dollars have lost nearly $4 billion. This seems certain to have an important impact in undermining the willingness of foreign businesses, governments and banks to hold American dollars as a key currency. The American government will doubtlessly do everything within its power to maintain the international status of the dollar, but the era of nearly costless financing of America's military empire and her global economic take-over, appears to be coming to an end. It may, however, take a considerable period of time before another currency (or currencies) is able to displace the American dollar.

The important issues, which are not yet resolved at this writing, are whether the United States will return to a fixed exchange rate once the dollar is devalued sufficiently, and whether fluctuations in the demand and supply of American dollars will permit an orderly devaluation. Many economists and businessmen believe that a freely fluctuating exchange rate may become unstable. If this instability becomes sufficiently severe, it could reduce world trade drastically.

The prospect of a significantly reduced volume of international trade raises the question of the merits of such trade. Why do nations engage in trade? In the next section we shall attempt to answer this question.

the gains from international trade

The most obvious reason why nations engage in foreign trade is that many commodities cannot be grown or produced in certain regions of the world. Without foreign trade, Americans would be unable to purchase coffee, cocoa, tea, coconuts, bananas, or any of a large number of commodities that cannot be produced in the United States. In addition to these consumer commodities, the United States depends heavily on imports for many of the most important minerals. In the late 1960s, for example, imports of iron ore were 43 percent of that which was mined domestically; for copper, the figure was 18 percent; for lead, 131 percent; for zinc, 140 percent; for bauxite, 638 percent; and for petroleum, 31 percent. This partial listing alone indicates how crucial imports of agricultural products and minerals are to the American economy.

The United States can also gain from importing manufactured commodities if the *relative costs* of producing two commodities differ between the United States and some other country. To illustrate this, let us return to the example of beer and Coca-Cola.

Assume that the United States and Germany each produces all of the beer and Coca-Cola that they consume domestically. Assume further that in the United States, the average annual production per worker of beer is 5,000 gallons and of Coca-Cola is 7,500 gallons. Assume further that in Germany the figures are 4,000 gallons (beer) 3,000 gallons (Coca-Cola). Table 32.3 shows hypothetical prices for the two commodities (German prices are given in dollars for easier comparison) in the two countries. These prices reflect ratios of labor productivity.

From these figures, we see that the United States is more efficient in the production of both beer and Coca-Cola. Economists would say that the United States has an *absolute advantage* in the production of both commodities. It might seem that the United States would be better off not to import either beer or Coca-Cola from Germany because it can produce both more efficiently. This is not true, however. It would pay the United States to import beer and export Coca-Cola because the United States has a comparative advantage in the production of Coca-Cola and Germany has a comparative advantage in the production of beer.

The existence of a comparative advantage depends on the *relative* costs of the two commodities, not the absolute efficiency in producing them. In the United States, beer costs 50 percent *more* to produce than Coca-Cola, whereas in Germany, beer costs 25 percent *less* than Coca-Cola. Therefore, relative to the cost of producing

| TABLE |
| 32.3 |

price per gallon of beer and coca-cola in the united states and germany before trade takes place (in dollars)

UNITED STATES		GERMANY	
Beer	$0.60	Beer	$0.75
Coca-Cola	0.40	Coca-Cola	1.00

Coca-Cola, Germany is more efficient in producing beer. Similarly, in the United States, Coca-Cola costs 33 percent *less* than beer, whereas in Germany, Coca-Cola costs 33 percent *more* than beer. Therefore, relative to the cost of producing beer, the United States is more efficient in producing Coca-Cola.

Assume that the United States persuades Germany to exchange beer for American Coca-Cola *at the prices prevailing in Germany.* Some American workers will be shifted from beer production to Coca-Cola production. For each worker who is transferred from producing beer to producing Coca-Cola, the United States will lose 5,000 gallons of beer (which the worker will no longer produce) and gain 7,500 gallons of Coca-Cola (which he will begin to produce). This Coca-Cola can be sold in Germany for $7,500 (because the price of Coca-Cola is $1 per gallon in Germany). Then, paying the German price of 75 cents per gallon for beer, the United States can use the proceeds to purchase 10,000 gallons of beer.

The final result of this series of events will be that for every worker in the United States shifted from beer production to Coca-Cola production, the United States will lose 5,000 gallons of domestically produced beer but gain 10,000 gallons of German produced beer. Obviously, the United States will be better off after the trade. But the prices at which the two countries traded are identical to the German before-trade prices. This means that the United States received all of the gains from trade and Germany received no gains at all.

Assume now that Germany persuades the United States to trade at the prices prevailing in the United States. Then Germany will receive all of the gains from trade. When the Germans shift a worker from the production of Coca-Cola to the production of beer the worker will produce 4,000 gallons of beer (rather than 3,000 gallons of Coca-Cola). This beer will be sold in the United States (at 60 cents per gallon) for $2,400. With the proceeds of this sale, the Germans can purchase 6,000 gallons of Coca-Cola (at the rate of 40 cents per gallon). Thus, if trade occurs at the U.S. prices, the Germans will shift men from the production of Coca-Cola to the production of beer which they will export to the United States. In doing so, they will lose 3,000 gallons of domestically produced Coca-Cola for every man so shifted, but they will gain 6,000 gallons of American produced Coca-Cola. Obviously, this situation benefits the Germans.

From these examples, two conclusions can be drawn: (1) If the relative costs of producing two commodities in two countries differ, then trade can benefit one or both of the countries, and (2) if the prices at which trade takes place are the same as those prevailing in one country before trade began, then that country receives none of the gains from trade and the other country receives all of the gains.

We can draw a third conclusion which is undoubtedly obvious from the preceding discussion: If the ratio of prices at which trade takes place lies somewhere between the price ratios in the two countries, then both countries will share in the gains from trade. If, in the beer–Coca-Cola example, the United States and Germany traded at the rate of one gallon of beer equals one gallon of Coca-Cola, then both countries would benefit from trade. The reader can calculate the gains in each country as workers are shifted to export production. Such a calculation will verify the fact that both countries would benefit from trade at a price ratio that lies between the two domestic price ratios.

When two countries engage in trade, the one that is able to exert the greater bargaining power will succeed in pushing the trade prices closer to the ratio of prices and production costs of the other country. In doing this, the more powerful country will reap most of the gains from trade. Many economists have collected evidence to show that in the trade that takes place between advanced, industrialized countries and underdeveloped, agricultural countries, the industrialized countries reap nearly all of the benefits.[7]

the case for free trade

To what extent ought a country to engage in international trade? Nearly 200 years ago, the classical economists (particularly David Ricardo) developed the analysis of comparative advantage and correctly identified the economic gains that two trading partners can secure. On the basis of this analysis, they concluded that as long as any persons in either of the two countries desired to engage in further trade, then it was possible to reap more gains from trade. In practice, this meant that the government ought to place *no restrictions on trade*. People should be free to trade to any extent they wished. This conclusion was an integral part of the general laissez-faire policy advocated by the classical economists.[8]

Over the past 200 years, most orthodox economists have advocated free trade. They have extended and refined their analyses of comparative advantage and the gains from trade, but they have not altered the essential argument. They have consistently contended that any restrictions on international trade will reduce the volume of

[7] See, for example, U.N. Economic Commission for Latin America, *The Economic Development of Latin America and Some of Its Problems* (New York, 1949); Raoul Prebisch, "The Role of Commercial Policies in Underdeveloped Countries," *American Economic Review* (May 1959); and Hans Singer, "The Distribution of Gains Between Investing and Borrowing Countries," *American Economic Review* (May 1950).

[8] See Chapter 4.

trade, and that any reduction of volume will reduce the gains from trade. Therefore, most economists have concluded that restrictions on international trade reduce a nation's economic welfare.

This consistent advocacy of free trade might seem surprising in view of the fact that only rarely during the past 200 years have the governments of the major capitalist countries pursued such a policy. Most of the time, they have erected a wall of tariffs to keep out foreign goods. A tariff is a tax on an import, which forces the importer to charge a higher price to the general public in order to pay the tariff. Thus, the tariff is really a tax paid by the consumer of the import.

Tariffs have usually been imposed for two reasons. First, in the nineteenth century, the American government used the tariff as its chief source of tax revenue. Second, industries that must compete with foreign producers for the domestic market have lobbied for tariffs to protect their monopoly power from foreign competition. Because neither of these reasons would be particularly appealing to the general public, many arguments with greater popularity have been put forward. Historically, there have been three very common arguments for tariffs in the United States. Economists consider them all to be fallacious. We shall examine each.

1. It is often argued that tariffs protect American workers from competition from foreign workers who are paid very low wages. This argument concludes that tariffs maintain higher wage rates for American workers. While free trade may hurt the workers in industries that are undersold by foreign competitors (the workers will probably have to transfer to new occupations), it should raise the overall wage level. This is because, as we have seen, the total output available for consumption increases after trade. It seems unlikely that workers would not share in this increase.

2. It is sometimes proposed that tariffs are ideal taxes because the foreign exporter pays the tax. As we have already noted, however, the American importer is forced to raise the price he charges his American customers. Therefore, the American general public pays most of the tax in the form of higher prices for the commodities it consumes.

3. Finally, there are the campaigns to "buy American products" to "keep money in the United States." This simplistic argument assumes that when imports are purchased, money leaves the country, and that if they had not been purchased consumers would have bought American-produced commodities. It is argued that purchasing foreign products deprives American businessmen of sales and American workers of jobs. The problem with this argument is that it ignores the fact that when the United States engages in foreign trade commodities are *exported* as well as imported. The foreign demand

for U.S. exports increases the sales of American businessmen and creates jobs for American workers.

There are other arguments for tariffs, some not so obviously fallacious as those discussed above. Most economists agree, however, that in a powerful, industrialized economy such as that of the United States, there are really no convincing arguments for tariffs. The few problems that tariffs might help to solve (e.g., industrial relocations, regional economic depressions, and general underemployment) could certainly be solved more efficaciously by other, more direct government policies.

What is true for industrialized countries, however, is not necessarily true for underdeveloped countries. Many underdeveloped countries have become suppliers of raw materials and agricultural products for industrial countries. They generally receive such low prices for their exports that their standard of living remains abysmally low. If they engage in free trade, small local manufacturing industries cannot hope to compete with foreign giants. As a consequence, industrialization takes place very slowly, if at all. These countries would certainly be justified in placing some kind of restrictions on imports as an aid to industrialization. The issues involved in the relationship between advanced, industrialized countries and underdeveloped countries will be considered in the next chapter.

summary

International economic transactions differ from those within national boundaries. The two main differences are (1) different currencies are involved and must be exchanged, and (2) differing economic and political relations exist among nations, with some dominant, others subordinate, and others in intermediate positions.

The balance of payments is an accounting of all transactions between the residents of one country and the rest of the world. It summarizes the country's sources of foreign exchange and the uses to which the foreign exchange is put. The fact that the American dollar has been widely used as an international currency has helped to finance a worldwide military network as well as an ever-increasing private economic empire acquired through American investment abroad. However, recurring deficits in the American balance of payments forced President Nixon to take steps, on August 15, 1971, which have led to a devaluation of the American dollar in relation to other major currencies. This is likely to reduce the acceptability of the American dollar as an international medium of exchange.

Economists have shown that if the ratio costs of production (or prices) differ between two countries, then both of the countries can gain from trading with each other. Most arguments for tariffs in powerful, industrialized countries are either fallacious, or fail to point out that economically more efficacious means can be used to achieve any end for which a tariff was intended. In underdeveloped countries, a stronger case can be made for trade restrictions.

chapter 33
economic underdevelopment: natural causes or imperialism?

In Chapter 31, the problems of economic growth in developed industrial economies were considered. In economies that have not industrialized, the problems of economic growth are substantially and qualitatively different from those examined in Chapter 31. Before meaningful growth in per capita output and income can take place in these economies, they must undertake industrialization.

The economic, social, and political obstacles to industrialization are different from the problems of advanced industrial countries. Economic growth in the developed countries means mere incremental additions to output within an established structure. Development of the underdeveloped countries means basic social, political, and structural economic changes to lay the foundations for growth.

It is, therefore, necessary to devote an additional chapter to the question of economic development. The countries of the world are commonly divided into three groups: (1) socialist countries, (2) industrially developed capitalist countries, and (3) underdeveloped capitalist countries, or the *Third World* countries. It is with the latter that we shall be concerned in this chapter.

facts of economic underdevelopment

There are at least two generally accepted definitions of an *under-developed* country, one based on an economic index and the other based on certain distinguishing characteristics. The economic index generally employed is average income per person (GNP divided by population). According to this criterion, a country with an average income per person of less than some amount, say, $200 or $300 per year, is classified as underdeveloped.

The word *underdeveloped,* it must be emphasized, has misleading sociological connotations. For example, there is no correlation between level of income and level of cultural or social development. Obviously, ancient Greece or Egypt or China had very highly developed cultures and very low average income levels. Further, an average may hide wide disparities in individual incomes. For example, Kuwait has one of the highest levels of average income per head; but most of the income is concentrated in the hands of a few very rich persons, and there is an enormous gulf between the very rich and the very poor (despite Kuwait's much-publicized welfare handouts). The high average income per Kuwaiti is solely the result of this little country's oil resources, and, therefore, one cannot assume that it is highly developed in an overall sense.

Dissatisfaction with the use of a single, purely economic measure of underdevelopment has led some students of the subject to suggest a definition based on several distinguishing characteristics of under-developed countries: (1) low income per person, (2) the existence of a very high proportion (often 80 percent or more) of the population engaged in agriculture, (3) a low level of techniques used in production, (4) a low level of education, and (5) a low level of capital formation.

According to any definition of underdeveloped and developed, *the fact is that more than 50 percent of the population of the capitalist, or private-enterprise, world live in countries that can be classified as underdeveloped.* The enormity of the problem is indicated by the estimate that to raise the incomes of that portion of the world's population living in these countries to an average of only $200 per person per year (less than one-tenth of the average American income), about $85 billion of aid per year would be needed.[1]

[1] See Frederic Benham, *Economic Aid to Underdeveloped Countries* (London: Oxford University Press, 1961).

Among private-enterprise, or capitalist, countries in the lowest category, with income per person less than $100 a year (and mostly agrarian and lacking in technology, education, or capital) fall India, most of Asia, and most of Africa. In the second category, with income per person between $100 and $300 a year (and still very underdeveloped in all other indexes), are most of Latin America, North Africa, Indonesia, and the Philippines. In the third category ($300–$600; still very poor, but slightly developed in some aspects) are a few Latin American countries, the Union of South Africa, Greece, and Spain. The fourth category ($600–$1,500; well developed in many aspects) includes Israel, Australia and New Zealand, Japan, and most of western Europe. In a category by themselves are Canada and the United States with over $2,500 income per person per year. (Kuwait and Qatar are also listed in this category, but these are tiny areas sitting on top of oil wells with most of the income going to a few sheiks.)

In the advanced capitalist countries, workers' wages have grown greatly in the last 100 years. But conditions in most of the capitalist world, its underdeveloped part, have shown little or no improvement, and incomes remain at incredibly low levels. Most African and Asian incomes are less than one-tenth, and most Latin American incomes are about one-fifth, of the average incomes in the advanced capitalist countries. In fact, many of them are not only below poverty but also below subsistence levels. "Two-thirds of the inhabitants of the underdeveloped countries of the Third World do not get the essential minimum of 2,500 calories per day; the expectation of life for many of them is less than half that in the highly developed countries."[2]

The gap between rich and poor is reflected in the fact that in 1964, two-thirds of the world's population produced only about 25 percent of world output. At the same time, the United States alone (with only 6 percent of world population) produced about 30 percent of world output.

And the gap is widening.

In the whole period 1953–1964, the advanced capitalist countries showed rates of growth twice those of the underdeveloped capitalist countries.[3] Thus, the advanced capitalist countries outproduced the underdeveloped ones (in product per person) by 10:1 in 1950, but by 11:1 in 1960, and by almost 12:1 in 1969.[4]

[2] Perre Jalee, *The Pillage of the Third World* (New York: Monthly Review Press, 1965), p. 8.

[3] Ibid., p. 11.

[4] Jalee, loc. cit., and current U.N. data.

colonialism and neocolonialism

It will help us to understand the current economic, social, and political conditions of underdeveloped countries if we examine, briefly, some aspects of their history. In particular, we are interested in their relationships with the economically more advanced countries over the last several centuries.

From the fifteenth century onward, the developing capitalist economies of Europe grew economically and militarily at a rate then unparalleled in human history. From the fifteenth to the nineteenth centuries, they slowly came to dominate much of the rest of the world. They plundered, enslaved, and ruled so as to extract the maximum from their subjects.

Such havoc was created that ancient and culturally advanced civilizations disappeared, as in Peru and West Africa; and progress was set back hundreds of years by the destruction of native industries, as in India. On the other side, the plunder was so great that it constituted the main element in the formation of European capital and provided the foundation for prosperous trade and eventual industrialization.

By the end of the nineteenth century, almost all of the present underdeveloped countries were under the colonial rule of the more advanced countries. The imperialist countries invested in the colonial countries at astoundingly high profit rates, primarily because of a cheap labor supply and an enforced lack of competition. The capital was mainly invested in extractive industries, which exported raw materials to the imperial country. In the imperial country, the cheap raw materials were profitably turned into manufactured goods, part of which were exported back (tariff free) to the colonial country.

The tariff-free imported finished goods generally completed through competition the destruction (often begun by plunder) of the colonial country's manufacturing industries. An example of this may be seen in colonial India, especially in its textile industry:

> Foreign trade statistics best show the effects of "deindustrialization."
> India, still an exporter of manufactured products at the end of the
> eighteenth century, becomes an importer. From 1815 to 1832, India's
> cotton exports dropped by 92 per cent. In 1850, India was buying
> one quarter of Britain's cotton exports. All industrial
> products shared this fate.
> The ruin of the traditional trades and crafts was the result of
> British commercial policy.[5]

The development of the colonial areas was thus held back by the imperialist countries, while the development of the imperialist countries was greatly speeded up by the flow of plunder and profits from the colonies. The exception that proves the rule is Japan. Japan escaped colonialism as a result of several more or less accidental factors. Thus, she was able independently to industrialize and develop her own advanced capitalist economy. Japan achieved this alone among the countries of Asia, Africa, and Latin America because the others had all been reduced to colonies and had their further development prevented.

The half-century from 1890 to World War II was the peak period of colonialism, when all the world was divided amongst the western European and North American powers. In the late 1940s and 1950s, a new era began, with formal independence achieved by hundreds of millions of people throughout Asia and Africa as the result of struggles fomented by the impact of two World Wars, the Russian and Chinese revolutions, and the long pent-up pressures for liberation. The day of open colonialism is over, but the pattern still holds by which the ex-colonial countries export food or raw materials. In fact, the underdeveloped countries are often dependent mainly on exports of just one product, and they still import most of their finished goods. Foreign investment still dominates their industries. Moreover, most foreign capital invested in the less developed countries still goes into raw-materials production.[6] Because of the continuance of the underlying colonial economic pattern, we are justified in describing this situation as *neocolonialism,* in spite of formal political independence.

In fact, formal independence has changed the essential economic relationships very little. On the one side are all the underdeveloped newly independent countries, still under foreign economic domination, still facing all the old obstacles to development. On the other side are the advanced capitalist countries, still extracting large profits from the dependent Third World. The imperialist group includes all those who extract profits by trade and investment. Thus, it includes most of western Europe, Japan, and the United States. Neocolonial profits from the underdeveloped countries flow even to countries such as Sweden and Switzerland that never held colonial power over any underdeveloped country.

[5] Charles Bettleheim, *India Independent* (New York: Monthly Review Press, 1968), p. 47. Also see Romesh Dutt, *The Economic History of England* (7th ed.; London: Routledge & Kegan Paul, 1950), pp. viii–x.

[6] See, for example, United Nations, *International Flow of Private Capital, 1948–1952* (New York: United Nations, 1954).

Although there are still cases of direct occupation (e.g., the Portuguese colonies in Africa), most neocolonial control comes through economic and monetary penetration. This ranges from blatant forms such as subsidies and military supplies to highly complex monetary agreements. It also seems to be characteristic that independence is granted to small territories, tiny divisions of former colonial domains. Thus, they have no political or economic power with which to resist continued domination.

It should also be noted that the economic control is often not direct but built up in a complex pyramid. For example, some American companies directly invest in Northeast Brazil. More control of that area, however, is achieved through American domination of major southern Brazilian companies which, in turn, buy controlling interests in companies in the Northeast. Still more control is achieved through American domination of some western European companies which, in turn, own most of some major Brazilian firms or directly own some of the local firms in the Northeast.

obstacles to development

Is overpopulation the primary obstacle to economic development? This view is widely held by the average man in the street, many newspaper reporters, even some university professors. Little systematic evidence is presented to substantiate it. Most generally, proponents merely point to the vast number of poor and starving people in India as an example. Even such an eminent "economist" as Robert S. McNamara (former president of Ford Motor Company and former U.S. secretary of defense) asserts that: "The greatest single obstacle to the economic and social advancement of the majority of the peoples in the underdeveloped world is rampant population growth."[7]

The important point to note about McNamara's ideology is that it tells the hungry people that the "greatest single obstacle" to their development is their own animal sexual desires. The function of this ideology is thus identical to that of the theory that underdevelopment is due to racial inferiority, the laziness and/or stupidity of "the natives." It provides the perfect defense to the suspicion of these peoples that their problems are due to antiquated social systems,

[7] Robert S. McNamara, "Introduction" to H. Gray and Shanti Tangri, eds., Economic Development and Population Growth, A Conflict? (Lexington, Mass.: Raytheon/Heath, 1970). All of the Western experts in the collection simply assume (or present inadequate proofs of) McNamara's ideology.

rapacious ruling classes, and, above all, foreign domination and exploitation.

If one turns to the facts, there is no evidence that high population density is the prime cause of underdevelopment. More precisely, there is *no* statistically significant correlation between high population density and low income per person. On the contrary, many countries with high incomes per person also have high population densities. For example, Belgium has 816 people per square mile, West Germany has 624, and the United Kingdom has 588. India has only 406 people per square mile, and most of the underdeveloped countries have much lower population densities.

In fact, we find many cases of concomitant successful development with rapid population increase. The highest recorded rate of population growth over a long period occurred in the United States during the years 1850–1950, but because U.S. production also grew at record rates America not only became a developed country but also had record growth rates of output *per person,* and thus individual welfare improved.

Of course, if a country is standing still economically, any growth of population is a terrible problem. We do not deny that overpopulation can be a problem, but only maintain that it is always *relative* to growth of output. The basic problems are seen when we try to explain why output is rising so slowly in the undeveloped countries. Although population is a problem, it is secondary to these larger problems, and exclusive focus on it tends to hide the more important problems.

Moreover, it turns out that the key to reducing population growth is development of industrialization and urbanization. A rural family with a primitive technology finds young children useful for many tasks. An urban family in an industrialized country sees children as an economic burden until they have undergone a long education. Furthermore, birth-control information is much more effective in an urban setting in which a woman may find cultural interests outside the home and needs family planning to develop her own independent life. Thus, all the developed areas from the United States to the Soviet Union have witnessed rapid declines in birth rates as the agrarian sector has shrunk and education and culture have spread, as a result of economic development.

Another theory of underdevelopment claims that the underdeveloped nations are all those that by accident have relatively few natural resources on their territories. Yet the underdeveloped countries in 1965 provided 37.5 percent of the total output of raw materials in the capitalist world, including the bulk of many strategic materials. This is certainly a large enough absolute amount for a solid industrial base. But the underdeveloped countries do not produce anything like 37.5 percent of manufactured goods. In fact, most of their raw materials are taken away to the advanced capitalist countries, and are there manufactured into finished goods (some of them being sold back at a high profit to the underdeveloped countries).

It appears, therefore, that the main obstacles to development are *not* natural or biological factors inherent in the underdeveloped countries. The main obstacles are *not* sexual desires and procreation, laziness, low intelligence, or lack of natural resources. The obstacles reside in the present social relationships of man to man: the fact that all of the peasants' and workers' surplus over immediate needs is extracted from them by the landlords, moneylenders, tax collectors, and foreign corporations. We shall show that the native ruling classes use their high incomes for luxury consumption and that most of the foreign corporations' enormous profits are removed from the country.

As a result there is a lack of capital for investment in development. The lack of capital (and lack of nonhuman power per person) *is* correlated with low income per person.[8] The lack of capital means not only little construction but also little new equipment, little technological improvement. It also means few funds available for education and training, let alone research. The lack of capital also means that millions of workers cannot be employed at a sufficient rate of profit and thus are left unemployed or underemployed. Thus, it is the social relations (and their consequences) that are the real obstacles to development.

As an example, consider the present revolution in agriculture in several underdeveloped countries. In this "green revolution," new types of grains have been introduced, especially in India and Pakistan. They have brought much higher yields, and thus one of the technical barriers to feeding the population seems to be falling. To make efficient use of the new processes and output, however, requires large mechanized farms. Indeed, small peasants are being evicted in growing numbers to make way for large agricultural enterprises. The dispossessed peasants are swelling the ranks of the unemployed in the cities. At the same time, complaints are heard from the large farm owners that there is overproduction of grain relative to the small money demand of the poor. Thus, the social relationships form a barrier to technological development.

It is a mere truism to say that growth would be faster if the underdeveloped countries had more capital, more technology, and more education and training. In fact, for many underdeveloped capitalist countries, the problem is not a low rate of growth of income

[8] See David Landes, *The Unbound Prometheus* (Cambridge: Cambridge University Press, 1969).

per person but no growth at all. Aggregate income does not grow much faster than (and maybe not as fast as) the population. Moreover, a complete change is needed from a rural, agrarian economy to an urban, industrialized economy. The issue, then, is how to *begin* to develop, how to start from little or no growth at all, and how to change the whole economic structure.

We shall argue that the obstacles are mainly institutional: (1) an internal ruling class that spends much of its income on luxuries and government revenues on unnecessary public monuments or military expenditures, (2) foreign trade on very poor terms, which creates an exploitative economic dependence and which imports the wrong items for development, and (3) foreign investment in low-priority areas with high profits sent abroad. Notice that this is quite opposite to most Western views. Some, we have seen, argue that the trouble is too much sex and too much population, or laziness, or stupidity.

internal obstacles to development

Let us begin with the internal obstacles to development created by the underdeveloped countries' social systems. The typical situation finds millions of peasants engaged in subsistence farming, obligated to pay high rents to landlords, high interest to moneylenders, and high taxes to local and national governments. From his original small net product, the peasant usually pays more than one-half to meet these obligations, thus retaining hardly enough for his bare subsistence and none for major improvement or investment.

The landlords and moneylenders take much of the surplus from the peasant and spend it on conspicuous luxury consumption. If they reinvest any, their extreme conservatism prompts them to invest in more land or to send it to some safe foreign country; little, if any, is invested in industry. The governments are mostly dominated by a small elite of wealthy landlords and merchants (in turn, often foreign dominated), who have little motivation to invest government funds in constructive projects; in fact, the advent of industrial capitalism would undermine their power. Most government revenues are spent on military goods and services for the purpose of internal repression. Governments spend some on showcase projects (e.g., sports arenas) or, as in Venezuela, in beautification of the capital city. The little that is invested constructively is usually for roads or ports to serve the needs of foreign investors.

The reactonary ruling groups in the underdeveloped capitalist countries are generally supported by the advanced capitalist countries (including the U.S. State Department). It is *not* that the U.S.

State Department *wants* backwardness and governments dominated by reactionary landlords and military cliques. On the contrary, the U.S. government would undoubtedly be happier with rapidly developing liberal capitalist countries (with American firms having most of the development investments). The problem is that these areas have only very few and very weak native capitalists who are linked by blood and marriage to the landlords and militarists. The countries are very much a part of the international commercialized capitalist market, but they have no steam to develop their own dynamic capitalism and thus they remain appendages of the advanced capitalist countries.

Not only is there no strong group willing to build a liberal capitalism in these countries, but also the real political alternative is usually a left-leaning socialist government. Plans for rapid development have been an essential part of socialist programs, as with the new socialist government of Chile. But these socialist development programs have been violently attacked by the U.S. State Department. In Brazil and Greece and several other countries, very mild socialist governments (whose practical measures only *helped* native small capitalists and were not yet even contemplating socialism) were overthrown by military coups supported by the CIA. Thus, the real choice in the underdeveloped countries has not been between landlords and militarists versus liberal capitalists, but between landlords and militarists (and a few native capitalists) versus socialist movements (composed of workers and peasants and students). In every case so far, the United States has chosen to support reactionary landlords and militarists such as Franco or Ky or Thieu.

the effects of foreign trade on underdeveloped countries

The colonial era left the economies of the Third World countries very dependent on foreign demand, and consequently very sensitive to the foreign business cycle of expansion and depression. It is also a fact that international investments and trade in primary products (i.e., in raw materials, both agricultural and mineral) show the greatest fluctuations. "It follows that any country whose economy is intimately dependent on foreign investment or whose trade is greatly dependent on primary commodities will be seriously affected by swings of business arising outside its own borders."[9]

9 League of Nations, *Economic Stability in the Post-war World* (Geneva: League of Nations, 1945), p. 103.

This dependence is recognized in the underdeveloped countries. The government of Ceylon states: "The economy of Ceylon depends almost entirely on its export in tea, rubber and coconut products. . . . About 80 percent of the people are employed directly or indirectly in the production and handling of these exports."[10] The government of Burma says explicitly: ". . . the most important source of unemployment in Burma is a decline in prices of raw materials caused by the depression generated elsewhere."[11]

The statistics for many countries, both developed and under-developed, show that (1) a high proportion of the demand for their national product is the demand for exports, and (2) the exports to the United States constitute a high proportion of the total export demand. Thus, the United States often absorbs more than one-half, and always more than one-third, of the exports of Canada, Brazil, Chile, Mexico, the Philippines, and others.[12]

In addition to the special place of dominance of the United States vis-à-vis the underdeveloped Third World, there is some data bearing on the trade relations of all the developed capitalist countries with the Third World.[13] First, in the underdeveloped countries, there is rapid growth in production *only* of those raw materials and food products exported to the imperialist countries. Production of goods for internal use in the Third World grows very slowly, if at all.

Second, 73.5 percent of the total trade of the developed capitalist countries is with each other. The continued dependence of the underdeveloped countries, however, is reflected in the fact that fully 74 percent of *their* total trade is with the developed countries. Between 1948 and 1964, there were three important trends: "(1) The commercial growth of the imperialist countries was much greater in value than that of the Third World . . . , (2) the imperialist countries have come to depend less on the Third World for their exports, and (3) the latter has become more dependent on the countries of the capitalist group."[14]

These data also confirm the picture of the underdeveloped countries as raw-material exporters and finished-goods importers. Detailed examination "shows that the trade of the Third World is wildly out of balance: 85 percent of its exports consists of raw materials and another 5 percent of common metals, products of the first state of smelting. Only 10 percent of the total consists of

[10] United Nations, Department of Economic Affairs, *National and International Measures for Full Employment* (New York: United Nations, 1949), p. 42.

[11] Ibid., p. 21.

[12] See annual reports for all countries in International Monetary Fund, *International Financial Statistics.* (Washington, D.C.: IMF, published annually)

[13] Jalee, op. cit., pp. 25–55.

[14] Ibid., p. 32.

manufactured goods, most of which are textiles. Imports, on the other hand, are predominantly manufactured goods (60 percent of the total)."[15] Because most of the manufactured imports are consumer goods, such a pattern can never lead to development, only to continued dependence.

The situation of dependence is still more exaggerated for each underdeveloped country taken by itself. Each tends to export only one or two goods and to trade with only one or two buyers (so that the buyers can easily exert monopoly power). "For the vast majority of Third World countries the range of products is as narrow as possible; one, or two, or three products often providing three-quarters, or even more, of the trade of a country. The number of countries selling and buying is also very restricted; a single imperialist country usually occupies such a dominant position that it can exercise every kind of pressure."[16] It should be emphasized that the only cases where the former colonial master has not retained control of the Third World countries are cases where control has shifted to the United States, for example, all of Latin America, Vietnam, and parts of Africa.

In contrast, in recent years the developed capitalist countries' exports are only 30 percent raw materials and 70 percent manufactured goods.[17] In fact, the international division of labor is becoming more and more pronounced, rather than equalized. That is to say, the developed countries are producing a larger and larger percentage of the manufactured goods of the capitalist world, and the underdeveloped Third World countries are producing a larger and larger percentage of the raw materials.

There is also a trend toward a worsening balance of trade for the Third World. This trend results from the fact that in the last fifteen to twenty years international prices of most products have risen, but prices of most primary products have fallen. Because Third World countries mainly export primary goods, they are receiving lower prices, or less and less in each exchange of goods. The developed capitalist countries are receiving higher prices for their finished goods, or more and more in each exchange. Hence, the foreign exchange of the underdeveloped countries is drained off, their development is retarded, and their balance-of-trade positions are further deteriorated.

Another aspect of the worsening international-payments situation arises from Western control of so-called invisible trade, or services. Over 90 percent of world shipping is controlled by the developed

---

[15] Ibid., p. 33.

[16] Ibid., p. 43.

[17] United Nations, *Statistical Yearbook* (New York, U.N., published annually).

capitalist countries. Between 1951 and 1961, they increased the shipping rates paid by underdeveloped countries by about 60 percent. The countries of Asia, Africa, and Latin America pay over $2 billion a year in shipping costs and insurance payments. Most of this money accrues to the developed capitalist countries.

We have noted that in recent years the value of the trade among the industrialized capitalist countries has grown much more rapidly than their trade with the Third World. As a result, the Third World's share in the trade of the developed capitalist countries fell from 32 percent in 1948 to 23 percent in 1964.[18]

Do the developed capitalist countries really need the trade of the underdeveloped world as much today as previously? The percentage decline in trade suggests a lessened importance. This was a period, however, of rapidly rising world trade; the absolute amount of trade between the two groups *rose* from $12 billion in 1948 to more than $25 billion in 1964. Furthermore, almost all of the increase in trade among countries in the industrialized capitalist bloc was in manufactured goods. While some of these exchanges are urgent, most of them merely increase efficiency; more expensive substitutes could easily be arranged (and, of course, there is a heavy flow of luxury consumer goods, which could be ended without causing permanent damage).

The situation is quite different in the trade of the industrialized capitalist bloc with the underdeveloped Third World. This trade is vital and irreplaceable. When developed capitalist countries import major food products and raw materials, they realize that these imports are very important. The food products are essential parts of the diets of Westerners, and the raw materials are indispensable for their factories. The manufactured goods which the underdeveloped countries buy are needed desperately because these countries do very little manufacturing themselves.

foreign investment

Much the same picture emerges if we look at American foreign investment. It is often argued that this investment channels American dollars into underdeveloped countries. These dollars, it is claimed, can then be used to finance industrialization in the underdeveloped countries. The data, however, do not confirm this argument.

The U.S. Department of Commerce has provided a partial breakdown of U.S. investment in different geographical areas. Interesting

18 Jalee, op. cit., p. 53.

differences are documented for the period 1950–1965. In Europe, U.S. corporations made direct investments of $8.1 billion and transferred $5.5 billion of profit from their European investments to the United States, for a net flow of 2.6 billion U.S. dollars into this advanced capitalist area. Similarly, U.S. corporations invested $6.8 billion in Canada and extracted $5.9 billion of profit, for a net flow of 900 million U.S. dollars into this advanced capitalist area.

In the underdeveloped Third World, the situation was different. In Latin America, American corporations invested $3.8 billion but extracted $11.3 billion, for a net flow of 7.5 billion U.S. dollars from that area to the United States. Yet profit rates were so great that at the same time the value of U.S. direct investments in Latin America *rose* from $4.5 to $10.3 billion. In fact, in the period 1957–1964, only 11.8 percent of direct U.S. investment in Latin America came from the United States; 74.1 percent was reinvestment of profits or depreciation funds from Latin American operations. Similarly, in Africa and Asia in the period 1950–1965 American corporations invested only $5.2 billion but transferred to the United States $14.3 billion of profits, for a net flow of $9.1 billion to the United States. Yet, enough profit remained for reinvestment that U.S. direct investments in Africa and Asia rose from $1.3 to $4.7 billion.

Two facts are blatantly obvious from these data: (1) The rate of profit in U.S. investments abroad is several times higher in the underdeveloped than in the advanced capitalist countries; and (2) that the underdeveloped neocolonial countries generously make a good-sized contribution to U.S. capital accumulation.

In addition to the basic fact that high profit rates squeeze more capital out of the underdeveloped countries than foreign investment puts in, there is the problem that most foreign investment goes into areas that are least helpful to industrial development. We saw that in trade the underdeveloped countries mainly export raw materials and import manufactured goods. This trade pattern is supported by the pattern of foreign investment.

On the whole, the investment is mainly in the primary industries producing raw materials. But the materials are then shipped back to the developed capitalist countries for manufacture. On the one side, this discourages real industrial development. On the other side, it means that the underdeveloped countries are limited to production of the least valuable types of goods in international trade (since the relative price of raw materials has been declining). The fact is that the foreign capitalist firms in the underdeveloped countries are largely located in the export sectors of the economy, exporting those goods that are easiest to sell in the international markets.

The International Monetary Fund report for 1963 states, "Much of the foreign product capital investment in the underdeveloped countries takes the form of direct investment in primary production for export, especially in the oil industry."[19] The U.S. Department of Commerce figures show that in Latin America, Asia and Africa, a large majority of all U.S. investment is in the extractive industries, especially petroleum. Only in Europe and Canada is the majority of U.S. investment in the nonextractive industries, mostly in manufacturing.

It is true that in the last decade there has apparently been a strong shift of the pattern in some underdeveloped countries. In several countries, such as Peru, there has been a sharp rise in the percentage of foreign investment going into manufacturing rather than agriculture or extraction of raw materials. These investments take advantage of the extraordinarily cheap labor to move part of the U.S. and other foreign firms' operations within the underdeveloped countries themselves (thus, the "multinational" firms discussed below). Some economists—even radicals—argue that the trend toward more manufacturing investment is a fundamental change, an aid to development, and an attempt to integrate the underdeveloped countries into the capitalist world.

Unfortunately, this change in the statistics has so far not been much of a help to development of the underdeveloped countries (although it has meant that the foreign-directed multinational firms control ever more of their economies). It has not been much help for three reasons. First, although it has increased, manufacturing is still a much smaller percent of all foreign investment than agriculture and extractive industries. Second, almost all the manufacturing investment is in light or consumer goods rather than heavy, basic, producer goods. Third, most of the investment in consumer goods industries is not in production, but only in assembly. Thus, a U.S. firm may produce refrigerators or cars, ship the parts to Brazil, and have its subsidiary there assemble and sell them. This does not seem much of an aid to Brazilian industrial development.

multinational firms

The ways in which American firms extract profits from underdeveloped countries have changed since World War II. It used to be that most investment was in the form of loans or stock purchases in existing companies or the setting up of brand new companies (with or without native participation). Today, such purely financial movements are less important. Rather, the capitalist corporation simply

[19] International Monetary Fund, op. cit., 1963 Report.

establishes branches of its own firm or completely subordinate satellite firms. The day of the multinational firm is here.

The very dramatic example of Standard Oil of New Jersey typifies the trend. By 1962, Standard Oil of New Jersey had 33 percent of its assets abroad (20 percent in Latin America and 13 percent in Europe and Asia). Furthermore, the importance of these areas is shown by the fact that Standard's profit on investment in the United States amounted to only 7.4 percent, in Canada and in Latin America, 17.6 percent, and in Europe and Asia, 15 percent.

Not only does the giant multinational firm operate equally well in the United States and abroad, but also its board of directors, and its sphere of influence, usually reflect an inseparable mixture of financial and industrial interests. In the fantastic size and complexity of their structure, which includes both finance and industrial capital, and the multiplicity of their interests, which includes both domestic and foreign sales, the giant corporations of today are very different from either earlier banking or earlier industrial interests.

Through multinational corporations, American capital thus directly owns a large chunk of western European industry, and the capitalists of all the developed capitalist countries together own the major industrial enterprises of the underdeveloped capitalist countries. "There are no reliable figures for the Third World as a whole which measure the extent of foreign economic intervention, but it is certain that many, perhaps even most, of the industrial undertakings of the underdeveloped countries are foreign-owned or controlled."[20] A careful investigation of one important neocolony concludes: "Foreign capital can . . . be said to share the control of the Indian economy with domestic capital on what is very neary a fifty-fifty basis."[21]

It should also be stressed that most of these multinational firms are none other than our old friends, the few largest American corporations. In the last official survey by size of firm (using data for 1957), it was found that 45 giants (each investing over $100 million abroad) had 57 percent of total American direct foreign investment, that 163 firms had 80 percent, and that 455 firms had 93 percent.[22] Certainly, any survey today would show increased concentration.

The concentration of profits is much greater. In 1966, more than one-half of American profits from abroad went to but 16 firms (all among the top 30, according to the *Fortune* listing).[23] Moreover, these profits were not a small sum, even in terms of total American profits.

[20] Jalee, op. cit., p. 22.

[21] Charles Bettleheim, *India Independent* (New York: Monthly Review Press, 1968).

[22] U.S. Department of Commerce, *United States Business Investments in Foreign Countries* (Washington, D.C.: U.S. Government Printing Office, 1960), p. 144.

[23] Arthur MacEwan, "Comment on Imperialism," *American Economic Review* (May 1970), p. 246.

From 1950 through 1969, profits from foreign investments were about 15 percent of total American corporate profits; so one-half of that was still a tidy sum for a handful of giant corporations.[24]

One of the most important recent trends is the differential growth of domestic U.S. sales and sales abroad. These sales abroad do not include export sales, but are only the sales of the affiliates and subsidiaries of American corporations in foreign countries. From 1957 to 1962, total American domestic sales in manufacturing rose from $341 to $400 billion; the sales of foreign affiliates of these same manufacturing corporations rose from $18.3 to $28.1 billion. Hence, foreign sales were and are growing much more rapidly than domestic sales.

Thus, the United States is able to compete abroad not only with exports, but even more importantly with the output of its foreign-based subsidiaries. This trend is reflected in the fact that the sales of American-owned plants abroad rose by 140 percent from 1950 to 1960, while exports from the United States went up by only 55 percent. And this trend has certainly continued since 1960 as may be seen in the fact that in 1961 only 460 of the thousand largest U.S. companies had a subsidiary branch in Europe, but in 1965 over 700 of them had a branch in Europe. This means, of course, that there is amazing concentration of capital in the few largest American firms, not only the capital of the United States but also that of the entire capitalist world.

All of the largest American firms are on the road to being truly multinational, thinking from a viewpoint based on their worldwide investments. Therefore, they are not merely interested, as was the earlier industrialist, in the export of commodities, or, as the earlier banker, in the export of capital. Rather, many have some of their major assembly plants in foreign countries, and they export a great deal from those subsidiaries in foreign countries. In fact, many foreign subsidiaries are large-scale exporters to the U.S. market. For example, in 1967, the total sales of all U.S. enterprises abroad was $32 billion, of which 11 percent was exported to the United States. That 11 percent constituted a total of $3.5 billion of goods, or 25 percent of total U.S. imports that year!

As noted earlier, this especially means that profits can be transferred around within the corporation, from a subsidiary in one country to a subsidiary in another. Therefore, the reports of total profit remittances from the colonial areas to the United States can no longer be trusted as more than a general indicator. An entire corporation's total profits are the crucial point, and they often include hidden profits in one subsidiary by reason of another selling to it

24 Ibid. Also data in Magdoff, *The Age of Imperialism* (New York: Monthly Review Press, 1969), p. 183.

more cheaply, or hidden losses in one subsidiary by reason of another selling to it more expensively than market price. For example, it appears that in 1961, bauxite production in Jamaica, Surinam, and Guyana yielded to American corporations a rate of profit of from 26 to 34 percent. Yet this does not really give the total picture. Much of their costs "on materials and services" turn out to be exceedingly high payments to American corporations, also subsidiaries of the same major corporate group. On top of that, between 1939 and 1959, the price of bauxite in the United States almost doubled, but the price of bauxite exported from Surinam and Guyana remained almost the same throughout the whole period. Thus, these firms' West Indian subsidiaries overpaid greatly for their materials and services and were underpaid for their finished product. (Notice that this also means more corporate taxes going to the United States, but much less going to the West Indies.)

It follows that the multinational companies may have conflicting interests when it comes to terms, export subsidies, foreign investment, and so forth. They are absolutely united, however, in desiring there to be as many nations as possible whose laws and institutions are favorable to the unhampered development of private enterprise. Thus, there is much intracorporate conflict over economic details, but there is no conflict over the main political and strategic issues concerning the defense of imperialism.

The United States, of course, is not alone in making foreign investments, yet its role has changed tremendously and it is certainly dominant at the present time. Thus, in 1914, the United States had only 6.3 percent of the capital-exporting countries' foreign investments; in 1960, it controlled 59.1 percent of all foreign investments. Canada's share has also increased, but most major Canadian industries are owned or controlled by American firms.

At the same time, the investments of the United Kingdom fell from 50.3 percent to 24.5 percent of the total (although Britain remains the largest foreign investor on a per capita basis). France's fell from 22.2 percent to only 4.7 percent, and Germany's, from 17.3 percent to 1.1 percent. Clearly, total western European control of foreign investments has fallen drastically and American and Canadian investments have risen sharply.

What are the consequences of multinational firms? On the political side, there is an important and expected change. Under the old system, there was conflict, direct and inevitable, between each of the investing countries. Under the new system, at least some of that conflict is eliminated. Thus, a multinational firm has the interests of many different countries and many different investment bases to consider. Still, most multinational firms have their home office in the United States. This, of course, greatly increases the dominance of the United States in the world scene.

neocolonial "aid"

From 1951 to 1959, average annual donations from the advanced countries to the underdeveloped countries amounted to $1.304 billion per year. The long-term public loans of capital amounted to $748 million per year. This gives a total of $2.052 billion per year.[25] As these data include some aid and loans from the socialist countries, they overstate the amount provided by the advanced capitalist countries. For the year 1965, the Organization for Economic Cooperation and Development calculates that public aid from the advanced capitalist (imperialist) countries to the underdeveloped countries was $6.270 billion. Even including private investments and loan funds, which were only $3.879 billion, the total comes to $10.149 billion for the whole year 1965. This is only 0.99 percent of the national income of the imperialist countries.[26] Furthermore, this is a very generous estimate using extremely exaggerated figures. Such a small amount, certainly less than 1 percent of the national income of the countries giving the aid, could not be considered much of a burden. And also, unfortunately, it is not much of a help.

As we saw, the private investment part is itself more than offset by the profit and interest returns on the investments. The small public aid does not even offset the capital extracted by imperialism. That public aid which is (1) nonmilitary and (2) in the form of official donations or grants may be some help, but it is not a large total amount. Even this "help" has extreme qualifications in that it is used to bolster repressive governments, to subsidize foreign investments, "to subsidize foreign imports which compete with national products, to introduce technology not adapted to the needs of underdeveloped countries, and to invest in low-priority sectors of the national economies."[27] The long-term public loans for nonmilitary purposes may also be some help, but the necessity to return principle and interest is rapidly becoming a main worry of the underdeveloped areas. Thus the United States officially admits that for all underdeveloped countries receiving U.S. aid: "The cost of maintaining such large indebtedness is at present eating up approximately 30 percent of all new assistance."[28]

25 United Nations, *The International Flow of Long-Term Capital and Official Donations, 1951–1959.* (Table 7)

26 Jalee, op. cit.

27 Theotino Dos Santos, "The Structure of Dependence," *American Economic Review,* Vol. 60 (May 1970), p. 233.

28 Committee on Foreign Relations, U.S. Senate, *Some Important Issues in Foreign Aid* (Washington, D.C., 1966), p. 15. Also see Magdoff, op. cit., pp. 52–57.

It is the declared policy of all of the American agencies, for example, the Agency for International Development, that the countries that receive the aid shall use it primarily to beef up the private enterprise sectors of their economies, and shall not use it for public investment, which is often the most necessary in these countries for rapid development. Obviously, it goes without saying that the aid of the United States is directed to shore-up these countries against communism, and is not given for any pure idealistic reason. In fact, the American aid agencies often point out that: "(1) Foreign aid provides a substantial and immediate market for U.S. goods and services. (2) Foreign aid stimulates the development of new overseas markets for U.S. companies. (3) Foreign aid orients national economies toward a free-enterprise system in which U.S. firms can prosper."[29]

The U.S. Agency for International Development boasts that, "Private enterprise has greater opportunities in India than it did a few years ago . . . fertilizer is an example of a field which is now open to the private sector, and was not in the past. This is largely a result of the efforts which we have made, the persuasion that we along with other members of the consortium have exerted on the Indian government."[30] A more blatant case of political pressure occurred in Brazil, where American aid fell from $81.8 million to $15.1 million from 1962 to 1964 because the U.S. disliked the Goulart government. When "good" reactionary military officers overthrew Goulart, American aid jumped to $122.1 million in 1965 and $129.3 million in 1966.[31]

Nor are all the rewards of foreign aid purely ideological and in overseas areas. Just as the aid agencies claim, large parts of U.S. business benefit directly from the foreign aid program. Thus, 24.4 percent of U.S. exports of iron and steel products are financed by the U.S. Agency for International Development. Similarly financed are 30.4 percent of fertilizer exports, 29.5 percent of railroad equipment exports, 11.5 percent of nonferrous metal exports, and 5 to 10 percent of the U.S. exports of machinery and equipment, chemicals, motor vehicles and parts, rubber and rubber products, and textiles.[32]

29 Magdoff, op. cit., p. 13.

30 Reported in Committee on Foreign Affairs, House of Representatives, *Hearings on Foreign Assistance Act of 1968,* p. 185.

31 Statistics and Reports Division, Agency for International Development, *U.S. Economic Assistance Programs, 1943–1966* (Washington, D.C., March 30, 1967), p. 28. Also see Magdoff, op. cit., pp. 39–47.

32 Charles Hyson and Alan Stout, "Impact of Foreign Aid on U.S. Exports," *Harvard Business Review* (January–February 1968), p. 71.

impact of imperialism
on the united states

The impact of military spending on the United States was discussed
in Chapter 27. Most U.S. military expenditures at home and abroad
serve the aims of imperialism: protecting raw materials, foreign
markets, commercial routes, spheres of influence of U.S. business,
and U.S. investment opportunities (as well as capitalism in general).
The profits from U.S. foreign trade, U.S. foreign investment, and
from the military production to defend U.S. interests amount to about
25 to 30 percent of all profits. And recalling that most military and
foreign profits go to the same few giant corporations, we begin
to have some idea of the importance of American imperialism.

Conservative economists would object to lumping military profits
with the profits from imperialism, but we believe it is impossible to
separate the two. By 1969, the United States had a total of 1,517,000
military personnel in 1400 foreign bases of all types, in 70 to 80
foreign countries (not including Korea and Vietnam).[33] The major
reason for this multibillion dollar allocation of resources is the need
to maintain control over the vast American overseas investment
empire. Note also that the decision to fight for a given área does *not*
depend on the profits to be made from that area alone, but even more
on its military–strategic importance to the structure of imperialism in
a wider area. "Understood in these terms, the killing and destruction
in Vietnam and the expenditure of vast sums of money are not balanced in the eyes of U.S. policy-makers against profitable business
opportunities in Vietnam; rather they are weighed according to the
judgment of military and political leaders on what is necessary to
control and influence Asia, and especially Southeast Asia, in order
to keep the entire area within the imperialist system in general, and
within the United States sphere of influence in particular."[34]

We may now make an evaluation of the costs and benefits of
imperialism and militarism to the United States. On the benefit side,
military production and military service do increase employment,
assuming that the nation begins from a position of major unemployment. On the harmful side, the flow of capital to the United States
(profits and interest from foreign investment less current investment) must have a negative effect on domestic profit rates and em-

[33] Data from Harry Magdoff, "Militarism and Imperialism," *American Economic
Review* (May 1970), pp. 237–242.

[34] Magdoff, op. cit., pp. 14–15.

ployment through the competition of more capital. Still, the net effect on employment is probably positive.

The public at large, the taxpayer, pays the direct costs, including $115 billion for six years of fighting in Vietnam.[35] Non-Vietnam military expenditures continued throughout the period at about $50 billion a year. Because America entered the war with a low level of unemployment, unemployment was not reduced (although *perhaps* a major depression was avoided at some point); but employment and demand remained high enough that monopoly power brought about price inflation which lowered the public's real income.

More than 45,000 Americans have been killed in Indochina, and more than five times that many wounded. (About 1 million Vietnamese civilians have been killed, but that is, presumably, not a cost to America.)

The necessary climate of racism against the "inferior" Indochinese has also worsened racism at home (as racism learned and practiced by the soldiers in Vietnam is brought back to the United States). The need to limit opposition to the war has increased repression and denial to civil liberties, and has especially undermined academic freedom in the colleges. The attempt to curb inflation by cutting all welfare spending increases the costs to the poor. For the public as a whole, therefore, the costs in blood and money are vast, and outweigh any slight employment benefits.

For the largest corporations, however, the balance is very different. They do pay some added taxes for the war, but they are able to pass on most of these to consumers and workers. They do have some higher costs from inflation, but their own prices rise faster. We speak here of the whole military-imperialist effort, not just the war in Vietnam. Some sections of big business find that the Vietnam War has overheated the economy too much or is a tactically "bad" (that is, losing) war, and so oppose it. Aside from that specific tactical situation, their interests are clear: Profits from military production and from foreign investment represent about 25 to 30 percent of all corporate profits.

Furthermore, the largest 100 corporations receive more than one-half of that very large amount, or the difference between depression and very high profit rates. Therefore, for the giant corporations the benefits of the military–imperialist effort clearly outweigh the costs (although whether they dribble down some of these benefits to the very top strata of labor, to keep labor content, is still highly controversial). Because these same corporate interests are dominant in the capitalist state, it is no wonder that militarism and imperialism continue to be American policy, regardless of the tremendous cost to the American people.

[35] U.S. Bureau of the Budget.

summary

The underdeveloped capitalist countries are not only poor, but also are growing more slowly than the developed ones; the gap is increasing. While too much population is obviously a problem for underdeveloped countries, the question is what holds back their development. The most important barriers seem to be (1) reactionary ruling classes that waste much of the product in unproductive ways, (2) a trade pattern in which the underdeveloped countries export mainly raw materials and import most of their finished goods, and (3) imperialist investment at such high profit rates that the profit outflow is greater than the current investment inflow.

Imperialism and militarism have both benefits and costs for the United States. Imperialist wars (such as Vietnam) and military spending for them do create some jobs, but they also create inflation, high taxation, reduction in welfare services, more racism, and thousands of dead and wounded Americans (and there are more rational and constructive ways of creating employment). On the other side, there are vast benefits for a small number of giant corporations that make very high profit rates on foreign investments and on military production.

part four

socialist economic systems: a radical introduction to comparative economics

chapter 34
varieties of socialism

The word *socialism* has been used to mean a great many different things. To begin with, it refers to (1) a system of ideas, (2) a political movement, and (3) an economic system of actual institutions. In Chapters 5 and 6, the early socialist ideologies and the Marxist socialist theories were discussed. These were systems of ideas. To complicate matters, there are now many varieties of Marxist socialist ideas alone, not to speak of other socialist ideas. Different views within the general set of Marxist ideas are currently expressed by the Russians, the Chinese Maoists, the outlook of Cuba's Castro and Che Guevara, and many others. We shall not develop each of these, but refer to them from time to time when relevant.

In the second category, political movements, there also falls a wide variety. In fact, most systems of socialist thought have generated socialist political movements. Today, there are many parties calling themselves Socialist or Labor parties. Many of these, such as the Social Democratic party of West Germany, specifically do *not* advocate a fully socialized economy, but urge a mixture of capitalist and socialist economic forms (mostly the status quo, as it now exists in West Germany). The other main political branch of the socialist movement is tenanted by the parties calling themselves Communist. Curiously, these parties say they advocate socialist economic systems rather than communist ones (defined below). So Socialist parties mostly do not advocate a fully socialist economy, and Communist parties do not advocate an immediate communist economy.

Of course, the Communist parties are also split into warring groups, particularly the group following the Soviet party versus the group following the Chinese party. Finally, there are many radicals in the United States and elsewhere who advocate socialism, but do not belong to any of the Socialist or Communist parties.

So much for socialist thought and socialist political movements. Most of this part of the book is devoted to actual economies calling themselves socialist. Each of these economies reflects, of course, the socialist ideas of the particular variety of socialist party in power in that country, but we are going to discuss the actual economic structures, referring to the systems of thought or the party politics to a much lesser degree.

THE WESTERN EUROPEAN MODEL OF SOCIALISM

Many western European countries have at times had Socialist or Labor parties in power, and they have initiated a certain degree of socialism. These include England, France, Germany, and all of Scandinavia. Each has strongly supported traditional institutions of political democracy, changing only certain economic structures. In fact, the same forms of political democracy are found in some countries predominantly socialist and in some predominantly capitalist, and the same is true for the forms of political dictatorship. Radicals would generally argue that the conditions of a socialist economy are more likely to produce more genuine political democracy than the conditions of a capitalist economy. The issue, however, is surely very controversial, and it is settled only in the minds of those people who define it away, making socialism or capitalism *by definition* either a democracy or a dictatorship.

Thus in western Europe (excluding the capitalist-oriented dictatorships of Spain, Portugal, and Greece), we find the forms of political democracy to a considerable degree, although to what degree the content of these forms is genuine is another hard question. Most of these western European countries also claim to have a considerable degree of socialism. While there are immense differences between them, they generally seem to mean two things by *socialism*. One element is the nationalization of several industries, or public rather than private ownership. The second element is a very wide area of welfare payments and free goods, including health and education, and other attempts to distribute income more equally (though their income distribution is still very unequal and shows little change).

The industries nationalized have often been near bankruptcy, with their owners very willing to be nationalized—with extensive compensation. Moreover, many basic industries have not been nationalized. On the whole, therefore, it appears that most of these economies still act as and fluctuate as capitalist economies (except for the usual monetary and fiscal policies). At any rate, to an outside observer, it seems that the capitalist sectors still predominate in the economies of western Europe.

THE SOVIET MODEL OF SOCIALISM

The Soviet ideology distinguishes between *socialism* and *communism*. In their view, socialism means public ownership of all economic enterprises. In socialism, however, consumers still must pay for goods with money; and workers still work for wages, which differ according to the amount and difficulty of work accomplished. This is the situation in most of the Soviet economy.

The Soviets say they wish ultimately to reach the goal of communism. Then there will still be public ownership of all enterprises, but there will be neither wages nor money: All goods will be free. Only a small part of Soviet goods and services are presently free.

Two other characteristics should be added. First, the Soviet economy is all centrally planned and is supervised by a large bureaucracy. Second, they are ruled by a one-party dictatorship; all parties but the Communist party are prohibited.

Soviet economic history is discussed in the next chapter, and its economic system and problems are examined in Chapter 36. The decentralization reforms of the 1960s are presented in Chapter 37, and political and social factors are explored critically in Chapter 38.

THE CHINESE MODEL OF SOCIALISM

China, like the Soviet Union, claims to have socialism with most industrial enterprises publically owned. It differs in certain respects. Particularly, the Chinese admit that wages are still necessary, but claim that their wage-income distribution is much more equal than in the USSR and that they rely more on moral and collective incentives. Details of their economic development, operation, and outlook are given in the next chapter.

THE YUGOSLAV MODEL OF SOCIALISM

The Yugoslavs also claim to have a socialist economy. Its main feature, however, is *not* central planning, but independent operation by each enterprise. Moreover, the manager of each enterprise is not appointed by the central government (as in the Soviet Union), but by a workers' council, which is elected by all the workers in the enterprise. Details of this system are discussed in Chapter 37.

THE CHILEAN MODEL OF SOCIALISM

Chile has only recently elected a government committed to socialism.
We do not know what its economic model will be. But it is one case
in which everyone (even conservatives) admits that a left-wing socialist
government committed to establishing full-scale socialism *and* maintaining full democratic political forms has been elected in a free
election.

THE AMERICAN RADICAL MODEL OF SOCIALISM

Probably every radical in the United States has his own view of
exactly what socialism should be like. All agree that there should be
no private profit, that it should be decent and human, that it should
be based on a genuinely democratic political process. But beyond
that, there is disagreement on every particular.

Those who argue that no existent model even begins to approach
the goal of full participation and an end of alienation usually emphasize a preference for economic and political decentralization down
to the level of small (self-sufficient?) communities in harmony with
the surrounding ecologies. Other radicals criticize this as a return to
the impossible utopian visions of the nineteenth century (see Chapter
5). They argue that most economic activity is irrevocably nationwide
and that ultimate control, therefore, must also be exercised through
nationwide democratic processes (with local participation encouraged).

chapter 35
socialist development in russia and china

Marx and most of his nineteenth-century disciples believed that the end of capitalism was near, at least within the next several decades. The capitalist system proved to have considerably more staying power than they imagined. Lenin attributed much of this prolonged viability to the gains made through imperialism. Ironically, this same imperialism led, indirectly, to the demise of a great European power, Russia, which was only in the infant stages of capitalist development. A socialist revolution overtook the fallen giant, and power was seized, in the name of Marxism, by Lenin and the Bolsheviks.

the bolshevik revolution and the civil war

The general competitiveness of nineteenth-century imperialism created an international climate of tensions and distrust. With the crumbling of the once powerful Ottoman Empire, the major European powers scrambled to seize territory over which the Turks were no longer able to maintain hegemony. The predictable result was open armed conflict: World War I. The war so weakened the economic and political structure of Russia that the tsarist government collapsed in

1917. It was replaced by a provisional government which also proved unable to cope with the chaotic situation.

Finally, in October, 1917, the Russian Bolsheviks, in an almost bloodless coup, seized power. For the first time, socialists had the reins of power and could attempt to create a society without the many evils of capitalism they had consistently denounced. The problems that had overcome the tsar and the provisional government, however, were of an overwhelming magnitude, so the Bolsheviks, who were mostly intellectual, utopian dreamers and political amateurs, had no easy road to trod.

The new government found itself in the midst of a war that had devastated the foundations of the economy, slowed transportation and communication almost to a halt and created something approximating social anarchy. One of the chief sources of Bolshevik power was the support of the mass of peasants who were revolting against centuries of ruthless exploitation. In an elemental revolutionary thrust, the peasants seized the holdings of wealthy landlords and rich peasants (*kulaks*). They divided the land up into millions of tiny plots. When, as one of their first acts after taking power, the Bolsheviks announced a land reform, they were merely putting an official stamp of approval on an event that was a fait accompli, about which they could have done nothing had they so desired. Nevertheless, the new, small and inefficient peasant holdings made it exceedingly difficult for the Bolsheviks to secure the food to feed their armies and urban dwellers. Moreover, the newly independent peasants wanted to consume the little they produced.

In the cities, most important enterprises and industries were in the hands of capitalists who were hostile to and distrustful of the Bolsheviks. A very large percentage of the physical capital of these enterprises had been destroyed, and the allocation of raw materials and supplies had been severely disrupted. The Soviets had hardly begun to extricate themselves from the war with Germany when a group of reactionary pro-tsarist and pro-capitalist generals launched a military drive to destroy the new government.

The reactionary forces were supported by the major capitalist powers. Not only did their army (called the *White Army*) receive financial and material aid, but also, most of the major capitalist governments sent armed troops to destroy the Soviet government. Few Americans realized it at the time, but President Wilson sent thousands of American soldiers and spent millions of tax dollars on a war that, like the Vietnam War nearly a half-century later, was undeclared.

war communism

Thus, in a period of bitter and extensive warfare, while the economy and whole society were approaching a state of total anarchy, the Bolsheviks were forced to take extreme measures in order to survive. The policies followed during the period from 1918 to 1921 were called *War Communism.* The Communist government was driven under the exigencies of war, hunger and chaos to attempt to impose centralized control on all economic processes.

In May, 1918, the government gave one of its agencies the power to obtain and distribute food. It became necessary to use brute coercion to wrest food from some of the richer peasants (kulaks). Workers' detachments were sent to find and confiscate hoards of grain. Poorer peasants also attacked the kulaks and confiscated their hoards. The kulaks resisted bitterly and the result was almost a second civil war. Ultimately, however, the threat of a triumph of the White Army and a return of the old landlord class kept most peasants loyal to the communists; their support was instrumental in the communist victory in the civil war.

Being unable directly to secure sufficient resources to keep the economy going and fight the civil war, the government created large sums of money with which to buy resources in the market. The result was an inflation so drastic that money became almost worthless. Many state enterprises ceased using money in transactions among themselves. In 1919 and 1920, most workers' wages were no longer paid in money but rather in products or services. Many essential commodities, including municipal services such as public trains and tramcars, were free to workers.

The government was forced to nationalize almost all industry from the largest factories down to enterprises employing only a few people. This was the only way in which they could gain the required amount of control over industry. It was made necessary, not only because of the confusion, but also because most capitalists and managers had a deeply ingrained hostility toward the communists, and many actively attempted to sabotage the government's efforts. The nationalization drive ultimately became an attempt to eliminate all privately owned manufacturing enterprises.

There was also a drive to ban all private trade. Middlemen and tradesmen were said to be parasitic and to depend upon exploitation of both producers and consumers for their profits. All trade and selling was to be transacted by government agencies. The government was never very effective at enforcing this ban, especially in a number of critical areas in which severe shortages existed.

By 1920, when it became obvious that the White Army would be defeated, the peasants began to resist the government's confiscation of their surpluses. Other pressures against the total regimentation of economic life began to assert themselves. In early 1921, the sailors at the Kronstadt Naval Station revolted against the miserable conditions of their life (ironically, it had been a revolt of the sailors at this some Kronstadt Naval Station that had helped the Bolsheviks seize power three and one-half years earlier).

the new economic policy

Under these pressures, the government abruptly abandoned many of the policies of War Communism and inaugurated what was called the *New Economic Policy* (NEP). The government continued to own and operate heavy industry, power, transportation, banking and some wholesale trade. Many small businesses and most retail and wholesale trade, however, were returned to private ownership and private profit-making.

The economy responded very rapidly to NEP policies. By 1928, the crises were over and the economy had been restored to its prewar levels of output in most industries. But the prewar levels were woefully inadequate. The USSR was still primitive and backward by Western standards. Furthermore, "instructed" by the earlier armed intervention by the great Western powers and the continuing barrage of anticommunist pronouncements and propaganda from most Western governments, the Communists felt threatened by the West. Believing that the USSR would eventually be attacked by hostile Western powers unless she achieved such strength that they would be reluctant to do so, the Communists accepted the fact that rapid industrialization would be absolutely necessary. Apart from the threat which they believed existed, their socialist goals also required an industrialized economy.

the industrialization debate

With all Communists accepting the necessity of a rapid industrialization, a debate raged in the late 1920s over the most efficient method of financing this industrialization. In order to feed and clothe the workers producing capital goods, and to spare the material resources necessary for the construction of factories and machinery, large surpluses had to be appropriated by the government. Foreign capital goods could also be purchased if the surpluses could be marketed in the West. With the overwhelming majority of the Russian work force employed in agriculture (and a large percent of these in subsistence agriculture), it was obvious that most of the surplus would have to come from agriculture. But Soviet economists and political leaders were divided on the question of how best to appropriate this agricultural surplus.

One group of conservative Communists (or *right-wing deviationists,* as Stalin called them) were led by the economist Nikolai Bukharin. He believed that industrial planning should emphasize increased production of agricultural machinery and consumer goods to be sold to the peasants. The peasants should be paid high prices for their grain and should be offered consumer goods and agricultural machinery at low prices to induce them to expand output and market a continually larger surplus. Industrial development, Bukharin believed, was limited by the rate of expansion of agricultural production.

A second group of *left-wing* communists was led by Leon Trotsky, ex-commander of the Red Army and Lenin's chief lieutenant during the civil war, as well as Eugene Preobrazhensky, the leading Marxist economist of the period. They favored extracting a maximum surplus from agriculture by paying peasants low prices for produce (with heavy taxes) and charging them high prices for manufactured goods. Agriculture should be more efficiently organized, they believed, by the formation of large-scale collective farms. Many sectors of the economy should be purposely neglected or short-changed, in order to devote a maximum of resources and manpower to the rapid expansion of heavy industry which, when fully operational, would efficiently produce the capital necessary to catch up in the industries neglected in the initial phases of industrialization.

Joseph Stalin used the antagonisms created in the debates as a means of achieving power for himself. At first, he aligned himself with the conservatives to form a coalition that ousted Trotsky and his left-wing sympathizers. He then turned on Bukharin and his followers and successfully stripped them of their power, leaving himself in full control. Having thus gained power, he began to move along lines that had been advocated by Trotsky and Preobrazhensky, although he moved more rapidly and more harshly than they had ever advised.

collectivization

In November 1929, the government announced a policy of promoting collectives as a means of increasing agricultural production (during that same month Bukharin was expelled from the Politbureau). At first, the collectivization was to have been voluntary. Suddenly, however, in early 1930, the government decided to force collectivization as widely as possible and eliminate the richer peasants or kulaks by turning their holdings over to collectives. This was called the drive to "liquidate the kulaks as a class." The resulting change was so profound that a careful expert could say: ". . . the events of 1929–34 constitute one of the great dramas of history."[1]

Only the poor peasants could be persuaded to join the collectives voluntarily; but they owned so few animals and so little capital that collectives could not succeed with them alone. The middle and rich kulaks resisted forced collectivization with bitterness and ferocity. At times, this resistance was so widespread as to constitute what could almost be called a second civil war. When the kulaks and other recalcitrant peasants realized they could not defeat the government directly, they began to burn buildings, destroy equipment, and slaughter animals. By 1931, one-third of all cattle, one-half of all sheep and goats, and one-fourth of all horses had been slaughtered.

The drama of the battle over collectivization was one about which many books have been written. Here it will suffice to say that an immense social cost was incurred, but that it did bring about the revolution in Soviet agriculture that made industrialization possible. Collectivization succeeded in drastically increasing the government's collections of grain. The 22,100,000 tons from the 1930–1931 harvest were more than twice the tonnage collected by the government in 1928–1929.

industrialization and war

When collectivization placed a large economic surplus in government hands, Soviet industrialization proceeded at a striking rate during the five-year plans of the 1930s. Industrial growth at such a rapid pace had never before occurred in history. Official Soviet figures for the 1930s show an average annual growth rate in industrial production of about 16 percent. Studies by Western economists using

[1] Alec Nove, *An Economic History of the USSR* (Baltimore: Penguin, 1969), p. 160.

different methods of arriving at indexes of industrial production show somewhat lower rates (ranging from about 9 percent to about 14 percent), but by any of these estimates the performance was without historical precedent.[2]

This spectacular rate of growth was interrupted by World War II, during which Russians suffered unparalleled losses. Estimates of the number of Russians killed in World War II are generally around the 20 million figure, although some experts place the figure at 30 million. Early in the war, Hitler rapidly conquered an area which contained over one-half of the USSR's prewar productive capacity. The German-occupied territory had accounted for 70 percent of Russian coal mining, 60 percent of iron-ore production, 50 percent of steel capacity, and 33 percent of the area sown in grain.

When the Germans were subsequently pushed back, they pursued a scorched-earth policy, destroying everything of value as they retreated. Especially hard hit were factories and houses. In addition to killing more than 20 million Russians, the Germans destroyed the homes of another 25 million, totally razing about 2,000 towns and 70,000 villages. (Many of the productive facilities had previously been destroyed by the Soviets themselves to prevent their use by the Germans.)

The destruction of these millions of people, homes, factories, untold millions of animals, and railroads, transportation and communications systems left Russia an almost totally devastated "victor" in World War II. The economic progress of the 1930s, which had been purchased at a high social and human cost was, in large measure, erased by the fascist attempt to conquer the USSR.

Despite these losses, however, the Russians retained their economic organization and general skills, and with their experience with economic planning gained during the 1930s, they recovered with miraculous speed. By 1950, gross industrial production was actually substantially higher than it had been in 1940 and agricultural production had almost recovered to its prewar level.

the post–world war II situation

During the 1950s, the Soviet economy continued to grow at an impressive rate. From 1950 through 1958, its average growth rate was over 3.5 times that of the United States according to official Soviet estimates, and nearly 2.5 times the U.S. rate according to most

2 For a short discussion of various estimates of Soviet industrial production, see Howard J. Sherman, *The Soviet Economy* (Boston: Little Brown, 1969), pp. 79–99.

American estimates.[3] The growth rate slowed down during the late 1950s and early 1960s, but the Soviet economy still appears to have done better in its leanest years than the American economy did in the booming prosperity of the early and middle 1960s. This slowdown led to a series of reforms launched in 1965 and still being implemented as of this writing.

The Soviet experience has proven that their model of central planning can achieve industrialization at a very rapid pace. But has their record led to any conclusions about the ability of a socialist economy to overcome the difficulties socialists have traditionally attributed to capitalism? The question is very difficult to answer because most socialist criticisms of capitalism have assumed that socialism, when it came, would be superimposed on the productive structure of an industrial capitalist economy. Many of the worst evils found in the USSR during the last 50 years have represented the social costs of industrialization and should not be compared with conditions under capitalism during the same period. A more appropriate comparison would be with England during the industrial revolution.[4]

Conditions of work were harsh and the worker's standard of living was low throughout the 1930s. After the first five-year plan had provided the impetus toward industrialization, many leading Communists argued that more attention should be given to the working and living conditions of the laborers. Increasingly, as the decade passed, the regime became less and less tolerant of such requests. Protests against prevailing conditions were often met with repression and terror.

The Stalinist purges of the late 1930s constitute one of the bleakest chapters in Russian history. They are certainly the nadir in the history of the Soviet Union. Stalin's paranoid excesses were barbarously harsh. Framing any real or imaginary opponent as a traitor, Stalin eliminated three-quarters of the men who had been elected to the Party Central Committee in 1934, 90 percent of the Soviet Army's generals, and many others of lesser status. In all, probably 500,000 persons were jailed or executed in the purges, in addition to the recalcitrant peasants who were dislocated and often sent to forced labor camps in the collectivization drive.

In 1953, Stalin died. By that time, economic progress had made political liberalization possible. Since the execution in late 1953 of Stalin's chief executioner, Beria, violence has not been used to settle political issues in the Soviet Union. Leaders have come and gone, but no one has been executed, jailed or legally disgraced as a

[3] See Sherman, op. cit., p. 105.
[4] See Chapter 5.

consequence of political differences. Accompanying this decrease in coercive force has been a general increase in political and intellectual freedom. At present, there is reason, although somewhat uncertain, to be optimistic about future Soviet prospects in this vitally important area. (Although recently there has been some reversion to coercive methods, due, in part, to the increased international tensions created by the Vietnam War.)

recent economic reforms

In the more liberal atmosphere since the mid-1950s, Soviet literature on the problems of economic planning under socialism has increased immensely. The basic problem under investigation has been the question of evaluating various output mixes and input costs. One of the most important issues with which the Soviets have been dealing is that of the relation between the market and the plan. Specifically, the economists have debated the issue of the appropriate extent of centralized versus decentralized economic decision-making. In 1962, the economist Evsei G. Liberman published an article in *Pravda,* which initiated a debate on decentralization. This "great debate" eventually led to a series of economic reforms beginning in 1965.

The *Kharkov incentive system* (which was what Liberman named his plan) called for important changes in the planning process only at the level of the firm. For the entire economy, "the basic levels of centralized planning—prices, finances, budget account, large capital investments . . . all the value, labor and natural indices of rates and proportions of production, distribution and consumption will be determined entirely at the center."[5]

Liberman proposed that enterprises be assigned only their final output mix. The appropriate technology was to be determined by each firm. The more efficiently a firm used its inputs, the lower would be its costs. The lower its costs, the higher would be its net revenue, or profits (total sales revenues minus total costs). Therefore, the size of a firm's profits would be an index of its efficiency. Bonus payments were to be given to firms that made profits above some profitability norm established for the industrial sector in which the firm was a part.

From 1962 to 1965, the Kharkov system was supported and attacked in a lively and penetrating debate. Critics pointed out that cost and profit calculations do not mean a thing if prices and costs do not accurately reflect a normative, or ethical, evaluation of social

5 E. G. Liberman, "Plan, Profits and Bonuses," in M. E. Sharpe, ed., *The Liberman Discussion: A New Phase in Soviet Economic Thought* (White Plains, N.Y.: International Arts and Science Press, 1965), p. 79.

values and social costs. The Liberman proposal did not contain any new insights into the solution of this problem. Supporters argued that by giving the individual firms more autonomy and responsibility, there would be greater economic maneuverability and stronger individual initiatives. These, they asserted, would lead to greater efficiency regardless of whether prices accurately reflected social values. The greater individual freedom in making production decisions and the lure of profit bonuses would lead to more enthusiastic and conscientious application of productive effort.

Critics countered by pointing out the long socialist tradition that rejects, on moral grounds, any economic system that depends upon acquisitive, greedy, pecuniary motives. They insisted that Marx's analysis of alienation proved that the root cause of alienation was the use of human beings by other human beings as mere objects to be utilized in the quest for more profits. What, these critics wondered, would differentiate a socialist factory manager, who hired laborers solely to maximize the factory's profits, from his capitalist counterparts?

In September 1965, it became obvious that, for the time at least, the Liberman supporters had won the day. The Soviet government proposed a major organizational reform which was adopted as law by the Supreme Soviet on October 2 of that year. Although the reform did not make profits the only criterion of productive efficiency (as Liberman had proposed), profits did become the principal one among several criteria. Firms were given much more autonomy in purchasing and organizing inputs in the productive process. And bonuses were paid out of profits to managers who were successful under the new system. (The debate and the reforms are considered in more detail in Chapter 37.)

summary of the soviet experience

The Soviet Union industrialized with truly phenomenal speed despite obstacles many economic and political systems probably could not have surmounted. Judged strictly from the goal of rapid industrialization, Soviet socialism has been a spectacular success.

But most socialists, in the nineteenth and early twentieth centuries at least, envisioned a socialist society that would be superimposed upon the productive base of an advanced, industrialized capitalist economy. Capitalism was objectionable, in their eyes, because production was undertaken for profits and not for human welfare. Prices in a market economy merely reflected, for them, an index of the capitalists' ability to exploit workers and consumers in order to maximize profits. Such a system was, in their opinion, thoroughly irrational from top to bottom. They wanted it to be replaced by a socialist system in which human beings would live to their fullest potential in a decent environment. The problems involved in assessing social values and social costs in order to plan rationally were hardly touched upon by these socialists. Their goal was the replacement of capitalism with a humanist socialism. The problems of rational planning they left to be solved after socialism was achieved.

During the reign of Stalin, the goal of rapid industrialization overrode all others. The harsh intellectual repression, commencing with the purges of the late 1930s and lasting until Stalin's death in 1953, resulted in a nearly total eclipse of meaningful intellectual endeavors to solve the economic and philosophical problems of humanistically oriented socialist planning.

After this long period of intellectual stagnation, Soviet economic thought came to life after 1956. The problems of social evaluation, rational planning, and decentralization of economic decision-making have all received thoughtful, penetrating analyses since then. No definitive answers to these problems have emerged from the Soviet debates, but the fact that official dogma has not precluded a broad and thorough intellectual campaign to come to grips with these issues is cause for optimism. The Soviet Union has certainly not achieved anything resembling the socialist system envisioned by the great thinkers in the socialist tradition. But with industrialization successfully behind them, and having initiated some beginnings of political and intellectual freedom, they may well be starting on the path to such a socialist system. Only time will tell.

socialist development in china

Since World War II, socialism has been established in several countries. In some, it has developed along lines quite different from the Soviet Union's version. China is the largest country in which socialists have triumphed. The Chinese experience differs from that of the Soviet Union in many ways. For these reasons, we shall briefly examine some of the main features of Chinese economic development since 1949.

During the period between 1911 (which marked the fall of the Manchu dynasty) and 1949, the Chinese economy had been ravaged by revolution, civil war, foreign invasion and exploitation, and flood and famine. When the Communists took over in 1949, they inherited an extremely poor and backward economy.

The industrial sector was very small and mostly foreign owned. In the major urban centers, most industry and commerce had ground to a near standstill. Dams, canals, and irrigation systems were in a dilapidated condition. The fighting had destroyed most of the railroad lines. Inflation had nearly ruined the money system. And, worst of all, the population that had survived the preceding disasters was abysmally poor, half-starved, and exhausted.

The Chinese economy was basically feudal, with about 80 percent of the population employed in agriculture. The coastal cities had become enclaves of foreign capitalist industry, but in 1949, there was less industry in China than existed in Russia in 1914, or in India when it became independent in 1947.

The first step taken by the new government was to begin a massive land reform. In 1949, landlords and rich peasants, who constituted less than 10 percent of the population, owned 70 percent of the land.[6] By 1952, the land reform had been completed; over 300 million poor peasants had benefited.

Other policies undertaken between 1949 and 1952 were designed to restore the economy to its pre-1949 level and to create the necessary economic, political, and social prerequisites for a successful planned economy. Accomplishments during this period were impressive. The government suppressed the banditry that had been rife during the period of social turmoil, restored the dilapidated railroad system, and repaired and extended the irrigation systems. An extensive system of public health, preventive medicine, and sanitation was initiated. Perhaps most significant of all, they undertook to provide a relatively equal distribution of the available food and clothing.

By 1952, the government believed that conditions justified launching their first five-year plan, to cover the years 1953–1957. The slogan was *Learn from the Soviet Union.* Ministries, each responsible for an industry were established in Peking. Planning was centralized, with the ministries fixing prices and output targets. A high priority was given to the major capital-goods industries.

In education, public health, and industry, most of the plan's targets were achieved. By 1958, the educational system had graduated 431,000 students, including 130,000 engineers, more than twice the number produced in the previous twenty years. The public health program virtually eliminated such diseases as cholera, typhoid and plague, which had previously decimated the Chinese population regularly.

[6] E. L. Wheelwright and Bruce McFarlane, *The Chinese Road to Socialism* (New York: Monthly Review Press, 1970), p. 32. Most of the statistics in this section are from this source.

Considerable increases in the output of heavy industry also were achieved: "Crude steel output increased from 1.35 million metric tons to 5.35 million; coal from 66.5 to 130.7 million; petroleum from 0.44 to 1.46 million; cement from 2.9 to 6.9 million; sulphuric acid from 190 thousand metric tons to 632 thousand; and electric power from 7.3 billion kilowatt hours to 19.3 billion."[7]

There were failures during the first five-year plan. The size and complexity of the Chinese economy made it extremely difficult to plan everything from the center. Inevitably, there were inefficiencies, wastes, dislocations. Light industry was growing very slowly. And there were problems in the agricultural sector remarkably similar to those the Soviet Union had encountered in the 1920s. As a consequence, in 1956–1957 the Chinese stepped up the process of agricultural collectivization. By the end of 1957, almost all peasant households were in collectives.

The second five-year plan was never undertaken, for in 1958, the Chinese launched their *Great Leap Forward,* an all-out effort to transform radically the most basic social and economic institutions. This transformation involved a complete rejection of the planning model of the Soviet Union and, ultimately, an almost complete break with the Soviet Union.

The first and most basic change was the establishment of *people's communes.* China's 752,000 collective farms were reorganized into 26,500 communes. The collectives had included an average of 158 households; in the new communes, the average was 5,000 households. The new organizations were designed to permit the effective mobilization of the massive rural labor force to facilitate the construction of many labor-intensive capital projects and to increase the production in small-scale industries. These functions were, of course, in addition to the households' more basic role as producers of agricultural products.

The communes undertook such important projects as the construction of new irrigation systems and water-conservation systems and programs of afforestation. They also organized small-scale production in several industries, including cloth weaving, machinery repair, simple tool-making and the manufacture of many other industrial products. (The "backyard" smelting of pig iron that was widely ridiculed in the Western press never did have the importance attributed to it in the West.)

The communes established schools for technical training, research institutes, and spare-time facilities for general education. They also served to ration and distribute food and other consumer goods, and

7 Ibid., p. 36.

maintained communal kitchens, laundries, and children's nurseries. In general, they were integrated social units performing many social, political, and cultural functions for the people.

In late 1957 and early 1958, there was a widespread attempt to decentralize industrial decision-making. The central authorities continued to control the capital-goods industries, but consumer-goods industries were put under the control of provincial authorities.

The years 1959–1961 were years of crisis. Innumerable problems were encountered in the communes where radical social reorganization was occurring simultaneously with the introduction of new systems of production and education. The primary cause of the crises, however, was disastrous harvests. Many Western observers believed that China was on the brink of social collapse.

Gradually, however, as Western scholars gathered more information, they realized that, along with the failures, the Chinese had achieved many successes. The Great Leap Forward

> familiarized millions of backward peasants with industrial techniques at great immediate cost, but at an equally great potential benefit. It liberated China from excessive reliance on the Soviet developmental model which, whatever its strengths, was not suitable to a populous Asian land. . . . It achieved a strategically and economically significant dispersion of industry and an increase in the number of home-made scientists and technicians. . . . By 1962 China's meager army of scientific and technical personnel had almost doubled; important inroads had been made on illiteracy; and the number of types of steel, rolled steel, and nonferrous metals had increased by 200 percent, and those of machine tools by 150 percent. . . . Contrary to the oft-repeated assertions in the West, the commune system of socio-economic organization was not jettisoned, merely made more rational.[8]

During the 1960s, several changes were made in Chinese economic priorities. First, increased emphasis was given agricultural production and light industries in the national-investment program. A larger share of the output of heavy industry was devoted to agricultural machinery, chemical fertilizers, insecticides, fuel, electric power, irrigation equipment, and building materials. Second, much greater stress was placed on improving the quality of all goods produced. Third, there was a general reorganization of the communes aimed at increasing their effectiveness. Between 1958 and the late 1960s, the average number of households per commune fell from 5,000 to about 1,600.

---

[8] Jan S. Prybyla, "Red China in Motion: A Non-Marxist View," in Harry G. Shaffer, ed., *The Communist World* (New York: Appleton-Century-Crofts, 1967), p. 176.

the accomplishments of chinese socialism

Since the Great Leap Forward, the Chinese have not made general
production statistics available to the West. Thus, we lack quantitative
evidence with which to evaluate their economic performance since
1958. Judgments about China's progress must be made from firsthand
observations of the general conditions under which the people are
living. Many contemporary economists have visited China. When an
economist visits China and wants to evaluate their performance, he

> studies the official statistics and publications put out by the
> government and other institutions. He talks to the country's
> economists. He moves around as much as he can, visiting various
> units of production over as wide a field as possible. In his travels,
> . . . he utilizes his previous experiences and observes the condition
> of the people—whether they appear well fed and healthy, whether
> there appears to be substantial unemployment (real or disguised), the
> absence or presence of beggars, standards of cleanliness and
> hygiene, the quality and range of consumer goods in the shops,
> other products exhibited in trade fairs and elsewhere, the standard
> of public housing, the clothing of the people, the leisure habits of the
> people, and so on.[9]

Before making such judgments, the economist should keep in mind
the conditions prevailing in China after World War II. Over the
previous several decades, approximately 100 million people had
perished in floods, famines, war, and revolutions. The overwhelming
majority of those remaining were starving, poverty-stricken,
demoralized people. Intestinal and lung diseases were endemic; the
country was regularly devastated by epidemics of various
communicable diseases.

Economically, China was much more backward than Russia had
been prior to the Revolution. Russia's petroleum production in 1913,
for example, was over 27 times as great as was China's in 1943. Steel
production in prerevolutionary Russia was 3½ times that of China. On
the eve of collectivization, the Soviets had 210,900 tractors; in 1949,
the Chinese had 400. Russia's 1913 railroad mileage was approximately 45,600; China had 13,600 in 1949 and most of her railroads
went inland only far enough for foreign capitalist powers to bring her
raw materials to the seaports to be shipped abroad.

In agriculture, chemical fertilizers had virtually never been used

9 Wheelwright and McFarlane, op. cit., p. 13.

prior to 1949. Reckless deforestation and soil erosion had made a large percentage of cultivable farmland subject to periodic devastating floods. Agricultural techniques were abysmally backward. It is only against this background that we can evaluate the Chinese economic performance since 1949.

Agricultural accomplishments are perhaps most important because of the massive, starving population that existed in 1949. The Chinese reorganized agriculture. They increased the degree of mechanization, produced and used substantially more chemical fertilizers, and greatly expanded the supplies of eggs, vegetables, fruits, poultry, fish, and meat. Today, China feeds her entire population and exports more food than she imports. One American economist has gone so far as to state that "it would not be farfetched to claim that there has been less malnutrition due to maldistribution of food in China over the past twenty years than there has been in the United States."[10]

In education, there have also been important achievements. Virtually all urban children and most rural children attend school. Illiteracy, which before the Revolution was almost universal, has nearly been eliminated. A wide variety of schools and technical training centers exists at all levels throughout China.

The gains in the medical and public-health fields are very impressive. A Canadian doctor recently reported on his visits to Chinese medical colleges, hospitals, and research institutes. He reported that they had high medical standards, used high-quality equipment, and dispensed excellent medical care, which was almost all comparable to Canadian standards.[11] A member of the United States Public Health Service has written that "the prevention and control of many infectious and parasitic diseases which have ravaged [China] for generations [was a] most startling accomplishment." He also asserted that "the improvement of general environmental sanitation and the practice of personal hygiene, both in the cities and in the rural areas, were also phenomenal."[12]

In the area of industrial production, China is definitely still a backward nation. Nevertheless her achievements have been much more impressive than other comparably situated underdeveloped countries, and this despite the abysmally low starting point, which precluded successful industrialization within a period comparable to that of the Soviet Union.

Considering all of the facts, we can conclude:

[10] John W. Gurley, "Maoist Economic Development: The New Man in the New China," *The Review of Radical Political Economics* (Fall 1970), pp. 34–35.

[11] G. Leslie Wilcox, "Observations on Medical Practices," *Bulletin of the Atomic Scientists* (June 1966).

[12] Quoted in Gurley, op. cit., p. 35.

The truth is that China over the past two decades has made very remarkable economic advances (though not steadily) on all fronts. The basic overriding economic fact about China is that for twenty years she has fed, clothed, and housed everyone, has kept them healthy, and has educated most. Millions have not starved; sidewalks and streets have not been covered with multitudes of sleeping, begging, hungry, and illiterate human beings; millions are not disease ridden. To find such deplorable conditions, one does not look to China these days, but, rather, to India, Pakistan, and almost anywhere else in the underdeveloped world. These facts are so basic, so fundamentally important, that they completely dominate China's economic picture, even if one grants all of the erratic and irrational policies alleged by her numerous critics.[13]

chinese economic philosophy

Any country undergoing industrialization must devote massive amounts of resources to the building of industrial capacity. This means, of necessity, that the average worker must remain relatively poor for a long period of time. Yet the low standard of average consumption can be achieved in either of two ways.

The first method is the one used by the Soviet Union. There, the few skilled technicians, engineers, and managers were offered material incentives. Thus, egoistic drive for more material benefits was manipulated to achieve industrialization, just as it had been during capitalist industrialization.

The second method, used by the Chinese, attempts to develop other types of incentives. Materialistic incentives are discouraged. Ideological propaganda emphasizes the importance of overcoming selfish, egoistic behavior. The well-being of everyone, the development of socialism and other social, nonindividualistic motives are stressed.

Education and training are less specialized. Each person is trained to do a number of jobs and may rotate from manual to mental labor, from urban to rural employment, and from rank-and-file positions to leadership positions. The Chinese emphasize the notion that narrow specialization prevents an individual from achieving his or her mental, emotional, and creative potential.

Many Western observers have noted that the income differential between factory worker and factory manager is quite small. Furthermore, the factory manager is expected to take his turn at tedious or

[13] Ibid., p. 34.

menial labor such as sweeping out the factory floor with a broom. As a consequence, workers and managers have much closer and more amiable personal ties in China than they do in most other countries.[14]

Some economists have criticized this policy. They assert that it is inefficient and retards the training of the large number of highly skilled technicians desperately needed for industrialization to be successful.

The Chinese reject this criticism on two grounds. First, they argue that they consider the making of well-rounded, intelligent, and creative human beings to be the final goal of industrialization. Rigid specialization, they assert, treats the individual as a *means* and not as an *end* because it stunts his or her development in the interest of greater productive output. Second, they believe that even though rigid specialization may bring short-run advantages in production, in the long-run, it is disadvantageous. Over the longer period, a broadly educated, creative, and happy population, whose motives are social rather than individualistic, will be much more productive. Further, they assert that this is the only concept of human development that is consistent with traditional ideals of socialism.[15]

The Soviet and Chinese models of socialist industrialization are certainly strikingly different. At present rigorous attempts to compare and evaluate the effectiveness of the two models would be premature. The two countries have so many differences in their histories, cultures, and general economic circumstances that one cannot generalize from the experience of the one to evaluate the other. Nevertheless, they do present contrasting approaches for any country that, in the future, might wish simultaneously to industrialize and to build a socialist society.

summary

The first revolution calling itself socialist occurred in 1917, in Russia. Against incredible odds, the Russian Communists ended the tsarist autocracy; won a civil war in which 14 foreign countries intervened against them; socialized industry; collectivized agriculture; carried through a successful change from a rural, illiterate, and under-developed economy to a predominately urban, highly educated, and advanced economy; and defeated the onslaught of Hitler's fascist

---

[14] See, for example, Barry M. Richman, *Industrial Society in Communist China* (New York: Random House, 1969), chap. 9.

[15] For a good discussion of Chinese economic philosophy, see Gurley, op. cit., pp. 29–38; Wheelwright and McFarlane, op. cit., pp. 197–240; and Edgar Snow, "Mao's Attributes," *The Listener* (May 29, 1969).

armies. Income is distributed more equally than in the United States, and the Soviet rate of production growth exceeds the U.S. rate. Unfortunately, Russia paid for all of this not only in decades of hard work and postponed consumption, not only in blood and millions of lives lost, but also in a political dictatorship that formerly executed its enemies, and often represses intellectual life, even today.

In 1949, the Chinese Revolution ousted the old, corrupt regime of Chiang Kai-shek, after decades of fighting against Chiang's forces and resisting Japanese imperialism. In less than a quarter of a century, they have had remarkable successes in raising living standards and hopes in the once most backward of all large countries. Their industrialization drive apparently has appealed even more than did the Russians' to social consciousness and less to immediate individual money incomes. It is still too early to undertake a detailed evaluation or evaluate their performance (although some other underdeveloped countries are already very much influenced by the Chinese model of development). Thus, in the next two chapters, we turn to the Soviet experience.

chapter 36
problems of socialist planning

We assume for the time being that the centralized, dictatorial Soviet model represents a kind of *socialism*. Although many socialists would argue that the Soviet Union is not really socialist, the Soviet case is considered here simply because it is the record of the longest experience with some kind of planning under some kind of socialism.

the soviet economic model

In the capitalist United States, most land and factories are privately owned. In the socialist Soviet Union, most land and factories are publicly owned, with the government claiming to represent the public. Public ownership, of course, tends to mean public direction and therefore usually means planning. The principal type of household income in the Soviet Union is wage income for labor. On the other side, in the United States, income consists not only of wages but also of profits, rent, dividends, and interest. These latter incomes are derived basically from private property; thus, most U.S. planning is necessarily limited in scope to the confines of single enterprises, in which decisions reflect the search for private profit.

In the Soviet Union, the only exceptions to public ownership are a very small percentage of cooperative industrial enterprises, mainly composed of handicraft workers. There are also many collective farms that are supposed to be cooperatives but are subject to considerable central control (but each farmer does also have a small private plot of land).

In the publicly owned enterprises, the Soviet government, or some agency of the government, appoints a manager. He is solely responsible for the performance of the factory, and his bonus is based on how well it performs. His performance and his conduct are checked by numerous agencies, and he may be promoted, transferred, or fired at any time. In turn, he hires and fires all the other workers at the enterprise.

The government grants the enterprise its plant and equipment and initial working capital, although they are now beginning to charge interest on capital. After the initial grant of capital, however, the enterprise is then made financially independent. It must meet all costs of wages and materials out of revenue from sales and must also replace or repair depreciated and broken capital out of revenues from sales. And it is normally expected to show a profit above all of its costs.

The Soviet economy is centrally planned. The most important economic orders originate from the USSR Council of Ministers, but additional orders to the enterprise may come from regional or local governmental bodies. Further orders may originate in or be transmitted through the agency directly supervising the enterprise, whether that agency is associated with a regional governing body or with the ministry directing some industrial area. Finally, all of these orders from governmental or supervisory bodies are supposed to be in accord with the plan, which emanates from the Central Planning Commission or its subordinate agencies. The enterprise manager is solely responsible for the performance of the factory, then, only in the sense that he must execute all of the orders he has received within the constraint of the resources allocated to him.

The Central Planning Commission first collects information up the ladder, from enterprise through agencies, in order to evaluate the last year's performance and the present conditions and possibilities. Then the Commission is told by the Council of Ministers what goals it must strive to meet. On these bases, it draws up a general plan for the whole economy, although production and allocation details are provided only for, say, 2,000 commodities. The draft plan is then shown to all agencies on down the ladder to the enterprise. After all these units have added their detailed modifications and suggestions, the Central Planning Commission draws up the final draft.

The plan is supposed to provide sufficient investment for the desired rate of growth, guarantee balance among all the industrial needs and outputs, and choose the *best* assortment of goods. At any rate, the Central Planning Commission hands the plan over to appropriate government bodies to enact into law. It is then passed on with detailed commands, expanded at each intermediate level, until the enterprise receives a formidable document which is supposed to tell the enterprise for a year (or some other period) exactly what to produce, how to produce it, what prices to charge, and what funds it may use. Again, the manager is judged on how well he follows these commands, though he has always had some decision-making power over details. The economic reforms of 1965 augmented the manager's decision-making power (discussed in Chapter 37).

planning for growth

In the case of a centrally planned economy such as the Soviet Union, it may be assumed that *aggregate* effective demand always rises as rapidly as aggregate supply, although *particular* goods may be unsalable for various reasons. Thus, there are no retardations or depressions caused by lack of demand. If the problems of demand are thus eliminated, then growth will depend simply on how fast output can be expanded. The supply problem may be resolved into two questions. (1) How much of each input (labor, capital, natural resources, and technology) can be procured under existing circumstances for use in production? (2) how much output can be obtained from these inputs in the production process?

These questions can be most usefully analyzed in terms of the growth formula explored in Chapter 31. It may be repeated here:

$$\text{Rate of growth of output} = \frac{\text{increase in output}}{\text{investment}} \times \frac{\text{saving}}{\text{output}}$$

If saving equals investment, as it does in the Soviet Union, then this formula is true by definition. The ratio of saving to output then indicates how much new capital is invested per year, and the ratio of increased output to investment indicates the amount of product produced by the new capital invested. Of course, that productivity is affected by changes in the labor force and in natural resources and technological improvements.

Consider the following application of the growth formula. If the ratio of saving to output is 9 percent, and if the ratio of increased output to investment is 1:3, then we find:

$$\text{Rate of growth} = \frac{1}{3} \times .09 = .03, \text{ or 3 percent a year}$$

This has been approximately the performance of the U.S. economy since the Civil War.[1]

[1] For empirical data on the ratios and the average growth rate, see Simon S. Kuznets, *National Product Since 1869* (New York: National Bureau of Economics Research, 1946).

For the years 1950–1970, conservative U.S. estimates place Soviet GNP growth at 6 percent a year; official Soviet figures indicate 9 percent a year.[2] (It is worth noting that China, in spite of political upheavals, also achieved a 6 percent growth rate each year from 1949 to 1966.[3]) Even the conservative American estimate is still high enough to call for an explanation in terms of the growth formula. If it is assumed for the moment that the Soviet ratio of increased output to investment is the same as the U.S. ratio, then in this simple analysis, the higher rate of growth can be explained by a higher ratio of saving and investment from current output (or income). Thus, if the Soviet ratio of increased output to investment is also 1:3, then a 6 percent growth rate can only be explained by an 18 percent ratio of saving to output. According to the formula:

$$\text{Soviet growth rate} = \frac{1}{3} \times .18 = .06, \text{ or 6 percent a year}$$

One reason for the high Soviet growth rate is that there is always sufficient aggregate demand in the Soviet Union for full employment of labor and full use of capacity. Therefore, all Soviet saving is used for investment because the planners can always find a use for new capital. In fact, Soviet planners usually complain of a *scarcity* of capital because they attempt to invest more than the entire available amount of savings. In the United States, however, when businessmen cannot find a profitable investment for all of their savings, some planned saving does not become investment in new capital. American economists often complain of *too much* planned saving, while planned investment in additional capital is less than it could be. In some years "too much" supply of all goods (in terms of money demand) even causes a decline of American production and a depression situation, not any growth of output.

Another reason for the high rate of Soviet growth is the enormous amount of resources invested in education and scientific research. By this means, their output per unit of capital has been greatly increased. First, education has given them a highly trained work force, capable of very productive labor. Second, education and science have given them a rapidly rising level of technology.

It is obvious from the formula, however, that the Soviet people have to pay a price for their high rate of investment and growth of output. If the Soviets save 18 percent and the United States saves only 9 percent of national output, and if both begin with the same $100

2 The data used in this paragraph are discussed in detail in Howard J. Sherman, *The Soviet Economy* (Boston: Little, Brown, 1969), chap. 5.

3 See the testimony by John Gurley in U.S. Congress, Joint Economic Committee, *Mainland China in the World Economy* (Washington, D.C.: U.S. Government Printing Office, 1967), p. 188.

output, then in the first year, U.S. consumption would be $91, while the Soviet consumption would be only $82. It is impossible to have both higher consumption and higher investment out of the same output (assuming we begun with full employment); the Soviets have sacrificed some present consumption for more investment. Furthermore, in reality, total Soviet output is still far below the U.S. level, and thus the Soviet consumption level is even lower. In purely human terms, moreover, we must stress that when the Soviets began their rapid industrial expansion, their consumption was at a miserably low level. Therefore, each percent of national product taken from consumption in order to make investments meant a very great amount of present human misery accepted as the cost of future growth.

However, the simple growth formula also indicates that if the Soviet Union continues to grow twice as fast as the United States, after some years, both their total output *and* their consumption will be larger than those of the United States. That is true, however, only *if* they continue to build new capital at the same rate and *if* they maintain the same increase of output per unit of new investment (by more education and more scientific research). It is no wonder that a major *political* issue in the Soviet Union has been and continues to be, how much of national output should be devoted to present consumption. Conversely, how much should be taken away from present consumption and put into investment in order to increase future consumption?

aggregate balance versus inflation

The question of aggregate balance in the Soviet economy is mostly a reflection of the growth problem already discussed. Basically, the resources supplied for invesment must just equal the amount required or demanded for investment, while the amount supplied to consumers must just equal the amount they will demand at present incomes and prices. The capitalist economy of the United States has been plagued frequently by lack of adequate demand for the products of private enterprise. In the planned economy of the USSR, there has *always* been sufficient aggregate demand since the planning period began in 1928, and there has never been general or aggregate unemployment. In the USSR, however, the problem has usually been that the government has demanded much more for investment than could be supplied, and has failed to provide enough consumer goods to satisfy household demand.

Because aggregate demand has always more than equaled the amount of available resources and manpower, aggregate unemployment has been nonexistent since 1928. Of course, the Soviet Union does have a considerable amount of frictional and structural unemployment. *Frictional* unemployment may be defined as ordinary labor turnover. *Sructural* unemployment occurs when the structure of industry and technology changes, so that millions of workers must change jobs from one place to another, from one industry to another, or from one skill to another. These changes require large amounts of retraining and moving expenses. Many observers recently have reported significant unemployment from this source. The Soviet Union may also have some seasonal unemployment which occurs because in certain industries, especially agriculture, demand for labor varies over a year. It may not be profitable for a society to transfer these workers to another job for only a few months, although the Chinese now use them to build dams and roads.

As implied above, the main problem of aggregate balance in the Soviet economy has not been unemployment created by lack of demand but rather inflation caused by excessive demand for labor and all goods. The main reason for the inflation of the 1930s and 1940s was the excessive increase in government demand for investment goods, military supplies, and free, or nonpriced, welfare services, which created an excess demand for all inputs, including labor. The excess demand for labor pushed up wage rates much faster than productivity, and thus workers' demand for consumer goods rose faster than total production and much faster than the output of consumer goods.

The excessive wage payments (which resulted in inflation) occurred as a result of decisions both at the national level and at the level of each firm. In the initial industrialization and wartime periods, the planners called for much larger increases in investment and military goods than in consumer goods; and the discrepancy was usually even greater in the fulfillment of plans. Related to the high level of investment and military spending was the practice of overfull employment planning mentioned earlier. At the level of the enterprise, overfull employment planning meant that managers were given output targets that, for most firms, were essentially unachievable with the amount of labor and other inputs legally available to them.

In order to meet their production plans, therefore, Soviet managers found themselves competing strenuously for materials and labor. Material-goods prices were effectively controlled at the enterprise level, and most deliveries of goods were ordered by direct central priorities and rationing. Workers, however, did move from job to job according to the incentive of higher wages, and thus this was the path followed by managers competing for labor inputs. In the 1930s and 1940s, managers were able to overspend their payrolls with few if any penalties, but were under extreme pressure to meet output targets. They would bid notoriously high to obtain the scarce supply of workers, and even hoarded unneeded workers against future needs.

As a final result of this process, the workers attempted to spend their rapidly increasing wages on the much smaller increase in consumer goods. The consequence was too much money chasing too few goods in the consumer-goods market, and steadily rising prices until 1947. This is the basic pattern of prewar and wartime inflation: excess demand for labor as a joint result of the high rate of investment and overfull employment planning; and excess demand for consumer goods as a result of wages rising faster than productivity and faster than the output of consumer goods.

In the face of these extreme inflationary pressures, Soviet policy was always to maintain constant or declining prices by administrative fiat. In practice, the pressures forced them to raise prices for long periods in the 1930s and 1940s. These reluctantly imposed increases did not soak up the full demand, however, and the result was *repressed inflation,* or regulation of prices below the free-market level. Repressed inflation showed up in shortages and long queues for many goods. Because their wages often could not be spent for any goods (because none were available at any price), workers' incentives to labor declined.

Only since 1947 has the problem been brought under some control (although a smaller degree of repressed inflation still exists). Since that time (1) the State Bank allows enterprises to pay wages above the planned amount *only to the extent* that they increase output above plan, and (2) the degree of overfull employment planning appears to have been sharply reduced (because the most urgent military demands have lessened).

relations between industries: microbalances

We have examined the aggregate (or macro-) balances between the major parts of the economy, such as consumption and wages, or saving and investment. Now the analysis must turn to the individual (micro-) balances required between different industries. In this context, each *industry* is defined as a collection of enterprises producing a single product for which no close substitute exists.

Soviet planners have been using a fairly simple approach called the *method of balances* to state macro- and microbalances. The following example at least roughly approximates how they would record the disposable personal income of all Soviet citizens (some details are omitted here) as a balanced budget of income and expenditures.

a. Workers' budget:

Wages + Pensions	Consumer spending + Personal saving
Source of disposable income	Spending disposable income

Next, government income and spending:

b. Government budget:

Taxes Profits + Loans	Investment Welfare Military + Surplus (deposited in State Bank)
Total income	Total spending

The same method of establishing a balanced intake and outgo is used for microbalances in each product or industry. Thus, the balance for the iron industry would appear as

c. Iron industry:

Imports Reduction in inventory + Production listed by plants or regions	Exports Increase in inventory + Uses by other industries, usually listed by region
Total sources	Total uses

Of course, it is only the totals that must balance. But somehow, enough iron must be available to meet each use or need in each area of the country.

This method runs into many problems. It is very difficult to achieve such a balance among all the conflicting needs and available materials in any one industry. Moreover, the balances are all related because each industry relies on others for supplies. For example, more steel is needed to produce more blast furnaces, but more blast furnaces are needed to make more steel. Recently, consideration has been given to adopting the input–output method developed in the West (by which a computer can estimate all the balances, *if* it is given the correct information).

prices and economic planning

One of the most important issues in Soviet planning is the question of how the planners are to decide which outputs society should produce. A related question is which technology is the cheapest for society to use in production.

Under capitalism, the search for profits dictates what is produced. Socialists have been persistent in pointing out that this method of deciding what to produce gives a higher social priority to trinkets, useless gadgets and other trivia for the wealthy than it does to the necessities of life for the poor. Socialists have always rejected the notion that market prices reflect meaningful social values.

Yet price offers a convenient basis for comparing goods and services that are not directly comparable. If a capitalist determined that he could produce several alternative "bundles" of commodities with, say, the $1 million of resources at his disposal, deciding which bundle to produce would be relatively simple for him. Given the resources at his disposal, he would produce the bundle of commodities that had the highest dollar *value.* He does not claim to be making a philosophical or moral judgment. He is merely maximizing his profits.

But when socialist planners are faced with the same situation, a fixed group of resources from which several possible combinations of outputs can be attained, theirs is a far more difficult task. They are not attempting to maximize profits. It is the general social welfare they wish to maximize. In order to choose the combination of commodities that maximizes social welfare, the *prices used for calculations must reflect perfectly the goals of a socialist society.*

Until the 1950s, this was not a terribly important problem for Soviet planners. The USSR's was still a backward economy in the 1930s, and therefore rapid industrialization could be achieved simply by copying the product mix and technologies of the most advanced capitalist countries.

During the 1940s, the war and the necessities of reconstruction dictated the product mix to the socialist planners. But by the mid-1950s, they had achieved a reconstructed industrial economy with immense productive capacity. Many more possibilities were technologically feasible. Furthermore, although rapid growth was still important, it had lost much of its urgency, while the goal of increasing the general welfare and providing more comforts for consumers had assumed much more importance. Under these circumstances, the question of how to evaluate the different possible commodity mixes became a central issue of socialist controversy in the Soviet Union. To understand these issues, we must first reexamine some debates in the West.

rational planning under socialism

In the 1920s, the possibility of rational socialist planning was denied by Ludwig von Mises.[4] Mises argued that the calculation of economic

4 See Ludwig von Mises, "Economic Calculation in the Socialist Commonwealth," in F. A. Hayek, ed., *Collectivist Economic Planning* (London: Routledge & Kegan Paul, 1935). A brief history of the whole debate appears in Abram Bergson, "Socialist Economics," in Howard Ellis, ed., *A Survey of Contemporary Economics* (Philadelphia: Blakiston, 1948), vol. I, pp. 412–448.

choices requires a knowledge of "rational" prices for both inputs and outputs. For example, if a farmer wishes to know whether to produce oranges or apples, he must know their relative prices at the time in order to maximize his revenues. Or if a planner wishes to decide whether railroad locomotives should use coal or oil, he must know the relative prices of coal and oil in order to minimize costs.

In socialism, however, the government owns the coal and oil as well as the locomotives. Therefore, according to Mises, because there is no market and no competition between producers there can be no rational prices. If the coal and oil producers are merely commanded to turn over a certain physical product to the locomotive-makers, no one can know which kind of fuel will cost more. In short, Mises argued, if there is no free market in socialism, there are no rational prices, and thus there can be no meaningful calculation or rational planning of allocation of resources.

The answer to Mises was pointed out long ago.[5] It is that *economic calculation of optimum allocation does not require* prices *in an actual market.* Only three kinds of information are required: (1) availability of resources, including men and machines as well as raw materials; (2) the preference scale of consumers, whether they are individuals or planners or politicians or some weighted sum of the three; (3) the production function of each output—that is, the combination of resources necessary to produce each output at the present level of technology.

As a concrete example, assume that the Soviet economy produces only two kinds of outputs: apples and oranges. The planners must have information on the given technology of apple and orange pro-duction, and they must know the given amount of labor and capital inputs available. Assume next that the economy can produce *only* either (A) 5 apples and 10 oranges or (B) 10 apples and 5 oranges. Which output mixture should be produced to maximize output? That obviously depends on the price of each output relative to the price of the other. The planners will set some relative prices according to their knowledge of consumer preferences (and social goals). If con-sumers like apples twice as much as oranges, their price should be twice as high. If the prices (calculated according to preferences) are 2 rubles an apple and 1 ruble an orange, then social value, or output, is maximized by choosing mixture B, 10 apples and 5 oranges. But if the prices (reflecting different preferences) were 1 ruble an apple and 2 rubles an orange, then we would maximize value by choosing mixture A, 5 apples and 10 oranges. (This is simple arithmetic; the reader should do it to prove it to himself.)

5 The clearest statement is in Oskar Lange, *On the Economic Theory of Socialism* (New York: McGraw-Hill, 1964 [written in 1938]).

INFORMATION FOR PLANNING

As was noted, planners must be informed about resource availability, consumer preferences, and technological possibilities. In both a private-enterprise economy and in socialism, the third kind of information (about alternative production possibilities) is furnished by engineers, although the final choice among technologies is an economic problem relating to the costs of various inputs. In a competitive private-enterprise economy, however, market prices *automatically* reflect the first and second types of information—that is, the relative scarcity of different resources as well as the relative preference of consumers for different products. Under socialism, the planners have to collect this information themselves. *If* it can be obtained, then socialist planners will be able to calculate rational prices for all resources and for all products. These prices would be data for planners to use, and need never be paid anybody.

If the planners of socialist industry had access to the same information available to the private-enterprise managers, presumably they could then calculate the optimum mix of technology and resource allocation for the maximization of social welfare in much the same way that private-enterprise managers calculate for the maximization of profit. The problem is that collecting the necessary information and calculating the necessary equations is very difficult, and hence planning is far from perfect. However, the Soviet economy has performed reasonably well, and the deviation from optimal allocation may be less than it is under oligopoly conditions in the capitalist market. The relative inefficiencies of bureaucratic planning and oligopoly price-setting cannot be reliably evaluated on the basis of available data.

summary

Soviet economic planning faces various economic problems, although they are very different from American economic problems. The Soviets have full employment because their planners can always use excess funds for more projects. However, they have had inflation problems because they have tried to produce even beyond their physical capacities and have paid out more wages than there were consumer goods available at current prices.

There is also a constant political fight over producing more consumer goods versus producer goods (for growth) versus military goods versus welfare goods (including education, which also contributes to growth).

Moreover, there is need for balances between individual products; each industry must produce enough to meet the need for its product from every other industry.

Finally, the planners must decide how much of each product to produce and how to produce it. These decisions depend on information about (1) resource availability, (2) consumer and social preferences, and (3) technological possibilities. Getting this information is difficult, but the imperfect planners may still do as well or better than the imperfect markets of capitalism.

chapter 37
use of the market
under socialism

In the modern world, socialism has usually meant central planning.
In this chapter, we shall examine the Soviet debate and reforms,
which decreased the degree of centralized power over economic
decision-making, and the Yugoslav experience with extreme
decentralization of economic decision-making.

marxism and
decentralization

Marx himself wrote very little about the details of socialist planning;
he always emphasized that it would be utopian to discuss such
details before the advent of an actual socialist economy. But clearly,
Marx and Engels disapproved of the planlessness of capitalism.
In addition, they felt it to be an important cause of the periodic crises
of depression or inflation. Nevertheless, this does not indicate that
they would necessarily disapprove of the market device under
socialism because socialism provides a very different economic
environment.

recent soviet experience

Soviet planning reforms may have been generated partly by the increasing complexity of the economy and partly by the shortage of labor. The argument is that rational planning and decentralization are more necessary in relatively advanced than in less developed countries. Technical innovation, which is now one of the most important Soviet goals, depends mainly on continuous local initiative at the production point. By contrast, throughout the 1920s and 1930s, the main problem was putting to work in industry the resources that were unemployed or less profitably employed in agriculture. For that purpose, central control was very efficacious.

soviet managerial behavior before the 1965 reforms

The Soviet debate pivoted on the behavior of the manager under the old system. Critics argued that attention to cost-cutting and profit-making could hardly make him act more in a greedy, bourgeois manner than he had behaved for decades. Under the prereform system, if the manager fulfilled or overfulfilled his plan each month, he received an additional large bonus, which generally ran from 25 to 50 percent of his salary. Some of the rewards to the successful manager were speculative and hard to measure, but it was certain that the unsuccessful manager would lose bonuses and ultimately his job or be demoted to a less important operation.

Because the manager was under great pressure to produce, he resorted to many evasions. His performance was judged by several criteria, including wage and raw-material costs per unit and other indicators of productivity and efficiency. But the principal index of success, the one he strove above all to achieve, was simply the value of the gross output produced. If he did not achieve the planned value of output, he received no bonus at all. If, however, he exactly met the planned target, he might receive as much as a full 40 percent bonus, although the average bonus was somewhat less. For each 1 percent overfulfillment of the plan, managers in high-priority industries received an additional 4 to 6 percent bonus.

The Soviet manager brushed aside bureaucratic regulations and controls when they conflicted with the achievement of output goals. To a great extent, he evaded specific regulations only in order to meet his plan. This was not always to the national benefit. For example, the manager sometimes circumvented red tape in order to obtain materials that should have been his anyway. On other occasions, however, he may have illegally obtained materials that could have been better used by a higher-priority enterprise. Unfortunately, some of the manager's devices (e.g., lowering quality in order to produce greater output) yielded a bonus for an *apparent* plan fulfillment. Such behavior constituted, in fact, an antisocial act not dissimilar to the well-known evasions of the corporate income tax or antitrust laws by managers of American corporations.

Practices that reformers called attention to include the following:[1]

False reports   Obviously, if his production for the month had fallen short of 100 percent of the planned target, and thus the manager had lost his bonus, he might have padded his figures with waste or unfinished goods or "shifted" enough production from a very high to a low month. Some managers, but not many, actually resorted to outright falsification (the system forced them to do so if they were to survive). Of course, falsification was dangerous because the manager had to submit a very large volume of related reports which were examined for internal consistency by bank auditors or his superiors.

More important, there were many different channels of control over the manager, and these channels were sufficiently independent to make collusion by all agents at best very difficult. First, there was the superior agency that controlled the enterprise, whether it was under an industrial ministry or a regional council. Second, there was the Communist party which has cells in each enterprise, and these had certain rights to inspect and suggest improvements on enterprise projects. Third, there were the trade unions, one of whose functions was the stimulation of production. Fourth, there was the State Bank, in which every enterprise kept accounts. Fifth, there also were agents of the Ministry of State Control whose sole function was to check on the legality of enterprise actions. Finally, there was the Central Statistical Agency. Because each agency carried its information to a different place, cross-checking was very difficult. Moreover, bribery, direct and subtle, reached everywhere, and controllers at the local level tended to form a coalition with managers.

Easier plans   The manager himself played an important role in formulating the plan. He naturally bargained for a lower output target and a higher amount of required supplies. In this way, output targets were more easily overfulfilled.

Poorer quality   If a plan could not be met in the necessary

---

[1] See, for example, Harry G. Schaffer, "Ills and Remedies," *Problems of Communism* (May–June 1963), pp. 27–32; also David Granick, *The Red Executive* (New York: Doubleday, 1961).

quantities by producing what was supposed to be produced, it could often be fulfilled by producing a poorer quality of good. Some Soviet consumer goods have been of notoriously poor quality.

Fewer styles   It was much easier to produce a large amount of one homogeneous good than it was to produce small quantities of many different goods. The manager therefore had an incentive to produce all of one type of good rather than a variety, although the latter might lead to more consumer satisfaction. Because the price was fixed the manager did not depend on demand. However, managers sometimes introduced a new style just to get assigned a higher price.

Easiest mixture   The type or style on which production was concentrated may have been chosen, not on the basis of usefulness to the economy, but because it was the cheapest method of achieving the output goal.

Extra supplies   It is a well-known fact that managers kept on their payroll men whose only function was to expedite the flow of supplies or to find new sources of supply outside of the planned sources. These men were known as *pushers,* although they had some other title on the official payroll. They often enjoyed pleasant lives on expense accounts, wining and dining officials from other firms and various higher organizations, who may have been able to furnish scarce supplies (by barter or bribery). They were the counterpart of the American *expediters* of World War II, who hung around Washington trying to get scarce materials for their firms.

Hidden reserves   A wise Soviet manager piled up inventories of any goods he could get his hands on, regardless of whether he happened to need them at the moment. When his output target was raised, he could use these extra reserves if he was unable to procure more supplies legally. Thus, a large amount of resources may have been wasted, frozen in an unproductive storage stage of the productive process.

Extra labor   The manager had a plan for labor and for the total amount of wages he could spend. Overspending on wages, however, was usually very lightly punished, if at all. Of course, meeting, and especially exceeding, the output target cleansed him of all crimes.

High-priced raw materials   The manager was penalized very little for high costs and was given a great reward for overfulfilling his output target; thus, he had no reason not to use high-priced raw materials. Moreover, he was judged not by the value added by the enterprise, but by the gross value of the product *including* the value of the raw materials which were merely bought from other firms. Therefore, the higher the price of the raw materials he bought, the higher the value of his gross output and the greater his own reward.

Naturally, Soviet managers had considerable incentive to buy the most expensive raw materials.

Resistance to innovations   The manager frequently did not react with enthusiasm to innovations that *may* have increased his productive capacity at lower costs. First, innovations are risky because they may actually lower output for some months while the transition is being made to new machinery. Managers seldom took the long-run view because they were often switched to other jobs on fairly short notice. Frequent reassignment may have prevented or reduced corruption and collusion (or "familyness"), but it also motivated managers to focus their attention on immediate production gains, so that they were unwilling to gamble on higher bonuses from greatly increased production at some future date.

Second, the manager knew that if the innovation succeeded in greatly increasing his capacity to produce, his production targets would be increased, and thus he himself might gain nothing. If the plan were overfulfilled by a large margin, targets were apt to be raised in the same proportion. Therefore, a manager was likely to try for a steady 103 percent or 105 percent, but not more.

The tendencies we have just described did exist (and still do to a lesser extent), but they should certainly not be taken to mean that Soviet managers were completely inefficient. The Soviet economy *has* produced higher peacetime growth than the American economy despite these inefficiencies. This dysfunctional behavior does imply that the growth achieved was at greater cost and sacrifice than necessary, or that growth could have been faster with the same amount of effort. The fact that some degree of inefficiency did exist in the old system of central planning was the driving force behind the recent decentralization reforms and the continued fight for further modifications.

course of the debate

In the atmosphere of increased freedom for scientific inquiry after 1956, there arose a faction of economists whose approach was pragmatic. They analyzed organizational matters and very concrete policy issues; through experimentation they hoped to develop solutions for limited problems. During the 1950s, criticism of the malfunctions of the enterprise-incentive system flowed largely from their evidence and conclusions.

Kharkov Professor Evsei G. Liberman was one of these critics. In fact, he was not the most important critic, but was chosen by the political leaders to spark the public debate. Liberman published three papers in Soviet journals during the 1950s. He argued that specific problems created by existing success indicators could be overcome by appropriate changes in the operational constraints on enterprises. The reforms he advocated in 1959 were essentially those that touched off the 1962 controversy. However, until 1962, both the man and his recommendations were ignored by other writers as well as the general public.

The debate was given urgency when the Soviet political leadership became alarmed over the retardation in growth rates apparent in the early 1960s. As already noted, these difficulties and the need for reform may have been due to the growing complexity and inter-dependence of Soviet allocations, which made it increasingly difficult to devise priority rankings and balance the plan. The opposite argument by some American economists, that the problems may have been purely temporary and unconnected with the level of development, should be noted. These more noneconomic factors include poor weather, the enormous manpower losses of World War II, extravagant foreign-aid programs, and increased spending on military and space ventures.

the essentials of the liberman plan

In September 1962, the Communist party initiated a public discussion by allowing Liberman to publish his plan in *Pravda.* His *Kharkov incentive system* calls for structural changes in the planning process, but only at the level of the firm. All investments, prices, and outputs are to continue to be centrally planned. The relationship of the planning apparatus to the individual enterprise, however, is to be fundamentally changed.

To encourage greater flexibility and initiative, the large number of indicator targets presently passed down to the firm is to be stream-lined to "key indices" only. Liberman recommends assigning enter-prises just those targets that pertain exclusively to their final output mix: quantity and assortment of production, product destinations, and delivery dates. The *input* mix is to be determined by each individual firm: the planners will then presumably sum up all the enterprise needs and provide them through the centrally planned system of material allocation (this would be quite difficult).

How well an enterprise fulfills society's demand for maximum productivity is to be assessed solely on the basis of an evaluation of its efficiency. *Profitability,* which is defined to be profits expressed as a percentage of total capital, is to serve as this inclusive evaluator, and is to be estimated in yearly plans submitted by all firms. Once the stated output goals are attained, the rate of profitability achieved becomes the sole determinant of the amount of bonus funds awarded to the firm and its employees. Liberman depicts the central planners as "relieved from petty tutelage over enterprises" and from "costly efforts to influence production through administrative measures rather than economic ones."[2]

Bonus payments are to be computed by comparing the profitability rate of a particular firm with a profitability norm established for the branch of industry within which each firm is to be included. This is an attempt to set a "single standard of profitability for enterprises in roughly the same natural and technical conditions."[3] Norms also are to vary with the proportion of new products in a firm's production program; they will be raised, for example, when no new products are being introduced. Different incentive-payment scales will then be set up for the different branches of industry. The bonus premiums earned by the firm under this system will be utilized, as the manager directs, to (1) pay salary bonuses to management and workers, (2) provide new housing, nurseries, kindergartens, and recreation facilities for workers' families and (3) finance small, decentralized investments.

To motivate directors to attempt as ambitious a plan as their productive potential allows, Liberman advances three proposals. First, incentive premiums per ruble of capital invested are to rise as the rate of profit increases. Second, the firm is to benefit more from fulfilling its own profitability plan than from overfulfilling it. Third, the norms of profitability are to be established for an extended period of time (from two to five years or more). This will prevent the harmful practice of raising norms whenever a firm surpasses its planned targets. In this way, the firm's directors can count on reaping benefits from successful innovations or particularly effective cost-saving programs. The concern for profitability is also supposed to stimulate the manager to search for cost reductions and to produce the output mix demanded by his consumers.

soviet controversy, 1962–1963

Both moderate and active Soviet supporters of the Liberman system agree that a rational price system is a necessary precondition for a profit-based index to serve as an effective evaluator of enterprise efficiency. Although Liberman himself has been somewhat indefinite

[2] Evsei G. Liberman, "Plan, Profits, and Bonuses," in M. E. Sharpe. ed., The Liberman Discussion (New York: International Arts and Sciences Press, 1965), p. 79.
[3] Ibid.

about the changes in pricing methodology that would be necessary to achieve this rationality, others (e.g., V. S. Nemchinov) have taken a strong stand for many years. Because profits derive from selling prices and cost prices, profitability will be a measure of real, and not merely paper, efficiency only if prices reflect the relative values of all inputs into production. Consequently, as a Soviet commentator asserts, a substantial price deviation "above or below the socially necessary outlays, results, regardless of the operation of the enterprise, either in an unjustifiably low profitability, and even loss, or in excessive profitability."[4]

One group of Soviet writers argued further that the existing material supply system was too complex and inflexible to give enterprises the freedom of input determination envisioned in Liberman's incentive scheme. Therefore, they advocated replacing administrative allocations with a system of state trade, in which enterprises would negotiate independent agreements with suppliers and customers. Nemchinov boldly argued that all planning of intermediate goods should cease; the state should decide only what final products it needs.[5]

The majority of responses to *Pravda*'s 1962 request for discussion, however, were characterized by either total hostility to Liberman's scheme or considerable criticism. For example, Zverev, former Minister of Finance, denounced the theory he sees lurking behind Libermanism: that profit is created not only by the worker's labor, but also by fixed and current capital: "It is hardly necessary to prove the erroneousness of such a theory."[6] (Notice that he may be confusing the productivity of capital with the productivity of capitalists, while none of the reformers says that capitalists are productive, nor do any of them advocate paying profits to individuals.) Zverev also rejected the premise that the central planners are less informed as to the capabilities of enterprises than the enterprise itself. They "are obligated to know, and actually do know, the production capacities of enterprises."[7] The former minister challenged too the profitability norms to be established for branches of industry, asserting that they would not be objective for all firms in a grouping, and predicting that constantly changing technical conditions among firms would cause persistent pressure on any norm-setting govern-

[4] L. Gatovskii, "The role of Profit in a Socialist Economy," translated in *The Soviet Review* (Summer 1963), p. 20.

[5] See V. Nemchinov, "Plan, Assignment and Material Incentive," in Sharpe, op. cit., pp. 107–113.

[6] A. Zverev, "Against Oversimplification in Solving Complex Problems," *Problems of Economics* (April 1963), p. 18.

[7] Ibid., p. 16.

ment agency to revise the norm. The only way to keep norms fair, he concluded, would be to revise them continuously.

A full measure of hostility was focused on the increase in decentralized investment likely to occur with the adoption of a Liberman-type scheme. Convinced that existing defects in "capital construction" are due to insufficient centralization, several writers emphatically decried the proposal to leave an increased number of investment decisions with the enterprises. They claimed that enterprises are "ignorant of the various national economic interrelations," so that the effect would be to increase "parochialism" and to multiply "disproportions in the national economy."[8] (Actually, Liberman never advocated decentralization of major investment decisions.)

Professor Liberman's reply in 1962 to his critics made some interesting points.[9] First, he attempted to clear away the confused notion held by some that profitability alone would be the single index to regulate enterprise behavior. The production goals that society demands of enterprises, including the quantity and assortment of output, are still to be centrally planned and individually assigned to firms. Only after meeting the output targets does profitability take prime importance for the firm. Second, he countered the charge that successful enterprises will be able to rest on past efficiency achievements, asserting that "even a small increase in incentive payments is of some interest" and that "every manufacturing enterprise must constantly introduce new production . . . or its incentive scale will drop."[10]

By May, 1963, however, controversy had died down considerably. The government gave no further indication of its readiness to alter the basics of its system of minutely detailed planning and supervision of enterprises. Yet during the lull in public debate, which lingered through mid-1964, problems with unsold consumer goods became critical. It was apparently the unwanted inventory increases that precipitated the first Soviet experiments with profit incentives and direct ties to consumers.

Specifically, the drastic situation of soaring inventories of textiles and clothing goods stirred the government in early 1964 to place two large garment manufacturing associations, the *Bolshevicka* in Moscow and the *Mayak* in Gorky, under the rules of a new system. This system had at least some of the general characteristics of Liberman's scheme. The two producers were to work out their own output plans on the basis of orders from retail outlets, and their

8 Quotations in this paragraph from K. Plotnikov, "E. G. Liberman: Right and Wrong," translated in Sharpe, op. cit., pp. 161–165.

9 E. G. Liberman, "Reply to Critics of the Profit Proposal," *Current Digest of the Soviet Press* (December 1962), pp. 18–20.

10 Ibid., p. 18.

performance was to be judged by sales rather than output, although not by profit as in Liberman's scheme. They were to negotiate their own contracts with principal suppliers, and financial penalties were to be levied for failure to make deliveries according to contract. In spite of a number of predictable difficulties, especially with surrounding bureaucracy, both associations overfulfilled output and profit plans for the year. The USSR Council of National Economy decided to extend the experiment to 400 associations in the textile, clothing, leather, and footwear industries during 1965. There were even trials of the new system among a few factories manufacturing producer goods.

the resumption of debate: 1964–1965

Shortly after this initial experimentation with greater incentives began, public discussion was again requested by the editors of *Pravda*. The inference is that desires for economic reform from within the party had significantly grown in the interim. The party was probably influenced by the intensification of the Soviet economy's problems between 1962 and 1964, including the rapidly mounting inventories of consumer goods, the grain-crop failures in 1963, and the declining growth rate. The Soviet party was surely also influenced by the virtual stagnation of the Czech economy in 1963, the inception in 1964 of profit-sharing and a charge on capital in Hungary, and the continued success of the decentralized Yugoslav system.

In 1964, another lead article by Liberman in *Pravda* reiterated his position and, in addition, advocated a charge on capital. Within six months, the newspaper received 600 articles and letters in response. Most indicated a substantial shift from the tone of the 1962 controversy. A *Pravda* columnist concluded that the overwhelming majority of writers felt it necessary to "intensify sharply the role of economic levers in the management of the national economy to expand the rights of enterprises, to enhance the importance of profit . . . and to put price formation in order."[11] Expressions of total hostility were practically nonexistent. And an expanded and vocal group of economists, research workers, and enterprise managers became increasingly insistent in their demands for the adoption of widespread change.

The degree of enterprise autonomy urged by some of the writers now went considerably beyond the Liberman plan and its 1962 extensions. Arguing that output plans should be based on orders

11 "Survey of Readers' Letters," *Pravda* (February 17, 1965).

from customers, they asserted first, that enterprises "should be given the right to amend the output plan with the consent of the customer" and second, that when an enterprise is producing a product "with higher consumer properties than are stipulated by the standards, it should be given the right to fix the price with the agreement of the customer."[12] One Soviet author even proposed that central price-setting be replaced by competition ruled by consumer demand.[13]

The goals of most hopeful reformers, however, did not at first include changes that would decentralize price-setting. Their main new demand was for the introduction of direct links with suppliers in order to supplant the unwieldly system of central supply allocations. They were also loud in urging a price calculus with capital charges. Nevertheless, complete central control over national parameters (including prices) was still regarded as integral to the preservation of economic balances and a high rate of accumulation. Only after the reforms actually began in 1966 and 1967 was considerable sentiment voiced for price decentralization as well as output decentralization.

official reforms

Although "economic experiments" were extended and given more varied trials during 1965, it was not until that September that the government responded with a major organizational reform in industry, which moved somewhat in the direction of the Liberman proposals. Adopted as law by the Supreme Soviet on October 2, the stipulations of the Kosygin Reform were conservative and tentative, yet they did begin the process of reform. The section pertaining to the individual enterprise contains four significant new policies. First, and most important, managers' bonuses are to be paid for fulfillment of planned targets for sales, profit or profitability, and physical output. The scales of bonuses will be designed to provide relatively higher rewards for fulfillment of targets. Moreover, to evaluate the amount of sales, the *gross value of output* indicator is to be replaced by *output sold,* which implies the necessity to produce what the consumers desire. Numerous target directives will be eliminated, including the norms for labor productivity, number of workers and employees, and average wages.

Second, the enterprise will be permitted to retain and utilize a large proportion of profits (and some portion of depreciation allow-

12 V. Belkin and I. Berman, "Independence of the Enterprise and Economic Stimuli," translated in Sharpe, op. cit., pp. 225–230.

13 O. Volkov, *Pravda* (August 23, 1964).

ances) for bonuses, welfare purposes, and decentralized investment. This may turn out to be a very significant measure, giving financial muscle to the decentralization reforms. Third, one-half of decentralized investment is to be financed by repayable and interest-bearing loans from banks, and interest charges are to be levied (in the form of a tax) on all fixed and working capital put at the enterprise's disposal. Fourth, contracts between enterprises are to be more strictly enforced, prohibiting superiors from changing enterprise plans at will during the plan period.

Some of the reform measures do approach the spirit, if not the letter of Liberman's scheme. Attention to what has been left out of the Kosygin system, however, gives us a more pessimistic view of the possibility that the reforms will implement the kind of changes Liberman sympathizers have been proposing. For example, it has been pointed out numerous times that any attempt at a greater reliance on profitability criteria would be useless (or even harmful) without a rational price system. Yet the wholesale price reform has been very slow in coming, and the more drastic changes requested by Soviet reformers have not been made. Furthermore, the new committee charged with price policy has been told no more than that prices should reflect costs, a remarkably insufficient suggestion considering that economists and planners have been arguing the basic principle for at least ten years.

Moreover, the new economic system continues to maintain the method of direct material allocation (there are recent reports of some attempts to replace or modify it by the introduction of large wholesale-warehouse type establishments in which enterprises can buy anything they need). As long as the system of direct material allocation is continued, the reforms certainly will not result in the Liberman objective of enterprise freedom to vary inputs. Notice that the reformed system also keeps the central limits on total payrolls and allows managers to choose the labor mix only within those limits. At the same time, the apparent intent to allow more decentralized investments may result in a significant decrease in central control over the determination of future output. Indeed, we note again, the allowance of a large amount of decentralized investment may turn out to be one of the most important practical features of the reform.

It must be admitted that even these limited reforms have already run into bureaucratic obstruction and sabotage. Thus, there have been numerous reports of continued extralegal interference by government and party organs in the day-to-day operations of enterprises, including those on the new system. The undoubted difficulties of the new system will be resolved eventually either by retrogression (renewed centralization) or by further reform (toward real market socialism). Which direction is taken will depend on many factors, including external ones such as peace in Vietnam.

the yugoslav model

The Yugoslav experience revealed to the whole world that a socialist economy could be largely decentralized and directed mainly by the market. Although it was at first denounced with the usual Stalinist unanimity, later, when the anti-Stalinist tide began to rise, the Yugoslav economy became a model to investigate.

The Cominform (or Communist Information Bureau) was established in 1947 by Stalin primarily as a means of keeping eastern Europe, and perhaps especially Yugoslavia, on a tight leash. In 1948, however, Yugoslavia broke with the USSR and advocated complete independence and equality for all socialist nations. The Yugoslavs complained that the Russians had attempted to dominate their army, to exploit their economy through joint companies, to use secret agents to investigate and blackmail important Yugoslavs, and to threaten the cutting off of all trade should Yugoslavia take any independent action. In reply, the Cominform excommunicated Yugoslavia, charging that she had slandered the USSR and was no longer Marxist because she had stopped pushing collectivization.

The Yugoslavs eventually answered that the USSR had deviated further and further from socialist democracy toward bureaucratic overcentralization. As a concrete reaction, by 1950, the Yugoslavs began to decentralize their economy and create their own socialist democracy, focused on *Workers' Councils* in each factory. During this period, the Yugoslavs advanced the economic theory that central or administrative planning may at first greatly help the progress of an underdeveloped or war-torn socialist economy. As the economy becomes more built-up, complex, and interrelated, however, such extreme central direction "turns into its opposite," and becomes a barrier to further progress. Some variant of this theory has become the basis for reforms in much of eastern Europe and even the Soviet Union.

framework of the yugoslav economic system

After 1950, farming in Yugoslavia reverted to private ownership (as it did in Poland after 1957). There are few Yugoslav collectives today, although the goal of collectivization supposedly remains. In fact, the government is very, very gradually buying up individual pieces of land as farmers retire. There is also a private-business sector, mostly in the areas of trade and handicrafts. Private businesses and farms may hire up to five persons, but this limit apparently has been exceeded in practice. Farmers may acquire land up to ten hectares. The private sector thus plays a very small role in industry, but constitutes almost the whole of the farming sector. Private enterprise also plays an increasing role in the catering and service sector.

In the socialist sector of industry, each factory is run as a producer's cooperative under the control of its own Workers' Council. The Workers' Councils are a feature unique to Yugoslav socialism. Many other eastern European countries are slowly directing their economies toward fully independent activity by each enterprise. Yet none of them presently intends to institute workers' councils as a basic feature, preferring control by government-appointed managers. (When the revolutionary tides ran strong, workers' councils *were* temporarily introduced in Poland in 1956–1957, and Czechoslovakia in 1968–1969.) Today, only the Yugoslavs consider Workers' Councils the most vital part of their economic structure. They not only praise its allegedly democratic aspects, but also claim that it motivates workers and managers to the highest efficiency. Some Yugoslavs even assert that the Workers' Councils are responsible for their high rate of growth, which skeptics attribute primarily to a high rate of investment.

How does the system of Workers' Councils operate? The workers elect a council. The manager is then appointed by the local government, but the Workers' Council has a veto power over the appointment of the manager. The council can also fire the manager; set wages, within limits established by the central government; set prices, also within limits defined by the central agencies; set production targets and determine technology; and dispose of its profits after taxes through additions to wages, collective welfare projects, or reinvestment. Taxes collected by the national government are used to finance major investment projects as well as defense and welfare.

Because all firms compete in the market, prices set will be rational from the viewpoint of neoclassical economics, provided that there is pure and perfect competition. Nevertheless, because a large percentage of investment is still under central control, capital cannot freely flow to areas of higher profits. This constitutes a barrier to entry of other firms and may allow monopoly or oligopoly to arise in any area in which the central government sets an optimum firm size that is very high in relation to the total market. Because Yugoslavia is a small country (of medium size in eastern Europe) and the total market for many commodities is limited, there are many industries in which optimum firm size demands only one or a few producers. As the result of such monopolies, (1) price relationships are distorted away from the socially "rational" price, (2) resources are therefore allocated wrongly from the social viewpoint, and (3) consumers are exploited in the sense of paying higher prices to these particular firms.

Expansion and new investment by a particular firm also have some peculiar aspects under this system. If an entirely new firm is organized, it has its own council to look after the benefits of its own workers. New firms are often, but not always, set up by old firms. However, a new Workers' Council does not return any profits to the firm that set it up, although it is obligated to pay interest to the government on the capital it has been given. Some of the "sponsored" new enterprises are treated legally as mere subsidiaries of the old firms, and the additional profits are divided amongst the workers of both the old and new firms. In either case, the way that a council evaluates a new investment project outside its own plant is far more complicated than the usual profit calculus of a capitalistic competitive firm. One would expect some tendency to limit projects to those that might be considered a legitimate part of the old firm.

In addition to these microeconomic aspects of investment, there is something new in this system with respect to the question of aggregate investment. What is to keep a particular firm's workers from deciding that all of their profits should go into current wages or welfare projects rather than reinvestment and expansion of the productive base? Legally, the only constraint is that the firm must first pay its taxes to the central government. The central government does take a very large tax bite, and much of this revenue has been used for investment, which has contributed significantly to Yugoslavia's impressive rate of economic growth. Yugoslavs also claim that the workers are generally very willing to make many large reinvestments, supposedly being content to wait for the large future returns.

The Communist party group within each enterprise also strongly encourages collective welfare projects and reinvestment for expansion of the productive base. And the manager of the enterprise exerts a somewhat independent pressure, in most cases advocating expansion of the enterprise's capital. Actually, it appears that the balance of power over the distribution of income between workers and managers and higher authorities varies from plant to plant as well as from year to year. For example, Yugoslav as well as Western economists agree that in 1961 workers' wages increased more than productivity, causing inflation in the consumer-goods market. At present, the ratio of investment to national income is very high. Therefore, a large percentage of all investment, especially that going into new enterprises, must be and is still done by the central government, but an increasing percentage is coming under the control of existing firms and local governments.

It should be noted that the revenue of the enterprise must pay (1) interest on loans from the banking system, (2) depreciation allowances, (3) interest to the central government on the initial capital investment, (4) the turnover tax on sales, (5) miscellaneous taxes and fees, and (6) the income tax on profits. After the firm has paid these expenses, it is then free to divide the rest of the revenue between wages and new investment. Yet the workers still must pay an additional social insurance tax on their wages. It is also required that at least 24 percent of investment funds go to a housing fund and to communal investment projects such as recreation centers. One further restriction lies in the fact that the government enforces a minimum wage for each worker.

For some time, the total of all taxes, including profit tax, turnover tax, and interest on initial capital, amounted to about one-third of GNP. In 1961, about 50 percent of government revenues were spent on defense, 35 percent on welfare, and 15 percent on investment. But allocations by enterprises pushed gross investment up to 35 percent of GNP.

In other areas too, decisions are not made by the enterprise-level Workers' Councils. Central planning is responsible for (1) all of the most important investment projects, (2) most research and development, and (3) the education of skilled and professional workers.

some problems of the yugoslav system

Prices of products in Yugoslavia are set by the enterprises (to the extent allowed by government price control), and the enterprises have every reason for increasing prices at every opportunity. If output demanded does not fall proportionately, then higher prices give the Workers' Council an opportunity to pay higher wages. Furthermore, as was noted, a small country such as Yugoslavia inevitably has many monopoly producers because a single large-scale, optimum-size enterprise takes such a huge slice of an industry. This problem is mitigated, in part, by foreign trade because foreign competition helps keep the monopolies in line. The result of the strong wage position and monopoly structure has been a chronic tendency toward price inflation. One interesting consequence of the monopoly pricing is that socialist Yugoslavia has passed an antimonopoly law against combinations in restraint of trade or conspiracies to raise prices.

In addition, the natural reaction of a central government with a planning tradition was the imposition of a large number of price controls. It was noted above that by 1967 a large percentage of Yugoslavia's industrial sales were of price-controlled goods (this is supposed to be a temporary situation). Firms either may set prices only within certain limits, or they must get agency approval for any price change. Bureaucracy thus returns to the price-setting stage via the back door, although the enterprises are still the formal sources of all prices.

Another Yugoslav problem has been the continuing importance of regional or national rivalries. This is especially significant in the investment process, in which the allocation is achieved partly by local and regional agencies. Some of the allocation is by central planners, but they themselves may be afflicted by regional biases. Moreover, it is not just a matter of regional rivalries; the regions are in vastly different stages of economic development. To achieve equality in the level of development, it still is necessary to invest, say, in Macedonia, despite the fact that the project could do much better in a more advanced region. This is a profound problem; in the short run at least, it causes a great loss from investment allocation that is inefficient in terms of what might be done were there no extra-economic regional considerations.

Another problem arises from the attempt to give real power to Workers' Councils over the specific plants and enterprises. This tends to result in the splitting up of industries into units of a size small enough for democratic participation. But the political objective may conflict with the economic goal of achieving enterprises large enough to utilize all possible economies of scale. Thus, the railways of Yugoslavia have been divided into a rather loose association of more than 160 autonomous enterprises, far too many competing firms in an industry that requires integration. Similarly, Yugoslavia has five factories producing entire radios; considerable economies of scale might be obtained by having each factory specialize in a single radio component. In recent years there has been a strong trend in some industries toward merger of enterprises, in spite of the obstacles presented by entrenched Workers' Councils.

Another problem that socialism was supposed to have avoided, but that is found in Yugoslavia today, is a certain degree of job insecurity and unemployment. It is theoretically possible that a system of market socialism such as Yugoslavia's might be subject to a certain degree of aggregate unemployment. In the past, this has generally been overcome by a sufficient amount of central investment and by exportation of about 400,000 workers, mostly to West Germany. Nevertheless, there is a continuing problem of frictional unemployment to the degree that inefficient enterprises are allowed to go bankrupt, although there is some noneconomic pressure against this. Moreover, there was a significant amount of aggregate unemployment in 1966 and 1967.

In addition to the regional biases mentioned earlier, investment allocation under the Yugoslav system is subject to certain distortions due to the limited outlook of individual enterprises operating on purely profit criteria. Because workers are only attached to the firm for a limited time (at most during their lifetime), the Workers' Councils tend to neglect many long-run considerations in favor of short-run rapid returns. Furthermore, some individual Yugoslav firms like those under a private enterprise system, tend to overlook the possible social benefits and damages of their investments. For example, each firm does not consider fully the effects of creating smog in the community.

A quite different problem is posed by the private nature of Yugoslav farming. Because it is not only private but also of low productivity in general, with low yields per worker, this sector tends to conflict with the socialized and rapidly modernizing industries. The official Yugoslav remedy is that farming itself will eventually be socialized, but the lack of significant movement in this direction may leave one skeptical about the political feasibility of the move at any time.

Finally, consider the left-wing, Chinese criticism that the Yugoslav system will eventually revert to capitalism. This is based on the notion that workers and managers in particular plants are coming to have a vested economic interest in those plants. It is hard to see, though, how the workers of a given plant in the Yugoslav system can ever use their possession of the plant either to exploit other workers or to pass on their position as an inheritance to their children.

Related to the allegation just described is the charge that the Yugoslav economic psychology is reverting to a bourgeois obsession with profit-making. This may certainly be the case to some extent, but it is not easy to see that the central-planning alternative produces less of a money-making psychology on the part of workers and managers. Moving in a different direction, the Chinese have retained central planning, but have drastically reduced the income differentials between unskilled workers, skilled workers, and managers. Thus, while the Yugoslavs are relying more and more on individual material incentives, the Chinese claim to be relying more on collective moral incentives. There is still no good study of the economic impact of different incentive systems.

summary

For several years in the 1960s, a debate raged in the Soviet Union over how far to decentralize the economy. In 1965, the government passed limited reforms which increased the freedom of action of the plant manager in several areas and made his bonus dependent more on maximizing profits than on following a detailed output plan. The central plan is still very important, and the profits still go to the public rather than to any individual.

Since 1950, Yugoslavia has pursued an extreme form of decentralization and use of the market, leading many observers to question whether she has retained any planning or any socialism. All major decisions in the enterprise are made by a Workers' Council, which is directly elected by the workers. It appoints the manager (jointly with the local government), decides how much income is to be reinvested, how much is to be distributed, and who shall get the income distributed. Thus, ownership is no longer really public in Yugoslavia; rather the ownership resides with all the workers in the enterprise, as a collective or cooperative venture. A basic criticism leveled by some radicals has been that this wide use of the market and money incentives instills a more bourgeois psychology and leads back toward capitalism.

chapter 38
political and social problems under socialism

So far, only the core of purely economic problems under socialism
has been discussed. Socialist countries, it has been demonstrated,
can plan in a rational manner for the whole economy; they do achieve
the necessary balance for full employment (although with some
inflation problems); and by using a high rate of saving and investment,
they have usually achieved very high rates of growth. Further, there
are attempts to overcome some of the problems of overcentralized
planning, partly through the application of better economic theory
and advanced computer analysis and partly through some decentralization of decision-making.

Now we must examine the impact of socialism on the more general
problems of equitable income distribution, free social services,
racism, sexism, pollution, dictatorship, imperialism, and alienation.
Obviously, a book could be devoted to each of these problems, so in
this brief chapter, we shall do no more than pose some problems and
note some trends in the socialist countries.

exploitation or equitable income distribution?

The distribution of income in the Soviet Union is very similar to the
distribution of wage income in the United States. The difference is

that there is no upper end to the distribution; there is no private profit income, no rent income, no interest income (except on savings lent to the government). To the extent that only wage income is given to Soviet citizens, we may say that there is no exploitation in Marx's sense of the term.

However, some Soviet income that is supposedly wages paid for labor may be exploitive income in disguise. The incomes of the top government officials, top Communist party officials, and the top military men are known to be very high, but are state secrets. Officially, they are paid labor income, but because they set their own wages, these "wages" may be considerably above an income based on labor alone. To the extent that this is so, it is fair to question just how socialist is the Soviet Union. It may be added that most observers believe the income distribution in China (and Cuba) to be much more equalitarian, as was Soviet income distribution immediately after the 1917 Revolution.

free social services

In any event, it is a long way to the complete equality, or payment according to "need," that is promised for communism. Still, the highly differential wages paid in the Soviet Union are made considerably more equal because of the very large sector of free goods and services available to everyone. Of course, all goods and services are produced by human effort and therefore they are not free in that sense. But the Soviet government chooses to give many goods and services to its citizens without payment.

The Soviets are particularly proud of their very extensive, excellent, and free medical services. They are also proud of their completely free educational system, from elementary school to graduate school. Good students are also given scholarships enough to live on without outside work. Their retirement system is comprehensive, as is the right to a paid vacation each year. Paid maternity leaves with job security are also mandatory under the law. The area of free goods and services provided by the public is clearly far larger than in the United States, although just how large is controversial (the Soviets claim that it amounts to one-third of the real wage). Presumably, under full communism all goods and services will be free, but the present Soviet leadership is certainly not rushing in that direction (and the leaders with high incomes have a vested interest in the present system).

racism

The Soviet government has always propagandized against racism, and there is little or no perceptible prejudice against black people in the Soviet Union. But there are very few blacks there, and it does appear that some racial prejudice has been used as a political weapon to get popular support in the verbal struggle between the Russians and Chinese (and it has been used on both sides apparently). There also used to be much propaganda against anti-Semitism, but Stalin used anti-Semitism as a weapon against his political opponents, and Hitler brought propaganda against the Jews with him when he invaded Russia. As a result of these two sources of prejudice, and because the Jew continues to be a convenient target for prejudice, the Soviet leaders still make many anti-Semitic statements. (Many racist statements are made under the guise of anti-Zionism, which is a perfectly legitimate political position that is grossly misused in this case.)

One should not overestimate Soviet use of anti-Semitism. Many Soviet authors are allowed to attack it, if they do not criticize top leadership. Moreover, Soviet Jews have much *higher than proportional* numbers of students and faculty in higher education, scientists, actors, concert artists, and journalists. This by no means results from discrimination in their favor, but it does indicate lack of discrimination in certain educational and economic areas; their high proportions result simply from an urbanized, education-oriented tradition. Only in political positions are Jews almost completely unrepresented.

sexism

In this area, the Soviet system has shown its most striking successes. Women are close to equality in numbers of college students and have a rapidly rising number of PhD's (now over one-third of the total). They constitute about 20 percent of associate professors. More than 50 percent of all doctors and lawyers are women, and in the sciences and all other professions the percentages are very high (even one-third of all engineers). Women comprise more than 50 percent of the total Soviet labor force.

On the negative side, it must be admitted that the attitudes of Soviet men have changed very little since pre-Revolutionary days. Or, more precisely, the social situation of Russian women was so low that, even with fantastic upgrading, it still appears poor by the standards of the Women's Liberation movement. Men and women do take it for granted that the average Soviet woman has a job appropriate to her abilities, and *at equal pay* (and that she is entitled to a lengthy maternity leave, while being paid and retaining her job). *But* men also assume that when the woman returns from a hard day's work, she takes the children from a child-care center (which service is very well developed in the Soviet Union and is free to all), and is exclusively responsible for their care. She is also expected to cook and clean the house, while the man, who worked the same number of hours in the day, relaxes and does nothing. This situation has not changed at all in the countryside; it is beginning to change *very* slowly among educated urban men and women.

pollution

The Soviet Union has much less pollution than the United States, but that is partly a consequence of less economic development (particularly because there are vastly fewer automobiles). Yet the reduction of pollution is also due to the fact that private profit has been replaced by social control. All new facilities (including whole cities) are carefully approved by a sanitation inspector who is pledged to strict protection of the environment. There also is a new set of very strict antipollution laws.

Nevertheless, many cases of environmental destruction have been reported, in loud and agonized voices, by Soviet newspapers and journals. The reasons for this pollution, in spite of social planning and laws, can be traced to the continued private interests of Soviet managers and some bureaucrats. The manager's bonus depends on how much he produces and how low his costs are; but he can produce more at lower costs by paying no attention to pollution. As a countermeasure, fines are beginning to be applied to polluting managers. Yet some managers are protected by higher bureaucrats because their performance too is judged on the basis of how much their district produces and at how low a monetary cost. Under Stalin, *production* was the sole goal *at any cost,* monetary, human, or environmental. That set of priorities is only slowly changing. (And that is natural. People at very low income levels before economic development need more food, clothing, and shelter; worry over polluting the environment is a luxury they cannot afford. With affluence, pollution becomes a major problem, which can and must be attended to.)

dictatorship

One reason for the Soviet disregard of human feelings and environmental destruction during the period of rapid industrialization was the lack of democratic control over the leadership. Stalin ruled as a sole and arbitrary dictator. Even at present, decision-making is only partially shared with the Central Committee, which has a few hundred individuals. A considerable amount of freedom of discussion and criticism does exist now, but it is still very much limited to safe subjects and the criticism of local leaders. Thus, there was vast public discussion of educational reforms and new marriage and divorce laws, but no dissent at all was allowed on the invasion of Czechoslovakia, and intellectuals are still carted off to jail for criticizing basic policies of the top leadership.

The Soviet trend to dictatorship over the working class (rather than democratic representation of it) began during the emergency situations of civil war and foreign intervention. The new Soviet government not only was menaced by a violent uprising of the old reactionary forces (tsarist military men, landlords, and so forth), but also was invaded by 14 foreign countries, including the United States. All this in a country with very little democratic tradition, grinding poverty, and 70 percent or 80 percent illiteracy. Still, there was considerable revival of free speech and debate in the 1920s. This was stifled, and Stalin became absolute dictator only later when the all-out industrialization program was launched.

Rapid industrialization implies, as we have seen in previous chapters, a vast concentration of the country's resources in invest-ment in new factories and machinery. These resources for investment could only come (because there was no foreign help) from the effort and sweat of a population provided with very few consumer goods. Because over 70 percent of the population were peasants in agriculture, this meant squeezing out every bit of agricultural product from them above their minimum survival needs (and sometimes, in the early years, even that was taken). The food was given to the industrial workers or exported to buy foreign machinery. Thus, most of the population was hostile to the government, and would not have backed this drastic program in any democratic vote. Hence, *it was the attempt to overcome economic backwardness rapidly by heroic means at the expense of the present generation that led inevitably to the terrorist Stalinist dictatorship.* In the recent period, with greater affluence, a reduced industrial pace, and the spread of general education, it is possible to see a long-run trend toward political liberalization (but the trend often gives way to very regressive steps).

imperialism

We saw in an earlier chapter that imperialism has tended to flourish under capitalism because it has brought vast gains to the owners of a few large corporations, even though it has meant taxes and inflation and deaths and wounds in wars for most of the population of the imperialist countries. The Soviet Union has no private owners of large corporations, nor can anyone make private profit from an overseas investment or from a military contract. In fact, Soviet planners recognize military spending for what it is, a drain on their ability to produce more consumer and producer goods for the society.

Still, it is a fact that the Soviet Union has taken aggressive actions against Czechoslovakia and Hungary and has militarily occupied them in spite of the will of their peoples. It is a fact that the Soviet Union and China have clashed on their borders. What are the ultimate causes of these actions if they are not related to private profits? Partly, at least, the causes would seem to be related to the continuing undemocratic character of the Soviet government, and to the fact that top leaders make high salaries and have vested interests in maintaining their positions. It is often easier to keep political power at home by putting people's minds on foreign adventures, and always reminding them of the possibilities of foreign intervention. It also means further extension of the Soviet leaders' personal political control over eastern Europe.

The most succinct analysis of Soviet foreign policy has been provided by Andreas Papandreou, a man whose country (Greece) was taken away from him by a military coup known to be backed by the CIA.[1] Professor Papandreou says: "While the expansionist-capitalist dynamic is absent in the Soviet Union, the bureaucratic-militarist dynamic is very present indeed. . . . Thus, while the Soviet Union lacks an imperialist dynamic that springs from its economic organization, it does not lack an expansionist dynamic which reflects the needs of its establishment to consolidate its world position. . . . There is the old saying, that the best defense is a good offense."[2]

[1] Professor Papandreou was Chairman of the Department of Economics at University of California, Berkeley, before he returned to join the cabinet in the last Greek democratic government (of which his father was premier).

[2] Andreas Papandreou, *Man's Freedom* (New York: Columbia University Press, 1970), p. 49.

alienation

Legally speaking, the Soviet worker is one of the owners of all the factories in his land. Nevertheless, in his own factory, he must still take orders from the foreman, must still arrive on time, and must still often do tedious routine work for many hours. Thus, although one kind of alienation has been eliminated or reduced by socialism, other kinds still persist because of the needs of any modern industry.

The alienation in the factory is reinforced by the lack of democratic control over national political and economic policies. The Soviet worker is ordered about by the foreman, by the manager above him, by the higher economic agencies, by the police and secret police, by several layers of bureaucracy, and ultimately by the top political leaders, who are self-perpetuating. Thus, he still has the feeling of facing a huge faceless machine. Undoubtedly, greater democratic participation in national decision-making would reduce some of this alienated feeling.

Perhaps some greater feeling of control over his life would also be contributed by a wide area of workers' control in the factory. In Yugoslavia, where Workers' Councils do have full legal control over the manager and the enterprise, some of this type of alienation may have been eliminated. Still, we noted that the Yugoslavs achieved this control at the expense of other kinds of alienation. Specifically, elimination of centralized bureaucracy means substitution of the marketplace as the arena of economic decision-making. It thus means even more reliance on purely material motivations, on local gain (sometimes by monopoly profit) at the expense of the rest of society, and on highly differentiated individual incomes.

Both the Soviet Union and Yugoslavia (and to a lesser extent China) retain highly unequal income distributions. The Soviet income distribution is, however, many times less unequal than the American, mainly because the Soviets have no private income from ownership of capital. And the Soviets do have a much wider area of free public goods and services. Nevertheless, they are far from the communist principle of "payment according to need." In a society with this range of income distribution, even though it has socialist ownership of production, there are workers with relatively low incomes who feel left out of the growing affluence. And there are top leaders with very large individual incomes (only vaguely associated with their labor contribution), who have a vested interest in preserving their economic and political privileges. Hopefully, if and when the socialist countries achieve 70 percent or 80 percent of their distribution in free goods and services, workers will feel less alienated, the political structure will give up its coercive powers, and the whole attitude of people toward work and power will change. But for the present, that is only science fiction speculation.

summary

This is a chapter of summaries, so it cannot easily be summarized. Suffice it to say that from the viewpoint of most American radicals the Soviet Union has been much more successful in solving economic problems (such as full-employment, growth, and income distribution) than social and political problems (such as the elimination of alienation and dictatorship). The other countries calling themselves socialist are still too new to make any definite evaluation, except to point out that they have evolved a remarkable variety of social, political, and economic models, many of which are strikingly different from the Soviet model.

Socialist movement (*cont.*)
and capitalist system, 5
contemporary, 561–562
and imperialism, 120
and Judeo-Christian ethic, 5
in 1930s, 133
Socialist nations. *See also* Chinese
economy; Soviet economy;
Yugoslav economy
and income distribution, 615–616
and international trade, 516
and production decisions, 592
and racism, 617
social services in, 616
Socialist revolution, 71
Marx on, 87–88
Socialist theory. *See also* Marxism
of Babeuf, 67–68
and Fourier, 70–71
and Godwin, 68–69
and neoclassical theory, 154–155
of Owen, 64–66
and Saint-Simon, 69–70
of Winstanley, 66–67
Socialists. *See also* Socialism; Socialist movement; Socialist theory
and industrial revolution, 43
pre-Marxist, 66–73
South Sea stock speculation bubble,
338
South Vietnam, inflation in, 324
Soviet economy, 563
and aggregate balance versus inflation, 588–590
and collectivization, 570
compared with Chinese economy,
579–580
and decentralization debate, 613–614
and economic planning. *See* Economic planning in USSR
evaluation of, 574–575, 583
and free social services, 616
growth rates in, 340, 511
and income distribution, 615–616
and industrialization debate, 568–569
and information for planning, 594
and New Economic Policy period,
568
in 1930s, 133
and pollution, 618
and price-fixing, 196
and War Communism policies, 567–
568
and microbalances between industries, 590–591
as model for Chinese, 576
pre-World War II, 570–571, 571–573
recent reforms of, 573–574
and World War II, 571
Soviet Union. *See also* Economic planning in USSR; Russian Revolution; Soviet Economy
and imperialism, 620
and political democracy, 619
and sexism, 617–618
and Yugoslavia, 608
Spain: and bullionism, 25

and U.S. imperialism in Cuba, 124,
125
Speehamland system of poor relief, 61–
62
Spencer, Herbert, 100
Spending flows, 350–353
and maximization of utility, 202–205
Stability of Prices, The (Patten), 113
Stackelberg, H. von, 261
Stage of production concept, 455–456
Stalin, Joseph, 569, 572, 575, 617, 619
Standard of deferred payment, money
as, 334
Standard of living: and British imperialism in India, 124
and consumption, 392
and industrial revolution, 56–60
and poverty line, 217–218
of Soviet workers in 1930s, 572
in underdeveloped nations, 326
of welfare recipients, 293
of workers, 85–86, 117–118, 227
Standard Oil Company of New Jersey,
550
Standard Oil Company of Ohio, 104–
105
Starvation. *See also* Poverty
in China, 580
and Malthusian population theory,
50–51
State. *See also* Government control;
Government role
and enforcement of Christian corporate ethic, 28–33
Fabian view of, 118–119
Proudhon on, 72
State Bank of Soviet Union, 590, 598
Statue of Artificers (1563), 27, 32
Statute of Monopolies (1624), 32
Steam engine, development of, 42–43
Stock market: and monetary policy, 487
in 1929, 347
Stock ownership, concentration of, 220,
274
Store of value, money as, 334, 335
Structural unemployment, 589
Subsistence wage, in underconsumptionist theory, 446
Suicide rates of black and white compared, 305
Supply. *See also* Supply and demand
changes in, 191–194
and costs of production, 234–237
definition of, 184
elasticity of, 210–211
and marginal cost, 208–209, 213
in market system, 183
and prices, 184–189
Supply and demand, 216
circular flow of, 350
and market as allocative device, 195–
199
and money and prices, 375–377
and price and output, 209–210
and Say's law, 328–329
Supreme Soviet, 574, 606
Surplus value, 80–81